JACK LYNCH

A Biography

JACK LYNCH

A Biography

DERMOT KEOGH ～

Gill & Macmillan

Gill & Macmillan Ltd
Hume Avenue, Park West, Dublin 12
with associated companies throughout the world
www.gillmacmillan.ie

© Dermot Keogh 2008
978 07171 3469 4

Index compiled by Helen Litton
Typography design by Make Communication
Print origination by Carole Lynch
Printed and bound in Great Britain by MPG Books Ltd,
Bodmin, Cornwall

This book is typeset in Linotype Minion and
Neue Helvetica.

The paper used in this book comes from the wood
pulp of managed forests. For every tree felled,
at least one tree is planted, thereby renewing
natural resources.

A CIP catalogue record for this book is available
from the British Library.

5 4 3 2

This book is dedicated to
William and Maureen Keogh

to
Ann, Eoin, Niall, Aoife, Clare, Elizabeth, Marco,
Caroline, Abi, Aisling and Luke

to
Matthew and Madelaine MacNamara

to
Michael Mills, Dick Walsh, Kenneth Whitaker,
Patrick Hillery, Eamonn Gallagher

and to
Chief Superintendents John Fleming and
Phil McMahon.

CONTENTS

PREFACE

The late Ombudsman Michael Mills is responsible for first encouraging me to write this book. His rationale was quite simple. As the political correspondent of the *Irish Press* for more than thirty years he had reported on historic events that shaped Ireland in the second half of the twentieth century. He wanted a narrative written by an insider to place events, and interpretations of those events, on the record before they were lost to history. To that end, he had unsuccessfully sought to persuade Jack Lynch to write his memoirs. When that failed he asked him to tape extensive and comprehensive interviews with himself and Dick Walsh of the *Irish Times*. The idea was to put Jack Lynch on record. The content, if sensitive, could be embargoed for decades if the former Taoiseach so wished. Lynch preferred to keep his silence, allowing history to judge him. But, as Michael Mills realised, there were competing narratives and interpretations. Without the voice and testimony of Lynch, he feared that the recasting of interpretations of the period would not prove to be fair or favourable to the former Taoiseach. History is not an impersonal and impartial judge.

In retirement, Lynch remained an intensely private figure. After a lifetime in politics, from 1948 until the early 1980s, he valued the belated and precious free time he then had to spend with his wife, Máirín. They had both lived through difficult times. Lynch had led his country through, arguably, the most testing years since the early post-Civil War years of the 1920s. The years 1969–73 were particularly demanding. He had experienced Irish politics at their most stressful and most dangerous, and the writing of a memoir—or the commissioning of an official biography—would have mired him in controversy and public debate.

The temptation to do so was great as Lynch found himself being systematically airbrushed out of modern Irish history by Charles Haughey and his entourage. Showing considerable self-discipline, he stoically resisted being provoked into retaliation. In truth, Lynch was tired of national political life. Confident about the part he had played, he was willing to let his reputation be judged by future generations of historians. Máirín Lynch supported his vow of silence, to which—with two exceptions—he remained faithful.

Without the persistence of Michael Mills, I would not have embarked upon this eight-year research assignment. I had become very friendly with him between 1970 and 76 when I worked as a journalist in the *Irish Press*. Living through that very confused and violent period, he helped a number of young journalists, such as myself, John Banville and others, to make sense of what was happening in national and international politics, Anglo-Irish relations and Northern Ireland. He was very much part of a counter-culture in the paper, which had no sympathy with the ascendant editorial line on Northern Ireland. He was a very strong supporter of the constitutional line taken by the then Taoiseach, Jack Lynch, from the outbreak of the crisis in 1969. It was an unglamorous position to hold at a time when passion and raw emotion demanded more direct methods for 'solving' the problem of partition 'once and for all.'

I was a recent history graduate from UCD and—thanks to the generosity of the editor, Tim Pat Coogan—had joined the paper as a sub-editor on the same day as a classmate, Stephen O'Byrnes. Working on the sub-editors' desk, it was John Banville's nightly task to take the reams of copy on Northern Ireland and craft the jumble into a narrative that would usually form the lead story. A strong opponent of the necrophilia of the Provisional IRA, I recall the difficulty encountered when both of us put forward a motion condemning the Birmingham bombings in our branch of the National Union of Journalists. If memory serves me correctly, the motion was not allowed on the agenda, as, it was ruled, the NUJ did not take a position on political matters. It was difficult at the time to understand such detachment.

The *Irish Press* was a microcosm of Irish society, and, not surprisingly, political tensions manifested themselves in the news room and at the editorial level. Unwaveringly, Michael Mills wrote daily on national politics and on Anglo-Irish relations. Quite how his daily by-lined reports appeared in the *Irish Press* often depended upon the duty editor. On numerous occasions I witnessed the sub-edited copy being placed in the out tray by one duty editor in particular. What sometimes appeared under his by-line was not exactly as he had written it. Depending on your point of view, that was either a form of censorship or a corrective to ensure a consistent editorial line. I had no doubt that it was censorship.

I left the *Irish Press* and Ireland in 1976 to pursue my studies for a doctorate at the European University Institute in Florence. A year later I drove back from Italy to Dublin, arriving on the day after polling in 1977. The evening newspapers declaimed Fianna Fáil's sweeping return to power. Lynch was hailed as a hero and a saviour. Returning to Ireland in 1979, I worked as a journalist with RTE, where I observed at close quarters the final year of Jack Lynch's leadership. In 1980 I took up a position as a lecturer in University College, Cork.

More than a decade and a half later, Michael Mills asked me to consider writing a biography of Jack Lynch. He knew that there were a number of potential biographers waiting to take on the task, but he felt that I might receive favourable treatment from Jack Lynch and win his co-operation. I was reluctant to embark on such a task. In 1992 I had interviewed Lynch when commissioned by Seán Dunne to write a profile of the former Taoiseach for his book *A Cork Anthology*. On that occasion I found Lynch to be cautious but helpful and co-operative. After we had completed the interview I enquired whether his biography was being written. Lynch mistakenly thought that I was interested in doing so; he told me that there were a number of people before me in the queue. Some years later Michael Mills visited University College, Cork, at my invitation. He stressed again that there was a lacuna in Irish historiography because of the absence of a major study on Lynch. He said he had in his possession the papers of Gordon Lambert, which he would allow me to consult.

Lynch died in 1999. When I went to work on the Lambert papers, Michael offered to introduce me to Máirín Lynch. Earlier, I had some contact with Dr Kenneth Whitaker and with the late Dr Patrick Hillery.

Without knowing anything of what I have described above, the senior commissioning editor with Gill & Macmillan, Fergal Tobin, approached me in 2000 to write a biography of Jack Lynch. He proved to be persuasive, and I signed a contract. I was invited to meet Máirín Lynch in 2000 and on a number of occasions was asked back to her home in Garville Avenue, Rathgar, Dublin. She found it hard to understand why there would be an interest in writing a biography. Jack and herself were just ordinary people, she said. She would not do an interview, but she was very helpful. When I enquired about personal papers she said she had asked a former civil service secretary of her husband to go through what was in the house. Later I learnt that a large number of documents had been returned to the Department of the Taoiseach. Later still Máirín Lynch phoned me to ask whether Jack Lynch's desk diaries should be kept or thrown out. I was also asked about other material. My response was consistent: throw nothing out.

On my third visit to Garville Avenue I was presented with three sacks containing what remained of Jack Lynch's personal papers. Máirín Lynch did not think the material was of any historical value. She probably had not read the documents; her eyesight was very bad. But she undervalued the historical importance of what she had given me. I was told to keep them for as long as I wished and then to deposit what I thought might be of interest in the library of University College, Cork.

Máirín Lynch also set up meetings for me with a number of people who worked closely with her late husband. She continued to be helpful to me until shortly before she went into hospital to confront her final illness. I also received a number of letters from her and regular phone calls. She deposited her own personal papers in the National Library of Ireland, and these proved to be immensely valuable. She also sent me three scrapbooks of newspaper cuttings and photographs that had been lovingly assembled over the years by a nun who was a great admirer of the Lynches.

I have been stimulated rather than deterred by the publication of two Jack Lynch biographies during my time in the archives. The studies by Bruce Arnold and T. Ryle Dwyer provided me with a framework in which to situate my own investigations.[1]

I delivered the manuscript to Fergal Tobin in 2007. He had kept faith in the project, despite the many delays in delivery caused by the burden of university administration. What follows will, I hope, go some of the way towards meeting the challenge set down for me by Michael Mills a few decades ago.

ACKNOWLEDGEMENTS

This biography has taken nearly a decade to research and write. I was first prompted to undertake the work by the former Ombudsman, the late Michael Mills, who stressed—in the absence of Lynch memoirs—the necessity of writing a monograph that would analyse the life and times of a political leader of great importance in the development of the Irish state. I was reluctant to undertake a project that would take me away from my main research areas. I changed my mind when, independently of Michael Mills, Fergal Tobin of Gill & Macmillan persuaded me in 2000 to write a book on the life and times of Jack Lynch. The delivery date was set but proved too ambitious in the light of the volume of material to be covered.

Ironically, Mrs Máirín Lynch, who, through Michael Mills, I met on a number of occasions in 2000 and 2001, was sceptical of the idea that there would be much public interest in the details of the couple's lives. 'We were not very political people, but had great admiration for Éamon de Valera, and [were] deeply committed to God's will and to each other,' she wrote to me on 11 March 2003. Those sentiments were not based on any false modesty. She stressed in her conversations with me that neither of them had come from a partisan political family background. Máirín Lynch was convinced that both herself and Jack Lynch had merely done their duty as Irish citizens, nothing more and nothing less.

Up to the time of her final illness Máirín Lynch took an interest in the progress of my work. I was able to reassure her that there was much to occupy the professional historian in studying their life and times. I am very grateful to her for her interest, for her support and for providing me with access to archival material and scrapbooks and with contact with those who knew her late husband. It is very easy to see why she was universally liked and regarded as a formidable ally during a shared lifetime in public life. She was steeped in the values of the Irish parliamentary tradition, Irish Ireland and public service. She is deserving of a biography, as are Sinéad de Valera and other partners of leading male politicians, whose roles have been neglected by historians.

In Cork, members of the Lynch family were most helpful to me while I was beginning my research. I interviewed Jack Lynch's brother Finbarr on two occasions and spoke to him on the phone a number of times. Ms Eileen Compagno, who is related by marriage to Jack Lynch, also interviewed, on my behalf, his two sisters, Irene (Rena) and Eva, a cousin, Jim Crockett, and T. Ryle Dwyer. Captain Dan Harvey, a nephew of Jack Lynch, helped me track down the family history and was very supportive of my efforts to come to terms with the intricacies of the role of the Irish army during 1969 and 1970. I am also grateful to the O'Sullivans, the O'Donoghues and other members by marriage of the extended Lynch family. I am very grateful to Mr James Crockett, Jack Lynch's cousin, and to Eileen Compagno, who helped with the research on the Lynch family.

I was greatly encouraged and assisted by many of Lynch's closest friends. I talked at a very early stage in my research to Dr Ken Whitaker, who had been very close to Jack Lynch when he was both a minister and Taoiseach. There is an extensive correspondence between the two men, which is very valuable in tracing the development of the Irish Government's Northern policy. The late Dr Patrick Hillery, a former President of Ireland, gave me an extensive interview and introductions to a number of people who knew Lynch well. Senator Des Hanafin also gave me an interview. Neville Keery, a former senator, deposited his personal archives at University College, Cork; he also gave me an interview and answered many questions by e-mail. I spoke at length on the phone to Pádraig Faulkner and derived much enlightenment from his memoir, as I did also from my conversations with Michael Mills and in reading his reminiscences (see bibliography). My thanks also to Anne Colley for giving me an interview. Thanks also go to Brian Crowley MEP.

I met Desmond O'Malley on a number of occasions over the years but never had the opportunity to interview him about Jack Lynch. He was very helpful on the history of Fianna Fáil. Paul Mackay, a former member of the National Executive of Fianna Fáil and a founder-member of the Progressive Democrats, gave me a detailed account of life inside the former party during the period 1969–70. In the 1980s this accountant was expelled from Fianna Fáil following a drumhead court-martial as a consequence of his refusal to sign off on the accounts in Charles Haughey's constituency. Stephen Collins, a former colleague from the *Irish Press*, has, as a journalist, produced works of a much more enduring quality than 'the first draft of history.' I owe him a great debt of gratitude.

Jim Dukes, a former civil servant, gave me an interview and wrote an *aide-mémoire* about his time as Lynch's private secretary in the Department of Education. I am grateful to Dermot Nally, former secretary-general of the Department of the Taoiseach, for his help while I was working on the late 1970s period. I am also grateful to a number of diplomats, Eamonn Gallagher, Seán Donlon, Padraig (Paddy) MacKernan and Frank Cogan, for their observations on the formulation of Irish foreign policy during the Lynch period.

Stephanie Walsh, the daughter of Lynch's lifelong friend and Fine Gael TD

Stephen Barrett, gave me many insights into the Lynch couple that are based on her childhood memories. She also shared with me correspondence in her possession relating to Jack Lynch and, in particular, details of the occasion when he received an honorary doctorate from the University of Limerick in November 1995.

Three former Lord Mayors of Cork—Toddy O'Sullivan (Labour), Michael Ahern (Labour) and Donal Counihan (Fianna Fáil)—gave me valuable help.

Judge Tony Murphy, a lifelong friend of the Lynches, spoke to me at length about Lynch as a barrister. I am grateful to Dr Miriam Hederman O'Brien and Anthony Hederman O'Brien. Marcella Murrin, who nursed both Jack and Máirín Lynch during their final illnesses, gave me a good insight into the characters of the couple. I was assisted early in the research by Máirín and Ita Quill. They gave me valuable advice and contacts and remained actively in contact with me throughout the project. My thanks to Con Murphy, a contemporary of Jack Lynch's at the Mon. The vice-principal of Gaelcholáiste Mhuire, North Monastery, Mr Tony Duggan, was most generous with his time and knowledge. He secured access to the roll-books for Jack Lynch's time at the Mon and allowed me to take copies of a number of historic team photographs.

Members of the staff of the *Irish Examiner* have also helped me in research. I am grateful to Ted Crosbie and the late Suzanne Crosbie. Liam Moher proved a great source of support. My thanks to the family of Jim Hurley, who let me see the family archive.

I also acknowledge the help of Denis Owens of Glen Rovers, Father Ralph Egan, retired parish priest of Mount Argus, Angela Devlin O'Donnell, and Edward O'Driscoll, solicitor, Bandon.

Special thanks to Kay Hart, Mirco and the staff of the Farmgate where my ideas on Jack Lynch fell into place amid the din of this special restaurant.

I acknowledge the help of the staff of the National Archives of Ireland and in particular Ms Catriona Crowe and Tom Quinlan. Dr Gerard Lyne, keeper of manuscripts at the National Library of Ireland, secured for me access to the uncatalogued Máirín Lynch papers. Commandant Victor Laing, officer in charge of Military Archives, and his staff were most helpful and co-operative, particularly in obtaining a number of archival fragments in response to my queries. My thanks to my fellow-editors on the Documents on Irish Foreign Policy project: Prof. Eunan O'Halpin, Prof. Ronan Fanning, Ms Catriona Crowe, Dr Michael Kennedy and Dr Kate O'Malley.

I am very grateful to the archivists and library staff of the following institutions: Cork City and County Archives; Cork Northside Oral History Project; Trinity College, Dublin; University College, Dublin; Queen's University, Belfast; National University of Ireland, Galway; National University of Ireland, Maynooth; European University Institute, Florence; Irish College, Rome;

Vatican Archives; National Archives, Washington; National Archives, London; Georgetown University, Washington; Library of Congress, Washington; Boston College; University of New South Wales, Sydney; University of Sydney; University of Melbourne; Archdiocese of Dublin; and Archdiocese of Armagh.

While writing this book I also visited archives in Britain and the United States. I am grateful to Mike Lacey in Washington State and Patrick Goggins in San Francisco. While working in the Library of Congress and Georgetown University in Washington I stayed with Paul and Susan Nugent and Tom and Marguerite Kelly. Dr Paula Wylie, a former UCC postgraduate student and an expert on Irish foreign policy, shared with me the archival work she had undertaken in a number of presidential libraries. She also surveyed the debates of Dáil Éireann and helped me come to terms with on-line sources. I am grateful to her and to her two children, Brooke and Callan, for their help and hospitality.

Another postgraduate student, Paul Loftus, helped me find material in the Lyndon B. Johnson Presidential Library, Austin, Texas, on Ireland and the Viet Nam war. Dr Robert McNamara worked as a researcher in the National Archives, Dublin, on files of the Department of the Taoiseach. John Paul McCarthy was very helpful. Dr Emma Cunningham also helped in the early stages of the research, ordering and advising on material I was accumulating from different sources. Dr Niall Keogh and Aoife Keogh helped me throughout the process, obtaining a number of documents from the National Archives in Dublin and London. Brona Allison helped find files in the PRONI on the period 1969–73. Dr Mary Harris, NUIG, also helped. Assistance was also provided by Dr Jérôme aan de Wiel of the Department of History, UCC. More recently Patrick Kiely, also a postgraduate student, assisted me in completing the manuscript. Dr Bernadette Whelan, University of Limerick, helped me with a number of queries.

When embarking on the biography I had little understanding of the magnitude of the undertaking. I made my first great strides with this book while I was a visiting Jean Monnet professor in 2001–2 at the European University Institute, Florence, where I had completed my doctorate in 1980. I am grateful to Angela Schenk, Prof. Alan Milward, Prof. Robert Wokler, Prof. John Horgan and Prof. Arfon Rees. Later that year I went as a Fulbright professor to Boston College, where I continued my research at the Center on Wealth and Philanthropy, directed by Prof. Paul Schervish. I am grateful to Mary O'Mahony, the staff of the John J. Burns Library and Prof. Tom Hachey and Prof. Robert Savage of the History Department at Boston College.

More recently, Prof. Peter Kuch, University of Otago, Dunedin, was responsible for bringing me to the University of New South Wales in 2007, where Prof. John Gascoigne and his colleagues made me very welcome. Erin Riley, the departmental administrator, played an important role as a computer expert and supporter. I am grateful to John McCarthy, chancellor of the

University of Sydney, Jeff and Robyn Kildea, Michael and Gary Kildea and the Aisling Society for their support while my wife, Ann, and myself were in Sydney. We were shown equal hospitality in Melbourne by Prof. Elizabeth Malcolm, Elizabeth and Brendan Pierce, and Dr Val Noone.

I owe a great debt to my UCC colleague Dr Andrew McCarthy, who helped my research in three areas. He provided a study of the social context in which Jack Lynch was raised on Cork's north side in the 1920s and 30s. One of the country's leading economic historians, Dr McCarthy worked earlier as a research assistant on the chapters covering Lynch's time as Minister for Industry and Commerce and Minister for Finance. He helped me to under-stand the world of finance and budgetary control. His scholarship, friendship and support were also expressed in another tangible way: he generously shared his unrivalled computer skills and expertise during the long gestation of this book. My apologies to his wife, Deirdre, for the many occasions on which he returned home late as a consequence of agreeing to help me resolve research and computer difficulties.

Equally, I acknowledge the support of my colleague Gabriel Doherty, who took over the headship of the Department of History at a critical juncture in 2001/2 and for a term in 2007, which enabled me to take leave in order to complete the writing of this book in the seclusion of the University of New South Wales. He has been an immense support as a colleague, and I have relied upon his judgement throughout my work on the book. He is a leading authority on Irish cultural and social history in the nineteenth and twentieth centuries, and I have worked with him in the organising of conferences and in editing a number of books. I acknowledge warmly his great generosity of spirit and his willingness to share ideas. He has built up an extraordinary press archive of the *Irish Times* that even the arrival of the digital archive will not eclipse in usefulness.

Moreover, all my colleagues in the UCC Department of History have been very helpful and supportive. In particular I thank Dr Hiram Morgan, Dr Mervyn O'Driscoll and Dr Dónal Ó Drisceoil for sharing with me their insights into modern Irish history. Dr David Ryan, Dr Damian Bracken, Dr Diarmuid Scully, Dr Diarmuid Whelan, Dr Finola Doyle O'Neill and Dr Larry Geary contribute to the vibrant intellectual environment in the department that helps sustain my research, as did Sir Adrian Beamish, Ms Liz Steiner Scott, Dr Jason Harris and Dr Jennifer O'Reilly. Rory O'Dwyer, who is writing a doctoral thesis on Frank Aiken, shared files on the premature retirement of the veteran Fianna Fáil politician in 1973 over the nomination of Charles Haughey as a candidate in the general election. I am grateful to the adminis-trative staff in the Department of History: Déirdre O'Sullivan, Geraldine McAllister, Charlotte Holland, Norma Buckley and Veronica Fraser. Both

Margaret Clayton and, latterly, Sheila Cunneen helped at various stages in the preparation of the final manuscript. Ms Cunneen was there at the critical final part of the submission operation and helped prepare the bibliography and to draw my attention to the tiniest of details.

Over nearly thirty years working at UCC I have been supported in my research by the staff of the Boole Library. I am grateful to the staff of Special Collections and the head librarian, John Fitzgerald. My thanks also to Donal Kingston of the Computer Centre.

A former president of UCC, Prof. Gerard Wrixon, gave me support and encouragement. His successor, Prof. Michael Murphy, continues that support for the advancement of the study of history at UCC. The vice-president for planning, communications and development, Michael O'Sullivan, notwith-standing being a dyed-in-the-wool Blackrock supporter, was a source of prac-tical and personal help. I am grateful to Prof. David Cox, head of the College of Arts, Celtic Studies and Social Sciences, for the research funding that made the writing of this book less burdensome on family finances. Thanks also go to Prof. Áine Hyland for her assistance, and to Fiona Kearney, director of the Lewis Glucksman Gallery, UCC. Feidhlim Ó Súilleabháin, Séamus Nicholson and Pádraig McCarthy supplied me with answers to queries about Lynch's sporting life.

I am grateful to Séamas Ó Brógáin, who sub-edited the text and made many useful suggestions. I also wish to thank Finbarr O'Shea, who read the text at page proof stage.

My friends Prof. Matthew and Madelaine MacNamara, Angela Cahill and her late husband, Edward, Maureen Brady and Brian and Laura Lennon were a constant source of support throughout my many academic projects, as were each member of my family in Dublin. Joe Lee has remained a mentor and friend for over thirty years. He has provided great support, encourage-ment and advice throughout that period. His enthusiasm and good humour are infectious.

Finally, my thanks to Clare, Aoife, Eoin, Caroline, Niall, Elizabeth, Marco, Abi, Luke and Aisling.

Ann, who has shared the trials and tribulations of being married to a mendicant researcher, must take the lion's share of the credit for ensuring the completion of this work. However inadequate the phrase, thank you.

I dedicate this book to Ann, to my late parents, Maureen and William Keogh, and to Michael Mills and those others mentioned with him on the dedication page who showed judgement and courage at a very difficult time in the history of the Irish state.

Chapter 1 ～

FROM SHANDON TO
DÁIL ÉIREANN

History turned on the toss of a coin, or so it would appear. In early 1948 Máirín and Jack Lynch were standing inside the main door of Cash's, a well-known department store in Patrick Street, Cork. The country faced a general election on 4 February. With only half an hour left before the deadline for the handing in of nomination papers, the couple appeared hesitant and undecided. Would the holder of six all-Ireland medals go forward as a Fianna Fáil candidate for the constituency of Cork City, or would he turn his back on public life and devote himself exclusively to his career as a barrister? It was quite apparent, however, that there was more hesitancy on her part than on his. 'We'll toss a coin,' said Máirín as a way out of the impasse. They did, and fortune favoured his standing. That was how Máirín Lynch, more than fifty years later, remembered making the fateful decision that sent her husband into a lifetime in national politics.[1]

The reality may not have been quite so unclear, or so dramatic. Despite some personal misgivings, the uncertainty of his wife and the opposition of his father, Jack Lynch had a strong wish to enter national politics. But he would not have done so had he not first gained the unqualified support of his wife. The willingness to consult and decide together characterised their lifetime partnership. Within two weeks of tossing the coin Jack Lynch, aged thirty-one, was elected a member of Dáil Éireann on his first attempt. He held that seat until his retirement on 21 May 1981, an unbroken parliamentary career of thirty-three years, during which time he served as a parliamentary secretary (assistant to the minister), as Minister for Education, Industry and Commerce, Finance, and finally as Taoiseach.

But who was the neophyte parliamentarian? John Mary Lynch was born on 15 August 1917 in the family home in Shandon Churchyard.[2] Still standing, the house has been renovated by the state and bears a plaque in his honour. Now officially known as Bob and Joan's Walk (though not to local people), the

laneway ran down to a graveyard and to the back entrance of what was then
the mortuary chapel of the North Infirmary. Skiddy's, a home for the elderly,
was nearby. Jack Lynch was born and lived until his early teens in Shandon,
literally under the bells of the landmark Cork clock-tower known as the 'four-
faced liar.' Exchequer Street was around the corner from his home, and the
Butter Market (known locally as the Buttera) was close by, as was also T.
O'Gorman and Sons' Cork Cap Factory, to which Lynch gave patronage all his
adult life.

POVERTY AND SOCIETY IN THE SHANDON AREA

What was the social milieu into which the future Taoiseach was born? Some
77,000 people were living in Cork, according to the 1911 census, taken six years
before his birth. The city engineer, J. F. Delany, reporting in 1918 on social
conditions, estimated that 18,645 city residents were living in 'undesirable
conditions' in premises 'approaching a condition of unfitness for habitation.'
That represented nearly a quarter of the city's population.[3] An estimated 8,785
were living in tenements and 9,860 in cottages or single houses.[4] In relation to
the 'very poor' Delany suggested that 'it is clear that the care of this section of
the community, which is on the lowest scale of living, cannot be met by the
erection of houses.' The reason was straightforward: such people would not be
able to meet the rents on new premises.[5] Delany indicted the government for
its inaction: 'The state is not meeting the case of Irish Housing as it ought to
do.'[6] He was not hopeful that the British Government would provide a new
housing programme and noted: 'Derelict areas are not so numerous as on the
North side'—the area of the city where the young Jack Lynch was living.[7]

The state had not been effective in its interventions, and wartime conditions had exempted local authorities from expenditure on public housing.[8]
However, the Notification of Births (Extension) Act (1915) empowered local
authorities to provide maternity and child welfare (up to the age of five); but,
as the historian Ruth Barrington noted, 'the legislation was permissive, not
mandatory.'[9]

Local effort was encouraged instead, and Cork was one of the early respon-
dents. The lord mayor, T. C. Butterfield, convened a public meeting in City Hall
on 12 February 1918, which was 'largely attended', to 'consider what steps should
be taken to inaugurate a child welfare scheme in Cork.'[10] The Bishop of Cork,
Daniel Cohalan, moved the motion 'that in order to reduce and as far as
possible prevent infantile mortality in Cork City and to promote a healthy
race, an association be and is hereby formed to be called the Cork Child
Welfare League.' Prominent citizens duly filled the posts.[11] The Child Welfare
League quickly determined that a health centre should be created, and that
it would be 'sufficient to have one whole-time nurse,' with the assistance of

nurses from the Maternity and Erinville hospitals—provided they received grants. They approached the Public Health Committee of Cork Corporation (city council) for this support, suggesting a levy on the rates of one penny in the pound (0.4 per cent); the proposal was accepted by the corporation, provided it had representation on the proposed twelve-member committee.[12]

The Child Welfare League continued its work throughout the 1920s until it was gradually subsumed into the restructured and centrally directed health structures of the Irish Free State, established in 1922.[13] In 1931 Dr Jack Saunders, medical officer of health for the county borough (city) of Cork, paid tribute to its work in the following terms:

> A voluntary body to whom the citizens generally are greatly indebted for inaugurating and carrying on in spite of great difficulties a scheme which was the first of its kind in the city and of which it may be said that the results of its work are reflected in the marked reduction in infant mortality which has characterised the statistical tables during its period of existence.[14]

Those same statistical tables point to a patchy record. Saunders, however, smoothed difficulties to assist with the transfer of some remaining functions from the Child Welfare League to the newly instituted Maternity and Child Welfare Scheme.[15] He produced his first annual report in 1931, covering the previous year, in which he pointed out that the last annual report had been produced in 1922.[16]

The material suggests something of the environment into which Jack Lynch was born. August 1917, the month of his birth, was the wettest August in Cork since 1905.[17] In normal circumstances that would be unremarkable, except that for the Lynch family it meant the confinement of the children indoors just after the home birth of Jack on 15 August. The year 1917 saw a birth rate of 20.2 per 1,000 in Cork, the lowest in the fifty-year period 1881–1930 and only slightly higher than for the 26 counties for that year.[18] There were 1,552 recorded births in Cork in 1917: of these 169 died under the age of one, a rate of 108 per thousand, compared with the national rate (26 counties) of 84. The total number of deaths in Cork in 1917 was 1,340; the principal causes were tuberculosis (280), respiratory diseases (127), cancer (62) and deaths attributed to violence (24)—an unusually high number. There were great risks, however, for newly born children, as shown by the figures for deaths from such causes as pneumonia (74), diarrhoea (34) and whooping cough (14). Remarkably, there was no death from measles in Cork in 1917; but the following year the city was struck with an epidemic that claimed 88 lives. Pneumonia was also rampant in 1918, claiming 247 lives and the following year 248.

In 1919 also a severe outbreak of diphtheria hit Cork, claiming 32 lives, equal to the total for the previous four years.[19] Diphtheria, a horrible throat infection inducing asphyxiation, was by far the most prevalent of infectious diseases in Cork throughout the 1920s, though the mortality rate was consistently lower than in Dublin. It claimed 345 lives between 1920 and 1930. Given its principal epidemiological characteristic, mainly affecting schoolchildren, the majority of those deaths occurred in children up to the age of ten.[20] Enteric fever, or typhoid, let loose on Cork in 1920 what was the 'biggest epidemic of the disease in the history of the City [and] was clearly traced to infection of the water supply just above the source at which it was drawn.' There were 244 cases that year, resulting in 13 deaths.[21] The possibility of a recurrence, according to Dr Saunders's report for 1930, was remote, though it would hardly have been reassuring to learn that the first systematic bacteriological survey of the city's water was not undertaken until 1928, the year in which the rapid gravity filtration plant was commissioned.[22]

According to the historian Ruth Barrington, 'Irish sanitary authorities had been obliged since 1919 to organise the medical inspection of children in national schools but the act was a dead letter over much of the country.'[23] The meeting of the city's Public Health Committee on 26 September 1916 heard a report from the medical superintendent regarding Coley's Lane (just off the Old Market Place) in the parish of St Mary in Shandon. He stated that in his opinion numbers 3–16 were 'not fit for human habitation' and proposed that they 'be closed up unless they are put into habitable condition, and that steps be taken to reduce the overcrowding in No. 17, 18 and 19 . . . and to have general repairs carried out to same and the kitchens concreted.'[24] In 1927 the school medical services officer, Dr Annie M. Sullivan, reported that the follow-up on defective children was hampered by having only one nurse allocated to general hygiene in schools. She felt that 'it is truly deplorable that such conditions should exist in our schools.'[25]

DANIEL AND NORA LYNCH

Jack Lynch, the fifth of seven children, was born into one of the poorest districts in the city.[26] He was fortunate to avoid having to live in destitution, but those images of the tenements of his childhood would have a lasting impact on him in his later public life. The family in descending order were: Theo, Charlie, Finbarr, Jimmy, John (Jack), Irene (Rena) and Eva. Theo trained as a primary school teacher at De La Salle College, Waterford, and returned to teach in Cork. Charlie entered St Patrick's College, Maynooth, and was ordained for the Cork diocese. He served in London during the Blitz, later returning to the Cork diocese, where he was a curate and later parish priest of Ballinlough. Finbarr became a civil servant and worked in the Departments of Agriculture and

Health in Dublin until 1963, when he was posted to the Department of Defence in Cork.[27] Jimmy died in childhood. Eva worked with the Irish Dunlop Company and married Dr John Harvey. Rena worked with Browne and Nolan, the booksellers,[28] and married Gerard Dunne, principal of Cork School of Commerce.[29]

Jack's father, Daniel, was raised on a small farm in Baurgorm in Bantry. The original family home had been at Kealkill. His grandfather's name was Thady and his grandmother was Nan O'Sullivan Lámh. Daniel had two brothers; one emigrated to California, while the other, according to Rena, went to Dublin and worked in insurance.[30] T. Ryle Dwyer writes that one brother stayed on the farm.[31] Jack Lynch remembered his father as 'a tall, dignified looking man, quiet and modest in all his doings. He liked a drink occasionally, and was interested in sport.'[32] When he was young, Lynch remembered that his father's main recreation was walking and occasionally throwing a bowl, which, of course, is still a favourite pastime in Co. Cork.[33] Lynch recalled: 'In his day he played football, first in west Cork and then for a Cork City team, Nil Desperandum, now defunct whose members were associated with the drapery trade in Cork.'[34] Known for short as the 'Nils', Nil Desperandum (meaning 'Never despair') was the football team of the tailors, garment workers and drapers' assistants.[35] Finbarr Lynch recalled that his father was on a winning cup team around 1908.[36] As a boy, Jack Lynch had been told that his father played junior football in Croke Park.[37] I have found no record of this in published sources. Daniel was interested in all sports and attended soccer and rugby matches as well as Gaelic football and hurling. Despite being a member of the Gaelic Athletic Association, Lynch's father showed a healthy and lifelong disregard for the ban that prevented its members from playing or attending soccer, rugby or cricket matches and other foreign or 'garrison' games.[38]

On arriving in Cork, Daniel became an apprentice in Daniels and Sons, merchant tailors, of 81 Grand Parade.[39] There he met his wife, Nora O'Donoghue. She and her sister were employed as seamstresses when the young west Cork man arrived to begin his apprenticeship. 'Nora, come upstairs, a country boy has started work,' she was told by her sister.[40] It was a fateful encounter. Jack Lynch's mother was one of seven sisters: Sis, Elizabeth, Cathy (Kate), Anastasia (Statia), Madge and Josephine.[41] They were a close-knit family. Nora and Daniel were married on 30 September 1909 in the North Cathedral, known locally as the North Chapel.[42] Ninety years later Jack Lynch's own funeral service would be held there.

The couple went to live first in Dominic Street and then to Shandon Churchyard, to a well-appointed house in a poor area owned by Nora's grandmother.[43] Daniel and Nora Lynch, helped by the grandmother, who lived with them, raised their family surrounded by, but not living in, poverty.

Life as a tailor was precarious in the early years of the Irish Free State. 'In those days,' Jack Lynch remembered of his father, 'he wasn't always able to get a full week's work. Even though he was regularly employed, his employers didn't have sufficient work. He was often on short time.'[44] He was taking home six pounds a week when Daniels' closed in 1929. At that point Daniel Lynch must have gone to work for Ross's, near Cash's[45]—the shop in whose doorway his son allegedly tossed a coin in 1948 to determine his future career. There, Daniel rose to the top position as head cutter.

The area in which the family lived was 'quaint', as Finbarr Lynch described it. However, by the standards of the time the Lynch family was, as Rena put it, 'never short of food.' This was not the lot of the majority of families living in the area. Her brother Charlie recalled: 'We were comfortable enough for the time. There was always enough on the table, and we were well dressed with our father a tailor.'[46] Finbarr described the family as having been 'comfortable by the standards of the time,' and 'we were reasonably well off. We had a decent standard of living and we met de Valera's definition of frugal comfort.'[47] Jack Lynch too recalled: 'Because my father was a tailor, we could always claim to be reasonably well-dressed, though nothing extravagant. Our clothes were usually hand-me-downs. My mother's training as a seamstress made her fussy about our clothes and appearances.' However, he further recalled that with 'six of us in the house and all going on to secondary education, it wasn't easy. A couple of us won secondary school scholarships, so that helped out a lot.' But, he added, 'there was never any sign of wealth in the house, but the quality of life was good.'[48]

Nora continued to work as a seamstress after her marriage. When the first child arrived she remained at home but took in some sewing to help pay the bills. The young boys carried the unfinished garments from the tailors to her home, where she stitched in buttonholes and finished basted garments.[49] The reason for the additional work will be obvious to those who experienced the precariousness and unpredictability of working at trade in the earlier part of the twentieth century. 'That was a much-needed supplement to my father's earnings,' Jack Lynch recalled.[50] Nan Walsh, a local woman, used to come in regularly to help Nora in the house.[51]

Finbarr remembered that his father was allegedly the 'boss' in what appeared to be an Edwardian household. But appearances were deceptive: the Lynch family was very much a matriarchy. Finbarr had no doubt that his mother was the dominant personality; she made all the major decisions, he said. She was 'a major force' even among her own sisters. Her word was respected and carried weight. Finbarr remembered a phrase she repeated when chastising her children: 'Upon my song, I'll change your tune.'[52]

The Lynch family was not untouched by tragedy. Jimmy died at the age of three in 1914 from either diphtheria or suppressed scarlatina. This had a devastating effect on Nora, a woman who was strong and outgoing, forceful and resourceful[53] and acknowledged by the O'Donoghue family to be the leader of the sisters. Nora and other women of her generation, without medical help, often had to contend with the sorrow of such loss. Then it was called melancholia; today it is known as depression.

Jack Lynch recollected of his mother that 'naturally I was very close to her growing up.'[54] She was known in the family as an 'outer', somebody who liked to go out to the theatre or to a show. Nora shared her love of music with Jack in particular. She regularly attended concerts in the Opera House on Thursday nights, usually bringing a number of the children with her.[55] Finbarr, a year older than Jack, recalled seeing the Abbey Theatre players perform on a number of occasions.[56]

Rena and Finbarr remembered that their mother kept an open house. Relatives, in-laws and friends extended and enlarged the Lynch household, which became known as 'Grand Central Station'. Finbarr said: 'They were part of our lives.' Rena recalled the countless occasions when, on returning from school, she found the house full of people from around Bantry up in the city for a day or for a few days' shopping. The country people who stayed overnight usually found it impossible to sleep under Shandon's Bells. Nora's sister Elizabeth and her husband, Fred Crockett, were also long-staying guests at the Lynch household: they came in 1929 and remained for a few years.[57] Daniel's brother John also stayed with them for a time.[58]

Finbarr recalled that his parents were ecumenical long before the term was generally known or became fashionable. They lived close to a Protestant church and school. Two Protestant families, the Batemans and the Merediths, were regular callers. George Meredith was the sexton of the local church and the two Bateman sisters were teachers in the local school.[59] Residents of the nearby Skiddy's Home, a retirement home for both Catholics and Protestants between St Anne's, Shandon, and the North Infirmary,[60] dropped in often for a cup of tea and a chat.[61] In the late 1960s the old building was saved by Jack Lynch when he was Taoiseach.[62]

POLITICS AND THE LYNCH FAMILY

Jack Lynch always stressed that independent-mindedness was one of his father's main characteristics. His son was similar in temperament and character. Daniel was an active trade unionist, probably a member of the Amalgamated Tailors' Union, to which William O'Brien, a founder of the Irish Transport and General Workers' Union, originally belonged. According to Finbarr, his father took an active interest in trade union affairs and on one occasion represented his branch at a conference in Leeds.[63] Daniel, according to oral sources, was a follower of another William O'Brien, the long-standing

MP for Cork, land agitator, outstanding investigative journalist and author of note and was at one time secretary of the Blackpool branch of O'Brien's All-for-Ireland League. When he first came to the city Daniel shared digs with J. J. Walsh, who in 1922 became Minister for Posts and Telegraphs in the first government of the Irish Free State.[64]

Political events moved swiftly towards independence in the wake of the 1916 Rising. Jack Lynch was only a year old when the Sinn Féin movement contested the general election in 1918 and its 73 newly elected MPs (out of Ireland's 105 seats) seceded from the British House of Commons and established Dáil Éireann. On the first day of the Dáil, 21 January 1919, the Democratic Programme was adopted, which, among the more radical social objects, committed the republic to abolishing 'the present odious, degrading and foreign Poor Law system, substituting therefor a sympathetic native scheme for the Nation's aged and infirm.' Provision would be made for the physical, mental and spiritual well-being of the children of the nation so that they would want for nothing.[65] These were aspirations worthy of any revolutionary movement, but, as is often the case, the execution of this policy did not match the rhetoric.

How did national politics and the War of Independence impinge upon the Lynch family? After the general election of 1918 Daniel supported Sinn Féin and the independence movement. He was almost certainly sympathetic to the Labour Party, which did not put forward candidates in the general election.[66] Jack Lynch was three in 1920, when Cork city and county were in the eye of the political storm. The Lynch house in Shandon was a place where the IRA could find refuge, a 'safe house'. There was good reason, therefore, for Daniel to send the older boys to different relatives near Bantry for the summer holidays. Jack remained at home, being too young.[67]

In 1921 Jack, then four, and his three brothers went on summer holidays to Bantry, where they were divided among relatives and friends. Jack stayed with Big Dan Sullivan, not a relative but a close friend of Daniel Lynch's family in west Cork. He was deeply political. His son Jimmy, who was a noted republican and political activist, lived in the Lynch home from the early 1920s until 1927, when Jack was ten. He chose the anti-Treaty side during the Civil War. Finbarr remembered visiting his Uncle John in republican headquarters in the city centre in 1922. He survived the Civil War, remaining in close friendship with Daniel Lynch and his children. On Lynch's mother's side, Mick Donoghue, an uncle of Nora's, was active in republican and labour politics.

EARLY CHILDHOOD, EDUCATION AND SIGNS OF SPORTING PROMISE

In 1921 Jack Lynch began school in St Vincent's Convent, Peacock Lane, run by the Sisters of Charity.[68] Finbarr, who had almost died of whooping cough the previous year, began the same day. He was put in high infants, while his brother started in junior infants. The headmistress, Sister Bruno, was a formidable figure, known for her ability to remember the name of every child in the school and to continue to recognise them by name for many years after. Finbarr remembers many children coming to school in bare feet.[69]

Teddy Forde at that time was Jack's closest friend. His mother, Mary Forde, remembered that they used to play with another boy, Dinny Sullivan, in Johnny Collins's field; neighbours scolded them regularly for destroying their shoes in the muddy field. Mrs Forde further recalled that Jack Lynch used to visit their house to swap books. As Lynch grew older he used to speak in Irish to Mrs Forde's parents, who were Irish-speakers from Baile Bhuirne.[70]

Rena remembered Jack as having a great sense of humour. 'Jack was always the wild one of the family, always getting up to some devilment and, because he was the youngest of the four boys, always getting away with murder at home.'[71] Jack and his brothers swam in the open-air Lee Baths, as did tens of thousands of Cork children. The Lynch brothers also cycled out of the city to the sea.[72] Theo recalled that Jack was a very strong swimmer.[73] Rena said that Jack also used to spend a good deal of time on wet days in the 'big cellar'— one of two cellars in their house—playing hurling with his brothers and friends.[74] Finbarr was certain that playing in such cramped surroundings enabled him to develop the skill used to such effect in his later sporting career, being able to pick a ball up amidst a crowd of players. Jack was a natural left-handed player who taught himself to hurl equally well with his right, and he could also kick with both feet.

Jack Lynch remembered that he first held a hurley while playing on 'a little bit of a garden (or earthen patch) attached to our house and a lane or passage way dividing the graveyard at Shandon. We were forever flicking a ball around and the skills picked up then certainly came in useful in later days.'[75] That was also where his brothers Theo, Charlie and Finbarr 'first got their grip of a hurley.' Lynch remembered 'my frequent visits to O'Connell's sawmills in Leitrim Street, a three-penny bit clutched in my grubby hand, looking for shape-outs. From these we fashioned our first hurley.'[76] The graveyard next door was also a place for the children to play. The laneways around the area served as practice grounds, as did O'Gorman's cap factory wall, known locally as the 'blockie'.[77]

Playing hurling on the street was against the law, and it was necessary to maintain a constant watch for the approach of gardaí. Local knowledge of the labyrinth of lanes usually guaranteed escape. Jack Lynch was usually among the swiftest of his peers when being chased. On one occasion a garda nearly caught him as he climbed over a wall. The future Taoiseach chose to leave his coat in the hands of his pursuer rather than risk the consequences of being caught.[78]

While sport and study took up most of Lynch's time, he caught his first glimpse of politics during the general election of 1932, which brought Éamon de Valera and Fianna Fáil to power. Lynch took part in an old-style election rally in Shandon. He was fifteen. According to Finbarr, Jack carried a torch made of a burning sod of turf in the procession, accompanying de Valera through Blackpool into the city, and later formed part of the large crowd that heard him speak. The *Irish Press,* reporting under the headlines 'Reunion of national forces' and 'Not such enthusiasm since 1917,' stated:

> Bonfires and tar barrels illuminated Blackpool to-night where Mr. de Valera was accorded the greatest reception extended to any public man for several years. The crowd that awaited him at this point was estimated at twelve thousand. Many motor-cars attended. Headed by a torchlight procession of great length and three bands—Blackpool National Band, Erin's and Volunteer Pipers—the Fianna Fáil leader was escorted to the Grand Parade, where a crowd awaited him which extended from the National Monument to the Fountain. On reaching the Grand Parade Mr de Valera was taken from his motor and shouldered to the platform outside Fianna Fáil election premises amid scenes of great enthusiasm. Mr de Valera was unable to speak for some time owing to the loud and prolonged cheers which greeted him.[79]

When the applause died away, de Valera spoke of 'enemies' who divided the Irish people and said that 'we have been marching in opposite directions for years.' He said that Fianna Fáil had been formed to bring the two strands together again, and the huge gathering before him showed that that had been achieved.[80] His party had no fleet of motor cars to bring people to the polls, he said—a reference to the 'opulence' of Cumann na nGaedheal. He said he took heart from the presence of young people at the pre-election rally:

> Thank God we have young Ireland with us again. I know that the young people here tonight will come to the polls. I believe they will do as they did in the Roscommon election, when they brought the old people on their backs to the polls when the snow was on the ground.[81]

De Valera gained power; but that did little to alleviate the harshness of life for those living in Ireland in the 1930s.

DEATH OF NORA LYNCH
In October 1932 Jack Lynch suffered a devastating personal blow. His mother had been admitted to the North Infirmary (which was practically next door to

the Lynch home) for what was not thought to be a serious or life-threatening illness. She was forty-eight and had enjoyed relatively good health. Rena recalled that the children were not allowed to visit her in hospital. 'So, every day, at a specific time the children would wait outside the building and our mother would come to wave to us from a window.' Finbarr, after seventy years, still vividly remembered the details of the Thursday when she died. Cruelly, he recalled that she was to have been discharged the following day, and his two sisters were in town with two aunts buying clothes for her homecoming. In 2002 Rena too could still remember that day 'as if it were yesterday.'[82] A neighbour, not knowing that they were unaware of Mrs Lynch's death, stopped the children and their aunts to express condolence.[83]

Finbarr and Jack were at home alone when there was a knock on the door. Jack recalled: 'A nurse rushed up to the house from the North Infirmary to tell us that she had died.' Finbarr immediately went to his father, who was at work, to break the terrible news. 'He was devastated,' he recalled. Jack had gone to the hospital. He summed up years later what so many have felt in similar circumstances: 'I was absolutely shattered. I walked around the streets in a daze for hours before coming back home and for years later I was deeply affected by the loss.'[84] In 2002 Finbarr said simply, 'Our world collapsed.'

The death notice in the *Cork Examiner* records:

On October 5th 1932, at the North Infirmary Nora wife of Daniel Lynch and daughter of the late James and Margaret O'Donoughue, St Anne's Shandon. Deeply regretted R.I.P. remains removed from hospital this Friday evening at 7.30 o'clock. Funeral arrangements later.

The funeral Mass was held in the Cathedral Church at 2 p.m. on Saturday 7 October. Nora was buried at Caherlag.[85]

In the circumstances of that time, the Lynch family might have expected to be broken up, the brothers and sisters being sent to an orphanage or to an industrial school. Daniel struggled to keep his family together, and he had the support of his wife's extended family. The O'Donoghue sisters stepped in at that point. Daniel was out all day at work; who would take care of his six children? Jim Crockett remembered that Nora's sisters took over the washing and ironing and the care of the children. Statia, who lived nearby in 34 Roman Street, went every day to clean the house and cook for the children. He also recalled that the sisters met regularly in the Lynch house to discuss the future of their late sister's children. They were extremely ambitious for them, he said.[86]

But practical steps had to be taken to provide for the long-term maintenance of the Lynch children. Statia and her husband, Michael O'Reilly, an accountant working for Egan's jewellery shop, bought a bigger house at

Palaceanne Terrace, South Douglas Road (popularly known as Back Douglas Road), in order to provide a home for the two families. It was not an ideal solution and least of all for Daniel Lynch. One of Jim Crockett's most vivid memories of the time was of seeing 'Pappy' at night with a small ironing-board on his lap. He was always working to earn extra money. Sharing the house of his sister-in-law, while less than ideal, was a small price to pay for keeping his family together.

The move to the south side of the city lasted only about six months. Finbarr said that the children of the combined families felt 'like fish out of water' living in Douglas. They were supported now by two incomes, and the decision was taken to return north of the River Lee. Their new address was 'Clonard', 22 Redemption Road—a semi-detached house with four bedrooms. The last house in the Bishop's Field, at the top of Waters Lane,[87] it was a crowded but nevertheless a 'very happy home.'[88] The actor Niall Tóibín lived nearby.

NORTH MONASTERY AND SPORTING STARDOM
Jack Lynch had moved in 1925 from the convent school to the North Monastery school, run by the Christian Brothers. There he completed his primary and secondary education. After his Primary Certificate he com-peted for a corporation scholarship, in which he tied for tenth place. An additional grant was made that year to ensure that both boys received an award.[89] In all, he was at the North Monastery for eleven years.[90] He followed in the scholarly footsteps of his three brothers and was a member of the A class. There were, according to the roll-book, thirty-nine in his sixth and final year, 1935/6. His name was recorded as Seán Ó Loingsigh, his date of birth was recorded as 15-8-17, and his address was given as Clonard, Farranferris. His school attendance was 199 days. (The best recorded was 205.)[91] Michael Twomey was among Lynch's best friends at the North Monastery.[92] Tadhg Carey, a future president of University College, Cork, was also a member of that class.

While there was a strong emphasis on discipline in the school, Finbarr—who was in the class ahead of his brother—recalled the lay teachers and brothers as being fair. While corporal punishment was used, he did not remember the strap being used to excess. Brother Byrne (Irish and geography) was among the teachers who made a strong impression on that generation. An English-teacher, Dan Moore, and his brother Seán 'Pal' Moore, who taught maths, were greatly respected. Dan Moore was regarded by that generation of pupils as being a gifted and exceptional teacher. Jack Lynch developed his love for and competence in Irish from Father Tadhg Murphy, who used to bring classes to Baile an Fheirtéaraigh, later building a house there so the pupils might have more access to the Irish-speaking areas of Co. Kerry.[93] The school was noted for high academic achievement, and Lynch was among the best in the best class.

The North Monastery also had a high reputation for excellence in track and field sports, particularly hurling and football. During those early years in secondary school Jack Lynch followed his brothers Theo, Charlie and Finbarr as permanent members of the school teams, laying the foundations for a future legendary career as a player for Glen Rovers and as a dual star on the Cork hurling and football teams of the late 1930s and 40s. His many sporting honours included being on the North Monastery team in 1934, 1935 and 1936 that won the Harty Cup colleges senior hurling championship. He was also part of the school team that won the Munster colleges senior football cup in 1935 and 1936. He was captain in 1936 of the winning inter-provincial colleges senior hurling championship. He also won the Cork county schools and colleges 120-yard hurdles in 1936.

While still at secondary school, Jack also played for St Nicholas's Gaelic Football Club. This was a sister club to Glen Rovers, with which he was also playing at the time,[94] and there was a considerable overlapping of players in the two clubs and two games. The Lord Mayor of Cork, Tomás Mac Curtáin, murdered on 20 March 1920, had an association with St Nicholas's, as had also— but in a less direct way—Terence MacSwiney, who succeeded Mac Curtáin and died on hunger strike in Brixton Prison, London, on 25 October 1920.[95]

Jack Lynch's success as a hurler must be attributed as much to his membership of Glen Rovers as to the North Monastery.[96] Theo was the first of the brothers to join the 'Glen', and Charlie and Finbarr followed. Paddy O'Connell, known as the 'Father of the Glen', who worked in Goulding's fertiliser factory, trained the four brothers. Jack Lynch recalled:

> I was only ten years of age when I joined Glen Rovers in 1927. Paddy O'Connell, a member of the senior team himself, was in charge of all the Glen's under-age teams and took me under his experienced wing. He taught me so much that I figured on the Glen minor team when I was eleven, and managed to get my place on the Cork senior team when I was still in fifth year in the North Mon.[97]

O'Connell, who took Jack Lynch through street leagues and from juvenile to minor ranks, brought him at fourteen to his first all-Ireland game in Croke Park in 1931. 'I saw the first and third of the three matches between Cork and Kilkenny, although I believe that the second was far the best,' he said.[98] When reminiscing about those who influenced him at that time, Lynch remembered Mickey 'Wrennie' O'Brien, the trainer, Billy 'Ceann' O'Connor, a most competent chairman and a strict disciplinarian, and Capper Mullins, who repaired the hurleys. The Glen heroes of the day were Fox Collins, the first member of the club to win an all-Ireland, and Josa Lee and Willie 'Shelley' Hyland.[99] At the Glen, Lynch soon befriended his team-mates Jim Young from Dunmanway and Dan Coughlan from Ballydehob, once school rivals from Farranferris. They were joined by Joe Kelly.[100]

Jack Lynch's first senior game for the Glen was in 1934 at left half-back. He played in the semi-final of the championship against Seandún in the Mardyke. He did not have an inspiring game and afterwards was taken up before the chairman of the club, Billy O'Connor, who knew from his sluggish play that Lynch had been swimming as well as trying to play field sports. He was instructed to concentrate on hurling.[101] In the final Jack Lynch was brought on to replace the injured captain, Josa Lee. He won his place the following year and thereafter held it during a famous era in the history of the club. Beginning in 1934, Glen Rovers teams won eight consecutive county senior hurling championships. Lynch's career is recalled comprehensively in Liam Ó Tuama's collaborative commemorative volume, *The Spirit of the Glen*.[102]

In 1935 Jack Lynch made his debut for Cork in hurling in the National League. Lining out against Limerick, he was pitted against no less an opponent than the great Mick Mackey.[103] Lynch found him to be 'a fair though tough opponent.' At one point in the game Lynch fell in pain as they both went for a ball. His team-mates, thinking that Mackey had struck him, 'were about to take a course of action that they thought to be appropriate' when Lynch shouted to them: 'He did nothing to me. It's a cramp.'[104] His intervention came just in time.

Known primarily as a mid-fielder, Lynch moved later in his career into the half-forward line, where he partnered Jack Barrett and Con Cottrell. His Munster championship debut was in 1936, when Cork lost heavily in a replay to Clare. They were eliminated in 1937 and lost to Waterford in 1938.[105] But great sporting honours were to follow.

LEAVING CERTIFICATE, 1936: FROM FIRST JOB TO STUDY OF LAW

Jack Lynch sat his Leaving Certificate examination in 1936. He also did the examinations for teacher training, for clerical officer in the civil service and for the Electricity Supply Board. While he was awaiting the results, Finbarr, who was working in the Department of Agriculture in Dublin, heard about a temporary position that might suit Jack. Finbarr's former superior in the civil service, Seán Brennan, had become chairman of the newly established Dublin District Milk Board.[106] He was also chairman of the Civil Service Hurling Club and, according to Lynch, was 'as anxious to recruit new talent to the club as he was to the new Milk Board.' Finbarr contacted Jack, who was delighted to take the temporary job.[107] He lodged at 140 Cabra Road in Dublin; he later went back to the same digs when he returned to Dublin during the war. Finbarr rented a flat at 46 Upper Mount Street, ten doors from the offices of the Milk Board. That was to be a gathering place for all their Cork friends.[108]

Jack, who was accepted into the permanent civil service later in 1936, liked his temporary job and enjoyed living in Dublin. Yet Cork remained the centre of his sporting life. He was a star of the highly successful Glen Rovers and county teams while also playing football for Civil Service and St Nick's. He continued to work in Dublin until Christmas, 1936, when he received news that he had been accepted into the civil service, which meant that he would be assigned to a government department and would probably stay permanently in Dublin. However, good fortune made possible his return to Cork in a new position.[109] Following a minor scandal in the State Solicitor's Office in Cork, a decision was taken to staff the local courthouse with three civil servants.[110] Jack Lynch was among the 'three Cork boys' sent down to fill those positions, joining the court service on 29 December 1936.

> The County Registrar asked me to sit with him in court and after a while he let me take over as acting registrar, sitting in the court on my own until 1943. In the six to seven years I worked in the Circuit Court, I gained a knowledge of law and legal procedures and naturally developed an interest in it.[111]

In 1937 Lynch kept to his winning ways. He retained his place on the Cork county senior hurling championship team and on the Cork county intermediate football championship team. The following year, 1938, he was on the Cork county senior hurling championship team, the county senior football championship team and the Railway Cup inter-provincial hurling championship team. In his book Ó Tuama describes the place of that hero in his own childhood in the late 1930s and early 40s: 'To us as youngsters listening to what was being discussed around us about hurling, it seemed that Jack Lynch was just as important as the nightly rosary and took second place only to God.'[112]

Lynch contributed to that near-mythical reputation on 27 November 1938 while playing in the Cork county senior football championship in Inch field, Bandon. It had rained for three days and the pitch was 'quite a quagmire'. A large crowd, braving the elements and disregarding a soaking, saw the action through the 'muck and slush'. Jack Lynch was named twice in the *Cork Examiner's* report of a game described as being 'fast and furious'.[113] But the real drama in the match went unreported. With a few minutes to go, Clonakilty had no hope of catching their opponents. It is said that Mick Finn of Clonakilty either inadvertently or deliberately kicked the ball—the only ball available on the day—into the river in order to have the game abandoned. This interpretation is hotly disputed; but, according to the meta-narrative,

Lynch, spotting the danger of having to abandon the game and force a replay, jumped into the river and waded out to catch the precious ball as it was being swept downstream. A sodden Jack Lynch returned the ball to the field of play and finished out the game.[114] The Blackpool side beat Clonakilty by 2-1 to 0-2.

In 1939 Jack Lynch brought his extraordinary sporting career to new heights. Made captain of the first Cork hurling team to get to the all-Ireland final since 1931, he was on the losing side against a great rival, Kilkenny, in a final that is still being talked about and fought over. Played on 3 September, the day war was declared in Europe, it became known as the 'thunder and lightning' final. The second half of the match was played in a downpour. The *Irish Independent* reported:

> The game had just restarted when the crowd and players were startled by a clap of thunder. It was a portent of things to come. What followed was a thunderstorm of extraordinary proportions with thunder and lightning accompanying a heavy downpour. So bad did conditions become that spectators could not make out the identity of some of the players, leading to confusion immediately afterwards over the identity of the Kilkenny player who scored the winning point.[115]

After falling behind in the first half by 2-4 to 1-1, the Cork players, according to the same report, 'had found their feet and mounted a spirited fight-back. Lynch started with a goal . . .'[116] Lynch recalled that, 'Yes, it was a raging storm, and rain came down like stair rods. At times, it was impossible to see more than 20 yards away from you. Conditions were almost unplayable.'[117] In the game he found himself straight in front of the goal.

> The ball came right across in front of the square but just exactly on the line, and I hit it on the ground, angling the hurley downwards to make sure I wouldn't skew it over the bar. That's exactly what happened. I remember Jimmy O'Connell, the Kilkenny goalkeeper, looking around the back of the net for the ball, and then when he saw the white flag going up he looked around and kind of laughed at me, as if to say, 'you didn't expect that one!' or something like that.

The final score was Kilkenny 2-7, Cork 3-3, a margin of a single point. Was the 'seventy', as the legendary commentator Mícheál O'Hehir maintained, taken from the wrong line? Was too little time played? Thus the controversy raged and continues to provoke discussion.

Lynch was again on the Cork team in 1940. They were knocked out in the Munster final by Limerick, and the epic struggle was settled by a single point after a replay. Con Murphy, who had been a few classes behind Lynch in North Monastery, played with him on the county team for a number of years. He recalled Lynch's calm authority and toughness. He remembered playing in a Munster final in Thurles (not 1940) and recalled John Mackey of Limerick moving from the full-forward line back towards centre-field. He returned a few minutes later with a cut to his face and told his opponent, Con Murphy, 'Lynch gave me a poke,' and added: 'But what in the name of Jesus was I doing out there anyway.'[118] Lynch was respected on and off the field.

After a wait of ten years, Cork won the first of the four-in-a-row all-Irelands in 1941. It was a most unusual year, as the normal pattern of qualification had been disrupted because of a severe outbreak of foot-and-mouth disease. Travel restrictions were imposed as a result, in addition to wartime fuel shortages. Lynch found himself during those war years travelling to a game down the country by taxi paid for by the GAA. He would pass many of his civil service colleagues going to the game on bicycles and found it absurd that he was not allowed to give any of them a lift.[119] Played at a time of travel restriction and petrol shortages, the game attracted a small attendance of 26,150. Connie Buckley of Glen Rovers captained Cork against Dublin on that occasion. It was a one-sided affair, Cork winning by 5-11 to 0-6. The star of the day was a twenty-year-old called Christy Ring, who scored three points.

Jack Lynch was named Cork captain in 1942. But they had great difficulty getting beyond the Munster championship. The game against Limerick was the most memorable of that campaign. Cork snatched a two-point victory in the closing seconds of what was described by Jim Young of Dunmanway as 'the greatest game of hurling I ever played in.' The score was Cork 4-8, Limerick 5-3. Cork went on to beat Tipperary in the Munster final by 4-15 to 4-1.[120] Beating Galway easily in the semi-final, they went on to face Dublin in the all-Ireland final for a second year in a row. One commentator wrote of Lynch's performance: 'All through this half the challengers were outclassed at centre-field where Jack Lynch ruled the roost, and it was a splendid performance to hold the champions to so close a margin with this handicap.'[121] They won by 2-14 to 3-4, Jack Lynch and Christy Ring each scoring three points.

A future political correspondent of the *Irish Times*, Dick Walsh, recalled watching Lynch on a much later occasion playing against Limerick.

Taut as a coiled spring in a red jersey as he shot a point for Cork which set the crowd in Limerick's Gaelic Grounds reeling with admiration. The best of it was that as he crouched by the sideline 40 yards out, he knew he could depend on wrist and eye; he wasn't going to miss. 'There you are,' said my father, 'and he's a TD and a barrister to boot.' 'Or not to boot,' said the cool Corkman beside us. 'Didn't he throw the boots away at half time.' You could tell the story about many another player-turned-politician—if they were good enough—but only in Lynch's case is it close to being the whole truth.[122]

Lynch deserved his reputation as a great athlete. In one day he turned out for Civil Service in a senior league hurling match in the morning; he then dashed to Croke Park to play on the winning Munster side against Ulster in the Railway Cup hurling semi-final; and immediately after that game he lined out with the Munster footballers. He scored in all thee games.[123]

However, Lynch was not merely a sports star. He had set out to study law. David Marcus, author and literary editor, wrote of first meeting Jack Lynch in the autumn of 1941. As he was walking up the main avenue of University College, Cork, to sign on to study law,

> a man drew abreast of me on a bicycle, stopped, dismounted, and said, 'You're David Marcus?' 'Yes,' I answered. 'I'm Jack Lynch,' he said. 'I'm doing the Bar with you.'

Knowing nothing about Gaelic games, Marcus was one of the few people in Cork who did not recognise such a great sports star and local hero.[124]

> What struck me immediately about Jack was his athletic build—not until I later learned of his sporting fame did I see the reason for it. In addition, his firm facial bone-structure gave him a handsomeness that was often enriched by a warm smile. And he was an easy talker.[125]

Together they formed the entire UCC law class for 1941.

Lynch sometimes went home to the Marcus house in the evening to study. David Marcus recalled in a letter that his father was 'a very keen talker,'[126] and he wrote in his memoirs:

> Jack would arrive on his bicycle on one or two evenings most weeks, and we would spend a few hours together on our books before adjourning to the kitchen for cocoa and sandwiches, where Jack and my father would chat like old friends on the ways of the world.[127]

Marcus and Lynch went on to Dublin together to study and qualify at King's Inns.[128] The two then went their separate ways, Marcus to London and Lynch to a career at the bar and into politics. Their paths crossed again nearly thirty years later at one of the most critical points in the political life of Jack Lynch.[129]

MEETING WITH MAIRIN O'CONNOR

Lynch had personal as well as professional reasons for wishing to return to Dublin. In the summer of 1943 he had met Máirín O'Connor, a Dubliner who joined the civil service as a clerical officer in 1934[130] and worked in the Department of Industry and Commerce.[131] She went on summer holidays with a friend, Beryl Fagan, to Glengarriff, Co. Cork.[132] They booked into the Golf Links Hotel and were given a room over the bar. There was a terrible row every night from below, Máirín recalled. Upon enquiring, she discovered that prominent members of the Cork hurling team were among those taking part in the nightly festivities. In fact there were four in the party: Jack Lynch, Jim 'Tough' Barry, Pat Donovan and Frank Casey. Jack Lynch was in the holiday party but he was also training for the coming all-Ireland final against Antrim.[133]

When Máirín O'Connor heard them speak together she was hardly able to understand a word any of them said. Try as she might, it was impossible to follow their conversation. Only later did she discover that Jack Lynch and his three companions had agreed to speak with the 'Coal Quay' accent and vocabulary for the entire stay (the Coal Quay being the site of a famous street market in Cork). That did not deter her. She had observed Jack Lynch's swift, easy and elegant style on the training field on previous days. He moved with grace, she recalled after his death. Her curiosity and interest grew, and one day she casually asked his name from one of the group. 'Don't you know?' was the amazed reply. 'That's Jack Lynch.'[134]

Without knowing many of the details about his legendary sports career, Máirín's interest burgeoned during that summer holiday. One evening, as people gathered around the piano, Máirín said that her friend would like to sing. She could be quite forthright when the occasion demanded (as Lynch would learn, to his benefit, later in life). The friend in question, Beryl Fagan, was a fine singer and played the piano.[135] A strong friendship between Máirín and Jack Lynch developed during that holiday. 'It was love at first sight,' Finbarr recalled in 2002. Throughout their later life together Jack would occasionally tease Máirín by lapsing into 'Coal Quay' argot.

Máirín, for the first time in her life, was in Croke Park in September 1943 to watch Cork and Antrim play in the all-Ireland hurling final. A crowd of 48,000 watched Jack Lynch and the Cork team win by 5-16 to 0-04. The world of the GAA was foreign to the future Mrs Jack Lynch. Born in Dublin on 14 August 1916, Máirín O'Connor was an only child. Her mother, Margaret Doyle, was from a farm in Co. Meath. She married Arthur O'Connor, a medical student from Dublin; Máirín's birth certificate lists his profession simply as 'gentleman'. They lived at 5 Abercorn Terrace in Inchicore. Máirín heard from her mother that her father was a great lover of music and sang with the Rathmines and

Rathgar Musical Society. According to Máirín, her father had joined the British navy during the First World War and was lost in action. She has only one fragmented memory of her father coming down the stairs in uniform in their family home. He held her in his arms while she played with the shiny buttons on his jacket. But how reliable is such a memory?[136]

Her mother did not remarry. She worked as an administrator with the Irish Industrial Development Association,[137] which was renamed first the National Agricultural and Industrial Development Association and then the Federation of Irish Manufacturers. Mrs O'Connor worked with Elizabeth Somers, a formidable driving force. She also worked with Erskine Childers, who served first as secretary to the NAIDA and then as secretary to the FIM before he became a minister in 1944.[138] She dedicated her professional life to promoting the products of Irish industry and to the 'buy Irish' campaign. Máirín recalled visiting as a child the head office in O'Connell Street, where 'all the great people of those days would wander into my mother's office. Maude Gonne McBride—she was very beautiful. Madame [Charlotte] Despard, in big boots and tweeds. Lord Ashbourne in his green kilt.'

Because there was nobody to look after her in their flat, Máirín would accompany her mother to the annual dinners of the association.[139] In the early 1960s the president of the FIM, Gordon Lambert, presented a prize in her honour to the organisers of the annual St Patrick's Day industrial parade, the Margaret O'Connor Perpetual Trophy.

Máirín was raised in a strongly nationalist household, with an emphasis on industrial nationalism. The 'buy Irish' philosophy permeated her childhood and political formation. When growing up she always wore Irish-made clothes. Generations of Irish people will remember the rough vests manufactured in Cork by Sunbeam Wolsey. She would jokingly remind Jack Lynch in later life that she had 'scratched for Ireland' and that the GAA was not the only patriotic organisation in the country.[140] Mrs O'Connor was 'an ardent Devite—though not at all a party woman.'[141] Through the influence of her mother, Máirín voted Fianna Fáil.

Máirín spent thirteen years during the 1920s and early 30s being educated by the Dominican nuns at Muckross Park convent school in Donnybrook. She was a weekly boarder, returning home to her mother at weekends. One of her classmates, who later joined the Dominican order, recalls how the boarders used to visit Mrs O'Connor in her office. There was a shop attached that sold Irish produce. 'Mrs O'Connor never allowed us go back to school unless each of us received gifts of the sample jams and marmalades,' the nun recalls.[142]

Máirín was a good pupil, with an aptitude for mathematics but not for languages. She was independent-minded and not afraid to defend her point of view in public. In religion class on one occasion she told her teacher that she did not understand the three-in-one concept of the Trinity. Notwithstanding the fact that the mystery of the Trinity has defied explanation for centuries, the religion teacher ordered her out of the class, not readmitting her for a number of weeks.[143] She was a high-spirited, hard-working pupil with an independent cast of mind. Her education strengthened her interest in dressmaking and fashion and developed in her a strong attachment to music and an appreciation of modern art.

She was an accomplished sportswoman, playing hockey and tennis in school to a high competitive level. Hockey was her first love. She was also among the pupils who introduced camogie to Muckross. However, she came late to the game. She recalled: 'It was just that the few of us were so bad and awkward trying to learn it, after playing hockey for so long.' But, according to a girl who played with her, 'they had a good team.'[144]

On leaving Muckross Park, Máirín would have liked to go to university or to study dress design. Even if the family's financial situation had been better, she had no wish to leave her mother to pursue her studies outside Dublin. She attended the Dominicans' commercial college in Eccles Street, where she further developed her interest in camogie. The school had a 'wonderful camogie team,' she recalled in 2002. 'They won everything, were like greyhounds and a dream to watch—like Jack Lynch playing hurling. How I miss him!'[145]

In 1934 she successfully sat the examinations for the civil service and had a choice between the Department of Industry and Commerce and the Department of External Affairs. Because of the family interest in the promotion of Irish goods and her closeness to her mother, she chose the former and worked there from 1934 until the marriage bar obliged her to leave her post in 1946. Jack Lynch would later serve as Minister for Industry and Commerce between 1959 and 1965.

In her leisure time Máirín played tennis as a member of Kenilworth Square Tennis Club. She continued to play hockey with Maids of the Mountain. There she first met Gordon Lambert, who was later to become managing director of Jacob and Company, the biscuit manufacturers. In the 1960s he became a close friend of Jack and Máirín Lynch. Lynch made him a senator in 1977. He recalled in 1979: 'Come to think of it, Máirín and I used to play mixed hockey on Sundays, she for the Maids of the Mountain and I for Three Rock Rovers.'[146] In 1945 Máirín captained Maids of the Mountain to victory in the Leinster intermediate league.[147] The same year she led the team to victory in the H. M. White cup, played between the winners of provincial leagues at junior level.[148]

Working in Dublin in 1943, Jack Lynch became private secretary to the secretary of the Department of Justice, Stephen A. Roche. The two men got on very well together. Roche allowed Lynch off early from work in order for him to be on time for his law lecture at 4:30. In the congenial environment of the Department of Justice he gained further administrative experience at a high level. He was a popular member of the staff—unlike his slightly older contemporary and later secretary of the department, Peter Berry.[149] Lynch was called to the bar in 1945.

Meanwhile his relationship with Máirín developed. On the first occasion that she brought him home to meet her mother, little did he realise that he would be secretly subjected to the 'buy Irish' test. Beforehand, the formidable Mrs O'Connor told her daughter—perhaps not entirely without an element of seriousness—that it would be the end of a beautiful relationship if her new friend was wearing a foreign-made hat. Lynch innocently handed Mrs O'Connor his hat in the hallway. Upon examination, it was discovered that it had been made by T. O'Gorman's Cork Cap Factory, a firm to which Lynch gave lifelong loyalty.[150]

Jack and Máirín were married on 10 August 1946. The couple remained close to Mrs O'Connor throughout their life. When she was in her eighties, in the 1960s, her only daughter persuaded her to give up her flat and live with them at 21 Garville Avenue, Rathgar, and she lived there until she was admitted to the Rehabilitation Centre, Dún Laoghaire, after suffering a stroke. She died on 23 November 1967.

HIGH HONOURS AND THE END OF A DISTINGUISHED SPORTING CAREER

Máirín O'Connor was in Croke Park in September 1943 to watch Jack Lynch, playing again in mid-field, help defeat Antrim convincingly. In 1944 Lynch missed the semi-final against Galway because of injury; but he resumed his place at mid-field for the all-Ireland final against Dublin. His performance won him praise in the *Irish Press*: 'At centre-field Lynch and Con Cottrell struck up a marvellously successful partnership and their sound and spectacular feats paved the way for the forwards to the all-important scores.'[151]

Although Lynch was one of the stars in Ireland's sporting life during the war years, he did not receive the type of pampering bestowed on high-profile sports people of later generations. Evidence of this is to be found in a letter he wrote to the former Cork star and selector Jim Hurley in July 1945:

I wrote to Seán Óg [Murphy] last Monday and asked him to mention to you that I had hurt my ankle in the last few minutes of the game in Thurles last Sunday. It was very sore then but it must have been only a knock as it has improved considerably. If the improvement keeps up I think it will be alright for next Sunday. The question of travelling is my main difficulty now. My leave allowance has suffered considerably of late—a week for the exams, a day for my call to the bar and a day last weekend. The trip to Killarney would mean two further days and all this out of my 21 days total allowance is pretty serious, particularly in view of the fact that I haven't had my summer holidays yet.

Lynch wondered whether it would be possible

to get a lift back to Dublin on Sunday. If you know of any car you might enquire for me. There are no journalists going from Dublin and I've been trying to contact Paddy Kennedy [of Co. Kerry] without success for the past few days to see if he has a car. It would be far too expensive to hire a car. Since I wrote the last time I've just rung up a pal in the Dept. of Supplies who tells me that a permit is being issued to P. Kennedy for himself Garvey and Lawlor. I'll make it my business to contact him tonight and ask him for a lift. I suppose I may pay him a reasonable sum for the seat if I'm successful.

But he then asked:

What about Crone? I'm sure I'd be lucky to get a seat for myself without asking for a second. However I hope to hear from you by Saturday morning. Ps. ask the trainer to bring along a supply of cotton wool—it would be helpful to my ankle if I'll be required to play.[152]

Hurley wrote on the letter: 'Lynch, seven Brigton Rd., Rathgar, cost of seat assured.'[153] Lynch got his lift and, if he was lucky, may also have got the cotton wool.

Knocked out in the Munster hurling championship in 1945 by Tipperary, Lynch was not starved of honours that year. The Cork football team reached the all-Ireland final, beating Cavan by 2-5 to 0-7. Lynch helped his county regain their first football title for thirty-four years. In 1946 he won his fifth all-Ireland senior hurling championship medal when Cork beat Kilkenny by 7-5 to 3-8 before a crowd of 64,000 (with 5,000 locked outside) in an epic game in which Christy Ring scored one of the greatest goals of his career. 'Ring's wonder goal kept title in Cork,' announced the *Cork Examiner* headline.[154] Cork were back in the all-Ireland hurling final in 1947 to face Kilkenny before a crowd of 61,000. It was a classic final and regarded as one of the best ever played. Many years later Lynch recalled: 'I had the equalising of the game twice in the closing minutes but hit wide on both occasions. It was the end of an era.'[155] Kilkenny won by 0-14 to 2-7. Nine players had appeared in Cork's four consecutive hurling all-Ireland victories. Lynch won six all-Ireland titles in a row, making him one of the all-time greats.

Con Murphy, who played behind Lynch on the Cork team for many years, was in a good position to assess the sporting prowess of the future Taoiseach.[156] He described him as being extremely competitive, courageous and a great athlete. He had limbs and bones like tree trunks and was a great reader of the game. In man-to-man marking he never saw Lynch beaten by an opponent in all those years of playing at the highest level.

> I never saw him outclassed or out-played. He had a natural quality of leadership that brought him automatically to the fore. He had charisma but he never pushed himself forward. He took decisions on the field. Players came to rely upon his judgment and followed his instructions. He was intelligent and articulate. He conveyed the impression that he was in charge. I was struck repeatedly by his shrewdness in being able to judge the performance of his own team. He would give advice at half time and it was always well received. He never put people down or belittled them. What he had to say would be said in a few words and he would say it kindly. He was a good judge of players and I never once heard his decision being questioned by a fellow player.[157]

In 1950 Lynch won another hurling county championship with Glen Rovers against their arch-rivals, St Finbarr's. In a somewhat one-sided game Lynch took a pass from his team-mate Christy Ring and scored a goal. The final result was 2-6 to 0-5. It was a sweet victory against the traditional rivals and a fitting end to a great sporting career. In 1951 Lynch showed wisdom when he refused an invitation from the captain of Glen Rovers, Seán O'Brien, to play in the county semi-final against Blackrock.[158] He promised: 'But I'll be there to cheer you and the boys on to yet another County Final.' Here was a frank but firm admission that his competitive career in field sports was over.

Foolishly, he allowed himself to be persuaded to tog out one more time. On his way from a meeting in Ottawa he visited Gaelic Park in New York in 1952 and was persuaded by Paddy Barry of Glen Rovers to play for only ten minutes for the visiting Cork side. Watching a ball he had sent towards the goal, Lynch received 'a charge with a hurley in the ribs.' He went down in pain but played the whole match. When he was travelling home the ship's doctor diagnosed a few broken ribs. 'That was the last hurling match I ever played,' he said.[159] Lynch's competitive career stretched from 1929, when he was twelve, until his retirement in 1951 at the age of thirty-four. He played in no fewer than seventy-nine championship and league finals.[160]

At the end of his life Jack Lynch decided to donate his medals and trophies to the GAA museum at Croke Park. 'His career with St Nick's, Glen Rovers and Cork', according to Dave Hannigan, 'yielded five all-Ireland hurling medals (four in a row, of course), one all-Ireland football, ten Cork county senior hurling championships (eight in a row), three National Hurling Leagues, three Railway Cups, two Cork county senior football championships and a Dublin senior football title with Civil Service.'[161] In February 1996 Con Murphy went with Liam Ó Tuama and Liam Mulvihill to Lynch's home to collect his impressive collection.[162] Murphy recalled that Lynch, now enfeebled by serious illness and only a shadow of his former self, betrayed uncharacteristic emotion as he handed the unique collection to his visitors: 'Take good care of them. They were hard won.'[163]

Chapter 2 ～

JOURNEYMAN POLITICIAN: BACKBENCH TD AND PARLIAMENTARY SECRETARY, 1948–57

O n stepping down as Taoiseach in 1979, Jack Lynch said that the warm praise given to him belonged more properly to his wife, Máirín, for her pivotal role in his success in public life. Máirín Lynch was a partner of great depth and solid judgement, from whom he constantly drew strength in his political battles.[1] They were a formidable partnership, and only a rank sexist would diminish her significance.[2] She revealed in 2000 that her husband never stopped her from saying anything in public. He might say to her casually, 'You should give this matter some more thought.' Máirín Lynch married a very calm and controlled person. But, she said, 'he was no saint.'[3]

The couple began their married life together in Cork, where Lynch was making his way as a newly qualified barrister. They lived in a rented flat in the South Mall. Jack and Máirín Lynch quickly learnt that they could not have children. They considered adoption and took the first steps in the process in 1947[4]; but that did not happen, for unknown reasons. The friendship of a fellow-barrister, Stephen Barrett, and his wife, Betty, proved to be a great support. Betty took Máirín under her wing, introduced her to Cork 'society', and helped her to settle in to the city. The couple regularly visited the Barrett household in Douglas. Always interested in dressmaking, Máirín made her own clothes and taught the Barrett daughters, Stephanie and Colette, how to cut out patterns.[5] Lynch and Barrett were young barristers, relatively new to the circuit. When one or other had secured a brief, which paid one guinea, the two couples often celebrated together by going to dinner at the Oyster Grill and then wondering about tomorrow's dinner, Máirín said.[6] She admitted in a press interview that she wished her husband had continued his law career, because 'she had never wanted to be a political wife.'[7] The two men remained steadfast friends, despite in 1948 one becoming a TD for Fianna Fáil and the other for Fine Gael.

Lynch's decision to seek a nomination for Dáil Éireann was neither pre-ordained nor inevitable. His sister Rena said that he had no overt interest in politics as a young man. Because of his sporting prowess, however, the members of different parties 'had a path worn to the door trying to get him to join various political parties,' she said.[8] In June 1946 Fianna Fáil asked him to stand in a by-election. Maurice Forde, Pat McNamara, Bill Barry and Garrett McAuliffe of the Brothers Delaney Cumann of Fianna Fáil in his native Blackpool made the offer in the Lynch flat in Summer Hill.[9]

After fourteen consecutive years in power Fianna Fáil faced a backlash over the prolongation of wartime rationing, a wage freeze and general fiscal austerity. However, that was not the reason why he refused to stand. Lynch knew that his friend Patrick 'Pa' McGrath, a Civil War veteran and lifelong member of Fianna Fáil, was seeking the nomination. Declining the offer, he said he might stand the next time.[10] Lynch canvassed on behalf of his friend, making his first recorded political speech in Blackpool on a platform shared with the candidate and a founder-member of the party and Minister for Finance, Frank Aiken.[11] The latter's attack on Fine Gael was extensively reported in the *Cork Examiner*.[12] The Minister for Lands, Seán Moylan, also spoke in support of the candidate. Two sitting Fianna Fáil TDs for Cork City, Seán MacCarthy and Walter Furlong, gave short speeches, the latter stating that Fianna Fáil was 'a workers' government, interested in John Citizen, his wife and family.'[13] The *Cork Examiner*, in the final line of its report, stated: 'Mr. J. Lynch, B.L. presided.' He had confined himself 'to extolling the virtues of "Pa" McGrath,' but his exact words went unrecorded. McGrath won the seat on the second count.[14]

Seán MacBride, a former chief of staff of the IRA and well-known defence counsel, founded Clann na Poblachta in 1946. Lynch was invited to join the party and was offered a nomination in the next general election.[15] His brother Finbarr said that the approach had come through Con Lehane.[16] There were also unsubstantiated rumours in Cork at the time that Lynch was sympathetic to Fine Gael,[17] though Finbarr was unaware of any offers to his brother from that party. At one point Lynch sought advice from a senior legal colleague about a career in politics. The Fine Gael barrister told him bluntly to stand for Fianna Fáil, as that party 'looked after its own.'[18] Seán Casey, who later became a Labour Party TD, may also have asked him to stand for that party.[19]

With the approach of the 1948 general election, the Brothers Delaney Cumann and Tom Crofts, chairman of the Fianna Fáil comhairle ceantair (district council), approached Lynch to go for a nomination. Tim Barry, the Cork trainer and a strong Fianna Fáil activist, also approached him on the same topic. Lynch allowed his name to go forward to the Fianna Fáil convention, which took place on the same evening as a law dinner he attended in the

Metropole Hotel. At that time he was not a member of Fianna Fáil, but he soon joined the Brothers Delaney Cumann and remained a lifelong member.

His Cork team-mate Con Murphy remembered being a little surprised to hear about Jack Lynch's decision to enter national politics, but he knew that 'he would make a go of it' once he had set his mind to it.[20] Daniel Lynch was most unenthusiastic about his son's decision to enter politics. 'Have you not achieved enough already as a sportsman and a barrister?' one of the family overheard Daniel ask him as he tried to persuade him not to stand. Once he had been elected to the Dáil, his father called the family together and gave instructions that none of them was ever to ask him for any political or personal favours while he was in public life.[21]

The calling of a general election for 4 February 1948 had been expected for some time. Despite the Dáil having a year to run, there had been rumours for some months that Fianna Fáil might go early to the country. But, facing two difficult by-elections, de Valera tried unsuccessfully to use the tactic of surprise employed in 1933, 1938 and 1944 and dissolved the Dáil on 11 January 1948. Facing a dreaded winter campaign, Fianna Fáil ran on its post-war record. Unemployment was at a high level throughout the country, and there was increasing emigration to the newly established welfare state in Britain. Wages were kept under strict control. Wartime rationing continued, though in a less severe form. The country also faced bad summers and severe winters in 1946 and 47.

The redrawing of the constituency boundaries had created considerable uncertainty and apprehension among candidates in the Cork area. The two four-seat and one five-seat constituencies were changed to one five-seater in Cork City and four three-seat constituencies in the county.[22] Fianna Fáil needed to win extra seats in the city. Jack Lynch, a man of great popularity, was a welcome addition to the ticket for the party but not for his Fianna Fáil running-mates, Walter Furlong, Patrick 'Pa' McGrath and Seán MacCarthy. The constituency had an electorate of 62,626.[23] Fianna Fáil had polled 14,230 in 1944 to Fine Gael's 9,707, socialist (Michael O'Riordan) 3,184 and independent (Tom Barry) 2,547. In the presidential election in 1945 Seán T. O'Kelly had won 13,875, Seán Mac Eoin 9,025 and Patrick McCartan 4,714.[24] Fianna Fáil had won a by-election in 1946.

There were sixteen candidates for Cork City's five seats. Lynch was running with three other Fianna Fáil candidates. Fine Gael brought in the party's deputy leader and sitting TD for Leix-Offaly, Dr T. F. O'Higgins, to win back the Cork City seat held by William T. Cosgrave until his retirement from public life in 1944. It also put forward three other candidates: Stephen Declan Barrett, David Allen and Michael Sheehan. Patrick McCartan, John F. Fennessy and Liam Stack were put up by Clann na Poblachta. The Labour

Party put up Richard Sidney Anthony and Seán Casey, while James Hickey and Seán Ó Dubhghaill were the candidates for the rival National Labour Party.[25] The lord mayor, Michael Sheehan of Ballintemple, stood as an independent.[26] Polling day was 4 February and the new Dáil was to meet on 18 February 1948.

Jack Lynch enjoyed many advantages. He was a sports hero with a growing legal practice. He had a warm personality and a winning way with people from all social backgrounds. He had a very astute and supportive wife, and he could rely on his friends in the sporting world to campaign enthusiastically for him. Many members of Glen Rovers, with whom Lynch had played since the early 1930s and continued to play at the time of the election, took an active part in the election 'and did a personalised canvass for me.' When that caused trouble in the Fianna Fáil camp Lynch requested his club-mates not to continue with the canvass, but 'they argued that it was purely a private matter for them and didn't involve the Fianna Fáil party.' Lynch 'went so far as to impound the personal canvass cards but they got another supply.' He finally persuaded those supporters to ask for support for the other Fianna Fáil candidates at the doors.[27]

Lynch's first electoral campaign was not widely reported by either the *Cork Examiner* or the *Evening Echo*. At the foot of the page, under the heading 'Irish workers returning in big numbers,' he was quoted in the *Cork Examiner* on 9 January 1948 as saying: 'A general election is the essence of democracy.' Defending the record of the outgoing Government, he said that it had recently been forced to introduce new taxes. Fianna Fáil, he said, could easily have waited for better times and the end of those taxes and then, its popularity restored, asked for an election. But the party did not choose that course, because it respected the democratic system. Lynch spoke of wartime emigration as having been inevitable when Britain was short of labour. Now Irish workers were coming home, he said, in ever-increasing numbers and our industries were returning to normal and expanding.[28]

On 11 January 1948, the day of the dissolution of the Dáil, Lynch returned to the question of emigration. Speaking on a platform with the three other Fianna Fáil candidates at North Gate Bridge, he said that about 27,000 people annually had emigrated from Ireland before Fianna Fáil came to power. That annual number, he said, had dropped in 1938 to 8,000. During the war, he said, emigration was inevitable, but even now people were coming back in considerable numbers.[29]

Lynch was not a very good public speaker during that campaign. Máirín recalled: 'I always remember the first time he was asked to stand for election. He was on the back of a lorry in Cork and I was outside the cathedral, hidden at the back. He couldn't get a word out edgeways. I was stuck to the railings! To this day I get hot under the collar when I think of it.'[30] Despite her criticism of his oratory, Máirín observed at the time that her husband had the common touch. Door-to-door canvassing gave her the first insight into the deep respect that ordinary people had for him, and for her too, she said. She could see how much he respected the people of the city.[31] Dr Patrick Hillery said that campaigning with Lynch in Cork was like being in the company of Cú Chulainn.[32] Toddy O'Sullivan, a Labour Party TD for many years, said that fighting an election against Lynch was like taking on the whole of Glen Rovers.

Fianna Fáil, after sixteen years in power, had money to spend on newspaper advertising. The *Cork Examiner*, despite its editorial hostility to the de Valera government, received a good share of the party's campaign revenue. One advertisement read: 'Fianna Fáil has the capacity for leadership, the unity, and the know how.' The text defended the party's industrial policies over the previous sixteen years, emphasising the help given to private enterprise and the placing of factories in secondary, medium-sized towns. 'Every city and town will be helped to develop a variety of industrial employments which Fianna Fáil regards as necessary for the growth of healthy social conditions.' The party's policy was to provide 'wider and more varied opportunities of employment for men and women.'[33]

Fianna Fáil sent its most influential campaigners to Cork. Éamon de Valera came and stayed in Blackrock with his friends the Dowdalls. On Saturday 17 January, a few hours before the public meeting, Lynch met his party leader for the first time in the home of his friends. He found that de Valera was anxious to find out the local issues before his speech. Lynch confessed: 'I had a reverential awe for him but at that meeting I found him very human.' Candidate and party leader went together to the big election rally in Patrick Street, the main street in Cork. In the course of that speech de Valera touched on a sensitive local issue. The president of University College, Cork, Dr Alfred O'Rahilly, criticised the outgoing Government's failure to address 'the exodus of nationals and the invasion of non-nationals,' accusing the Government of not wishing to fight an election on such an issue.[34] De Valera depicted O'Rahilly as an armchair critic, living inside an academic ivory tower, composing homilies for angels.[35] O'Rahilly, in his defence, recalled that the *Irish Independent* had published on 15 February 1932 a Cumann na nGaedheal advertisement stating: 'The Communists are voting for Fianna Fáil.' He had defended Fianna Fáil and de Valera vigorously on that occasion, as he was now defending that party's opponents against identical charges. He called for an end to the degradation of public life through 'this campaign of mud-slinging,' concluding, 'Arguments, gentlemen, please.'[36]

There was a high turn-out on 4 February in the Cork Borough constituency. The *Evening Echo* reported: 'Although it is impossible to say at such an early stage who are the likely successes, candidates who appear to have polled heavily were the Lord Mayor (councillor M. Sheehan), Ind., Mr. J. Lynch, B.L., Fianna Fáil and T. O'Higgins, Fine Gael.'[37] The *Cork Examiner* reported on 6 February:

> In Cork City, the first count took five hours, but there were sixteen candidates. Dr. T. F. O'Higgins, Deputy Fine Gael leader, headed the list in Cork and after him came the well known All-Ireland Gael, Mr. Jack Lynch, B.L. whose first election campaign this is. The Lord Mayor of Cork, Mr. Ml. Sheehan was also near the top of the list.[38]

When all the votes were counted, the results were as follows:

GENERAL ELECTION TO THE THIRTEENTH DAIL, 1948 (147 SEATS)[39]
Polling day: 4 February 1948

Constituency and number of seats	Electorate and quota	Candidates	Affiliation	First preferences
Cork Borough (5)	62,626 Quota 7,480	1. Thomas Francis O'Higgins (sen.)	FG	7,351
		2. John (Jack) Lynch	FF	5,594
		3. Patrick (Pa) McGrath	FF	5,092
		4. Michael Sheehan (Ballintemple)	Ind.	4,898
		5. James Hickey	Nat. Lab.	4,507
		Walter Furlong	FF	3,601
		Seán MacCarthy	FF	2,747
		Richard Sidney Anthony	Lab.	2,688
		Patrick McCartan	C. na P.	2,346
		Stephen Declan Barrett	FG	1,496
		John J. Fennessy	C. na P.	1,423
		Seán Casey	Lab.	987
		David Allen	FG	911
		Liam Stack	C. na P.	565
		Michael Sheehan (Blackrock)	FG	409
		Seán Ó Dubhghaill	Nat. Lab.	260

It took fourteen counts to complete the constituency. O'Higgins was the first to be elected, on the sixth count. The *Cork Examiner* reported:

The closeness of the voting was further emphasised by the fact that eleven counts were necessary before another candidate was elected, who was Mr. Jack Lynch B.L., youngest member of the Fianna Fáil team and one of Cork's best known exponents of Gaelic games.[40]

Pa McGrath was also returned. Michael Sheehan (independent) won a seat, as did James Hickey of the National Labour Party. Three sitting deputies,Seán MacCarthy, Richard Anthony (Labour Party) and Walter Furlong (Fianna Fáil), lost their seats. That represented a gain for Fine Gael at the expense of Fianna Fáil and a gain for National Labour.[41]

When the votes were counted nationally, Fianna Fáil lost power to a five-party alliance of Fine Gael, Labour, National Labour, Clann na Poblachta and Clann na Talmhan.[42] Out of 147 seats, Fianna Fáil got 68, Fine Gael 31, Labour Party 14, Clann na Poblachta 10, Clann na Talmhan 7, National Labour Party 5, and independents and others 14.[43] On the day that John A. Costello was elected Taoiseach, Paddy Lindsay, a future Fine Gael minister, drove into Tuam, Co. Galway, and asked a member of the Garda Síochána the result. He replied: 'At ten past five this afternoon, Mr John Aloysius Costello was elected Taoiseach of this country.' When offered a drink, the garda replied: 'We'll have two.' As Lindsay had parked awkwardly, he asked the garda to wait while he parked the car. 'Leave it where it is. We have freedom for the first time in sixteen years.' Both men had more than one drink that day.[44]

BACKBENCH TD

Jack Lynch entered Dáil Éireann as an opposition backbencher. He spoke often in the chamber and his frequent interventions brought him to the attention of Éamon de Valera, who persuaded him to take on the jobs of party researcher and secretary to the parliamentary party. Lynch, who still had his legal practice in Cork, held both posts for his first year in Dáil Éireann. During that time he also helped draft speeches for de Valera, prepare briefs for members of the front bench and index newspaper reports and Dáil debates. When he pointed out to de Valera that the work load was far too heavy, Fianna Fáil employed Pádraig Ó hAnnracháin as a private secretary.[45] Lynch, who was also a member of Cork Corporation, returned to the city most weekends. He paid great attention to his constituency work and less and less to his legal career.

Lynch made his name in Dáil Éireann as an effective rather than an eloquent parliamentarian. His interventions were well ordered and the arguments structured usually under three or four headings. His manner was mild, on occasions disarmingly mild, and frank. He spoke extensively on external affairs, social welfare, justice and law reform, agriculture, industry and commerce, and education. Perhaps he had the advantage of being under-estimated by those who felt that his talents lay exclusively on the playing-field.

His interventions showed that his political philosophy, while nationalist, was not jingoistic or ultra-republican. He was a strong supporter of Irish and of its restoration but was not an extreme cultural nationalist. He favoured economic protection and he showed great impatience with the inter-party Government's alleged policy of industrial centralisation. He favoured a policy of rapid job creation and economic modernisation. He repeatedly displayed a social radicalism, identifying with and speaking on behalf of the poorer sections of Irish society.

Lynch's first speech was delivered on 13 May 1948 during a debate on the first budget of the new Government. He defended the interests of the 'ordinary man' and of the 'poorer sections of the people' by drawing attention to the increased duty on petrol and oil. He felt this would lead to an unnecessary increase in transport costs. Singling out the budget measure to withdraw the subsidy on sugar, tea and butter for hotels and catering establishments, he said:

The only food, or anything akin to food, which has been reduced in cost as a result of this Budget, and of the accession to power of Fine Gael, are wines and champagne . . . I am dealing at the moment with wines and champagnes. I think it is a character in Shakespeare who says that 'if music be the food of love, play on and let me have excess of it,' but if wines and champagne are the food to which the Parliamentary Secretary was referring on that occasion, I am afraid the ordinary person in this country will not say to the Minister for Finance: 'play on, let me have excess of this kind of food and of this kind of reduction' because, as far as I can see, it is a fact that the cost of none of the ordinary foods consumed from day to day by the people has been reduced since this Government came into power. On the contrary, the price of many of them has gone up . . .[46]

On 25 November 1948 Lynch made a statement that revealed, uncharacteristically, his ideas on nationalism. Speaking in Irish, he chided the Taoiseach, John A. Costello, for his failure to use Irish in the debate on the Republic of Ireland Bill.[47] He spoke about his growing up in Cork, where he had not been born at the time of the 1916 Insurrection. He was too young to appreciate fully what was going on around him as a young boy, but on the basis of his examination of the past he had decided 'that the adoption of the Treaty in 1921 was a stop-gap and an obstruction to the onward march of this nation.' He felt that Cumann na nGaedheal had based its policy on 'the repulsive terms of that Treaty,' and 'we were nationally static for the ten years that followed the signing of that Treaty.' He also referred to the 'passive spirit' of the Cosgrave government between 1922 and 1932.[48]

Lynch felt it was not until Fianna Fáil attained power in 1932 that 'then and only then, the nation proceeded on the onward march towards the attainment of our national ideas which had been stated in 1919.' Among Éamon de Valera's achievements he listed the abolition of the oath of allegiance to the king, the retention of the land annuities and the return in 1938 of the Treaty Ports. At the age of twenty, he recalled, 'it was to me a source of great joy when our ports were finally handed back on that Monday evening in June, 1938.' Reflecting on his younger days, he said, 'I was, as a young boy, playing around the shores of Cork Harbour and I saw the badge of subjection, the Union Jack, flying over part of our own territory to which we were denied admittance. Young as I was, I appreciated the significance of that particular attainment.'[49]

Lynch regarded the Fine Gael change of policy as being very recent. Quoting from Costello's Dáil speech in 1936 on the Executive Authority (External Relations) Act (1936)—commonly called the External Relations Act—he referred to the Crown as simply the symbol of Irish free association within the Commonwealth. Fine Gael policy had been up to recently, Lynch claimed, that 'the Treaty was part of the development and evolution of our national progress' and that 'the onward march of the nation was full membership of the Commonwealth.' He stated: 'That is a position that I consider no nationally-minded people could tolerate,' adding that 'down through the years, since 1937, we have listened to a malicious form of propaganda about dictionary republics.' As far as Lynch was concerned, 'we have been a republic since the enactment of that Constitution . . . The republic was created and was there since 1937 and it needed no enactment by any Government to declare it.'[50] This was an unremarkable recitation of the orthodox position of Fianna Fáil, but it provides an insight into Lynch's early political formation and his understanding of recent history.

Lynch took a progressive line as a backbencher on educational matters. On 21 February 1950 he used a debate on the Transport Bill to air his concerns over the eligibility of shed and shop clerks in CIE to be promoted to the clerical grades, and he proposed an amendment to allow for such promotion. The Government had argued that the clerical grade required a higher standard of education; Lynch countered:

> In many cases the attainment of a high standard of education takes money and while I do not like to show the poor mouth and use it in order to make a case on this particular amendment, I can well visualise young men who have poor fathers or who maybe have not got fathers being very glad to get a job as a messenger or some other immediate occupation on the railways

in order to help to support their family at home. If such a young man had the chance to continue at school he might attain as high a standard of education as any man in the clerical grade.[51]

'They might have been able to self-educate themselves in later years,' he ended.[52]

Lynch, who became Minister for Education in 1957, often debated educational issues during his early years as a TD. He used question time to extract embarrassing admissions from the minister. On 25 April 1950 the Minister for Education, Richard Mulcahy, told him there were 206 classes in Dublin with more than sixty pupils.[53] On another occasion Lynch asked if the minister was aware that Glasheen Boys' National School was 'in a very dilapidated condition with completely inadequate amenities for the school boys, and if he will state when it is proposed to have a new building erected.' Mulcahy conceded the point about the building being in 'a very dilapidated condition. The building is overcrowded and I am advised that the premises fall short of modern standards.'[54] Lynch kept a keen eye on constituency needs.[55]

Predictably, Lynch displayed an expertise in debates on legal questions. He showed himself also to be a reformer and a strong defender of the right to equal access to justice. On 3 November 1949 he spoke on the Criminal Justice Bill, stressing the need for the inclusion under its terms of a free legal aid scheme. He spoke of many who would have witnessed

> unfortunate accused persons coming for trial on indictment before the Circuit Court without being legally represented and, as the charges are being read to him—several charges, possibly, in connection with a single offence—on being arraigned, that undefended accused person pleading, possibly, guilty to a succession of charges of varying degrees of criminality or arising out of the one offence.[56]

He also spoke out against punitive sentencing.

> Where the offences are purely minor in character, I suggest that 12 months is too serious a punishment to impose . . . We are dealing with minor offences and in those circumstances a period of imprisonment extending over two years could not be said to be commensurate with a minor offence.[57]

On 7 July 1950 Lynch defended the right to free legal aid in a debate on the Department of Justice.[58]

> In this country it is limited to cases of murder, and I suggest that the Minister should take immediate action to see whether he could not extend,

to some extent at least, the scope of free legal aid in this country. I have seen people accused of crime, whether serious or otherwise, coming into court and listening to a long list of indictments. Anybody who has listened to these indictments knows that it is difficult for even the experienced practitioner to differentiate between the various forms of indictment referring to a single criminal act. These people, when unrepresented, plead guilty parrot-like, to every indictment on the sheet whereas, in many cases, they may not be guilty at all.[59]

He also called for the early release of prisoners to employers who were willing to look after their well-being.[60]

Among the arguments he made on 11 May 1949 was the case for greater tax relief for working widows, a subject that was not merely of academic importance to him. 'I feel that a woman who, by reason of the death of her husband, has to work for her living is entitled to more relief, particularly if she has children, than the ordinary single man.'[61] Lynch remained vigilant in his defence of the rights of widows throughout his political career.[62]

While debating the weightier issues of the day, Lynch did not neglect Cork and matters local. He stoutly supported the idea of building an airport at Farmer's Cross, on the Kinsale Road, against opposition from Aer Lingus.[63] On 18 November 1949 he wanted the Minister for Industry and Commerce to urge CIE to build the same bus shelters in Cork as they had in Dublin. On 9 December 1949 he requested the authorities to ensure that more telephone kiosks were erected in areas of increasing population in Cork; their absence had caused great hardship, particularly late at night, when doctors needed to be called to sick children.

During the budget debate on 11 May 1949 Lynch spoke on rising un-employment and the increases in emigration.

No matter what statistics are brought forward, it cannot be denied, so far as the rural areas are concerned, that the number emigrating is mounting considerably. That is true of many places with which I am familiar. I am told that in remote parts of the country they cannot get enough people to organise dances. The young people are not there because they are emigrating. It is a sad state of affairs that young people should be allowed to emigrate.[64]

It was obviously a matter of immediate concern for a Cork city deputy that his young constituents were being forced into emigration because of a lack of employment, and he asked on 14 June 1950 about the number of factories opened in Cork city and county.[65]

In a debate on the estimates on 22 March 1950 he again attacked what he described as the excessive travel plans of ministers.

Some people are travelling all over the world, Ministers and other members of the present Government, at the State's expense . . . People are commenting adversely on it. It is little wonder if people nowadays change the old saying 'Join the navy and see the world' to 'Join the Coalition and see the world.'[66]

Lynch rejected tit-for-tat politics. 'To criticise one side and to eulogise another side is not a reasoned approach to any measure or debate in this house. I do the best I can even though I may not be taken notice of in certain respects.'[67] Lynch had earned the respect of his peers by the time the inter-party Government self-destructed in the spring of 1951.

GENERAL ELECTION AND PROMOTION TO PARLIAMENTARY SECRETARY, 1951–4

As a consequence of the Mother and Child controversy, the inter-party Government was weakened by the resignation of the Minister for Health, Noël Browne. The Dáil was dissolved at the end of April. Nominations closed on 17 May 1951, polling day was 30 May, and the new Dáil was scheduled to meet on 13 June. A Fianna Fáil election advertisement in the *Cork Examiner* on 26 May read: 'Look Ahead—This time—Fianna Fáil.' The candidates listed to run for the party in the Cork City constituency were Alderman Walter Furlong, Alderman Jack Lynch, Alderman Seán MacCarthy (lord mayor) and Alderman Patrick McGrath. The illustration was of a father with his son by the hand, striding away as the sun rose behind them. The text of the advertisement spoke of the immediate future: 'Peace or war—whatever the next five years bring—Ireland will need a government with a clear policy, and capable of effective leadership. Fianna Fáil can establish it.' The alternative, according to the advertisement, was a Government divided against itself, 'with conflicting and ever-shifting policies based on day-to-day expediency.' Fianna Fáil promised an efficient government 'and fair play for every citizen and section without fear or favour.'[68]

An earlier Fianna Fáil advertisement on 14 May quoted inter-party election promises from 1948 to reduce radically the cost of living, bring down taxes and introduce price control. 'How have they been kept?' it asked.[69] The following day another advertisement in the *Evening Echo* reproduced quotations from Government ministers. Dr T. F. O'Higgins, who was again standing in Cork City, was quoted as having said:

'Our Party advocates a frank acceptance of this country's membership of the Commonwealth of Nations [1/1/48].' Ireland declared herself a republic and left the Commonwealth in 1949. You know NOW what they were worth.[70]

The main issues in the election in Cork were unemployment, emigration and the rising cost of living. On 29 May an advertisement in the *Evening Echo* showed four prominent inter-party ministers looking out through curtained Georgian windows at a woman in a shawl knocking on the unopened door: '1948—STILL WAITING!' read the caption.[71] That advertisement appeared again on polling day.[72]

De Valera was scheduled to arrive in the city on Monday 28 May, two days before the election. A party advertisement for his visit gave the route through Great William O'Brien Street, Clarence Street, Shandon Street and North Main Street to Patrick Street. 'Bands will not play passing the cathedral,' it read.[73] De Valera, showing great energy, toured the country and was in the south towards the end of May. On 26 May he spoke in Bandon and Bantry and the following day in Cóbh, Mitchelstown, Mallow and Charleville.[74] He spent the 28th canvassing Cork, and in the evening he was driven outside the city to Dublin Hill to join a procession in his honour. He turned to Lynch, who was beside him in the car, and asked him what he was going to speak about. Lynch replied that he was thinking of having 'a go off' Bishop Cornelius Lucey, who had been very critical of Fianna Fáil in his recent public statements. De Valera quickly replied that that would not be very wise.[75]

Transferring from his car, de Valera rode into the city in a horse-drawn carriage in the company of the lord mayor, Seán MacCarthy. A second carriage took the other three Fianna Fáil candidates, including Jack Lynch. They were led by a motorcycle escort and large numbers of motor cars covered in party slogans. 'Four bands added tone and hundreds of banners colour to the procession which reached huge dimensions by the time it arrived in Patrick Street,' according to a press report.[76]

Flanked by Lynch and the other candidates, de Valera delivered a strong address in which he stated that Fianna Fáil had received the largest number of first-preference votes in the last election. He wanted a clear majority in this election. He made a strong attack on the outgoing Government; he gave it credit for its house-building policy but said the Fianna Fáil record of building 17,000 houses in one year was ahead of that of the outgoing Government. He denied that Fianna Fáil was a party wishing to extend state control. 'We stand as a matter of fact very much more than some of the elements in the Coalition Government for free enterprise, giving the individual the fullest freedom he can be given, consistent with the rights of his neighbour.'

If the Fianna Fáil candidates for Cork City spoke at length, this was not reflected in the press coverage. The lord mayor, Seán MacCarthy, opened the speeches.[77] Lynch spoke last. He was quoted as saying that Seán MacBride had stated that Fianna Fáil was bereft of a policy, 'but they could ignore that; for Mr MacBride was a man bereft of a party.'[78] The *Cork Examiner* reported: 'At the close of the meeting a surge of people in the direction of the platform resulted in the breaking of a plate-glass window in one of the nearby shops. Nobody, however was injured.'[79]

The 'Chief' travelled on triumphantly to north Cork later that night, where he was met on the outskirts of Fermoy by another torchlight procession. On 29 May, the eve of polling day, he returned to address a large rally in Dublin. The *Cork Examiner* reported that de Valera was greeted in O'Connell Street with 'wonderful enthusiasm' by 'a huge gathering.' The Fianna Fáil organisation, the paper reported, 'put all possible into a big demonstration in the way of bands, banners, slogan-bearers and a contingent of old I.R.A. which formed up in Bachelors Walk and escorted Mr de Valera to the platform in front of the G.P.O.'[80] De Valera laid emphasis on his party's wish to unify the country, restore the national language and develop the land and industry. In all things, it was actuated by one thing only: the common good, the welfare of the people, and it would do it not by resorting to manoeuvres such as diminishing the estimates by £4 million.[81]

There were ten candidates for five seats in the Cork City constituency.[82] Polling day, 30 May, saw a reported 75 per cent turn-out in the city, compared with 72 per cent in 1948 and 70 per cent in 1944. Polling in Fermoy and Dunmanway was between 80 and 90 per cent and in Timoleague there was a 97 per cent turn-out. Despite reports of apathy, people in Cork turned out in large numbers to vote. Summer-like weather helped to get people out. Cars were in plentiful supply to transport voters to polling stations. By noon one experienced polling-booth official said it was the heaviest he had known for many years. Old people were among those who voted earliest, it was noted. That evening, at the close of the polls, 46,953 people had voted out of a total register of 62,336, a turn-out of 75 per cent. There was also a record postal vote in the constituency, 253 voting out of 282.[83]

Alderman Pa McGrath for Fianna Fáil and Dr T. F. O'Higgins for Fine Gael were elected on the first count. It then took nine counts to complete the election in the constituency. Lynch was the third candidate to be elected; he was followed by his party colleague and lord mayor Seán MacCarthy and by the Labour Party candidate James Hickey, who was separated by only twenty-three votes from the next eliminated candidate.[84]

GENERAL ELECTION TO THE FOURTEENTH DAIL, 1951 (147 SEATS)[85]
Polling day: 30 May 1951

Constituency and number of seats	Electorate and quota	Candidates	Affiliation	First preferences
Cork Borough (5)	62,336 Quota 7,733	1. Patrick (Pa) McGrath	FF	8,923
		2 Thomas Francis O'Higgins (sen.)	FG	7,858
		3. John (Jack) Lynch	FF	6,233
		4. Seán MacCarthy	FF	5,096
		Walter Furlong	FF	4,359
		Stephen Declan Barrett	FG	3,434
		5. James Hickey	Lab.	3,376
		Richard Sidney Anthony	Lab.	3,018
		Michael Sheehan (Ballintemple)	FG	2,442
		Seán Casey	Lab.	1,657

At the national level, Fianna Fáil had 69 seats, a gain of one seat on the 1948 result. The combined other parties had 78. There were fourteen independent deputies in the new Dáil, and the formation of any future Government hinged on secure majority support from that quarter. De Valera was elected Taoiseach on 13 June 1951 by 74 votes to 69. He did not resume the External Affairs portfolio, giving it instead to Frank Aiken. Seán MacEntee, another founder-member of the party, was made Minister for Finance, while Seán Lemass returned to Industry and Commerce. Dr James Ryan, who had also been present at the creation of Fianna Fáil in 1926, was given the sensitive portfolio of Health. Gerry Boland returned to Justice; Oscar Traynor went to Defence; Paddy Smith took over in Local Government; Tom Walsh was given Agriculture and Tom Derrig Lands. Erskine Childers, whose father had been executed during the Civil War in November 1922, was made Minister for Posts and Telegraphs. The North Cork TD Seán Moylan was made Minister for Education. But for a few exceptions they were the same old faces.

Jack Lynch returned to Leinster House to be present for the opening of the new Dáil. Checking his pigeon-hole, he was handed a letter by his namesake, Jack Lynch from North Kerry, which the latter had opened in error.[86] It contained good news: de Valera wished to see him. He was to be appointed a parliamentary secretary, with special responsibility for the Gaeltacht and what was known as the Congested Districts. He was to report directly to de Valera, and he was allocated an office in Leinster House, off a corridor known to TDs as the Burma Road. His division was made up of a head of department, three executive officers and a small typing staff.[87]

Lynch's primary responsibility was chairing an inter-departmental committee representing Finance, Industry and Commerce, Agriculture, Local Government, Lands, and Education. Each of those departments had some responsibility for the Gaeltacht and Congested Districts. Lynch explained:

Attached to Oifig na Gaeltachta was an inter-departmental committee, composed of officers chosen from each of the Departments listed above. They were senior officers who knew their business in relation to the administration of affairs in the Gaeltacht. They came together and were presided over by me as Parliamentary Secretary. They met once in three weeks and more often twice in every three weeks.

Lynch's job was to fashion a strategy for infrastructural development and the creation of jobs.[88] Having done the final two years of his secondary schooling through Irish at North Monastery, he had a good grounding in the language. He had also gone to the Irish-speaking districts of Béal Átha an Ghaorthaidh and Baile an Fheirtéaraigh in his young days. But it was only after he had become a TD that his speaking knowledge of Irish improved. He had many dealings with the Fianna Fáil chief whip, Donnacha Ó Briain, who 'used to speak Irish to me and I responded not very well.' But he persisted. 'I felt that as one of the new generation who had learned Irish at school, I should use Irish in debates and I did from time to time. It began to come easy to me after that.'[89]

Lynch consulted widely, travelling throughout the country, where he saw at first hand the profundity of the problems facing any government hoping to attract industry to such areas. His first major parliamentary test in his new role came on 29 November 1951, when he faced a debate on the Gaeltacht. He spoke at length in Irish, explaining his duties and the provisions of the Undeveloped Areas Bill. The latter would help him discharge his new responsibilities.

The opposition, while full of good will towards Lynch personally, gave him a difficult time. James Dillon wished him well.

So far as I am concerned, I wish him all the luck in the world and I hope he will have great success in the position to which he has attained at so early an age.

But he continued:

Since Eusebius the Eunuch put up the provincial prefectures of the Roman
Empire of the East for sale I do not think any more indecent proposal has
been brought before Dáil Éireann than this Estimate coupled with the Bill.
Fianna Fáil lost seats in nine counties in the last election . . . What are the
undeveloped areas? The nine constituencies that Fianna Fáil lost a seat in.
Can you imagine the dirty fraud of identifying Connemara, the Rosses and
West Kerry with County Roscommon? Look at me. I am a congest.

Lynch defended himself vigorously against charges of party bias. He told
the Dáil on 4 December 1951 that he had taken every precaution 'to ensure that
no political tinge whatsoever would be given to any visit I paid to any part of
the country.' His statement that he had notified every deputy in the areas
before his visits was greeted by a remark by Deputy John Mannion (Fine Gael):
'The parliamentary secretary is telling a deliberate lie.' He withdrew that
serious charge when cautioned by the Ceann Comhairle. The passage of that
legislation was a baptism in blood.

Lynch was an alderman of Cork Corporation (city council) from 30
September 1950 until his resignation on 14 May 1957. An examination of the
minutes reveals that he attended fairly regularly when his schedule allowed.
He represented his Dáil constituency of Cork City with great energy. For
example, on 8 May 1951 he referred to the announcement by the Minister for
Posts and Telegraphs of an accelerated postal service between Ireland and
Britain by the carriage of mail by air between Dublin and Manchester. Lynch
moved that the minister be requested to inaugurate an air mail service
between Cork and Britain and that the Minister for Industry and Commerce
be requested to license the airfield at Farmer's Cross, outside Cork, for this
purpose. The motion was carried.[90]

His new appointment as parliamentary secretary meant that he could not
give as much attention to the corporation. At a meeting on 25 September 1951
he resigned as a delegate of Cork Corporation to the Association of Municipal
Authorities of Ireland. On 28 September 1954 he proposed that the corporation
submit to the Housing Committee a list of those living in overcrowded or
unhealthy conditions for rehousing.[91]

Between 1951 and 1954 Lynch continued to refine his skills as a parliamentarian. He would never achieve a reputation as one of the leading orators in
the Oireachtas; but he was very effective in the chamber and he developed a
new sense of confidence, as can be seen in the following exchange with James
Dillon on 12 July 1951. 'Carry on,' Lynch said to the Fine Gael deputy, only to
be told by Dillon: 'It will be a bad day when I want leave from Deputy Lynch
of Cork to carry on in the house. I put down bigger men than he and down
he will go too if he thinks fit to usurp the functions of the Ceann Comhairle.'

Lynch and other Fianna Fáil deputies were on their feet. 'Are we supposed to sit down while you insult us?' Lynch asked. On 20 March 1952 he referred to Dillon as being 'volatile' and said that the deputy's exhibition of 'ranting and raving' reminded him of the words of Robert Burns:

O wad some Power the giftie gie us
To see oursels as ithers see us!

When the Government was asked by Deputy Seán Keane (Labour Party) on 10 June 1952 about the provision of a helicopter for spraying crops against the wheat midge in Co. Cork, Lynch asked whether, if a spray gun was found, the deputy would 'take a job as a rear gunner.'

Lynch was not afraid to speak out strongly against racism, intolerance and anti-Semitism on the rare occasions on which such prejudices were manifest in the Dáil. Lynch, it may be remembered, was a friend of David Marcus and was also friendly with other members of that Cork Jewish family. Patrick McGilligan, a veteran Fine Gael TD and former minister, made an ugly and intemperate speech on 11 July 1952 with reference to the Fianna Fáil TD Ben Briscoe:

It is very hard to have to listen to Deputy Briscoe parading himself as a patron saint of Irish nationality. It is a rather distorted and objectionable appearance he presents under these circumstances. One does get the feeling of ease when the Deputy slips over to being the profiteers' pal . . . It is nauseating to hear Deputy Briscoe preaching about Irish flags and Irish crews. When I hear him in this national mood, it takes my mind back through the mists of history to search out the area behind the present Iron Curtain where that voice had its origin.[92]

Lynch interjected at that point: 'That is a most degrading remark.' Lemass followed: 'Leave him alone. Personal abuse is his only argument.' McGilligan then turned on Lynch: 'If the Parliamentary Secretary has anything to say, would he please not mumble?' Lynch repeated his remark as the Ceann Comhairle called on McGilligan to withdraw. Deputy Briscoe was not in the chamber at the time.

But McGilligan continued to argue the point, and Lemass said: 'Every Deputy here is a representative of the Irish people and Deputy Briscoe has as much right to be here as Deputy McGilligan.' 'He has not,' replied McGilligan. Lemass again intervened: 'He has as much right to be here as Deputy McGilligan, and I am sure that there are some decent Deputies on the opposite benches who do not like this muck.'

McGilligan appeared to have completely lost his temper. 'I want to say with regard to Deputy Briscoe that it is nauseating to hear him lecturing me on Irish nationality. It is sometimes nauseating to hear the Minister doing it, too.'

When Lemass said that they should let the Irish people decide, McGilligan retorted: 'We will, and we will let people talk of nationality who have a proper right to talk about it.'

Lemass again came to the defence of Briscoe. 'A Deputy who has given such long national service as Deputy Briscoe has given has a right to speak here, without being abused in that personal way.' But McGilligan refused to bow. 'I am entitled to say that I am a better national of this country than Deputy Briscoe is, in my origins. My origins are clearly Irish and always were, not like some other Deputies—and I do not mean exclusively Deputy Briscoe.'

Lemass urged a return to the subject of the debate—the estimates—'and leave out the muck. We are sick of that type of muck here and the Irish people are sick of it, as they have shown.'

McGilligan then turned his fire on Lynch.

I have complete scorn for that office and for the Parliamentary Secretary, who allows himself to be put into a dead-end of an office where he knows he has no power and no likelihood of doing any good, and where he is being used for the purpose of bribing certain parts of the community. We know how his office came into being, since it has been introduced into this debate. Talk about the midge pest down in Cork! A bigger pest of Parliamentary Secretaries hit the West of Ireland in the summer of last year than any plague that ever descended on it. After several of them had gone down there, Deputy Lynch's office was set up, and it was rather amazing that, in the 25th year of its period, Fianna Fáil discovered the Gaeltacht. It ought to be ranked with one of the great explorer's victories, after the discovery of America.[93]

Lynch ignored what McGilligan had said about him personally. He said that the deputy had made a most degrading remark by the standards of any party or any deputy, 'and the fact that it referred to that Deputy's nationality and the country of his remote origins was more degrading still.' Without losing his composure, Lynch continued with the debate on the estimates.

Reviewing Fianna Fáil's record in office between 1951 and 1954 did not provide much ground for optimism. The Government of 'old men' had no answers for halting the outward march of the younger generation to seek work in Britain.

OPPOSITION AGAIN: THE 1954 GENERAL ELECTION AND THREE YEARS ON THE BACK BENCHES

When the Government fell, polling day was fixed for 18 May 1954, and Lynch faced his third general election in six years. Pa McGrath, Jack Lynch, John Galvin and Dónal Daly stood for Fianna Fáil in Cork Borough. 'Vote for the men who will stand by you,' stated the party advertisement, chastising the opposition for claiming falsely that they would reduce the price of foodstuffs. But the electorate was not being told how it would be done. 'Fine Gael fooled you then. Don't let them fool you again,' read the advertisement.[94]

Speaking during the campaign in Béal Átha an Ghaorthaidh on 9 May, Lynch referred to the three remedies put forward by the Bishop of Cork, Cornelius Lucey, for bringing about the restoration of Irish: reasonable prosperity for farmers, tradesmen and shopkeepers in Irish-speaking districts; industry in the region where Irish would be the language of the work-place; and decentralisation of the civil service. Lynch claimed that the Fianna Fáil Government had met the first two through the provision of grants and the setting up of industry. The terms of the Undeveloped Areas Act were of benefit to the Gaeltacht, and Gaeltarra Éireann had decided to extend its activities to Béal Átha an Ghaorthaidh.[95]

On 10 May he defended the Government against charges that Fianna Fáil had brought only austerity and hardship. He argued that the consumption of every type of food had increased considerably, while savings had also increased significantly.[96]

Both de Valera and Lemass campaigned in Cork; but the political tide was running against the outgoing Government. Stephen Barrett, Lynch's friend and fellow-barrister, headed the poll for Fine Gael. The following table (*p. 46*) shows the first-preference votes in the Cork Borough constituency.

Nationally, Fianna Fáil obtained 65 seats, Fine Gael 50, the Labour Party 19, Clann na Talmhan 5, Clann na Poblachta 3 and others 5.

The inter-party Government, headed by John A. Costello, was returned to power. Costello reshuffled his front bench and shared power with the Labour Party, but many of the old names reappeared as ministers: Richard Mulcahy (Education), James Dillon (Agriculture), Seán Mac Eoin (Defence), T. F. O'Higgins (Health), William Norton (Tánaiste and Industry and Commerce), and James Everett (Justice). Gerry Sweetman (Fine Gael) took over Finance, and Liam Cosgrave was given External Affairs. Lynch was out of office; responsibility for his duties was given to the Minister for Education, Richard Mulcahy. A Department of the Gaeltacht was set up in 1956, and on 24 October Patrick J. Lindsay from Co. Mayo took up the new portfolio.

GENERAL ELECTION TO THE FIFTEENTH DAIL, 1954 (147 SEATS)[97]
Polling day: 18 May 1954

Constituency and number of seats	Electorate and quota	Candidates	Affiliation	First preferences
Cork Borough (5)	63,325 Quota 7,987	1. Stephen Declan Barrett	FG	16,393
		2. Patrick (Pa) McGrath	FF	9,190
		4. John (Jack) Lynch	FF	6,125
		James Hickey	Lab.	3,244
		5. Seán Casey	Lab.	3,052
		John Galvin	FF	2,904
		Dónal J. Daly	FF	2,149
		3. Anthony Barry	FG	1,911
		John William Reidy	Ind.	1,108
		Laurence Neville	FG	816
		John Bermingham	FG	572
		Seán Patrick Twomey	Ind.	452

Lynch had little option but to return to Cork to pick up the traces of his much-neglected legal career. Having been away from the bar, he found it hard to catch up on recent case law and he had the strong feeling that he should not again absent himself for so long from his profession.

Judge Tony Murphy, who qualified as a barrister and returned to Cork to practise in 1955, was a lifelong friend of Jack and Máirín Lynch. He recalled that Lynch 'was on his uppers' at the time. The pay of a parliamentary secretary was very poor, he recalled.

Judge Murphy recalled travelling in the same car as Jack Lynch, Dónal Crosby and the Fine Gael TD Stephen Barrett. The *Cork Examiner* journalist Jack O'Sullivan was another of the passengers. Barrett and Lynch used to take turns at driving. As they approached the town where the court was sitting, the one who was not driving would get out and walk to the courthouse, to allay the fear of the litigants that two barristers, on opposite sides in court, could be so friendly as to travel in the same car.[98] The fact that one was a Fine Gael TD and the other a Fianna Fáil TD was less relevant.

Judge Murphy remembered that Lynch was very sociable. When they stayed overnight while on the circuit he would sing, accompanied by Dónal Crosby on the piano, smoke his pipe and drink Paddy whiskey. But the friendships went further. Murphy recalled the many occasions on which he and his wife shared a table at a function with the Barretts and the Lynches. They did not discuss politics. Both Lynch and Barrett, if called upon to speak, would stand up and criticise the rival party for about five minutes. When both men resumed their seats at the table the conversation continued as before, without any reference to politics. Indeed after every election the Barretts and the Lynches would go to the Oyster Grill and have a meal.[99] The venue was sometimes the 44 Club, where dinners were held a few times a year. Jack and Máirín Lynch were present in later years as often as official commitments in Dublin permitted. Murphy recalled that Lynch had a pleasing light baritone voice. His party piece was 'The Rose of San Antone.'[100]

Judge Tony Murphy recalled that Lynch was very popular and much sought after by the public. He also said candidly that, given the short time that Lynch was at the bar, he did not have the opportunity to gain the necessary experience to reach the top of the profession. He pointed out, moreover, how difficult it was to make a living in the law in Cork in the mid-1950s. There was very little work; there was hardly any serious crime. In his recollection there was only one judge for Cork city and county and only four criminal sessions of a fortnight per year. When Judge Murphy started to practise in Cork in 1955 the judge was handed a pair of white gloves by the registrar for five sessions in a row, signifying that there was no indictable crime. Disputes between landlords and tenants were among the most frequent cases heard, together with workmen's compensation claims. It was a matter of celebration on the South Mall if a barrister won a settlement of four pounds ten shillings per week for a client, he said.[101]

Judge Murphy mentioned another reason why Lynch might not have been best suited to the law. 'Lawyers are a peculiar tribe,' he said. 'It is a necessary quality for a solicitor and a barrister to have empathy with the lowest of the low.' It was necessary 'to put yourself as low as they are' in order to build a defence. He did not feel that Lynch could do that. 'In bad times in politics, Lynch often expressed regret at having left the practice of law,' the judge recalled; but he was certain that Lynch had made the correct vocational decision.[102]

When starting to rebuild his legal career, Lynch was supported by both sides of the political divide, receiving briefs from Fine Gael supporters such as Michael Powell, Michael Ronnie Boland of Skibbereen and John Field.[103] Martin Harvey, a strong supporter of Fianna Fáil, also kept him well supplied.

While living in Cork between 1954 and 1957, Lynch played an active part in the life of the city. He and Máirín were members of Muskerry Golf Club, but a recurring hurling injury limited his ability to play to a high level. He won 'a remote competition' at the club, for which he was docked a stroke. His handicap was reduced to seventeen, at which it remained. Máirín was a more accomplished player, winning the president's prize in 1954. Jack Lynch became president of the club in 1970, but his political duties during that year did not permit his attendance at many functions.[104]

Between 1954 and 1957 Lynch continued to attend meetings of Cork Corporation and its committees. On 27 September 1955 he said he had been informed that some difficulty had arisen regarding the issue of summonses under the School Attendance Act (1926) in the Spangle Hill (present-day Farranree) and Garranabraher districts, which had been added to the county borough (city) of Cork in April, so that the clerks for both Cork and Blarney District Courts declined to accept summonses issued against defaulters in those districts. It was agreed to draw the attention of the Minister for Justice and Minister for Education to the matter and to ask them to clarify the position. In reply to this question, details were given of convictions from both district courts, with fines of between 2 shillings and 20 shillings being imposed on those convicted under the act.[105]

On 13 December 1955 Lynch proposed to the corporation:

> In view of the number of tragedies caused in recent years by motor cars being inadvertently driven into the River Lee, this Council demands that a survey be carried out jointly by the Corporation and Cork Harbour Commissioners as soon as possible, of the quays and riverside under the joint or respective areas of administration with a view to obviating such occurrences in the future and that the costs of such survey and of works carried out consequent thereto be borne by the Corporation and the Harbour Commissioners in such proportions as may be required by law or as may be agreed.[106]

The Harbour Commissioners replied on 10 January 1956 that they could not accept the proposal but would agree to meet representatives of the corporation to deal with the issue. Councillor Healy proposed that the corporation establish a committee that would meet the Harbour Commissioners, and this was duly seconded by Alderman Lynch.[107]

This is not the complete record of Lynch's activities as an alderman; but local government was neither his major political strength nor where his interests resided.

Back in Leinster House, Lynch in opposition had a greater opportunity to question the Government about constituency matters. He took a strong interest in the educational needs of the Cork area. But despite his energetic performance, opposition proved to be a fallow and difficult time for him. However, his legal practice was picking up. The very week in which he was invited to join the new Government in 1957 he said he had to forgo £800 in briefs; 'and that was a lot of money at the time.' But a general election in 1957 provided Fianna Fáil with an opportunity to return to power and Lynch with the offer of a seat in the Government.

Chapter 3 ∿

MINISTER FOR EDUCATION, 1957–9

The outgoing Minister for the Gaeltacht, Patrick Lindsay, referred with warmth in his memoirs to Lynch, Barrett and another Cork deputy, Denis Murphy. All three, he recalled, had 'helped many a lame dog over difficult stiles.'[1] Jack Lynch would continue to be sympathetic to such hard cases throughout his life in politics. By the time of the 1957 general election he had already established a good name as a constituency worker. Fianna Fáil won 78 seats in that election, Fine Gael dropped to 40, the Labour Party got 12, Clann na Talmhan 3, Clann na Poblachta 1, Sinn Féin 4 and independents and others 9.

In Cork the outcome was quite predictable. Lynch was returned comfortably with 7,107 first preferences. His friend Stephen Barrett headed the poll, with 8,600.

GENERAL ELECTION TO THE SIXTEENTH DAIL, 1957 (147 SEATS)[2]
Polling day: 5 March 1957

Constituency and number of seats	Electorate and quota	Candidates	Affiliation	First preferences
Cork Borough (5)	63,495 *Quota* 7,177	1. Stephen Declan Barrett	FG	8,600
		2. John Galvin	FF	7,647
		3. John (Jack) Lynch	FF	7,107
		4. Seán Casey	Lab.	6,074
		Seán Ó hÉigeartaigh	SF	4,789
		5. A. A. (Gus) Healy	FF	3,519
		Dónal J. Daly	FF	2,747
		Anthony Barry	FG	1,663
		John Bermingham	FG	911

That general election is notable for another result. The son-in-law of Seán Lemass, Charles J. Haughey, was elected to the fourth seat in the five-seat Dublin North-East constituency, knocking out the veteran Henry Colley. The latter's son, George Colley, a future Government minister, had been at school with Haughey in St Joseph's, Fairview, Dublin. That schoolboy friendship did not last.

While working on St Patrick's Day in his office in Cork, Jack Lynch received a phone call from Éamon de Valera, requesting that he go to Dublin to see him. When the two men met Lynch 'wasn't very keen' about taking on a ministry, because he was at that point 'doing fairly well at the Bar.' His wife, he explained, would prefer him to stay at the law. He added that he was 'flattered to be offered a ministry at all.'[3] He felt he had an obligation to accept the offer once it had been made; but he told de Valera he would give him his decision when he had had an opportunity to discuss the matter with Máirín.

Driving to a court session the following day with his legal colleagues, Lynch told them that the Chief had called him up to Dublin to offer him a ministry. There was immediate speculation over the portfolio he might be offered. Tony Murphy suggested that it would be either Justice or Education. Jack O'Sullivan felt it would be either Education or Industry and Commerce. Lynch, who was the driver, replied that he did not know much about education and less about industry and commerce. At that point the car hit a hump-backed bridge and he temporarily lost control; all he could do was aim the car at an open gate into a field. Driving through it, he reversed and got back out onto the road again. Though nobody was injured, the incident ended specu-lation about Lynch's ministerial future.[4]

On 26 March 1957, after two further meetings with de Valera, Lynch was given a ministry. He explained many years later: 'As I hadn't got a family I felt I wasn't risking too much by going back into politics full time.' He was given the Department of Education and responsibility for the Gaeltacht. A few months later a Co. Mayo solicitor, Mícheál Ó Móráin, was made Minister for the Gaeltacht.[5]

Because of his new responsibilities, Lynch had to review his commitments in Cork. His bar practice was at an end. On 9 April 1957 he also resigned from Cork Corporation.

> I wish to take advantage of this occasion of expressing through you to the Lord Mayor and my other colleagues on the Corporation my appreciation of the painstaking, unselfish and co-operative manner in which they undertook the administration of the City's affairs. I feel sure that the high standard of conduct and co-operation will be maintained in the future. I wish to also express to you, to the officers of the Corporation and to the

staff of the City Hall my sincere thanks for the ready assistance always given to me and for the unfailing courtesy shown me during the period of my membership.[6]

Lynch was one of a handful of new faces in the Government after the 1957 election. De Valera did not reappoint Gerry Boland. His son Kevin, however, was made Minister for Defence on his first day in Dáil Éireann. Blunt and plain-spoken, Boland was immersed in the early lore of Fianna Fáil. He remained uncomfortable with the emerging affiliation between Fianna Fáil and the building industry and developed a fondness for resigning on matters of principle. Neil Blaney, first elected in 1948 and also the son of a TD and founder-member of the party, was given Posts and Telegraphs but changed in November 1957 to Local Government. He was a rough diamond, who believed that what was good for Co. Donegal was good for the country. He was a difficult task-master and was not popular with his civil servants. He lacked respect for authority and also for those who did not share his republican views.

Despite the introduction of new blood, the 'old guard' continued to dominate de Valera's final Government. Lemass was Tánaiste and Minister for Industry and Commerce. Seán MacEntee was given Health, and Dr James Ryan was sent to Finance. Frank Aiken returned to External Affairs. Oscar Traynor was assigned to Justice, Erskine Childers to Lands and Paddy Smith to Local Government. With the exception of Childers, all had been founder-members of Fianna Fáil in May 1926.

Jack Lynch became a Government minister at forty-one; but he had only two years in Education before being moved. That was a very short time to make an impact, and his performance must be set in historical context. Firstly, the depressed state of the economy in the 1950s militated against bringing forward any ambitious plans for widespread reform in primary and secondary education. Secondly, the Department of Education remained predominantly conservative at the top and resistant to radical change.[7] In the more junior administrative grades, however, innovative educational ideas emerged to challenge the status quo. Patrick Lindsay has left a withering profile of the 'top brass' in Marlborough Street. He described the then secretary, Larry Murray, as

a gentleman, very mild of manner but like so many of the other heads of departments in those days, he was content to let things slide. You can do no wrong, you can make no mistakes, if you do nothing. That seemed to be the prevailing philosophy of the day.[8]

A new secretary, Tarlach Ó Raifeartaigh, was appointed shortly before Lynch took up office. Seán O'Connor, who was secretary of the department between 1973 and 1975, was a principal officer when Lynch became minister. Reflecting on the portfolio many years later, he wrote:

> Education was not an important ministry nor did it offer any great scope for conspicuous achievement, but it was a good starting point for a young man at the beginning of his ministerial career. Nobody expected anything exciting from it, given that power resided elsewhere.[9]

O'Connor wrote that after the 1957 election in the Department of Education there was a 'general feeling of good will towards him [Lynch] as a young man who might set things right.'[10] Civil servants were happy to welcome him. They did not expect him to stay long; 'Education was a staging post in his career with Industry and Commerce as his next immediate objective,' O'Connor wrote.[11]

Richard Mulcahy was the darling of the more traditional Department of Education civil servants. His perception of being a minister, he told Dáil Éireann in July 1956, was 'that of a kind of dungaree man, the plumber who will make the satisfactory communications and streamline the forces and potentialities of the educational workers and educational management in this country.'[12]

In contrast, Lynch did not see his ministerial role as being confined to that of a maintenance man. Firstly, his own experience taught him the social importance of improving and expanding the educational system. He knew about the poor state of many national schools in his own constituency. As a former civil servant in the Department of Justice he had personal experience of working in a hierarchical administrative environment. Secondly, he had refined his political skills in the office of parliamentary secretary. Thirdly, he was fortunate that de Valera 'was very sympathetic to any demands I made' in the Government. De Valera used to phone him 'every now and again to enquire how things were going.'[13] Fourthly, he was a good Irish-speaker, a skill much appreciated in the Department of Education. Finally, his mild manner was disarming. He was not suspected of harbouring innovative educational ideas. Appearances would prove to be deceptive.

Lynch was fortunate to have Jim Dukes (father of a future leader of Fine Gael, Alan Dukes) as his private secretary. 'Not many Private Secretaries have survived a change of Government,' Dukes recalled.

> When he first arrived he said he would need three weeks or so to select a Private Secretary but asked me to carry on until he could make a decision. At the end of the period he asked me to carry on indefinitely.

Dukes, who went on to serve Dr Patrick Hillery,[14] developed a high regard for Lynch. 'I must say at once that he was the most considerate "boss" I ever had in nearly 46 years as a Civil Servant.' He recalled that in their two years working together

> we never had a difference of opinion, about anything. I can only say that he was the easiest Minister to get along with provided you knew enough to point out any difficulties that just might arise in any particular case.[15]

Lynch was 'invariably meticulous about appointments and about his preparation for meetings and interviews with the various educational bodies.' He kept to a strict weekly schedule.

> One knew he would depart for Cork at 4.00 p.m. on a Friday and be in the Office by 09.15 a.m. on Monday with sheaves of notes he had taken from constituents while in Cork which it would be my job to sort out to his satisfaction through my contacts with the private secretaries of the Ministers concerned. This was not as difficult as it may sound. We all depended on each other and had to give of our best when called upon.

Lynch and Dukes remained friends. 'I used to look forward to meeting [him] at All-Ireland Finals in Croke Park for many succeeding years.'[16]

Despite the quality of the individual officials, Lynch took over a relatively poorly staffed department in a decade of deep economic depression, high unemployment and mass emigration. Seán O'Connor has described the dissatisfaction with the educational system during the late 1950s in a series of articles in *Studies*. He wrote that there was strong criticism of the methods being used to restore Irish and to reform secondary and third-level education.[17] But he felt that the critics were 'unaware that they had the wrong targets.' The public showed little interest in debate on education, while neither the teachers nor the Catholic Church offered any support to the critics, 'perhaps because they felt that the attack was in part directed at themselves.' Lynch took over Education, according to O'Connor, in a climate of 'underlying unease that all was not well.'[18]

Lynch had an opportunity on 1 May 1957 to set out his policy in a speech on departmental estimates for the year 1957/8. The inter-party Government had introduced a cut of 10 per cent in the capitation grant paid to secondary schools and a 6 per cent cut in the annual grant to vocational education committees. Speaking in Irish, Lynch announced that he would not revoke the proposed cuts but he hoped not to have to continue them beyond the current year. He stated that more schools and smaller classes were needed. He also said he would consider the bar on married women teachers in primary schools and emphasised the necessity for the extension of technological education. He described the educational system as a co-operative in which the state did not hold all the shares.[19]

The following figures will give an insight into the size of the educational system in Ireland in the late 1950s. In the school year 1958/9, Lynch told the Dáil, there were 4,878 national schools, with 505,363 pupils enrolled. There were 13,753 teachers, 2,079 of whom, or approximately 20 per cent, were untrained. There were 69,568 pupils at the post-primary level, attending 494 secondary schools, which employed 3,542 full-time and 1,490 part-time teachers. There were 272 vocational schools, attended by 23,675 pupils in whole-time courses. There were also 929 pupils in whole-time technical courses and 2,761 in part-time apprenticeship courses. However, many left school at a very early age. It was difficult to encourage pupils to remain in secondary school until the Leaving Certificate. In 1959, 15,205 pupils took the Intermediate Certificate examination and 7,309 sat for the Leaving Certificate.[20]

On 8 April 1959 Lynch reported the amount being spent *per capita* on education as follows:[21]

	National schools	Secondary schools	Universities
1950/1	£15	£23	£67
1951/2	£17	£25	£67
1952/3	£18	£26	£76
1953/4	£20	£27	£104
1954/5	£20	£32	£76
1955/6	£20	£32	£71
1956/7	£22	£33	£87
1957/8	£21	£36	£80

In 1958 Jack Lynch had an education budget of slightly less than £14½ million. This was increased by a million the following year.[22]

Just how badly was the primary school system in need of reform when Lynch took over the Education portfolio? Firstly, the physical condition of many schools gave grave cause for concern. On 19 February 1958 Dr Noël Browne TD obtained the following information from Lynch:

There were, in December, 1957, 821 schools which it was considered were defective in various respects and should be replaced by new schools. Grants had been sanctioned by my Department for the erection of 136 of the required new buildings. The cases of those 821 defective schools are of varying degrees of urgency . . . The total number of new schools completed in the years from 1947 to 1956 was 435.[23]

At that rate of school building, the minister said, it would take at least fifteen years, or until 1973, to provide new schools in all the necessitous cases.[24]

The second and perhaps gravest problem was the use of so many untrained teachers in the primary system. On 19 February 1958 Lynch again told Dr Browne:

(a) Approximately 20 per cent. (i.e., 2,079 teachers) of the lay teachers in national schools are untrained (the figure 2,079 includes 1,256 teachers in the category Junior Assistant Mistress normally an untrained class). (b) Approximately 32 per cent. (i.e., 927 teachers) of the religious in national schools are untrained (282 of these i.e., about 10 per cent. of the total, are awaiting entry to the training college, some having already undergone the first year of training). (c) the present output rate of trained lay teachers from the training colleges is 418. (d) The annual wastage rate of trained lay teachers at present is 334. (e) On the basis of current enrolment approximately, 3,100 additional teachers would be required to implement the recommendations of the Council of Education in regard to the staffing of national schools.[25]

The last statistic put into context the level of the educational crisis in the 1950s.[26]

Browne drew attention to a third problem in primary education when he asked Lynch on 20 March 1958 if he would state the number of classes in schools in the city of Dublin that were overcrowded. Lynch replied:

In the circumstances I feel it should suffice if I tell the Deputy that by reference to enrolment for the year 1956–57 and the number of classes operating on 30th June, 1957, the average number of pupils to a class in national schools in Dublin county borough was 47.[27]

He evaded giving a precise answer. There were fifty-seven in my own fourth class in Raheny National School in Dublin in 1955. That was not unusual in many new suburban areas of an expanding city in the late 1950s. Therefore, many schools in Dublin had classes far in excess of the average of forty-seven pupils.

There was a further problem at the primary school level. In practice, the majority of pupils left national school on or before the age of fourteen; but they could be maintained on the roll-books until they reached the age of eighteen. According to the report of a committee in 1947 on the raising of the school-leaving age, the statistics available showed that there were 215,000 children in the country between the ages of twelve and sixteen. Some 144,000, or two-thirds, were already in whole-time attendance at school. Almost half the number, 107,000, were in national schools. The report acknowledged the inadequacy of the national school system for that age group.[28] Many pupils remained for as long as possible in primary school before becoming part of the more than 400,000 who emigrated to Britain during the 1950s.

The debate on primary schools must be set in the context of the contemporary discussion provoked by the Council of Education's report on the function and curriculum of the primary schools. Published in 1954, it was the subject of much discussion.[29] However, according to Seán O'Connor, Lynch ignored the report as far as that was possible, 'which was probably the best thing to do with that lacklustre and most conservative document.'[30] His successor, Dr Patrick Hillery, received a report from the same body on secondary education. Both Lynch and Hillery were quietly opposed to any philosophy that failed to link education with the struggle for economic modernisation and development.[31]

While Lynch did not resolve the fundamental problems of the educational system during his two years as minister, he did succeed in having the Government lift the ban on employing married women as primary teachers. In retrospect, that may appear to be a rational if not obvious change to make in the 1950s, with so many untrained teachers in national schools. The ban, however, had been introduced by Fianna Fáil on 1 October 1933. It had its origins in a process begun under the previous Cumann na nGaedheal government. Under the direction of the Minister for Education, John Marcus O'Sullivan, the secretary of the Department of Education, S. Ó Néill, sent a letter to each of the Catholic bishops on 25 January 1932. He outlined the proposal that 'women National Teachers (including Junior Assistant Mistresses) who became qualified as such on or after a certain date, shall, on marriage, cease to be eligible for recognition in any capacity in a National School.' The Church of Ireland and other church bodies were also consulted.[32]

In a memorandum dated 28 April 1958 the Department of Education recorded that the bishops who replied in 1932 had expressed 'conflicting views.'[33] The Catholic hierarchy decided to place the matter before the general conference of bishops. On 24 March 1932 Ó Néill wrote in the light of that decision to the secretary of the Bishops' Conference, Bishop O'Doherty, setting out the reasons for such a policy from 'the ordinary official point of view.' He said it was the rule that a married woman teacher absented herself from school for two months during the period of childbirth, and a substitute was employed for that period.

This is a considerable upset to the school and the position is aggravated by reason of the fact that there is at present no margin of unemployed women teachers sufficient to supply an adequate number of suitable substitutes. In some cases it is impossible to get any substitute at all to go to a remote part of the country for the short period of two months—with the result that there is in such cases no teacher to do the work during the period.[34]

He then asked:

There is also the question as to whether the employment of married women teachers in mixed schools is desirable. Of 5,400 schools in the Saorstát, approximately 3,300 are mixed schools.[35]

Further, the bishops were told: 'The continuance of women on marriage must inevitably mean some loss either to the school or to the home.' It was acknowledged, however, that 'the service of married women teachers during the latter period of married life is satisfactory.'

The letter pointed out that the average age of women teachers on marriage was about thirty-one or thirty-two, giving them about ten years' service. On financial grounds, the bar was justified.

The average amount saved in salaries as a result of substituting teachers at the minimum of the scale for women compulsorily retired on marriage would, after the first few years, be more than adequate to cover the cost of marriage gratuities.[36]

Ó Néill also pointed out to the hierarchy that the existing practice limited

the opportunity of entering the teaching profession in the case of a large number of young people who have aptitude for the work and, in consequence, tends to restrict the diffusion of employment generally.

The number of suitable women candidates wishing to enter teaching was more than twice the number that could be admitted. Finally, Ó Néill also pointed out that the presence of families with a double income in the countryside was 'a cause of considerable local irritation.'[37]

The incoming de Valera Government did not give the marriage bar any policy priority. The response of the Catholic hierarchy is not recorded. But the Department of Education, believing that it was in the best interests of the country, kept the issue alive for nearly two years. The new Minister for Education, Tom Derrig, accepted the arguments for the bar. It was taken to the government, approved, and introduced on 1 October 1933.

The bar covered both primary and the recently established vocational schools. After ten years in operation the Department was obliged to seek a relaxation of the rule. In 1944 Derrig was given permission to accept women who had been retired from teaching on marriage in national schools as temporary teachers where the manager was unable to find a qualified teacher to fill a vacancy. The period of employment of a Catholic woman teacher after retirement on marriage was restricted to one quarter. The minister had discretion to allow a longer period of employment to a Protestant woman teacher.[38]

That did not resolve the problem, any more than the policy decision in 1946 to replace untrained junior assistant mistresses with trained national teachers. The latter remained no more than a pious aspiration.[39] But, despite the damage done to schools, the policy was deeply entrenched in the conservative culture of the Department of Education.

In 1953 the Minister for Education, Seán Moylan, went to the Government with the following recommendation:

The Minister for Education accordingly desires to recommend to the Government that the rule requiring woman national teachers to retire on marriage should not be rescinded or modified and that the proposal made by him in his memorandum of the 11th October for the provision of extra Training College accommodation for women should be approved.[40]

The rationale for the retention of the status quo was laid out in a memorandum dated 14 February 1953. It deserves to be quoted in full.

MEMORANDUM FOR THE GOVERNMENT
THE RULE REQUIRING WOMEN TEACHERS TO RETIRE ON MARRIAGE
1. In accordance with the arrangement made at the Government meeting of the 3rd November last, the Minister for Education submits this memorandum on the question of a modification of the Rule, introduced in 1934 (copy attached), requiring women teachers to retire on marriage.

2. The number of women N.Ts. who retire compulsorily on marriage is at present between 60 and 70 per annum; this number will probably grow with the increase in the number of women in the service to whom the Rule applies.

3. The arguments in favour of the Rule are:—
   (a) the care and direction of a home, and the rearing of a family, constitute a whole-time assignment sufficient to tax the strength and energy

of the normal woman. The addition of another arduous avocation, involving extended daily absences from the home, must impose a physical and mental strain on the woman herself, and she could not be expected to reach a high standard of efficiency in both spheres of activity.

(b) Marriage involves for most women child-birth. The present Rules require that a married woman teacher shall absent herself from school for two months i.e. a month before and a month after child-birth; and employ a substitute. There is a distinct loss of teaching power, even where a fully qualified substitute is available, and, a fortiori, where, as so often happens, a non-qualified substitute has to be accepted. There are also inevitable short and slight illnesses and inconveniences necessitating absence without a substitute and contributing still further to the loss of teaching power.

(c) There is bound to be comment and a degree of unhealthy curiosity in mixed schools of boys and girls and even in schools for girls only, during the later months of pregnancy of married women teachers.

(d) Ordinarily, it would be expected that a man should be willing and able to maintain a wife and family without the addition of a second income in the shape of a salary earned by his wife. Women teachers usually marry men of substance and as a consequence two substantial incomes find their way to one house. This causes unfavourable comment in a country where incomes are small and ready cash not easily available. Under the present salary scales, husband and wife, both teachers, can have a joint income of £1,175, exclusive of principals', children's and rent allowances.

(e) There is a more than ample supply of suitable candidates seeking entry to the profession. The effect of depriving over 60 girls annually (see paragraph 2 above) of the opportunity of becoming teachers and acquiring a livelihood would be serious. Already the complaint is made that there are too few outlets for the 2,000 girls who obtain the Leaving Certificate each year and that too many of these have to go abroad. If marriage is a sufficient career for the normal woman then, when a woman teacher marries, she should make way for the young unmarried woman, who has as yet not other career.

(f) Women civil servants and vocational teachers are required to retire on marriage, and in most cases secondary schools dispense with the services of women teachers when they marry.

4. The arguments advanced against compulsory retirement of women on marriage are given under, with, for convenience of reference, comments thereon.

ARGUMENTS	COMMENTS
(*a*) The State and the teacher herself are not adequately recouped, by way of service given and remuneration received, for the money, time and energy expended in the process of preparation for the profession.	(*a*) As far as the State is concerned a saving results from compulsory retirement on marriage, even if allowance is made for payment of marriage gratuity and cost of training of successors (including capital cost of providing extra Training College accommodation.)
(*b*) Women Teachers marry after ten years' experience or so when they are physically and mentally at their best. They are replaced by young and immature teachers with a resultant loss of educational efficiency.	(*b*) The efficiency of the older teacher, against that of her young successor, can be easily overrated. Much depends on the personal equation. There is no clear evidence that the marriage rule results in a loss of efficiency.
(*c*) The rule must militate against the chance of attracting the best candidates. Parents will hesitate to enter their girls for a "temporary" profession.	(*c*) In point of fact, the supply of suitable candidates for teaching is more than ample (par. 3(*e*) above). The marriage rule in the civil service does not deter girls from entering that service.
(*d*) Married teachers who have children of their own are more likely to sympathise with and understand their pupils, and to treat them with a motherliness that could not be expected from single women.	(*d*) This consideration is greatly exaggerated. No person has an inexhaustible fund of these emotions and, if it is being used up both at home and at school, it is likely to run out on occasions. These emotions are inherent in women as regards children and it could be argued that if they are not being drawn on at home they are more likely to be available in school.

(*e*) The woman teacher having marriage as her object will regard her teaching work as of secondary importance.

(*e*) The teacher, like any other woman, realises that marriage may, or may not, come her way, and she is unlikely to alter her attitude towards her profession because, if she does marry, she would have to retire. Were it otherwise the standard of efficiency amongst women teachers would not be as high as it is.

(*f*) The marriage rule is contrary to the spirit if not the letter of the Constitution, which gives the same rights, privileges and status to women as to men in that it places an impediment on women which is not placed on men.

(*f*) The Constitution stresses the supreme importance of the family. The wife has her duties and obligations as well as the husband in the creation and maintenance of the home, and anything that hinders the fulfilment of those duties and obligations would be contrary to the Constitution.

(*g*) Married women teachers have been employed for over 100 years; no case had ever been made that their efficiency was impaired by their married responsibilities; and no representative body had asked for the present rule.

(*g*) That case could not be made without a personal investigation into the lives of the women concerned, and that is not feasible. The Rule stands on the logic that the woman cannot with full efficiency serve both the home and school. If the Minister should act only on representations from outside then he would be deprived of all initiative. No representative body, other than the I.N.T.O. has called for the removal of the rule. The Bishops were consulted before its introduction. Collectively they refused to pronounce showing that they were not prepared to oppose.

(*h*) The rule operates as a barrier to marriage. A woman with a continuing income is more likely to receive offers of marriage than one who has to resign. She who has to retire will be disinclined to sacrifice her independence and her comfortable income for the cares and responsibilities of marriage and will postpone the step as long as possible. A regulation which prevents or postpones marriage has serious moral implications.

(*h*) This is tantamount to demanding that women teachers should have a privileged place in the matrimonial field without regard to any other consideration. A similar claim could be made for women civil servants and all those required to resign when they wed. The issue would then arise that the State should provide marriage gratuities for those girls who have no dowry, no income, and no job. It is submitted that the State has met the needs of the situation fully by the payment of marriage gratuities to women teachers.

5. The rule was introduced on the basis of specific educational moral and social considerations, and to remove it would be to announce that these are no longer valid. If the Rule were to be abrogated even as a temporary measure to meet a shortage of teachers, it would be extremely difficult if not impossible to re-impose it, owing to pressure from those affected. (There are of course certain types of case (small remote schools, etc.) where married women have to be accepted temporarily and in a non-pensionable capacity). Furthermore teachers' salary scales have since 1946 rested on a marriage differentiation, based on the fact that in due course the position would cease to occur wherein a man teacher would have a special married scale whilst his wife also a teacher, would have a woman's full salary. The granting in 1951 to teachers of children's allowances would make that situation more anomalous still; at present the payment of the two salaries and of children's allowances is justified only by the fact that the incidence of such duality is gradually disappearing.[41]

The Department of Finance did not accept that recommendation. In a memorandum dated 19 February 1953 it rejected the proposal for the establishment of a third training college for women teachers, favouring the employment of graduates to meet the shortage and suggesting the 'temporary relaxation of the marriage bar.' The department did agree, however, that the rule requiring women teachers to retire on marriage was 'desirable in principle'; but it suggested that the bar would be affected if the employment of women in other callings, such as medicine and commerce, continues to increase, as the position may be reached where young women would choose a career in fields offering continued employment after marriage and would be drawn away from entering on a career as a teacher.[42]

According to the memorandum, the Minister for Finance, Seán MacEntee, informed the Government that he

would not regard the modification of the ban for a short period to meet a temporary shortage of teachers as impairing the validity of the rule of preventing the application of the rule when circumstances no longer require its modification.[43]

As a way out, the Government sought to increase the number of primary teachers entering training colleges. But it did not provide an answer to the growing problem of having to employ more and more untrained teachers.

The inter-party Government between 1954 and 1957 refused to make any change in the policy. In a reply in the Dáil to the Fianna Fáil TD Michael Davern on 11 May 1955 the Minister for Education, Richard Mulcahy, repeated the official position that 'the continuance in operation of the rule requiring women national teachers to retire on marriage is a matter of general policy involving considerations of a social and economic as well as of an educational nature.' He did not think it would be appropriate to rescind or modify this rule for the purpose of dealing with a shortage of teachers.[44] The policy reflected a popular prejudice against the employment of women in general in Ireland in the 1950s.

Soon after coming into office Lynch set up a committee of six senior officials in his department to make recommendations on how the problem of untrained teachers could be solved. With one dissenting voice, the committee recommended the abrogation of the marriage bar.[45] Arguments were set out in an appendix to the memorandum that Lynch brought to the Government at the end of April 1958. The report was a comprehensive rejection of the 1953 Department of Education memorandum on the same subject. The committee estimated that the educational loss in the operation of the marriage bar in primary schools was approximately 105 trained women teachers every year. They worked on average eleven years before being obliged to leave their posts. It was felt that the great majority were likely to remain in employment if the bar were revoked. Such women were being obliged to leave the profession 'just when they had reached the peak of their efficiency.'[46] The committee estimated that the educational loss involved was 'very considerable' and was compounded by the fact that motherhood is likely to give a woman teacher a special understanding of and sympathy with children in their relations with their fellow-pupils and with their parents. A married woman, in addition, developed a poise and a maturity of outlook in her relations with adults as well as children, and a capacity to help and advise parents which can be of great value to a local community.[47]

The committee held the view that 'many a rural community has derived great benefit from the devotion and influence of a husband and wife teaching together in the local school.' It held that the marriage bar had deterred 'some women teachers from marriage and that their efficiency is affected on that account.'

Rejected out of hand was the once-cherished argument that the pregnancy of a teacher might occasion 'unhealthy' curiosity and comment among pupils. The committee stated politely that it did not find the argument 'a compelling one today.' It commented further:

> There has developed a more natural, open and healthy attitude to matters of this kind and, for that reason there is less danger of the morbid curiosity which Victorian pseudo-gentility tended to foster in children's minds. Furthermore, many pupils have seen their own mothers during pregnancy.[48]

It was felt that the removal of the marriage bar would lead to greater stability in the teaching profession, as married women would not be inclined to change schools frequently. School managers had found it a constant source of anxiety that young women in rural areas tended to change jobs frequently and to gravitate towards urban areas.

The committee was also quick to despatch, as having lost its validity, the argument that the combined income of husband and wife might have occasioned local irritation where both were teachers or where the husband of a woman teacher was well off. The committee pointed out that

> the Republic of Ireland is probably unique among those countries in the world which are associated with the International Labour Office in the matter of the imposition of a marriage ban on teachers, both primary and vocational.

Based on an examination of the ILO's annual report for 1957, it was apparent that 'apart from ourselves, none of the associated countries has imposed or continues to impose, a permanent marriage ban on teachers.'[49]

The committee reported that women were now employed in factories and in offices, while women in business and in the professions continued to work in their respective fields after marriage. The report conceded that objections could be raised to the employment of large numbers of women in industry, 'but the fact must now be faced that such is now the pattern of life in many countries.' That made the argument in favour of the ban all the more difficult to sustain. Women teachers, with short hours and long holidays, were in a better position to look after their families than other women employed in factories and in industry.

The committee made the connection between a good educational system and economic progress.

> Education is vitally important to the welfare and progress of a country: the less favourable its economic position the more enterprising it needs to be in providing adequate education for its people. The retention of married women teachers offers a ready and immediate means of staffing with trained teachers many of the schools now staffed with untrained and/or unqualified teachers.[50]

The committee concluded that the shortage of teachers was 'having a detrimental effect on hundreds of primary school pupils.' The employment of a large number of unqualified teachers was 'wholly indefensible on educational grounds.' Additional teacher training places would not solve the problem. The gravity of the existing situation 'brooks no such long delay,' it concluded.[51]

The Department of Education sent a memorandum to the Government towards the end of April 1958, together with the committee's report and other statistics and documents. The memorandum stated that 'the Minister is in agreement with the committee's views and conclusions.' The Government was informed that the minister was 'keenly aware' that it was 'precisely in those parts of the country where facilities for post-primary education are almost non-existent that the majority of the untrained and unqualified teachers are serving.'[52] It repeated a number of the arguments outlined in the original committee report. But most compelling were the figures. On 30 June 1957 there were 6,866 lay women teachers serving in recognised posts in national schools, of whom 2,027 were untrained, although 1,339 of those had qualifications as junior assistant mistresses. The figure would have been higher were it not for the fact that 180 teachers had been retained in the service until they had reached the age of sixty-eight. Moreover, on 30 June 1957 there were 235 married women working in primary schools. Almost all were fully trained national teachers, but they were ineligible for recognition because of the marriage bar.

The lifting of the ban, the Government was informed, would bring two hundred married teachers back into the service, in addition to those already employed in a temporary capacity. It was estimated further that the lifting of the ban would affect about ninety women teachers annually who, on marriage, would continue to teach. Therefore, the lifting of the ban would diminish the need for untrained teachers and help eliminate the problem thus created in the long run. The change in policy would also help reduce class sizes. The costings were laid out, and it was estimated that the removal of the ban would be a saving to the state.[53]

The minister, the memorandum added, did not intend to submit the proposed policy change for the consideration of the Catholic hierarchy. It was noted that the hierarchy had declined to express an opinion in 1932. 'It may be stated, however, that several leading members of the Hierarchy and many other prominent clergymen have recently expressed the view privately that the ban on married women teachers should be removed.' Lynch sought the permission of the Government to abrogate, with effect from 1 July 1958, rule 72 (1) of the Rules and Regulations for National Schools, the rule requiring women teachers in national schools to retire from the service on marriage.[54]

Amid much press speculation and questions in the Dáil, on 11 June 1958 Lynch announced the lifting of the marriage bar, with effect from 1 July. He pointed to the problem of unqualified teachers. Even the provision of more training facilities, he said, would not resolve that problem.

> Approximately 105 trained teachers retire each year. These teachers, on their retirement, have an average of 11 years' service. I gave it as my opinion before that many of them retired when they were coming to the peak of their teaching capacity. I thought, and still think, that it represented a serious loss to the State of so much teaching capacity at an age when women are best able to teach.

He rejected an argument that had been used by his department since 1932.

> With regard to the objection to mothers teaching in school, on the contrary, I think that a mother has poise and maturity that give her a special advantage in teaching; that give her a special advantage in relation to the children she controls and, in particular, in dealing with parents and helping and advising them as to the progress of their children and as to the careers their children might well follow. In the past, as we all know, many rural communities revolved around the married teachers, the husband and wife, teaching in the same schools. It was a wonderful advantage to a locality . . . Therefore, the removal of the ban, I believe, will lead to greater stability and less frequent changes. In addition, a woman who could look forward to teaching, if she so wished, after her marriage would in the early

years apply herself much more effectively to her profession and even in the early years would become a more efficient teacher. The fact remains, also, that some 235 married women teachers are already accepted into the service in different parts of the country in a temporary capacity.

The lifting of the marriage bar on primary and vocational teachers may appear to people living in the twenty-first century to have been a routine administrative decision. But an entrenched policy had to be overturned. Without fanfare, Lynch changed that policy. In 1979 he outlined his record in education as follows: 'I was Minister for Education for only two years but during that time I was responsible for removing the marriage ban on women teachers. I also decided on a major building project at the training college in Drumcondra . . .' Seán O'Connor also singled out for note the minister's decision in 1959 to recruit candidates to the primary teacher training colleges on the grounds of an interview and not on results alone.[55]

In the same interview in 1979 Jack Lynch recalled that he had removed the 6 per cent and 10 per cent cuts introduced by the inter-party Government (1954–7) in vocational and secondary education *per capita* grants. He had doubled the rate of primary school building and also introduced the idea of an oral test in Irish for the Leaving Certificate.

> I established a commission to review accommodation and grants. As a result there was a considerable increase in university grants. I asked that the committee should investigate whether Earlsfort Terrace [UCD] should be expanded but it was felt that the acquisition of new property in that area would be very expensive, therefore, they would have to build upwards. It was then that the massive Belfield project got under way.[56]

In the light of Lynch's review of his record, did he make an impact during his brief spell in Education? Professor Séamas Ó Buachalla offers the following assessment: 'Lynch's term of office did not witness any major changes in the system yet his two years are significant in that they ushered in the beginning of some of the policies which dominated the succeeding decades.'[57] He also argues that the new minister 'had not available to him the resources to initiate major changes.' Yet he points out that Lynch 'was among the first to link the functioning of the educational system with the social reality of Irish society.'[58]

Seán Farren argued that Lynch had made no impact on the secondary school system but continued 'to express the same complacency and satisfaction about the education system as his predecessors had.' Lynch described the system as 'sound' and argued that the role of the state was merely 'to allow the

conductors of schools the widest possible freedom compatible with the protection of the State's interests arising from expenditure undertaken by it.'[59]

Seán O'Connor, who knew the strength of conservatism in the civil service
from the inside, provided a more rounded understanding of Lynch's tenure in
Marlborough Street. He agrees with Farren that Lynch 'eschewed interference
in secondary education.' He made some improvement in the vocational
schools, he said, but 'did nothing to remove the disadvantages under which the
vocational system laboured.' Nonetheless, O'Connor argued that Lynch 'initiated reform and his contribution to Irish education, particularly at primary
level, was substantial.' He concluded that 'the removal of the marriage ban, the
ending of recruitment of untrained teachers, the initiation of a sequence of
improvements in the teacher-pupil ratio, and the reform of the inspection
system added up to no small achievement in a two-year span.'[60]

Chapter 4 ～

MINISTER FOR INDUSTRY
AND COMMERCE, 1959–65

The 1950s had been, in the words of Cormac Ó Gráda, 'a miserable decade for the Irish economy.'[1] Joe Lee wrote that 'no other European country . . . has recorded so slow a rate of growth of national income in the twentieth century.'[2] The following table shows growth rates for selected countries from the 1960s to the 1980s.

EUROPEAN GROWTH RATE AVERAGE (SELECTED COUNTRIES), 1960–70, 1973–83[3]

Country	1960–70	1973–83	Country	1960–70	1973–83
Austria	4.5	2.8	Italy	5.3	2.2
Belgium	4.8	1.8	Netherlands	5.5	1.5
Denmark	4.7	1.8	Norway	4.9	3.7
Finland	4.6	2.7	Portugal	6.2	—
France	5.7	2.5	Spain	7.1	1.8
FR Germany	4.4	2.1	Sweden	4.4	1.3
Greece	6.9	3.0	Switzerland	4.3	0.7
Ireland	4.2	3.2	United Kingdom	2.9	1.1

Between 1951 and 1961 the population of the Republic declined more rapidly than in previous decades, so much so that the 1961 figure of 2.8 million was the lowest on record.[4] The following table shows Ireland in the 1950s and early 60s to be in a pre-modern phase of development, with the largest category of the work force in agriculture, forestry and fishing.[5]

Despite being independent for more than three decades, Ireland had failed to reduce significantly its dependence on the British market. In 1959 approximately 47 per cent of Irish imports came from Britain and approximately 4 per cent from the North; in 1965, 55 per cent of imports came from Britain and almost 7 per cent from the North.[6] The destination of exports was almost reciprocal: in 1959 almost 60 per cent went to Britain, another 14 per cent to the North; in 1965, 58 per cent still went to Britain and almost 12 per cent to the North.[7] Trade in 1959 saw imports at a 'record level' of £212.5 million, an increase of 6.8 per cent over the 1958 figure of £199 million. Exports, despite a drop of £8.4 million in the export of live cattle, were valued at £130.7 million, only 0.4 per cent less than the 1958 total.[8] The United Kingdom was clearly the Republic's primary trading partner. Something had to be done to increase the number of industries and to extend the range of trading partners.

EMPLOYMENT IN IRELAND BY INDUSTRIAL GROUP, 1951–71[9]

	1951	1961	1966	1971
Agriculture, forestry and fishing	497,802	379,919	333,527	273,079
Building and construction	85,790	59,587	74,140	84,533
Other production industries	194,768	197,585	219,593	238,216
Commerce, insurance, finance, business services	162,958	159,086	166,144	172,278
Transport, communications, storage	59,744	54,167	57,246	60,122
Public administration and defence	39,745	40,543	43,189	48,869
Professional services	75,316	84,821	93,774	109,078
Other	100,983	76,831	78,374	68,664
Total	1,217,106	1,052,539	1,065,987	1,054,839

The secretary of the Department of Finance, Dr Ken Whitaker, had outlined a blueprint for recovery in 1958 in his document *Economic Development* and subsequently in the *White Paper on Economic Expansion*. A shift in national leadership coincided with, rather than precipitated, a strategy for change. On 15 January 1959 Éamon de Valera announced to a Fianna Fáil party meeting his intention to resign as Taoiseach.[10] That would not be the end of his role in public life: on 17 June he was elected President of Ireland, to succeed Seán T. O'Kelly. He was then aged seventy-seven.[11] Seán Lemass was proposed by two party elders, MacEntee and Aiken, for the leadership of the party,[12] and on 23 June 1959 he was elected Taoiseach.

Lemass, who was sixty, knew that the country needed an immediate and radical change away from protectionism.[13] He called Lynch to his office in the Department of Industry and Commerce, telling him: 'I want you to sit at this desk.'[14] Feeling that he was on the verge of achieving something important in the Education portfolio, Lynch's first inclination was to say No. When Lemass insisted, he accepted the portfolio.[15]

The incoming Taoiseach did not make many changes to his Government. Most notably, the Clare TD and medical doctor Patrick Hillery succeed Lynch in Education. He shared Lynch's ideas on the need to accelerate reform of the educational system. The two men became good friends during the years that followed. James Ryan, then aged sixty-eight, continued in Finance. Charles Haughey, Lemass's son-in-law, became parliamentary secretary to the Minister for Justice.

Shortly after his appointment Lynch told an audience in Dublin that

there is widespread acceptance that the government's proposals outlined in the White Paper for Economic Development, are both realistic and imaginative and that, properly and assiduously executed, this programme, with suitable adaptations as the need may arise, is well suited to our economic advance.

Lemass had put Lynch in his old ministry for the precise purpose of bringing about a shift to free trade.

At the inaugural meeting of the Technical Students' Debating Society on 11 November 1959 Lynch stated:

In a free-enterprise economy the government's duty is primarily, insofar as it can, to create the conditions which make for prosperity and to encourage but not to dictate to the free citizen how he should use his opportunities. The citizen's duty on the other hand is to have confidence in his own ability to make progress, to be able to appraise the problems and difficulties that he must overcome and to use the best means at his disposal or within his procurement to tackle these problems. He must realise that he has his own part to play in the working of the complex national scheme.[16]

That was new language for a Minister for Industry and Commerce. The espousal of that philosophy placed him on a potential collision course with his new department, which had carefully husbanded the policy of protectionism since the 1930s.

While the shift from protection to free trade was Lynch's goal, he had to face on his first day in his new post the stark reality that the Department of Industry and Commerce was more a combination of satellite departments than a single entity. The secretary of the department, J. C. B. MacCarthy, was supported by four assistant secretaries: P. Ó Slatarra (chairman of the Fair Trade Commission), A. Ó Coinneáin, T. Cahill and J. Murphy. J. Gannon was the new minister's private secretary.[17] The department was organised into six divisions: Finance, Establishment, Industries and Foreign Trade, Commerce, Labour, and Cereals. Industries and Foreign Trade, which included the responsibility for exports and duty-free licensing, was the largest. Most of the divisions had one principal officer and an assistant principal officer; however, Exports and Industries had three principal officers and six assistant principal officers. The Registry of Friendly Societies, the Industrial and Commercial Property Registration Office, the Geological Survey, the Weights and Measures Office and an Industrial Inspectorate were also under the jurisdiction of the new minister. Other agencies coming under the department's umbrella were the Labour Court, the Industrial Development Authority, An Foras Tionscal and the Fair Trade Commission.[18]

The economic development picture when Lynch took over the department in 1959 was as follows. An Foras Tionscal—the statutory body established in 1952 for the purpose of making grants to industry—received 81 new applications in the year to the end of March 1959. Of these, 19 had been approved, 20 were pending and 42 were rejected, mainly on the grounds that it would be unfair to existing industries producing for the home market. From 1952 to March 1959 An Foras Tionscal had approved investment grants of £2,232,740 (£1,110,684 actually granted) to eighty separate projects that employed an estimated 3,875 people (2,007 male, 1,868 female).[19] Significantly, the approval of nineteen projects in 1958/9 alone represented almost a third of total approvals from 1952 to 1958. This upsurge in activity had not really been seen since the halcyon days of the agency's foundation.[20]

The Industrial Development Authority, established in 1949 to attract industries to Ireland, was not empowered to award grants until the enactment of the Industrial Development (Encouragement of External Investment) Act (1958). The authority's total commitment from 1956 to 31 March 1960 amounted to £1,092,850 in respect of twenty-two projects. Actual payments made by the IDA in that period were £236,900. That had generated an estimated 2,818 jobs.[21] Under the Industrial Grants Act (1959) the grant-awarding function of the IDA was transferred to An Foras Tionscal from 26 August.[22]

The Economic Development Branch, which had emerged in September 1959 under the umbrella of the Department of Finance, was strong evidence of a shift in power away from the Department of Industry and Commerce. Chaired by a future secretary of the Department of Finance, Charles Murray, the EDB set about its work with great vigour and determination. Lynch, on taking over Industry and Commerce, found himself very much in the centre of that demarcation controversy. The development bodies, under the auspices of his department, were among the first objects of interest to the EDB. The IDA and the grant-awarding Foras Tionscal were not very happy with this new development. Dr J. P. Beddy, chairman of the Industrial Credit Corporation, of the IDA and of An Foras Tionscal, fought his corner very well but ultimately had to learn to live with the new situation. Lynch had the responsibility of acting as peace-maker between the two departments.

LYNCH AND THE LEGISLATIVE BACKLOG

Lynch inherited a bewildering array of incomplete legislation, consisting of seventeen bills at various stages of formation. In the first instance there were four bills to be enacted in the current session: the Air Navigation and Transport Bill, the Export Promotion Bill, the Electricity (Supply) (Amendment) Bill and a bill to amend the Industrial Grants Act (1956). It was also planned to circulate and introduce three new bills in that session: the Transport Bill, a bill to finance the Shannon Free Airport Development Company, and the Petroleum (Exploration and Development) Bill.

A further ten bills were proposed for the following session. These concerned hire purchase, mines and quarries, a new Companies Bill, explosives, an amendment to the Restrictive Trade Practices Act (1953), the protection of performers of dramatic and musical works, an amendment to the Harbours Acts, a Mercantile Marine Bill and amendments to the Truck Acts and to the Industrial Research and Standards Act (1946). The Export Promotion Bill and the amendment of the Industrial Grants Act were among the priorities.[23]

Lynch pushed forward his policy on apprenticeship for An Cheard-Chomhairle, the statutory body for regulating apprenticeship, and it was published in December 1960. The policy required that there be a suitable educational qualification for entry to apprenticeship, a reasonable but realistic approach to the intake of apprentices, a programme for training on the job that would ensure that apprentices reached a proper standard of skill, the release of apprentices from work for attendance at technical school courses, a review of the length of apprenticeship in the light of improved arrangements for practical and theoretical training, and supervision of the progress of apprentices, particularly by a system of tests in trade practice and theory during and at the end of apprenticeship. An Cheard-Chomhairle brought the trades of motor mechanic and electrician and the trades in the furniture industry under the scope of the Apprenticeship Act (1959) and established statutory apprenticeship committees for them. It also appointed supervisors for those trades—technical experts whose functions included assisting in the preparation and implementation of suitable training programmes. The statutory apprenticeship committees and An Cheard-Chomhairle agreed on minimum educational qualifications for entry into apprenticeship in the trades with which the committees were concerned.[24]

Lynch also pushed forward legislation to take account of changing economic circumstances in the fields of consumers' rights and company law. He moved the second stage of the Hire-Purchase (Amendment) Bill in February 1960. The bill contained provisions intended to protect consumers' rights, attempting to protect them from the often hidden 'small print' relating to terms and conditions.[25] It entitled the minister to regulate the minimum

deposits and maximum periods of payment for HP and credit sale transactions.
The handling of such legislation was part of the unglamorous side of being a
Government minister.

LYNCH AND THE INDUSTRIAL UNREST OF THE 1960s

Lynch's portfolio also gave him responsibility for labour at a period of
unprecedented industrial unrest. 'There were', he recalled, 'a number of occasions during which I was called back from holiday because of strikes and my
wife and I lost a few holiday deposits during that period.' The demands of the
job 'virtually shattered my private life.'[26] The following table will support that
assertion.[27]

	Number of disputes	Number of firms affected	Number of people involved	Work-days lost
1960	49	60	5,865	80,349
1961	96	342	27,437	377,264
1962	60	112	9,197	104,024
1963	70	114	16,067	233,617
1964	87	339	25,245	545,384
1965	89	227	38,917	552,351
1966	112	175	52,238	783,635
1967	79	237	20,925	182,645
1968	126	801	38,880	405,686
1969	134	368	61,760	935,900
1970	134	159	28,752	1,007,714
1971	133	153	43,783	273,770

Charles McCarthy pointed out in his retrospective overview of industrial
unrest in the 1960s that strikes during that decade had two distinguishing
features: they occurred at all social levels, blue-collar and white-collar, and
they were protracted in character.[28] Industrial relations continued to be regulated by free collective bargaining and by custom and practice. Exceptionally,
the Agricultural Wages Board was empowered to set down the statutory
minimum wages for farm labourers.[29]

In November 1959 officials of the Department of Industry and Commerce
considered alterations in industrial relations machinery to remove the necessity for intervention by members of the Government in future disputes. Lynch
had been dragged into the petrol strike in November 1959, as the Labour
Court declined to allow its conciliation officers to intervene after its initial

recommendations had been rejected. He was consequently anxious that con-ciliation services be available at all stages of a dispute and tentatively raised the desirability of removing the necessity for intervention by members of the Government in future disputes. However, as Lynch informed his advisers, the matter had been discussed informally and 'the general feeling of the Government was that it was not necessary to make any change,' and any pro-posals for alterations were unlikely to be acceptable.[30]

The Employer-Labour Conference was established in 1963 to provide a national forum for the discussion and review of all major industrial relations problems. It was reconstituted under the chairmanship of Professor Basil Chubb in 1970.[31] Free collective bargaining helped secure agreement on the eighth (1961), ninth (1964), tenth (1966) and eleventh (1968) national wage rounds. Sustained industrial unrest cost the economy dearly in the 1960s. Lynch held responsibility for the labour area until he was moved to the Department of Finance in 1965.[32]

TOURISM AND MINING

As Minister for Industry and Commerce, Lynch was constantly challenged to balance Irish industrial interests against the risk of entering into agreement with foreign consortiums wishing to invest in the country. The outside inter-ests consistently drove a hard bargain, knowing how desperate the Government was to provide jobs and to build up new areas of employment in disadvantaged areas.

In moving the second stage of the Tourist Traffic Bill on 9 July 1959, Lynch earmarked additional funds for Bord Fáilte Éireann 'to enable the Board to operate a programme of financial assistance for the development of major tourist resorts and the provision of additional bedroom accommodation in tourist hotels.'[33] In brief, the bill provided that Bord Fáilte would be able to draw from the exchequer £1 million over ten years to assist 'local authorities and other agencies who are willing to prepare and execute suitable schemes for the improvement of local amenities.'[34]

When looking back at progress over two years, Lynch took satisfaction from his contribution to the development of that industry. He said in 1961 that income from visitors in 1960 had reached a record figure of £42.4 million, compared with £37.8 million in 1959, and since 1957 that represented a 30 per cent increase in earnings from the industry. He also pointed out that his ini-tiative in January 1960, allowing new grant and tax incentives, paid dividends and alleviated possible bottlenecks in the provision of accommodation. During 1960 seventy-six hotel projects were undertaken, providing more than six hundred new bedrooms. The total capital investment involved in those projects was of the order of £1 million.[35]

In November 1959 Lynch had to deal with a proposal supported by Bord
Fáilte for a 350-bed hotel in Dublin backed by Intercontinental Hotels
Corporation. Two additional hotel projects were in prospect, in Cork and
Limerick, contingent on approval of the Dublin application. But Lynch,
unimpressed by the particularly small contribution from foreign investors,
wanted at least 50 per cent of the total capital. He referred the matter back to
Bord Fáilte with a message

> that he would be willing to consider proposals from other groups for the
> construction of this hotel. It should also be brought home to Bord Fáilte
> that it was important that nothing should be done which might give the
> impression that special treatment was being given to the foreign interests
> which had put up this proposal, or that they were being given terms more
> favourable than those which might be available to an Irish group.[36]

He insisted on leaving the door open for an Irish-led proposal.

Intercontinental duly submitted a revised proposal, which envisaged a
total investment of £1.428 million, down from the original £2 million, comprising £600,000 in sponsors' money and assumed eligibility for a further
£105,000 in bedroom grants from Bord Fáilte. That left an application for the
balance of £723,000, or 54 per cent, to be provided by guaranteed loan. While
normal practice was not to approve loans greater than 50 per cent, Bord Fáilte
recommended an exception in this case. The hotel would be owned by an Irish-
registered company and managed by Intercontinental, which would be entitled
to 25 per cent of gross profits. Assuming 60 per cent occupancy, an annual gross
profit of £176,000 was forecast, giving a projected profit of £44,000 per year to
Intercontinental Hotels. The consortium requested a thirty-year lending period,
which was twice the normal period. While the minister could not approve
that position, he would not object if they got the finance elsewhere.

The Department of Industry and Commerce recommended approval, subject to certain considerations. Firstly, the Gresham Hotel proposed to build a
230-bed hotel in the city centre, and it would require terms and conditions
comparable to those granted to Intercontinental. Secondly, as both projects
would increase Dublin's single-bed availability to approximately eight
hundred by 1962, the department wondered whether demand would be sufficient to warrant the investment. Lynch approved, subject to the consortium
raising the full amount of £600,000 from non-public funds.[37]

When Intercontinental failed to secure the desired site, Bord Fáilte stated
that it was inadvisable to insist on £600,000 being raised from funds other
than public. Lynch bided his time.[38] The director-general of Bord Fáilte had
no precise details but envisaged that the capital would comprise £210,000 in

shares and £500,000 in guaranteed debentures—repayable in full after twelve years. Lynch felt that this new information made the project undesirable. He was disturbed by the lack of definite information available from Bord Fáilte concerning the capital structure. He had no difficulty with participation by Aer Rianta in the consortium, or the loan guarantee, but the consortium would have to produce more satisfactory arrangements for its share capital.[39]

Bord Fáilte reported that Intercontinental was upset over the refusal of the application. The group's European representative was despatched to Dublin for a meeting on 22 March 1960 with the secretary of the Department of Industry and Commerce, J. C. B. MacCarthy, and the assistant secretary of the Department of Finance, Sarsfield Hogan. This meeting resolved the impasse, and Lynch directed that the proposal be submitted to the Government at the end of March 1960.[40]

There was a further snag. Bord Fáilte had a letter from one of the private investors, Pan-American Airlines, outlining conditions under which it would provide a second mortgage loan of £400,000 for the project. This stipulated that there be a moratorium on repayments of the Government loan covering the period of the Pan-American loan. Intercontinental's European representative placed a similar letter before the March meeting in Dublin. Those conditions were unacceptable to Lynch. He was prepared to guarantee a loan for thirty years, giving debentures priority in the early years, but Pan-American wanted to amortise its loan in eight years.

The Department of Finance also found it unacceptable that private investors could withdraw their money during the period of the guaranteed loan. On those grounds, Lynch refused to recommend the project to the Government.[41] Intercontinental then considered reapplying, incorporating the Gresham plans, and in July a proposal emerged to proceed with projects in Dublin, Cork and Limerick. The revised project would cost £2.2 million and envisaged finance on the following basis:

Guaranteed loan	£1,100,000
Bord Fáilte	£165,000
Bank loan	£285,000
Aer Rianta	£250,000
Intercontinental Hotels	£250,000
Gresham Hotel	£100,000
Prince Sadruddin	£50,000

The bank loan would be repayable over the first five years, after which the thirty-year Government-guaranteed loan would be paid. Lynch decided on that basis to recommend the proposal to the Government. He further stated that he would expect Irish workers, materials and manufacturers to be used to the maximum in the construction, equipping and operation of the hotels. In November 1960 he directed that the project be pursued 'vigorously' if the economic study proved favourable.[42] Although it took some time, Lynch had achieved his initial objective with determination, decisiveness and a willingness to override official advice.

Lynch was happy to share responsibility in this area in 1961 with Erskine Childers and the Department of Transport and Power.[43] That transfer drew a wistful comment from James Dillon TD that 'shortly there will be nothing left of the Department of Industry and Commerce but the minister and the building in Kildare Street.'[44] Tourism in the 1960s, as Fergal Tobin remarked, 'became a major Irish industry, and by the middle of the decade it was already the country's largest single source of revenue.'[45]

Lynch was equally tough when dealing with funding for St Patrick's Copper Mine in Avoca, Co. Wicklow. After a licence had been issued in 1956 there had been a slump in the world copper market. In 1958 the Canadian company Mogul Mines Ltd sought Government-backed loans of £1.36 million.[46] In October 1959 Lynch reviewed an application for a further state guarantee of £550,000 to proceed with development. A draft memorandum submitted to the Department of Finance noted 'all the unattractive features of the proposal' but concluded that, despite those features, the minister

> still felt that the guarantee sought should be provided. This step had been taken as it was considered essential that the risks involved should be fully set out for the government; the government could then decide whether, despite these risks, the loan should be made in view of the general social and economic considerations involved.

If the loan were approved it would be the last instalment of state assistance, Lynch said. He proposed that further state aid be on the condition that 'this capital [$600,000] should be allowed to remain in the business.'[47] In early November the reply from the Department of Finance warned that 'it was undesirable that the state should become financially involved in speculative enterprises of this nature.' Lynch pointed out that there was 'the danger that this would give the workers the impression that they were employed by a semi-state body; this might lead to demands for improved pay and working conditions.'[48] Copper-mining in Co. Wicklow did not turn out to be a major long-term economic success.

ATTRACTING INDUSTRY TO CORK

At the opening of Whitegate Oil Refinery on 22 September 1959 Lynch spoke of Cork's advantages as a site for new industry. It had a natural harbour and a new dockyard; a new airport was under construction. He said Irish Steel was planning a major expansion and Goulding's new fertiliser factory was on the way, while funding for the Opera House had gathered momentum. He returned to the same theme when addressing the Cork Chamber of Commerce the following February: 'You have, indeed, good reason to be optimistic about future prospects when one examines them against the background of the principal economic events in the Cork area during the past year.' Yet, he believed, 'Cork might have done better in the attraction of new industries.'[49] Thus, while he avoided any personal approaches on job creation in Cork, he took a keen interest in the industrial welfare of his constituency.

The rebuilding of the Opera House was a cherished project. In November 1959 Lynch met the solicitor acting for the committee and trustees of the Opera House to review some points that the Department of Finance had raised on financing the project.[50] The previous month he had been called on to assist another Cork establishment, St Patrick's Woollen Mills, which sought financial assistance to stave off the effects of an American tariff quota. Córas Tráchtála, the statutory export board, confirmed that the situation was genuine and affected all Irish woollen exporters, while their competitors had assistance with meeting interest charges. The Department of Industry and Commerce, however, baulked at the idea of subsidising exports but conceded that the case had merit. The amount of money involved in covering the cost of bank accommodation until August was small—estimated at £5,000. Lynch felt that if Córas Tráchtála could not help it should consider raising the matter with the Department of Finance. Córas Tráchtála suggested establishing an export bank to provide cheap capital, but that was not pursued; it then proposed an assistance package but one in which Lynch would have to guarantee loans, and that opened up unlimited possibilities for applications from other exporters and even non-exporters.[51] Lynch continued to confront similar difficulties elsewhere.

In October 1959 the Ford Motor Company completed a feasibility study for the assembly of car engines in Cork. The chairman, Sir Patrick Hennessy, stated that the 'problem had been fully reviewed and that it was finally considered that technically and economically the proposals were not feasible.' Lynch felt there should be a fresh examination of the matter. He took that position in the knowledge that Ford was able to recondition engines in Cork; therefore he felt that it 'should be a practical proposition for the company to assemble new ones.' The matter was taken up with the new managing director of Ford in Cork, T. J. Brennan. Ford replied that to undertake that work it would need to invest £10,000 in equipment and would need more floor space, giving rise to a 'substantial increase in the cost of producing cars at Cork.' Lynch did not pursue the matter.[52]

Lynch introduced the second stage of the Irish Steel Holdings Limited Bill on 27 October 1960. Its purpose was to enable the Minister for Finance to hold £1½ million in the establishment 'and thus put that company in a position to purchase plant and put other work in hands in connection with its expansion plans.'[53] Those plans envisaged two new mills and the adaptation of the existing plant to increase capacity. All told, the expansion would increase employment by more than 200, to over 700, and would cost approximately £3½ million, of which all but £99,000 would be provided or guaranteed by the state. Lynch, with the consent of the Department of Finance, authorised borrowings of up to £½ million. All in all it was a generous package, which Liam Cosgrave supported as a 'desirable project,' though he wondered why the company did not use more of its own resources in the expansion programme.[54]

There was a proposal in October 1959 for a new tannery in Bandon, initiated by Charles Robson of the Canadian firm Robson Leather Company. In full production it proposed to employ 250 people and to be entirely geared to exports to Britain. Bandon Town Commissioners applied to have the town scheduled as an 'undeveloped area' in order to secure the tannery investment. The IDA, however, was concerned with the impact the new factory might have on existing exporters to Britain and whether the efforts to attain the ambitious export targets might have 'other undesirable consequences in our trading relations with that country.' Lynch mentioned to the IDA that the chairman of the town commissioners had made representations to him recently; a site was already purchased, for a considerable figure. The chairman of the IDA, Dr Beddy, supplied him with an interim report. Lynch advised that his reply to the chairman of the town commissioners should state that the IDA was examining the issue.[55]

Lynch might have been accused of favouritism in relation to Cork were it not for the fact that he was open and consistent about his intentions in relation to rescheduling areas. He would later assure his advisers, in private, that 'if the necessity should arise' he would 'implement any undertaking given to schedule under the Underdeveloped Acts [Undeveloped Areas Acts] areas from which suitable industrial proposals may come forward as projects in respect of which Foras Tionscal would be prepared to make a grant to the promoters.'[56] The Irish Tanners' Association registered objections to the Bandon project,[57] and the British appeared to be apprehensive.[58] Lynch learnt that the British Board of Trade had little power to prevent Irish exports, though there was a danger that it might invoke an argument on dumping, given the tax concessions Irish exporters enjoyed. There was only a limited possibility of progress.

In November 1959 Lynch considered a proposal from the Dutch entrepreneur Cornelis Verolme, who ran a dockyard in Cork, to import steel free of duty. The minister had to consult the Taoiseach over what had allegedly been agreed verbally between Verolme and Lemass during the latter's visit to the Netherlands. The IDA supported the Verolme case that that it had received an assurance that it would be given licences to import steel for any works required. Irish interests were directly concerned with such concessions.[59]

The same month Lynch faced a delicate task in relation to balancing shipbuilding requirements. Irish Shipping would be placing an order for a vessel with Verolme to initiate large-scale shipbuilding in Cork. Lynch had the power to refuse Verolme the contract for a commission from Cork Harbour Commissioners for a vessel that could be built in the Liffey Dockyard. (Cork was the second-cheapest in its tender; Liffey Dockyard had been placed eleventh in the original tenders.) Lynch justified his position on the grounds of safeguarding jobs in both Cork and Dublin.[60]

After the Minister for Transport and Power, Erskine Childers, announced the order for the Irish Shipping vessel, Verolme argued that he could proceed with the Cork vessel only in April 1960 and the Irish Shipping vessel in June. Therefore, the loss of the Cork vessel would not be a setback to him. Lynch needed to persuade Verolme to withdraw from the tender for the Cork vessel. Under Verolme's new-manufacture licence he was precluded from building smaller vessels.[61] It emerged in January that Irish Shipping and Verolme were in detailed negotiations only on specifications; price would not be negotiated for some time. Lynch was 'not prepared to waive the condition in Verolme's New Manufacture Licence about the manufacture of small vessels.'[62]

In March 1960 Verolme was reported to be negotiating an agreement with the Polish authorities. The Polish government would buy a ship from Verolme in return for imports of Polish coal. J. P. Reihill of Tedcastle's Oil Products had been approached by Verolme to influence the securing of such an order, but he was worried about the implications of such an agreement for British coal supplies.[63] Lynch's department refused to enter into any commitments on the Polish proposals. Verolme's defence of his barter proposal with Poland was that the Department of Industry and Commerce could make no commitments to pressure importers.[64] In the end the proposal fell through, as Verolme could not comply with the delivery time of nine to twelve months. But the issue still left a general question for the Government: should powers be available to restrict imports from communist countries in order to enforce the acceptance of Irish exports?[65]

Verolme proceeded with the contract for the Irish Shipping vessel, with Lynch's blessing. It would be built at a higher cost than the British tenders. The minister directly concerned, Erskine Childers, was reluctant to allow the gap to climb to more than £40,000. Verolme defended his position by stating that a first ship would incur abnormal costs. In a letter to Lemass, he cited Brazil's case of 75 per cent accepted overrun.[66]

During negotiations for building his first ship in Cork, Verolme was involved in an unsuccessful proposal to build a ship for Israel. At one point the Department of Industry and Commerce agreed in principle to provide export credit for the project. Consultations with the British rated Israel sound, despite a high political risk category. The British mentioned that Verolme 'tended to sell credit where he could not sell ships.'[67] This was perhaps Lynch's first inkling that Verolme was a colourful entrepreneur.

Lynch flatly turned down a request in 1963 from Verolme to extend his new-manufacture licence to cover all items in his company's articles of association.[68] At the same time the Department of External Affairs forwarded a copy of a letter Verolme had sent to the chairman of Nigerian Shipping Lines, in which he made the

> exaggerated claim that his company had the backing of the industrial and financial powers of Irish and Netherlands Authorities; the implication being that this would facilitate the Verolme plans for Nigeria. It was felt that something would have to be done to restrain Mr. Verolme from making such extravagant claims.

Lynch directed the chairman of the IDA, Dr Beddy, to look into a proposal to build twelve ships in a new Nigerian dock, with Cork as the main contractor and part construction in all three countries.[69] That did not come to pass.

Lynch took a mild view of what were deemed 'technical offences' committed in Ireland by Verolme. The Department of Posts and Telegraphs complained in 1964 that Verolme was reported to be providing offshore platforms for pirate radio and television operations. Enquiries established that the secretary of Verolme Cork Dockyard Ltd had confirmed that the company was making drilling rigs. Multi-purpose equipment of that kind could be used for anything; Verolme had no knowledge of intentions to use the product for pirate television.[70] The Department of Posts and Telegraphs proposed to take action against the company over the alleged possession of an illegal wireless transmitting apparatus imported by Verolme and intended for use in a floating platform that would constitute a pirate television station. Verolme, it was alleged, hoped to complete the structure and export it on 6 April. The Industry and Commerce view was that

> even if there has been a technical offence, it does not appear that punitive action by the Post Office would be warranted, having regard to the fact

that the apparatus would not be used in this country. It was proposed to write to the Department of Posts and Telegraphs suggesting that a temporary licence be given in respect of the short period remaining before the structure leaves the country.

Lynch would have 'a word with the Minister.'[71] Such were the vagaries of attracting foreign industry and capital to Ireland.

GENERAL ELECTION, THE ROAD TO FREE TRADE AND MEMBERSHIP OF THE EEC

In 1961 there were 96 strikes, affecting 342 firms and involving 27,437 workers. The number of work-days lost that year was 377,264. In that climate of social unrest, Lemass went to the polls on 4 October 1961. In power since 1957, Fianna Fáil dropped from 48 per cent to 44 per cent of first-preference votes, with a decline in the number of seats from 78 to 70. Despite the slippage in the party's electoral performance, for the first time Lynch headed the poll in Cork and was returned on the first count, together with his close friend and Fine Gael rival Stephen Barrett.

GENERAL ELECTION TO THE SEVENTEENTH DAIL, 1961 (144 SEATS)[72]
Polling day: 4 October 1961

Constituency and number of seats	Electorate and quota	Candidates	Affiliation	First preferences
Cork Borough (5)	55,022 Quota 6,216	1. John (Jack) Lynch	FF	9,929
		2. Stephen Declan Barrett	FG	9,515
		3. Seán Casey	Lab.	5,616
		4. John Galvin	FF	4,257
		Dáithí Ó Conaill	SF	1,956
		A. A. (Gus) Healy	FF	1,846
		5. Anthony Barry	FG	1,637
		Dónal J. Daly	FF	1,281
		Seán Patrick Twomey	Ind.	794
		Dominic Joseph O'Brien	FG	462

While it was an outstanding election for Lynch, Fianna Fáil now formed a minority Government. Relying on abstentions, Lemass was voted in as

Taoiseach by 72 votes to 68. The Government survived until 1965.[73] In the new Government, Lynch retained Industry and Commerce; Hillery remained in Education. The old guard—Ryan, MacEntee, Aiken and Smith—stayed in Finance, Health, External Affairs and Agriculture, respectively. Blaney kept Local Government, and Mícheál Ó Móráin the Gaeltacht; the latter was also given Lands. Kevin Boland was moved from Defence to Social Welfare. Erskine Childers dropped Posts and Telegraphs but retained Transport and Power. Charles Haughey was brought into the Government as Minister for Justice.[74]

Much had changed in the country since 1959. Ireland had applied for membership of the EEC in mid-1961. Lynch continued to play a central role in the struggle to win people over to the philosophy of free trade in anticipation of entry. Ken Whitaker in the Department of Finance and Con Cremin in External Affairs took the lead. Senior officials in the Department of Industry and Commerce spent much of their time in late 1961 and 1962 preparing supporting documents for Brussels. Lynch, in line with the tone set by Lemass on Europe, began hammering out the message that the EEC was the correct option for the country.[75] In January 1962 he exhorted industrialists to face the future with confidence and adopt modern procedures and techniques.[76] When addressing the annual dinner of the Federation of Irish Industries in 1962 he warned that industrialists who 'squatted behind the wall of protection' could expect neither sympathy nor help.[77] Launching an Irish Management Institute course in March 1962, he asserted that the 'fundamental question the manufacturer must ask himself was not "What can I most easily make?" but rather "What do people want to buy?"'[78] The EEC would present a challenge for Irish distributors too, as they would need to combine and adapt to new circumstances in the 'race for customers.'[79] On another occasion he argued that exporters should move quickly also to establish themselves in the British market, or extend their operations, before tariffs came down.[80] Again and again it was the same message going out, more refined with each delivery and modified for selected audiences.

With EEC membership in mind, Lynch set out in May 1962 to review the situation regarding grants to industry. A memorandum put before the Government in May noted:

The existing legislation is due to expire on 31 December 1963, but, having regard to the provisions of the Rome Treaty relating to aids for economic development, the minister considers that, if there is to be a reasonable prospect of the retention in Common Market conditions of a scheme of assistance for economic development, any necessary legislation should be enacted before the accession of this country to the EEC. The emergence of problems in relation to capital-intensive projects (i.e., projects with a relatively high capital and low employment content) also make it necessary to seek amending legislation.[81]

Much debate followed in the relevant bodies. On 23 November 1963 the secretary to the Government, Nicholas Nolan, outlined its approval for proceeding with a draft bill on the grounds of the need for Government approval for projects over £250,000 and a reduction to £1,000 per worker in the value of grants. Also, the restriction of 50 per cent outside 'undeveloped areas' stood, with scope for An Foras Tionscal to decide up to two-thirds in cases below £250,000. The Department of Industry and Commerce proceeded on the assumption that Lynch would have the authority to approve above the £250,000 and £1,000-per-job limits. On 11 December Nolan clarified what the Government approved that day: in effect, An Foras Tionscal could be authorised to breach the limits set by the Government, and the Minister for Industry and Commerce could authorise grants above £500,000 within the guidelines set out. The Department of Finance immediately sought a veto on the Minister for Industry and Commerce on the upper limit, and on 15 January the Government agreed.[82]

When the Committee on Industrial Organisation, set up by the Government in 1961, produced its interim report on industrial grants in December 1962 Lynch's response was tempered by the preceding negotiations with the Department of Finance. He was therefore non-committal on the question of abolishing the distinction between 'undeveloped areas' and the rest of the country, as recommended by the CIO. The latter felt that if the decentralisation of industry continued there should be selected areas of concentration, in line with trends of decentralised industrialisation in the EEC. The CIO called for grant differentials in favour of 'conversion' centres—areas not quite undeveloped but in transition. Lynch was in full agreement but not specific on details. While the CIO favoured the implicit inclusion in legislation of a provision that firms receiving grants should be capable of surviving and operating in conditions of free trade, Lynch considered the selection criteria of An Foras Tionscal already sufficient.

He agreed with the CIO's call for equality in access to grants for those intending to compete on the home market; he held that it was a matter of administration. He also agreed with the CIO's suggestion that training grants for new firms should be available to all, irrespective of location, pointing out that legislation already existed. Similarly, he felt that new legislation met the CIO's desire that no obstacles should impede capital-intensive industry, with flexibility on grant limits.[83] In its interim report the CIO had a number of useful findings. Actual jobs realised in 'undeveloped areas' were 93 per cent of the number forecast. Estimated capital investment per job in undeveloped areas was £1,107 and in the rest of the country £1,134; grants per worker were £586 in undeveloped areas and £390 elsewhere.

A survey of 172 grant-aided firms up to 31 March 1962 showed that a total of £10,582,322 had been granted. The size of individual grants, however, was small: 22 grants were less than £5,000, 40 were between £5,000 and £20,000, 46 were between £20,000 and £50,000, 30 were between £50,000 and £100,000, 28 between £100,000 and £250,000, and only 6 over £250,000. About one-eighth of the grants in undeveloped areas exceeded £100,000; in the rest of the country that proportion was about one-third.

While those discussions were going on in Ireland, the application for EEC membership was put in abeyance in January 1963 following President Charles de Gaulle's speech in which he blocked British entry. There was unconcealed disappointment in Government circles in Dublin over that development. Following the collapse of the negotiations, Lemass led a delegation of Aiken, Whitaker, MacCarthy, Nagle, McCann and some officials from the Irish embassy in London on a two-day visit to Britain. On 18 March they met the Prime Minister, Harold Macmillan, and the Secretary of State for the Commonwealth, Duncan Sandys, followed by a meeting with Sandys, Edward Heath and an array of British officials. J. C. B. MacCarthy attended from the Department of Industry and Commerce, but Lynch did not: it was too soon and would have been presumptuous. These were exploratory meetings, sounding out the British on their intentions in the aftermath of the collapse of talks and suggesting an interim trading arrangement with Britain until presumed eventual membership of the EEC. Lemass was interested in offering greater access to the Irish market for British industrial goods in return for better terms for Irish agricultural exports. This was followed by a letter from Lemass to Macmillan on 27 March—which went through painstaking drafting—giving more substance to the exploratory talks.

On the prospects of Lemass's proposals, Cremin reported on 25 April to the secretary of the Department of External Affairs that it was unlikely that the British would be able to engage in further discussions before the end of May. However, Duncan Sandys arranged to see Lemass in Dublin in mid-May.[84]

While de Gaulle's rebuff to Britain was interpreted as a setback for Ireland, it did not alter the general view on Ireland's economic future. In the bigger picture, Lynch still exhorted the Federation of Irish Industries to 'plan on the basis that the world is moving into an era of freer trade, and that our economy can prosper only if we are able to compete successfully in world markets.' Lynch advised industry to combine; urging a 'unity-is-strength' principle, he advocated major rethinking in adapting all aspects of relatively small-scale industry to large-scale market conditions. Inevitably, this would call for decisions on specialisation, variety reduction, product redesign and marketing.

To facilitate these efforts Lynch had earlier established a new division within his department, the Industrial Re-organisation Branch, which would encourage and assist industry as advised by the Committee on Industrial Organisation. But, Lynch warned, 'only industry itself can initiate action. In the final analysis this responsibility rests on individual firms and individual persons within such firms.'[85] In October 1963 he expressed his disappointment to the Dublin Chamber of Commerce. With eleven CIO survey reports published, only eight adaptation councils had been formed; only a few industries had proved to Lynch why such councils were unsuited to their business, while others merely dragged their feet on the issue. But Lynch warned that 'no sectional interest was entitled to be obstructive about the change for progress only because the adoption of new methods might prove a little painful at first.'[86] The adoption of new methods, or adaptation, was in progress, and the number of adaptation grants or loans approved by the Government up to 10 December 1963 came to a hundred, representing a total capital investment of more than £13 million, of which the state's contribution was £2½ million.[87] Moving forward a few years, the position on 31 March 1967 was that a total of 1,393 definite applications had been received for Irish grants under the auspices of either An Foras Tionscal or the IDA (1956–9). Of these, 739 were for undeveloped areas, of which 282 were approved, but 178 was the number realised (less drop-outs). Outside undeveloped areas, 654 applications had been received, 186 approved and 130 likely to be realised.[88] Approximately 34 per cent of applications did not proceed: some were subsequently activated in Dublin but it appeared that 'most of them have been lost to the country.'[89]

An analysis of 62 lapsed projects showed that 5 were wholly Irish-owned, 27 German, 14 American, and 10 British.[90] The IDA believed that many promoters may simply have been shopping around for locations. The reasons given varied: 26 alleged a failure to raise capital, 15 were dissatisfied with the size of grants, some said interest rates on loans were too high, 9 found depressed markets, and 3 were abandoned because of the uncertainty of Ireland's future regarding the EEC (these were in 1961–2).[91] On balance, the unevenness of the performance in attracting industry from abroad underlined the thesis that membership of the EEC would guarantee the country the 'economic take-off' necessary to achieve an elusive economic modernisation.

Between 1959 and 1965 Jack Lynch dealt with the exhausting Industry and Commerce portfolio—second only in complexity to that of Finance—with energy, skill and versatility. He handled a bewildering array of files, widely different in content and complexity, had gained wide experience and had done his job well. The spinal column of combined interests was the necessity to wean industrialists away from the womb-like comfort and security of protectionism. Lynch had to change the philosophical ethos within a department that had devoted itself to implementing a protective tariff system since 1932. The decision to join the EEC was not revised in 1963 when de Gaulle blocked the application of Britain. Ireland's application remained active but Brussels parked the process, pending a change in the ascendant politics of the French. Nonetheless Lynch used the hiatus to wrench Irish industry away from protection. The process was slow and, at times, frustrating.

In the end there were few in the country who believed that continued protection was a national option. There was no unanimity in favour of EEC membership: the Labour Party opposed it, as did the trade union movement; Sinn Féin and the IRA also rejected EEC membership. But that issue was not resolved until the referendum on May 1972. In the meantime, Lynch had moved from Industry and Commerce to Finance and then to become Taoiseach.

Chapter 5 ❧

MINISTER FOR FINANCE, 1965–6

Two years before Seán Lemass retired as Taoiseach he took a policy initiative that was to have an unforeseen impact on relations with Northern Ireland. The appointment of the urbane Terence O'Neill as Prime Minister provided a unique opportunity to make progress in a formerly intractable area. Behind the scenes the secretary of the Department of Finance, Ken Whitaker, had worked with like-minded friends in Belfast for a diplomatic breakthrough. Lemass, a politician of flint-like realism, agreed to cross the border to meet O'Neill in Belfast in January; a return visit to Dublin took place in February 1965.[1] This resulted in the first faltering steps towards cross-border economic co-operation.

Too much ought not be read into the practical outcome of those initial North-South contacts. But the meetings broke a psychological barrier, providing an answer to anti-constitutional elements among nationalists and unionists alike.[2] The personal contacts that Whitaker continued to have with a small but significant circle of professional and personal friends in Northern Ireland were of long-term importance to the reframing of the Government's Northern policy. Lynch and Whitaker, who had been friendly from the late 1950s, worked closely together in the years that followed. They shared ideas on how to lay the initial foundations for a North-South *rapprochement*. But that did not mean that Lynch and Lemass abjured their strongly held aspiration to bring about a united Ireland. Lynch was certainly not 'in some way, the father of modern Irish political revisionism.'[3] He is quite undeserving of such a burdensome 'accolade'.

The Irish state was not about to forget its revolutionary past. On 1 March 1965 an unidentified *Irish Times* reporter wrote on the state funeral of the remains of Roger Casement, who had been hanged in London in July 1916 for his actions in support of Irish freedom:

It was a day of pride, not of grief. The time for tears was half-a-century ago and yesterday Dublin watched with joy as much as reverence, as they

carried through her streets and over her bridges the remains of Roger
Casement, the man whose name will be remembered and honoured as
long as the Liffey flows.[4]

More than 65,000 people filed past the coffin at Arbour Hill. Crowds lined the
streets as the Tricolour-draped coffin was taken with military honours to the
Pro-Cathedral, where President Éamon de Valera and the Taoiseach waited.[5]
On 2 March, Seamus Kelly of the *Irish Times* completed the report of the
funeral:

> The mourners remembered a long journey—from Dublin to Antrim,
> where there was happiness; to the Congo and the Putumayo, where there
> was misery to be cleansed; from Norway and Berlin to Banna Strand where
> there was frustration and defeat; from Banna to the Old Bailey,
> Pentonville, and ignominious death, and then, after a needlessly bitter
> half-century, the repatriation to the Pantheon of Ireland . . . It was a bitter
> black wind that blew flurries of snow across Glasnevin yesterday. It cut to
> the bone with surgical remembrances of mortality that were perhaps
> appropriate enough to an age that has little time for the idealism of
> Casement and the men who died with him.[6]

This was a great moment in the calendar of Irish nationalism. But the high
emotion associated with that event was not easily translated into votes.

On 10 March 1965 the people of the Mid-Cork constituency were due to go
to the polls in a by-election that had the potential to topple the Government.[7]
Fianna Fáil put great energy into winning. On 5 March 1965 Lemass told a
party meeting in Carrigaline that he would consider it his duty to call a
general election if Fianna Fáil was defeated, so that the whole people could
decide whether they wanted the present Government to fulfil its programme.[8]
On 7 March he said that Ireland might be joining the Common Market soon
and that talks with Britain were important. The Minister for Industry and
Commerce, Jack Lynch, speaking at one of more than a hundred political
meetings in the constituency on the weekend of 6/7 March, expressed
frustration at the idea of an unnecessary general election, saying that it 'would
be a disruption of national development.' He promised that £11 million in
industrial development was planned for Co. Cork, which would bring with it
six thousand new jobs.[9]

In the Mid-Cork by-election the Fianna Fáil candidate topped the poll on
first preferences but the party vote dropped by 1,100 votes, despite Jack Lynch's
best personal efforts to rally the faithful. Eileen Desmond won the seat for the
Labour Party.

True to his word, Lemass announced on 11 March that the Dáil was to be dissolved.[10] He had no choice, as his party had been reduced to seventy seats. (There was a seat vacant in Longford-Westmeath because of the death of the Fianna Fáil TD, M. J. Kennedy.) The *Irish Times,* in an editorial, stated that the news would be greeted by the rank and file of Fianna Fáil with 'scant enthusiasm'. It felt that a general election was 'not the best thing for the country.'[11] Polling day was to be 7 April 1965.[12]

The *Irish Times* reported, tongue in cheek, that many budget-conscious politicians were grateful for the timing of the general election, as many of their workers were 'on the dry for Lent.'[13] On 15 March 1965 a 'special corre-spondent' wrote about the emergence of the back-room boys who appear at every general election to plan and strategise the campaigns of the candidates.

The day of the Baluba is at hand. [For the benefit of any African reader, this is a purely technical political term, as is the frequently used 'Mafia'.] Yesterday, like mushrooms after a shower of July rain, he sprang up in importance as he held his council of war outside a breezy chapel gate, in a smoky snug in Clare, in a suburban £9,000 house where Peek Frean biscuits were served with coffee, the carpeted lounge of Searson's of Baggot Street or the indolent comfort of the doctor's waiting room . . . The Baluba is the power behind the TD.[14]

Charles Haughey, a man with a growing reputation within the party, was made director of elections. Despite feeling the pressure, Lemass led his party into the contest with a distinct advantage. Brendan Corish, leader of the Labour Party, declared against coalition. The leader of Fine Gael, James Dillon, who harboured an acute antipathy for the left, presided over a divided party. Throughout the campaign Lemass poured scorn on the idea of coalition. He told a meeting on 24 March that his party would go into opposition rather than join a coalition; he had no intention of leading a 'yo-yo' Government, to be jerked on a string held by Mr Corish.[15] The party programme emphasised Irish membership of the EEC. Lemass stated that the 'primary purpose of the Fianna Fáil government after the next general election will be to maintain, and if pos-sible to speed up, the present drive of economic expansion embracing all the activities that can contribute to the national wealth.' There were also references to more traditional party objectives, such as the restoration of Irish.[16]

As politicians around the country intensified their campaigning, the first site meeting was held at Ballymun, Dublin, to start the building of 'semi-skyscrapers' that would house twelve thousand people.[17]

The election marked the retirement of two senior ministers, Dr Jim Ryan (Finance) and Gerald Bartley (Defence). The veterans Seán MacEntee and

Frank Aiken stood again. Three long-sitting Fianna Fáil TDs, Paddy Lenihan, Con Meaney and Seán MacCarthy, announced their retirement, leading the *Irish Times* to speculate that when all was over there would be an upheaval in the party that would make the Night of the Long Knives look like a picnic party.

Seán MacEntee, at seventy-six, was in fine form on the hustings. He told voters at a rally in Rathfarnham, Co. Dublin:

> I have looked death in the eye for Ireland. I have been in penal servitude for Ireland and many times in prison. I have served my country without self-seeking. I have devoted all my powers—and they are not inconsider-able—to that service. I can look back on almost fifty years of an active and arduous public life. Yet no man can say that . . . I did not serve them honourably and well.[18]

Lemass, also a veteran of the 1916 Rising, though ten years MacEntee's junior, announced that it might be the last election in which he would lead Fianna Fáil.[19] Tired and in failing health, he nevertheless provided determined leadership.

Fianna Fáil won the election with seventy-two seats, the party vote having increased to 48 per cent. It had not had three consecutive general election victories since 1944.[20] In the Cork City constituency Jack Lynch headed the poll, taking 12,852 first preferences.[21] Fine Gael lost a seat in that constituency to Fianna Fáil, which was of decisive importance in determining the outcome of the election. Lemass had a slender majority, which was strengthened by support from one independent, Joseph Sheridan from Longford-Westmeath. The Ceann Comhairle, Patrick Hogan, was a member of the Labour Party.

Unable to change radically the composition of his Government in 1961, Lemass took advantage of his new mandate in 1965 to promote younger TDs to Government positions. Frank Aiken became Tánaiste while retaining his External Affairs portfolio. In contrast, Seán MacEntee, who had been re-elected, moved to the back benches. Predictably, Jack Lynch succeeded Dr James Ryan as Minister for Finance. Dr Patrick Hillery replaced Lynch in Industry and Commerce but on 13 July 1966 was changed to the new Department of Labour. George Colley was then given Industry and Commerce. Neil Blaney went to Local Government, Charles Haughey remained in Agriculture and Kevin Boland went to Social Welfare. A young and mercurial Limerick TD, Donogh O'Malley, was given Health.

Fianna Fáil had a young Government with an old Taoiseach. Lynch, at forty-eight, was part of an in-between generation. He was Fianna Fáil's first non-founder-member appointed to Finance. He may have pondered the fact that his two immediate party predecessors in Finance, Jim Ryan and the outgoing Tánaiste, Seán MacEntee, had between them nearly twenty years' service in the department in Merrion Street. Both were elder statesmen, the former renowned for his diplomatic tact, the latter for many things, including strong economising convictions bordering on parsimony. Lynch would require an almost equal measure of both approaches in the months that lay ahead.

Frank Aiken, now the elder statesman of the party, was unlikely to succeed Lemass. The new Minister for Finance lacked a revolutionary pedigree, and the scions of that first generation—Colley, Boland and Blaney—were strongly represented in the Government. But while it was premature to speculate about succession in early 1965, Lynch was a likely candidate.

He had little time to ponder the historic nature of his preferment, or the various styles of his predecessors. He too had been responsible in the Cork by-election for making extravagant promises. Lemass had allowed decisions to be taken about the public finances in the previous months that had created a serious problem for the new Minister for Finance. On 22 April, the day after Lynch's appointment, the secretary of the department, Ken Whitaker, submitted to the minister an overview of the financial situation. It began ominously:

I am sorry that my first submission to you as Minister for Finance makes rather cheerless reading. The fact is, however, that there are serious difficulties looming up from which we have happily been free since 1956. Excessive pressure on resources is reflected in a growing trade and payment deficit. This is still a manageable problem and is best tackled by moderate measures in good time rather than by drastic action later. Since we overcame the last balance of payments crisis of 1956 we have enjoyed a period of unprecedented economic growth. It is essential to safeguard this growth and avoid the 'stop-go' policies which have impeded British progress, if we are to carry the Second Programme through to success. Any unpopularity associated with exercising some restraining influence on the balance of payments in the interests of steady growth will be much less than the unpopularity which would arise from a recurrence of the 1956 situation.[22]

Whitaker further outlined developments since 1956, referring to a 'virtual equilibrium' in the balance of payments from 1957 to 1961, followed by an increasing deficit, which was 'more than covered by an inflow of capital.' External reserves had therefore increased from £225 million at the end of 1961 to £242 million by the end of 1964. However, the reserves were steadily decreasing from early 1965 and would not be bolstered by continuing capital inflows. Restrictive measures on capital outflows in London and New York were likely to curtail inflows to Ireland, suggesting that the rate for 1964 was 'unprecedentedly high' but was nonetheless unsustainable. While others, such as the governor of the Central Bank, Maurice Moynihan, advocated a substantial reduction in the balance of payments deficit, Whitaker counselled that it should not get bigger in 1965.

Whitaker then advised that the most appropriate action lay in restraint in the financial field. 'The budget of 1965 should be constructed so as to have less of a deficit on current account than last year and no bigger increase in capital expenditure than was envisaged in the Second Programme, allowing for the fall in money values between 1960 and 1965.' The capital budget for 1965/6 should therefore be reduced from £111 million to £100 million, though this would show an increase on the previous year, but 'there can be no adverse public reaction to modifications of which the public will be unaware.' Nevertheless, the 'cuts must be real and not just presentational.'

The second area requiring restraint was that of credit creation. Whitaker felt that the Central Bank's advice to the banks, that credit creation in 1965 should not cause the balance of payments deficit to exceed the 1964 figure and that priority be given to credit for productive purposes, was appropriate.

The third field for restraint lay in incomes. While it was accepted that there was difficulty in preventing pay increases from outrunning productivity, action in the financial and credit areas would assist here. These lay down the road somewhat, as he concluded by returning to the fundamental pressing problem: 'The immediate need is to get Government agreement next Tuesday to a restriction of the 1965/66 capital programme to £100 million. We need decisions early next week if the Budget is to be ready for 11 or 12 May.'[23]

That was not what an incoming Minister for Finance wanted to hear. However, much of that advice appeared in Lynch's first financial statement on 11 May 1966. Facing into his first budget, he was given the clear message to cut and make more cuts. Such action was not going to make him popular with his Government colleagues, who were in an expansive and spending mood.

Lynch and Whitaker, from his previous ministries, worked together daily. On occasions the two men travelled together on official trips to Britain, the Continent and the United States. Over the following years, while Lynch was Minister for Finance and then Taoiseach, their friendship grew into a unique working relationship. Lynch valued Whitaker's judgement in a wide range of areas, extending to Northern Ireland. That relationship would have important, if not profound, historical consequences, which have yet to be fully realised and documented.

In April 1965, with less than three weeks to go to the budget, Whitaker continued to speak bluntly to his new minister. He stressed that the country's financial problems had been looming for some time. There had been a clearly discernible background to problems on both the current and the capital budget, problems that Lynch inherited and had to manage immediately on assuming office. On the current account, the Department of Finance had warned the Government in November 1964 that there was likely to be a deficit of £5–6 million in prospect for 1964/5 and a deficit of at least £12 million in framing the 1965/6 budget.[24] The department warned further, in February 1965, that the latest estimates confirmed the prospect of the 1964 deficit, without including the cost of aid to industry arising from the British surcharge on imports.

Despite the Government's decision of 8 December 1964 that each minister should submit proposals for reducing expenditure, the results proved disappointing: only the Minister for Defence proposed any savings, amounting to £141,000. Further problems were anticipated with the 1965/6 budget. On the current account, the estimate for the non-capital supply services was almost £194 million. While the Department of Finance had managed to secure reductions of about £4.1 million, it still proposed further savings of about £3 million. Even if the Government managed to bring down the estimate to about £187 million, 'considerable increases in taxation will still be unavoidable.'[25] Problems also loomed on the capital side. Total estimates for voted capital services, as submitted to the Department of Finance, were £37.8 million, or more than £6 million more than the figure in the Second Programme. Agreed reductions of £3.28 million still left an overrun. The Department of Finance insisted on the implementation of the Government's decision of 8 December that capital expenditure be kept within the Second Programme figures for 1965/6.

In a memorandum of 12 April 1965 from the Department of Finance for the Government[26] it was again pointed out that difficulties had already been experienced in financing the capital budget for 1964/5, and that the estimates for 1965/6, 1966/7 and 1967/8 were already considerably above the Second Programme figures.[27] Exchequer provision for capital purposes in 1964/5 was estimated at £71.5 million, comprising £31 million from loan repayments, small savings and departmental funds, leaving £40.5 million to be provided from a national loan. However, the exchequer had to provide more than £73 million and could raise only £59.5 million from these sources, leaving £13.5 million to be found 'elsewhere.' The 'elsewhere' in this case was at the commercial banks, in the form of three-monthly bills. That brought the total short-term indebtedness to the banks to an unsatisfactory £29 million. This situation provoked comment a month earlier from the governor of the Central Bank, Maurice Moynihan, who insisted that it was neither prudent nor possible to continue borrowing on such a scale.[28]

Despite the explicit Government direction on 8 December 1964 that capital expenditure in 1965/6 should remain within the Second Programme estimate of £95.57 million, it already threatened to overshoot by £15.5 million, to more than £111 million.[29] There was an expected shortfall of £21 million in funding such expenditure, and the commercial banks were unlikely to increase the Government's short-term debt to £50 million—leaving aside possible implications for bank credit facilities. In addition, the Department of Finance estimated a deficit in the balance of payments of £30 million for 1964 and possibly higher in 1965, while 'dependence on a continued capital inflow of the unprecedented size of 1964 would be too hazardous.' In the circumstances, the department understandably urged caution, not least because the situation, if left unchecked, could cast doubt on the viability of programming.

This was the position Lynch faced before the first meeting of the new Government on 27 April 1965. His first task, as Whitaker advised, was to ensure that the public capital programme for 1965/6 be reduced to £100 million. The Government accepted that proposition in principle, leaving the precise details of the cut-backs for negotiations between Finance and individual departments. Those negotiations were concluded within two days, by the evening of 29 April 1965. They resulted in reductions of £7.224 million, a figure that included a reduction of £1.874 million on the voted capital services already published in the estimates for 1965/6.[30]

Difficulties arose, however, in relation to how the cut-backs in the voted capital services were to be communicated to the Dáil. The revision of the Department of Agriculture's estimate for capital services, involving a cut of £350,000, was agreed on 27 April. The Department of Finance directed that the Minister for Agriculture, Charles Haughey, announce the revision in his estimates speech on 29 April. However, a note for Lynch simply stated that 'the Minister for Agriculture was not prepared at that stage to announce the revision' and considered that the announcement was a matter for the Department of Finance.

Haughey's un-cooperative attitude was an act of gross insubordination. But Lynch was not in a strong enough position to be confrontational at that time, knowing that other ministers might adopt the same attitude. In that situation 'it was felt [in the Department of Finance] that there would be no point in making similar requests to the other Ministers who were due to introduce Estimates which had also been affected by the voted capital revisions.' Two further estimates were due within a week: the Forestry vote, which had been cut by £100,000, and the Industry and Commerce vote, pared back by £500,000.[31]

The Department of Finance duly informed the Government on 3 May 1965 that, following the decision of 27 April to reduce the capital budget to £100 million, it had only proved possible in the short time to reduce it to £103.75 million. This was, the department stated, still £3.75 million above what had been projected in the Programme for Economic Expansion.[32] The Second Programme, as published in July 1964, envisaged expenditure on the public capital programme as follows:

1964/5	1965/6	1966/7	1967/8	1968/9	1969/0
£96.11 million	£95.57 million	£94.23 million	£93.2 million	£92.82 million	£97.32 million

Source: *Second Programme for Economic Expansion, Part II* (1964), table 4, p. 270.

However, the programme elaborated:

> The figures in Table 4 for 1965/6 and subsequent years are tentative. Furthermore, when expenditure on individual items is large . . . a change of timing can considerably alter expenditure in the year concerned. It would be theoretically desirable that the pattern of capital spending should start from a lower base and show a regular increase in conformity with the projected general rise in GNP, but in practice the timing of capital spending must be determined by the needs of the particular service, subject to availability of resources.[33]

That last sentence was undoubtedly influenced by Lemass, to offer flexibility to cope with developments, not least of which was the matter of a general election. Nevertheless, the Government decision of 8 December 1964—that capital expenditure remain within the Second Programme limit of £95.57 million—showed clearly that both the Department of Finance and the Government were aware of what was required. The slippage occurred between December 1964 and May 1965, and Lemass had to take the full responsibility for letting the general financial situation drift in the period before the election.

On 29 April 1965—shortly before Lynch's first budget—Lemass gave the opening address to the conference of the Irish Management Institute in Killarney. He stressed the danger of complacency in relation to the national economic position and suggested that there was a need to 'look again at our national situation as a whole and attempt in a realistic way to assess our economic and social development possibilities, and the difficulties which may impede progress.' He predicted that it would be a 'fairly tough year,' noting that 'already there are some warning signals which we must heed,' but he did not wish to cause 'undue alarm.'[34] Lemass's speech was the first post-election acknowledgement that all was not exactly rosy with the country's finances. It set a pattern for his last months in office.

Behind the scenes, the Department of Finance was engaged in the difficult task of trying to craft a budget speech. An introductory economic survey noted that the prospects for 1965 were for a continuation of growth in the economy, although a balance of payments deficit of £25–30 million was expected. But 'as the capital inflow is likely to continue at a high level, any impact of this deficit on the external reserves should be small.' That prompted a revised draft to note that the appearance of a variety of publications recently forced the minister to give only 'a very brief summary' and to concentrate on 'some major problems.' Some of those might be gauged from the comment on the balance of payments. While reserves were still strong, 'one must recognise the vulnerability of an expansion programme which is dependent on a continuation of a capital inflow of the recent unprecedented size.'[35]

The explanation for the emerging discrepancy offered in the capital budget for 1965, published on 10 May 1965, was very lame. Paragraph 7 stated: 'Since the Estimates Volume (Pr 8172) was published, the actual detailed figures for last year's capital expenditure became available and it was possible, in the light of these figures and other up-to-date information, to arrive at closer estimates of the amounts needed to carry out this year's programme.' *Second Programme for Economic Expansion: Progress Report for 1965* outlined the position on the capital programme for 1965/6. The estimated out-turn for the year was £103.72 million, on a Second Programme projection of £95.57 million.[36] The differences were accounted for by housing (£2.1 million), schools (£1.2 million), agriculture (£1.6 million), agricultural credit (£1.4 million), telephones (£1 million), fuel and power (£0.6 million) and industrial credit (£0.95 million)—all approximate figures. The explanation then given was:

The White Paper on public capital expenditure, which was published by the government in October 1965 . . . explained the need, as part of the corrective economic measures announced by the Taoiseach on 13 July, 1965, to adjust the capital programme and gave details of alterations which would have the net effect of reducing capital expenditure by £3.44m to £100.28m. Provisional figures for 1965/66 show the outturn to be of the order of £104.25m.

Additionally, there was a deficit of slightly more than £4 million on the current account for the year ending 1965, and an anticipated 'sizeable deficit on the current account in 1965/66.'[37]

Lynch's first budget did not bring joy to the citizens of Ireland. But it might have been much harsher if a more conservative line had been taken. Non-contributory old-age, blind and widows' pensions were increased by 10 shillings per week for those with annual means of less than £26 and by 5 shillings for others. Unemployment assistance was increased by 5 shillings per week; maternity and disability benefits went up by 10 shillings per week; infectious diseases maintenance allowance and disability increased by 10 shillings per week. More favourable means tests for smallholders in 'congested districts' were proposed, while public-service pensions were adjusted to compensate for the increase in the cost of living between 1959 and 1964. The budget also brought tax increases: 3½ pence on twenty cigarettes, 2 pence on a glass of spirits, 1 penny on a pint of beer, 1 shilling on a bottle of wine and 3 pence on a gallon of petrol.[38]

Lynch did what was required of him. But it did not make him popular within the Government. The Dáil went into committee stage on 13 July to consider the estimates for the public services. Lemass opened with a defence of the measures the Government had taken, and announced that he intended making a general review of policy.[39] 'We have decided to rectify the adverse economic trends which are developing,' he said. That statement drew the comment from James Dillon: 'This is like Alice in Wonderland.'[40] Nevertheless, Lemass advised the Dáil of the unfolding situation: a substantial increase in imports and decline in exports; a reduction in net capital inflow; a slowing down in the rate of growth of industrial production and exports. Other unfavourable trends were discernible too, such as the increase in personal consumption, the rise in the consumer price index and the unsettling nature of continuing wage demands.[41] The Waterford deputy Thaddeus Lynch responded sardonically: 'We now have a programme of economic contraction.'[42]

On 9 September 1965 Lynch opened on the motion 'that Dáil Éireann approves of the measures taken by the Government to deal with the economic situation.'[43] Liam Cosgrave moved an amendment to add 'but regrets that the Government failed in time to inform Dáil Éireann and the country of the situation and neglected to take adequate steps to prevent the economy reaching its present position.' He traced the national economic troubles back to the white paper of February 1963, *Closing the Gap*, and the subsequent introduction of turnover tax.[44] The leader of the Labour Party, Brendan Corish, followed with a similar amendment and accused Fianna Fáil of having 'lulled people into a false sense of security.'[45] He also attacked the specifics of the Second Programme, pointing out the embarrassing fact that it forecast gains in employment of 78,000 by 1970 yet they had managed a net gain of only 4,000.[46]

In response, Lynch addressed the overall picture: the development of free trade in Europe and Ireland's position relative to the EEC and EFTA. 'We can accede to GATT [General Agreement on Tariffs and Trade] only if we have such an agreement with Britain that amounts to a free trade area agreement as defined by GATT.'[47] On the general economic situation he sidestepped the debate nicely, mentioning that Lemass had already outlined the difficulties; he would address the steps necessary to overcome the situation.[48] He stated that the economic problems in 1965 'may be fairly summed up by saying that we have been spending more than we have been earning.'[49] He continued through a stormy session with several interruptions, mainly from Gerard Sweetman and T. F. O'Higgins of Fine Gael.

There was no room for complacency. The follow-up from the Department of Finance stressed that some serious work still needed to be done to bring the public finances back into line. On 22 October 1965 Dr Whitaker advised Tadhg Ó Cearbhaill, then an assistant secretary in the Department of the Taoiseach, that

> the economic situation is more serious than we have been admitting officially. We have deliberately not been too pessimistic in public for fear of undermining confidence and also in the hope that as the months went by things would show a sufficient turn for the better. This hope is not being realised—indeed, it was not soundly based—and we now have to increase the corrective measures. We should also, without being alarmist, be more forthright about the nature and extent of our problems. We would be deluding ourselves if we continued to make reassuring comments on their temporary nature . . . There is a basic difficulty of a more lasting character and it is time we did something more effective about it.[50]

That difficulty was the gap in external payments and recourse to reserves to plug the gap. Whitaker felt that 'money is not only likely to be tight *but must be kept tight* if the balance of payments deficit is not to get worse.' He also warned that they would have to be vigilant in guarding against any departments looking for money from foreign sources, thereby aggravating the balance of payments gap and undermining the position of the Minister for Finance. He called for a 'holding operation': holding down public expenditure, holding existing jobs and living standards and holding costs. 'People must be asked to be content with their present degree of comfort unless they want themselves or their neighbours to be put out of employment.'[51]

Lynch then circulated the Government with proposals to reduce the public capital programme for 1966/7 to the projected £94.23 million outlined in the Second Programme. Lynch's position was in fact strengthened by the report of the eight-member Interdepartmental Committee on the Public Capital Programme. In its second report it conceded that as the need for cutbacks was urgent, 'the speediest and most effective way to meet the situation would be for the Minister for Finance to formulate recommendations to the government after bilateral discussions with departments.'[52] The challenge was significant. The committee had noted that total forecast expenditure was of the order of £121.5 million—well above the estimated resources of £95.75 million. A week later, on 2 November, the Government approved Lynch's proposals.[53]

However, Neil Blaney in the Department of Local Government submitted a note through the secretary to the Taoiseach's private secretary on 22 November. It dealt with Lynch's seeking a commitment in the white paper on public capital that every effort be made to secure a reduction of £1.36 million in expenditure on construction. The Department of Finance had stated that £1.25 million of this reduction should come from housing and sanitary services. Neil Blaney argued that his department was tied to 'inescapable commitments.' He continued:

> It is clear, therefore, that not alone is there no scope for a saving of £1.25m in these services but that the full amount provided in the budget to finance the works will fall short by £1.13m of commitments maturing for payment before 31 March 1966. This shortfall is due to the cut of £2.5m made in February 1965, in the estimates prepared by the Department of Local Government.

The effect of further cuts would be to reduce any new works and even involve curtailments of existing ones. Blaney concluded:

> In the circumstances, it would be unthinkable to reduce the 1965/66 capital provision by £1.25m or to restrict expenditure in 1966/67 to the amount suggested in the White Paper.

Blaney proposed circulating his note at the Government meeting the following day. Lemass, alarmed at the wider implications of the Blaney note, blocked its circulation.

Notwithstanding the tension between Lynch and the other ministers, he proceeded to implement the Government decision of 2 November to reduce the public capital programme. At the end of November he circulated a 41-page memorandum to the Government, the net effect of which was to reduce the forecast total of capital expenditure by £25.8 million, down to approximately £95 million.[54] Even then this was considered some £20 million more than the estimate of resources—necessitating the raising of that £20 million by borrowing from the banks and abroad, on top of the £44 million already raised by borrowing in 1965. Lynch pointed out that 'borrowing on this scale from these sources involves serious economic and political dangers.' He did not propose reductions below £95 million, because of the 'impracticality, without serious dislocation of the economy, of effecting so drastic a change suddenly and because he has not abandoned hope that resources may become sufficient or nearly sufficient in 1967/68 if public expenditure is stabilised at the £95m level, with some readjustment within that total in favour of directly productive expenditure.' He requested the Government to direct ministers to make the reductions.

Lynch admitted it had been difficult making decisions. However, '[the] settlement of specific long-term priorities involves radical policy decisions and is not a matter, in the opinion of the Minister, to be decided in the short time available to define the capital programme of the Departments of State for next year.' In effect, no project would have complete priority, and all expenditures would have to be adjusted. Allowances would be made for contractual obligations and for work in progress.[55] However, Blaney's department, Local Government, was the first lined up for the cut. It was pointed out that the estimate was almost £11 million over the figure of £21.96 million in the white paper. 'These estimates ignore the realities of the financial situation and are at variance with the statement in the White Paper that it was hoped that it would be possible to maintain the public building programme next year *close to* this year's level.'[56]

The general cut-backs outlined by Lynch can be viewed in columns 4 and 6 of the following table:

[1] General department	[2] Second Programme estimate (000)	[3] Latest forecast (000)	[4] Reduction suggested (000)	[5] Recommended provision (000)	[6] (4) as percentage of col. 3	[7] (5) as percentage of col. 2
Local Government	£22,885	£32,893	£10,000	£22,893	30.4%	100.0%
Education	£5,994	£7,368	£1,785	£5,583	24.2%	93.1%
Health	£3,200	£3,500	£500	£3,000	14.3%	93.8%
Office of Public Works	£3,645	£3,363	£663	£2,700	19.7%	74.1%
Gaeltacht	£312	£815	£378	£437	46.4%	140.1%
Lands	£1,954	£2,176	£176	£2,000	8.1%	102.4%
Agriculture and Fisheries	£11,455	£13,555	£2,023	£11,532	14.9%	100.7%
Industry and Commerce	£3,250	£6,338	£2,000	£4,338	31.6%	133.5%
Transport and Power	£27,209	£31,938	£5,346	£26,592	16.7%	97.7%

Posts and Telegraphs	£6,450	£8,000	£1,400	£6,600	17.5%	102.3%
Finance	£7,882	£10,792	£1,557	£9,235	14.4%	117.2%
Total	£94,236	£120,738	£25,828	£94,910	21.4%	100.7%

Notes

Column 6 is the amount by which the proposed reductions would have reduced the latest forecast for each head.

Column 7 is the amount by which each head deviates from the original forecast in the Second Programme.

What remained to be seen was whether the Government would accept the cuts. November 1965 was a crucial period for Lynch in Finance. He needed to ensure that the Government would agree to and implement cut-backs on both the current and the capital accounts. Blaney made it clear, however, that he would not be reducing his 1965/6 capital budget by the desired amount, nor accepting the recommendations for 1966/7.[57]

If that was not bad enough, Lynch faced further headaches on the current account side from all quarters. The Minister for Health, Donogh O'Malley, was a particular source of concern. Lynch was under pressure to get O'Malley to withdraw his proposal for a white paper on the extension of the health service. On 3 November 1965 he told O'Malley:

Since I wrote to you on 12 October, I have given further thought to the advisability of publishing, in present circumstances, a White Paper on the Health Services. The White Paper on Public Capital Expenditure has been published in the meantime and paragraph 31 refers to current expenditure. It says there must be measures to contain such expenditure and relate it to the expected revenue, even if this, in the Taoiseach's words of 13 July, 'involves putting back until later many improvements of the public services with which we would prefer to be able to proceed quickly.'

I may say, in confidence, that revised estimates for the current financial year show that current expenditure will exceed revenue by several millions of pounds. That makes it certain that extra taxation will have to be imposed in next year's budget to finance existing commitments. We will also have to look for retrenchments in existing services to close the gap.

Your Department has stated that an extra expenditure of £400,000 approximately will fall to be met by the Exchequer next year to finance existing commitments on Health Services. As it will be difficult enough to find this sum, I could not agree to changes in the financing of the Health Services which would cost a further £400,000 in 1966–67.

Having regard to the foregoing . . . the present time is inopportune for the publication of a White Paper proposing costly changes in the Health Services. We must be realistic and defer consideration of such changes until there is a reasonable prospect that the economy will be able to afford them. I trust that you will agree with this conclusion.[58]

Lynch, or Whitaker, correctly anticipated trouble with this issue, and on the following day, 4 November, a copy of this letter was sent to Lemass. In addition, Lynch advised the Taoiseach that

the proposed improvements and changes in the Health Services would impose an extra charge on the Exchequer amounting to £406,000 in 1966–67. The extra charge would rise to £2,476,000 in 1967–68 and to £3,926,000 in 1969–70.[59]

O'Malley rejected Lynch's appeals to defer proposals and stated: 'I am, accordingly, making my submission, incorporating in it your views.'[60] Furthermore, it is clear that O'Malley was appealing to Lemass rather than to Lynch when seeking justification for his action. He continued:

I should mention that the Labour motion on the Health Services came up for discussion last Wednesday in the Dáil. It is being supported by Fine Gael but from the introductory remarks made by Deputy Kyne it seems likely that, if in speaking on it I were in a position to promise a definite statement on our policy for the future of the health services, the Motion might not be pressed . . .

I do not agree that the present time is inopportune for outlining future plans for developing the health services. As will be clear from the time-table sent to your department, no substantial expenditure—except for a transfer of £400,000 from local to central taxation—is projected until the year 1967–68, and this is on the basis of a very tight time-table. I am not aware that we should be expecting the present financial stringency to continue as far ahead as that. If we are at all to plan for future developments in the health services, that planning must start now if it is to become effective in the next three or four years . . .

You will note that that will bring us up to the probable date of the next General Election. I need not say anything more on this except to refer you to the capital made out of the deficiencies in the Health Services at the last General Election, which caused the Taoiseach to make his statements, at the time, in relation to the introduction of a choice of doctor and the extension of the scheme for providing drugs in hardship cases for the middle income groups.[61]

O'Malley had in fact prepared his ground in relation to Lemass since the summer. On 20 July he told the Taoiseach that he was

arranging to have the draft White Paper ... sent to the other departments for their views. I do not expect that I will be seeking to have it before the Government until the Autumn, but I thought that I should send you a copy of the draft now for your information, in view of the rather intense public interest which has been shown in the topic.[62]

O'Malley proceeded with a memorandum to the Government four days later, 8 November, and on 19 November the Government agreed to the submission of a further memorandum from the Department of Health incorporating other departmental views.[63] Lynch had numerous objections and, lest he give any hostages to fortune in what was now emerging as a white paper on the health service, he attempted to limit commitments, suggesting that if his objections were not approved by the Government

then any reference in the White Paper to the Government having 'decided' on proposals should be deleted and replaced by a less definite reference, having regard to the recent indication by the Taoiseach that the White Paper was being put out for discussion before final decisions were taken.[64]

Decisions were duly taken and, as Ruth Barrington has shown in her study on the health service, the white paper was published in January 1966.[65] However, as she also pointed out, 'Mr O'Malley's promise [on 1 March 1966] of legislation to implement the White Paper by autumn 1966 proved optimistic.' In August of that year O'Malley was transferred to the Department of Education, where he continued his strategy of rebelliousness, with more success.

Lemass's position throughout was most interesting. While he appeared to support O'Malley over Lynch in allowing the white paper to proceed, his decision to replace him in Health before any changes could be implemented suggests clever management of an intractable problem. His decision to transfer O'Malley to another 'spending' department, Education, was imaginative. His successor in the Department of Health, Seán Flanagan, was 'less enthusiastic about the choice of doctor scheme.'[66] He was a more placid soul and far more respectful of the Department of Finance.

O'Malley, irrespective of his portfolio, was beyond being contained. He had the opportunity to engage in an even bolder solo run—by introducing free secondary education—in his new department, as will be seen later.

In December 1965 the Government began its preparations for the 1966 budget. Having considered Lynch's memorandum on the prospects for the current account, on 2 December the Government decided that it would run a deficit of not more than £4 million for the two financial years 1965/6 and 1966/7 and towards this end requested reductions of a little more than £0.5 million in various departments in the current year. No matter what spin was placed on the issue, it was deficit financing, planned, albeit covertly and not published. In the circumstances, unless there was a substantial turnaround in the public finances, a formal decision to unbalance the budget could not be too far away.

On 2 December a further major decision was taken at the Government meeting: 'The Minister for Finance should introduce the Budget in respect of 1966–67 in mid-February 1966, or as early as possible thereafter.'[67]

Problems deepened for Lynch before Christmas. Whitaker informed him that following a meeting with the Revenue Commissioners on 17 December 'the position has worsened,' as they were forecasting a slight drop in revenue for 1965/6, but the drop anticipated for 1966/7 was approximately £1¾ million. The reductions were based on revenue loss from motor-car duties, tobacco and beer. The prospects were not promising: 'In general, little revenue buoyancy can be expected next year in view of the disappointing receipts this year and the indications of a deceleration in the expansion of the economy next year.'[68] The Revenue Commissioners estimated that the most they could take from extra taxes in 1966/7 was £8.75 million, which might be topped up to £10 million with a 'raid' on the Road Fund.

In those circumstances the Department of Finance anticipated a deficit of about £9 million on the current account for 1965/6 and 1966/7—more than double the amount authorised by the Government earlier that month. Further increases in turnover tax were ruled out, because of their knock-on effect on wage claims. The department suggested that 'there is little if any scope for increasing the Estimates limits.'

In parenthesis, the Anglo-Irish Free Trade Area Agreement of December 1965 gave Irish industry immediate tariff-free access to the lucrative British market. Ireland won a higher quota for butter and a guaranteed market for store cattle. A 10 per cent annual reduction of tariffs on British goods was also agreed. 1975 was set as the target for achieving full free trade.[69] This was an important preparatory step on the road to achieving Lemass's primary economic and foreign-policy goal: full membership of the EEC.

Lynch strongly supported the Taoiseach's EEC policy. In supporting the Anglo-Irish Free Trade Area in the Dáil on 6 January 1966 he pointed to four main factors that anchored Irish moves towards freer trade: (1) a satisfactory rate of growth depended on expansion of the industrial sector; (2) because of competition in export markets the economy could not achieve the expansion unless it was competitive itself; (3) this competitiveness could not be achieved without lowering protection: the choice then was between doing this unilaterally and as part of a free-trade area with reciprocal arrangements; (4) if the state didn't face the challenge it would incur the penalty of economic stagnation and face much graver burdens down the road, whenever the opportunity of EEC membership presented itself.[70]

But that agreement did not solve the immediate problems of the Minister for Finance. His department continued to battle for greater control on Government spending. On 14 February 1966 the department circulated a revised memorandum on the public capital programme. It was now increased to £97.63 million, from £95 million, and additional allowances for Erin Foods and the Nítrigin Éireann fertiliser factory increased it by a further million to £98.68 million—or £3.5 million more than available resources.[71] The same day a secret Department of Finance memorandum for the Government warned that

> recent indications are that there will be a deficit of £8.6m on the current budget for 1965–66. This deficit, which is the largest ever incurred, will have to be financed by borrowing at the expense of the limited amount of capital available to finance the public capital programme.[72]

And it forecast a deficit of £15.3 million for 1966/7.

The gravity of the financial situation had already prompted Whitaker to arrange a private meeting with Lemass on 28 January 1966. Lynch 'outlined the situation generally, and the causes of anxiety,' and then left Whitaker to wrestle with the Taoiseach. Whitaker

> . . . began by saying that for almost a year now the government and the Department of Finance and the Central Bank have been trying hard to bring the economic and financial situation under control. It was obvious that we couldn't live with the size of the deficit that confronted us in the spring of 1965 and we still had a good way to go to be really secure on the external payments front. It had to be admitted that one of the chief causes of trouble was the over-rapid rise in government expenditure. A lot of effort in Departments, in the Government and in the Dáil had gone into formulating and explaining means of overcoming our difficulties. A great deal of government time had recently been spent in trying to fix manageable limits to expenditure, both current and capital, in 1966–67. The limits fixed were, however, on the generous side having regard to the resources we had at our command. We were taking big chances about the continuance of the capital inflow and the possibility of external borrowing. It was absolutely essential, therefore, that the limits should not be exceeded and that proposals having this effect, such as the Minister for Local Government's intention

to invite special tenders and finance for housing in Cork and Limerick should be rejected. The housing needs in these cities, even if they lent themselves to special treatment on the Ballymun lines, would have to be fitted financially into whatever allocation was made for housing in the Capital Budget of 1966–67 and later years. There was no point in having limits if they could be side-stepped. Indeed, to allow liberal expenditure limits to be breached in this way would be in direct conflict with the economic policy which the government was trying so hard to have understood and carried into effect. All the trouble taken to correct the present position would be for naught if this kind of contradiction crept in.[73]

In the culture of the Department of Finance, this ought to be read as a strong rebuke. Whitaker 'placed a great deal of emphasis' on the point that if the Government 'were seen to be in control of the economic and financial situation' it would work to their advantage at home and abroad. The implication was clear: the Government was not perceived to be in charge. Resources were tight: they were facing a shortfall of £45 million in normal domestic resources to finance public expenditure, meaning they would have to borrow £20 million from the Central Bank, £7 million from the International Monetary Fund and £17 million from the commercial banks. However, the total amount available from the commercial banks for lending in Ireland was £29.2 million, but central and local government had borrowed all but one million pounds of it. 'Such a complete disproportion in the credit absorbed by the public as against the private sector would be certain to come under most unfavourable notice and clearly was indefensible in the long run,' Whitaker commented.

Whitaker also mentioned that the executive director of the Bank of England had informed him that recent 'shopping around of so many of the London [finance] houses had been to our disadvantage.' This referred primarily to Neil Blaney's attempts to raise finance. Blaney had proposed providing foreign builders with a Government guarantee on which to borrow money to support their tenders for work in Ireland. Lemass stated that no advertisements for such conditions would be issued until they had first secured government borrowing, and the possibility of such backed loans 'would be reconsidered only if proof could be produced that finance so raised would not cut across the normal sources or be more expensive.'

Less than three weeks later, on 16 February, Whitaker wrote to the chairman of the Revenue Commissioners, Seán Réamonn, stating:

The Taoiseach has expressed the view that the estimates of tax revenue for 1966–67 are rather low in relation to a projected growth rate of 3% in GNP at constant prices and has asked that they be reconsidered with a view to

View of Shandon church from Shandon Street, Cork, in 1928, with O'Callagans's shop (right).
(*Irish Examiner*)

Jack Lynch with his sister Rena when he was about four. (*Courtesy of Eileen Compagno and Crockett family*)

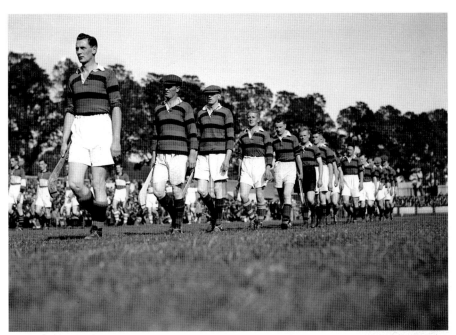

Lynch leading Glen Rovers in the county senior hurling final at the Athletic Grounds in 1940. (*Irish Examiner*)

A star sportswoman: Máirín O'Connor (*front centre*) with the school hockey team in the early 1930s. She attended St Mary's College (Muckross Park), Donnybrook, Dublin, throughout her school years. (*Máirín Lynch Papers*, NLI)

The victorious captain with the Liam McCarthy Cup in 1942. (*Irish Examiner*)

Two photographs of Jack and Máirín on their wedding day, 10 August 1946. (*Máirín Lynch Papers, NLI*)

On honeymoon: Jack and Máirín (*right*) at the Gap of Dunloe, Killarney, 14 August 1946. (*Máirín Lynch Papers, NLI*)

Máirín's mother, Margaret O'Connor (née Doyle). She worked all her life promoting 'buy Irish' for industrial development authorities and the Federation of Irish Manufacturers. The Margaret O'Connor Perpetual Trophy was established in her honour in the 1960s. (*Máirín Lynch Papers, NLI*)

In a thoughtful mood: Máirín in the mid-1940s. (*Máirín Lynch Papers*, NLI)

Back at his alma mater, the North Mon, as Minister for Education in the late 1950s. (*Irish Examiner*)

revision upwards. I have explained that any increase that might be hoped for on grounds of 'buoyancy' will be more than offset by contingent liabilities on the expenditure side which have not been included in our estimates.[74]

Whitaker meanwhile advised Lynch not to run any deficit on the current account for 1966/7. He suggested that the

public mood is . . . in favour of realism. Let them know the worst and they will respond. Better acknowledge frankly that we have over-reached ourselves and present this early 1966 budget simply as a correction of the budget of May last.

He then advised against handing out 'bonanzas to any section' and rounded on the claims of farmers.

To 'provide' extra money for farmers would be an unnecessary and indefensible extravagance. The year 1966 is likely to bring farmers a sizeable increase in incomes. The government has done quite enough for them this year by negotiating a Trade Agreement which enables them to get more from the British government and British consumers by producing and selling more. Remember that, even if they do this, the Irish Exchequer will, on the *present* subsidy basis, have to make automatically a large extra contribution to their incomes.[75]

The options available to Lynch in trying to present some sort of balance on the current account for 1966/7 also diminished that February when Blaney politely but sternly declined a proposal to 'raid' the Road Fund to the amount of £2 million.[76]

Faced with ever-increasing problems, Lynch took Whitaker's advice and decided to let the public know what had been happening. On 9 March 1966 he presented the Dáil with his second financial statement. In opening his budget, Lynch stated that it was earlier than ever because of the Easter Rising commemorations in April, but this was not the principal reason. 'In fact,' he admitted, 'we are dealing with a supplementary rather than a new budget. What went wrong with the budget introduced last May?' he asked. The answer was straightforward: they were approaching a deficit of £8 million instead of balance. Revenues were down, expenditures were greater than budgeted and errors arose in estimations. 'But one cannot justify it on financial or economic grounds and that is why early correction is necessary,' he said.[77]

The main budgetary changes involved tax increases on beer of 2 pence per pint, on spirits of 4 pence a glass, on table water of 4 pence a gallon, on tobacco

of 2 pence on a pack of twenty cigarettes, all with immediate effect. Road tax
on private vehicles was increased by 25 per cent, petrol and diesel (buses
exempted) by 4 pence a gallon. The turnover tax on dances was increased to
10 per cent. Income tax saw an additional 8 pence on the standard rate, mod-
erated by granting an extra allowance of £30 for every child over the age of
eleven. Estate duty relief for widows and dependent children extended from
£15,000 to £25,000 and abatement was increased to £350 and £250, respectively.
The special import levy—introduced the preceding November in response to
the British levy and due to expire on 31 March—was extended until 30 June.

Lynch had little to give away. In social welfare gains, those with no means
received an increase of 5 shillings per week, as did pensioners, the blind and
widows and the personal and adult dependant rates of unemployment assistance. Infectious diseases and disabled allowances were increased by the same
amount. With the trade agreement coming into force from 1 July, consultations
with manufacturers would begin regarding how they would handle discrimi-
natory reductions: either over five years from 1 July or in ten equal annual
instalments.

The March supplementary budget was not sufficient to take the
Government out of its dilemma, and Lynch found himself delivering his third
financial statement in a little over thirteen months on 14 June 1966. Despite
the fact that on 9 June he advised the Government that he 'cannot recommend the introduction at this stage of a selective wholesale tax,'[78] that was
precisely what was introduced. The budgetary changes involved increases of
2 pence per gallon on petrol and oil, 2 pence on a packet of twenty cigarettes,
and a new tax at the rate of 5 per cent on all goods currently affected by
turnover tax, except food, clothing, fuel, medicines, drink, tobacco, petrol and
oil. About one-seventh of total consumer expenditure was expected to be
liable for new tax, with all categories of goods, from industrial and agricultural machinery, already exempt from turnover tax to be exempt from the
new tax. The new tax was a selective wholesale tax.

The budget was a corrective. But it was not enough to keep government
finances regulated to the satisfaction of the Department of Finance.

CLOSING IN ON SPECULATORS

The building boom of the mid-1960s provided a challenge to the Government
to regulate the possibility of windfall profits caused by transforming agricultural land into building land. Agricultural land in the outer suburbs of
Cork and Dublin, by the standards of the twenty-first century, was ripe for
development. Lynch inherited some work in progress from Dr Jim Ryan on
the subject of taxing profits from land deals and speculation. In February 1965
the chairman of the Revenue Commissioners, Seán Réamonn, responded to

exploratory probing by the Department of Finance on the prospects of introducing capital gains tax with the view that they were not in a position to move
on it yet. On 12 March, however, Whitaker indicated that while his minister,
Dr Ryan, 'would like to leave the general issue of capital gains tax open for the
present he would like to have examined, as a matter of urgency, the possibility
of taxing gains arising from increases in [the] value of unimproved land.'[79]

This position was confirmed in a draft memorandum for the Government
in April 1965, which stated that capital gains were under consideration and that
the Minister for Finance was interested in taxing speculative profits on lands or
business premises that were escaping tax. It was argued that most of the profitable lands suitable for development were adjacent to urban areas. Speculators
were not engaged in the trade of buying or selling land and therefore were not
liable to income tax. The minister wanted the profit on the disposal of land to
be treated as income tax, surtax or corporation profits tax in the case of a
company, and to be subject to tax in the year the profit arose. Liability would
arise in cases of sale, transfer, gift or death or the sale or transfer of shares in a
company owning land. This would bring builders into the tax net.[80]

These efforts came to fruition in section VII of the Finance Bill (1965) and
merit some attention because of the controversy surrounding them.

In practice what had happened was that pre-1935 legislation was challenged
in the Supreme Court. The respondent acquired by lease certain plots of
ground, each for a term of five hundred years and subject to ground rent.[81] He
built houses on the plots, which he disposed of by way of sub-demise for periods
varying from 450 to 495 years, for 'fines' (the selling price of the houses) and
ground rents. Then, for the purposes of assessment under schedule D, the fines
were brought into computation, and added to them was the capitalised value
of the difference between the ground rents reserved by sub-demise and the
original ground rents. However, the Supreme Court held that the respondent
was not liable to be assessed under schedule D on the amount of the fines or
of a capitalised value of the ground rents received by him. It had not been
denied that the respondent was a builder by trade, that he built houses on land
he owned or occupied, and disposed of them by way of sub-demise in consideration of rents and fines. But the respondent contended that those facts did
not justify assessment under schedule D on his profits from these transactions.

The Supreme Court held that he derived no profits from any source other
than his ownership of lands and tenements. He took lands upon lease for a
long term at a rent, and on these lands he built houses. But if those profits
exceeded the annual poor-rate valuation on which he was assessable under
schedule A (which covered profits from the ownership of land) his partial
immunity was due to the inadequacy of the machinery for estimating the
annual value of the property to be taxed.

The Supreme Court held that the respondent traded with and not upon the tenements he owned. And the profits derived from trading of that description—if it could be called a trade—were covered by and taxed upon an annual valuation of the tenement as ascertained by the Commissioner of Valuation.

The problems in relation to taxing builders' profits went back to particular weaknesses in section VI of the Finance Act (1935). To establish liability to tax under that legislation it was necessary to show that the person concerned acquired the land with the intention of reselling it or developing it. The difficulty lay in proving intent at a previous time. While the 1935 act declared that references in schedule D to profits from a trade were to include profits from building operations, it contained a defect: it did not specify that building was to be a trade chargeable under schedule D. In practice, the provisions of the act were easily defeated. If a builder acquired a freehold of land, built houses and sold them freehold—thereby disposing of the entirety of his interest—there was no doubt about liability under schedule D. But that was regarded as unusual. More commonly, a builder, on disposing of the houses, reserved an interest in the form of an annual rent and was thereby exercising his ownership of the property. Thus schedule A assessment, relating to land, exhausted his liability.

What the Finance Bill (1965) proposed to remedy was the situation arising from a builder disposing of only a part of his interest in the land and incurring liability under schedule A assessments as a landowner only. It also sought to remedy another subtle tax avoidance mechanism relating to property whereby the buyer did not purchase in the ordinary way but acquired shares in the company that built the property, thereby acquiring the use of the property.

The new proposals sought to redefine 'development' and to shift the liability to income tax under schedule D on any profits derived from dealing in or developing land. However, any person, including a farmer, who sold land in the ordinary way without stipulation or condition about development was not caught. But the typical builder was covered. The builder would lease an area of land, lay out roads and divide it into sites, on which houses would be built, and the site would then be disposed of for a fine and ground rent. Section 39 (2) (a) of the 1965 bill was intended to bring them into the net, dealing with persons having an interest in land who disposed of that interest or of 'an interest which derives therefrom.'

However, section 39 (3) provided for certain conditional exemptions. Firstly, the person in question must not have carried on a business of dealing in or developing land for the previous three years. Secondly, the sale must not have occurred earlier than six years after the erection of a building that was throughout in the sole occupation of the person building it, or the individual had erected a house as a residence for himself. This was intended to catch speculative builders who lived in one of their houses for a period and sub-sequently sold it at a profit. In the past, builders had lived for short periods in houses they built and successfully avoided tax on the profits of the subsequent sale of houses. However, because a builder was in the business of dealing in or developing land, he would not be eligible for an exemption.

The ring was being closed on speculation in commercial property also. An obvious device for defeating existing legislation was for a builder to form a subsidiary company that would contract with him for the construction of a building, conduct business in the premises for a short period and then sell. Under the new proposals, a building acquired for use for trade and sold with-in six years would be liable to have any profits deemed to have derived from a distinct adventure in the nature of trade, as it would prove impossible to dis-tinguish between intentions to use the building for ordinary trade and selling it for profit. There would be no exemption for persons who constructed a building, let it on a yearly tenancy and then sold it. Profit on the sale would be taxable at the time of sale, to prevent speculators initially leasing an office block to would-be purchasers on the understanding that the block would be sold when the period of immunity from tax was past.

Fianna Fáil's close proximity to the building industry in the 1960s removed the political will to tackle such problems. While Lynch had pursued the matter vigorously during his short tenure in Finance, the measures taken had been defeated by a court ruling. This would remain a difficult area and almost certainly a source of conflicting interests between a Government seeking revenue to balance the books and a vested interest willing to pour cash into party coffers and the hands of individual politicians. As Minister for Finance, Jack Lynch tried to stop that drift and failed, for the reasons given.

FINAL MONTHS IN FINANCE

While Lynch sought to cope with deteriorating Government finances in April 1966, the country celebrated the fiftieth anniversary of the 1916 Rising. Some historians, and I include myself among that group, have tended to interpret those events in all too stark nationalist terms. However, at another level politi-cians such as Lemass and Éamon de Valera had liberated themselves from the shibboleths of an earlier generation. They viewed the challenge to end partition as something other than a matter of restoring lost territory.[82] Lynch was of that same school of thought. Ireland was changing. Even the sole sur-viving commandant of the 1916 Rising, who was so prominent at the fiftieth anniversary celebrations in April, was fortunate to be returned in June when he stood for re-election as President of Ireland.

Lynch was not in the Department of Finance for enough time to make a strong impact on the direction of the national finances. However, he showed himself to be a quick learner. He did not show rebel tendencies. He accepted the analysis of the national economy presented to him by the Department of Finance. Persuaded by Ken Whitaker's logic, he went to the Government determined to get agreement from his ministerial colleagues on a policy of retrenchment. He usually met with a very unsympathetic response from ministers equally determined not to make cuts in their own estimates. His ministry gave him an insight into the difficulties Lemass faced as Taoiseach from powerful and strong-willed ministers and which he failed to contain. Ministers had already learnt bad habits during the Lemass years. They knew they could get away with insubordination. If they could do that with a member of the GPO garrison in the 1916 Rising and a founder-member of Fianna Fáil, what respect would they show to a leader recruited from a new generation? Lemass passed that legacy on to his successor.

In the autumn of 1966 Lynch faced a spectacular 'solo run' by the Minister for Education, Donogh O'Malley. It was not out of line with the insubordination of other ministers but it was by far the most audacious. Without seeking Government approval, O'Malley announced at a dinner of the National Union of Journalists the introduction of free secondary education. Lynch and the Department of Finance had not been consulted; he may not have discussed the matter even within his own department. It is possible that the Taoiseach may have been aware of his minister's plans, though I now consider this to be most unlikely. On 12 September, Dr Whitaker wrote to the Taoiseach expressing astonishment that 'a major change in educational policy should be announced at a weekend seminar.' He continued in a clinical tone:

> This 'free schooling' policy has not been the subject of any submission to the Department of Finance, has not been approved by the Government, has certainly not been examined from the financial (whatever about the educational) aspect, and, therefore, should have received no advance publicity, particularly of the specific and definite type involved in Mr O'Malley's statement.

He felt that the Minister for Education

> must be aware, as other members of the Government are, of the enormous increase in taxation in recent years and of the fact that, despite this increase, even existing current services are not being financed completely from current revenue.

Whitaker then became even more pointed in his comments.

Mr O'Malley should have had all the more reason for caution since the Ministry of Health, which he vacated only recently, is gravely insolvent in the sense that the current year's provision for health services is now reported as being almost £2 million short of what these services are costing.

That was a barbed and pointed reference to the runaway financial style of O'Malley in his previous department. Whitaker said it would be the 'negation of planning' if substantial commitments were announced by individual ministers without the consent of the Department of Finance or the approval of the Government. It would become 'increasingly futile to be drawing up 5 or 7 year programmes, and even the financial and economic policy of the Government in the short-term will be seen to bear no relation to what the country can afford.'

While it was accepted that priority 'should be given to education in the allocation of national resources,' that should be done 'in the light of a proper assessment of the trend in these resources and of the cost of educational and other desirable improvements.'[83]

O'Malley received a rebuke from Lemass. He replied unrepentantly on 14 September 1966: 'I believe that it is essential for a government from time to time to propound bold new policies which both catch the imagination of the people and respond to some widespread, if not clearly formulated, demand on their part.'[84] Between 1966 and 1969 the number of pupils attending second-level education rose from 104,000 to 144,000.[85] The initiative was long overdue. Northern Ireland had had free secondary education since 1945.

Lemass had either lost the will to face down the recalcitrant members in the Government or had grown weary of standing in the way of 'progress'. It was time to hand the reins of power to a younger person. He resigned as Taoiseach in November 1966.

Chapter 6 ~

NEITHER A 'CARETAKER' NOR A 'RELUCTANT' TAOISEACH, 1966–9

In the late summer of 1966 Seán Lemass decided to step down after seven years as Taoiseach and as leader of Fianna Fáil.[1] He was sixty-six. Jack Lynch, aged forty-nine,[2] recalled that the retiring Taoiseach had 'put his raddle-mark on me early on.'[3] Lemass called him to his office and told him of his intention to retire very soon and asked him whether he was interested in the job.

There are two apparently contradictory versions of what happened next. Lynch recalled in 1979: 'I told him emphatically that I was not and he seemed to accept it.'[4] Bruce Arnold quotes a conversation between the secretary of the Department of Finance, Dr Whitaker, and Lynch in the latter part of September 1966. The two men were in New York, attending a meeting of the International Monetary Fund. They had made the sea crossing together and had ample opportunity to range over different topics. They had become very friendly from working together since April 1965 in the Department of Finance, and they also knew each other from Lynch's time in Industry and Commerce. One evening as they relaxed after seeing a performance of *Hello, Dolly!* on Broadway, Lynch related to Whitaker the content of the conversation he had had with Lemass a few weeks before. He had given no immediate answer, simply saying that he needed time to reflect. When Whitaker asked what Máirín would think, Lynch replied: 'I'll talk her round.'[5]

Lemass raised the question of his retirement on 21 September at a meeting of the parliamentary party. He did so in the context of his swingeing criticism of the party's morale and its financial state, a diagnosis he repeated at a meeting of the National Executive on 26 September.[6] Lynch, who had returned to Dublin, was asked to meet the Taoiseach again in the company of George Colley and Charles Haughey. He told all three that they should be thinking about the future leadership of the party. Lynch remained circumspect, while the other two expressed a keen interest in the job. Haughey, then aged forty-one, had talent and proven ability, matched only by his overweening ambition.[7] He was part of a new Dublin smart set, living life in the fast lane, in the company of self-made entrepreneurs, who were doing very well out of the building boom. Haughey had his champions within the Government. However, senior members of the party, such as MacEntee and Aiken, were neither amused nor edified by his antics and his zest for the good life. Neither did Lemass show his son-in-law the slightest preferment.

George Colley, then aged forty, would emerge as a contender for the leadership. He had been made Minister for Industry and Commerce on 13 July 1966, having served as Minister for Education.[8] He was supported by Frank Aiken. Neil Blaney, then aged forty-four, was another potential candidate. The son of a Fianna Fáil veteran and founder-member of the party, he came into the Dáil in 1948 on the same day as Lynch. He was supported for the leadership by Kevin Boland, aged forty-nine, another son of a founder-member of Fianna Fáil. Both were choleric in temperament, very nationalistic and dedicated to preserving the 'core values' of the party, which had been dipped in aspic.

Lemass knew that a leadership contest would reveal the divisions within Fianna Fáil. He preferred an agreed successor, therefore, and wanted Lynch to succeed him. Lynch had proved a success as Minister for Industry and Commerce and Minister for Finance. He suffered from one major disadvantage: born in 1917, he was between the generations: not old enough to have been part of the revolutionary wave and not young enough to be counted a member of the 'young Turks'. But he was a unifying force.[9] Moreover, he enjoyed unprecedented national popularity, reflected in the general election of 1965, in which he polled 12,852 first-preference votes in the Cork Borough constituency.[10]

In the last days of October 1966 George Colley flew to the United States to lead a promotional drive by the Industrial Development Authority. Donogh O'Malley was in Paris; Charles Haughey was in London. Lemass contacted Colley, asking him to return home immediately on the grounds that there was to be a major development in Irish politics. Haughey made a speedy return from London, to be greeted at Dublin Airport by supporters carrying placards stating 'Charlie is our darling.'[11] O'Malley also returned home. The leadership campaigns were in full swing, and Lemass had not yet formally declared that he was going to retire.[12]

At the beginning of November the political correspondents in Leinster House saw the succession as a two-horse race: Colley versus Haughey. Speculative prognostications gave Haughey a slight edge; Colley was later perceived to be four votes ahead. But the political correspondents had installed Jack Lynch as 6-4 favourite if he agreed to run.

Then, besides Colley and Haughey, there was Neil Blaney, who was being supported by Donogh O'Malley. One commentator wrote in retrospect:

To many the choice was on a simple basis. It was between a man who was too-clever-by-half, who was mistrusted even by some of his immediate colleagues, and a man who was safe, traditional and unostentatious. The legend of the man who wanted to be Taoiseach, who was ironically not clever enough—or did not care enough—to conceal his own cleverness was the greatest single factor against Charles Haughey. Colley trailed some of the clouds of glory of the de Valera myth; many who did not share his Irish-Ireland views nevertheless lent towards his simpler style and had faith in his solidity.[13]

The *Cork Examiner* reported on 3 November that a 'dark horse', in the person of Haughey, was still very much in the contest.[14] Blaney was also in the race, as was Colley. On 1 November, Lemass had met Haughey and Colley; he promised neither of them his support. While it appeared that there would be a contested succession,[15] Lemass behind the scenes still hoped and worked to get Lynch to stand. A delegation of TDs from Cork and the south met Lynch in a hotel in Charleville to persuade him to run. Seán Ó Ceallaigh, a running-mate of Dr Patrick Hillery from Co. Clare, was prominent in the group.[16] Hillery recalled seeing on another occasion a group of TDs—probably Ó Ceallaigh from Clare, Seán Ormond from Waterford, Tom McEllistrim from Kerry and Martin Corry from Cork—waiting outside Lynch's office in Leinster House.[17] The date may have been 2 November. According to the *Cork Examiner*, when they got in to see him they assured him that his election would be unanimous. The same day Lynch received requests from other quarters to stand for the leadership.[18] According to Lynch, Lemass 'again invited me to his room, informed me that several backbenchers wanted me to run and that the party generally favoured me as his successor.' Lemass 'pointed out that I owed the party a duty to serve, even as leader.' Lynch was given to understand that the other contenders, to whom Lemass had already spoken, were prepared to withdraw in his favour. He said he would reconsider his position and discuss the proposition again with his wife.[19]

In a letter to the *Cork Examiner* on 10 September 1973 Máirín Lynch wrote:

It has been said that my husband was a reluctant Minister and a reluctant Taoiseach. I wish to make it perfectly clear, that any reluctance shown by him in accepting these offices derived from his consideration of my preference not to be involved prominently in public life. It is a continuous source of surprise to me that so many knowledgeable people in their assessment of political affairs forget, or perhaps do not wish to recognise, the human side. Is it too much to expect that the feeling and reactions of a woman should be taken into consideration? Are these feelings not accepted as being a factor in her husband's endeavours to accomplish whatever his tasks in life may be? . . . The real fact is that I know my husband enjoyed the challenge of the various Ministries that he held and that he felt privileged to be elected Taoiseach: thus in his different offices he was in a favoured position to help create a better life for our people.[20]

She added, with reference to the situation in 1973: 'Knowing that my husband wishes to continue to lead the Fianna Fáil Party, any support I can give him will be gladly given.'[21]

She did not mention the circumstances that lengthened Lynch's reflections on the decision to go forward. His mother-in-law, Margaret O'Connor, was very ill at the time. A fiercely independent person, she had reluctantly, in her eighties, agreed to give up her flat and move into 21 Garville Avenue.[22] In poor health, she suffered a series of strokes. Jack and Máirín kept her at home for as long as possible; she was then moved to Our Lady's Hospice, Harold's Cross, where she died on 23 November 1967. Any hesitancy Lynch had about taking on the role of Taoiseach primarily arose out of concern for the well-being of his wife at the time of the grave illness of her mother. He talked over the matter of his candidature with Máirín twice in one day, once over lunch and then later in the afternoon. He recalled: 'We decided after a long and agonising discussion that I would let my name go before the party.' Returning to Government Buildings, he told Lemass of his decision to stand. He was somewhat overawed, however, by having to 'assume the mantle of the likes of Éamon de Valera and Seán Lemass.'[23] But he was never a reluctant leader of Fianna Fáil.

Once Lemass got the news that Lynch was prepared to stand, he immediately phoned Blaney, who agreed to withdraw,[24] as did Haughey.[25] Lemass then sent for Colley. Instead of stepping out of the race, Colley told Lemass that he would like to talk the matter over with Lynch before making a decision. He phoned Lynch and they agreed to meet the following day. That evening Colley was astonished to hear a report on the news that Lynch would be elected unanimously and that the other candidates had withdrawn. Requesting RTE to issue a correction, he issued a statement later on 3 November that he was not withdrawing.[26] When he and Lynch met the following day he said that an election was in the best interests of the party. At that point neither Blaney nor Haughey would have been able to re-enter the race, as they had already given their word to Lemass that they would stand aside.[27]

The political correspondent of the *Cork Examiner* reported on 4 November that a Corkman was expected to become Taoiseach, for the first time in the history of the state. This was being regarded as a 'certainty'. An editorial stated that Fianna Fáil had acted wisely in turning to Lynch. It felt that, despite not having said anything to confirm his candidature, he had been 'drafted', and such was the 'magnet of his personal popularity and dedicated service to the party' that 'there now remains only a formality of selection before Mr. Lynch assumes the mantle of his distinguished predecessor.'[28] That paper had good sources. On the evening of 4 November 1966 Lynch told a reporter from the *Cork Examiner* in Waterford that he had agreed to go forward only after 'prolonged and insistent pressure.' He said it was 'the greatest decision I have had to make in my life.' That was the first time that he commented in public on the leadership.[29]

Lemass's departure from public life was as swift as it was lacking in drama.[30] On 8 November he announced that his relinquishing of office was 'a political decision, uninfluenced by any personal considerations.' There was, he said 'no question about my general health, which is quite good.' He announced that he was convinced that 'it is in the interests of the country, the Government, and the Fianna Fáil Party that responsibility should now pass to a younger man.'[31]

The Fianna Fáil parliamentary party met to decide the leadership at 11:30 a.m. on 9 November. There were two candidates: George Colley and Jack Lynch. While the outcome was a foregone conclusion, the debate was divisive and acrimonious. Seán MacEntee attacked Lemass for leaving the leadership at a time when Fianna Fáil as an organisation was at 'its lowest ebb' and 'the state was tottering towards anarchy.'[32] While this was vintage MacEntee, there was discomfort and disappointment in the room at the tone and tenor of the address. Later in the meeting MacEntee announced that he would support Lynch. Frank Aiken, who nominated Colley, criticised the manner in which Lynch had been put forward. Kevin Boland launched a tirade against the veteran politician. Robert (Bobby) Molloy, a young Galway TD who seconded the Colley nomination, recalled that Boland's 'barrage of abuse' had 'astonished' him. 'I had never seen this side of things in Fianna Fáil up to then.' But Aiken was not distracted from his task.[33] Paddy Smith, a veteran and an opponent of Lemass, spoke in favour of Colley. Tom McEllistrim, Kerry North, proposed Lynch.

Only the seventy-one TDs voted, members of the Seanad not being eligible. The ballot papers were placed in a shoebox, prompting Lemass to comment later: 'A queer receptacle for such a momentous decision.'[34] The outcome was 52 to 19 in favour of Lynch. The announcement, accompanied by loud cheering, came at 1:15 p.m.[35]

In his acceptance speech Lynch praised his predecessor:

He set very high standards for his successor. Mr Lemass knew and understood what high standards are. I will do my utmost to maintain these
standards. I am conscious that I am the second successor of Fianna Fáil to
Mr de Valera and in my opinion no greater honour could fall on any man
than to be one of this great man's successors.[36]

'If anything, a tougher individual than I am' was Lynch's summing up of
Lemass. Lemass announced to Dáil Éireann on 10 November: 'I have resigned.'[37]

Before the job of managing the affairs of the state began, Lynch had the
pleasant task of returning in triumph to Cork. The new Taoiseach had been
scheduled to return to his native city on Saturday 12 November. It was a
triumphal homecoming. The *Cork Examiner* described it as 'historic, memorable and packed with emotion,' reporting that 'tens of thousands of people
cheered him as he drove at snail's pace in an open American-built Cadillac
from Blackpool to the heart of Patrick Street.' There was 'a succession of bands
to lift the hearts with their rousing music,' and the route 'was brightened by tar
barrels and bonfires. Singing, cheering crowds were everywhere to welcome
their Taoiseach and age-range was from babies to octogenarians. There were
fireworks, flags and streamers.'[38]

Lynch looked pale and strained, according to the press report, but all his
feelings seemed to erupt when he stood to wave to the crowd in Blackpool,
outside the Glen Rovers hall. His words were lost in the huge roar of welcome.
'Up the Glen!' was what he had undoubtedly said. His brother Theo, a vice-
president of the club, was in the crowd, which responded in song. Then the
car moved on very slowly, making its way to the top of Gerald Griffin Street,
where, stopped at traffic lights, he saluted the nuns of the North Presentation
Convent.[39] The parade then freewheeled down Shandon Street, making a stop
outside Molly Owen's pub, Jack Lynch's traditional haunt, where a flaming tar
barrel had been placed.

The crowds became thicker as the car made its way down North Main
Street and into Washington Street and then the Grand Parade, where the
people on both sides were so compressed that the car had difficulty getting
through to the platform outside the Savoy cinema. 'The cheering, surging
people closed in from all sides when Mr. Lynch got out and mounted the platform,' according to the report. In a brief address, punctured by persistent
cheering, Lynch said that his aim would be to try to generate good will among
the people generally. But, he added, 'I am not going to be the quiet mouse
politician either.' He thanked those from a non-Fianna Fáil background
who had turned out to welcome him. In conclusion, he said he felt that the
country was almost out of the economic troubles of the previous twelve
months. The measures taken by the Government had secured that turnaround

'and, with the grace of God and the firmness of purpose of all Irish people, we can resume that advance again.'[40]

Later that night Lynch attended the annual dinner of the North Monastery Past Pupils' Union in the Imperial Hotel. His brother Finbarr was the president. Theo and another brother, Father Charlie Lynch, were also in attendance.[41] Jack and Máirín Lynch were in Croke Park the following day to watch Cork play Wexford in the all-Ireland under-21 hurling final.

Speaking in Dáil Éireann on 16 November, Lynch told deputies that he had personal reasons for being reluctant to allow his name to go forward for the position of Taoiseach. 'They are now irrelevant and have been put aside,' he said, assuring the Dáil that 'I am not going to be a reluctant Taoiseach': he was going to be a 'vigorous and progressive one.' Neither was he 'in a caretaker capacity. I am going to stay here as long as I can hold down the job.'[42] He set out his policies, laying emphasis on the need to preserve Ireland's independence and individuality. He wanted to secure adequate economic progress, accompanied by the moral and intellectual development of all the individuals comprising the Irish community. Education was a priority. He challenged the notion of 'free education', as the community had to pay for it. 'The important thing to be done is to see that inability to pay the cost of such education does not debar any child who can benefit from it from receiving it,' he said. He stressed the need for early access to the EEC as a full member. He wanted to increase foreign investment, curb wage rises and improve the external trade balance. On Northern Ireland he said he would promote co-operation and relations with Stormont. The objective of unity would be pursued through agreement, toleration and equality of status.[43]

The Dáil voted 70 to 64 in favour of the motion nominating the members of the Government. At a glance it can be seen that Lynch had held on to many of the Lemass team. Frank Aiken, then aged sixty-eight, was Tánaiste and Minister for External Affairs. George Colley remained as Minister for Industry and Commerce. Lynch moved Charles Haughey from Agriculture to Finance. Mícheál Ó Móráin retained Lands and the Gaeltacht. Neil Blaney was moved from Local Government to Agriculture; his former portfolio was given to Kevin Boland. Brian Lenihan remained in Justice; Dr Patrick Hillery retained Labour; Donogh O'Malley was confirmed as Minister for Education. Erskine Childers held on to Transport and Power, while Michael Hilliard retained Defence.[44]

WHY HAUGHEY WAS PROMOTED

On the surface, the hand-over was smooth; Lynch's election had not created disunity. Division already existed within the Government. Lemass had allowed too much latitude to Blaney, Boland and O'Malley in the running of their portfolios. As Minister for Finance, Lynch had been seen as a soft touch. He had personal experience of the actions of the spendthrifts in the Government. Perhaps he made Haughey Minister for Finance in order to keep those ministers in check. The new Taoiseach needed a strong hand to guide the parlous and perilous finances of the country. Therefore, it is most likely that he put the accountant Haughey in Finance to rein in the undisciplined spending of the wild boys in the Government.

Blaney had been given Agriculture to soften his cough. Boland, another big spender, was now in Local Government. O'Malley, who had played ducks and drakes with the Department of Finance when he was in Health and Education, required strict supervision. Haughey, once a poacher, had been given the role of gamekeeper. As Minister for Finance he would be obliged to curb the reckless enthusiasm of his friends.

However, neither Blaney nor Haughey abandoned their own leadership ambitions. They had to confront lingering and gnawing feelings about what might have been, if only they had not allowed themselves to be thwarted by the wily Lemass. Haughey and Blaney were not natural allies but they were united by a strong and unrequited ambition to wrest the leadership from a man neither of them considered to be of authentic republican timbre. They bided their time for the right opportunity to make their separate moves for the top job.

Lynch made another decision that would have unforeseen consequences. While in the Department of Finance he had worked well with James Gibbons as his parliamentary secretary. Gibbons, who was a prominent supporter of Colley for the leadership, was reappointed to Finance as parliamentary secretary, where he worked under Haughey until after the 1969 election.[45] That relationship, particularly in the primary Department of Finance, was very much a junior-senior one, and the residue of that dynamic would carry over into 1969 and 1970, when Gibbons was Minister for Defence.

Haughey was a strong and capable minister. He brought in four budgets, expanding public spending each time. He was a strong supporter of the Second Programme for Economic Expansion as Minister for Finance. Economic planning was not a restriction on freedom, Haughey said, but 'a means of exercising it purposefully.'[46] But he operated in troubled economic times. The British Government devalued on 18 November 1967; the Irish Government quickly followed.

Haughey captured public attention with his flair for self-publicity and his openly flamboyant life-style. He was controversial and larger than life. He employed a public relations consultant, who made sure that the media were well supplied with copy.[47] This was unheard-of behaviour in the staid Department of Finance, where anonymity was a way of life. John Healy,

'Backbencher' in the *Irish Times*, numbered Haughey among his favourite politicians and wrote about him regularly in a flattering light.[48]

Haughey's flamboyant style must have jarred with senior officials, such as Whitaker, whose more reserved manner was viewed as being the norm in Merrion Street. In contrast, Haughey took the credit for introducing free travel and subsidised electricity for people over the age of sixty-five. He introduced tax concessions for those suffering from disabilities. He received international acclaim in 1969 when he introduced a tax exemption for artists who produced original, creative work of 'cultural and artistic merit'. The Revenue Commissioners were invited to consult those 'competent to advise them.' The result was a tax-free environment for artists, writers, composers, musicians and singers, and more than three hundred people qualified for exemptions in the first three years of the scheme, 70 per cent being writers and 20 per cent artists.[49]

Haughey was also Minister for Finance when the National Science Council was set up on 4 January 1968. On its inauguration he recognised the necessity for a radical improvement in the education of successive generations of Irish people in that vital area.[50]

Haughey was a patron of the arts. The architect Patrick Scott made him the first president of Rosc, an exhibition of modern art, in 1967. Held in the Great Hall at the RDS grounds in Dublin, it brought the participation of leading artists from all over the world.[51] At the opening, on 12 November 1967, Haughey stressed that Dublin would become 'an international forum of artistic discussion.' This would serve as a 'stimulus for our own artists by putting them in direct contact with the best modern paintings and confronting them with shining examples of the high artistic traditions of the past.'[52] The exhibition was held again in 1971, after Haughey had been sacked from the Government.

How the secretary of the Department of Finance, Ken Whitaker, worked with Haughey and evaluated his administrative performance is difficult to assess with accuracy. On the surface it was correct and productive. However, it is safe to state that Whitaker's relationship with Lynch was more harmonious. The *Irish Times*, in a profile of the Minister for Finance, reported that there were rumours that the two men were at loggerheads. That was denied, and they appeared to continue to work fruitfully together.[53] There were tensions between the two past pupils of the Christian Brothers, in both substance and style. That relationship cries out for a careful comparative study.

Before he replaced Maurice Moynihan as governor of the Central Bank on 1 March 1969, Whitaker witnessed what he would have considered to be worrying trends in the finances of the state. He wrote about the resumption in the rise of public expenditure, capital and current, under the tenure of Haughey (1966–70) and Colley (1970–3):

Total expenditure, which had been 25 per cent of GNP in 1956, had reached 40 per cent by 1972 and the Exchequer borrowing requirement had risen from 4 per cent to 7 percent of GNP. Moreover, the rate of increase was accelerating.

He wrote that one bulwark remained: 'No one had yet undermined the disciplinary safeguard of not deliberately incurring deficits in the current budget.' That was to change in 1973.[54]

TACA AND CONTROLLING FIANNA FAIL

The closing years of the 1960s proved challenging for the new leader of Fianna Fáil. His party had been in office since 1957, and a number of Government ministers exuded an arrogance, triumphalism even, unlikely to win electoral support and popular respect. The battle over the development of Fitzwilliam Square, Dublin, symbolised the clash of the modern in Ireland under Lemass and Lynch. Sixteen late-eighteenth-century houses were at the centre of the controversy, which dated from 1961, when the Electricity Supply Board sought to demolish numbers 13 to 28 Lower Fitzwilliam Street and build a new office block. The Old Dublin Society, the Irish Georgian Society and An Taisce joined forces with other conservationists to prevent the destruction of one of the finest Georgian streetscapes in the world. The Minister for Local Government, Neil Blaney, gave the ESB planning permission to go ahead with the plan. The replacement building was completed in 1970.

This was, according to the journalist Frank McDonald, a signal for the widespread demolition of historic Dublin, most marked around the area of St Stephen's Green.[55] Here was a state in an almighty hurry, with little regard for history or architectural heritage. Large sections of Dublin were reshaped and rebuilt in the 1960s. With the approval of Charles Haughey, the Central Bank sought to build a fifteen-storey skyscraper in a centre-city area where buildings were under a preservation order. Turned down by the city council, the Central Bank then sought and received permission for a thirteen-storey building. However, Kevin Boland withstood pressure from Haughey to allow the plans to go ahead. An Taisce, the conservation lobbying organisation, campaigned against it, and the Minister for Local Government upheld its objection. His successor in that department, Bobby Molloy, was in office for the construction of a building almost thirty feet higher than it should have been. In the process a number of buildings of historical and architectural value were also demolished, and brute architecture overshadowed the Corinthian porticoes of the neighbouring Bank of Ireland.[56] It was not one of that Government's better decisions.

The building boom of the 1960s offered opportunities for making profits on a scale never before encountered in the more sluggish economies of the

1920s to the 1950s. Lynch, as Minister for Finance, had attempted to close the door on loopholes providing windfall profits for speculators and large builders. There was a sense of unease among a number of ministers in 1967 over the growing closeness of Fianna Fáil and the building lobby. In February the Minister for Local Government, Kevin Boland, made a strong attack on property speculation. He was concerned at the preference for commercial over domestic building, and he felt that speculation in land was driving up the price of houses for ordinary people. George Colley, the Minister for Industry and Commerce, did not disagree with an opposition TD's view that speculators were crooks engaged in highway robbery.[57] Both politicians were witnessing the acquisition and the rezoning of land around Dublin and other cities for the building of vast housing estates.

Charles Haughey was among those ministers who displayed his wealth most ostentatiously. He represented the new generation of ministers in the mohair suits sitting all too comfortably in an official Mercedes. He suffered the ire of more traditional party members because of his outings—top hat and all—with the Ward Union Staghounds. In 1964 a stag jumped over him at the end of the hunt, knocking off his hat; the incident made the *Irish Times*. His more traditional party associates were 'bitterly offended by Haughey's enthusiasm for such "Ascendancy" past-times.'[58]

Haughey was close to the builders of the new suburban Ireland. In the 1960s he bought a house and land from Matt Gallagher at Raheny in the northern suburbs of Dublin. The sale of that land back to Gallagher in 1969 for £205,500 provided the liveliest of exchanges in the general election of that year.[59]

Lynch viewed with anxiety the trend of Fianna Fáil growing all too close to the building industry. The transfer of money from that industry to the coffers of the party required careful scrutiny. The Fianna Fáil fund-raising agency Taca appeared to have free rein. The unbridled donations of cash to the party alarmed Lynch, and he tried to make the process of receiving donations more transparent. He asked a party member in Co. Tipperary, Des Hanafin, to take control of the fund-raising operation. Hanafin moved the operation from Fianna Fáil head office to a centre-city hotel, a move that did not meet with universal approval either from Taca critics or from the supporters of closer links with big business and men of property. Hanafin said the new arrange-ment gave him the privacy in which to conduct the fund-raising in accor-dance with party norms. He kept a strict record of each donation received, and Jack Lynch, he said, had no hesitation in returning donations that he felt might compromise the freedom of the party. Nevertheless, party elders remained decidedly ill at ease about the fact that the 'men of no property' had become too closely identified with the men of immense and expanding property. This too is an area that urgently requires extensive research.

Lynch's Government confronted widespread industrial unrest in the latter years of the decade. The 1960s had been the 'decade of upheaval.'[60] It was also a decade of rising expectations. The tenth national wage round had been entered into in 1966. That recommended a maximum increase of £1 per week. During 1967 the practice began of negotiating two-year comprehensive agreements, and this was a feature of the eleventh round in 1968. The increase, in two or three phases, was between £1.75 and £2 per week for men, while women would receive 75 per cent of that.[61] There had been industrial unrest in the maintenance sector in the latter part of 1968. On 28 January picketing began; on 5 February the strike spread, and strikers placed pickets throughout the industry. Some other workers, prevented from going to work, placed counter-pickets; but the general principle of refusing to pass a picket held, and that caused widespread chaos. The president of the Irish Congress of Trade Unions, Jimmy Dunne, was one of the sternest critics of the strike. Maintenance workers wanted the same reduction in working hours that had been granted to craftsmen. The employers would not yield. The situation was complicated by the fact that there were eighteen unions involved. By the end of February, employer solidarity began to crack and individual deals were done to bring about normal productivity. Finally, the employers caved in.

Work did not resume until about 10 March. But so dangerous was the precedent that there was a common resolve on both sides to end such disruptive practices. The Minister for Labour, Dr Patrick Hillery, worked hard to encourage consensus. That was reached in the 'very sophisticated national agreements in 1970 and 1972.'[62]

Ireland in the late 1960s continued to cautiously develop a greater sense of openness. On 11 July 1967 the Censorship of Publications (Amendment) Act came into force, removing a ban on books that had been published for more than twelve years. It was a step in the right direction. Brian Lenihan, as Minister for Justice, presided over that significant change, the achievement of which should not be underestimated. To have attempted to preserve the status quo would have been impracticable. Young people would have ignored the law. That new assertiveness was demonstrated in May when students staged a sit-in on 19 and 20 May at University College, Dublin.

In the wider community a division of opinion had emerged over certain teachings of the Catholic Church. On 29 July 1968 Pope Paul VI issued the encyclical *Humanae Vitae,* which reaffirmed the traditional Catholic teaching on the use of 'artificial' forms of birth control. The Lynch Government did not address the legalisation of the sale of contraceptives. Neither did the Taoiseach, at that point at least, take up the recommendation of the Constitutional Review Committee to hold a referendum on article 44 of the Constitution of Ireland, regarding the 'special position of the Catholic

Church.' The issue of divorce was not even on the horizon. Lynch was cautious in his handling of such divisive issues. His first three years as Taoiseach were devoted to the major issues, such as achieving membership of the EEC.

FOREIGN POLICY, MEMBERSHIP OF THE EEC AND ANGLO-IRISH RELATIONS

While Lynch was still Minister for Finance, the Government had sought meetings at the ministerial level with the EEC Commission.[63] Those meetings took place on 20 September 1965. The Minister for External Affairs, Frank Aiken, attended, as did Lynch. The European Commission was represented by Jean Rey (External Affairs), Sicco Mansholt (Agriculture) and Robert Marjolin (Economic and Financial Affairs). The Irish delegation sought to reaffirm the country's active and continued interest in full membership. The Government followed through with a series of ministerial meetings, which began in January 1966.[64] The focus of the discussions was on the swift opening of negotiations with the EEC. Five of the original six members were still in favour of enlargement. France remained the obstacle. Lynch emphasised Ireland's wish to join as a full member of the EEC simultaneously with Britain. He urged close contact between officials of the two countries and frequent personal contact at the prime ministerial level. The meetings ended on a note of cautious and guarded optimism.[65]

In July 1966 the Government accredited a separate mission to the three European Communities. (Up to that point the Irish ambassador in Brussels had been assigned to Belgium, Luxembourg and the three European Communities.) This was in anticipation of a new drive to gain EEC membership. The British Prime Minister, Harold Wilson, reaffirmed on 10 November 1966 Britain's intention to join the EEC, subject to safeguards. Wilson and George Brown, the Foreign Secretary, made a tour of the capitals of the Six between January and March 1967,[66] and Wilson was impressed by the level of support he encountered for British membership.[67] The Department of External Affairs prepared an analysis of the tour. Dated 29 March 1967,[68] it concluded: 'There is wide support for the view that the British Government will decide to request the reopening of negotiations and that the decision will be announced within the next month or so.' Referring to the attitude of the French, the document states frankly: 'The question of the continued existence and intensity of French political objections to Britain's membership remains an imponderable.'[69] Nevertheless it was concluded that Wilson seemed to be increasingly optimistic and was giving the impression that progress had been achieved, and the momentum generated by his tour of the capitals was unlikely to be lost. The department recommended arranging a meeting with the British as soon as possible.[70]

Shortly after Lynch became Taoiseach the Government committed itself to publishing another white paper on Ireland and the EEC in early 1967. The Committee of Secretaries of the relevant departments met on 29 March 1967 to decide how the Government should proceed in preparation for Anglo-Irish discussions due to take place in April or early May 1967.[71] The secretary of the Department of External Affairs, Hugh McCann, summarised the position of his department. A meeting between Wilson and Lynch was not likely to take place until the second half of April 1967 at the earliest. Doubt lingered whether the deadline of 1 July for the submission to the Government of a comprehensive report on Irish admission to the EEC could be met, because a number of the officials directly involved were working on the Kennedy Round and the negotiations on accession to GATT.[72]

The white paper on the EEC was published in April 1967. It differed strongly in content and emphasis from the previous one, published on 28 July 1961, which had focused on trade and specifically Ireland's adhesion to the EEC.[73] The 1967 white paper covered the implications of EEC membership extensively. It described membership as 'boarding a moving train.' The document was principally used as a way of informing the public on the EEC's legislative framework.[74]

Meanwhile the Department of External Affairs put forward a proposal to improve informal liaison between Dublin and London regarding EEC membership. This involved the setting up, at the official level, of continuing contacts on EEC matters, in particular with regard to technical questions. This matter was raised by the Taoiseach in talks with the British Prime Minister.[75] On 1 May 1967 Lynch met Wilson in London.[76] He was accompanied by Dr Whitaker and by the assistant secretary of the Department of External Affairs, Dónal O'Sullivan. The significance of these talks was underlined by the fact that the Irish delegation met the entire British Cabinet.[77] Wilson spoke about his recent tour of the six capitals of the EEC and of the six Cabinet meetings he had chaired since returning to London. He crushed rumours that there were deep divisions in his Cabinet over EEC membership.[78] He emphasised that a final decision had not been taken, so his discussion with the Taoiseach—according to the Irish record of the exchanges—would have 'to be on the hypothesis that a decision to apply would be made.'[79] Wilson revealed to Lynch that a decision was likely to be taken the following day. Regarding negotiations, he informed Lynch that it was 'almost certain that the British would decide on a completely fresh start.' In view of the previous negotiations, he doubted whether it was a good idea to work on the basis of reviving the dormant 1961 application.[80] He recommended that the Irish consider getting advice on the status of their existing application before settling the form of a new approach. He told Lynch that a formal application was likely to follow quickly upon the promised debate on the issue in Parliament, and he would like negotiations to begin with a minimum of delay before the EEC summer holidays in August.[81] Wilson told the Irish delegation that 'ratification could be a fairly long-drawn-out process.'[82]

Lynch and Wilson agreed that, because of the similarity of the legislative systems in Britain and Ireland, close liaison between British and Irish officials would be of great advantage when the time came.[83] Detailed discussion followed concerning the transitional arrangements the British would be seeking following entry. The two men agreed that there ought to be an early meeting of officials on both sides to discuss the matter in greater depth. At several points in the discussion Lynch stressed the need for the closest consultation between the two countries,[84] particularly with regard to the recent Anglo-Irish Free Trade Area Agreement. The Irish side regarded that agreement as 'an interim arrangement pending the admission of both countries to the EEC.' Wilson, according to the Irish note, fully accepted that point and 'expressed the understanding of the Irish view that our negotiations should, as far as possible, proceed *pari passu* with those of Britain.'

Wilson acknowledged Lynch's concern over Ireland's special position of dependence on British markets and confirmed that the point 'was fully recognised, not only in Europe but in Britain.'[85] He enquired whether any problems existed between the Republic and Northern Ireland in the context of EEC membership. Lynch gave the reassuring reply that 'the greater the freedom of trading and equality of economic conditions which would result from both of us being within the Common Market would undoubtedly be a considerable help in our relations with the North.' He said he could see no problem on the economic side.[86]

After a photo call at 10 Downing Street and dinner at Marlborough House, the British and Irish Governments issued an agreed communiqué that stressed that the discussions had been 'cordial' and were a continuance of those that had taken place when the two had met in December 1966. It was agreed that there be continuing consultations between the two governments on relations with the EEC.[87]

The day after the conclusion of the talks Wilson made a significant speech, strongly advocating a fresh application for membership of the EEC.[88] The House of Commons debated the proposal until it was agreed by majority vote on 10 May, and the British Government submitted its application for membership of the three communities on 11 May 1967. The previous day the Irish Government had made its application. The Taoiseach wrote to the president of the Council of the EEC, Renaat van Elslande, requesting the opening of negotiations on Ireland's application, pursuant to article 237 of the Treaty of Rome. He assured Brussels that 'the Irish Government fully share ideals which inspired the parties to the Treaty and accept the aims of the Community as set out therein, as well as the action proposed to achieve those aims.'[89]

The Irish application differed from Britain's by referring to Ireland's original application in 1961, drawing attention to the Council's decision in October 1962 to open negotiations.[90] Lynch's letter referred explicitly to the European Coal and Steel Community, the EEC and Euratom, as recommended by the Committee of Secretaries (in 1961 the Irish application made reference only to membership of the EEC); this further demonstrated to Brussels Lynch's interest in all aspects of the European communities, even if they were not to Ireland's immediate benefit.[91]

While the Government awaited a reply, the Committee of Secretaries met on 23 May 1967. Discussion centred on a proposed tour of the capitals by the Taoiseach to win support for Ireland's application. Whitaker advised the meeting that 'haste should be avoided in this matter,' as he felt that 'precipitate action now could leave the Government in an embarrassing position if negotiations did not get under way.' That cool-headed reasoning contrasted starkly with Ireland's rushed application to join the EEC in the summer of 1961.[92] Whitaker suggested that the Government should 'envisage a long-drawn-out process,' the immediate aim being to arrange a meeting with the French government in June; the meetings with the other governments could 'extend into the months following.' He also told the meeting that 'if the French showed signs of not being co-operative, their attitude could be taken as indicative of an unfavourable outcome for the British application.'[93]

The secretary of the Department of External Affairs, Hugh McCann, reinforcing the belief that discussions should first be with the French, also thought it important that, as it came near to the time for discussions with the Six, Ireland 'should not be overtly in close contact with the British': it should demonstrate a certain degree of independence from Britain.[94]

The EEC Council replied on 6 June 1967, stating that it had decided 'to put in train the procedure envisaged by the Article of the Treaty.'[95] Ireland's application for EEC membership having been reactivated, the Government's new priority was to ensure that formal negotiations would open as quickly as possible. Nobody wanted a repeat of 1961–3.[96] The Government laid down a careful strategy for persuading the Six to open negotiations to achieve simultaneous accession with Britain.[97] In spite of the international uncertainty following the war in the Middle East, the Department of External Affairs succeeded in organising the Taoiseach's tour of the Five, beginning in the Hague from 21 to 23 June; a visit to Bonn was to follow, from 26 to 28 June. However, before their departure no news had been received from Paris regarding the Taoiseach's requested talks with President de Gaulle and the French Prime Minister, Georges Pompidou.[98] In the autumn Lynch made an overdue visit to de Gaulle and his senior ministers. Although the Irish received a cordial reception, there was no melting the President's opposition to British membership, and French reservations again brought the process of integration to a grinding halt. The Danish, Irish, Norwegian and British applications remained on the table.[99] Despite failure, at least it showed that France and Germany were prepared to contemplate interim arrangements with applicant countries.[100]

Meanwhile Lynch met Wilson on 14 February 1968 for an exchange of views concerning the Council meeting of 18 and 19 December 1967.[101] Wilson told Lynch openly that the British Government would prefer if Ireland did not accept any interim arrangement. The two discussed the Benelux plan, the German-French declaration and the Italian memorandum. It was agreed that the two countries should concentrate on the Benelux proposals, which showed 'the best prospect for progress in the existing circumstances.'[102]

On 9 March 1968 the EEC Council discussed the various proposals for interim arrangements between the Six and the Four. Deadlock loomed as all arrangements were rejected. The Council did agree, however, to put forward proposals for an agreement that would prepare the way towards membership. There would be a preparatory phase of limited duration, providing a procedure for consultation, co-operation in trade and scientific and technological development. Following the preparatory phase the Commission would state whether the conditions for membership were satisfied and would decide under article 237 of the Treaty of Rome whether to enlarge. In the meantime the Council would also strengthen its structure to be prepared for enlargement.

The Commission's proposals were accepted by the Council on 5 April 1968, and enlargement was discussed at successive monthly Council meetings. It was scheduled to come before the Council in May or June 1968.[103] To keep the matter alive, the Council recommended that it continue to be discussed in Brussels among the permanent representatives of the individual states.

However, the Irish Government viewed progress as being very slow. EEC enlargement was the subject of a Department of Finance report covering the period January–March 1968, and a second report was prepared to review developments during May.[104] On 23 May, Whitaker wrote to McCann, enclosing a copy of the second report. 'The interpretative comment is deliberately pessimistic in tone, but not, I think, excessively so.' He added that the document had been prepared before 'the recent developments in France, which could have quite unpredictable consequences for the Community.'[105] The student riots and street unrest in Paris contributed indirectly to the resignation of de Gaulle in April 1969[106]; but in mid-1968 few could see such a development.

In November 1968 Harold Wilson was forced to introduce a series of measures to correct Britain's adverse balance of payments.[107] That action breached the Anglo-Irish Free Trade Area Agreement, according to Jack Lynch, and he requested an immediate meeting with Wilson.[108] Wilson told Lynch that he could not look indulgently on Ireland, because that would 'bring down the wrath of Britain's other trading partners particularly EFTA partners with which full free trade in industrial goods had been achieved.' Wilson also stated that its EFTA partners did not enjoy duty-free access to the British market any longer but that Ireland's access was protected by the AIFTA.

Despite the vicissitudes of Anglo-Irish relations over Northern Ireland after 1969, Dublin and London had worked out a *modus operandi* to ensure wide co-operation and collaboration in discussions and negotiations on joining the EEC.

IRISH FOREIGN POLICY AND VIET NAM

Lynch also followed the Lemass doctrine in the sphere of Irish-US relations. Ireland's neutral status did not interfere with a usually high level of co-operation between Dublin and Washington. Dr Robert McNamara has argued that a protectionist Ireland in the late 1950s allowed Dublin greater freedom to express its attitudes on international issues. The switch to free trade in the 1960s 'was geared to attracting foreign multinationals, many of them US-owned.'[109] In that context, he argues, Irish policy was much more sensitive, particularly in relation to the defining issue of the Cold War in the 1960s: Viet Nam. Lynch merely followed the Lemass policy line, which had taken a strongly pro-Washington stance throughout his time in office. He continued to support the US Cold War stance, to attract American investment to Ireland and to hold out against granting landing rights to American airlines at Dublin, because of the need to develop the Shannon Airport region and the tourist industry in the west and south-west.[110] His refusal to condemn the Viet Nam war[111] helped to soothe disagreement over the landing rights issue at Dublin.[112]

The Government was viewed in a favourable light by the Johnson White House. A senior member of the Johnson staff, Walter Rostow, was told on 23 January 1968 in a memorandum: 'On Vietnam, the Irish Government has steadfastly supported the United States Government even while public and opposition criticism of its position has increased.'[113]

On 24 January 1968 Rostow told the President: 'U.S.-Irish relations have traditionally been close and cordial. There are no significant problems, which might disturb this relationship with the exception of the long-standing Dublin Landing Rights question.'[114] The conclusion was firmly that, despite growing public and opposition party criticism, 'the Irish Government continues to support our Vietnam policy.'[115]

In that policy context, RTE reversed a decision in April 1967 to send a team to North Viet Nam to report on the war; Lynch had taken the unusual step of telephoning Montrose to express the Government's concerns on the matter.[116] T. Ryle Dwyer, in his biography of Lynch, states that Lynch's 'decision to thwart RTE's proposed investigation was entirely in line with his policy on the matter.'[117] The *Irish Times* felt that the intervention revealed much about Government fears that such an endeavour 'would be an embarrassment . . . in relation to its foreign policy.'[118]

As the vortex of Viet Nam increasingly sapped the energy of the Johnson administration, Lynch took a more explicit position on the war. In April 1967 he told the RTE television programme 'The Person in Question' that he was not in favour of the bombing of North Viet Nam. However, 'he did not feel that the stopping of the bombing of North Viet Nam would necessarily result in bringing the parties to the conference table.'[119] The Government's proposal that countries in the south-east Asia region organise themselves into a neutral area of law, guaranteed by the great powers, was based on a similar proposal by Aiken towards Europe and the Middle East in the late 1950s.[120] There was a consistency, nonetheless, in Government statements on the need for a dual cessation of hostilities.[121] Both a consistency and a vagueness remained in Lynch's statements, particularly in his response to the protest by the House of Bishops of the Church of Ireland at the Government's inaction on the issue. Lynch replied:

> It is hardly necessary to say that the Government deeply deplore the continuance of the war in Vietnam which for so many years has brought death, destruction and misery to the Vietnamese people. Ireland's representatives in the United Nations and in the Capitals in which Ireland is represented have accordingly advocated the complete cessation of all armed hostilities in the area in order to create the atmosphere necessary for the success of negotiations aimed at establishing lasting and stable peace in Vietnam and South East Asia.[122]

In June 1968 Lynch led an Irish delegation to attend the funeral of Senator Robert Kennedy. He made a hastily arranged visit to the White House to meet Johnson after an earlier meeting with the Secretary of State, Dean Rusk.[123] The Department of State memorandum of the conversation noted that the 'participants had an informal and friendly discussion of current affairs and mutual friends for approximately twenty minutes.'[124] The Irish ambassador, William Fay, reported that 'the Taoiseach deliberately avoided the discussion of any issue of political importance, either in the international or national field.' Despite Lynch's insistence on the need to show face and represent the Irish people at Robert Kennedy's funeral, 'the result politically [was] to add one more link to the chain of friendship which binds our two countries together.'[125]

The Department of State noted with satisfaction in 1968 that 'Irish-American relations have traditionally been friendly, and during the Johnson Administration the same close and cordial relations were maintained with the Government of Prime Minister John Lynch[126] . . . as with that of his predecessor, Mr. Sean Lemass.'[127] The same policy continued through the period of the Nixon administration. Lynch played down Viet Nam in his meetings with Nixon during his visit to Ireland in October 1970 and subsequently during the Taoiseach's return visit to Washington the following year.

VISIT TO TERENCE O'NEILL

Largely as a result of the behind-the-scenes work of Ken Whitaker, Lynch continued the policy of greater openness towards the Government of Northern Ireland. He visited the Prime Minister, Terence O'Neill, in Belfast on 11 December 1967, when he also met members of the Northern Ireland Government. He was accompanied by Ken Whitaker and by the secretary of the Government, Nicholas Nolan. Unlike the secrecy that surrounded the Lemass visit, a press release on the visit had been put out as Lynch's car crossed the border, giving Ian Paisley and some of his clerical and lay followers an opportunity to lie in ambush for the Irish Government party, and the reverend gentleman and his supporters snowballed the Taoiseach's car as it rounded the statue of Edward Carson on the drive leading up to Stormont.[128] As Whitaker, Nolan and Lynch got out of the car they were greeted with shouts of 'No Pope here!' 'Which one of us', Whitaker asked, 'does Mr Paisley think is the Pope?'

Lunch was held in the Prime Minister's residence, prepared by a daughter, Anne O'Neill. Mrs O'Neill, all the members of the Northern Ireland Government and the Attorney-General were present. O'Neill later recorded in his memoirs that the meal and the meeting appeared to drive Paisley and 'some of today's leading extremists' into 'paroxysms of pleasure.'[129]

A general discussion in Stormont Castle followed the meal, at which the two prime ministers and officials, the Minister of Commerce, Brian Faulkner, and the Minister of Agriculture, James Chichester-Clark, took part. Faulkner's main interest, according to Whitaker's minute, was in obtaining further concessions for the admission of Northern manufactures to the South at a preferential rate of customs duty. He singled out furniture and carpets—furniture being the main category that had been identified in the first Lemass-O'Neill talks. Footwear and ropes were also raised, together with a list of specific products, ranging from watch-straps to ceramics, which were before the Department of Industry and Commerce for consideration. Faulkner made a special plea for consideration of the request by the British Customs for a concession road across the border between Belcoo and Garrison, Co. Fermanagh.[130]

Whitaker recorded that Lynch had mentioned that he had under consideration the possibility of granting concessions on a purely voluntary and, perhaps, progressive basis to Northern firms in relation to tendering for public contracts. The position regarding co-operation in the fields of tourism and electricity supply was reviewed and was considered satisfactory by both sides.[131]

In the area of cultural co-operation, Lynch raised the difficulty of maintaining two symphony orchestras without one bidding against the other for instrumentalists; that had happened to some degree when the City of Belfast Orchestra was enlarged in 1965 or 66. The Taoiseach suggested that when the occasion required the supplementing of an orchestra it should be possible to arrange for a loan of personnel from one centre to the other.[132]

On another cultural matter, Lynch referred to the exchange of interesting exhibits between the National Museum and the Ulster Museum. He said Dublin was grateful for the co-operation of the Northern authorities in lending objects for the Rosc exhibition. 'He explained the legal difficulties which lay in the way of lending to the Ulster Museum objects in the possession of the National Museum which had come originally from the Royal Irish Academy collection' but added, according to the Whitaker note, that as far as objects purchased by the National Museum were concerned the Government would be happy to make periodic loans to the Ulster Museum. This would apply to such purchases as the recent Killymoon Hoard, Lynch said.[133]

After afternoon tea Lynch and his party met the Northern Ireland parliamentary secretaries. Arrangements were made for a visit by O'Neill to Dublin early in the new year, the date to be agreed later. Lynch wrote a note of thanks on 15 December. He spoke of the courtesy and hospitality extended to his party and added: 'It was a particular pleasure for me to meet you again and to have the opportunity of meeting the members of your Government. Our talks were very useful and I am certain they will be fruitful.' He was pleased that they had been joined for lunch by Mrs O'Neill and their daughter, who had 'so expertly' prepared the meal. He also expressed his thanks and those of his wife for the beautiful Irish linen handkerchiefs they had been given and offered renewed good wishes for Christmas and the New Year. He concluded that he looked forward to greeting O'Neill in Dublin some time.[134]

That return meeting took place on 8 January 1968. Replying to the Taoiseach's welcome and toast, O'Neill remarked that the series of meetings of prime ministers, which had begun three years before, had been a bigger break with the past than many people realised. In the North there had been a rigid policy of 'no meetings before recognition.' It was possible to interpret Lemass's agreement to come to Stormont as 'a kind of recognition.' While he knew the Irish Government had its problems too, he hoped it would be able, in the interest of improving relations, to use and promote the terms Northern Ireland and Northern Ireland Government, instead of Six Counties and Six-County Government, in all publicity, including radio and television.[135]

At the conference afterwards, which was attended by ministers and officials as well as the two prime ministers, Lynch initiated a general discussion with the remark that, apart from the proposed extension by Aer Lingus of its transatlantic jet service to Belfast, there seemed to be little fresh to add to the review conducted a few weeks previously in Belfast. He asked the ministers present to outline the position on matters of interest to them. The Minister for Transport and Power, Erskine Childers, referred to the satisfactory co-operation that was proceeding on tourism. The Minister for Agriculture, Neil Blaney, dealt mainly with the need for continued vigilance in both parts of Ireland to keep out foot-and-mouth disease. The Minister for Finance, Charles Haughey, said that, because of Brian Faulkner's special interest in the Belcoo–Florencecourt Road, he had instructed the Revenue Commissioners to agree to the request of the British Customs that it be classed as a concession road. He recalled that the exchange of objects of interest between the two museums had been mentioned at the Stormont meeting on 11 December and suggested that, as the Rosc exhibition was coming to an end, it would be an appropriate time to lend the Ulster Museum the Killymoon Hoard and any other objects of special interest. O'Neill said that the minister had 'taken the words out of his mouth,' as he intended raising this general matter of cultural exchanges, the holdings of the National Museum and National Gallery being much richer than anything in the North. The Northern Ireland Government would be very appreciative if at least the Killymoon Hoard could be lent for a period right away. Lynch said that that would be arranged. O'Neill also wondered whether the Lane pictures might not spend a while (say, six months) in Belfast on their way back to London and was assured that, as far as the Irish Government was concerned, they would be agreeable to such a change in the arrangements if the trustees of the British National Gallery also agreed. The six months could be taken out of the Irish entitlement.[136]

A television interview and a press conference followed the meeting. Worrying news had reached O'Neill while the meeting was in progress. Advised by Irish officials that the IRA had laid an ambush for O'Neill's party somewhere along the main Dublin–Belfast road, he followed Garda advice and returned home via Armagh—only to be heavily criticised the following evening by the *Belfast Telegraph* for lacking the courage to use the main road.[137] But courage O'Neill did not lack.

What emerges clearly from the visit is the centrality of the role of Ken Whitaker in bringing the meetings to pass in the first place. He received a thank-you letter on 19 January 1968 from O'Neill.

I cannot tell you how grateful I am for all your explanations and trans-
lations. You will note that I have used Turlough or Terence's seal on this
envelope. My wife and I are hopeful we might be able to persuade you both
to come and spend a weekend here with us—Jim will ring you. We might
do a little antiquarian visiting with Paddy Shea who is in charge of the
Works Branch of the Ministry of Finance.[138]

Whitaker had a wide range of contacts in Northern Ireland among his
counterparts in the civil service and had formed strong friendships as a result
of meeting them regularly at conferences in London or further abroad. He
also had good relations with his counterparts in the Treasury and in the Bank
of England. Both professional contact and networks of friends would be of
great service in the troubled years of 1968 and 69.

CONFLICT IN NORTHERN IRELAND

By the autumn of 1968 the policy of long-term peaceful economic co-operation
was threatened by the serious disintegration of political stability in Northern
Ireland. Demands from nationalists for a range of reforms spilled over into
confrontation on the streets. The cockpit of conflict was Derry. On 5 October
1968 between two hundred and four hundred civil rights marchers assembled
at the railway station in the Waterside district of Derry. The protest, against
discrimination in the allocation of houses and in the provision of jobs, was
banned by the Minister of Home Affairs, William Craig, ostensibly because of
a fear of a clash between the civil rights protest and the annual parade of the
Apprentice Boys of Derry. The leader of the Nationalist Party, Eddie McAteer,
and the civil rights activist Austin Currie led the marchers. Gerry Fitt,
Republican Labour MP at Stormont and Westminster, and three British
Labour Party MPs joined the front of the demonstration. The latter had ring-
side seats for a lesson in Northern Ireland-style democracy in action and
inequality before the law.

Scuffles broke out when the marchers reached an RUC roadblock. Fitt,
McAteer and Currie were arrested. The crowd sat down and sang 'We Shall
Overcome'. At that point the police gave the order to disperse, and the
marchers were caught between two police lines, being unable to go forward or
to retreat. Despite orders to halt, the police showed indiscipline and advanced
on the demonstrators.[139] That day television viewers in the South saw the
vivid film taken by the intrepid cameraman Gay O'Brien, who recorded the
gratuitous and indiscriminate use of the baton on law-abiding marchers.

Another section of the civil rights group assembled at the Guild Hall. They
were forced into the Diamond and were dispersed by the police. Rioting broke
out and there were pitched battles between the police and youths from the

nearby Bogside area. The violence continued for two days as the police used armoured cars, high-pressure hoses and baton charges. About a hundred demonstrators and a number of RUC men were injured. Clashes between police and demonstrators went on for almost two weeks.

The Taoiseach laid the blame for the trouble on 8 October on partition and 'on the methods necessary to maintain Partition against the wishes of the vast majority of the Irish people.' He called for all men of good will to strive to obtain better community relations, eliminate discrimination and bigotry and establish the full exercise of democratic rights. His speech was distributed through Irish embassies abroad. At the same time the Minister for External Affairs, Frank Aiken, instructed senior diplomats not to engage in debates and public controversy over Northern Ireland.[140] Eddie McAteer, as a protest against the violence of the RUC, announced on 15 October that his party would not continue to act as the official opposition in Stormont. That decision dismantled one of the outcomes of the Lemass visit to Belfast in 1965, as McAteer had agreed to allow his party to play that role in response to the Dublin *démarche*.[141] While nationalists believed that the actions of the RUC had demonstrated that they were not equal before the law, leading members of the Unionist Government read what was happening as the fruits of a communist-led IRA infiltration of the civil rights movement.

The conflict in Northern Ireland increased throughout October. There were student demonstrations in Belfast on 9 and 16 October, and in Derry on 19 October there was a sit-down protest in the Guild Hall.

Against the background of a deteriorating situation, Lynch was scheduled to meet the British Prime Minister, Harold Wilson, on 30 October. Wilson had been shocked by the actions of the police during the Derry march. The Home Secretary, James Callaghan, was asked for a full report. What was the British Government to do in such delicate circumstances? Pressure from London, which O'Neill felt was inevitable, might only strengthen the hand of the growing body of anti-reformers inside the Northern Government.

Whitaker was very much alive to the sensitivity of the situation. In a note to the Taoiseach on 22 October 1968 he suggested that it would be desirable before the meeting to make 'some contact' with O'Neill. He thought such a message should be oral, not written, and that it might suffice if he (Whitaker) or someone else carried the message to O'Neill. He advised that 'it would be desirable that you should let the Minister for External Affairs see the lines of the proposed message,' a draft of which he included.

The Taoiseach has no intention of adopting, in public or private, a policy of asking the British Government to put pressure on the Government of Northern Ireland. He will confirm to Mr Wilson that his views on the root

cause of the recent trouble in Derry were as publicly stated by him in
Kilkenny on Sunday 6 October 1968 ... The British Government may take
whatever course they judge appropriate but it will not be at the behest of
the Irish Government.

Whitaker returned in the draft to the position on the North-South problem
as previously stated by Lynch and Lemass.

The solution of the problem of Partition is one to be reached by agreement
in Ireland between Irishmen. What we expect from Britain is benevolence—
at least no British interest in maintaining Partition when Irishmen, north
and south, want to get rid of it. Our hope is that the causes of social
discontent in Northern Ireland will be eliminated as quickly as possible so
that people of different religious and political convictions may be able to
live together in peace and harmony, free to exercise and enjoy their lawful
democratic rights. The need for improvement in social conditions, particularly for the Catholic population, is urgent; and positive evidence that
a progressive programme will be followed would be a great help in reliev-
ing grievances and tension, improving community relations in the North
and creating better North-South relations. It is our hope that in good time
agreement will be reached on arrangements which will bring all Irishmen
together as collaborators in developing their native land as an economic
and political entity. Meanwhile, we are most anxious to maintain a spirit
of co-operation and goodwill. This need not involve the abandonment by
either side of its political principles.[142]

It is probable that contact was made, directly or indirectly, with O'Neill.

On 23 October Dr John O'Connell TD of the Labour Party put Lynch
under pressure in the Dáil regarding a meeting with O'Neill. His reply did not
show any departure from existing policy: 'No arrangements have been made
for a meeting with Captain O'Neill and myself although I would hope that the
practice of periodic meetings initiated four years ago will be continued.' He
confirmed that no representations had been made to O'Neill, 'as he is aware
of my views from a public statement made following the recent incidents in
Derry.' Lynch told the Dáil that he proposed to call on the British Prime
Minister 'during my visit to London next week and to restate my views as to
the root causes of the Derry disturbances.'[143]

When Lynch and Wilson met, on 30 October 1968, they had a very broad
agenda to cover. Lynch's briefing document advised him to concentrate on the
remedying of the political situation that permitted the existing injustices and
not to get caught up in details about discrimination in housing and jobs. He

was advised to urge Wilson to permit the expression of political opinion within the United Kingdom that would help bring pressure for a change, rather than urge him to bring direct financial or other pressure on O'Neill. He should stress that the convention in the British Parliament that they not discuss the affairs of Northern Ireland should be dropped: London, not Belfast, had the responsibility under international law for the protection of human rights. The Taoiseach ought to mention the need for the reform of local government and for the ending of gerrymandering in such places as Derry. 'The Taoiseach's aim should be to have the underlying disease cured rather than to have some of the symptoms relieved.' That would mean the setting up of a royal commission to redraw the boundaries of the local government, Stormont and Westminster constituencies on a just and equitable basis. In the discussion the Taoiseach was reminded to tell the British Prime Minister that since he came into office the North must have cost the British Exchequer half a billion pounds.[144]

On 30 October, Lynch and Wilson met for nearly ninety minutes in the House of Commons. Following the talks Lynch gave a press conference at the Irish embassy in London, where he told journalists that he had given the Irish Government's views on the situation in Northern Ireland and regarding Derry in particular. He laid emphasis on the need to introduce a reform of the franchise for local government.

His words angered Unionist politicians, and on 4 November O'Neill travelled to London with William Craig and Brian Faulkner. Lynch also supported the call by O'Neill for early changes in the local government franchise. Behind closed doors, Wilson told O'Neill that the pace of reform was too slow, and he urged movement in all the disputed areas: housing allocation, the appointment of an ombudsman and the reform of the local government franchise. Wilson announced that such reforms would be introduced in the House of Commons on 5 November. While he renewed the 1949 pledge that there would be no transfer of Northern Ireland to the South without the consent of the Northern parliament, he told the Dáil that he wanted to set up an impartial inquiry into what had happened in Derry in 5 October.

Whitaker wrote for Lynch on 11 November 1968 a six-page note on North-South policy.

1. Long since, we abandoned force as a means of undoing Partition, and rightly so because (1) the use of force to overcome Northern Unionists would accentuate rather than remove basic differences and (2) it would not be militarily possible in any event. We were, therefore, left only one choice, a policy of seeking unity in Ireland by agreement in Ireland between Irishmen. Of its nature this is a long-term policy, requiring

patience, understanding and forbearance and resolute resistance to emotionalism and opportunism. It is none the less patriotic for that. This is the
policy enunciated and followed by Mr Lemass as Taoiseach and it under-
lies the contacts made by him and by the present Taoiseach with Captain
O'Neill and the members of his Government.[145]

His second point stated without qualification:

> De facto, at any rate, we have recognised that Northern Ireland is at present
> part of the United Kingdom and that the Government of Northern Ireland
> exercises responsibility there to the extent of the devolution granted by
> Westminster. The British Parliament has determined and guaranteed the
> constitution of Northern Ireland.[146]

He wrote that Dublin did not envisage that the British Government or
Parliament would repeal the 1920 and 1949 acts and expel Northern Ireland
from the United Kingdom against the wishes of the majority in Northern
Ireland.

> The British are not blameless, as far as the origins of Partition are
> concerned, but neither are they wholly to blame. Nobody can read the his-
> tory of the past century in these islands without some understanding of
> the deep, complex and powerful forces which went into the making of
> Partition. It is much too naïve to believe that Britain simply imposed it
> on Ireland. For the Northern Unionists the main motive binding them to
> the United Kingdom is fear rather than loyalty—fear of loss of power,
> property, privilege and even religious independence if they were subject to
> a Dublin Parliament. They are also conscious (as are many Nationalists,
> too) of the superior financial advantage, in terms of agricultural subsidies,
> social services, etc., of being part of the United Kingdom rather than an
> independent dominion or part of an Ireland receiving no annual subven-
> tions from Westminster. At present, the annual subsidy from Westminster
> (over and above entitlements based on N.I. tax contributions) is of the
> order of 90 million pounds.[147]

Whitaker argued further:

> We have already drawn the conclusion that all we can expect from the
> British is a benevolent neutrality—that no British interest will be inter-
> posed to prevent the re-unification of Ireland when Irishmen, North and
> South, have reached agreement. This, of itself, will be cold comfort if we
> cannot, in addition, achieve a good 'marriage settlement', in the form of a

tapering-off over a long period of present British subsidisation of N.I. Otherwise, we in the South will be imposing on ourselves a formidable burden which many of our own citizens, however strong their desire for Irish unity, may find intolerable. We cannot lay certain social ills in the North at the door of Partition without acknowledging (at least in private) that conditions for the Catholics in N.I. would be far worse if Partition were abolished overnight. We could not for a long time offer more than partial compensation for the loss of the enormous U.K. grants and subsidies.[148]

Whitaker wrote that it was unwise to suppose that the reaction of the British Government and Parliament, of the press and public opinion to evidence of discrimination in housing and jobs and an inequitable local franchise would favour the ending of partition.

The concern aroused is rather about the image of Britain and the reaction will be to hasten the righting of social and political injustice in the local jurisdiction. The British merely want to clean up what they regard as an unpresentable back-yard.

Whitaker felt it was possible that some British Labour Party members would like to see Northern Ireland cut adrift from the United Kingdom in order to reduce the Conservative-Unionist vote and, perhaps, save money for other purposes.

But these are probably a minority even in the Labour Party; and such British saving would, in any case, be at our expense in the South; and there can be no doubt that the British Parliament would overwhelmingly refuse to expel a 'loyal' N.I. from the U.K. We must treat all British manoeuvres in relation to N.I. as being inspired by (1) short-term political party motives and (2) the longer-term desideratum of cleaning up a 'back-yard' which gives Britain a bad image in the eyes of the world. We should, above all, be most careful, bearing in mind both our own long-term interests in 'reaching agreement in Ireland between Irishmen' and our short-term economic incapacity, never to appear to suggest to the British that N.I. could be brought to heel by financial sanctions, such as the reduction or withdrawal of present grants and subsidies.[149]

Whitaker felt that the mere suspicion in the North among Catholics, no less than Protestants, that Dublin was trying such tactics would be very damaging to Irish Government interests. If tried, those tactics would prove ineffective, he wrote.[150]

The meetings between prime ministers and other ministers, north and south, had been

> directed towards fostering good-will and co-operation. They have expressly had no constitutional or political content. Neither side has in any way abandoned its political principles or ideals. Mr O'Neill and his Government remain Unionists.

Their aim, he argued, was to reduce tensions between nationalists (north and south) and unionists and to make Northern Ireland a thriving, efficient entity within the United Kingdom in which all the inhabitants, regardless of religion or political loyalties, would be happy to live together.

> We, for our part, remain dedicated to the ideal of a united Ireland. We need not torment ourselves by the thought that Mr O'Neill's policy might succeed, that even Northern Nationalists would some day be seduced, by the elimination of discrimination and satisfaction of employment and housing needs, into becoming happy citizens of a N.I. within the U.K. We should rather remind ourselves how Mr O'Neill's policy, besides being best for our Nationalist brethren in the short-run, is the most likely to loosen the roots of Partition and prepare the way for agreement between North and South on some from [sic] of re-unification.[151]

Whitaker felt that the longer-term factors were working in favour of the Irish Government.

> So far as Partition (and Northern 'loyalty' to the U.K.) rest on fear, the grounds for this will be progressively removed by the growing prosperity of both parts of Ireland, the approach to full employment and satisfaction of housing needs, the disappearance, in other words of the root causes of discrimination. All the modern trends are towards liberalisation, towards greater concern with human rights and conditions, towards looser regional political grouping, towards greater tolerance (or indifference) in religious matters. There is also a growing desire, even within the U.K., for greater local autonomy and there is little doubt that the N.I. Government envies our distinctive statehood as shown by our independent representation on international bodies and our comprehensive responsibility for administering our own affairs and following our own economic and fiscal policies.[152]

In the approach to North-South relations it was important that Dublin not be the prisoner of old ideas, even as to the form that re-unification might take. Some of these ideas are no doubt still fruitful but we may have to be more original and ingenious if we are to accommodate ourselves to the realities of the present day and more particularly to the conditions that may exist when the question becomes a live one. The recent emphasis on the need for fresh thinking is timely. Our minds should be open to explore all kinds of possibilities, confederation, federation, external association, condominium, the Benelux arrangement, the political integration principles evolved in EEC. The financial subsidisation problem is only one of the reasons why a very special formula may have to be found. It need not involve any surrender of our present independence. From the standpoint of North-South relations it is unfortunate that our 1937 Constitution appears to claim for Dublin such a premature and dogmatic right, without reservations as to form, to rule the whole of Ireland. But there is nothing we can do about this, in present circumstances.[153]

Whitaker concluded:

The most forceful argument in favour of the patient good-neighbour policy aimed at ultimate 'agreement in Ireland between Irishmen' is that no other policy has any prospect of success. Force will get us nowhere; it will only strengthen the fears, antagonisms and divisions that keep North and South apart. Relying on Britain to solve Partition is also futile; the very most we can expect is generous goodwill, financial and political. Trying to get Britain to put pressure on the N.I. Government will pay no dividends politically; they are interested only in cleaning up their own image, while we will incur the antagonism of both Unionists and Nationalists if we seem to be exploiting the social rights issue for our own political ends. There is, in fact, no valid alternative to the policy of 'agreement in Ireland between Irishmen;' any other policy risks creating a deeper and more real partition than has ever existed in the past. We were in real danger that such a partition would be created during the IRA raids when the people North and South almost ceased visiting one another and the Border resembled the Berlin wall. Misunderstanding and suspicion can be broken down only by friendly and frequent contact, just as discrimination can be abolished only by working together to create better prospects of jobs and houses for all. We can leave it mostly to public opinion and to pressure from the British Parliament and Government to prod the N.I. Government into more vigorous and effective reforms regarding social conditions and the local franchise. If progress continues to be slow, we might consider what we could do vis-à-vis the Belfast, in preference to the London, Government.[154]

As a means of introducing a further note of sobriety into Dublin's Northern policy, Whitaker estimated that the Northern Government's own income of £200 million a year was topped up by a further £100 million from the British exchequer. He estimated that if all British assistance, direct and indirect, were stopped the figures would be as follows:

Transferred revenue	£54.7 million
Residuary share of reserved taxes	£171.3 million
less	
Amount by which the estimate of yield of reserved taxes is thought to be inflated by present method of calculation (est.)	£16 million
	£155.3 million
	£210.0 million

The obvious conclusion was that an end to partition was not financially viable in the short or medium term.

While Lynch assimilated the Whitaker memorandum, Craig announced a one-month ban on all marches. On 16 November fifteen thousand people from a broad front of nationalist groups defied the ban and marched in Derry. There was another march by nationalists on the 18th.

On 22 November the Government of Northern Ireland issued a five-point programme for reform. The package promised a new system for the allocation of local government housing; an office of ombudsman would be established to investigate complaints; a development commission would replace Derry Corporation (city council); and the Civil Authorities (Special Powers) Act (Northern Ireland) (1922)—commonly called the Special Powers Act—was to be abolished. Within the Northern Government the announcement provoked serious disagreement.[155]

On 30 November there was a confrontation between loyalists and civil rights marchers in Armagh. Ian Paisley was sent to jail for three months for unlawful assembly. There was violence also in Dungannon on 4 December between civil rights marchers and loyalists.[156] In an effort to stem the spread of protest, on 9 December O'Neill made a direct appeal on television to the people of Northern Ireland. He appealed for calm, saying that 'Ulster stands at the crossroads.' Reaching out to all sections, he said: 'I made it clear that a Northern Ireland based upon the interests of any one section rather than upon the interests of all could have no long-term future.

What kind of Ulster do you want? A happy and respected province in good standing with the rest of the United Kingdom? Or a place continually torn apart by riots and demonstrations and regarded by the rest of Britain as a political outcast?

Catholic leaders received the speech very favourably. O'Neill sacked Craig on 11 December. Unionist MPs gave O'Neill strong support.[157]

On foot of such decisive action, Whitaker wrote a note of congratulation to O'Neill. On 18 December O'Neill sent Whitaker a personal note, addressed to 'My Dear Ken' and signed 'Terence', acknowledging 'such a kind letter' and saying:

> You will have been close enough to politics to know very well that it is often an art of compromise. There comes a time, however, when one simply must stand up for the things one believes in and as Winston Churchill once said—'Put these grave matters to the proof.' I am encouraged to think that there are in truth far more sensible people in Northern Ireland than the other kind.[158]

Much depended on the future course of events in Northern Ireland and on O'Neill's ability to win support for compromise and to retain at the same time the loyalty of his Government ministers. He was given little time to deliver his reforms.

About forty members of the student-based People's Democracy set out on 1 January 1969 on a 'freedom march' from Belfast to Derry; their numbers grew to a few hundred en route. Militant Protestants attacked the marchers on 4 January at Burntollet, near Claudy, Co. Derry. The bloodied marchers arrived to a warm reception in Derry. What followed was the most serious rioting since the troubles began when the police entered the Bogside area and spread havoc. Street protests and unrest spread from Derry to Newry. On 11 January a civil rights march was banned from entering Derry. Nearly thirty protesters and ten members of the RUC were injured in the confrontations.

On 9 January O'Neill returned to London to brief the British Prime Minister and the leader of the opposition, Edward Heath. The setting up of the Cameron Commission to investigate disturbances in Derry[159] was the straw that broke the camel's back, and Brian Faulkner resigned from the Government on 24 January. His departure was a significant blow to North-South functional co-operation. Ultimately, the commission found that the RUC was 'guilty of misconduct which involved assault and battery.'[160]

The Fianna Fáil ard-fheis was held at the end of January, a week after the Government had celebrated the fiftieth anniversary of the founding of Dáil Éireann. 'We are living in exciting and challenging times,' Lynch told delegates. He warned against change that was based on

ideologies which are anathema to the Irish people, that are incompatible
with our Christian heritage and inconsistent with the dignity and freedom
of the individual for which Irish men and women fought so hard a mere
fifty years ago.

This was a reference to the rise in support for socialism in Ireland.[161] On
Northern Ireland he sought to blend his reaffirmation of party orthodoxies
with the language of conciliation. He asserted that the first aim of the party
was the same as when it had been founded in 1926:

> the re-unification of the Irish people as one nation; to secure by agreement
> the unification of the national territory; and towards that end to continue
> to work for the removal of the barriers of suspicion, animosity and
> mistrust which have divided Irishmen in the past, so that unity can be
> founded on tolerance and goodwill, and to achieve the maximum possible
> measure of cooperation in practical matters of public concern between the
> two areas into which Ireland is now divided without sacrifice of principle
> in regard to political constitutional issues.[162]

He sought to balance the territorial claim with a more conciliatory
approach.

> I do not wish that any word of mine would, in any way, tend to inflame the
> present situation in the Northern area. We want to see basic human rights
> granted—and granted in full—to our Northern brethren who are now
> denied them. We want to see discrimination in the North in every form
> ended.[163]

He wanted to see the fundamental rights and freedoms enshrined in the
Constitution of Ireland enjoyed by every citizen in Northern Ireland, regardless
of class or creed: 'Good neighbourliness should, we believe, have no boundaries.' He concluded by stating that nobody should be under any illusion that
the sentiments he expressed and his Government's efforts to promote good
relations between North and South indicated the abandonment by his
Government of 'our just claim that the historic unity of this island be
restored.'[164]

The Lynch-led Fianna Fáil policy on Northern Ireland was far too opaque
for Neil Blaney and Kevin Boland. Somewhere just beneath the surface,
tensions ran high in the parliamentary party on Northern Ireland.[165]

O'Neill, facing a growing rebellion in the Unionist Party, called a general
election for 24 February. Lynch remained silent on the sensitive issues during

the course of the campaign; but on 22 February Blaney said on television that 'there will never be any real peace in the country, north and south until [partition] is [gone].'[166] In the Dáil, Lynch faced questions on 27 February from members of the opposition on whether or not Blaney's speech was in line with Government policy. He was muted in his answer, much to the anger of opposition TDs.[167] Not long afterwards Blaney made a conciliatory speech, clothing himself in the rhetoric of Éamon de Valera. He did not recant: he merely made a tactical withdrawal.

When the election results were announced, O'Neill held the majority of Unionist Party MPs—24 out of 39. There were two undecided and three unofficial Unionists, who supported the Prime Minister. In Derry a new force in the leadership of northern nationalism, John Hume, won a seat at the expense of Eddie McAteer.

There were two sinister developments showing evidence of loyalist paramilitarism. On 30 March an electricity sub-station was blown up at Castlereagh, near Belfast. The damage was costed at £500,000. On 20 April there was an explosion at the Silent Valley reservoir in the Mourne Mountains; the target was the main water supply to Belfast. An electricity pylon was blown up at Annaboe, near Armagh. All were the work of loyalist paramilitaries.

There were riots in Derry on 19 April, and a series of attacks on public utilities forced the deployment of 1,500 British soldiers to guard vital installations. But when the Northern Government announced its acceptance of universal adult suffrage in local elections, the Minister of Agriculture, James Chichester-Clark, resigned, protesting against the timing of the decision.

Meanwhile, on 1 March 1969 Whitaker had replaced the long-serving Maurice Moynihan as governor of the Central Bank. He was succeeded in the Department of Finance by Charles H. Murray. Whitaker withdrew from trying to influence the direction of Northern policy. He sent a note to the Minister for Finance, Charles Haughey, on 21 April 1969. On Central Bank stationery and marked 'Personal,' it outlined his thinking on the Northern situation. It recommended that

Government action here should be on following lines:
(1) Do nothing to influence situation further, eg. over-reacting to use of British troops, but aim to impress and encourage the moderates on both sides, Catholic and Protestant.
(2) Avoid playing into the hands of extremists who are manipulating the civil rights movement and who wish to stir up trouble and disorder. Civil war, or anything near it, would make real N.S. unity impossible by destroying goodwill and creating fierce new enmities and divisions.

(3) Deplore recent turn of events, especially the desire or failure to protect, the right of peaceful protest and the recourse to disruption and violence.

(4) Appeal for a period of restraint—for abstention from all forms of protest on the streets for a few weeks.

(5) At same time, emphasise the desirability of the N.I. Govt. taking early and positive steps to remedy the social and other grievances against which the civil right movements is campaigning and which are the immediate causes of the present disturbed situation.

(6) Convey to U.K. Govt. our anxiety that they should (1) act with the greatest care so as not to add to an inflammatory situation which might easily spread to the whole of this partitioned island and (2) use their influence to secure early and effective remedying of the immediate (and at least long-term remedying of the ultimate) causes of the present crisis.

(7) Take early opportunity for a full and authoritative statement by T. [Taoiseach] of Govt. policy on partition i.e. peaceful solution based on agreement between N and S and British support and goodwill.[168]

A decision was taken at a meeting of the Government on 21 April 1969 that the Taoiseach should seek an immediate meeting with the British Prime Minister, Harold Wilson. It was also decided that the Tánaiste and Minister for External Affairs, Frank Aiken, should seek an appointment with the secretary-general of the United Nations, U Thant. The British were not willing to meet Lynch at that time.

On 23 April, Aiken met U Thant and immediately afterwards held a press conference. This was a new and unwelcome departure in Irish policy, and Aiken's intervention angered the British. The leader of the opposition, Edward Heath, sought out Aiken at a Foreign Office reception in London on 5 May 1969. The Irish ambassador, J. G. Molloy, was asked to make the introduction. Heath expressed his extreme concern,

in a somewhat hectoring tone, about what he described as the interference of 'Éire' in the situation there [in Northern Ireland]. 'Éire' had no right to interfere in the affairs of a part of the United Kingdom; to have brought the question to the attention of the United Nations was the very last thing the Irish Government should have done. 'Éire' interference could only have the effect of jeopardising the chances of peace in a part of the United Kingdom for which 'Éire' had no responsibility.

Heath went on to say that Northern Ireland was as much part of the United Kingdom as Yorkshire, and any interference there and in particular at the United Nations was 'unasked and unwarranted.' He emphasised that the Tory Party would form the next government and that Dublin's action had put any hope of good relations in jeopardy. He said the Tory government would seek to revise the terms of the Anglo-Irish Free Trade Area Agreement. Interference in Northern Ireland at the United Nations would put Anglo-Irish economic relations in danger. He added that the Irish Government seemed to be aiming at threatening the unity of the United Kingdom.

Aiken's reply was firm but non-confrontational. He asked the ambassador to send a copy of his press conference statement to Heath. He said further that he was acting on a decision of the Irish Government to advise U Thant of the developing situation in Northern Ireland. He also said that the Taoiseach would seek a meeting with the British Prime Minister. Aiken pointed out to Heath that he had not requested that any action be taken by the United Nations: no motion had been tabled. In fact since Ireland had become a member of the United Nations in 1955 the Government had not sought, by way of a resolution, to bring the question of partition before the United Nations. The question had been adverted to on a number of suitable occasions in ministerial speeches.

In reply, Heath maintained his position but 'spoke in a less upbraiding manner.' But he would not accept the principle that 'Éire' had any right 'to interest itself, or the United Nations, in the affairs of Northern Ireland, which was a part of the United Kingdom.' Aiken made reference to the need for electoral reform and an end to gerrymandering; and he said he could not accept Heath's view that the Irish Government had no right to interest itself in the situation and in recent developments in Northern Ireland. He told Heath that the Unionists should recognise that 'we are now living in the last third of the twentieth century and not in the middle of the nineteenth century.'

In response, Heath said that Bernadette Devlin MP was 'something from the last century,' her behaviour being 'appalling' and incredible in the case of such a 'young girl'. In the light of the thesis put forward earlier in the conversation, Aiken replied that Heath should realise that she 'is really your baby.'[169]

The Irish Government's initiative at the United Nations was an unwelcome departure for the beleaguered O'Neill, who was clinging to power by his fingernails.[170] His position no longer tenable, he resigned on 28 April 1969. Chichester-Clark replaced him as Prime Minister and as leader of the Unionist Party. Lynch, speaking in the border county of Cavan, wished the new Prime Minister success but was quite unapologetic for speaking out on behalf of all Irishmen in defence of right and justice. He asked all Irishmen to rededicate themselves to the union of minds and hearts, north and south.[171]

Neither Dublin nor London had much confidence in the ability of Chichester-Clark to deliver reform. In an effort to bring pressure on the new

Prime Minister, Lynch sought to meet Harold Wilson for talks on reform and
to review progress made since the two had last met in October 1968. Wilson
was anxious to meet first the new Prime Minister of Northern Ireland, and
Chichester-Clark went to London on 21 May. The conclusion in London after
the meeting was that the new man would deliver the necessary package
of reforms according to schedule but that the change in suffrage for local
government would not be introduced until 1971.[172]

Much had changed in Ireland since Lynch and O'Neill met in Dublin on
8 January 1968, when the ground had been firmly laid for functional co-
operation on a broad range of policy areas between Dublin and Belfast. But
Northern Ireland fell apart as a functioning political entity between April and
August 1969.

If Northern Ireland was a tragedy foretold, little was done by the
Government or by the media to prepare for likely developments and for the
impact that they might have on the South. In the areas of public diplomacy
and informing the public, RTE, the national broadcasting station, had no
resident full-time correspondent in Northern Ireland. None of the four
national daily newspapers—the *Irish Times, Irish Press, Irish Independent* and
Cork Examiner—had an office in Belfast. The Lynch Government did not
make contingency plans. Perhaps there was no realisation in the Government
of how bad the situation was likely to get. The Department of External Affairs
did not yet have a specially designated section devoted to Northern Ireland.
There was still in vogue the nebulous view that Northern Ireland policy was
the preserve of the Taoiseach. If that was so, the responsibility for a failure to
prepare for what was to follow must rest in that quarter.

Military Intelligence was not provided with additional staff for monitoring events in Northern Ireland. The Special Detective Unit of the Garda
Síochána (commonly known by its former name, Special Branch) was not
given more personnel to deal with the new contingencies. Liaison between the
Special Branch and Military Intelligence remained problematic, competitive
rather than co-operative. The army was not given any new equipment or
special training to cope with an unprecedented danger to the security of the
state. And in the late spring and early summer of 1969 the Government was
focused on preparing for a general election.

THE 1969 GENERAL ELECTION

If Jack Lynch had been picked for his electoral popularity, he did not dis-
appoint in his first three years as Taoiseach. There were seven by-elections
between December 1966 and May 1968. On 7 December there was an election
in Kerry South to replace the deceased Honor Mary Crowley. John O'Leary
held the seat for the governing party, polling 12,499 first-preference votes. On

the same day the electorate of Waterford South went to the polls to replace the late Thaddeus Lynch of Fine Gael; Patrick Browne took the seat for Fianna Fáil. Seán French took a seat in Cork Borough on 9 November 1967 from the Labour Party following the death of Seán Casey, polling 18,417 first preferences. On the same day in Limerick West, Gerard Collins won the seat held by his father for Fianna Fáil, receiving 14,384 first preferences.

There were two by-elections on 14 March 1968, in the Clare and Wicklow constituencies. Sylvester Barrett took the seat for Fianna Fáil from Fine Gael, polling 19,066 first preferences. In Wicklow, Fine Gael took the late James Everett's seat from the Labour Party.

The Minister for Education, Donogh O'Malley, had died suddenly on 10 March 1968 at the age of forty-seven. Brian Lenihan took over the Education portfolio. On 22 May a nephew of the deceased, Desmond O'Malley, was elected, securing 16,638 first preferences.[173]

Neil Blaney, on behalf of Fianna Fáil head office, had run a successful by-election campaign in Limerick, echoing the politics of the Civil War. A bemused candidate witnessed the politics of another era being acted out in a constituency far removed from border antagonisms. *Remember the 77*—a reference to the anti-Treatyites shot during the Civil War—was scrawled on the roads. Ironically, Desmond O'Malley's grandfather had been shot by the Black-and-Tans; but the thirty-year-old candidate was light years removed from the political philosophy of Blaney on Northern Ireland.[174] He had studied law at University College, Dublin, and then joined his father's legal practice in Limerick. By mid-1970 he had become one of Jack Lynch's most trusted friends and ministerial colleagues.

After such a good electoral run, Lynch made a bad decision. The report of the Constitutional Review Group urged the abolition of proportional representation and allowing a variation of one-sixth in the ratio of Dáil deputies to the population. Fianna Fáil had failed to abolish PR in a referendum in 1959; a decade later, Lynch would try again. Two Trinity College political scientists, Basil Chubb and David Thornley, estimated that Fianna Fáil would stand to win more than ninety seats if a general election were held under the straight-vote system. The opposition parties read the warning signs clearly, and Fine Gael and the Labour Party vigorously opposed the two propositions. Even within Fianna Fáil itself there was little enthusiasm for the proposed measures.

Charles Haughey was named campaign director. He was quoted at the time as saying, 'We're going to lose it, and they're going to blame me.' But his role in the campaign was cut short on 20 September when his official car hit a wall on the Co. Wexford side of Arklow. He lost a knee-cap, and his recovery was slow. He spent weeks in the Mater Hospital, Dublin, which gave him 'plenty of time to think.' According to a profile in the *Irish Times,* it was being said that he had changed: people close to him talked of a new 'maturity', a greater tolerance and a more detached view of his own limitations. It is almost, according to one of his associates, 'as if he had undergone some kind of mental plastic surgery.' He gave his loyalty to Jack Lynch but, according to the *Irish Times* article, Lynch's leadership did not impress him. Haughey saw Lynch as a compromise and believed that he himself would have made a better leader: 'He accepts that he must wait, but is sure his day will come,' still feeling that 'the tribe may yet decide to let him inherit the plume.'[175] He had not changed radically. Haughey was impatient for the leadership and to become Taoiseach.

As Haughey recovered, Seán MacEntee and Seán Lemass spoke from the back benches in favour of the referendum proposal; but support for the change was thin on the ground. Fianna Fáil workers simply did not turn out to canvass. The political correspondent of the *Irish Press,* Michael Mills, travelled around the country and found no sign of political activity. 'Is it not all a great illusion,' he mused. In the end there was a 65 per cent turn-out on 16 October 1968, and the Government lost on both propositions. Mills termed the outcome 'a shattering defeat' for Fianna Fáil. It was also a strong personal setback for Jack Lynch.[176]

However, defeat was also the spur to prepare for a general election in June 1969. Fianna Fáil was helped by the redrawing of the electoral boundaries, done under the aegis of the Minister for Local Government, Kevin Boland. The opposition dubbed it Boland's gerrymander.

Fianna Fáil had been in power for twelve years. There was a sense of euphoria within the Government party and of disorientation on the opposition benches. Under Liam Cosgrave, Fine Gael had made overtures to the Labour Party to form an electoral pact of a loose kind. But that had been spurned by Brendan Corish and his born-again Labour Party, which operated on a strategy that after the election they might hold the balance of power between the two major parties. The Labour Party would then be in a position to force the setting up of a coalition Government of Fine Gael and Fianna Fáil. The alternative was another general election, out of which the Labour Party might emerge as an actual or embryo Government. The logic was fanciful and the electoral mathematics impossible; the strategy was less practical than millennial. The naïve logic and clueless political analysis that lay behind the Labour Party slogan 'The seventies will be socialist' determined that the socialists would be seventy before they came to power as a single-party Government or as a majority party in a coalition Government. In 1969, neither of those possibilities had yet come to pass.

The redrawing of the electoral boundaries aided Fianna Fáil, and the party was well prepared to fight an election. It had ample funds, and its vote-winning machine had been tested in the recent rounds of by-elections. It had an attractive party leader in Jack Lynch. The political campaign was designed to suit the style and the strengths of the leader, and Lynch provided the party with a clean electoral persona. Haughey helped plan Lynch's triumphal, presidential-style election tour of the country in early June. He addressed large gatherings in many towns, went on walkabouts and pressed the flesh. Lynch was a major electoral asset. He had name recognition from politics and from his sporting days in the 1940s. The Fianna Fáil campaign was a well-organised one.

Much play has been made of Lynch's visits to convents. But were they any more than leading politicians in Fine Gael would have made?[177] Nuns too were citizens.

A rejuvenated Labour Party attracted a host of celebrity candidates from among the country's most prominent intellectuals. Dr Conor Cruise O'Brien, diplomat, academic, literary critic and historian, stood in Dublin North-East. The Trinity College political scientist and television presenter David Thornley stood in Dublin North-West. Justin Keating, also a television presenter, sought a seat in Dublin County North. The Labour Party refused to enter a pre-election pact with Fine Gael. Its electoral tactics were almost as inept as the political programme laid out in a 150-page policy statement that promised a massive housing programme, the nationalisation of building land and of land belonging to idle farmers, and workers' democracy.[178] Quite how that programme was going to be paid for was not satisfactorily explained. Here was a world of evangelical politics.

The Labour Party helped Fianna Fáil set the electoral agenda. The last 'red scare' election had been in 1932, when Éamon de Valera and his party were on the receiving end of a campaign mounted by Cumann na nGaedheal (Fine Gael after 1933). There was enough ammunition in the Labour Party manifesto to build an entire campaign of fear about land nationalisation and a command economy. Fianna Fáil had also received a generous propaganda present from Conor Cruise O'Brien. Speaking in January at the Labour Party conference, he suggested as an aside that Ireland should close its diplomatic mission in Catholic, authoritarian Portugal and open one in Cuba. Later, in Limerick, he called before a large audience for an end to the 'special position' of the Catholic Church as laid out in article 44 of the Constitution of Ireland. Fianna Fáil was not slow to exploit the fears engendered by the Labour Party manifesto and by the wayward rhetoric of Dr Cruise O'Brien.[179] Red-scare tactics distorted debate and dominated the election.[180]

Donald Akenson describes Lynch as being very shrewd yet often underrated by contemporaries as a political tactician.[181] His electoral leadership in 1969 proved this beyond doubt. His style was strongly populist, highly ideological and accusatory. In Limerick on 14 June he asked the leader of the Labour Party to define what was meant by 'New Republic'. Did Corish's new republic accept partition? Was it the kind of 'republic' where private enterprise would no longer be accepted and where the seeking of profit from investment in industry and commerce would become all but a criminal offence? Was it the kind of republic where decisions were handed down to people, who would have no voice in them? Was the Labour republic the kind of political entity that would confiscate private industrial concerns and bring them into the ownership and control of the state? Was it the kind of republic where land would be brought under state control? Was it the kind of republic where the individual would be ordained for the state and not the state for the individual? Finally, Lynch asked which ideology would be the inspiration of the 'new society' created within the 'New Republic'.[182]

At the final pre-election rally in Dublin on 16 June, Lynch told the large crowd that his party had scored two victories in the campaign: 'We have succeeded in driving the so-called Labour Party Leftists into full flight from the socialist Republic and the Cuban society which they launched with such a salvo of trumpets a few months ago and we have exposed Fine Gael as a divided party who are neither ready nor capable of providing the kind of Government which the country needs.' He asked what the leader of the Labour Party was afraid of: 'either he is for the Cuban society so dear to the hearts of his new-found friends or he is against it—which way is it?' He wanted to know what Corish meant by saying that the Labour Party would make the financial institutions serve the people. He asked whether Corish was going to nationalise the banks and the building societies. He wanted to know where the Labour Party intended to get the money to buy land to build hundreds of thousands of houses and to provide 100 per cent loans.[183]

This was the tone of many of the Fianna Fáil exchanges in the campaign. The governing party viewed such rhetoric as mere exposure of dangerous and destructive policies; the Labour opposition viewed much of those allegations as smear tactics.

On the other side of the argument the Labour Party received the gift of a major electoral issue by the untimely sale of Charles Haughey's home and lands at Raheny, Dublin, to the builder Matt Gallagher, from whom he had originally bought the property. The figure was over £205,500, or £5,000 an acre. Haughey promptly bought the nearby Abbeville estate and its 250 acres for £140,000. Designed by James Gandon in the eighteenth century, it was a fitting residence for a man who liked hunting, style and the sport of kings.[184] The Fine Gael politician Gerald Sweetman alleged that Haughey had benefited from an amendment that he himself had introduced as part of the Finance Act (1965), ensuring that he did not have to pay tax on the profit from the sale of his property. He referred the matter for adjudication to the Attorney-General but received a response that 'no liability to income tax or surtax would have arisen' under the 1965 act even if it had not been amended.[185] Not satisfied by this ruling, Sweetman proposed that an opinion be sought from an independent tax counsel to the Incorporated Law Society.[186]

Haughey and Cruise O'Brien faced each other in Dublin North-East. The latter gave speeches on the issue of a conflict of interest. He pointed out that planning permission was still needed to convert Haughey's farmland in Raheny into land for development purposes. But the issue was not as emotive for voters as the Labour Party might have thought. An editorial in the *Irish Times* on 13 June pointed out the stark fact: 'There is in Ireland today nothing for a socialist or the follower of any other party to be ashamed of in making money in a situation when not only the law permits but where certain considerations of conscience have also been observed.' Another editorial in the same paper on 14 June stated: 'We still live in a society of private property, and to attack a man for disposing of what is his own can be dangerous.'

There was a chronic housing shortage. Haughey had the gall to suggest that the sale of his farmland was for the benefit of young married couples seeking a new home; his public-relations team converted his acquisitive manoeuvre into the selfless act of a Robin Hood.

Both Haughey and Cruise O'Brien were elected. The latter polled 7,591 first preferences and his Fianna Fáil opponent 11,677.

During the campaign, news was leaked that a Labour Party candidate, Justin Keating, had recently sold land. This emerged in the course of a debate in Dublin on 6 June between party representatives. The Fianna Fáil representative, Anthony Hederman, claimed that the price had been £2,000 an acre. Keating issued a statement to clear his name: he had refused an offer from a developer in favour of selling at a much lower price to the city council.[187]

The intervention of the farm sale issue denied the electorate the opportunity to hear Cruise O'Brien and Charles Haughey debate issues of a more philosophical kind. Haughey had rejected the socialist vision in a speech on 29 May 1969 on the political philosophy of 1916. He asked:

Why should Ireland, which has been in the forefront in developing political philosophy, go back and adopt out of date socialistic themes which have failed in every country where they were tried? We do not need any other political motivation than the directive principle of the 1916 Proclamation— cherish all the children of the nation equally. We are now reaching the stage from which we will be able to move fairly rapidly towards achieving our goals.

He stated that the Irish economy had been progressing faster than most other European countries. But Fianna Fáil did not regard growth and development as ends in themselves. 'Fianna Fáil want to distribute evenly among the community the fruits of this development, to raise further the standard of living for ordinary men and women as much as possible.' In modern times, he argued that a government could not administer unless with the fullest consultation and co-operation. The Haughey message carried in his constituency.

The electorate was denied an alternative in the general election of 1969. The Labour Party's grand strategy flopped. Fine Gael got 34 per cent and moved from forty-seven to fifty seats. The Labour Party, ever confident that 'the seventies would be socialist,' dropped from twenty-two to eighteen. The combined strength of the two opposition parties was not sufficient to keep Fianna Fáil out of office. With 46 per cent of the first-preference vote, Fianna Fáil gained three seats, finishing with seventy-five.

The outcome was a personal victory for Lynch and a safe and comfortable majority for his party. Kevin Boland wrote of the election victory: 'Morale had never been higher; our enemies were confounded, a footstool under our feet and we were invincible again.'[188]

Between polling day on 18 June 1969 and the end of the month, speculation was rife about the composition of the new Government. Lynch had announced that there were going to be changes.[189] As all the outgoing ministers had been re-elected, did that mean that the Taoiseach-elect was going to make the kind of radical appointments he felt he could not undertake when he took over from Lemass at the end of 1966?

Lynch was in contact with all the members of his new Government. How many of his team were restive and rebellious at that point? Lynch, it is known, had great difficulty persuading Kevin Boland to stay on as a minister; he also met serious opposition when he asked him to change portfolios. The two men first spoke by phone, when Lynch may have offered him the Social Welfare portfolio. Boland wrote to Lynch on 27 June 'so that you will know fairly accurately how I feel.' Whatever misgivings he had, his first action was to declare his loyalty to the Taoiseach.

I want first of all to assure you of my own personal loyalty to you in all circumstances and to say that everything that has happened since you were selected as Taoiseach has strengthened my conviction that your decision to accept the role the party had already spontaneously decided you should have was the salvation of the party.[190]

The nub of the difficulty was Lynch's proposal to shift Boland from Local Government to Social Welfare, where he had served between 1961 and 1966.

The reason for the move was obvious: Boland had been a controversial and confrontational Minister for Local Government. He viewed his proposed change as a demotion, though he did not dispute the Taoiseach's right to move ministers around.

> I also want to assure you that it is my honest opinion that you should under no circumstances allow any Minister or Deputy to select his own post but that the Taoiseach's attitude should be 'Take it or leave it.'[191]

In normal circumstances, Boland would have welcomed a change to Social Welfare, a portfolio he regarded as being among the four most important. But in present circumstances he felt a shift from Local Government would be seen 'by friend and foe alike' as 'an indication of repudiation,' and to accept would exhibit 'a weakness of character which I hope I don't possess.' He was not prepared to appear to be 'interested only in office because that is in my opinion contemptible.' He requested Lynch to leave him out of the Government, as he had felt for some time that he would be of more use as a backbencher. He stated that there was a great danger 'for the future of the party in what appears to me to be a distinct tendency to move to the right.'[192] In that respect Boland was taking distance from his former schoolmate Charles Haughey and his friends in Taca, who represented a new wing of the party.

Referring to the developing problems in Northern Ireland, Boland added: 'You know also that I am not in agreement with the approach to Partition and to the stationing of troops outside the country in present circumstances.' That sentence demonstrated the burgeoning differences between Boland and Lynch on Northern policy. He went on to attack 'RTE's planned sabotage of our nationality.' This was presumably an indication of his wish to see RTE play a more constructive and patriotic role at a time of growing national crisis over Northern Ireland. Taking all this into account, Boland asked to be left out of the Government. He concluded, 'again assuring you of my personal regard and loyalty.'[193]

Lynch persuaded Boland to remain in the Government, but at a high price: he would retain Local Government in addition to being given Social Welfare.

Lynch outlined his team in Dáil Éireann on 2 July 1969. The new Government contained few surprises. Erskine Childers, then aged sixty-four, was named Tánaiste and Minister for Health. Haughey continued to hold Finance. Colley remained at Industry and Commerce but was given additional responsibility for the Gaeltacht. Aiken retired to the back benches, relinquishing his portfolio of External Affairs; Dr Patrick Hillery, who had added to his strong reputation by the manner in which he had handled the Department of Labour, replaced him. Lynch needed a strong pro-European negotiator

to lead the Irish team charged with securing Ireland's membership of the
EEC. Mícheál Ó Móráin held on to the Justice portfolio. Jim Gibbons was
promoted to Defence. Brian Lenihan was given Transport and Power.
Joseph Brennan was made Minister for Labour. Seán Flanagan was given
Lands, and Pádraig Faulkner took charge of Education. Paddy Lalor received
the portfolio of Posts and Telegraphs. Desmond O'Malley was promoted to
the position of parliamentary secretary to the Taoiseach and to the Minister
for Defence.[194]

An acrimonious debate followed as the opposition raised issues regarding
the suitability of a number of the appointees. There were references to smear-
ing, land deals, etc. The exchanges were bad-tempered as the opposition
sought to replay the general election. There were a number of important new
faces in the chamber. Dr David Thornley and Justin Keating strengthened the
Labour Party parliamentary team, as did Dr Conor Cruise O'Brien, who had
outstanding oratorical skills and a wicked turn of phrase.

Charles Haughey came under sustained attack from Cruise O'Brien in his
first speech. He twisted the knife at every opportunity in his constituency
opponent, claiming that Haughey 'had been associated with people who had
seemed to violate the law with impunity.' He repeated a charge levelled many
times on the hustings that

> Deputy Haughey as minister failed to disclose a conflict of interest when
> introducing a taxation change. It is true that Deputy Haughey was exon-
> erated on that charge by his colleague the Attorney General, the partner of
> his political fortune and by a couple of civil servants or a civil servant in a
> Department for which he is responsible.

Cruise O'Brien said he was trying to measure his words, 'but in most other
democratic countries in Western Europe a Minister who had been seen to act
in this way would not be renominated.'[195]

Dr Garret FitzGerald of Fine Gael attacked the appointment of Boland to
Social Welfare and had critical things to say about the reorganisation of the
other part of his portfolio, Local Government. He also attacked the reappoint-
ment of Mícheál Ó Móráin to Justice. He argued:

> It may be that he is a weak man who allowed civil servants to foist this
> [Criminal Justice] Bill on him but this would be a reason why he should
> be removed from the office. Another reason is that during the election
> campaign he was one of the Ministers most active in the smear campaign
> directed against my colleagues on the right.[196]

Kevin Boland also came under attack for his alleged gerrymandering and for his vigorous defence of Government tactics during the election. Boland repudiated any suggestion that he was in politics for position, saying, 'The sack doesn't worry me, boy. It doesn't worry me in the least. I'm not here for the sake of office. Let no-one think I am.' He rejected allegations that Fianna Fáil had got into power

> by various underhand means: by means of a smear campaign, by means of gerrymandering which I am credited with having carried out, and that it is because of those tactics that this proposition to appoint me and certain other members of the Fianna Fáil party as ministers has come before the house.

He denied smear tactics; he had merely responded to the programmes of Fine Gael and the Labour Party. He said the Labour Party had advocated a 'fraternal association' with Cuba. 'That is a public fact,' he said, to cries of 'That is not true' from the opposition benches.[197]

Boland lost the run of himself, but in the end Lynch came to his rescue. He explained that Boland had come to him to say 'if he did not want him on the front bench he was quite happy to go to the back benches.' The Taoiseach replied that he wanted the co-ordination of the country's building construction potential. Knowing it was going to be a difficult job, he thought that Boland was right for part of that portfolio. He also wanted to ensure that 'our social legislation would be as advanced as our resources could possibly make it.' He made up his mind 'that Deputy Kevin Boland was the man to take charge of Social Welfare and that Deputy Neil Blaney was the man to take charge of Planning and Construction.'[198]

In conclusion, Lynch vigorously defended his party against the charges that Fianna Fáil ministers were anti-intellectual. He recalled Noël Browne's jibe that the Labour Party was smaller in numbers but could beat Fianna Fáil in many respects.

> I knew what he was referring to, this so-called superior intellectual capacity. There are two attributions I just cannot stand. The first is an intellectual and the second is a worker. I regard everybody who is doing a job in this country a worker whether he works with his head, his hands or anything else. Whether a person is an intellectual or not often means that one has not had the advantage of going to a university or, having gone to a university, has not had the means or facility of taking a secondary degree. The intellectual capacity on this side of the house is as good as on any side of the house. The people have proved that by returning Fianna Fáil Governments in successive elections since 1932.[199]

Having listened patiently to the barbed comments of his opponents, Lynch summed up. He used humour to remind the opposition that the election was over.

Not long ago a man was playing a match. He got a knock on the head towards the end of the game. His team were beaten. He woke up in hospital a fortnight later, having suffered from severe concussion. He wanted to get back immediately on the field and finish the game. The nurse had difficulty in telling him that the match was over and that his team were well beaten. The parties over there are suffering from the same sort of shock. The match is over and well won.[200]

Chapter 7 ～

THE NORTHERN 'TROUBLES'
AND THE IRISH STATE

With the general election over, Lynch and members of the new Government turned their attention towards their well-earned summer holidays. But before they left Dublin the Government had continued to receive fresh reports about the deteriorating situation in the North.

The news of a violent death in 1969 had a profound impact on a society not yet accustomed to the killing spree that left more than 3,500 people dead in the Northern Ireland 'troubles' by the end of the twentieth century. On 13 July a 67-year-old pensioner, Francis McCloskey, had been found lying by the roadside, seriously injured, following a police baton charge against a crowd throwing stones at Dungiven Orange Hall.[1] About five thousand people attended the funeral of the first victim of the 'troubles', and his death became, as the Scarman Report noted, a *cause célèbre* in Northern Ireland and beyond. It was believed, with good reason, that the RUC had beaten an inoffensive elderly man with batons.[2] With very few Catholics serving in its ranks, the RUC was not regarded as a neutral force. Policing was heavy-handed in nationalist areas.[3] The 'marching season' was taking off with a great sense of menace.

In London, John Hume, who had emerged as a fiery apostle of non-violence, sought to bring home the gravity of the situation to his fellow-parliamentarians. Con Howard, an Irish diplomat in London, reported on 24 July a conversation between Hume, Stanley Orme MP and a couple of friends. Hume said that he had only three hours' sleep for some time past because 'he has had to act as "Police Chief" in Derry.' He considered himself very lucky 'to have been able to influence the situation at least temporarily towards calm to some degree.' He described his native city as 'a powder keg' and stated that the Northern Government had 'lost control' of the situation. He emphasised that there was 'bitter hostility towards the police and the situation was exacerbated by the bad unemployment situation' and that 12 August was so dangerous that he was going to tell Lord Stoneham, a Home Office minister with responsibility for Northern Ireland, that the British

Government should suspend the constitution of Northern Ireland and appoint a parliamentary commission backed by the British army.[4]

Hume felt that a growing polarisation was taking place in the North. In Belfast three or four families a day were leaving Protestant areas because of fear. A bloodbath, he said, was a real possibility, particularly in Derry, Dungiven and Belfast. There was a deepening split in the Unionist Party. He could foresee a situation where the Derry people would ask for protection from the Government in Dublin, and he wondered about the possibility of UN observers being deployed.[5]

On 24 July 1969 Hume spoke to Lord Stoneham for more than three hours. He stressed that the situation in Derry was grave and that there was a lack of awareness among MPs about the explosiveness of the looming confrontation. He knew that the Northern Government could not ban the parade, for political reasons, as it would split the party and tear the organisation apart. But he warned that Stormont had lost control of the situation in Derry. He urged the Prime Minister or the Home Secretary to visit the city before the parade and also requested the Home Office to send a team of observers and to consider deploying members of the London Metropolitan Police. The question of having UN observers also deserved serious consideration, he said, and he argued that U Thant, the secretary-general, would be agreeable to such a move.[6]

Howard did not think that Hume had great faith in the likelihood of the British Government agreeing to that step or to the suggestion that a joint British-Irish military force be deployed. On the question of deploying British troops, Hume felt that it would be a lesser evil than using B Specials (the part-time Special Constabulary).

At another gathering Hume discussed the deteriorating situation in the North with Hugh Delargy and other Labour Party MPs. Delargy said that he was going to see the Prime Minister, Harold Wilson, on the matter and that Wilson had asked him to put down a question on Northern Ireland in the House of Commons. Hume had repeatedly made the point that the Irish Government ought to have a person in Belfast who could send reliable reports on the situation as it developed.[7] The absence of a network of professional observers in Northern Ireland meant that Lynch was forced in the end to rely on alarmist reports coming from untested sources or sources that proved very partisan, if not untrustworthy. Hume was prescient in that regard.

On 29 July a Government memorandum reflected Hume's growing concerns for the safety of the nationalist minority in Derry. It warned of widespread violence if the Apprentice Boys' march of 12 August, representing the 'extreme Protestant element', was allowed to grow from seventeen to seventy-three bands. It predicted a turn-out of thirty thousand. The memorandum urged that the British Government 'should take all possible action in advance . . . to ensure that bloodshed does not occur.'[8] Dublin decided to apply diplomatic pressure.

HILLERY'S VISIT TO LONDON, 1 AUGUST 1969

Lynch sent his new Minister for External Affairs, Dr Patrick Hillery, to London on 1 August to meet Michael Stewart, Secretary of State for Foreign and Commonwealth Affairs. Hillery was accompanied by the secretary of the Department of External Affairs, Hugh McCann, and the Irish ambassador in London, J. G. Molloy. The talks would demonstrate how far the British Labour government was—echoing Heath's hectoring comments a few weeks earlier to Frank Aiken—from accepting that the Irish Government had any role to play in Northern Ireland.

Hillery opened the discussions by expressing his grave concern about the prospects of further violence in Derry, particularly around the Apprentice Boys' march on 12 August. In any other year, he said, it might be 'a routine annual celebration but this year it went far beyond that.' Its scale had been stepped up. Derry, which was predominantly a nationalist city, had become 'a veritable powder keg.' He suggested that the parade should be banned, or contained to its normal size. The holding of an excessively large parade deliberately routed through Catholic areas was 'sheer madness in present circumstances.' At the least, he said, the parade ought to be confined to Protestant areas. The B Specials, who he baldly described as 'partisan', should not be allowed to be present. He wanted the British Government to send observers to exercise a restraining influence on events.[9] Hillery stressed that his visit to the Foreign and Commonwealth Office was private and that he did not wish to publicise it, 'lest he might make matters more difficult for the British Government.' But he stated that if nothing were done as a result of the visit, a different situation might arise.

In reply, Stewart said that the press should be made aware of their meeting and the fact that they had discussed Derry, the EEC and Nigeria. He said that it was not correct to say that the Stormont government was afraid to ban the parade: its judgement was that it was better to control it than to ban it. He made reference to a similar situation in Bermuda, when the same line was followed with success. A British official told the meeting that the parade would follow the less provocative of two routes. Stewart said that, despite the threatening situation in the immediate future, there were certain hopeful signs that the Northern Ireland Government had taken steps towards reform.[10]

Hillery replied that there was a certain lack of credibility about the reforms. Could Stormont not do something now as an earnest of its intentions?

Stewart replied that that was a question of judgement for Stormont, which was primarily responsible for Derry. 'You accept, of course, that responsibility for this area rests with the Stormont and London Governments, and not with your Government.'

Hillery accepted that control was now in their hands but that there would be strong reactions in Ireland if things were to go wrong. He pressed Stewart later in the conversation: 'You expect the situation will not get out of hand?' 'Yes,' was the firm reply.[11]

However, that was not what the Irish Government was being told by its sources. Lynch met the leader of the Nationalist Party, Eddie McAteer, on 8 or 9 August. The veteran Derry politician was pessimistic. From all its available sources, the Government knew that the situation in Derry was spinning out of control.

GOVERNMENT MEETING AS NORTHERN CRISIS WORSENS

Exhausted by their exertions in the general election, the ministers dispersed for holidays. On 9 August, Lynch left for his holiday in west Cork. Despite the Fianna Fáil victory he was deeply troubled by what he believed to be the imminent catastrophe. Dick Walsh of the *Irish Times* reported on 11 August that it was likely to be 'one of the most trying weeks in the history of Northern Ireland.' He also wrote that the Prime Minister, James Chichester-Clark, was scheduled to brief his Government colleagues on his meeting with the Home Secretary, James Callaghan, at which the use of British troops to quell riots had been discussed.[12] In all churches in Derry, prayers were offered for peace. Some five thousand marchers were now expected and more than a hundred bands. An *Irish Times* reporter wrote on the eve of the march of a 'quiet, brooding calm' enveloping the city. That quiet was intensified by the fact that many thousands had left for the seaside on their holidays and was broken only by the hammering of workmen putting up a wire-netting shutter on a shop window on the traditional marching route.

There was a meeting of about a thousand people on Sunday afternoon in Celtic Park. John Hume lent his support to all groups seeking to ensure the peace of the community in the coming days and the protection of citizens. A message from the Bishop of Derry, Bishop Neil Farren, was read at all Masses, urging peace and the practice of the law of charity and love of neighbour.[13]

On the morning of the march the *Irish Times* made its lead story: 'Street fights rage in Dungannon.' Police with riot shields had baton-charged civil rights supporters after street fighting and stone-throwing between Catholics and Protestants broke out in the late evening and early morning. In the Bogside area of Derry barricades began going up about 2 a.m. on the 12th. The paper's reporter, Dennis Kennedy, said that ten thousand were expected to take part in the march on what would be no ordinary 12th of August. About eight hundred police with water-cannon, armoured cars and riot control vehicles were in the city. They would have to be deployed on the fringes of the Bogside, at Bishop's Gate and Butcher's Gate, beneath the walls and at Waterloo Place. In the Bogside the Citizens' Defence Group and Citizens' Action Committee had arranged for a 'peace corps group' to rush to any trouble spot in order to prevent conflict.[14] The *Irish Times* warned in an editorial: 'The stakes for the opposition in the North are very high. Lives are at risk. It is easy to be sanguine in Dublin. Derry today may be another turning point in history.'[15] It was.

The main headline in the *Irish Times* the following day was: 'Tear-gas used on Derry rioters—112 casualties as police battle against Bogside barricades—Two men shot in disturbances after Apprentice Boys parade.' The reporters witnessed a force of a thousand RUC men in the city charging and counter-charging youths who rained stones and petrol-bombs on them. Tear gas was used in abundance against the protesters. That was believed to be the first time that tear gas had been used in either Northern Ireland or Britain. Youths had commandeered a petrol station at the entrance to the Bogside, giving them an unlimited supply of petrol. A petrol bomb seriously injured one policeman. In all, ninety-one policemen and twenty-one civilians were taken to hospital. In the rioting two men received gunshot wounds. The press photographs showed the city as a war zone. Disturbances were also reported in Belfast, Dungannon and Newry.[16]

In response to the violence Lynch made arrangements from Cork on the evening of Tuesday 12 August to hold an emergency Government meeting the following day. There was no respite in the violence. Alarmist press and radio reports confronted Lynch as he drove from west Cork between 5 and 6 a.m. on 13 August. Reaching Cork, he received a phone briefing about the latest developments. A few minutes after 8 a.m. he continued by car to Dublin, arriving at 11:30. The remainder of the morning he worked in his office, being briefed by senior civil servants. The Government meeting was scheduled for 2:15 to give ministers time to get back to the capital. Senior civil servants were also summoned back to their desks.

The secretary of the Department of External Affairs, Hugh McCann, was instructed to have his Political Division prepare two draft speeches for the Taoiseach's consideration. The first (draft A) put the British Government 'on the spot publicly for not having taken appropriate action to prevent last night's events in Derry, and secondly, it commits the Taoiseach to seeking a meeting with Mr Wilson now.' The drawback to such a course of action could be that 'Mr Wilson might manoeuvre the Taoiseach into appearing to have asked for, or approved of, the use of British troops in the North.' That might lead 'to an adverse reaction from extremist elements North and South.'[17] The second text (draft B) was more conciliatory. Lynch received the drafts and minuted: 'Taoiseach, 13/8/69,' but the time was not registered.[18]

Meanwhile, efforts to contact holidaying ministers met with mixed results. Patrick Hillery was in the west of Ireland on a holiday. He recalled that there was a strict rule that no member of the painting group to which he belonged was to be disturbed when out for the day, and repeated calls from the Taoiseach's office failed to persuade the proprietors of the guest house where Hillery was staying that even a national emergency was a reason for disturbing the Minister for External Affairs. He got the news of his emergency summons to Dublin on his return that evening.[19]

Those who were present that day were part of a Government that was not well prepared for dealing with the unfolding crisis. While the official diagnosis had been accurate, the contingency planning was poor or non-existent. The atmosphere in the room was charged as reports continued to reach Dublin that violence and disorder were spreading.[20]

It is difficult to piece together the order of the discussion. The official record is not helpful; but various sources, some of whom were present, have been used to construct the following narrative.

Lynch began by discussing the contents of the two drafts as the basis for his proposed television broadcast that evening. It appears that many of his Government colleagues reacted strongly to the cautiousness of the two drafts. They were dismissed as mere civil service talk by Blaney, Boland and Haughey, who wanted a much tougher statement. Seán Flanagan was hawkish. Brian Lenihan was highly emotional and uncharacteristically militant. Childers, Gibbons, Faulkner and Colley strongly backed Lynch's moderate and calming line.[21] Further discussion on the text of the proposed statement was deferred to the end of the meeting.

After an hour the Government instructed the secretary of the Department of External Affairs, Hugh McCann, to deliver a message to the British Government. At 3:30 p.m. McCann telephoned Kevin Rush at the London embassy, instructing him to 'convey immediately to the British Government the request that they arrange for the immediate cessation of police attacks on the people of Derry.' In the absence of the Secretary of State, Michael Stewart, arrangements were made to meet the minister of state, Lord Chalfont, at 5 p.m.

While waiting at the Foreign Office for his appointment, Rush took a call from the Department of External Affairs to add to his instructions that the British Government was also requested 'to apply immediately to the United Nations for the urgent dispatch of a peace-keeping force to the Six Counties of Northern Ireland and [to say that] the Government has instructed the Irish Permanent Representative to the United Nations to inform the Secretary General of the foregoing.' Before leaving the Foreign Office, Rush confirmed that the Government was not intending to raise the matter at the United

Nations but was requesting that the British should do so. He confirmed that interpretation and reported accordingly by phone at 5:30 that evening.[22]

This fragment charts the course of events in the Government room that afternoon. But there had also been wild talk about cross-border intervention. Dick Walsh wrote that Haughey, Boland and Blaney had demanded that 'the Republic take a hand in the fighting.' They wanted the Irish army to go into Derry or Newry, or both. Haughey, according to that source, argued that an incursion by the Irish army would create an international incident and thus provoke the intervention of a United Nations peace-keeping force.[23] Stephen Collins noted that the call was not for intervention but for drawing up plans in the event of a doomsday situation.[24]

While I understand that Haughey raised the question of a military incursion, the Irish army was neither prepared nor equipped to undertake such an open-ended strategy. Pádraig Faulkner recalled in his memoirs that the question of an army incursion was raised but quickly dismissed: 'As far as I can remember the matter was raised in a rather haphazard way and was given little or no consideration.'[25] The Minister for Defence, Jim Gibbons, briefed the Government on the state of preparedness of the army.[26] According to military sources, it had fallen well below its peacetime strength. On 31 July 1969 the strength of the Permanent Defence Force was 8,113. The first-line reserve was 1,889; the FCA (second-line reserve) was 19,786. The number serving in Cyprus with the United Nations peace-keeping force was 403.[27] Low in numbers, the army was also poorly equipped for contemporary warfare, particularly with the forces of the British army. It had antiquated equipment and no soft-skin personnel carriers; when, in the days that followed, the army was deployed along the border it had to be transported, in some cases, in CIE buses.

Lynch discounted military intervention, but he secured the support of his Government for the setting up of field hospitals at strategic locations along the border. It was also agreed to prepare emergency accommodation on the southern side of the border.[28] Pádraig Faulkner remembers that Gibbons and Haughey were instructed to bring the army up to 'an acceptable level of readiness as soon as possible.'[29]

Faulkner's invaluable account of this Government meeting helps bring out further the drama of that afternoon. 'Kevin Boland proposed that we bring home Irish troops on UN peacekeeping duties in Cyprus and call up the second line reserves.' That was also rejected, and Boland 'verbally resigned from [the] Government.' Shouting of treachery and betrayal, he stormed out. He left a note of resignation and, gathering up his belongings, went home. President de Valera, on hearing news of the resignation, called Boland to Áras an Uachtaráin for a talk.[30] On 18 August, Boland was back in the Government for a meeting,[31] having been persuaded to reconsider.[32]

The official minutes of the Government meeting of 13 July reveal nothing of what had happened other than that 'the Taoiseach should make a statement on the lines indicated at the meeting.'[33] Des Hanafin recalled that he met a 'shook' Brian Lenihan shortly afterwards in Leinster House. Invited for a drink, Lenihan readily agreed, saying that he had just been through a 'brutal' meeting.[34]

Did Lynch lose control of the Government that day and capitulate to the hawks? According to this reading of the evidence, Lynch remained in charge. He succeeded in getting consensus and prevented the resignation of one of his ministers. But he did agree in the end to deliver a tough statement on television that night.

Lynch left the meeting and returned to his office to work on completing the text with Nicholas Nolan, secretary of the Department of the Taoiseach. A line from draft A, prepared by the Department of External Affairs, was omitted, but the discarded phrase somehow entered public discourse at the time and remains one of the most often misquoted passages from the Lynch speech. The discarded line read: 'However, we must point out that if matters continue to worsen and forces of reaction progressively gain ground in the future, this Government will not be able to sit idly by while Irish people suffer.' In the speech as delivered Lynch said: 'It is clear, also, that the Irish Government can no longer stand by and see innocent people injured and perhaps worse.' As other ministers dispersed, Lynch continued to work on the text, later leaving for home before going to the television studio.

LYNCH'S TELEVISION ADDRESS

Desmond Fisher, who was the senior editor on duty in the news room that night, accompanied Lynch to the hospitality area of the RTE studios in Donnybrook. He noticed immediately that the Taoiseach's text had been 'badly typed, with corrections in ink scrawled all over it.' That may have been because Lynch had made a number of last-minute changes at home. Pointing out that the Taoiseach could not possibly go on air with a script in that untidy state, Fisher arranged to have it retyped in large type and with double line-spacing. Lynch asked for the use of a phone, and Fisher overheard him consulting his wife on the final changes he was going to make. At one point Lynch asked Fisher what he thought would happen if he ordered the army into Northern Ireland, 'as some of his advisers had counselled.' Fisher replied that British soldiers would massacre them within twenty miles of the border. 'He smiled wanly at my answer and said he had come to the same conclusion himself.'[35] Thinking out loud, Lynch merely sought confirmation from an experienced journalist—and northerner—over what he knew to be the reality. 'He would have resigned rather than take that position,' said his friend Des Hanafin many years later.[36]

Fifteen minutes before going on air at 9 p.m. Lynch asked Fisher if he would find out whether his old hurling team, Glen Rovers, had won a recent game. He came back with the news that they had.[37] 'I don't know if it was this news or the stiffener of Paddy [whiskey] which helped him to give his speech flawlessly,' Fisher commented in 1999.[38] In reality, Lynch was a professional politician and he kept his nerve:

> It is with deep sadness that you, Irish men and women of goodwill, and I have learned of tragic events which have been taking place in Derry and elsewhere in the North in recent days. Irishmen in every part of this island have made known their concern at these events. This concern is heightened by the realisation that the spirit of reform and inter-communal co-operation has given way to the forces of sectarianism and prejudice. All people of good will must feel saddened and disappointed at this backward turn in events and must be apprehensive for the future.
>
> The Government fully share these feelings and I wish to repeat that we deplore sectarianism and intolerance in all their forms wherever they occur. The Government have been very patient and have acted with great restraint over several months past. While we made our views known to the British Government on a number of occasions, both by direct contact and through our diplomatic representatives in London, we were careful to do nothing that would exacerbate the situation. But it is clear now that the present situation cannot be allowed to continue.

Lynch said the Stormont Government was no longer in control of the situation:

> Indeed the present situation is the inevitable outcome of the policies pursued for decades by successive Stormont Governments. It is clear, also, that the Irish Government can no longer stand by and see innocent people injured and perhaps worse. It is obvious that the RUC is no longer accepted as an impartial police force. Neither would the employment of British troops be acceptable nor would they be likely to restore peaceful conditions, certainly not in the long term.

In those circumstances, Lynch said his Government had

> requested the British Government to apply immediately to the United Nations for the urgent despatch of a Peace-keeping Force to the Six Counties of Northern Ireland and have instructed the Irish Permanent Representative to the United Nations to inform the Secretary-General of this request. We have also asked the British Government to see to it that police attacks on the people of Derry should cease immediately.

He commented on the high number of casualties and of the need to provide assistance.

> Very many people have been injured and some of them seriously. We know that many of these people do not wish to be treated in Six County hospitals. We have, therefore, directed the Irish Army authorities to have field hospitals established in County Donegal adjacent to Derry and at other points along the Border where they may be necessary.

He then suggested talks with the British Government:

> Recognising, however, that the re-unification of the national territory can provide the only permanent solution for the problem, it is our intention to request the British Government to enter into early negotiations with the Irish Government to review the present constitutional position of the Six Counties of Northern Ireland.
>
> These measures which I have outlined to you seem to the Government to be those most immediately and urgently necessary.
>
> All men and women of goodwill will hope and pray that the present deplorable and distressing situation will not further deteriorate but that it will soon be ended firstly by the granting of full equality of citizenship to every man and woman in the Six County area regardless of class, creed or political persuasion and, eventually, by the restoration of the historic unity of our country.

Pádraig Faulkner, a strong Lynch supporter in the Government, wrote in his memoirs: 'Some commentators may now find part of the final version of the speech to be less than diplomatic but it must be remembered that it was a very emotive time and nobody raised any objections. In retrospect I think it was just as well that the speech was somewhat tough.'[39]

Lynch's speech was not a detached, philosophical statement written in a calm and serene atmosphere. His primary objective was to have the violence stopped immediately, without any further loss of life or damage to property. If necessary, he wanted to shame the British Government into discharging its constitutional responsibilities in Northern Ireland by drawing international attention to a deteriorating situation already being reported as if parts of the North were like a scene from the film *Mississippi Burning*.

The following day, Thursday 14 August, the *Cork Examiner* published as its main headline across the front page: 'Taoiseach demands u.n. force for North.' The sub-heading was: 'Irish army to erect field hospitals on border.' Other front-page headlines read: 'r.u.c. accused of using "war gas" in Derry' and 'Violence spreads to five towns.'

The British Government reacted to the speech in a short, dismissive statement issued in the early hours of the morning by the Foreign and Commonwealth Office. It reaffirmed that it had no intention of departing from pledges previously given that Northern Ireland should not cease to be part of the United Kingdom without the consent of the people of Northern Ireland. On the issue of bringing in the United Nations it was pointed out that Northern Ireland was part of the United Kingdom and that the affairs of Northern Ireland were thus an internal matter.[40] The Northern Prime Minister, James Chichester-Clark, called Lynch's speech 'a clumsy and intolerable intrusion into our internal affairs.' He said that the statement that police were attacking people in Derry was 'a complete and unpardonable falsehood,' and that he must hold Lynch personally responsible for 'any worsening of feeling which these inflammatory and ill-considered remarks may cause.'[41] The Home Secretary, James Callaghan, told the House of Commons that there was no question of UN intervention, as Northern Ireland was a part of the United Kingdom. Both Wilson and Callaghan were reported to be ready to break their holidays to return to London to deal with the crisis.[42]

Eamonn Gallagher, one of the most energetic and best-informed officials on Northern Ireland in the Department of External Affairs, reported on 25 September:

Major Chichester Clark must be well aware that an Irish Government could not stand aside on 13th August and not take any action when an absence of movement might well have resulted in a massacre by B Specials. That this was a real possibility is, I think, certain and that Mr Lynch's statement on 13th August helped to prevent its happening will probably be the verdict of historians.[43]

The night of 13 August and the early morning of 14 August witnessed the continuation of street violence and clashes with police in a number of towns throughout Northern Ireland. The Minister for Agriculture, Neil Blaney, phoned Hugh McCann at about 3:30 a.m. He had tried unsuccessfully to contact the Taoiseach, the Tánaiste and the Minister for Defence. He was seriously perturbed by reports he was receiving about a grave deterioration in the situation in the North, especially in Dungannon and Derry. The Nationalist Party leader, Eddie McAteer, had told him that the police were still attacking the people of the Bogside. In a new development, police and Paisleyites were attacking the Catholic cathedral. Shots had been fired and a number of people shot, but he did not know how seriously. In Dungannon, he said, the B Specials were out in force and some of them were armed with Sten guns (sub-machineguns). 'The situation there looked very ugly also,' he reported.

Blaney urged, in that desperate situation, that McCann should contact the British, urging them to take action on the Government's earlier request. The chargé in London, Kevin Rush, was contacted, and he got in touch with the Foreign Office. McCann phoned Blaney, to be told that the Minister for Agriculture had received confirmation from an army source about the seriousness of the situation in Derry and Dungannon and in other centres, including Newry, where it appeared that the civil rights demonstrators had taken over two-thirds of the town.

Rush phoned back at 4 and again at 4:15 a.m. The Foreign Office reply was to refer Rush to the official statement issued at about 1 a.m., which repeated the British Government line that there would be no departure from the pledge that Northern Ireland was part of the United Kingdom. Rush pointed out that the objective of his communication was to get the British Government 'to arrange for the immediate cessation of police attacks on the people of Derry.' The Foreign Office desk officer, Goldsmith, was reluctant to get his superior, the first secretary at the Irish Desk, out of bed a second time.

Rush persisted. At 10:30 McCann received a call from Rush. He learnt that his phone call had got action. At 5:30 the Home Office was contacted, which in turn contacted Stormont. Stormont 'pleaded that they were already doing all they could to control their own police. They were already pushed to the limit with this and could do little more.' Rush's earlier representations to Lord Chalfont had been communicated to Lord Stone at the Home Office at 5:30 p.m. and were in the hands of the Home Secretary by 6 p.m. Belfast had been contacted immediately. Rush expected to be called in to receive a formal reply to the points raised by the Irish Government later in the morning.

Riots had spread throughout Northern Ireland: to Belfast, Newry, Coalisland, Enniskillen, Lurgan, Omagh, Dungiven, Strabane and Dungannon. In Derry the battle with the RUC continued. There were fires in William Street and Little James's Street. The Stormont Government gave an order placing the 10,000-strong force of B Specials, hated in nationalist areas, at the disposal of the RUC.[44] British army units waited in readiness to be deployed.

South of the border, the army had begun to set up four field hospitals to treat the injured from various areas. There were three on the main road from Derry to Donegal and one in Co. Cavan. One, established right beside the Co. Derry border, had been completed at midnight and was ready to deal with casualties.[45]

The army also opened two refugee camps on the 14th, at Gormanston, Co. Meath, and Finner, Co. Donegal. By midnight four women and sixteen children had taken refuge in Gormanston. The wife and one-year-old daughter of Austin Currie were expected the following day, having been burned out of their home in Dungannon. There was a forward movement of army units to the border area in support of the field hospital initiative and as an aid to refugees. These were not manoeuvres primarily to position the army in an advantageous position for crossing the border in the event of a doomsday scenario.

THE GOVERNMENT'S FOLLOW-UP ACTION

An editorial in the *Irish Times* on 15 August supported the deployment of British troops on the streets of Northern Ireland. It felt that 'the people of Derry are, on this occasion, pragmatic.' But it warned that 'if the military units are seen to act alone, the situation may remain calm, but, if they are seen to work with the police or B Specials, the trouble may not be at an end.' It pointed out that the Government had clearly committed itself to an active role in pressing for decisive action by the British Government against the Stormont regime. It concluded with a question: 'While it is hard to see what more the Government could have done, are we proud of the fact—or even conscious of it—that the British have, to a certain extent, salved our consciences?'[46]

At 10:30 a.m. on 14 August, Lynch met the leader of the opposition, Liam Cosgrave, in his office, using the opportunity to brief him on recent develop-ments and to elicit his views. There was a Government meeting at 11 o'clock, at which a number of decisions with the most far-reaching implications were taken.

> That the Minister for External Affairs should seek an immediate meeting with the British Secretary of State for Foreign and Commonwealth Affairs or the Secretary of State for the Home Department.
>
> That the Minister for External Affairs should instruct the Ambassadors in countries other than Great Britain to inform fully the Governments to which they are accredited of the present grave situation in the Six Counties and to seek their support for the Government's proposals to deal with the situation.
>
> That, should the need arise, the Minister for External Affairs should arrange for a similar approach to the non-British member-States of the Security Council of the United Nations in cases in which Ireland has no diplomatic representatives.
>
> That the Minister for Defence should arrange for the provision of such troops as the Chief of Staff considers necessary for the protection of the field hospitals which are being established in the Border areas.
>
> That the Minister for Justice should expand the intelligence service maintained by the Garda Síochána in the Six Counties; and
>
> That a committee comprising the Secretaries of the Departments of Justice, External Affairs, Defence and Local Government should be set up

to keep the situation under continuous review and to advise the Taoiseach on the matter.[47]

After the Government meeting the secretary of the Department of the Taoiseach, Nicholas Nolan, wrote to Hugh McCann in External Affairs to inform him of the decision that the minister should inform the British Government that,

> in anticipation of their agreement to the proposal regarding a United Nations' Peace-keeping Force in the Six Counties, or failing that, to an alternative proposal which the Minister was putting to them regarding the provision of a joint Irish-British military Peace-keeping Force in the Six Counties, the Government had authorised the mobilisation of the First-line Reserve of the Defence Forces, so as to ensure that they would be in readiness at the earliest practicable date.[48]

After the meeting Patrick Hillery left for London to have talks at the Foreign and Commonwealth Office.

WHITAKER CALLED ON FOR ADVICE

Faced with the many difficulties and uncertainties, Lynch had made contact with his friend and unofficial adviser Ken Whitaker, now governor of the Central Bank, who was on holiday with his family in Carna, Co. Galway. Whitaker was taken by Garda car to the station in Carna, where he phoned Lynch at 10 a.m.[49] The contents of the conversation were not recorded. Later that day Whitaker posted a memorandum and a hurriedly typed letter to the Taoiseach, encouraging him to stand firm. His letter, in essence, suggested some modifications to Government policy as outlined in Lynch's speech of 13 August.

Whitaker identified 'a horrifying degree of teenage hooliganism and anarchy' in the unrest, organised, 'in part at least,' by 'extremists on both sides.' He warned Lynch:

> No Govt can benefit from appearing to support or condone this. Indeed, no Govt. can afford to be critical—without overwhelming evidence of misbehaviour—of police attempts to restore law and order. And some allowance must be made for the fact that the police are only human.[50]

He further warned against the 'terrible temptation to be opportunist' and 'to cash in on political emotionalism—at a time like this.' It should never be forgotten that 'a *genuinely* united Ireland must be based on a free union of those living in Ireland, on mutual tolerance, and on belief that the ultimate governmental authority will be equitable and unprejudiced.' He advised Lynch

> in any Govt. statement from Dublin [to] avoid identifying the Govt. solely with the Catholics or Nationalists of N.I. and make it clear that the aim of a United Ireland would be a scrupulously fair deal for all—indeed, that the position of N.I. Protestants would be particularly respected.

A special effort was needed, he wrote, to

> reassure the very *moderate* Protestants who otherwise may be driven to side with the extremists under threat, as they see it, of losing their 'freedom, religion and laws.'[51]

Whitaker warned Lynch that the 'govt. should not be driven before the emotional winds fanned by utterly unrepresentative and irresponsible organisations such as Sinn Féin.' He felt that RTE had given Sinn Féin's statements and telegrams 'quite disproportionate publicity.' Viewing the RTE television coverage, he said that 'an outsider would be misled into thinking they were the Govt. party or at least the main Opposition.' He urged Lynch to have close liaison with the main opposition parties. He felt that both Fine Gael and the Labour Party might 'help to abate the danger of purely short-term competitive and opportunist reactions to a situation which calls for cool headed, longer-term appraisal.'[52]

Whitaker assumed in relation to the British Government that the Government would stress in any public statement the failure of the experiment of devolution in Northern Ireland—

> a failure due *not just* [emphasis in ink added in original] to the unfairness and discrimination of the régime and its inability to maintain law and order without forfeiting the respect of a large body of its citizens, *but also* [emphasis in original] to the fundamental weakness of its constitutional position in that it was never accepted by the whole of Ireland, or even by a majority in each of the counties of its artificial composition.[53]

Asking about a future course of action for the Government, Whitaker wrote with candour: 'We can't take over Britain's financial contributions, nor do we want the terrifying task of keeping sectarian and anarchical mobs in order.' He felt it was better for the Government to confine itself to 'preventing groups from here intervening by strict control of the Border.' What had to be envisaged, he argued, was 'a slow-phased movement towards some form of unification,' where there should be 'no rigid clinging to pre-conceived formulae. Even condominium may be a useful transitional concept.'[54]

Lynch had not received the typed version of Whitaker's stern words of advice before he went into the Government meeting at 11:30 a.m. on Friday 15 August, a meeting that was reconvened at 8 o'clock that evening. But he did have the benefit of the phone conversation, and its content may not have diverged greatly from what was sent in the letter.

Lynch issued the following statement on 15 August:

> Through last night's tragic loss of lives in Belfast and Armagh our worst fears have, unfortunately, now been realised. On behalf of the Government and people of Ireland I wish to express profound sympathy with the families and relatives of the victims. What is needed now more than anything else is a period of restraint so as to create an interim situation of non-violence during which every possible channel may be explored so as to arrive at an acceptable solution of the immediate problems and, eventually, to reach a permanent solution of the basic issues involved. The Government are doing, and will continue to do, everything in their power towards this end.[55]

The events the Taoiseach was referring to were those described by the *Irish Times* in the headlines '6 killed in Northern shootings—Boy (9) one of five victims in Belfast, man dies in Armagh—Night of gun battles in several places as peace returns to Derry.' Herbert Roy, a Protestant, died on 14 August from wounds to the chest from shots fired by an IRA gunman as he stood on the corner of the predominantly Protestant Dover Street and Divis Street. A nine-year-old Catholic boy, Patrick Rooney, died after being struck by a tracer bullet fired by the RUC as he lay asleep in his bed in Divis Tower. Samuel McLarnon, a 27-year-old Catholic, was shot by a member of the RUC who fired through a window into the living-room of his house in Herbert Street, Ardoyne, during a fierce riot. Michael Lynch, a 28-year-old Catholic, was shot by the RUC as he crossed a street in Ardoyne near his home. A thirty-year-old Catholic, John Gallagher, was shot dead by B Specials in Cathedral Road in Armagh following a meeting of the Civil Rights Association. Two other people were wounded in the incident.[56]

On 15 August fifteen-year-old Gerald McAuley was shot dead by a loyalist gunman in Bombay Street, Belfast. He was the first member of the IRA's youth wing to die. The same day Hugh McCabe, a twenty-year-old Catholic serving in the British army in Germany, was shot dead by the police in controversial circumstances near his home in the Divis Flats.[57]

Meanwhile, Lynch kept an appointment at 3 o'clock with a delegation from the Nationalist Party consisting of Austin Currie MP and James O'Reilly MP. At the meeting, which lasted about twenty minutes, Currie described the situation in towns such as Dungannon and Coalisland as explosive. He had good personal cause to feel anxious, as his wife and one-year-old daughter had fled to the South to take refuge from the sectarian violence in Dungannon.[58] The two MPs urged Lynch to emphasise the word 'protection' for the Catholic people in all his speeches. The Taoiseach told the delegation of the Government's attitude towards the people of the North generally, 'that we regarded them all as Irishmen (with a view to long-term settlement of the national problem) and that he could rest assured that we were particularly anxious about the situation of the Catholic population.' Lynch recorded that both men appeared to approve of the actions taken so far by the Government.[59]

Immediately afterwards the Taoiseach met Brendan Corish, leader of the Labour Party. They discussed the situation in a general way, and Corish repeated his request for a recall of the Dáil. Lynch told him he would consider the matter, and the meeting ended after about twenty minutes.

Afterwards Lynch met Senator J. G. (Gerry) Lennon from Armagh, who had just arrived in his office. He told the Taoiseach of a shooting in Armagh the previous night in which a young man had been killed. He said that the B Specials had arrived in two unlighted cars and fired shots into the crowd standing around after the civil rights protest. One man was wounded seriously, another less seriously. He told Lynch he would produce affidavits to bear out what he had just related. Lynch said that Dr Hillery was at that moment in consultation in London with Lord Chalfont, minister of state at the Foreign and Commonwealth Office; he expected that he would have a phone call from Dr Hillery afterwards, when he would have the opportunity of asking him to convey a protest to the British regarding the shootings in Armagh.[60]

HILLERY IN LONDON AGAIN

In London on 15 August the Minister for External Affairs, Patrick Hillery, met the minister of state at the Foreign and Commonwealth Office, Lord Chalfont, who was temporarily in charge of the department. He was joined by Lord Stoneham, minister of state at the Home Office, Sir Edward Peck, deputy under-secretary of the Foreign and Commonwealth Office, and C. Lush, first secretary, Irish Desk, Foreign and Commonwealth Office.[61] The remainder of the Irish delegation were Hugh McCann, secretary of the Department of External Affairs, Kevin Rush, chargé d'affaires, London, and D. Hurley, Irish embassy, London. Chalfont immediately referred to the contents of the Irish aide-mémoire. He rejected the suggestion that there had been police attacks on the people of Derry 'as being without foundation.' He strongly rejected the suggestion that an international peace-keeping force be sent to Northern Ireland, which 'we regard . . . as an integral part of the United Kingdom,' and said the despatch of such a force was not 'necessary or relevant.' His Government did not propose to take any action on that request. At that point he handed over a formal reply to the Irish *aide-mémoire*.

Dr Hillery responded that it was 'not entirely realistic to say that this is a totally internal problem.' He referred to his visit to London in early August to warn about the danger of allowing the Apprentice Boys' parade to proceed. In normal years, he said, there were about sixteen bands, but on this occasion there were between sixty and seventy. The holding of the parade was 'sheer madness' and 'humiliating for the Catholics who comprise the large majority of the people of Derry.' He added: 'Ireland and the Six Counties are one island and cannot be separated, or treated is if they were a separate island.'[62]

He referred to the fact that 'there is trouble for all of us—serious, grave trouble.' He said that both governments could blindfold themselves with technicalities, but 'people are being killed now,' and a way had to be found of defusing the situation. As the RUC was not 'an impartial force' and the B Specials were 'a partisan, armed mob, such as is only found in dictatorships,' both Dublin and London needed to combine to find a solution. He proposed the setting up of a combined Irish and British military peace-keeping force or, alternatively, a UN force. He also said that he had been instructed by the Irish Government to say that 'there should be consultations between us regarding the constitutional position of N.I.'[63]

Chalfont resolutely rejected the fact that there had been an attack by the police on the people of Derry. The decision to allow the march to go ahead had been on the advice of the Government of Northern Ireland. He rejected the suggestion that London should consult the Irish Government 'on how to solve a problem which is essentially a problem of the United Kingdom.' He would take careful note of what the minister had said and they would continue to consider as useful normal diplomatic consultations. On the suggestion of abolishing the B Specials he said that 'it would be entirely improper for me to agree with a representative of a foreign Government to take action in our domestic sphere.'

Hillery pressed for further talks at the ministerial level or the embassy level 'in view of the gravity of the matter.' Chalfont replied that he could only dis-cuss legitimate foreign affairs matters. He could not 'undertake on behalf of Her Majesty's Government to enter into consultations with you about this problem. This is not a situation in which citizens of Ireland are involved.' Later he said: 'This is a domestic matter.' Hillery, who asked to meet the Prime Minister, was left to face the press with no positive results from the meeting.[64]

The answer was not satisfactory. Hillery was told that the content of what he had said would be reported to the Prime Minister and the Home Secretary, Callaghan. Chalfont said he did not hold out any hopes of talks with the Prime Minister, who was on holiday in the Scilly Isles.

Hillery returned to Dublin with the further news that the British had been informed that the secretary-general of the United Nations, U Thant, shared London's view on the deployment of an international force in Northern Ireland.[65]

The tone and tenor of those exchanges belong to a long since departed era. But it was the point of departure for Hillery in August 1969. London had treated Dublin as a government wishing to interfere in the internal affairs of the United Kingdom. That stance changed by 1973 under the full pressure of the horror of violence in Northern Ireland. In Dublin it was thought that the situation in Northern Ireland had spiralled out of control. The Government, for that reason, sought to internationalise the Northern crisis. Irish nationalists, before and after independence, had used the tactic for scores of years. In 1969 the United Nations provided the vehicle for such an initiative. Even if the appeal for an international force was not successful, the process was a mechanism by which global attention could be drawn to what was happening in Belfast, Derry and elsewhere.

GOVERNMENT MEETING OF 16 AUGUST 1969

On the morning of Saturday 16 August readers of the national newspapers were treated to further depressing headlines. 'Gun-battles renewed in Belfast violence—British troops use tear-gas on Protestant militants—Soldiers wounded by snipers' fire' was the headline across four columns in the *Irish Times*. There was a large photograph of a scene from Belfast with the caption: 'Against a background of a building burning after the rioting, a British soldier takes up duty in the Falls Road, Belfast, yesterday evening.'[66] However, the lead editorial in the newspaper supported Government policy: 'The Government must not be deterred by any rebuffs on the part of Britain from keeping up the pressure on her to intervene decisively in the affairs of Northern Ireland. Loss of face is nothing compared to the loss of life which hangs in the balance.'[67]

The papers also published reports of unrest the previous evening in Dublin city centre, outside the GPO. Sinn Féin held a meeting, attended by about three thousand people, and recruited 'volunteers' from the platform for 'service' in Northern Ireland. It was stated, to cheers from the crowd, that IRA units had defended with guns Belfast people under attack on Thursday night. The president of Sinn Féin, Tomás Mac Giolla, told the crowd that the IRA were the only ones to protect the people and that it was a time for action. He said the army and the FCA had the weapons needed to protect people in the North. If they were not prepared to use their weapons, 'then give them to us,' he said. He then challenged the crowd to accompany him to Collins Barracks, where, upon their arrival, Mac Giolla demanded that the garrison protect the people of Northern Ireland or else hand over guns to the 'volunteers' who were ready to do so and were waiting outside. Scuffles broke out in front of the barracks and one youth was taken away in an ambulance. Stones and bottles were thrown and fights broke out several times. The crowd shouted 'Give us guns!' and pushed forward several times. They then returned to the GPO, where a few minutes' silence was to be observed 'to shame the army,' a Sinn Féin spokesman said.[68] A new and sinister element had now entered the equation.

With reports of those disturbances in Dublin in the morning papers, the Government met at 11 on the Saturday morning. Dr Hillery reported on his meeting with Chalfont and the rejection of the Government's two requests— that the British Government apply immediately to the United Nations for the urgent despatch of a peace-keeping force and that, alternatively, there should be a joint Anglo-Irish peace-keeping force. He had returned empty-handed and had met only intransigence and behaviour that bordered on the insulting.

Following a discussion of the report, the Government decided, regarding the 'present grave situation in the Six Counties,' that the Minister for External Affairs should go immediately to New York with a view to having the question of a UN peace-keeping force raised with the Security Council at the earliest possible date. The Government also wanted an item, 'The situation in the North of Ireland,' included on the agenda of the next session of the General Assembly. Hillery was to state that the Taoiseach would attend the session at which the item was brought up.

At the same meeting the Government also decided that 'machinery should be established with the object of maintaining permanent liaison with opinion in the Six Counties.' It further decided that a sum of money, 'the amount and the channel of the disbursement of which would be determined by the Minister for Finance—should be made available from the Exchequer to provide aid for the victims of the current unrest in the Six Counties.'[69]

Michael Kennedy summed up the import of the day's decisions: 'Haughey distributing relief money with the amount to be set at his own discretion, Gibbons in charge of the actions of the army, Moran [Ó Móráin] in charge of Garda intelligence operations, and Blaney a key point of contact with Northern Ireland nationalists.'[70] That is a popularly perceived view of the outcome; but it is too reductionist in its assembly of the facts. Although Minister for Finance and chief accounting officer, Haughey was not solely in charge of designating the disbursement of Government emergency aid and relief funds. Theoretically, he would have to work through the framework of the Northern Ireland sub-committee of the Government; but he would ensure, as Michael Kennedy argues, that he would not be in any way constrained by such a measure. The following weeks and months would test the loyalty, the efficiency and the capacity of the Lynch Government to work under great pressure and at a time of unprecedented crisis.

Returning to the evening of 16 August, Lynch was scheduled to meet President de Valera at Áras an Uachtaráin at 5:30 p.m. Before he set out for this meeting the secretary of the Department of the Taoiseach, Nicholas Nolan, received two phone calls from Ivan Cooper MP and Paddy Kennedy MP, who claimed that the Ardoyne district of Belfast had been surrounded by Paisleyites and B Specials. Both men feared that the inhabitants were without any protection and felt that a massacre would take place without the intervention of British troops.[71] While the secretary of the Department of External Affairs, Hugh McCann, was briefing Lynch, the general secretary of the Labour Party, Brendan Halligan, phoned Nolan to give the same message about the critical situation in Ardoyne. The news had been received from two Labour Party deputies and two senators on a fact-finding mission. Nolan interrupted the Taoiseach's meeting with McCann to relay the latest news.

Just after 6 p.m. McCann phoned the chargé in London, Kevin Rush, and instructed him to pass on that information to the British Government. Rush phoned back at 6:20 to say that he had contacted the Home Office. They had been most reluctant to hear what he had to say but agreed, under protest, to pass on the message. Rush then contacted the Foreign Office and was given an assurance that his message would be conveyed without delay to the Home Secretary, James Callaghan. Nolan so advised McCann and Lynch.[72]

While Lynch and de Valera were meeting that evening there were ugly scenes in Dublin for the second night running. The National Solidarity Committee held a demonstration outside the GPO at 8 p.m., after which a crowd of nearly two thousand marched to the British embassy in Merrion Square, where there had also been a protest the previous night. The Gardaí cordoned off the street in front of the building, blocking it from the Merrion Square side and at Holles Street. As the marchers reached the cordon at Holles Street, bricks, bottles and stones began to fly. The Gardaí were ordered to charge, with batons drawn. The crowd dispersed down Holles Street and down Merrion Square to Clare Street, where a barricade was built of planks. A fire was started outside the Mont Clare Hotel, shop windows were broken and cars were vandalised. According to a Garda statement, two inspectors, two sergeants and twelve gardaí had been injured by petrol bombs, stones, bricks and other missiles. It stated further that sixty premises in the city centre had been attacked and eighty shop windows smashed. One business had been broken into and furniture removed. One car was vandalised. An automatic pistol had been found in the wake of the fleeing demonstrators.[73]

Meanwhile the assistant secretary of the Department of External Affairs, Seán Ronan, received a phone call at home at 10 p.m. from Dermot Gallagher to say that the duty officer had been in contact over the presence of three Northern MPs in Iveagh House (the offices of the Department of External Affairs in St Stephen's Green) requesting an interview with the Taoiseach for the purpose of obtaining arms for the Catholics in the Falls Road area of Belfast. The three MPs were Paddy Devlin (NI Labour, Belfast), Paddy O'Hanlon (Independent, South Armagh) and Paddy Kennedy (Republican Labour, Central Belfast). They were asked the purpose of their visit. Kennedy, acting as spokesman, said that the B Specials were on the loose in Belfast, that there was continuous sniping and that people were being shot. There was a growing concentration of refugees in the Falls, and those people were being forced further up the Falls Road. He said that soon the entire Catholic population of Belfast would be concentrated in that area and they would be massacred. He said that the Bogside area of Derry was mild by comparison. The Catholics of the area would have to defend themselves. They would not return to Belfast until they had seen the Taoiseach. If Irish troops were not to be sent to Belfast 'they wanted guns and they could not leave without definite answers to these questions.' Catholics in Belfast needed protection, he said, adding that, 'as regards guns, nothing need be done openly or politically—a few hundred rifles could easily be "lost" and would not be missed.'

Ronan said that the Taoiseach was not available for interview; that he had heard of the worsening situation in Belfast and of the appeal from Bishop Philbin for British troops to be sent to the Ardoyne area; and that appropriate action had been taken through the Irish embassy in London. It was later confirmed that British troops had entered Ardoyne and that the situation in Belfast was quiet. The official undertook to convey their request to the Taoiseach forthwith. They insisted on returning in three-quarters of an hour for an answer to their question regarding Irish troops or guns.

Ronan contacted the Taoiseach's private secretary, Bertie O'Dowd. They agreed on an answer similar to the one already given. The MPs returned at about 11:30 and were given the agreed reply, together with the answer that the 'request about troops or arms was a matter for Government and perhaps even for Dáil decision.' All three MPs reacted vehemently, saying it was a fobbing off. Devlin, who was more angry and emotional than the other two, made for the door, saying he would see the Taoiseach before he left Dublin. He returned 'muttering something abusive about the Government being responsible for deaths.' All three then left.

The official then took the precaution of phoning the Gardaí at Rathmines to warn them that an attempt might be made to contact the Taoiseach in his home. Sergeant Ryan assured him that additional security measures had already been established around the Taoiseach's house.[74]

Even the most experienced nationalists were alarmed at the deterioration taking place in the North. The diplomat and academic Conor Cruise O'Brien, a newly elected Labour Party TD, had been an eye-witness to the disturbances. On 18 August he was reported as saying that most Irishmen wanted to see a united Ireland but it was necessary to look for an immediate solution in Northern Ireland. 'It would be much better for Westminster to take control and to repeal the Acts which constitute the so-called Constitution of this area,' he said. 'There must be nothing less than the setting aside of the Stormont regime.' He called for the disarming and disbanding of the B Specials. That force was not seen to be protecting nationalists, 'rather are they felt to be oppressing them.' He denied that the trouble had been caused by subversive elements. 'No doubt there are some IRA men about, but they are very few,' he said. The use of the Irish army was unrealistic at present. 'There are circumstances in which a kind of intervention from across the border might be inevitable,' he said. He gave the example of the B Specials re-entering the Bogside 'for re-conquest' while the British army stood aside and there was bloodshed. Then, in those circumstances, 'pressure for entry by the Irish army would be strong.'[75]

On 19 August, after meeting for two days, the British and Northern Ireland Governments issued what became known as the Downing Street Declaration. The joint statement reaffirmed the pledges of successive British Governments that Northern Ireland would not cease to be part of the United Kingdom without the consent of the people of Northern Ireland. The border was not an issue, the document stated, and it reaffirmed that the affairs of Northern Ireland were entirely a United Kingdom matter and that the British troops would be withdrawn following the restoration of law and order.[76] The joint communiqué welcomed the determination of the Northern Ireland Government that 'there shall be full equality for all citizens.' The need to sustain the momentum for reform was reaffirmed and that 'every citizen of Northern Ireland is entitled to the same equality of treatment and freedom from discrimination as obtains in the rest of the United Kingdom, irrespective of political views or religion.'[77]

The British Government also announced the appointment of two senior civil servants, Oliver Wright and Alec Baker, to act as liaison officers at Stormont, and they arrived to begin work on 26 August. Already, on 14 August, Lieutenant-General Sir Ian Freeland had become director of operations in security matters.[78] The British Government had acted and sent in the troops.

The Irish Government decided on 21 August 1969, in consideration of the joint communiqué issued after the discussions in London,

> (a) that the Taoiseach should make a statement on the matter on lines indicated at the meeting.

(*b*) That the Minister for Defence should arrange to have statements taken by Intelligence Officers of the Defence Forces from refugees at present accommodated in the state regarding atrocities etc. endured by them in the Six Counties with a view to the preparation by the Chief State Solicitor of affidavits based on the statement and

(*c*) That the Minister for Finance should nominate an officer of his Department to be a member of the committee referred to in sub-paragraph (*f*) of the decision taken at the meeting held on the 14th August, 1969.[79]

Lynch also announced that he was setting up a Government sub-committee to keep the situation in Northern Ireland under review, made up of Charles Haughey and three TDs who were representatives of border constituencies: Neil Blaney, Joe Brennan and Pádraig Faulkner. Faulkner has recorded in his memoirs that a meeting of the sub-committee was held shortly afterwards. There was a general discussion on the North and on how to counter false and misleading press reports. A journalist friend and Blaney speech-writer, Seamus Brady, was appointed to help with publicity. But the role was not specified; later, Brady emerged as the editor of *The Voice of the North*. Before breaking up, a date was fixed for the next meeting.

That was the first and last meeting of the committee. Faulkner and Brennan turned up for the next meeting, but neither Blaney nor Haughey did so. According to Faulkner, the committee in effect had ceased to exist. Reviewing the episode with hindsight, he thought that 'it would be reasonable to assume that they [Blaney and Haughey] had come to the conclusion that Joe and I would not be suitable partners for their future plans.' Faulkner did not raise the issue of the committee with either man.[80] The Minister for Finance, without the scrutiny of the Government sub-committee, had taken personal control of the disbursement of £100,000 of taxpayers' money,[81] some of which would be spent on financing *The Voice of the North* and later on the illegal importing of arms.

PRESS AND PROPAGANDA STRATEGY AND OPERATION 'SILK PURSE'
Lynch was under great pressure in mid-August 1969 to provide a vigorous response to the British. His public diplomacy strategy was hurriedly put together and was, in part, ill-judged. It was strident and confrontational and at variance with the conventional diplomatic policy subsequently adopted.

Lynch found it very difficult to hold the different strands within his Government together. Public diplomacy was one avenue or vent through which negative energy could be channelled. On Saturday 16 August a brief had been drawn up for establishing an organisational structure to provide news to international agencies and foreign journalists. The Government Information Bureau was instructed to co-ordinate the strategy. Meetings were held with representatives of the Department of External Affairs, with the director-general and head of news in RTE, with the photographic agency Lensmen Ltd, which had 'international wire photo and multiple print facilities,' with the director of Military Intelligence, with the general manager of Aer Lingus, M. J. Dargan, and with Mr Scannel of the Department of Post and Telegraphs.

By Sunday 17 August the Department of External Affairs had prepared a background brief for foreign press and Irish missions abroad. The photo agency Lensmen was employed to operate a photo wire service to all parts of the world, concentrating in the first instance on the Security Council countries. The technical facilities for doing this were arranged with the Department of Posts and Telegraphs, and the charge was to be sent to the Government Information Bureau. Photographers were engaged to supply pictures, the 'financial details to be arranged later.' Aer Lingus agreed to carry material to selected countries. RTE agreed to supply 'tapes and film for distribution abroad' via Aer Lingus.[82]

RTE was instructed to investigate how television reception might be extended within the Six Counties. It was reported that the signal was being reasonably well received in the western parts of Cos. Derry, Tyrone and Fermanagh from a transposer station at Moville, Co. Donegal. The extreme eastern part of Co. Down (but not Belfast and its environs) also received RTE from Kippure, Co. Wicklow. With the exception of the city of Derry, the areas served in the North were sparsely populated. However, there were also 'black spots' in Cos. Wexford, Kerry and Donegal. The report concluded that it was technically possible to extend RTE coverage to the densely populated areas of the North within approximately two years by the provision of a transposer at Omeath, Co. Louth, and a booster at Moville. That would give 80 to 90 per cent coverage in the North. RTE had also to oversee the transfer from the obsolete 405-line system to 625-line colour transmission. The report also put forward a plan to extend the range of radio reception to the North and to Britain, including the greater London area. The coverage of the 26-County area was also not adequate. The time estimated for the necessary changes was two years. Those advances had to be set within the context of successful negotiations with the International Telecommunication Union and bilateral negotiations between the Department of Post and Telegraphs and the British Postmaster-General.[83]

By 18 August the Government Information Bureau had a system operational, and a campaign was being mounted to provide maximum publicity abroad in support of Government proposals. Government statements had been issued to Irish missions and to the foreign press. Basic materials were being prepared for distribution. Foreign journalists were being briefed. RTE agreed to send audiovisual material abroad with the widest possible circulation. All adverse criticism was being countered. The press campaign made it clear that Irish troop movements were related to the provision of hospital facilities and that the call-up of the reserve was intended for peace-keeping operations.[84]

The army and the Gardaí were also involved in the co-ordinated effort. The army had provided press officers for camps and hospitals, at the suggestion of the Government Information Bureau, and it was expected that the Gardaí would do the same. This was to be arranged with Peter Berry of the Department of Justice. The Department of External Affairs set up a co-ordinating committee to arrange for the printing and distribution of 'sustained outflow of background material and synopses of foreign (favourable) background material.'[85]

In the haste to produce sympathetic accounts of what was happening in Northern Ireland, decisions were not thought out fully. The employment of Lensmen was not very productive. The employment of Seamus Brady, who was a speech-writer for Neil Blaney, created serious problems for Lynch. After a Government meeting on 15 August, Haughey told the director of the Government Information Bureau, Eoin Neeson, that Brady was to be employed by the bureau at £200 a month—very good wages for a journalist at the time.[86] A Government Information Bureau memorandum, referred to above, stated that he

> is preparing detailed written material on Derry; esp. on what is happening in Bogside, role of B Specials, RUC provocation over recent months, injured/refugees and seeking responsible sources for affidavits which could be sent to Minister for External Affairs. Will also go to Belfast on further briefing to investigate situation there. Will supply written material for distribution abroad.[87]

He did just that. The following is an example from one of the reports received, written by Brady on 19 August:

> 27,000 people—more than half the population of Derry—are living in a state of siege behind barricades in the Creggan, Lecky Road, and Bogside districts of the city. This is the area that in the past week has come to be known as free Derry. These are the people who for three days in the past week—on Tuesday, Wednesday and Thursday, the 12, 13 and 14th of August 1969—defended this area against attacks by armed Royal Ulster Constabulary using armoured cars and tear-gas. What happened in Derry

during those three days and since is one of the most remarkable episodes in man's fight for fundamental rights and freedom.[88]

Although few nationalists could take exception to this, Brady did not prove to be very sympathetic to official policy. His appointment to the Government Information Bureau and his employment by Fianna Fáil were to have acrimonious repercussions.

There was yet another example of rushing into making decision that proved counter-productive. Through the Minister for Industry and Commerce, state and state-sponsored bodies were approached to provide information officers to be seconded to Irish missions abroad.[89] Seamus Brady writes in his book that he had been asked to return from Derry to attend a meeting in Government Buildings at which about a dozen PR officers, mainly from state-sponsored bodies, sat around a table and were briefed by George Colley. Captain Jack Millar, chief press officer of Aer Lingus and a northerner, was among them. They were quickly despatched to Irish missions in London, Liverpool, Washington, Canberra, Rome, Madrid, Paris, Bonn and Stockholm.[90] Each was given full accreditation as a press attaché. What results did the operation yield? One young diplomat serving in the United States at the time dubbed the plan, irreverently but accurately, Operation 'Silk Purse'.[91] On Ken Whitaker's recommendation, they were returned to the safety of their various departments a few months later.

The *Irish Times* headlined on 18 August: 'Shots disturb uneasy peace in Belfast—More British troops arrive—Tension remains high—Pleas by the Pope and churches.' A photograph, across six columns, showed the skeleton of a burnt-out double-decker bus in Divis Street, Belfast. According to the caption it had been 'commandeered by Catholics as a barricade against Protestant extremists.' The paper reported that the death toll had risen to eight when three more deaths had been reported on Saturday. That total included one victim of a shooting in Armagh. Civilian injuries altogether were 514, and 226 policemen had also been treated in hospital. The number of arrests stood at 161. It was reported that all flights and sailings out of Northern Ireland were fully booked. There was a stream of people across the border, a growing number seeking refuge in the centres set up by the army.[92]

HILLERY AT THE UNITED NATIONS

While the Government was flapping around to establish a public diplomacy strategy, Dr Hillery had left for New York in order to have a motion put on the Security Council agenda to have the United Nations send a peace-keeping force to the North. It was expected that a meeting of the Security Council on the issue could not take place before Tuesday the 19th.[93]

To reinforce the impact of the UN initiative, all diplomatic missions had been instructed to make representations to the respective governments. In Madrid the ambassador was also asked to see his Chinese counterpart. The ambassador in London was instructed to see the Pakistani ambassador and the Irish ambassador in New Delhi to see the Nepalese ambassador. The Taoiseach sent a cable on 16 August to President Kaunda of Zambia. In Dublin the Department of External Affairs held briefings for the French, Spanish and US ambassadors. The object was to secure the nine votes necessary to place the item on the agenda of the Security Council. That was on the assumption that the double veto did not operate. Cremin's estimate was that Ireland might get eight.[94] He saw the secretary-general in a personal capacity and briefed him informally on the Irish situation.

Between 17 and 20 August, Hillery conducted a canvass of each member of the Security Council in support of the initiative. On Sunday 17 August, Hillery and the Irish ambassador to the United Nations, Con Cremin, met the Spanish ambassador, Jaime de Piniés, who was the president of the Security Council, at his residence. He was very helpful to the Irish delegation and advised on the terms of the letter to be sent to himself as president of the Security Council. Cremin worked on the text throughout the day and it was submitted later that evening.[95] Meanwhile de Piniés had spent that Sunday consulting. He told Cremin later that night of his contacts and said there had been general agreement that a meeting should be called. But that was only a first step, as it did not necessarily mean that the council would agree to discuss the Irish proposal.[96]

Cremin also received a call from the British representative, Lord Caradon, the same evening; he lived on the floor below him. He was critical of the Irish initiative. He requested a meeting with Hillery, which took place on Monday 18 August. Cremin noted that the tone of the meeting was 'rather cold.' Having made the formal position clear, Caradon then reflected on how the Irish letter would receive worldwide publicity. That would meet one objective of the Irish Government. The letter would remain on file but it would not be discussed by the Security Council. He then presented another idea: Hillery might make a statement at the Security Council with a formal discussion.

A similar suggestion was made later that evening to Cremin by the Finnish ambassador to the United Nations, Max Jakobson. This experienced diplomat argued that Hillery should be allowed to address the council when it was deciding whether or not to allow a discussion on the request. De Piniés also agreed with this strategy, as he had ascertained by then that it was unlikely that the council would allow a formal discussion.

As the day progressed it became clear that Ireland would not get the nine votes necessary to get the request on the agenda.[97] De Piniés convened a council meeting on 20 August to take the Irish motion.

Cremin and Dr Hillery had used the intervening days to craft a statement together, with help from a young diplomat, Patrick MacKernan, drafted in from the Consulate-General in New York for the occasion. He remembers Cremin pacing the room as the text was being drafted and redrafted.

Surprisingly, Hillery had the opportunity to deliver its contents to the Security Council. On 20 August 1969, at midnight, Cremin phoned Hugh McCann to report on the outcome of the Security Council meeting. Caradon had objected to the adoption of the agenda, on the grounds that Northern Ireland was part of the United Kingdom and that it would be a violation of article 2.7 of the Charter of the United Nations. The Finnish representative proposed that the Irish minister be allowed to give his speech before a decision was taken on the agenda. The members accepted the proposal, 'which involved an almost unprecedented departure from the standard procedure.' Hillery delivered his speech. There was a statement of support for the Irish position from the Soviet representative. Caradon read a speech in which he put on record details of the recently announced British policy of reform for Northern Ireland. That proved to be a most useful development for the Irish delegation. The Zambian representative proposed a motion to adjourn without taking a decision.

This was a most desirable outcome for the Irish Government.[98] Cremin had predicted such an outcome the previous day in almost every detail. The result was the 'least bad' that could have been expected. At least Ireland was given an opportunity to explain the reasons for its application before a decision was taken. There had been a lengthy delay before the beginning of the meeting. This was due to London's determination to press Caradon to call for a vote. Had he done so, in Cremin's view, the British would have 'voted us down but also, of course, preventing the Minister from speaking at all.' Paraguay had gone back on its word to support Dublin, and all that Cremin expected was five or six affirmatives. He felt that Caradon's statement in the circumstances was 'reasonable', and it was noted that he had referred to the minister's speech as 'careful and restrained.' The general reaction to the speech had 'been quite favourable,' Cremin reported.[99]

The *Irish Times,* in an editorial on 21 August, praised Hillery for his 'pertinacious diplomacy,' using 'a combination of decorum, agility and perseverance which was greatly to his credit.' His visit had served the purpose of informing the international community on the North. 'Whatever else,' the editorial concluded, 'general ignorance of the situation will no longer be an obstacle to discussion on an international level.'[100] Cremin disagreed with the views of Dr Conor Cruise O'Brien, expressed on RTE, that, with the Security Council now 'seized' of the question, the General Assembly was prohibited by article 12 of the Charter from dealing with it. The permanent representative agreed with the department's rejection of the O'Brien interpretation.

While Dublin was muted about the outcome, it was a major diplomatic success. But that did not make the 'rafters ring' at home.

The Irish UN delegation pressed on, with Cremin and Hillery seeking a meeting on 21 August with the secretary-general. They would explore the 'personal aspect,' meaning U Thant's judgement of the position following the meeting of the Security Council.[101] Hillery met U Thant several times in 1969 and the latter offered, according to his memoirs, to mediate in the dispute. He proposed the nomination of a third party, suggesting Lester Pearson, a former Prime Minister of Canada, Earl Warren, retired Chief Justice of the United States, and Ralph Bunche, under-secretary-general and a Nobel Prize winner.[102] This did not come to pass.

Hillery returned to Ireland to brief Lynch on the outcome of his visit. His experience in New York had reinforced the need for moderation. The British Government, thanks in large measure to the prudence of Caradon, had shown that progress could be made through agreement and consensus.

Hillery returned to New York in the place of the Taoiseach. The Government continued to hold to its earlier position and sought leave to place the issue on the agenda of the General Assembly. On 17 September, Hillery appeared before the General Committee, composed of twenty-five people, including the president and vice-presidents of the General Assembly. Caradon again spoke against the proposal and urged the withdrawal of the Irish request while stressing the urgency with which the British were implementing reforms in Northern Ireland. In his reply Hillery did not use the occasion to speak in atavistic terms about Northern Ireland. He accepted Caradon's *bona fides* and the British Government's determination to carry out widespread reform. He said he would reflect on what had been said. The Nigerian delegate proposed that the Irish request for that agenda item be postponed and discretion left to the chairman in that regard. That was agreed.[103] The Irish motion remained on the table, not to be raised again. Honour was saved on all sides, and the basis for greater mutual understanding between Dublin and London was laid, albeit it in a very tenuous fashion.

But at least on 26 September Hillery, taking the place of the Taoiseach, had the opportunity to speak in the General Assembly debate.

THE IRA AND THE LYNCH POLICY OF 'NO FRATERNISATION'
From the outset of the 'troubles' Lynch showed no sympathy for revolutionary nationalist organisations. The IRA had made two public attempts in August at open recruitment in Dublin for 'active service' in the North. The chief of staff of the IRA, Cathal Goulding, was quoted in the press on Tuesday 19 August as saying that

units had been in action in defence of the lives and homes of the people which had been attacked by deliberately fomented sectarian forces backed up by B Specials intent on breaking up the natural solidarity of the working class.

He said that IRA volunteers had been placed on full alert, a number of fully equipped units had already been sent to the North and some had been playing a defensive role there. They had put their expertise at the disposal of the Citizens' Defence Association. Referring to Belfast, Goulding said that the IRA had helped

> hold up the terrorist forces of reaction which had been unleashed on peaceful men, women and children. The people of the Falls Rd. had gratefully acknowledged that assistance over the past few days.

He warned the British army that they would have to take the consequences if they allowed themselves to suppress the legitimate attempts of people to defend themselves against the B Specials. The IRA statement told the Irish Government:

> You must immediately use the Irish Army to defend the persecuted people of the Six Counties. You must then call an urgent meting of the United Nations Security Council followed by a meeting of the general assembly.

The statement further asked the people of the 26 Counties to put

> every pressure on the Dublin Government to support the victimised people of the North, and make Dublin justify its claim to sovereignty over the whole of the national territory.[104]

The Taoiseach prepared a statement on the morning of 19 August condemning the actions of the IRA. He spoke to Hugh McCann about 1 p.m. He wanted the British Government to be made aware of his intention to condemn the IRA and the wanton destruction of property and the looting that had taken place in Dublin and elsewhere in recent days. He also wanted McCann to convey 'some private information about the extent of the IRA activity which he had decided to exclude from the statement.' McCann asked the British ambassador, Sir Andrew Gilchrist, to meet him in his home at 1:45.

RTE had broadcast the contents of the Taoiseach's statement before the two men met. In it he said:

In connection with last night's statement purporting to come from the IRA, an illegal organisation, I wish to assert, on behalf of the Government and people of Ireland, that no group has any authority whatever to speak or act for the Irish people except the lawful Government of Ireland freely elected by the people. The government will not tolerate the usurpation of their powers by any group whatsoever. These powers of Government are exercisable only by, or on the authority of, the organs of the State established by the Constitution enacted by the Irish people themselves.[105]

Gilchrist expressed appreciation of the Taoiseach's action and, when given the additional information on IRA activity, said it was important that it be conveyed to the British Cabinet as soon as possible. He undertook to do so. He offered the personal comment that 'more should be done to discourage the IRA.' He also referred to the interview given by Goulding and to the publicity given in the press to the IRA's pronouncements.[106]

Gilchrist phoned McCann at 10:40 p.m. on 20 August. He had instructions to convey to the Irish Government the British Government's 'grave concern about the activities of the IRA.' It hoped and expected that the Irish Government would take every possible step to curb the activities of the IRA and in particular to prevent their crossing the border to attack the North. The British Government were appreciative of the Taoiseach's message. Gilchrist said that the Prime Minister, on 19 August, had in a few hours radically altered the whole situation in the North regarding security.

McCann replied that the Government, within the limits of the law, 'were doing everything possible to curb the activities of the IRA.' Gilchrist expressed appreciation for 'the expeditious and discreet manner in which he had been given yesterday's information.' He offered to convey, if he so wished, the Taoiseach's informal reaction to the British Prime Minister's statement on Northern Ireland.[107]

The political correspondent of the *Irish Times,* quoting Special Branch sources, estimated that that the IRA was weak in numbers, equipment and leadership. It was acknowledged, however, that a few armed men could do much damage. His sources revealed that only a few dozen IRA men had crossed the border and that they had not been engaged in physical-force activities there. Nevertheless, security along the southern side of the border would be strengthened to prevent any others entering the North. John Hume described the IRA intervention as unfortunate and ill-timed, strengthening the hand of the Stormont Government and adding weight to the argument that events of the past year had been an IRA plot. He said the only beneficiaries of the statement would be people like Craig and Paisley. His sources told him that there were no IRA in the Bogside.[108]

The Gardaí and the Department of Justice provided Lynch from the outset of the conflict with the best professional support for his determined policy against subversion. The secretary of the department, Peter Berry, was a long-serving civil servant; the two men had been contemporaries in that department for the latter part of the war years. Berry received regular visits and briefings from the Garda Commissioner, Michael Wymes, and the head of the Special Branch, Chief Superintendent John Fleming. The latter worked closely with a retired chief superintendent, Philip McMahon, whose service had been extended because of his unrivalled knowledge of the IRA.[109] He was also a friend of Jack and Máirín Lynch. Special Branch intelligence on the IRA was excellent, as events in subsequent months would prove over and over again.

The channels of communication between Berry and the senior officers in the Special Branch were excellent. However, a barrier emerged in the flow of information between the Department of Justice and the Government. This was due in large measure to the illness of the Minister for Justice, Mícheál Ó Móráin. He was an alcoholic and in a poor state of general health and was quite unable to withstand the pressure under which his ministerial duties placed him. Was he too susceptible to the blandishments of Blaney and Haughey? What if Lynch had replaced that minister in the autumn of 1969? These are some of the unknowns of recent Irish history.

The troubles in Northern Ireland stirred deep emotions south of the border, in a manner that had not been known since the foundation of the state. Moderate people sometimes became extremist in their views. Charles Haughey was among those who behaved somewhat out of character that summer. With a strong anti-IRA record as Minister for Justice in the early 1960s, he had demonstrated his toughness and shown that the security portfolio was in a safe pair of hands. Yet his maverick activities brought him to the attention of the Special Branch some time during the week beginning 10 August 1969. Chief Superintendent Fleming and Chief Superintendent McMahon visited the secretary of the Department of Justice, Peter Berry, in Rathgar near midnight on 19 August—the day Lynch made his trenchant attack on the IRA and handed over intelligence on that organisation's activities, through McCann, to the British ambassador in Dublin. So alarmed was Berry by what the two men had to tell him that he immediately set about preparing a handwritten report to his minister, running to several pages. Most prominent in the report was the news that the previous week a Government minister, left unnamed by the two gardaí, had had a meeting with the chief of staff of the IRA, Cathal Goulding, at which 'a deal had been made' that the IRA would have a 'free hand in operating a cross Border campaign in the North' if it called off its campaign of violence in the South. Berry's report recorded that the IRA Army Council 'could not understand the Taoiseach's statement of 19th August as it had been accepted that the Cabinet Minister was speaking to their Chief of Staff with the authority of [the] Government.'[110]

Mícheál Ó Móráin asked for the name of the minister concerned. Berry did not have it to give but when pressed, without any proof, mentioned the name of one minister who had 'a penchant for indiscretions.' Ó Móráin replied that it could be Neil Blaney or Kevin Boland. When he returned to his department after the Government meeting he told Berry that it was the last time he would read a statement of that kind to the Government. He would bring such matters directly to the Taoiseach. Ó Móráin reported that no minister had met Goulding. But he then went on to say 'that Charlie Haughey had mentioned that he had been asked to meet some fellow from the IRA but that he had not paid heed to what was said, that it was not of any consequence.'[111]

Berry, therefore, discounted the accuracy of the report: 'I was completely reassured when I heard of Mr Haughey.' Berry had been secretary of the Department of Justice when Haughey had served in that portfolio, from October 1961 to October 1964. He recalled how firm the minister had been in his action in reactivating the Special Criminal Court and in forcing the IRA into a ceasefire. Berry then stated to Fleming that there seemed to be no truth in the report of a meeting between a minister and the chief of staff of the IRA. He received the response that their sources had proved reliable in the past. Berry asked Fleming to keep checking their sources.[112]

As his minister was in his constituency, Berry reported about the same time to Lynch about recent IRA activities. The Taoiseach was informed that Goulding had instructed all volunteers from the 26 Counties to return home on a 'stand-to' alert. Select personnel and local units would continue operations for the present. Berry also told the Taoiseach on 25 August that 'an approach had been made to Gardaí on duty near the Border to turn the blind eye to the movement of men and materials (weapons and explosives).' He recorded that 'the Taoiseach instructed that that was out' and that there should be 'no fraternising.' That instruction was conveyed to the Garda Commissioner.[113] Lynch was consistent in that line.[114]

There is an entry in Lynch's desk diary for Wednesday 27 August showing that at 11:30 he was due to meet jointly Haughey and Blaney.[115] Whether the meeting took place or what precisely was discussed is not known. Perhaps he was advising them of what he was going to say in a speech the following day. He may also have been using such an opportunity to reaffirm to his ministers the peaceful nature of official policy towards Northern Ireland.[116]

On 27 August 1969 the British Home Secretary, James Callaghan, visited Northern Ireland. He went to Derry and Belfast, where his presence was seen to be reassuring. He held talks with the Unionist government and other groups. Callaghan and the Northern Ireland Government issued a joint communiqué pledging to accelerate the implementation of reforms, including the reconstruction of the police force under the Hunt Committee. A tribunal was set up under Lord Justice Scarman to inquire into the cause of the popular protests.

On 28 August, Lynch responded to the dramatic change of events in Northern Ireland. His first sentence reaffirmed the Government's position on the use of force: 'The Government agree that the Border cannot be changed by force; it is, and has been, their policy to seek the re-unification of the country by peaceful means.' Lynch agreed with Callaghan that an essential element of a democratic state would be to have a police force that was respected and accepted by all. 'For one thing, the minority in the North cannot be expected to live with a police force which they distrust and even fear.' But reform of the police was not sufficient in itself: Lynch stressed the need for fundamental constitutional change. 'There can be no return to the status quo,' he said: 'Distrust and fear must be banished and the barriers of suspicion and prejudice must be removed.' He used the example that people of all religions could live 'as equals in peace and friendship with each other in this part of the country and that the religious minority have no fears whatsoever of any discrimination against them.' Lynch said his Government was prepared to explore 'every reasonable prospect' for constitutional change. The federal model had been suggested many times. His Government was ready to discuss that possibility, even if it could be achieved only through interim stages. He spoke of not insurmountable economic and social problems and concluded: 'We want to see all Irishmen living in peace and harmony together as one community, as one nation.'[117]

On Friday 29 August the Government met at 11 o'clock. By that time tempers had cooled, and Lynch was not confronted by the same hostility from a number of his ministerial colleagues as he had been two weeks before. There were always strong voices within the Government supporting Lynch. The Tánaiste, Erskine Childers, sent an eight-page memorandum to him on 26 August on the Government's Northern policy. He sent another document on 2 September, which he described as being 'unconventional, most of it obvious to you whether desirable or practicable or entirely inadmissable [sic].' The first document was circulated to ministers at the Government meeting on the 29th. Commenting on the Government's double programme of reviving nationalism in the North and the winning of press and government support, it pointed out that between 1932 and 1947 'the Nationalist parties' policies have been weak, contradictory, unrealistic.' He wrote that Fianna Fáil policy 'has always made it clear that the 300 year old settlers were regarded as Irish, that Britain legalised partition but that agreement without recourse to arms would be essential to bring about unity.' He wrote about the impact of the Lemass-O'Neill initiative and the positive impact of the growth of ecumenism since the papacy of Pope John XXIII. Middle-class groups in the North were meeting socially 'on a basis unheard of ten years ago.' If that policy was to succeed, he suggested the need to have a 'policy for ending partition.'

Childers raised the question of the safeguarding of minority Protestant rights. There was the 'awkward problem of divorce.'[118] He did not know if the constitutional provision banning divorce would apply if there was an all-Ireland parliament. He also made reference to the *Ne Temere* decree. Childers stressed that 'the original need remains to get consent, grudging consent,' from the Unionist majority.

He asked a series of questions about how to treat with the Government in Northern Ireland. What were the conditions attached to a federal government solution? He noted that 'in 1932 we compromised our 1916 position as political realists.' Was there no case for taking a leaf out of the 1932–8 record? he asked.

> After forty-eight years of self-government in the Twenty-six counties would our electors not accept a gradualist policy? After six years of Fianna Fáil government under the 1922 Constitution (gradually revised); after ten years of Commonwealth membership as a Republic, 1938–48; after five years of extremely benevolent semi-neutrality in a world war; after 21 years of Republican government in increasingly close economic cooperation with the U.K.—there is at least a case for considering a new form of policy. If we were now joining the EEC the present official policy would look to some people extremely rigid.[119]

Childers said that, as an older member of the Government, he agreed with the ministers who months before had 'asked for a re-thinking of our unity policy.' He asked whether the British Government would alter its attitude to Dublin if 'a gradualist approach were adopted.' He reminded his colleagues:

> Everything that I have said presumes a tough control of the new IRA. Their incursion will spell disaster. The IRA can only destroy any reputation we have and discourage unity in the Six Counties.

He also warned that the use of the term 'our people' in the North could only be used 'in times of crisis, if at all.'[120]

Both papers by Childers were thought-provoking and helped raise a large number of questions about the consistency in the current Northern policy; but it is doubtful if the memoranda had a profound influence on the entrenched thinking within the Government. The Tánaiste's reflections did demonstrate, however, that he was resolutely opposed to the IRA and was prepared to put forward those views without any qualification or ambiguities. There was majority support for that point of view. However, the tactic of both Haughey and Blaney was to set up their own independent policy line, without reference to, or sanction from, the Government. That did not mean that the two men shared a unified approach. They shared a common antipathy and lack of respect for Lynch and for his Northern policy. That was yet to become fully apparent.

PUBLIC DIPLOMACY AND NORTHERN IRELAND

While Anglo-Irish relations had moved forward, thanks to subtle diplomacy at the United Nations, how was that in line with the big public diplomacy push from mid-August to mid-September 1969?

On 10 September the secretary of the Department of External Affairs requested reports from heads of mission on what the policy or aim of the Government should be in relation to the North of Ireland in the light of recent developments. The Irish ambassador in Bonn argued in favour of a clear distinction between short-term and long-term goals. The focus should be on the attainment of civil rights. In the long term, reunification could only take the form of federation and the southern Irish would have to settle for an entity that was not 'entirely Gaelic, or Catholic, in which the non-republican attitude of the majority in the North would have to be accommodated.' It was suggested that neutrality might have to be dropped. It was further suggested that the Government initiate a broadly based study of existing legislation on censorship, divorce and birth control as well as on the 'privileged position of the catholic church, especially in the field of education.' The ambassador also advised that the Government 'should take steps to take the IRA out of Irish politics,' as the Unionists would have most to lose from 'decisive handling of our extremist elements' and the Government was 'strong enough to resist being pushed around by the radical left.' The Government should press for talks with the British Government and seek the setting up of a Council of Ireland.[121]

The Irish representative to the EEC stated that the use of force 'should be disowned at frequent intervals or suitable occasions.' Emphasis should be placed on the denial of civil and human rights and fundamental freedoms. Consideration should be given to amending the Constitution of Ireland 'so as to delete provisions militating against the reconciliation of our people.' Greater cross-border contact was encouraged, as was the setting up of a bipartite or tripartite body for consultation.[122]

The ambassador in Canberra stated that Irish policies should remain based upon the principles of Wolfe Tone. He urged close educational, cultural and commercial contact between North and South, closer contacts with Welsh and Scottish nationalist groups, the amendment of article 44, replacing

'The Soldier's Song' with 'A Nation Once Again,' and revising history text-books to ensure that the stress was on the positive values of Irish nationalism. It was also recommended that once the period of crisis was over the whole question of propaganda and press work abroad should be reconsidered, as 'there is a danger that this could become counter-productive.' Diplomatic officers were best suited for work of that kind.[123]

The ambassador in the Vatican felt that reunion was essential as a long-term policy but that the federal solution should be closely examined. He wanted strong emphasis on support for civil rights through publicity abroad, especially in London, at the United Nations and in Strasbourg. He urged the de-escalation of tension by demobilising the reserve force and making no further effort to have a UN presence in the North; and public approval should be expressed for reforms that had been implemented. In that way it would be possible to create an atmosphere of co-operation. The Government ought to be prepared to make suitable constitutional and statute changes. He did not want to see an opt-out by the nationalist counties; that would only create a 'Northern Gibraltar.'[124]

From Ottawa the Government was encouraged to 'follow a persistent but discreet information policy and, in particular, avoid all suspicion of exagger-ated or emotion laden claims and accusations.' The ambassador stressed that the unionists, and not only the nationalists, were 'our people.' They should be seen as misguided rather than as 'rogues and ruffians.' An indication should be given of a willingness to revise the Constitution to ensure that it was suitable for a 32-county state. Serious consideration should be given to changing the flag and national anthem, as neither was acceptable to the majority in the North.[125]

The Irish ambassador in London, J. G. Molloy, wrote on 12 September that the policy adopted should not impede the speedy introduction of the necessary reforms in the North. Although the Government was convinced that partition was basic to the present unrest, that view had been rejected by the British Government and by the majority of well-informed commentators in London. The ambassador was of the view that the constant reiteration of the partition issue was regarded as being an impediment to the speedy intro-duction of reforms and as a pretext for delaying the process. He suggested that it would be advisable to play down further references to that issue in future statements. An emphasis on that issue 'could become progressively more detri-mental to our ability to exercise influence with London and Stormont.' Even the most well-disposed in London felt that it was unrealistic to emphasise partition, and 'our doing so has been regarded in some circles as opportunist and provocative.' The Government's action in setting up field hospitals along the border, in calling up the army reserve and bringing up the North at the United Nations was regarded in the same light, he said.[126]

Molloy wanted the emphasis placed on the achievement of civil rights at the United Nations and on Irish policy in general but not to go so far as to call for the abolition of Stormont. He felt that a reformed Stormont would improve the lot of the minority and enable it to increase its power and influence. He suggested a meeting between the Taoiseach and the British Prime Minister and he wanted Lynch to correspond directly with Wilson 'so that each would have full knowledge of the other's thinking before any tripartite talks took place.' Neither did he think it advisable to allow the question of the recognition of Northern Ireland to become a stumbling block to such talks, as it had not been so in the previous bilateral meetings between Lemass and O'Neill or between Lynch and O'Neill.[127]

Molloy advised that after the next election the Conservative Party might form a government in Britain. He suggested making contacts in that party. He was very critical of the Irish information policy. He cited two documents, 'The situation in the North of Ireland' and 'The story in pictures of the North's distress.' Both had been regarded in London as anti-British rather than anti-Stormont. The second in particular was regarded as 'casting unwarranted aspersions on the British troops.' He pointed out the condemnations of the Irish publicity campaign appearing in the *Guardian*, the *Daily Telegraph* and the *Sun*. There had been phone calls to the embassy from members of the public regarding the campaign. Aer Lingus, Bord Fáilte and Córas Tráchtála had also expressed concern that the effects of the campaign, 'with what appears to be an anti-British tinge, could so antagonise British people as to affect the major campaigns of the Irish tourist, travel, export and industrial development agencies.'[128] Molloy warned that if the British Government failed to deal successfully with the crisis in the North it might be obliged to suspend the rule of Stormont, 'and thereby "freeze" the Six Counties into a United Kingdom framework.' In that eventuality, and with the Conservative Party in power, 'the possibility would arise of a much more hard-line and reactionary solution being proposed.'[129]

WHITAKER AND THE SHAPING OF POLICY ON NORTHERN IRELAND

The advice received from most of the Irish diplomatic missions abroad, together with the ideas quoted earlier from Erskine Childers, dovetailed with what the Taoiseach was hearing from his close friend Ken Whitaker. Dr Whitaker wrote on 13 September 1969, making reference to a meeting on the previous Thursday, at which he and Lynch had had a full discussion on the Northern situation. Lynch had asked Whitaker to prepare a draft speech. In the covering note he stressed:

Unless there are strong reasons to the contrary from your intelligence services, I wd. like to see an indication in the speech of the possible early release to civilian life of the reservists. If this is accepted, wording on the lines of A attached might be added at the end of the speech.

He drew attention to the passage marked X below, saying that it was 'delicately phrased but is intended to meet your point that we shd. insist on our right to consultation.' He concluded: 'I shall be at the Bank every day next week, except Wednesday, and will be on call if you need me.'[130]

The draft text, handwritten, read as follows:

The Minister for External Affairs, Dr Hillary, will be presenting to the General Assembly of the United Nations late this month the Government's views, shared by the vast majority of our people, on the situation in the North of Ireland.

I would like in clear and simple terms to set out the basis of our thinking and policy. I hope this will help to reduce those tensions in the North which arise from misunderstandings or apprehensions about our attitude or intentions.

The historical and natural unity of Ireland was also a political unity until this was artificially sundered by the Government of Ireland Act passed by the British Parliament in 1920. That Act, in effect, provided for the partitioning of Ireland and the creation of a Government of Northern Ireland subordinate to Westminster. [The] partition was not expected to be permanent even by the authors of this legislation—the ultimate aim of 'one parliament and one Government for the whole of Ireland' appeared in the official summary of the Bill and provision was made for a Council of Ireland which according as powers were transferred to it by the two parts of Ireland, might develop into an all-Ireland Parliament.

[Quotations from Asquith, Churchill and King George V added here.]

I need not explain or justify the fundamental desire of the overwhelming majority of the inhabitants of this island for the restoration in some form of its national unity. This desire is not confined to Irishmen of any particular creed or ancestry. I want, however, to make it clear once more that we have no intention whatever of using force to realize this desire. I said as recently as 28th August that it is, and has been, the Government policy to seek the re-unification of the country by peaceful means. The unity we seek is not something forced but a free and genuine union of those living in Ireland based on natural respect and tolerance and guaranteed by a form or forms of government authority in Ireland providing for progressive improvement of social, economic and cultural life in a just and peaceful environment.

Of its nature this policy—of seeking unity through agreement in Ireland between Irishmen,—is a long-term one. It is no less, indeed even more, patri-otic for that. Perseverance in winning the confidence and respect of those now opposed to unity must be sustained by goodwill, patience, understanding and, at times, forbearance.

[Marked X] *The terrible events of the past few months have made it evident to all that, apart from disrupting the unity of Ireland, the 1920 devo-lution of powers has not provided a system of government acceptable as fair and just to many of the people in Northern Ireland.* [Line added] *Change there obviously must be. We are concerned that the grievances of so many of our fellow Irishmen and women be quickly remedied and their fears set at rest. We also have a legitimate and understandable concern regarding the dis-position to be made by the British Government in relation to the future administration of Northern Ireland. Our views on how peace and justice can be assured in this small island are relevant and entitled to be heard.* We have always believed, and recent events have in our view confirmed, that there can be no lasting solution which does not envisage the eventual re-unification of Ireland. [Last line dropped]

Let me make it clear, too, that in seeking this re-unification, our aim is not to extend the ['power or'* dropped] *domination of Dublin. We have many times down the years expressed our willingness to accept a solution on federal lines and in my recent speech I envisaged the possibility of intermediate steps in an approach to a final agreed solution.*

Whatever the constitutional setting might be—and we are prepared to explore the possibilities with London and Belfast—the united Ireland we desire is one in which there would be a scrupulously fair deal for all. The Protestants of the North need have no fear of any interference with their religious freedom or civil liberties and rights. This assurance is borne out by the fair treatment their co-religionists and other minority groups have received (even without any autonomy in Government) in this part of Ireland, as so often testified by them in public and in private. [Last sen-tence dropped]

Differences in political outlook or religious belief need not set people apart. They exist in most countries and are no barrier to effective and constructive co-operation of the various elements in the community in national develop-ment. Indeed, diversity of [cultural] background can exert a stimulating influence. The real barriers are those created by fear, suspicion and intoler-ance. Every responsible person must hope that early and adequate reforms will bring peace and security to the people of Northern Ireland so that they may live together in neighbourliness, without fear, sharing fairly in improving social and economic conditions, and with fading memories of past dissensions.

It will remain our most earnest aim and hope to win the consent of the majority of the people in Northern Ireland to means by which North and South can come together in a re-united and sovereign Ireland earning international respect both for the fairness and efficiency with which it is administered and for its contribution to world peace and progress. Meanwhile this Government intends to maintain the principle of co-operation between the two parts of Ireland in economic and other spheres for the benefit of the people of Ireland as a whole. [Last sentence dropped]

Finally, a few words on recognition. It is quite unreasonable for any Unionist to expect this, or any future Government, [slight rewording] *to abandon our belief and hope that Ireland should be re-united. It is also unnecessary to ask this because having foresworn the use of force, we are committed to peaceful means of seeking re-unification.* [Slight change in this sentence] *We are not seeking to overthrow by violence the Stormont Parliament or Government but rather to win the agreement of a sufficient number of the people of Northern Ireland to an acceptable form of re-unification. In any case, the Government of Northern Ireland, not being a sovereign authority with full powers, does not receive formal international recognition.* [Slightly changed]

It is also, for similar reasons, unreasonable and unnecessary to expect those living in Northern Ireland who share this desire for unity to renounce their deepest hopes. We and they have accepted as a practical matter the existence of a government in Northern Ireland exercising certain powers devolved on it by the British Parliament. We have had many fruitful contacts with that Government in matters of mutual concern. As I have said, I hope that this co-operation between North and South will continue. [Sections in bold not used] **Those within the area of the Stormont Government who desire the reunification of Ireland would, I am sure, find it much easier meanwhile to accept its authority and play their due part in public life if the régime were fair and just and protected their right to work democratically for a change of régime or a different political relationship with Britain and ourselves. Once force is excluded—as it should be on the Unionist side as well—no fear need remain, as change must then depend on a free consensus of responsible citizens.**

[Marked A] **The recent call-up of first-line army reservists constitutes no threat to the authorities, or to any section of the people, in Northern Ireland. On the contrary, the men were assembled to be ready to serve, if necessary, in a peace-keeping capacity in Northern Ireland, either under United Nations auspices or jointly with British troops. Difficulties about the right arrangements for peace-keeping have, however, not so far been resolved. The call-up has established the highly**

satisfactory extent to which reservists are available and the speed and efficiency with which they can be brought back into service. The Government, therefore, feel free to decide at any appropriate time that the reservists may return to their civilian occupations in the knowledge that, should the necessity arise, they can be recalled for their original purpose at short notice.

Lynch delivered the speech at Tralee on 20 September 1969. Virtually the entire Whitaker text was used, as may be seen from the italicised paragraphs above.[131] Lynch went from Tralee to west Cork to take a few days of his postponed holidays. It had been an exhausting summer.

On 22 September, Whitaker wrote to Lynch again. 'I am glad your speech got such a good reception (though it was somewhat less conciliatory than I wd. have liked).' That was a reference to the deletion of the draft paragraphs on which Whitaker had laid such emphasis: a conciliatory gesture to Unionism to stand down Irish army reservists. As befitted a senior public servant of his experience, he made no mention of the fact that the Taoiseach had used virtually his entire text, with little or no change.[132]

He encouraged Lynch to exert more discipline over statements made by leading party members on the North. 'If only public speaking on this extremely delicate matter could be reserved to yourself, and, subject to your approval, to the M/EA [Minister for External Affairs],' he wrote; and he ended by hoping that 'you are enjoying a few days rest.'[133]

Reaction to the Lynch speech had been quite favourable. In Derry, John Hume told Eamonn Gallagher of the Department of External Affairs that the Taoiseach was right to state long-term policy objectives. He felt that the Government should concentrate on obtaining bilateral communication with London. He remarked that Stormont would reject any suggestion of tripartite talks and that there was no point in inviting a sharp rebuff. Hume regarded such phrases as 'those living in the Six Counties who share our desire for unity' as giving ammunition to Paisley. Gallagher reported that Hume did not dispute the idea but simply regarded such a phrase as being 'unnecessary [and] impolitic in present circumstances.'[134]

Whitaker, in his letter of 22 September quoted above, made reference to longer-term planning on North-South relations. He sought an urgent examination of the kind of 'constitutional setting' that might prove acceptable to a majority in the North. Referring to a conversation between himself and the Taoiseach the previous week, he said: 'I emphasized the ingenuity required and you mentioned the possibility of an informal study group gathered around the Attorney General.' He had another proposal:

On reflection, I think that it would be quicker and more effective to have specific ideas come forward from Denis Fahy and Kevin Murphy (the two Finance men responsible for the constitutional paper you have already seen) and myself. One of the crucial elements in any plausible solution is how to keep the British £100m a year for the North and to work the requirement into a constitutional demands some knowledge of Common Markets, Customs Unions etc—economic information not normally possessed by lawyers.

He had talked to both men and arranged that

the constitution paper be quickly revised so as to indicate the possibilities subject to this constraint, namely the retention of the £100m. I think it might be possible to find a way of separating N.I. politically from Britain without severing the economic and financial links at least for a long time.[135]

He argued that 'a common market would solve the agricultural supports problem, leaving only the social service subsidy as the major difficulty.' Something in the nature of a Council of Ireland, to which representatives would be sent from both governments, might provide the apex of unity, he wrote.[136] He told Lynch that work was going ahead on this during his absence at the International Monetary Fund and that he would hope to see it on his return and discuss it with him. Then, if Lynch thought fit, the Attorney-General and others could look at it and dress it up fully, he wrote.

In a postscript he said that he had just had a phone call from Eamhain Macha (Armagh, meaning the archbishop, William Conway). The archbishop urged that there be no announcement of a Government decision on a referendum on article 44 until after the hierarchy's October meeting.[137] The constitutional review group in the mid-1960s recommended this change to the Constitution. Whitaker favoured making haste very slowly on constitutional change and urged that it be sectional—as for example the revising of article 44—and this accorded with Lynch's cautious approach.

Charles Haughey, Minister for Finance, was probably very sympathetic to the idea advanced by Whitaker. But his emphasis was distinct. On 25 September 1969 he wrote to Lynch enclosing a 'self-explanatory' letter that he might 'consider sending to the Ministers named in the programme of work attached.' He added: 'The object, briefly, is to complete as quickly as possible a dossier of the practical problems that would have to be solved in the context of any moves to evolve a new constitutional relationship between North and South.' This was concerned with the broad field of government administration. Those studies needed to be paralleled by an examination, possibly conducted by the Attorney-General, of the various possibilities for a new constitutional relationship between North and South, 'since on this would depend the framework within which solutions to the practical problems thrown up by the proposed departmental studies would have to be propounded.'[138] Haughey's draft letter to be issued by the Taoiseach spoke of the events of recent months having 'opened the possibility of changes in the existing constitutional arrangements in that area.' That called for a thorough examination in order to identify 'the practical problems that may have to be overcome if any worthwhile progress towards national reunification is to be made.' He had in mind an examination covering 'all major areas of government activity.'

Haughey's draft stated that a start had been made by the Department of Finance, which had completed a study 'of the financial implications of the ending of Partition' and had produced 'a first draft of a study on the constitutional position of Northern Ireland.' His letter asked departments to concentrate 'on the *comparative* aspects of the services, methods of financing, administrative arrangements etc., concerned with a view to identifying the main problems of assimilation.' The draft stressed the confidential nature 'of this whole exercise and would ask you to ensure that the officials of your Department who may be concerned are so advised.'[139]

The correspondence quoted above shows the gulf in outlook on the North between Haughey on the one hand and Lynch and Whitaker on the other. The Taoiseach sought to make haste slowly; Haughey, in contrast, was concerned with planning for 'assimilation' and 'reunification'.

The preparation of a paper on 'The constitutional position of Northern Ireland' continued discreetly in the Department of Finance during Whitaker's absence in the United States. Denis Maher and Kevin Murphy undertook the work. On 24 November 1969 Whitaker wrote to the Taoiseach enclosing a substantial document 'as revised by Maher, Murphy and myself.' He added that 'Maher will be sending the paper up the line in Finance i.e. to his Secretary and Minister, with an indication that I took part in its preparation. I hope the document will be of some use.'[140]

Although out of chronological sequence, it is worth emphasising here a number of the policy reflections. After an extensive review of comparative government structures, the writers concluded: 'The structure of government and administration as opposed to purely political characteristics, would pose no difficulty if harmonisation was ever envisaged.' In that context, the earlier section of the paper reviewed the history and evolution of official policy towards Northern Ireland. The conclusions drawn proved salient. On the question of the use of force the paper concluded that the Government had long since abandoned the use of such a method to solve partition. The reasons why the use of force should not be revived were identified as:

1 force would accentuate rather than remove the problem
2 force might not be militarily successful
3 we are committed to non-violence by our membership of the United
   Nations
4 from a humanitarian point of view it would be out of the question to
   engage in a policy of bloodshed.

The paper concluded that Irish action at the United Nations had also been
abandoned and should not be renewed, because

1 it is not an international problem
2 the ineffectiveness of the United Nations makes it pointless
3 and, we might lose our claim if the case were to be decided on strict
   international law.[141]

In relation to Anglo-Irish policy the paper acknowledged that it was
unlikely that the British Government would end partition without the
consent of the Northern Ireland Government, and it followed that any campaign designed to get them to do so was likely to be counter-productive. It was
accepted that the British would not stand in the way of unity if it were so
desired by the North, 'so we should aim at cultivating British goodwill for an
agreed settlement of the problem and at getting the British government to
assist, where possible, in facilitating North/South cooperation.'[142]

The paper restated what had already been accepted as policy by the
Government: that unity could be achieved 'by friendship and cooperation'
and by being prepared to accept a future structural set-up between the two
parts of Ireland that would allay Northern Ireland's fears and safeguard its
interests.[143]

The Whitaker-Maher-Murphy paper was a thoroughgoing examination of
North-South relations. The thinking was non-sentimental, factual and free
from republican yearnings. It also brought into the domain of the
Department of Finance a clear articulation of the reasons for continuation of
the Lynch line on the North.

REGAINING THE POLICY INITIATIVE
After the heady days of mid-August, Lynch had found a confident and
measured voice in which to speak about Anglo-Irish relations. He had to dis-
mantle the publicity apparatus and return the operations of government to a
state of normality. But that was not so easily achieved, as two of his most
senior ministers were not reconciled to his peaceful Northern policy. Events
had been set in train that had now taken on a life of their own.

On the surface, all appeared to be well. The British Labour Party conference had adopted a strong reform programme for Northern Ireland. Eamonn Gallagher reported extensively on this event and gained interviews with a number of prominent politicians.

Whitaker wrote to Lynch on 18 October 1969, lamenting the fact that a Dáil debate was being pressed on the Taoiseach during the following week at a very sensitive time for North-South relations.

> The Unionists are naturally finding it hard to swallow everything at once and Craig must have a good deal of support from those who think the RUC and B Specials have got a hard and sudden knock. It would be tragic if anything we said or did here just now built up new tensions and strengthened the Protestant extremists.

Could the debate not be held off for a fortnight or so? Nevertheless, he set about commenting on the draft of a 'piece' the Taoiseach was to deliver in Dáil Éireann on 22 or 23 October. He commented paragraph by paragraph, putting numbers in the margins.

> In the longer-term interest of persuading the NI moderates to listen to us, I would go easy on expressions like 'our claim to unity.' I think we cd. get the same idea across with less risk of provocation by some words like: 'continuing to assert, on behalf of the vast majority of the Irish people, our deep and legitimate desire for a united Ireland.'
>
> As you know, I think the continued mobilisation of the reserve is a mistake and I would urge the use now of the 'escape formula' I drafted a month or so ago. Under this, you could still keep them there for a week or two, to see if Craig's 'blood bath' is bluff or not. But you wd. have the credit of having done something to *abate* fear at a critical time.
>
> I would favour a 'mild tribute to Callaghan' as being politic in the context of your claim to consultation and his references, however cryptic, to lifting relations onto a new plane and to the 'inevitability, as the Catholics would say—and a great many others besides the Catholics—of the final unity of Ireland' (Brighton speech, Sept. 29).
>
> I think you should repeat the line taken in your Tralee speech— emphasising the peaceful approach, patient perseverance in winning the respect and confidence of those now opposed to unity, our claim and hope to win the consent of the majority of the people in N.I. to means by which the North and South can come together in a re-united and sovereign Ireland. I wd. be careful not to appear to back-track in any respect.
>
> I have considerable doubt about the wisdom of switching the GIB

[Government Information Bureau] team only immediately to propaganda vis-à-vis the Northern Unionists. This would be premature and could be counter-productive. They shd. be sent back for the time being to their ordinary jobs. None of these chaps has a clue—or could have—about the kind of complicated constitutional mechanism we may have to accept as a first step towards re-reunification; and by barging in now with diverse and half-baked ideas they are liable to spoil everything. It is of critical importance that the Government should first have formulated some ideas itself about the kind of proposition they will try to see to N.I. and U.K. and, at this stage, it is wiser to fly a few kites on this and hold back the public relations men.

I would go lightly on references to the Stormont Government, particularly of a depreciatory kind. It is, I believe, far better for us to have a representative Parliament there—the political opinion of which we, and Northern moderates, may hope to see altered in time—and a régime reformed in its policy towards Catholics, than to have no organs of public representation or government in the area and to be confronted with British administration.

We can, of course, stress, as you did in Tralee, our legitimate interest in any change in the British arrangements for the administration of Northern Ireland and re-affirm that 'our views on how peace and justice can be assured in this small island are relevant and entitled to be heard.'

This could lead to the final section of the speech in which you propose to outline our approach to an agreed solution—which must involve the UK as well as the two parts of Ireland.

This section should begin with a restatement of our aim—winning the agreement of a sufficient number of the people in the North to an acceptable form of re-unification.

As stated several times recently, we have no fixed ideas as to what the form of re-unification should be. We are, indeed, prepared to be very liberal on this point, recognising the need to overcome various apprehensions and the legitimate reluctance of the people of the North to forego material advantages. In this respect, there is room for a positive and helpful contribution from the British side towards the final solution of a problem for which they have had some responsibility—a solution which would make for ever closer and more valuable relations between the two islands.

Make clear again that we are prepared to explore all possibilities in constructive discussion; that our aim is a scrupulously fair deal for all; that we have no interest in extending the domination of Dublin: that we want to see religious freedom and civil rights and liberties protected for all

Irishmen. Suggest that we are prepared, as an intermediate stage on the road towards closer, agreed unity, to contemplate a loose federal or similar arrangement under which the North's financial and economic links with Britain might be preserved while we independently pursue our own development policies, though with an eye on eventual harmonisation of various standards. These and alternative possibilities are at present being studied. When the point is reached at which we can see clearly the various changes needed in our present Constitution to facilitate a re-unification settlement, I am sure that Dáil, Seanad and our people generally will not be reluctant to consider and approve the necessary changes.

In any case, we are (as stated in Tralee) anxious to maintain and develop the fruitful co-operation between North and South which in recent years had become more systematic in economic and other matters of mutual concern.

Our most immediate and earnest hope is a quick return to peace and progress in a just and acceptable environment in the North.

(I don't think we shd. promise equation of our standards with British or talk directly of early discussion with British on financial aspects: I wd. rather put it more delicately, as above).[144]

On 22 October, Lynch faced the first substantial debate in Dáil Éireann on Northern Ireland since before the summer recess. He had refused opposition requests at the height of the violence to recall the Dáil. That would only have added to the emotion of those difficult days and introduced another unpredictable variable into the situation. He used the occasion to review the course of events since August. He acknowledged the role played by a large body of PR staff recruited to cope with the crisis. Journalists and public relations people had been brought in from state bodies to fulfil the great need for personnel that the crisis in the North occasioned. He had decided some weeks previously to allow many of those so recruited to resume their duties with their own organisations.

He told the Dáil that he wanted to assert again that it was Government policy that 'our legitimate desire for a united Ireland will be realised by peaceful means.' He added:

First of all, we want to see peace and tolerance restored in the Six Counties so that Catholics and Protestants, minority and majority, can live side by side with co-operation and in understanding based on equal citizenship. Ultimately we want to see all Irish men and women in all parts of Ireland, irrespective of class, creed or politics, living in that same peace and harmony and unity.

Responding to unionist fears, he said:

> I feel it my duty to repeat again what I said on a number of occasions
> recently, namely, that the Government in this part of Ireland have no
> intention of mounting an armed invasion of the Six Counties. We could
> give a number of reasons for this attitude but the most cogent, in our con-
> viction, is that the use of force would not advance our long-term aim of a
> united Ireland. Nor will the Government connive at unofficial armed
> activity here directed at targets across the Border.

He wished to assert again also that

> we have a legitimate interest in any change in the British arrangements for
> the administration of the North of Ireland and to re-affirm that our views
> on how peace and justice can be ensured in such a small island as ours are
> relevant and entitled to be heard . . . Again, I want to say that we do not
> want to seek to impose our will on anyone by force. We do not wish, as I
> said before, to extend the domination of Dublin . . . Our aim is a scrupu-
> lously fair deal for everybody. We want to see religious freedom, civil rights
> and liberties protected for all Irishmen.

He also made public reference to the reforming of article 44 of the
Constitution, one section of which stated: 'The State recognises the special
position of the Holy Catholic Apostolic and Roman Church as the guardian
of the Faith professed by the great majority of the citizens.' (This section was
removed by referendum in December 1972).[145] Lynch delivered the speech in a
confident manner; he did not waver or equivocate.

Whitaker had pressed him to review one earlier decision and to withdraw
immediately the public relations specialists from state-sponsored bodies
whom he had ill-advisedly despatched to various embassies in August. The
Taoiseach received a memorandum, dated 6 October 1969, that estimated that
£5,000 per month was being spent on the campaign being run by the
Government Information Bureau and the Department of External Affairs. It
spoke of the fact that the four pros in New York 'should be able to stand
reduction after the departure for home of the Minister for External Affairs.'
Once the annual political conferences were over in Britain, it was suggested,
'the three pros may be excessive in London.'[146] The Government Information
Bureau and its newly acquired recruits had worked under the direction of the
Department of the Taoiseach. That cadre was very experienced in the world
of news management and liaison with the press within their individual
specialisations. The Department of External Affairs also had diplomats

working in Iveagh House and in the embassies and missions abroad capable of handling the dissemination of Government information. The effectiveness of the initiative awaits a formal study; but value and performance may have varied greatly from individual to individual and situation to situation. It would be difficult to disagree with the conclusion of T. Ryle Dwyer that 'the whole thing merely fuelled the paranoia of the Northern Unionists and aroused the nationalist sympathies and emotions of some Irish Americans.'[147]

Lynch accepted this advice, making the announcement in his Dáil speech on 22 October 1969. 'Operation Silk Purse' had proved itself to be a sow's ear.

The Voice of the North

Lynch's determined action had won the ascendant policy debate within Fianna Fáil. But that was merely a tactical setback for Blaney. He did not support party policy on Northern Ireland. He did not show any respect for Lynch. He was fundamentally anti-democratic, and his behaviour in the autumn of 1969 and spring of 1970 was in keeping with previous form. He did not feel bound by policy. Assertive and choleric, he was a formidable figure who could throw his weight about at a time when there were no formal codes of practice to preserve the right to dignity and respect in the work-place.

If Lynch devoted his energy to securing support for Northern policy, he also had a range of other portfolios to preoccupy him—not least access to the EEC. In retrospect, he should have paid more detailed attention to the day-to-day management of Northern policy. But the importance of certain issues appeared clear only in the light of hindsight. This point is exemplified by the confusion that surrounded the payment for and operation of the nationalist propaganda paper *The Voice of the North*. First published on 12 October 1969, it remained in circulation until before Christmas 1970. Seamus Brady, a scriptwriter and friend of Blaney, had been hired by Blaney and Haughey in mid-August to write eye-witness accounts of the plight of nationalist communities in Belfast and Derry. He rose to the challenge. He was also involved in the commissioning of two pamphlets on the situation in Derry and Belfast.[148]

Brady may also have been receiving funds from Fianna Fáil for work he was doing on behalf of Neil Blaney.[149] Heavily involved in the weeks following the mid-August crisis, Brady wrote that by the end of September he had retired from the 'Taoiseach's publicity unit'. He felt that 'the unit was a spent machine,' and he wanted to move on to publish a paper. Brady claimed that he also had discussions with Military Intelligence and the defence committees in the North about setting up a mobile radio transmitter along the border 'which would beam propaganda throughout the Six Counties.' He recruited a skeleton team and costed the production of material for broadcasting for four hours a night, but the project never got off the ground.[150]

But *The Voice of the North* did go to press, financed in part by taxpayers' money.[151] Its content was anti-unionist, Brady wrote, and 'overtly critical of his [Lynch's] policy of trying to unite Ireland by appeasement.'[152] In the second issue Brady was particularly critical of the Dáil debate in October 1969 on Northern Ireland. The editor had submitted to the Government Information Bureau a bill for £250 for each of the first two weekly issues. The third issue, on 26 October, published a reprint of a speech delivered by de Valera in 1939 in the Seanad.

It was ironic that Government and Fianna Fáil funding was being used to subvert official Government policy on Northern Ireland. *The Voice of the North* was prominently mentioned in an article on 30 October in the IRA's monthly paper, the *United Irishman*.[153] According to Justin O'Brien, Captain James Kelly gave Brady £5,100 between November and February 1970 to keep the paper going.[154]

By November, questions were being asked in Fianna Fáil about the prudence of subsidising a paper that followed an anti-Government line. Lynch became caught up in the management of this thorny issue when bills were passed on to him from the Government Information Bureau, with a strong recommendation that they not be paid. He passed them on to Haughey.[155] Here was yet another example of trying to control the outcome of policy decisions taken to deal with the particular contingency of mid-August 1969.

It is not easy to date precisely what happened next. Matters came to a head in Fianna Fáil some time in November. Paul Mackay, a member of the National Executive, explained what happened. The general secretary of Fianna Fáil, Tommy Mullins, had the practice of convening members of the National Executive at 7:45 p.m., fifteen minutes before the formal meeting began, to dispose of financial matters. The items of expenditure were read out, discussed, and approved or rejected. When details of a payment to Seamus Brady were read out, Mackay intervened to enquire why a journalist who was so hostile to Fianna Fáil policy on the North should be on the party payroll, at a cost of £200 a month. At that point Lynch intervened strongly, demanding an explanation and an investigation. He was disturbed by the item and demanded to get to the bottom of things.[156]

After the full National Executive meeting had ended, Mackay left the party office. As he was walking down Upper Mount Street he suddenly found himself being pinned against the area railings by Neil Blaney and a Dublin auctioneer friend, Louis Maguire. Mackay was asked in a crude and rough manner why he was sticking his nose into areas that should not concern him. Blaney told him, in no uncertain terms, to mind his own business in future.

Mackay squared up to them and, in vernacular Dublinese, told them both that they should take themselves off and that he would not be bullied or intimidated. Breaking free, he walked away.[157]

Although Lynch and the Government had travelled a long policy road since 13 August, Mackay's experience revealed that the victory had not been decisive. Blaney, in time-honoured fashion, and his associates had shifted terrain and were fighting a dirty war on Northern Ireland. There was another strategy, which was sympathetic to and supportive of physical-force nationalism.

Blaney's influence had a long reach. Lynch faced a significant but linked challenge from a most unlikely quarter: Military Intelligence.

MILITARY INTELLIGENCE AND NORTHERN IRELAND

Part of an emerging and so far undiagnosed problem in the autumn of 1969 revolved around the professional experience and the reliability of judgement of the Minister for Defence, Jim Gibbons.[158] Elected to the Dáil in 1957, he served as parliamentary secretary to Jack Lynch and then to Charles Haughey in the Department of Finance from 1965 to 1969, when, after the general election, he was promoted to Defence. He had very little time to find his feet before the tsunami of Northern Ireland broke in August 1969. Had the Taoiseach known what was about to happen he might have been better advised to leave the incumbent, Michael Hilliard, in Defence. Gibbons, new to his position as minister, worked in very unusual and challenging times. Hilliard, according to Patrick Hillery, would have been more familiar with procedures, no matter how emotional the times.[159]

Hilliard might also have been able to keep a stricter eye on the director of intelligence, Colonel Michael Hefferon. The Military Intelligence Section of Army Headquarters had a very small staff, quite inadequate to the new demands imposed upon it by the outbreak of widespread violence in Northern Ireland. Hefferon was a long-serving officer with a distinguished career who was due to retire in 1970.

Hefferon reported directly to the chief of staff, Lieutenant-General Seán Mac Eoin. Born in 1910 in Cooley, Co. Louth, Mac Eoin joined the Defence Forces in 1930 as a cadet. He was appointed commandant of the Military College in 1957 and chief of staff in January 1960 and the same year was appointed force commander of the United Nations Operation in the Congo (ONUC).[160] Known as a reformer, he was described by one retired officer as a man of the utmost integrity and honour.[161]

There was a great need in the summer of 1969 to minimise the traditional rivalry, and sometimes mistrust, between the Special Branch and Military Intelligence. That poor relationship was exacerbated, however, by the reports that Special Branch informants gave of the border activities of Irish military intelligence officers and the name of Captain James Kelly had cropped up again and again as allegedly consorting with known members of the IRA. It was further alleged that he was so forthcoming advocating the use of arms that doubts were entertained by his listeners as to whether he was, in fact, an Intelligence Officer.

Peter Berry obtained confirmation that Captain Kelly was working with Military Intelligence. He passed the information on to the Special Branch.[162]

James Kelly was born in Bailieborough, Co. Cavan, in 1929, the eldest of ten children. His father was a farmer and publican. Educated at St Patrick's College, Cavan, and Presentation College, Bray, he joined the army as a private in 1949 but later was admitted to the Cadet School and was commissioned in 1951. He was transferred to Kells, Co. Meath, where he was put in charge of FCA training. Promoted to captain in 1960, he worked with Military Intelligence before serving in the Middle East for three years as a military observer for the United Nations, based mainly in Damascus.[163]

Kelly had been released in 1968–9 from his position in Military Intelligence to attend a one-year command and staff course at the Military College in the Curragh. When civil order broke down in Northern Ireland in August 1969 he was on annual leave in Belfast, staying with his brother Martin, who worked there as a priest. The director of intelligence, Colonel Hefferon, had not assigned him to any duty in the North.

On 27 January 1971 Colonel Hefferon, who had been in his existing post since the early 1960s, described to the Public Accounts Committee the conditions in which his section found itself in August 1969. With a complement of about four officers, the section was geared more towards dealing with 'purely military intelligence in the sense of studies and all that kind of thing.' When violence broke out the army was suddenly faced 'with this situation of an involvement of some kind in Northern Ireland.' Irish soldiers were a few miles from the border, he said. He described 'a state of high public excitement for which our troops were not prepared.' It was necessary to get intelligence back from the border very quickly.

His staff had been increased from four to an unspecified additional number. He gave them a good deal of scope. 'The fact is that Captain Kelly had formed a certain liaison with the Northern people; he had their confidence.'[164] It was an expedient to leave Kelly in the North, therefore, where he remained until late September.[165]

Captain Kelly spent nearly six weeks travelling around the North. During some of that time he was accompanied by the journalist Seamus Brady. He met members of the defence committees in Belfast and Derry at a time when the lines were blurred between those who were members of the IRA and those who were nationalist activists. Kelly reported on his activities to Army Headquarters in Dublin verbally and in writing.

Captain Kelly found himself well positioned to provide eye-witness accounts of what was happening in the Catholic ghettos. Emotions were running high as people clamoured for action. Kelly was very much influenced by what he had witnessed; he could be said to have become less an observer than a partisan. That is the setting in which the following events need to be set and understood.[166]

Meanwhile Peter Berry had been admitted to Mount Carmel nursing home in Dublin on 27 September 1969. The previous day his son, Peter, had been involved in a serious car accident; he would die some years later as a consequence of his injuries. Berry senior had suffered a number of seizures and was under investigation for an aortic clot. He had a ground-floor room in Mount Carmel, and entrance to this room was possible directly from the garden through French windows.[167] If earlier reports on Captain Kelly's alleged activities had caused Berry alarm and disquiet, he was even more disturbed on Saturday 4 October to receive news in his hospital room from the head of the Special Branch, Superintendent John Fleming, and another garda that an army intelligence officer, Captain Kelly, had met the chief of staff of the IRA, Cathal Goulding, and 'that he had set up a meeting for that weekend in Bailieboro with persons from both sides of the Border with a known history in the IRA.'[168] Berry noted in his 'diary':

> From the information already communicated in recent weeks it looked as if an officer group in the Army were collaborating with members of an organisation which had been proclaimed by Government Order to be unlawful and who were engaging in violence contrary to the declared views of Government.[169]

Berry took immediate action when the gardaí left. He first phoned the Minister for Justice in his Co. Mayo constituency but failed to reach him. He then phoned the Taoiseach, but he too was out of town. Berry then succeeded in reaching the Minister for Finance, Charles Haughey, who promised he would be at the nursing home within the hour. He arrived at 3:30 p.m., causing great excitement among the staff. Berry told Haughey of the activities of Captain Kelly and of the planned meeting. 'He did not seem unduly perturbed about Capt. Kelly but was quite inquisitive about what I knew of Goulding. I felt reassured.'[170]

Berry would not have been so reassured had he known, as he learnt subsequently, that Haughey had had a meeting in his home with Captain Kelly and the director of intelligence, Colonel Hefferon, in late September and again on Friday 3 October—the day before he visited Berry to reassure him that nothing untoward was afoot. At the second meeting in Kinsealy, according to Berry's Special Branch sources, Haughey arranged for a cheque for £500 to be paid to Captain Kelly to cover the expenses of the Bailieborough meeting.[171] According to Michael Mills, the minister also told the captain that £50,000 was available for the purchase of guns.[172] Berry was not briefed fully about the Bailieborough meeting until 16 October.

In the intervening period concern grew over intelligence reports that a breakaway republican group, Saor Éire, was planning a series of bank robberies in the South. Efforts were made to build up the strength of the Special Branch. The Garda Commissioner, Michael Wymes, had gone to see Berry on 10 October, and he had raised with him the idea of strengthening the Special Branch. Berry was convinced, according to his diaries, that he had persuaded the minister to increase the strength of the Special Branch by thirty when they met in the hospital on 14 October.[173] This does not appear to have happened.

The Special Branch compiled a detailed account of what took place at the meeting in Bailieborough on 4/5 October. An officer reported the details to Berry in the hospital on 16 October. The venue had been a hotel owned by Captain Kelly's brother. Kelly had informed about fifteen members of 'defence committees' from Northern Ireland that a sum of £50,000 was available from Government sources for the purchase of arms.[174] In the absence of his minister, who was on holiday, Berry felt the contents of 'such an alarming report' should be made known to the Taoiseach.

Berry was not in any fit state to be working. He had not been given any food after 6 p.m., in preparation for the tests he was to undergo the following day. But he wanted to brief Lynch in person before he had to undergo his tests. Both Lynch and his private secretary, Bertie O'Dowd, were at a function. Berry left urgent messages in a number of places that he was to be contacted no matter how late the hour. O'Dowd visited him in his room after midnight. Berry requested that the Taoiseach come to see him the following day, 17 October.[175] That morning, at 8:30 a.m., he was given an injection and had tubing inserted through his nose into his stomach. When the Taoiseach arrived at about nine o'clock there were two doctors and two nurses in the room. As the two men attempted to have a confidential discussion they were repeatedly interrupted by the medical staff. Finally Lynch, according to Berry, said 'petulantly,' 'this is hopeless, I will get in touch with you again.' Lynch never resumed the conversation nor referred to it again, according to Berry,[176] who also admitted to not having 'a 100 per cent recollection of my conversation with the Taoiseach as I was a bit muzzy and bloody from the medical tests.'

Berry remained convinced to the end of his life that he had told Lynch on that occasion of Capt Kelly's prominent part in the Bailieboro meeting with known members of the IRA, of his possession of a wad of money, of his standing drinks and of the sum of money—£50,000—that would be made available for the purchase of arms.[177]

Lynch denied to his dying day that such a conversation ever took place. In his 'diaries', Berry wrote that

> no person with a scrap of intelligence could doubt that the Taoiseach was made aware by me on 17th October—the date of my medical tests is verifiable in the hospital records—of information of a most serious kind in relation to a plot to import arms and that he avoided making any more than a cursory enquiry. Indeed, I formed the impression from time to time that he was consulting me to find out how much I did not know and that he was not thankful to me for bringing awkward facts to his notice.[178]

Lynch and Berry disagreed fundamentally on the substance of what was said at that meeting. Both men are now dead; but neither changed his view on what he recalled as having happened. On the balance of probability, Lynch is more likely to have had the clearer recollection of what was said. Following the publication of the Berry 'diaries' in the news magazine *Magill* in May, June and July 1980, Lynch broke his silence and wrote: 'At no stage during this interview on this date, 17th October [1969], did Mr Berry mention the name of any Member of the Government nor did he try to implicate them in any way. I may add that there was no suggestion in *Magill* or otherwise that he did.' Colonel Hefferon, in evidence given in 1970, said he was sent for by the Minister for Defence, Jim Gibbons, and questioned about the Bailieborough meeting and Captain Kelly's part in it. Of the date of the meeting he said 'it could be November 1969.' But Hefferon was emphatic that he had told Gibbons of the meeting. Gibbons was equally emphatic that he had never been briefed on this meeting.[179]

Berry records that he was put on sedatives about 22 October and as a consequence his records were not kept 'in my normal fashion.' But he had a clear recollection of being told on that day of the involvement of the two ministers—Haughey and Blaney—in the importing of arms. He also recalled the next day that Wymes visited him and described what was happening as 'foul treachery to Government.' Berry remembers telling the commissioner on no account to put the names of the ministers on file, 'pending further checking.' He wrote: 'I still disbelieved that Mr Haughey could be involved.' His minister also visited him before the end of the month, 'and he approved of the suggestion that I had made to the Commissioner.'[180]

Why did Berry try to run the Department of Justice from his hospital bed? Had he been more professional he would have allowed the assistant secretary to handle the briefing for the Taoiseach. Berry appeared to be quite incapable— even when in hospital being investigated for a serious illness—to relinquish the reins of power. The word 'delegation' simply did not exist for him. At a critical juncture for the security of the country the Government had a dysfunctional Minister for Justice and a hospitalised secretary of the Department of Justice who could not delegate. The result was that the Taoiseach did not receive the details of a vital Special Branch report on the Bailieborough meeting or on the activities of Captain Kelly and two Government ministers.

Discharged from hospital on 3 November, Berry was given convalescent leave until 12 January 1970. In early December he phoned the Commissioner to suggest that he make a formal report to the Minister for Justice on the involvement of two ministers in a plot to import arms. The Minister for Justice appeared to be unconvinced by the reliability of the sources on which the allegations rested. There were further meetings between Ó Móráin and the Garda Commissioner and Chief Superintendent Fleming. Fleming, according to Berry, gave the minister a copy of an *aide-mémoire* that he had read to him and then asked him to read for himself. Although the minister may have been doubtful about the accuracy of the information, there was no follow-up, according to Berry. Ó Móráin wanted to make further checks. Incredibly, there the matter rested.

It must be stressed that this is an account based substantially on the Berry 'diaries', written probably in mid-1970 as he was facing being called as a witness in a court case and was also to appear before the Public Accounts Committee.

According to Michael Mills, Charles Haughey's brother Pádraig (known as Jock) went with a Northern republican, John Kelly (no relation of Captain James Kelly), to London in October to buy arms. Some arms were brought into the country. In December, John Kelly and another republican activist, Seán Keenan, went to America to discuss the importing of arms.[181]

OPEN CHALLENGE FROM NEIL BLANEY: 'FIANNA FAIL NEVER RULED OUT THE USE OF FORCE'

In the autumn of 1969 gun-running would not have been seen in a negative light by many members of the public, who would learn to abhor the violence perpetrated by the IRA a year or so later. Those who lived through that very difficult period will remember the rawness of emotion that supported unclear thinking regarding the use of violence or 'counter-violence'.

Neil Blaney was among those who placed an emphasis on the need to provide arms to defend the nationalist community of Northern Ireland. Lynch had repeated his hostility to the use of violence and argued for unity through peaceful means when he spoke on 3 November at Bray, Co. Wicklow, following the desecration by the UVF of the grave of the Protestant nationalist Wolfe Tone at Bodenstown, Co. Kildare.

> It has already been made clear that we have no intention of using our Defence Forces to intervene in the affairs of Northern Ireland. But the Irish Government have the clear duty imposed on them by the Irish people to guard the peace and security of the State. This is what the Defence Forces are for and this is a duty that the Government will discharge.[182]

Blaney's deep unease with the allegedly appeasing policy of Lynch became public on 8 December 1969 when he addressed the faithful at a function in the Golden Grill, Letterkenny, on the twenty-first anniversary of his taking his seat in Dáil Éireann.[183] He made his views very clear on his support for the use of force in certain circumstances in Northern Ireland.

> The Fianna Fáil Party has never taken a decision to rule out the use of force if the circumstances in the Six Counties so demand. The situation last August in Derry and Belfast was such that had the violence continued the question of the use of force in defence of our own people under attack would have had to be urgently considered. If a situation were to arise in the Six Counties in which the people who do not subscribe to the Unionist regime were under sustained and murderous assault, then, as the Taoiseach said on August 13th, we cannot stand idly [sic] by.[184]

Much contemporary reaction to Blaney's gospel of republicanism was negative. The lead headline in the *Irish Times* on 10 December was 'Blaney embarrasses Stormont opposition.'[185] One Unionist MP, Robin Bailie, called the speech a 'typical Blaney rant'. The Northern Minister of Development, Brian Faulkner, said that nobody could expect a responsible Northern Ireland Government to continue to participate economically with the Government of the South after such a speech.[186] The nationalist MP John Hume said it was totally irresponsible to talk of the use of force in the present uneasy situation. He said the speech was hard-line and emotional and that it was 'not really Irish to be talking of shooting Protestant fellow-Irishmen.'[187]

The Taoiseach's response made quite clear the policy divergence on Northern Ireland between himself and his minister. Referring to his speech of 20 September in Tralee and his Dáil speech of 22 October, Lynch said emphatically that he had ruled out the use of force and that Fianna Fáil had never taken a decision not to rule out force in Northern Ireland.[188]

Meanwhile Blaney and Haughey were in London with Patrick Hillery for talks on the Anglo-Irish Free Trade Area Agreement. On 10 December, Hillery had meetings with George Thompson, minister with responsibility for European Affairs in the Foreign Office. Although they were to discuss the Anglo-Irish Free Trade Area Agreement, Thompson was anxious to discuss the situation in Northern Ireland. Hillery, making reference to the recent statements by the Taoiseach and by Brian Faulkner, said that the policy of the Irish Government was not to attempt to use force to reunify the country. He confirmed that the Tralee speech represented the policy of the Government.[189] Thompson welcomed the assurance, stating that the Blaney speech had been 'rather silly.' Hillery replied that the Irish Government 'had a great deal to offer and a right to be consulted' in relation to Northern Ireland. The Government was well informed on such matters and on 'the strength of the reaction to be expected from the die-hards there.' He hoped there might be discussions between the two governments on the situation.[190] Thompson replied that 'there would be no difficulty in agreeing to [this] suggestion.' There was, however, a 'presentational difficulty,' and 'a number of tight-ropes had to be walked.' He suggested that meetings between Dublin and London to discuss Northern Ireland should be held 'only under the cover of more general talks, such as the trade talks which were taking place today.' There should be no public announcement of such talks, which could be held as a 'side issue' and through diplomatic channels. Thompson said that the constitutional differences between the two countries were well known. He felt that discussions should be confined to other problems, such as discrimination, reforms, etc. That could effect a new climate, he said.[191]

Hillery referred to the fear about a Paisley backlash. Although it was well armed, he said, the strength of the force might be exaggerated. He said that 'our own extremists' had been quietened by the actions of the Government.

There followed discussion on the reform of the police and the name of the new Ulster Defence Regiment. The British ambassador, Sir Andrew Gilchrist, who was also at the meeting, said that Blaney's reference in his speech to 'our people in the North of Ireland' was 'very unhelpful'. Hillery replied that 'such a statement as Mr Blaney has made was not in accordance with Government policy.' He urged consultation at the parliamentary level and co-operation in other fields, such as tourism, business and commerce. There were still extremists on both sides who were antagonistic to co-operation; but he felt that it would make the situation better between North and South. He was reassured that what had been done in the North by way of reform was irreversible.

In conclusion, Thompson looked forward to 'closer consultation between the two Governments on the situation in the North of Ireland by way of talks between Ministers and through diplomatic channels.'[192] That proved a highly satisfactory outcome to Hillery's visit. The tone of the meeting was far removed from the hostility he had experienced in London at the beginning of August. Northern Ireland had been discreetly put on the agenda of future Anglo-Irish ministerial and diplomatic talks. Both countries had agreed to focus on practical issues and matters for co-operation rather than rehearsing rival constitutional arguments.

In Dublin, Lynch encouraged Blaney to issue a clarification. The main story in the *Irish Times* on 12 December was headed 'Blaney rejects rift over policy—Conflict of views with Lynch on N.I. denied.' However, the text of the report stated that the minister had 'waved an olive branch and rattled his sabre in a neat bit of juggling in Dublin yesterday.' Blaney claimed that his speech was in perfect harmony with the Government policy on non-violence.[193]

On 15 December the second story on the front page of the *Irish Times* was headed: 'Blaney: I did not advocate use of force—No split in cabinet on Northern policy.' Speaking on RTE radio, Blaney said he had no regrets about making the speech, but he did regret the manner in which his words had been reported, with the word 'force' being highlighted. He denied that the Taoiseach had taken him to task over his speech and that there was a rift in the Government. Asked if he would like the job of Taoiseach, he replied that the question was mistimed, as Lynch was fairly newly elected and was young, able and vigorous. When pressed, he said:

If there was a situation in which a Taoiseach was being sought for the party and that the party wished to consider me, well then, in all probability, I would have to consider very seriously the implications of that and leave it to the party's best judgement, as has been done in the past in a fair selection, finally.[194]

An editorial in the *Irish Times* on 17 December 1969 described Lynch as being unsure of himself and Blaney as a 'fundamentalist'. It feared a relapse into the old stand of haranguing each other across the Border. Challenging directly Blaney's appeal for Catholics not to join the Ulster Defence Regiment, the editorial asked if it was wrong for Maurice Hayes, as a Catholic, to take over the chairmanship of the new Community Relations Commission. Were Catholics not to participate in other aspects of Northern life? That would be an odd concept for a republican government in 1969; but that, the leader-writer argued, was where an extension of Blaney's thought would lead the country. What was to be the relationship between North and South? It seemed to the editorial writer that 'we appear to be heading for a relapse into old and bad habits.'[195]

In the Dáil on 18 December, Lynch had less difficulty handling questions on the economy than on Blaney. John Healy's 'In the Dáil' column was headed 'A

night of humility as Taoiseach faces attack on Blaney affair.' It was an unwelcome end to the year for a Taoiseach who was suffering from exhaustion
and a heavy cold that lasted until after Christmas.

As Lynch sought to nurse himself back to health over the parliamentary
break, he had for his reading a Department of External Affairs memorandum
dated 28 November reviewing policy on the North. In part 1 the writer gave a
general historical overview and concluded that in the new circumstances
there were possibilities that 'could ease the way to the eventual realisation of
the reunification of Ireland.' That was not so much a prophecy as a suggestion
for a policy that would remove obstacles to co-operation and a sense of
mutual respect. The memorandum stressed that two things had always to be
present to the mind.

> The first is that a society whose origin is dishonourable and whose legiti-
> macy is constantly challenged is at a considerable disadvantage in dealing
> with its neighbours and remains fundamentally impotent.

The second consideration was that that same society 'contains a substantial
body of people ardently committed to the preservation of their own personality and peculiarities to the point of suicidal resistance if attacked direct.'[196]

In part 2 the memorandum suggested the setting up of a section in the
Department of External Affairs to co-ordinate various efforts and to

> act as a clearing house for the activities of other departments in relation to
> the North from the point of view of drawing attention to possible conflict
> with general policy and to encourage positive action where this is desirable.

The new section, which was to become the Anglo-Irish Division, would clearly
have to work in close liaison with the Department of the Taoiseach, as so many
issues in relation to the North were of direct concern to that department.

The memorandum made a number of detailed policy suggestions. The
basic approach was that the reunification of Ireland should be sought by
peaceful means, through co-operation, agreement and consent between
Irishmen. The use of force should be dismissed publicly, 'as frequently as may
appear necessary.' Gentle but firm persuasion was advocated to ensure
reform, and all care had to be taken to avoid any action leading to complete
direct rule, which would make the North a closer integral part of the United
Kingdom. The memorandum advocated the need to maximise discreet contact with London, both at the diplomatic and the ministerial level. Bilateral
talks were encouraged to deal with both the short-term and the long-term
issue. Meetings in the full glare of publicity were to be avoided. Talks on the

North should be bilateral rather than trilateral. Co-operation with the North in areas of mutual concern should be maximised. Encouragement should be given to contact between North and South in the private and official sectors. This would include academic, cultural, social and commercial contacts. Greater recruitment to the civil service from the North was advocated.[197]

The memorandum stressed the need for the Government to 'consider taking steps which would tend to convince the Northern Protestants that they would enjoy full civil rights and equality in a United Ireland.' It advocated a broadly based study on such questions as divorce, birth control and other disabilities and whether other reforms in the educational system were required. It had to be borne in mind that a united Ireland 'would be a pluralistic rather than a confessional society.' There was a need when teaching Irish history to stress positive aspects rather than aspects that tended to be divisive. There was also the need to envisage a changed role for the Irish language in a united Ireland. Care had to be taken not to condone the illegal activities of the IRA. There was a need to allay Protestant fears in the North and to educate the Irish public to the realities of the situation. The memorandum advocated a publicity campaign in the nature of 'a soft sell' to avoid exaggerated and emotion-laden claims. Officers with diplomatic training should carry out that campaign.[198]

When the memorandum was circulated within the Department of External Affairs, Eamonn Gallagher was among those who made substantial comments. He felt that with the Labour Party in power in Britain there was no need for the Government to take any action to prevent a collapse of the Stormont government, even if that meant direct rule. The public line should be against direct rule. In relation to co-operation between North and South, he did not recommend giving unasked concessions.

> The removal of troops from the Border has military and security aspects. There is the current recruiting campaign to be considered as well as the very obvious increased British military presence north of the Border. As a propaganda exercise the mollification of a section of Partitionist opinion in the North has to be weighed against possible dissatisfaction by sections of anti-Partitionist opinion here.

In relation to North-South intercourse, Gallagher suggested leaving the promotion of tourism in Northern Ireland to the authorities there, as 'the effect of a Sabbatarian Sunday in Portrush on a 26-county tourist were better not blamed on promotion from this side.'

On the proposal to set up machinery in the Department of External Affairs for study, co-ordination etc. Gallagher stressed that down through the years the principal objective of the Government—reunification—was the responsibility of the Taoiseach. Shifting responsibility to External Affairs raised a constitutional objection that 'it is not an external affair but an internal one.' He recommended that the essential thing was not to change the accepted view that the responsibility for reunification rested with the Taoiseach.[199]

THE FIANNA FAIL ARD-FHEIS, 1970

While Lynch was recuperating he received a phone call on 29 December from Peter Berry to say that a group of men armed with rifles had been arrested by uniformed gardaí in a disused house near the border in Co. Donegal. Berry informed his minister, who phoned back later to say that he had consulted the Taoiseach. Ó Móráin asked him to outline their choices. Berry replied:

1)—let them go as they had surrendered peacefully and confiscate their weapons.

2)—charge them with unlawful possession of arms and fine them £1. But they could not be held in custody.

3)—prefer charges of unlawful possession of firearms with intent to endanger life or property.

Ó Móráin spoke to Lynch again and returned to instruct Berry that 'the Taoiseach wants to throw the book at them, the indictable charges are to be preferred and they are to be lodged in Mountjoy Prison.' Berry gave the necessary instructions.

Within twenty-four hours Haughey was on to Berry, 'furiously inquiring who had given the Gardaí the *stupid* direction to arrest these men.' When Haughey was told that the instruction had come from the top, meaning the Taoiseach, Berry said that Haughey's 'language was not of the kind usually heard in church.' He told Haughey that the men would probably get off but that a complication would arise if they refused to recognise the court. Haughey replied that there would be no contempt. Berry recorded:

Subsequently, I consulted the Attorney General who, after consultation with the Taoiseach, instructed the local State Solicitor to appear at the District Court proceedings and the men were let go. Their weapons were held.[200]

Meanwhile the Army Council of the IRA met in December and voted to end its policy of abstention from Dáil Éireann and the British Parliament. That historic objective could be best achieved through the foundation of a national liberation front, involving the merger of Sinn Féin and the IRA.[201] Although the vote had been decisively in favour of the policy—a reported

39 to 12—it was achieved at a high cost to the unity of the movement. A split followed. The more left-wing element came to be known as Official Sinn Féin and the Official IRA. A rival 'Provisional Army Council' was established, as a result of which the dissidents became known as the Provisional IRA, later the 'Provisionals'.[202] The Goulding wing—the 'Officials'—allegedly leaked the news of the split to the press in late December 1969.[203] When the Sinn Féin ard-fheis met on 10 January 1970 the split became public. The vote to end abstention was carried on the 11th, but not by the required two-thirds majority. About a third of the 257 delegates walked out, reassembling in a hall in Parnell Square, Dublin. A caretaker Sinn Féin executive was established, and allegiance was given to the Provisional Army Council. The Provisional IRA and its political wing, 'Provisional' Sinn Féin, were thus born.[204]

By the end of 1970 twenty-eight people had died violently. That number included nineteen civilians, two members of the RUC and six members of the IRA.[205] What role Irish Government funds almost played in the arming of that ruthless organisation will be determined later in this chapter.

Over the New Year holiday Lynch worked at home on his notes for his speech to the Fianna Fáil ard-fheis on 17 January 1970. Blaney had openly threatened his position in the party; it was time the ball came down his end of the pitch again. He needed a very strong text on Northern Ireland to regain lost ground. Out of the blue Lynch called on the help of his former UCC law classmate David Marcus, who was at the time literary editor of the *Irish Press*. Máirín phoned Marcus with a message that the Taoiseach wished to see him urgently at their home. Marcus was taken by Lynch's car to Garville Avenue and shown up to the Taoiseach's bedroom. Marcus remembers him sitting up in bed, looking 'a bit tired but fully alert.' After welcoming him warmly, Lynch explained his dilemma. He had to write an ard-fheis speech, but he was feeling fatigued and was unable to concentrate. Requiring rest in order to be well enough to deliver it, Lynch asked his old friend to draft a text, 'basing it on the outline he would provide of the themes on which he wished to elaborate.'

With misgivings, Marcus agreed. He had never been a 'political animal' and since returning to Ireland from Britain had no more than scanned the headlines. He was given a sheet of Government notepaper, headed *Office of the Minister for Finance*, with a few themes sketched out. He worked through the night and into the following day. He found the section on Northern Ireland most difficult to draft. 'Appreciating the delicacy of the situation, it was of cardinal importance that I express Jack's attitude and policy with the strongest conviction and maximum sincerity.' He completed the text and sent it to Lynch.[206]

On 17 January 1970 the Taoiseach went to the fortieth ard-fheis of Fianna Fáil—the first held since the violence of August 1969. Seán Sherwin, a candidate for a forthcoming by-election in Dublin South-West, spoke in favour of the report of the honorary secretary (Kevin Boland) and endorsed Blaney as having expressed 'true Republican policy.' According to Boland, 'the delegates came seeking confirmation that the party was still Republican.'[207]

Boland gave a fiery speech, stating that the main objective of the party was to secure the unity and independence of Ireland and that

> every situation that arises in either part of the country must be assessed as to how it may affect this objective and must be handled accordingly— unhampered by pre-conceived ideas or pre-determined conditions as to the methods to be used.

Boland wrote later that that line was a paraphrase of what Blaney had said in Letterkenny about the rejection of force as a policy. But the political correspondents interpreted it as an attempt to defuse the situation. 'They couldn't have been more wrong,' he wrote. He was criticising to the Taoiseach's face

> his slavish acceptance, by his silence of Callaghan's and Wilson's jingoism and his failure to comment on the deployment of the British Army as being useful in the circumstances created by them but entirely unacceptable in principle. The Taoiseach knew exactly what I was doing.[208]

The speech, according to Boland, was 'received enthusiastically and apparently unanimously by the delegates.' When he sat down beside the Taoiseach he noticed that Lynch had already begun to amend his script.

> The truth was that he didn't agree with a word that I had said and he knew that I knew this but, in the circumstances of that Ard Fheis, he daren't disagree overtly.[209]

That evening, and without any direct reference to Blaney or Boland, Lynch delivered his address, not wavering in the section on Northern Ireland from what he had been saying since late August 1969. There was no room for force or coercion in Irish policy towards Northern Ireland.

> Without any doubt the most difficult, the most delicate and the most urgent problem which the Government had to handle during the past year was the outbreak of violence on a large scale in the Six Counties. This was a crisis, which developed into actual physical confrontation, culminating in despair, destruction and even death. It was of paramount importance for our Government to choose the right course of action to deal with this

situation. We had to make certain not to act in such a way as to exacerbate the hazards for the minority in the North nor to precipitate a worse tragedy for all our people. It was not enough for our hearts to be in the right place—our decisions, too, had to be made in the right way and at the right time.

Lynch took on the Blaney challenge in the following lines:

I think most people will now agree that the Government's decisions and actions during that crisis were the right ones—that what we did exemplified a sense of responsibility, a recognition of the vital need for restraint, and, above all, sound judgement.

Lynch had the ball in his possession, and he took full advantage of the situation.

No other political topic can generate more emotion in an Irishman's heart than the subject of Partition. Partition is more than just a Border, more than just an artificially made and artificially-maintained barrier, more than just an economically-disruptive division, more than just a culturally-divisive influence, more than just an historical affront. Partition is a deep, throbbing weal across the land, heart and soul of Ireland, an imposed deformity whose indefinite perpetuation eats into the Irish consciousness like a cancer. As I have said, it is impossible for true Irishmen, of whatever creed, to dwell on the existence of Partition without becoming emotional. But emotionalism and the brand of impetuous action or demands that it leads to cannot possibly solve, or even help in dealing with such a problem. The reasons for the distrust, the enmity, the hatred that exist in the Six Counties are far older than Partition. Partition's crime is that it gave them an official stamp and official backing and cemented them into a way of life.

He then turned to the resolution of the problem based on what had been learnt since the outbreak of trouble the previous August.

More people have come to realise the nature and magnitude of this problem and to face up to the fact that many of its aspects are not amenable to short-term solutions. We know what the long-term solution must be. Only re-unification can lift from our land the curse of history and restore to our people their natural birthright. But we also know, and the Government are firm in this conviction, that only peaceful means can achieve the abolition of Partition. Any other course must obviously carry with it the clear, the almost unavoidable, risk of a renewal of bloodshed.

Lynch repeatedly hammered home the message that peace was the only path to reunification and that this conclusion was

not arrived at as a matter of expediency. It is the result of a careful, balanced, realistic assessment of all the factors involved. While I reassert here Ireland's right to unity and reiterate our belief that the only lasting settlement to the recurring cycles of bitterness, violence and reprisals is the re-unification of our country, we must realise that we are not talking of a piece of movable property that has been taken from us and is ours to recover just for the taking. We are talking of land and people—and not of land and people alone, but of trust, goodwill, and brotherhood. Land and people can, and have been, grabbed by force but by force one cannot win the confidence, the co-operation, and the brotherhood that will make all our land and all our people united and happy.

Having again attacked the futility of the use of force, he continued:

Our initial objective must be to do all in our power to promote peace and goodwill among all the citizens of the Six Counties, to eradicate every vestige of hate, bigotry, and discrimination, to dispel distrust and suspicion, to eliminate all fears. And remember that though to us the fears held by many of the majority in the North are groundless, they are nevertheless sincerely held, and so it is up to us to prove beyond doubt that as citizens of a free, united Ireland they would have absolutely nothing to fear. Over and over again we have called to witness the complete equality and freedom of their co-religionists in this part of the country. Indeed, the latter, too, have constantly testified to the scrupulously fair treatment, which they have received from successive Irish governments.

His concluding paragraph was forceful and direct.

But people whose fears have been bred in them through generations cannot lose these fears overnight. Until the ugly blooms of mistrust and suspicion which poison the atmosphere have died and the ground is planted with the fresh, clean seeds of friendship and mutual confidence, re-unification can never be more than an artificial plant rather than a burgeoning, blossoming flower. And so, as I have said, our course is clear: amity, not enmity, is our ideal; persuasion, not persecution, must be our method; and integration, not imposition, must be our ultimate achievement.

Lynch's gamble had paid dividends. He had picked, out of the blue, a Jewish friend from his university days whom he had not seen for many years to write one of the most important speeches—if not the most important speech—of his political life as Taoiseach. The man of letters, David Marcus, had given the Taoiseach a forceful and persuasive text. His choice of words really mattered. The speech was delivered with strength and determination.[210]

The delegates were on their feet. Lynch had won the argument and gained the enthusiastic support of the majority of the delegates. 'Amity, not enmity, is our ideal' was in the headlines the following day.[211]

In the Jack Lynch Papers there is a note headed 'Taoiseach's address to Fianna Fáil Ard Fheis, Saturday, 17 January 1970—Additional material used by the Taoiseach when speaking on the situation in the Six Counties.' In it Lynch acknowledges that, whether Southern Ireland liked it or not, a high percentage

of the one and a half million people who make up the population of the Six Counties wish to be associated one way or the other with the United Kingdom . . . So those who preach force or military action to sweep away that wall may appear to some people to be advocating a heroic, romantic and decisive master-stroke. But let us be realistic. We may feel with our hearts but we must think with our heads—and when the heart rules the head, the voice of wisdom goes unheard. The plain truth, the naked reality, is that we do not possess the capacity to impose a solution by force. Even if we had that capacity, what would be the result? Would we want to adopt the role of an occupying conqueror over the million or so of the Six-County citizens who at present support partition. Would we compel them to flee the country altogether or else to live under our domination in constant opposition, feverishly nursing hatred and secretly plotting revenge. Thus we would have marched ourselves into the role of overlords, a role which would necessitate the imposition by us on the subjugated new minority of some of the hateful tyrannical practices which we and the world called an abomination when they were imposed on the Catholic minority in the North. Is this the Ireland we want? Is this the kind of Irishmen we want to be? Is this the kind of unity we seek to achieve? The answer is surely clear. And, because it is clear, the Government are determined to explore every peaceful means of removing the injustice of partition.[212]

The ard-fheis did not give Blaney an opportunity to launch a counter-offensive. Boland, probably echoing Blaney's views, wrote later that Lynch had defused the situation at the ard-fheis with a 'totally dishonest' speech. In his view Lynch was moving Fianna Fáil towards an 'old Cumann na nGael' policy on the North, using his 'own distinctive style, by staealth [*sic*], treachery and subterfuge.'[213]

Aware of the growing influence of the IRA, Lynch continued to help to reconstruct the constitutional nationalist alternative in Northern Ireland throughout the early months of 1970. The power vacuum had been quickly filled by the Provisional IRA. The mystique of a physical-force solution to partition was potent, all the more so in the context of the spread of sectarian violence. The civil rights activist and constitutional nationalist John Hume saw the Northern situation sliding out of control. The physical-force nationalists were perceived to be the answer. However, Hume sought to provide nationalists and Catholics—in spite of the political difficulties—with a democratic alternative to the emerging Provisional Sinn Féin and IRA. His analysis was shared by other courageous politicians: Austin Currie, Gerry Fitt and Paddy Devlin. They came together on 18 February 1970 to form the Social Democratic and Labour Party.

Eamonn Gallagher of the Department of External Affairs had already reported to Lynch on the 16th about that plan, two days after a meeting in Toome, Co. Antrim, at which the decision was taken and the title of the new party agreed.[214] Gallagher—whose source was Hume—reported that the 'colouration of the new party was left of centre.' The 'Labour' in the title was out of deference to Fitt and Devlin; but Hume wanted to assure Lynch that the new party would have no connection with the British, Irish or Northern Ireland Labour Parties. Gallagher reported that if the setting up of a new party succeeds 'it will be a most important political development as a coalition including Hume, Fitt and Currie will be very strong indeed and should eventually attract other opposition MPs.'[215]

Gallagher did not overstate the case. John Hume and the SDLP were central to the struggle to return Northern Ireland to the politics of non-violence and normality. Lynch sought to support the emergence of a constitutional nationalist party. That was a long-term strategy, strongly underpinned by reports of such officials as Eamonn Gallagher.

The announcement of the formation of the new party did not come until the summer of 1970.[216] However, the paramilitary element in Fianna Fáil was not allied to the SDLP. Neil Blaney's political contacts in the North were not primarily with John Hume or Gerry Fitt. He was quick to exploit the panic within nationalist circles in the early months of 1970, and he repeatedly conveyed the impression that the crisis in Northern Ireland was fast approaching doomsday. That meant the need to supply arms.

CONSPIRACY TO IMPORT ARMS

The 'autumn of 1969 provided fertile ground—and luxuriant cover—for conspiratorial politics,' wrote Dick Walsh, 'whether designed to hijack the party or to subvert the state, or to achieve both ambitions at once.'[217] He argued that the causes of the Arms Crisis in 1969–70 were

> the existence in the party of competing factions that were prepared to seize any issue as a vehicle for their ambitions and the party's failure to arrive at any clear definition of its first national aim and how it might be achieved.[218]

While Lynch had carried the party at the ard-fheis, there were those in the Government who only gave lip service to Government policy. Blaney, who would emerge as the leader of a shadowy 'parallel government', openly rejected the clear statement on non-violence repeated by Lynch. He sought, in a sinister and underhand manner, to weaken Lynch's leadership and to implement his private policy on Northern Ireland to arm militant nationalists in order to 'finish the job' and restore national unity.[219] The newly formed Provisional IRA embarked on a 'long war' to bring about a British withdrawal from Northern Ireland and achieve the goal of Irish unity. The illegal importing of arms, in such a combustible situation, had to be stopped by the state. Yet the Special Branch had passed on information to the Department of Justice in October 1969 that implicated Captain Kelly in a plan to use Government funds to purchase and import arms illegally for the purpose of distribution in Northern Ireland.

The secretary of the Department of Justice, Peter Berry, was convinced that he had given this information to his minister, having been informed about 22 October, while he was in hospital, about the involvement of both Blaney and Haughey in a plot to import arms.[220] While still on sick leave he attempted to remain in charge of the unfolding situation as evidence hardened about the plot. The argument presented earlier supports the view that Lynch had not been told, through Berry, that the Special Branch had received the proof. Berry remains responsible for the view that Lynch knew and had refused to act.

This unfounded belief gave rise to unnecessary confusion, suspicion and recrimination. Berry, who had been seriously ill and was coping with the news of the terrible injuries suffered by his son, ought to have handed over complete control of the running of the Department of Justice to the assistant secretary, Andy Ward. Yet while on sick leave he continued to try to run the department. This was all the more irresponsible and unprofessional in the light of the fact that the Minister for Justice was dysfunctional as a consequence of his alcoholism. There had been further confusion in early December before Berry resumed his duties in January 1970.

In mid-January, according to Berry, he had urged Ó Móráin to tell the Taoiseach of the involvement of the two ministers in the arms plot. The minister had temporised, requiring more evidence before he acted. Berry noted that the Minister for Justice 'was quite obviously not in good health from January onwards and it was difficult to get him to do ordinary Departmental work.'[221] By early February 1970, according to Berry, Ó Móráin had done nothing to inform the Taoiseach of developments regarding a conspiracy to import arms. Lynch had not even been told about the successful landing in December of a small quantity of arms for the IRA. In his confused state, according to Berry, the Minister for Justice allegedly told the Minister for Defence, Jim Gibbons, of the matter. (The precise date is not given by Berry.) Gibbons then allegedly questioned Colonel Hefferon, director of intelligence, about the Bailieborough meeting and Captain Kelly's part in it. Hefferon replied, according to Berry, that the information was 'pure poppycock'. When Berry conveyed this to the Special Branch, some time in February, the comment was: 'Christ, Hefferon must be in the swim, too.'[222]

Because of the gravity of the situation and of his minister's illness, which prevented him from doing his job, Berry's failure to contact the Taoiseach directly during February 1970 appears passing strange. It seems very unusual that Berry, knowing that Ó Móráin was ill, could not have taken a direct route to report so unprecedented a development. He had not been slow to phone the Taoiseach directly in the past, nor would he show reticence about phoning President Éamon de Valera a few months later.

Oblivious of any such developments, Lynch presided over a meeting of the Government on 6 February 1970. The Government discussed the 'situation in the Six Counties.' Amid continuing reports about the plight of Catholics in Northern Ireland, a general review was ordered of the state of preparedness of the army in the event of a rapid deterioration of events in Northern Ireland. That decision took on a sharp and specific focus when it was transmitted to the chief of staff. The Government 'informally agreed' that

1) sale of arms surplus to Army requirements, for which tenders were recently invited, should not now take place.
2) Minister for Finance, in consultation with Minister for Defence, would see how far he could go towards meeting cost of essential items of military vehicles and other equipment included in a recent application from Department of Defence for sanction of £13 m. for this purpose and Taoiseach, in consultation with Minister for External Affairs, would consider nature of an approach to British Government to inquire what they propose to do to meet present worsening situation in Six Counties.

In the climate of early 1970 it would have been irresponsible of the Government to sell surplus army rifles on the open market, which might find their way into the hands of extremists on both sides in Northern Ireland.

According to one account, the Minister for Defence, Jim Gibbons, on the same day as the Government meeting, 6 February, issued a directive on army contingency plans to the chief of staff, Lieutenant-General Seán Mac Eoin, and the director of intelligence, Colonel Michael Hefferon. The ministers also discussed on 6 February the purchase of about five thousand Belgian FN automatic rifles to replace the obsolete Lee Enfield models in current use.[223]

According to contemporary sources in Military Archives, Gibbons issued the following directive orally to the chief of staff, in the presence of Colonel Hefferon, on 6 February:

> The Government have instructed me to convey to the army a directive that plans be immediately put in train for operating in Northern Ireland, in the event of the situation (in the opinion of the Government) warrants interference. The Government further directs that training and planning programmes be directed to cater for such an eventuality.[224]

There is a handwritten record in Military Archives of a meeting on 10 February between Lieutenant-General Seán Mac Eoin (chief of staff), Colonel J. P. Emphy (adjutant-general), Colonel H. W. Byrne (assistant chief of staff), Colonel Michael Hefferon (director of intelligence), and Lieutenant-Colonel Adams. Dated 10 February 1970 and marked 'Copy no. five' and 'Top secret', it is headed: 'Ministerial Directive to Chief of Staff 16.30 hrs Friday 6 Feb. '70.'

1 *Present when conveyed* [*sic*] by CF [*ceann foirne*—chief of staff] 1700 hrs 6 Feb.
   AG [adjutant-general], ACS [assistant chief of staff], S. Fais. [*stiúrthóir faisnéise*—director of intelligence], Lt Col Adams.[225]
2 *Directive*
   a 'To prepare and train the Army for incursions into Northern Ireland.'
   b Respirators ?
   c Weapons and arms, surplus ?
   d The weak nature of the directive in regard to b and c was NOT mentioned by CF.
   e The following questions arise out of a.
      (1) the probable purpose of such incursions
      (2) when and in what circumstances
      (3) are ops to be 'large' scale or of a small hit and run nature

(4) are incursions to be overt or covert

(5) limitations or stipulations as to number of pers. [personnel] to be involved

(6) are ops to be with or without prejudice to all other tasks such as the security of posts and the protection of vital installations.

The document then recommended that

it would seem essential that the Minister and the Cabinet [Government] would make arrangements to hear the CF [chief of staff] on those aspects at 2 *e* above and on the critical state of the Army to undertake such a mission.

The document then laid out under various planning headings what needed to be done.[226]

There was a meeting on 11 February 1970 at which the chief of staff, the director of plans and operations and Lieutenant-Colonel Adams were present. The chief of staff

recapitulated on Minister's directive as follows:

a   'At a meeting of the Government held this morning (Friday 6 Feb 70) I was instructed to direct you to prepare the Army for incursion into Northern Ireland.'

b   'The Taoiseach and other Ministers have met delegations from the North. At these meetings urgent demands were made for respirators, weapons and ammunition the provision of which the Government agreed. Accordingly truck loads of these items will be put at readiness so that they may be available in a matter of hours.[227]

The minister asked the chief of staff 'what were the nature of critical deficiencies,' to which he replied: 'Manpower, AFVS [armoured fighting vehicles], TPT [transport].' The minister directed that the FCA be required to take on more security tasks in order to free army personnel for training and operations. The minister further instructed the chief of staff 'to hold himself in readiness *to discuss estimates* [marked *NB* in the margin] with Mr Haughey as soon as the latter was out of hospital.'[228]

The total strength of the Permanent Defence Force at the time was given as 8,860, including the Air Corps, Naval Service, units on UN duty, and back-up units. The sobering news for the Government was that from that number there 'would not be more than 2,500 line troops available to be mustered, organised into units and trained preparatory to undertaking incursions.' The paper stated bluntly that the combat effectiveness of that force would be low, as there were deficiencies 'in almost every type of armament, ammunition

Lynch throws in the ball in the Lough Rovers street league. (*Irish Examiner*)

Visiting the Metal Products factory in Cork in May 1961 as Minister for Industry and Commerce. (*Irish Examiner*)

With Seán Lemass outside 10 Downing Street in November 1964. (*Topfoto*)

Lynch phoning Máirín to tell her the news of his succession as leader of Fianna
Fáil and Taoiseach following the resignation of Seán Lemass (*background*). He had
just defeated his sole challenger, George Colley (*foreground*), by 52 votes to 19.
None of the trio was aware that this picture was being taken. (*Colman Doyle/NLI*)

Arriving at Áras an Uachtaráin to accept the seal of office as Taoiseach on 10 November
1966. (*Irish Examiner*)

With President Éamon de Valera, who is signing the official order confirming Lynch's appointment as Taoiseach, 10 November 1966. (*Topfoto*)

With the British Prime Minister, Harold Wilson, at 10 Downing Street. (*Topfoto*)

Lynch accompanies Jacqueline Kennedy to the parade ring at the Curragh for the Irish Sweeps Derby in July 1967. (*Topfoto*)

Lynch and the Minister for Transport and Power, Erskine Childers, arrive to attend church ceremonies for the victims of the Tuskar Rock air tragedy, 1968. (*Irish Examiner*)

With Máirín at the Taj Mahal. (*Topfoto*)

Meeting the Prime Minister of India, Mrs Indira Gandhi. (*Topfoto*)

The thaw in North-South relations immediately before the outbreak of the Northern Ireland Troubles was begun by Seán Lemass and Terence O'Neill, with whom relations also remained very cordial under the new Taoiseach. This photograph was taken during O'Neill's two-day visit to Dublin in 1968. (RTE *Stills Library*)

Opening the new playground attached to the Convent of Mercy, Passage West, Co. Cork, in June 1968. (*Irish Examiner*)

The Taoiseach and his wife entertain President Richard Nixon of the United States at Dublin Castle in 1970. (*Popperfoto/Getty Images*)

and military equipment.' Irish forces would be outnumbered by 16:1, facing 13,000 British troops and 8,600 police and armed reserves. The British forces could be strengthened by 20,000, with air and naval support.

The paper concluded:

> The armed opposition likely to be encountered by incursions into Northern Ireland is vastly superior in strength, organisation, combat training and equipment to those elements of the Defence Forces which could be mustered.

Lynch and his Government were warned, therefore, of 'disastrous consequences' if the army were to be ordered into Northern Ireland, leaving Catholic areas open to reprisals from Protestant extremists, without any prospect of those areas being reached by Irish troops.[229]

Incursion was not a policy option available to, or favoured by, Lynch. Any action precipitating an engagement across the border could result only in military disaster, glacial Anglo-Irish relations, international opprobrium, and the squandering of good will all over the world for the cause of human and civil rights in Northern Ireland.

On a 'Prime Time' television programme in April 2001 Captain Kelly claimed that a directive had instructed the army to prepare for a situation in which it would have to move into the Six Counties to provide people in the civilian population with arms to defend themselves. On the same programme Desmond O'Malley said that the scenario could happen only in a doomsday situation.[230] Clearly, the directive covered a hypothetical situation. Action would be taken only in case of a complete breakdown of law and order, in which the forces of law and order in Northern Ireland were 'unable or unwilling to protect the [Catholic] minority.'[231] Contextualised in that way, the decision was both responsible and prudent. The instruction, however, provided the chief of staff with an opportunity to advise against such a move and to demonstrate how ill-equipped the army was to undertake such an order.

THE DUNDALK ARMS SHIPMENT

In Derry on 29 March five thousand people marched to commemorate the Easter Rising of 1916. A section of the crowd attempted to storm the RUC barracks, in the course of which twelve British soldiers were injured and seventeen arrests were made. After further clashes with rioters the army sealed off the Bogside.

During the first three days of April there were serious clashes between British soldiers and people in the Ballymurphy district of Belfast. CS gas was used extensively. The officer commanding the British forces, Sir Ian Freeland, announced a 'get tough' policy with petrol-bombers, warning that anyone caught manufacturing, carrying or throwing such a weapon would be given a ten-year prison sentence. 'What's more, they are liable to be shot dead in the street if, after a warning, they persist.' The violence in Belfast also led to the expulsion of Protestants from the New Barnsley estate.[232]

Sectarianism was now a driving force in the conflict. During those days of panic in the first week of April 1970, Blaney put extreme pressure on the Minister for Defence, Jim Gibbons, to release arms he believed were stockpiled in Cathal Brugha Barracks, Rathmines, Dublin, for distribution in the North.[233] (Captain Kelly stated that the arms came from Clancy Barracks at Islandbridge, Dublin. That was correct.) Gibbons, in his evidence later in 1970, said he agreed to the movement of five hundred rifles to Dundalk, as requested by Blaney, in order to placate him and thus prevent him from doing something rash. Gibbons, therefore, instructed the chief of staff to release the weapons and to ensure the strictest security at all times. Despite the minister having the authority to issue such an order, alarm bells must have sounded in the office of the chief of staff. Precisely what action was taken at that level remains unclear.

On 2 April 1970 the consignment left Dublin. Travelling north, the lorries carrying the five hundred rifles, gas masks and other military equipment were headed for a monastery in Co. Cavan. According to one source they stopped at Gormanston camp in Co. Meath, where the garrison and the commanding officer became suspicious. The absence of a military escort immediately aroused concern. The commanding officer tried to get further information from the officer in charge of the convoy. There were no official documents to cover the movement of the arms. The officer commanding Eastern Command, Colonel James Quinn, was informed. He went through channels to have the shipment interdicted.

The Gardaí stopped the Taoiseach's car on the road to Cork, according to Michael Mills. He took a phone call from Dublin telling him about the shipment of arms destined for the North. He immediately contacted Gibbons and instructed him to countermand the original order, and an instruction was issued for the lorries to go directly to the army barracks in Dundalk.[234] A small number of regular soldiers had been stationed there since the 'troubles' broke out in 1969, but the local FCA unit had been its main user since 1958. The lorries were allowed into the barracks, the gates were locked, and the military authorities in Dublin were contacted. It was confirmed that there were no official documents to accompany the consignment, and the arms were impounded.

Meanwhile a demonstration organised by Sinn Féin gathered outside the barracks, demanding the release of the rifles and ammunition. When gardaí had dispersed the demonstrators, the arms were returned safely to Dublin.

Clearly, as Lynch's action demonstrated, it was never intended to ship guns in the existing circumstances in the North. The riots in Ballymurphy had not ushered in Armageddon.

This episode, which is well documented by the military authorities, requires further explanation and investigation.[235] It raises a number of unanswered questions, some of which were posed by Military Intelligence in a secret memorandum prepared in the latter part of 1970. With that context firmly in mind, the document acknowledged that the Minister for Defence, Jim Gibbons, was entitled to order the movement of arms within the state. (The shipment was destined for Northern Ireland.) Colonel Hefferon, in his evidence later in the year, said that

> a direction was received by the Chief of Staff to move rifles to Dundalk (a military post). On that evening, knowing that Captain Kelly was abroad and being worried about the situation should it be necessary to distribute the arms, I rang his wife and asked her to get in touch with him and have him return home immediately.

The memorandum raised the question of who had authorised Hefferon to plan for the distribution, through Captain Kelly, of arms to civilians in Northern Ireland. 'Was he party to a plot unknown to the General Staff?' it asked.[236] The evidence points firmly in that direction, even if the captain thought otherwise.

THE MURDER OF GARDA FALLON AND GUN-RUNNING

On 3 April 1970, the day after the Dundalk episode, an IRA splinter group, Saor Éire, shot dead Garda Richard Fallon during a raid on the Bank of Ireland at Arran Quay, Dublin. He was forty-two and unarmed and the first member of the force to be murdered since 1942.[237] A reward of £5,000 was offered for information leading to the arrest and conviction of the perpetrators. Despite a detailed investigation and a wide sweep of republican suspects, nobody was ever convicted of the crime.[238] The impact on the public was profound. Stephen Collins described the atmosphere at the time. 'In the days following Garda Fallon's funeral there was outrage among the Gardaí when stories of indiscriminate ministerial contacts with subversives, including Saor Éire, gained wide currency.' He continued:

> It was against this climate that Chief Superintendent John Fleming, the head of the Special Branch, and Superintendent Phil McMahon came to Berry with reports about the murder and outlined the connections they believed existed between Blaney and Saor Éire.[239] They also provided Berry with a full report on the progress of the plan to import arms.

Collins continued:

> By this stage Berry was becoming increasingly worried that the security of the
> state was being undermined by senior ministers. He was not sure what his
> own Minister, Ó Móráin, was up to and there were suspicions that he was tip-
> ping off colleagues about the Garda intelligence coming into Berry's hands.[240]

Perhaps Ó Móráin's serious drink problem made him an easy prey to those
who would have wished to extract information from him. But there is no evidence to support Berry's surmise. What is clear is that the minister was unable
to function to an acceptable professional standard.

Lynch had a responsibility as Taoiseach to pull the different strands of
Government policy together. The closing of the door for arms from official
military sources meant that the conspirators had to look elsewhere to fulfil
their requirements.

There was also the problem of the Minister for Justice, Mícheál Ó Móráin,
who appeared to be losing his grip on reality. At a Government meeting in
early April a proposal that the brother of the murdered garda be allowed to
join the force was approved. There was also a proposal to strike a special
medal in honour of a man who had died in the line of duty. The minister
had sanctioned a press announcement, which went out on the 1:30 news.
Ó Móráin completely lost control before Berry and the assistant secretary,
Andy Ward, and second assistant secretary. On his returning to the Department of Justice his reaction was alarming: 'Fuck you,' he roared five times
while thumping the desk in the Department of Justice. He claimed that the
press release was contrary to the wishes of the Government; the Government
wanted no publicity. Berry explained that he had approved the release. The
meeting ended with a half-apology. Berry then discovered that Ó Móráin had
not even raised the matter at the Government meeting. A gold medal was
posthumously awarded to Garda Fallon a year later.[241]

A historian must avoid the temptation to become over-reliant on the
'Berry diaries'. Until the files of the Department of Justice are released, they
must serve as a self-protective narrative written in the light of the two trials in
1970 and the hearings of the Public Accounts Committee in 1971. Those
papers, although in diary form, are reconstructions after the event—and they
were written to vindicate the writer from charges of any professional wrong-
doing or lapses in judgement. It is evident that relations between the Taoiseach
and Berry were strained during this period. The latter was a difficult personality, which has been acknowledged by those who worked with him. Lynch
had difficulties with Berry in the Department of Justice in the mid-1940s, and
he knew Berry's shortcomings.

Lynch's account of what was said on different dates should not be so readily discounted. Berry had the responsibility of informing the Taoiseach of the plot to import arms. The fact that he did not trust Lynch—as emerges later very clearly—may explain his reluctance to be explicit about the information he had in his possession. Lynch was emphatic that he had not been told about the activities of two senior ministers until 20 April 1970. Berry, in the account that follows, claims otherwise. It is my considered view that the Taoiseach had not been informed.

Lynch phoned Berry on 13 April, the first call in several months, according to himself. Lynch revealed that he was having difficulty getting in touch with Ó Móráin. Berry explained that as it was Monday the minister might not return to Dublin from Co. Mayo until the evening. Berry was asked to go over to the Taoiseach's office that evening to brief him on the IRA and Northern Ireland.

Before leaving the Department of Justice for that appointment in Government Buildings, Berry learnt that his minister had just arrived and was in his office. Berry told Ó Móráin that he could not properly brief Lynch without telling him of the involvement of Blaney and Haughey in the arms plot. According to Berry, the minister told him: 'Tell the Taoiseach whatever you feel you should tell him.' The secretary noted that the minister was fatigued and listless and 'scarcely conscious of what we were talking about.'[242]

At his meeting with Lynch, Berry told the Taoiseach about the meeting of the Minister for Justice with the Commissioner, Michael Wymes, and the head of the Special Branch, John Fleming. He told him of the involvement of the two ministers in efforts to supply arms to the IRA. He noted that the Taoiseach

> seemed genuinely surprised. (Up to then my feeling was that Mr Ó Móráin simply couldn't have kept the Taoiseach in the dark but that it was not polite to let me know.)[243]

That is a most extraordinary comment, coming, as it did, from the secretary of the Department of Justice. The gravity of the issue went beyond a matter of mere politeness. The system of cabinet government was being subverted. Two senior ministers were involved in a gun-running operation into Northern Ireland. Berry must share responsibility for his failure to report that Ó Móráin was guilty of gross dereliction of duty and of endangering the security of the state by not passing on vital information the previous autumn to the Taoiseach.[244]

The bulk of their discussion, according to Berry, was taken up with whether or not it would be possible to act on the advice of a senior churchman, probably Archbishop William Conway, to make a direct appeal to the leadership of the IRA to end the violence.[245]

Is it credible that the Taoiseach, hearing for the first time of a plot involving two of his most senior ministers to smuggle arms into the North, would spend most of the time discussing an appeal to the IRA leadership? Berry was at fault. Why and how such a state of affairs was allowed to occur ought to be the subject of a long and detailed study of the files of the Departments of the Taoiseach, Justice and Defence. The relevant files should not be held back. In addition, special attention must be paid to the extraordinary detective work of the Special Branch in the persons of Fleming and McMahon. The state owes both men a debt of gratitude, as will be demonstrated in the following section.

CAPTAIN KELLY AND THE 'GUN-RUNNING' PLAN

It is important at this point to clear up misunderstanding about two matters: official regulations governing the importing of arms for use by the Defence Forces, and the chain of command under which Captain Kelly worked. There is absolutely no ambiguity in the military record of either of those areas. Defence Force Regulations clearly laid down the procedure governing the importing of arms. According to a Military Intelligence memorandum, the Quartermaster-General's Branch co-ordinated any such transaction. The correct procedure involved the following stages:

a. Submission of case for purchase of arms through the Department of Defence to Finance by Quartermaster General's Branch, these arms having been approved for type and quality by the Army Ordnance Corps.

b. Issue of licence to import these arms by Minister for Defence under the Firearms Act of 1925.

c. Security at point of import and delivery to Military Magazines controlled by the Army Ordnance Corps under the direction of the Quartermaster General.

d. On reception arms and ammunition are stored and examined in accordance with Regulations by the Army Ordnance Corps before any issue is made to Units.

As a senior officer and the head of Military Intelligence, Colonel Hefferon was well acquainted with those strict procedures. The memorandum raises the question, Why did he permit Captain Kelly to be party to a procedure for the procurement and custody of arms so far out of line with the known and proper method, as laid down in Defence Force Regulations?[246]

Before we return to deal with this area, the second question posed above is also easily answered by reference to the same army memorandum. Colonel Hefferon was asked much later: 'Who was the person in superiority over

Captain Kelly entitled to give him orders as to his duties?' Hefferon replied: 'In this particular case I consider he was acting on a Government mission.'[247] He said later that the Minister for Defence was Kelly's superior officer. He also said that between January and April 1970 Kelly was under his own orders. But, according to the Military Intelligence memorandum,

a. Captain KELLY was properly and legally appointed Staff Officer (Captain) to the Director of Intelligence on 21st July 1965 in Gazette No. 13 of 1965. He was still so gazetted up to 28th April 1970. The Director of Military Intelligence has authority over all his Staff Officers. Colonel HEFFERON was, as Director of Military Intelligence, therefore, responsible for controlling Captain KELLY's daily activities and issuing orders to him up to the time of his (Colonel HEFFERON'S) retirement.

b. In the light of the above it was never officially and authoritatively arranged through the responsible officer, the Adjutant-General of the Army, that any Minister—Finance, Agriculture or Defence—would assume direct control over Captain KELLY and issue him orders, other than his official military superior, Colonel HEFFERON.[248]

That is a clear and unequivocal answer.

There is a subsidiary question that also needs to be asked. Who gave Kelly permission to travel to the Continent on more than one occasion in early 1970? This can be answered with the help of the memorandum cited above. Hefferon said in his evidence that

about the last week in March Captain Kelly told me that he wanted to go abroad and that he had been detailed for some regimental duties. He wanted to be relieved from them. I was not able to arrange this on my own authority and I asked Mr Gibbons to have Captain KELLY relieved from his duties . . .[249]

But Jim Gibbons in his evidence said he was not involved in a decision to excuse Captain Kelly from his normal duties over the weekend of 2–4 April to permit him to go abroad. The Military Intelligence memorandum commented further:

Whether it is a question of getting a Captain relieved from a Regimental Duty, such as Orderly Officer, or getting his permission to go abroad it is most unusual, if not indeed unprecedented, to have a Minister of State intervene in these routine matters, as the authority for both rested within Colonel HEFFERON's compass to arrange.[250]

As a high-ranking army officer, Hefferon would have learnt from the moment he had entered the Cadet School about the necessity to respect the chain of command and not to depart from established procedures. He was within a few weeks of retirement. He was very experienced. But it was a measure of the astuteness of both Blaney and Haughey that they could create the impression that in exceptional times it was necessary to depart from established procedure. Hefferon, an honourable man who had spent his working life in the defence of the state, was put under great pressure by senior ministers to take a course of action that cut across the chain of command. It was Government policy because Blaney said it was so. Hefferon's position was made all the more complicated by the weakness of the Minister for Defence, Jim Gibbons. Gibbons, who may have continued to see himself as a junior minister, was simply bullied and intimidated by Blaney and Haughey. Hefferon was also a victim of the ruthlessness of both men.

Before discussing the details of the plan to import arms it is worth examining a further set of questions governing the issue of communications at the top of Military Intelligence. Colonel P. J. 'Bud' Delaney, the new director of intelligence, had been posted to the Intelligence Section to familiarise himself with its operations for two months before Hefferon retired. During that time Hefferon did not tell Delaney of Kelly's activities, 'because it was a matter of great secrecy, in which some Government Ministers and in my mind acting for the Government were involved,' the Military Intelligence memorandum stated. Hefferon went on to say in evidence that if anyone should have informed Delaney of Kelly's activities it should have been Gibbons. Yet the memorandum states:

a.   Since the Chief of Staff who is the immediate superior of the Director of Military Intelligence saw fit to put Colonel DELANEY into Army Intelligence for two months before Colonel HEFFERON's retirement in order to take over these duties *fully* and *completely*, why did Colonel HEFFERON take it upon himself and consider it necessary to keep Captain KELLY's activities secret from the new Director?

b.   Why, if it were 'Government Policy':
      i. Did not Colonel HEFFERON seek a direction from the Minister as to whether Colonel DELANEY should be informed, or otherwise arrange that the Minister brief Colonel DELANEY on this matter?
      ii. Should not the new Director be *fully* briefed on Captain KELLY's activities?

c.   Was the Chief of Staff briefed by Colonel HEFFERON on the point that this was 'Government Policy'; if not, why not?[251]

However, in a number of publications Captain Kelly claimed that at all times he was acting under instructions from his superior, Colonel Hefferon, and the Minister for Defence, Jim Gibbons. With the assistance of Government money from a series of accounts (of which details will be given below) Captain Kelly wrote that he had been 'formally requested to assist in the proposed Continental purchase.' That, he wrote, was cleared by both Hefferon and Gibbons. He argued that Hefferon was wary of a serving officer becoming involved in an attempt to import arms. He alleges that he was 'secure in the knowledge that the Minister for Defence was fully briefed on this, my first direct involvement in the proposed arms importation.'[252] The memorandum quoted above flatly contradicts that interpretation of events.

The labyrinthine plans to import arms in the spring of 1970 have yet to be fully researched. There had been earlier but ineffectual efforts: Charles Haughey's brother, Pádraig (Jock) Haughey, had attempted to purchase arms in London in late September 1969 'in conjunction with a member of Saor Éire but this had come to the notice of the British Secret Service and was aborted.' A month later Jock Haughey and a Belfast republican, John Kelly, went to London to try again. It turned out to be a British intelligence sting operation, which almost ended in the killing by the IRA of a British agent in his room in the Gresham Hotel, Dublin. They then turned their attention to a more fertile source: the United States. While IRA sympathisers there successfully sent arms to Northern Ireland throughout the period of the 'troubles', on that occasion the plan was abandoned. Neil Blaney, through his friend Albert Luykx, had arranged an arms deal on the Continent. This involved visits to various countries by a leading Northern republican. The contacts introduced a series of characters who might have found their way into a script for a bad comic opera. There was a baron and a Hamburg arms dealer named Otto Schleuter. The cost of the arms shipment, manufactured mainly in Czechoslovakia, was £35,000; the suppliers promised about 350 machine-guns, 150 rifles, 200 pistols, grenades, flak jackets, and 250,000 rounds of ammunition.[253]

Under cover of going to see a sick sister in Frankfurt, Captain Kelly claimed that he travelled with £10,000 on his person. He returned to Dublin and alleged that he saw Gibbons on 3 March while the minister was entertaining a delegation from the North. He also met the minister the following day in his office; and a week later he was in Antwerp on the next leg of his 'mission'. When attempts to smuggle in the arms failed, the decision was taken to bring them into Dublin at the end of March on the *City of Antwerp*.[254] On 20 March the Minister for Finance, Charles Haughey, through his private secretary, Tony Fagan, directed the Commissioner of Customs and Excise that there was to be customs clearance for the cargo on the *City of Antwerp*.

The following is a statement given by Thomas Tobin, Customs and Excise Superintendent, Dublin Castle. Taken on 27 April 1970, it records the events leading up to the attempts to import arms:

On Sunday the 22nd., March, 1970 I was phoned by the Commissioner of customs and Excise—Mr Culligan—at my home that a container of allegedly mild steel plate, addressed to Wellux of Sutton, Co. Dublin was about to be landed off the ship—City of Antwerp on Monday the 23rd., March. It was believed to contain arms. Kelly of Military Intelligence was to be given every facility to collect this container and the container was to be cleared without Customs documents or Customs examination. Mr Culligan gave me the name of Mr Tony FAGAN of Finance. I phoned Mr Fagan on Monday the 23rd., and told him the Customs Surveyor whom Kelly should contact was O'Riordan at Alexander [Alexandra] Quay. I understand that Kelly did contact O'Riordan and that six bales of bullet proof clothing were landed off the City of Antwerp, and were taken possession of by Kelly. At the same time, Mr Muldoon—Assistant Collector, Customs House, Dublin informed me that there were 75 cases of ammunition—allegedly blank—held by the Dutch Customs in Antwerp or Rotterdam. When I had been speaking to Mr Fagan on 23rd., I asked him did he want the same type of operation mounted in Waterford as the boat was calling to Waterford before coming to Dublin. He said that he did not.

As stated above, the *City of Antwerp* arrived in Dublin and discharged bales of 'garments' (bullet-proof vests) for James Kelly and John Kelly. Two items relating to arms and ammunition were deleted from the manifest. James Kelly claims in his book that the arms consignment had been offloaded at Antwerp because of procedural technicalities.[255] By coincidence, an army detail arrived to supervise the unloading of an official consignment of weapons. Captain Kelly knew one of the officers, and they exchanged a few friendly words. The captain and his northern associates left; with the exception of bullet-proof vests, they were empty-handed.

Captain Kelly flew to Antwerp on 1 April 1970, accompanied by an 'interpreter', Albert Luykx, a naturalised Irish citizen and a friend of Neil Blaney. Kelly maintained to his death that he was 'on official business, which had the complete approval of the Minister for Defence.'[256] While in Brussels, Kelly received a phone call from his wife. Colonel Hefferon had issued instructions for his immediate return to Dublin because of the deteriorating situation in the North. Kelly got through to Blaney, who told him that the situation in the North had improved. The captain decided he would complete his mission on the Continent. 'I requested him [Blaney] to inform Colonel Hefferon of this decision.'[257] Is it not extraordinary that a serving army officer would disobey a direct order from his superior officer, and request the Minister for Agriculture to act as a messenger?

Ignoring Hefferon's order, Kelly travelled with Luykx to the office of Schleuter in Hamburg. There they learnt that the original consignment of arms had been sent back from Antwerp to Trieste. The two men were assured that the cargo would be sent on to Vienna and then by charter plane to Dublin. Kelly was back in Dublin on 4 April, where he wrote that he had another meeting with Gibbons to inform him of developments.

There was a critical shift in the command structure of Military Intelligence in April, which had a major impact on Captain Kelly's ability to travel. Colonel Hefferon was due twenty-eight days' pre-retirement leave but did not take it. In fact instead of going on leave on 12 March he stayed on in control of Military Intelligence up to 10 April, that is, one day after his official retirement from the army, the memorandum stated. Hefferon told Colonel Delaney, his successor, in February or early March that he would not take his pre-retirement leave at all but would serve in command of Military Intelligence for as long as possible.

However, when Colonel Delaney took over on 9 April, Captain Kelly's name appeared on the duty roster for regimental (i.e. routine) duty at Army Headquarters for 11 April 1970. He did not apply to be relieved from this duty. Colonel Delaney took the unusual step of instructing that Captain Kelly not be permitted to perform those duties, because, as orderly officer, he would have access to keys of the Intelligence Section offices and would be the recipient of possible intelligence reports from various sources.[258]

Captain O'Shea telephoned Captain Kelly on 10 April and informed him that he was relieved from regimental duty for 11 April 1970, without giving Colonel Delaney's reasons. Kelly confirmed with O'Shea that it was Delaney, and not Hefferon, who had had him relieved, according to the Military Intelligence memorandum. Up to 9 April—the date of Hefferon's retirement—Kelly at all times justified his actions on the grounds that he was carrying out 'Government policy'. From 10 April—the date on which Colonel Delaney became director of intelligence—Kelly was, in the eyes of his superiors, doing neither regimental nor intelligence duties, according to the memorandum. His superior, Colonel Delaney, gave him nothing to do, despite Kelly's efforts to have it understood that he was continuing to carry out Government policy. Delaney was 'forcefully urging his removal from Military Intelligence.' He succeeded in that objective on 28 April 1970.[259]

With those facts as a background, Kelly and Luykx flew to Vienna on 17 April to complete arrangements. There the matter rests for the moment; but the bizarre nature of the events might suggest that the attempt to buy arms may have been part of an elaborate British sting operation. The super-intendent of Customs and Excise at Dublin Castle, Thomas Tobin, recorded the following in his statement of 27 April 1970:

On or about the 10th April, 1970 Mr Fagan phoned my office and enquired about the names of the Preventive Staff at Dublin Airport, as it was expected that a chartered plane carrying arms would arrive at Dublin Airport. I gave him the names of the Preventive officers who would be on duty and told him to mention my name. Subsequently I told Fagan's Secretary that if Kelly mentioned my name to the Preventive Staff at the Airport he would be given every facility. I informed the Preventive Staff at the Airport that Kelly was from Finance.

At this stage in view of the instructions given me by the Commissioner—Mr Culligan, and Fagan being a Principal Officer in Dept. of Finance I naturally assumed that the consignment was being taken in by the Army on behalf of the Government. Some time during the week commencing 13th., April, I ascertained from Mr Connellan, Assistant Collector at Customs House, that Kelly had introduced himself to Mr Desmond—Surveyor, Dublin Airport as 'An Assistant to an Assistant of the Minister for Finance.'

On 18th April, Mr Sean Carpendale informed me of the approach made by Chief Supt. Fleming to him. Mr Carpendale gave me a telephone number at which Chief Supt. Fleming could be contacted. I phoned Mr Fagan at his home address before 3 p.m. on the 18th., and told him to phone Chief Supt. Fleming before 4 p.m., as the Gardaí were going to seize any arms that were landed at Dublin, Cork or Shannon Airports. I heard no more about the matter until I was approached by Chief Supt. Fleming on this date.

The Berry narrative, in which this writer does not have great confidence, provides further details about what was happening between the Special Branch and the Department of Justice. On 17 April intelligence was received in the Department of Justice of the imminent arrival in Dublin airport of 6.8 tons of arms. That news came during a meeting being attended by Berry, Andy Ward (assistant secretary of the Department of Justice), and the minister. First Ward was summoned from the room. Within minutes Berry was asked to leave the meeting. Ward told him that a call had been received from the Department of Transport and Power with news that a chartered plane was bringing a consignment of arms from Hamburg for the Gardaí and the army. The minister was informed and was 'in a quandary' as to what to do. He first wanted the consignment stopped at Hamburg. Berry favoured letting the arms arrive and then having them confiscated. The minister finally agreed with that proposal.

Plans to intercept the cargo upon arrival were made, and arrangements were also made to cover the contingency of a landing in any of the other four suitable airports. Berry wrote:

> From then on, I was in almost continuous telephonic communication with the Commissioner, C3 in Garda H.Q., the Head of the 'S Branch,' the Department of P and T [Posts and Telegraphs] as to what airports, other than Dublin, could land a plane with 6.8 tons of cargo and the answer was: Shannon, Cork, Farranfore in Kerry and Castlebar in Mayo. I also made enquiries as to the ceiling below which an approaching plane could divert to another airport without coming under radar notice.[260]

The following day, Saturday 18 April, Berry continued with the preparations to intercept the arms consignment. There were so many incoming calls until 12:30 p.m. 'that I was unable to receive a call from the Minister who was angry that I had not been in touch with him.' Ó Móráin had every reason to feel irked. He was the minister. Even if Berry could have informed his minister on that occasion that 'you can sleep easy to-night, there is a ring of steel around Dublin Airport,'[261] it was Ó Móráin's statutory responsibility to take the lead in making such arrangements. Yet how could any responsible minister leave Dublin at a time of such an unprecedented crisis?

At 6:30 p.m. on 18 April, Berry received a call at his home. He informs his readers that the phone rang as he was 'about to have a sauna and didn't have a stitch of clothes on.' The pips of the RTE time signal before the news sounded as he spoke into the phone. He recognised the voice of Charles Haughey and noted down the following conversation soon afterwards:

> Haughey: You know about the cargo that is coming into Dublin Airport this Sunday?
> Berry: Yes, minister.
> Haughey: Can it be let through on a guarantee that it will go direct to the North?
> Berry: No.
> Haughey: I think that is a bad decision.
> (I made no comment.)
> Haughey: Does the man from Mayo know?
> Berry: Yes.
> Haughey: What will happen to it when it arrives?
> Berry: It will be grabbed.

Haughey: I had better have it called off.[262]

Chief Superintendent Malone phoned Berry immediately after the
Haughey phone call. He told him that a principal officer in the Department
of Finance, Tony Fagan, had been in contact requesting that Chief
Superintendent Fleming phone either himself or Haughey at given numbers.
Berry gave instructions that there should be no such contact. He commented:
'It was as a result of that call that I came to realise the enormity of the attempts
that were being made to suborn the security forces.' Berry concluded, follow-
ing his conversation with Haughey, that his own minister did not know about
the cargo, and 'it was not likely to be a government sponsored effort.'
However, he had

> some lingering doubt that all this could not have gone on for several
> months without the knowledge of the Taoiseach unless he was wilfully
> turning the blind eye. But it now seemed evident that, at most, a caucus
> was involved and that Government qua Government were not behind the
> arms conspiracy.[263]

Written in retrospect and with the benefit of hindsight, Berry's admission of
lack of personal confidence in the Taoiseach supports Lynch's view that he
was not told about the plot to import arms until 20 April.

What happened next was extraordinary by any standards in a parliamen-
tary democracy. Without any reference to the Taoiseach, the secretary of the
Department of Justice phoned Áras an Uachtaráin, asking to speak to
President de Valera. When put through, Berry said:

> I have come into knowledge of matters of national concern. I am afraid
> that if I follow the normal course the information might not reach [the]
> Government. Does my duty end with informing my Minister or am I
> responsible to [the] Government by whom I was appointed?

De Valera asked him to repeat what he had said. 'Are you sure of your facts?'
he asked, and again 'Are you absolutely sure of your facts?' Berry replied that
he was absolutely sure of his facts. De Valera said: 'You have a clear duty to
Government. You must speak to the Taoiseach.' By way of explanation, Berry
wrote that his action meant that subconsciously he had 'lingering doubts'
about Lynch, and his phone call to de Valera meant that he was 'pushing the
Taoiseach towards an enforcement of the rule of law.'[264] If Berry, who appears
to have felt omnipotent, had been doing his job correctly he would have
known that Lynch did not need to be pushed to enforce the law.

The following day, Sunday 19 April, Berry was informed that Lynch was due back in Dublin late that night. He arranged to see him on Monday 20 April.[265] Berry was visited late that night by the head of the Special Branch, Chief Superintendent Fleming, who handed him the report quoted in full below.

Chief Supt's Office,
Detective Branch, C.S.
Dublin Castle.
19th April, 1970.

JOHN P. FLEMING. Ch/Supt.
19/4/70

Assistant Commissioner.

Re: Illegal Importation of Arms and ammunition at Dublin Airport

I am to report that as a result of a conference with the Commissioner on Friday 17th, April 1970 I interviewed Brendan Casey, Cargo Manager with Aer Lingus. This interview took place at Mr Casey's home 159 Shellmartin Road, Sutton on the night of the 17th, inst. Mr. Casey informed me that representation had been made to Aer Lingus by a man who stated he was Commandant Jimmy Kelly of Army Intelligence to have a shipment of arms and ammunition flown in from Vienna as soon as possible. Mr Casey was unable to give any further details as he said he only became aware of the incident through his Warehouse Superintendent in the Cargo Terminal of Aer Lingus—A Mr. Jack Ryan.

Later on same night I interviewed Mr Jack Ryan at his home in Portmarnock and ascertained the following facts:—On Wednesday last, the 15th., inst., Mr Ryan received a Telex communication from a Mr. Johnston—who is an Aer Lingus representative in Frankfort—to the effect that an Aer Lingus plane was required as soon as possible to convey a consignment of arms and ammunition from Vienna to Dublin. He stated there were ten cases of Luger Pistols, and Seventy-two cases of ammunition—approx. three tons in weight. Mr Ryan informed him that he would be prepared to take the pistols on a passenger plane, but that he would be contrary to regulations to carry the ammunition on a passenger plane.

Mr. Ryan then decided to call on Mr Andrew Desmond, who is a Customs and Excise Surveyor at Dublin Airport, to ascertain if there was official sanction for the importation of the arms and ammunition. He called to Mr Desmond's office sometime after 4.00 p.m. on Wednesday, the 15th., inst. There was another man in the office at the time and Mr Desmond introduced him to Mr Ryan as a Commdt. Jimmy KELLY of Army Intelligence. The three of them then discussed the shipment of the arms and ammunition and Mr Desmond stated that he was satisfied with the authenticity of Mr Kelly and that the importation in question was a genuine transaction and had Government approval. Kelly appeared surprised that the arms had not arrived on that date and became annoyed when Ryan told him he was not prepared to carry the ammunition on a passenger plane.

The Customs and Excise Surveyor—Mr Desmond—assured Jimmy Kelly that he would grant him a free entry for the consignment at the Airport, which meant that they would be free from scrutiny by Customs Officials. He stated that he himself was only at the Airport in a temporary capacity and would be finished there on Saturday, 18th., inst. He said he was being replaced by a Mr. McCLEAN and he then sent for Mr McCLEAN and introduced him to Jimmy KELLY. He told Mr McClean that Kelly was doing a 'Hush-hush' job for the Government, that he was satisfied this was genuine and had Government backing, and that he had granted Kelly a Free Entry which he asked Mr McClean to accept. Mr McClean agreed to this. Mr Desmond asked Kelly if he required any extra security at the Airport when the shipment arrived, and Kelly said No, that he wanted to take the crates from the plane onto a lorry, as quickly and unobtrusively as possible. Mr Ryan got the impression from Mr Desmond's conversation that the arms and ammunition were either for the Gardaí or Army authorities, but he cannot recall if either Department was specifically mentioned.

On Thursday, 16th inst., Jimmy KELLY again called to see Mr Ryan and stated that the amount of the shipment had now been increased to approx. 5.8 tons, (Five, point eight) and that the whole shipment would have to be taken on the one plane. That the question of separating the arms from the ammunition could no [sic] be considered. He said if Aer Lingus were not prepared to do this he would get in touch with Mr Squire of Aer Turas— which company also operates tes [sic] from Dublin Airport. He then told Mr Ryan that he didn't want the shipment to be listed as firearms on the Cargo Manifest, and that he intended to describe them as 'machinery.' At this stage Mr Ryan become suspicious that something was wrong and he decided to inform the Cargo Manager—Mr Brendan Casey—of the situation.

On Friday morning, 17th., inst Jimmy Kelly again telephone [sic] Mr Ryan and requested him to contact Mr Johnston in Frankfort, so that the latter could meet two men whom Kelly stated 'had gone to Frankfurt to bring in the stuff.' Kelly gave the men's names as Mr Albert and Mr Kelly.

Jimmy Kelly again telephoned Mr Ryan on Friday evening, same date, when he was told that the earliest time Aer Lingus could take in the shipment would be Monday or Tuesday of next week. He then said he would get in touch with Mr Ryan again but so far he has not done so. Mr Ryan got the impression that Kelly was acting as a 'go-between' and that he was not in a position to make decisions.

During my interview with Mr Brendan Casey he mentioned that he was on friendly terms with Mr Squire of Aer Turus, and I requested him to contact Mr Squire and ascertain if Jimmy Kelly had been in touch with Mr Squire but that the latter was not over-anxious to become involved in the transaction, as he said 'the whole deal smelled.'

At about 1.30 p.m. on Saturday, 18th., inst., with the approval of the Commissioner I visited the home of Mr Kilty, who is a Director of Customs and Excise, and informed him that a shipment of arms and ammunition was likely to arrive at Dublin Airport within the next few days, and I requested his assistance in having this shipment inspected by Customs Officials on arrival. I told him of Jimmy Kelly's arrangement with Mr Desmond regarding the Free Entry of the shipment, and that Kelly's story of having Government sanction for the operation was a pack of lies. Mr Kilty agreed to help in every possible way and suggested that the Inspector i/o of the Special Investigation Branch of Customs—Mr Sean Carpendale—should also be notified, as he was the person who would be dealing with the matter. I agreed to this and he telephoned Mr Carpendale, who arrived at Mr Kilty's home some time later. The three of us then discussed the manner in which the inspection and seizure should be made, and Mr Carpendale then said that his Superintendent at the Airport—a Mr Tobin—would also have to be informed of the matter. He said he would contact Mr Tobin as quickly as possible and would get in touch with me at 4.00 p.m.

As I had an appointment with Chief/Supt. Malone in the Garda Depot at that time I gave the latter's office telephone number (775203) to Mr Carpendale as a number at which to contact me. I remained with Chief/Supt. Malone until about 4.40 p.m. when I left to attend to other duties. Up to that time Mr Carpendale did not contact me. I arrived back to Chief Supt. Malone's office at approx. 6.55 p.m. when the latter informed me of the following developments:

At 5.30 p.m. Mr Sean Carpendale telephoned and asked to speak to me. When informed by Chief Supt. Malone that I was out on duty he left a message for me to ring Mr Tobin at 337515. He said that Mr Tobin had taken the matter out of his hands and had told him to mind his own business. Seeing that Mr Tobin had adopted this attitude I decided not to telephone him.

At 6.20 p.m. another telephone call was received by Chief Supt. Malone on 775203 line. This caller also asked to speak to me and when told I was not available he asked that I be given a message. He said his name was Fagan and that he was a Civil Servant and a Personal Aide to Mr Haughey, Minister for Finance. He said I was to telephone him—Mr Fagan—'about a very delicate matter' and gave his telephone number as 889595. He said he would be at that number up to 7.15 p.m. and that if I hadn't contacted him before that I was to ring Mr Haughey direct at telephone number 350111.

Chief Supt. Malone and I then endeavoured to contact the Commissioner to inform him of the latest developments and seek instructions but he was not available at the time. Having failed to contact the Commissioner we decided to contact Mr Berry, Secretary, Dept. of Justice and inform of the situation. The secretary then gave a direction on the matter. Observation is being maintained by members of s.d.u. [Special Detective Unit] on all flights arriving at Dublin Airport and this will continue until further instructions are received.

JOHN P. FLEMING. Ch/Supt.
19/4/70

Berry met Lynch shortly after noon on 20 April and handed him a copy of the Fleming report quoted above. He also gave the Taoiseach a full account of the events of the previous three days, including information about the complicity of two Government ministers. Lynch instructed Berry to investigate the matter fully and to report in detail to him at 9:30 the following morning. Lynch was hearing for the first time of the plot to import arms, involving two ministers, known about by the Department of Justice since the previous October.

The meeting was brief, as the British ambassador was waiting to see the Taoiseach, wrote Berry. However, Lynch in his account stated that he questioned Berry closely that day. He also requested further evidence that would enable him to act.

The following day, 21 April, Berry delivered to the Taoiseach a copy of a second report by Chief Superintendent Fleming, quoted in full below.

Assistant Commissioner,
Re: Illegal importation of Arms and Ammunition
at Dublin Airport.

Further to my report of the 19th., inst., in connection with above I am to state that on this date I received a telephone call from Capt. J Squire, Director of Aer Turas, Dublin Airport requesting that I call to see him. I subsequently called to his office where he related the following facts to me.

About three weeks ago he was approached by Mr Albert LUYKX, of Sutton House, Sutton who told him that he might be in a position to put some business his way regarding the freight of goods from Vienna to Dublin. Capt. Squire had known Mr LUYKX prior to this meeting as a man who was dealing in machinery, so he assumed that he was referring to the importation of machinery. He gave the matter no further thought until Thursday, 16th., inst. Then Mr LUYKX telephone him and asked if he could meet him in the Sutton House Hotel as he wanted to discuss some business with him.

Capt. Squire went to the Hotel, which incidentally is owned by a son-in-law of Mr LUYKX—a Mr Paul Drumm. On arrival there Mr LUYKX introduced him to a Capt. Jimmy KELLY and his brother, Seamus KELLY. He then drew Capt Squire aside and told him that Capt. KELLY was in Army Intelligence and that he had been commissioned by the Government to buy a large quantity of arms and ammunition on the Continent, which he understood was for use by the Army and the Gardaí. He also stated that these arms and ammunition had been purchased about a month ago, but that the Shipping Agent in Hamburg, who was supposed to forward them to Dublin had messed thing up, and that the arms, etc. were now in Vienna.

He stated that he (LUYKX) was a personal friend of Mr Neil Blaney and that the latter had asked him to assist in having the arms and ammunition taken to Dublin. He said he was travelling to Frankfurt on the following day with Mr Kelly, and that his job was mainly to act as interpreter. He asked if Capt. Squire would be prepared to send a plane to Vienna to collect the stuff, and the latter said Yes, providing the importation papers were in order.

He said the Government required strict secrecy in the matter, and that although the equipment was for use by the Army and Gardaí, neither of those Depts. had been told of the importation. He said that the shipment would be described as 'mining equipment' in the cargo manifest. Capt. Squire then asked him what type of guns were involved and he said 'Luger Pistols.' Capt. Squire thought this rather odd as he was aware that neither the Army nor the Gardaí used this type of weapon. He then asked Capt.

KELLY if he was in possession of what is known as 'An End Users Certificate', which would be required by the Customs Officials in Vienna. Capt. Kelly said that he never heard of such a Certificate, and this really convinced Capt. Squire that the deal was not genuine.

Jimmy Kelly then said that he would contact Capt. Squire again when Mr. LUYKX and himself returned from Frankfurt on Sunday night, but so far he has not done so. Capt. Squire telephoned Mr. Luykx home at 11 p.m. on Sunday night but was told that the latter was away on business.

A check of Aer Lingus records revealed that a Mr. A. LYKX and a Mr. J. Kelly travelled on Aer Lingus flight 650 to Frankfurt via Manchester on Friday last. They were both in possession of open return tickets.

Albert Luykx was born in Belgium in 1917 and came to Ireland on the 9/10/48 as a Political Refugee from Holland. At that time he was using the name 'Francis J. FAES.' He became a naturalised Irish citizen on 26/8/54. He was suspected of having Republican sympathies in 1952 when he was observed to associate with Thomas McCurtain of Cork.

Capt. Squire has promised that should he accept this contract he will let me know of the time of arrival of the arms and ammunition.

John P. Fleming. Ch/Supt.
20/4/70

In the course of the discussion Berry explained that security was so tight that there was no prospect of a shipment of arms being unloaded clandestinely at any Irish airport. Unburdening himself, he explained his dilemma over the previous few days and his reluctance to go over his minister's head to the Taoiseach. He said he had qualms about approaching Lynch, 'as I might be intruding on a secret Government mission.' In his dilemma, he told the Taoiseach he had spoken to the President, who had advised him that it was his duty to speak to the Taoiseach.

Lynch made no comment, and with good reason. He had worked with Berry in the Department of Justice in the mid-1940s and had his measure. Despite knowing Berry's failings better than most, he was angry beyond words at the secretary's presumption that he—the Taoiseach—could not be trusted. That could only have meant that Berry suspected that Lynch himself was directly involved in a conspiracy to import arms. When the two men met on 29 April the Taoiseach, according to Berry, said: 'When you said last Tuesday that you thought that the Government might be secretly involved I saw *red.* I was not able to speak to you I was so furious.'[266]

From a rereading of the 'Berry diaries' it is evident that the writer was attempting to provide a rationale for his actions. How was it possible for a conspiracy of such magnitude, involving two Government ministers, to reach such an advanced stage without the Taoiseach being kept informed? It is not sufficient to state that the Minister for Justice was dysfunctional. Berry was substantially to blame for the breakdown in communications that created so much unnecessary suspicion and mistrust between different strands of government, the Gardaí and Military Intelligence.

Following the publication in *Magill* in 1980 of the 'Berry diaries', Lynch spoke forcefully in Dáil Éireann on 25 November in defence of his integrity and honesty.[267]

My main reason for speaking in this debate is to restate what I said in Dáil Éireann in May, 1970, in the course of the debates touching on the Arms Crisis and which I reiterated in a short statement in July of this year [1980] after the publication of the last of the three *Magill* articles on the same subject and that is that Mr. Peter Berry first told me on 20th April 1970, of the alleged involvement of two Members of the Government in the alleged conspiracy to import arms illegally . . . I want to say that as far as I am concerned the main thrust of these articles seems to try to establish—

(1)   That I was made aware of a plot to import arms when I visited Mr. Peter Berry in Mount Carmel Hospital on 17th October, 1969, and

(2)   That Mr. Berry first told me on 13th April, 1970, and not on 20th April, 1970, of the alleged attempt at importation of arms which subsequently was the basis of a charge of conspiracy brought against two Ministers and two other defendants.[268]

I want to say categorically again to the Dáil that I was first informed by Mr. Peter Berry of the alleged involvement of the Ministers on Monday, 20th April. That was the first I heard of it from any source.[269]

With reference to my meeting Mr. Berry in Mount Carmel Hospital, I was told the evening before that Mr. Berry wished to see me at the hospital and I called there, as stated in the May issue of *Magill*, on the morning of 17th October, 1969. I called to the hospital in the ordinary way and was conducted to where Mr. Berry was in bed, as on any other occasion when I visited a patient in hospital. There was no attempt to keep my visit secret as the *Magill* articles seem to suggest.

To my lay mind, Mr. Berry was obviously a sick man and, as was indicated in the *Magill* articles, had a drip tube inserted in his nose. It is true that medical staff interrupted frequently during the 15 to 20 minutes or so that I was with him and, as far as I can remember, at one stage he was given an injection.

Mr. Berry spoke to me about alleged attempts at importation of small quantities of arms through Dublin Airport from time to time and that on

one occasion the gardaí were able to trace a delivery of one small consignment of arms to a location in the Dublin mountains. I asked Mr. Berry
why the gardaí, to use my own words, 'did not pounce' at that stage and he
told me that they would not do so because the quantity involved was very
small, that a probable result of their taking action would be to disclose the
identity of their source of information and thus cut it off.

He spoke generally in a rather confused manner, as could be expected
from a man who was obviously heavily drugged because of the tests which
he was undergoing that morning. I have no recollection whatever of his
informing me of a meeting in Bailieborough some time previously in
which a plot for the alleged arms importation was set and during which a
sum of money was alleged to have passed for this purpose. It may be that it
was Mr. Berry's intention the evening before to give me some information
on it before the drugs and injections were administered to him.

I would like to refer to Mr. Berry's own account of this interview, as
published in the June issue of *Magill,* and to quote from that issue what he
is alleged to have written in his diaries. 'I did not have 100 per cent recollection of my conversation with the Taoiseach as I was a bit muzzy and
bloody from the medical tests but I am quite certain that I told him of
Captain Kelly's prominent part in the Bailieborough meeting with known
members of the IRA.'[270] As I have already said, it may be that he intended
the night before, when he asked to see me, to tell me this and afterwards
when he was restored to health he may have believed that he had, in fact,
done so . . .'[271]

At no stage during this interview on this date, 17th October, did Mr.
Berry mention the name of any Member of the Government nor did he try
to implicate them in any way. I may add that there was no suggestion in
Magill or otherwise that he did.

As to the suggestion that Mr. Berry first told me on 13th April, 1970, of
the alleged involvement of the two Ministers in the attempt to import
arms, as I have already stated Mr. Berry did not mention anything to me
about the alleged involvement of the Ministers until Monday, 20th April,
when he called to my office at Government Buildings. He then produced
some documents and copies of statements taken from members of the
staffs of Dublin Airport and of the Revenue Commissioners which clearly
identified two Members of the Government as being involved. I questioned Mr. Berry very closely on that day. I asked him if, before I would
take action, he could produce some further evidence which I felt I
required. He left my office and returned the following day and produced
further documents.[272]

I will now briefly return to the reconstruction of a narrative for the days following Berry's encounters with the Taoiseach.

Having learnt all from Berry and the Special Branch, Lynch was determined to confront the two ministers concerned. His own account to the Dáil in 1980 confirmed what has been related above.

> I then made up my mind to question the Ministers alleged to be involved the following morning but, as is now well known, it was not possible for me to question one of them because of an accident he had met with earlier that morning.

Haughey did not report to the Department of Finance on the day of the budget, Wednesday 22 April, as he had been badly beaten up earlier that morning in a public house in unclear circumstances and for unconfirmed reasons. His injuries were so severe—an iron bar having been used by his attacker or attackers—that he had been admitted as an emergency case to the Mater Hospital. Lynch took over the duties of his absentee minister, read the budget speech and then reverted to his previous role. Too tied up with the debate to confront either Haughey or Blaney, Lynch had only found time on the day of the budget to reprimand Ó Móráin. The Minister for Justice had been told that he would be hearing again from the Taoiseach.

That evening, at a public function in the Gresham Hotel, Dublin, the minister appeared to have a panic attack at a dinner at which he was the guest of honour. He lunged for the exit, only to find himself in the kitchen. The following day, 23 April, Berry received a phone call from Ó Móráin, who 'seemed to be in great distress.' The minister asked him to get him into a nursing home. He was admitted to Mount Carmel on 24 April and detained for treatment.[273]

Lynch has left the following account of what happened when he tried to get in to see Haughey:

> Though I approached his medical adviser on a number of occasions, I was not given permission to visit him in hospital until several days later. I went to visit him in the Mater Private Nursing Home on 29th April but I found he was in a condition [in] which I thought it would be unfair to question him at any length.[274]

The new director of intelligence, Colonel Delaney, as has been seen, was highly critical of Captain Kelly's activities. He had written in a document of Captain Kelly's 'emotional reaction to events in Northern Ireland.' That pointed to 'his having lost that cool behaviour so necessary in an intelligence officer.' Delaney gave a verbal briefing to the Minister for Defence, Jim Gibbons, on 22 April, stating that from November 1969 Kelly had 'ceased to have any contact with the Security Sub-Section and no reports from him are on the record in the Intelligence Sub-Section.' There was an attempt to import arms illegally for subversive groups on both sides of the border. He stated that weapons should only be purchased for the forces of the state and 'NOT for illegal groups.' He pointed to the danger of such weapons being used 'against our own forces.' He argued that the giving of arms to untrained people was a most serious matter, and that if captured they could be traced to their source. Kelly's open contacts with illegal groups was a serious security matter, he wrote, adding that British Intelligence, sharing links with the CIA and European security agencies, would know about the attempt to bring in arms. 'The likelihood of these activities going undetected is small,' he said. He recorded that Gibbons agreed that the arms could be turned against Irish forces, that untrained people in Northern Ireland should not get arms, and that British Intelligence and the CIA could know about those activities. The chief of staff was given a copy of the report.[275]

On the morning of 28 April 1970 Captain Kelly was brought before Colonel Delaney, who said to him in the presence of Commandant O'Sullivan:

> You are now getting an order to desist completely and entirely from your present activities. You will make no more contact with anyone whomsoever either here or abroad in connection with these activities. You will engage yourself wholetime in the pursuit of your legal soldierly duties.

On 1 May 1970 Captain Kelly was arrested and was questioned in the Bridewell Garda Station in Dublin. That evening Berry received a phone call from President de Valera. He referred to the arrest of Kelly and the many rumours of arms imports. De Valera asked about the dependability of the Gardaí. Berry replied that the force was 100 per cent behind the Government. De Valera was also reassured that there was no fear of disaffection in the army and that only a small number were involved. As Berry did not have a minister at the time, he 'did not think it necessary to inform the Taoiseach.'[276]

The previous day, 30 April, Lynch had seen Berry in the morning and told him that he had seen both Blaney and Haughey (the previous day) and that 'the matter was ended.' That was Berry's memory of the conversation. But that interpretation of events was later rejected by Lynch, and his account was put on the record of the Dáil. He had said to both ministers 'that the information that I had would justify my asking for their resignation.' Blaney, who had been interviewed in the Taoiseach's office, protested his innocence and asked for some time to consider the position. Lynch went to see Haughey in the Mater.

He too protested his innocence. Because of his condition, Lynch felt that he could not continue at that time to pursue enquiries with him.

Lynch asked Berry on 30 April to have the head of the Special Branch, Chief Superintendent Fleming, at his home by eight o'clock. The Attorney-General and the Minister for Defence, Jim Gibbons, were there, as was the head of Military Intelligence, Colonel Delaney. After the meeting Fleming visited Berry's house and was present when Lynch phoned to say that he now had 'a better understanding of the position.' Berry said at the end of that entry: 'As a result of the misstatements already recorded, with more to follow, I lost respect for the Taoiseach's credibility.'[277] In turn, Lynch had good cause to have no confidence in Berry.

On 1 May 1970 Lynch addressed a meeting of the Government. He informed his colleagues that serious allegations had been made against Neil Blaney and Charles Haughey. He said they were accused of attempting to import illegally arms for use in Northern Ireland. Both had vehemently denied the allegations. The Minister for Education, Pádraig Faulkner, wrote:

> We were devastated and were under no illusion that if the allegations proved to be true this would not be the end of the matter. It could only result in the Taoiseach asking for their resignations ... Nobody made any comment and we turned to an item on agriculture.[278]

He further records: 'I can still clearly recall Neil Blaney, Minister for Agriculture, vigorously arguing a point on the subject. It was as if the Taoiseach had said nothing of any significance.' He was amazed that Blaney could ignore what had been said. 'Perhaps his attitude may have been to show contempt for Jack Lynch.'[279]

That contempt had been shown repeatedly at Government meetings. Patrick Hillery recalled a meeting in 1969 at which Blaney had been particularly disrespectful towards the Taoiseach. Hillery tackled Lynch afterwards and asked why he had not faced down his critic. Lynch replied: 'The ball will come down this end of the field again.'[280] (Lynch, a six-times all-Ireland winner, would not have displayed such patience with an opponent on the playing field.)

In May 1970 the ball was definitely in Lynch's end of the field. He consulted widely in the course of the following days. He visited the former Taoiseach, Seán Lemass, who told him: 'You're the Taoiseach: do what you have to do.'[281] Frank Aiken, now a backbencher, said:

> You are the leader of the Irish people—not just the Fianna Fáil party. The Irish people come first, the party second and individuals third. If you are asking me what I would do, the whip would be off these men as from now.[282]

On 4 May, Lynch went to Mount Carmel in the morning to see Ó Móráin, and in the afternoon he returned for his resignation. Faulkner, who had served as parliamentary secretary to Ó Móráin and had been on good terms with him, states: 'There is no question of his having been involved with, or supportive of, the illegal importation of arms.'[283] I am not so sure. Given his illness, there was diminished responsibility; but the ex-minister had to accept considerable culpability for not acting throughout the crisis in a more efficient manner. When Lynch announced the resignation to the Dáil on 5 May the leader of the opposition, Liam Cosgrave, asked: 'Can the Taoiseach say if this is the only ministerial resignation we can expect?' Lynch replied: 'I do not know what the deputy is referring to.'[284]

Cosgrave's remark was not inspired guesswork. He had received a tip-off from two sources about the plot to import arms. Stephen Collins states that the first came from the retired but still active Special Branch detective Phil McMahon. He received another on Garda notepaper, together with a list of names. But what was he to do with the information? Having consulted his senior colleagues in Fine Gael, he feared that the story might be printed in the *Sunday Independent*. He was advised that in the national interest he should go to see the Taoiseach that night. He did so later on 5 May. Returning to a small group of his closest Fine Gael colleagues he said: 'It's all true.'[285]

Lynch that evening again confronted Blaney and demanded his resignation. He refused. Lynch then phoned Haughey in hospital. He too refused to resign. Returning home, Lynch consulted a small number of his closest circle of advisers. He saw Berry at 2 a.m. on 6 May and briefed him on developments. He then instructed the head of the Government Information Bureau, Eoin Neeson, to issue a terse statement announcing the sacking of Blaney and Haughey.[286] That morning, 6 May, the city editions of the newspapers published the sensational news of the dismissal from the Government of two of the best-known and most senior ministers.[287]

When the Dáil met at 11:30 on 6 May, Lynch successfully requested a postponement of the sitting until 10 p.m. He informed the Dáil that he had not yet received the resignations, 'but the constitutional position is that I am entitled to act on my request.'[288] In the intervening hours Lynch had to carry the Government and—more problematical for him—Fianna Fáil. Hillery returned post-haste to Dublin, arriving after the Government meeting had started. Pádraig Faulkner has a vivid recollection of his looking around the table and 'seeing the four vacant chairs, like black holes, in the circle.'[289] The meeting was carried out in a businesslike fashion. Lynch proposed the immediate filling of the vacant posts. He named Desmond O'Malley, a young deputy from Limerick, as the new Minister for Justice. George Colley was given the Finance portfolio, and Jim Gibbons was given Agriculture and

Fisheries. Joseph Brennan was given the Department of Social Welfare. Patrick Lalor took over Industry and Commerce. Jeremiah Cronin was assigned to the Department of Defence. Gerard Collins took over in the Department of Posts and Telegraphs. Robert Molloy was given Local Government. The other ministers remained in their posts. David Andrews became parliamentary secretary to the Taoiseach and the Minister for Defence. Michael Kitt was appointed to the Gaeltacht, Liam Cunningham to Local Government and Michael O'Kennedy to Education.

There followed a discussion about how to handle the meeting of the parliamentary party later that evening. Hillery was clear in his mind that there should not be a vote of confidence in the Government or in the Taoiseach. 'Winning such a vote,' he said to the author, 'was never a victory': such a vote might 'only act to weaken the leadership in the eyes of the party.' Hillery proposed that a motion asserting the Taoiseach's right to appoint and dismiss ministers be placed before the party and later before the Dáil.[290]

Pádraig Faulkner described the unease at the parliamentary party meeting at 6 p.m. that evening as palpable. The motion was placed before the meeting and passed unanimously.[291] The parliamentary party then agreed to show unanimous support for the nominations of the Taoiseach. Kevin Boland spoke in a conciliatory tone. He asked Lynch if he had evidence against the dismissed ministers. Lynch replied that he had, and Boland softened somewhat. At the meeting there were those who believed that Boland regretted his precipitous action in resigning in the light of the facts of the case; but when the Dáil assembled at 10 p.m. Lynch announced that he had asked the President to accept the resignation of Kevin Boland.[292] He resigned on 7 May 1970. There was one further resignation at a junior level: Paudge Brennan quit as parliamentary secretary to the Minister for Local Government.

Lynch showed decisiveness, firmness and resolve when the Dáil met on 8 May and went into a continuous 36-hour session, until 10 p.m. on 9 May. It was a bruising affair. John Healy wrote that Fianna Fáil had taken a battering 'the like of which has not been seen in the House in this generation.'[293] In his 'Backbencher' column Healy stated: 'Honest Jack . . . when he's put to it, can give you the hurling stick in the ribs as good as the next.'[294] But what did the immediate future hold? Blaney returned, via Northern Ireland, to Co. Donegal and to a hero's welcome. Some seven thousand people turned out to greet him as his cavalcade took him through Lifford to Letterkenny. His speech was defiant.[295]

At the other end of the country, the mood in Cork was defiantly loyal to Lynch. A man in Patrick Street told a reporter: 'Jack is tough, boy, and we always knew that, even if they didn't in Dublin. He's his own man, and no daw [fool].' However, Fianna Fáil party organisers were not organising any public celebrations, because, as one said, 'Jack doesn't like that sort of thing.'[296]

The governments of the United States, Britain and other European countries viewed with concern what was happening in Dublin. That concern also extended to President Éamon de Valera. Originally, Berry had breached protocol by phoning him over the conspiracy. But in the wake of the cataclysm of 6 May, de Valera needed to be sure that Lynch had the resilience to stand up to the pressure. Maurice Moynihan, who had retired as governor of the Central Bank in early 1969, was called to the Phoenix Park to discuss the crisis with the President. They met on 17 May 1970 at the Áras. Just as in the old days (as private secretary to de Valera from 1932 and secretary of the Government from 1937 to 1960), Moynihan had prepared a minute for 'the Chief'. His style was characteristically direct, raising in the first instance the option of a policy of armed assistance from the South. That would do more harm than good, he wrote: it might lead to war over the whole of the island and might result in the reoccupation of the country by British forces. Blaney, in spite of those dangers, had argued that the Government should at least not prevent the supply of arms and ammunition for the defence of Northern Catholics. Moynihan speculated that Blaney might feel that the Government should connive at the supply of arms and ammunition or even allow armed force, though perhaps not the army, to go to fight in Northern Ireland.

Moynihan stated that there was a widespread belief that Blaney wished to displace Lynch as Taoiseach and that he saw the party as his means to the leadership. In that context, Moynihan believed that the country was going through a time of great danger. In those circumstances any head of Government had to steel himself to accept fully the responsibilities of his office. The Taoiseach was obliged to devote all his energies to carrying them out, regardless of any sacrifice to himself or to his personal feelings. Moynihan reported that there was one school of thought that Lynch would not be reluctant to relinquish the office of Taoiseach if he could do so honourably, for example by being the successful candidate at the next presidential election. Moynihan felt that there was a need to end all such speculation. If Lynch wished earnestly to provide a strong and stable Government he should announce at an early party meeting, his next if possible, that he was determined to retain the leadership and that he would not be a candidate in the next presidential election in any circumstances. As long as he remained leader, the Northern policy of the party would be that of peace.

Moynihan was of the view that nobody could remain a member of the party under Lynch's leadership unless he accepted that policy expressly and without reservations. Anyone speaking or acting at variance with that policy would be expelled. Lynch might challenge Fianna Fáil that if they did not wish him to remain as leader on those terms he would forthwith, as Taoiseach, make a statement on the position in Dáil Éireann and advise the President to dissolve the Dáil.

There is no evidence that de Valera acted on the advice laid out by Moynihan. But, given the unprecedented danger confronting the country, it appears very likely that the President spoke in those terms to the Taoiseach. Fears about Lynch were unfounded. He was determined to provide the necessary leadership to drive his way through the crisis. On a visit to Cork he rounded on a number of critics at a public meeting and told them that there was only one Government policy on Northern Ireland. That was the message carried throughout the summer of 1970.

'WE STAND ON THE BRINK OF A GREAT ACHIEVEMENT'

On 10 May, Lynch had 'handed to the Attorney General all the copy documents given to me by Mr. Berry for whatever action he, the Attorney General, decided. I had nothing further to do with the matter or with the subsequent trial.'

The law took its course. On 27 May, James Kelly, John Kelly and Albert Luykx were arrested on charges of conspiring to illegally import arms. Haughey and Blaney were held on similar charges the following day. The reverberations within Fianna Fáil were profound. Kevin Boland—who was not implicated in any way in the plot to bring in arms—accused Lynch of felon-setting and demanded a special meeting of the parliamentary party to remove him as leader. Lynch fought back. He strongly defended his stance against gun-running:

> Arms imported for defensive purposes could easily, in the tense situation which exists in the North, be used for offensive purposes, thus precipitating a situation which could escalate into civil war, not only in the Six-County area, but which could easily overspill into the Twenty-Six Counties.

He dispelled speculation about a general election.[297]

When the parliamentary party met on 3 June, Boland refused after a three-hour debate to withdraw his 'treachery' allegations. The meeting resumed on the 4th, when Boland was expelled from the parliamentary party in a secret ballot, by 60 votes to 11.[298] Lynch then faced a meeting of the National Executive of Fianna Fáil to remove Boland from his position as joint secretary. When the executive met on 22 June, the debate lasted four hours and twenty minutes, after which Boland resigned.[299] His father, Gerry Boland—a founder-member of the party—resigned in protest: 'I want no part of a party where an honourable man like my son appears to be an embarrassment.'[300]

Kevin Boland's departure was a personal tragedy. He had reluctantly taken his seat in the Government in the summer of 1969, being conflicted over Government policy on Northern Ireland. His departure was as unseemly as it was virtually inevitable. High farce was to follow at the ard-fheis in early 1971.

On 2 July, Blaney was carried shoulder-high from the Dublin District Court after the judge had refused informations against him on a charge of conspiracy to import arms and ammunition illegally between 1 March and 24 April 1970. Justice Dónal Kearney returned four other men—Charles Haughey, Albert A. Luykx, James J. Kelly and John Kelly—for trial to the Circuit Criminal Court. As the four men left the court they were loudly clapped by about a hundred supporters.[301]

Lynch, by way of reply to these developments, addressed the nation on Saturday 11 July on radio and television. It was one of the most important speeches of his career. Quoting John Montague's line 'Old moulds are broken in the North,' he told his audience: 'We stand on the brink of a great achievement.' He said to those who would try to stop the realisation of that goal on both sides of the border that there was no solution to be found

in shooting each other. There is no real invader here. We are all Irish in all our different kinds of ways. We must not now or ever in the future show anything to each other except tolerance, forbearance—and neighbourly love.

He added later: 'All Irish traditions are intertwined: let us cherish them all.'[302]

It was, by any standards, a lucid and a remarkable speech. 'The old order is changing,' stated an editorial in the *Irish Times*.[303] That was his answer to Blaney and the dissidents in the party.

Lynch participated in a three-day debate in Dáil Éireann that ended on 30 July. His Government survived. John Healy described it as being 'one of the sharpest' in the history of the Dáil. Blaney made wild allegations about spies and the phone-tapping of TDs. Boland attacked Lynch's speech of 11 July.[304] But the violence continued unabated in Northern Ireland. On 12 August, Lynch appealed again 'to all Irish people to turn their backs on violence so that a better future for us all may be secured.' He condemned the shooting of two RUC men near Crossmaglen, Co. Armagh, and the recent shooting of Daniel O'Hagan.[305] John Healy wrote: 'Fianna Fáil has survived. It may not look like that, with so much hanging fire, but it has survived the worst.'[306]

There was time to travel to west Cork for holidays and the recharging of lost energy. It had been a gruelling few months. Going into the new parliamentary session, Lynch had to face challenges from within his own party and from across the floor of the Dáil. On 28 August 1970 he wrote to his wife, who was on holidays in Majorca:

But to put you in the news. We had a meeting (party) last night ending at midnight. All 73 TDS present. Full support for supplementary Budget and prices and incomes legislation. Labour and FG have put down motion of no confidence in the govt. and me. I put to the party who was going to support us and in this—final result 70 to 3 in favour. Dail commences today and votes of confidence likely to be taken soon. If 3 votes against includes [?] K boland it could mean a 71-71 result in the Dail. At a press conference afterwards I said I would wait the result of the confidence motion before deciding on a gen. Election. I rang John Gleeson this morning. No change in Eileen. She is keeping fairly comfortable. Looking forward so much to your home-coming.

The Government survived.

THE ARMS TRIAL

Boland and Blaney kept up their attacks on Lynch in September. The former said in a speech that he did not want Fianna Fáil to turn into 'a party of Molly Maguires.' He stressed the need for adhering to the republican tradition. He warned against pragmatism and the lure of office.[307]

The funeral of a founder-member of the party, Dr James Ryan, provided an opportunity for a show of unity. The veteran of the 1916 Rising and War of Independence had died on 25 September. Lynch said he was 'a wise counsellor and a superb administrator; one could not wish for a more loyal colleague or for a more generous or enjoyable comrade than Jim Ryan.'[308] Lynch led the attendance at the funeral, which followed Requiem Mass in Greystones, Co. Wicklow. Ryan was given a state funeral with military honours. Members of the opposition from the Civil War period also attended. The graveside oration was given by a party elder and contemporary of Ryan, Seán MacEntee, who spoke of the deceased's love of Ireland, the land, and the people who worked it. President Éamon de Valera was in attendance.[309]

On 22 September the 'Arms Trial' began, Mr Justice Aindrias Ó Caoimh presiding. It was stopped on 29 September—the day following the James Ryan funeral—after an exchange of views between the judge and a defence counsel. The jury was discharged. A new trial opened on 6 October and lasted fourteen days. On 23 October, the four defendants were acquitted. The writer Tom MacIntyre described what happened.

The place flies asunder to a brute roar, timber, bodies, spin of faces, that roar, it dips, renews itself—but a cleaner poetry, abruptly, through the fury, beyond it, where, on a span of wall between Bench and jury-box, the sealed windowless weeks are in procession through two open doors.[310]

The four acquitted were carried shoulder-high from the court to cheers of 'We want Charlie' and jeers and catcalls demanding 'Lynch must go.' Inside the nearby Four Courts Hotel about five hundred supporters of the four sang 'A nation once again' amid roars of 'We are republican Fianna Fáil.' Haughey, caught up in the heat of the moment, told an impromptu press conference:

> I was never in any doubt that it was a political trial. There is some dis-satisfaction with the Taoiseach at the moment [laughter]. I will have to confine myself to that remark.

Earlier he said: 'The political implications will be far-reaching.'

He did not think that Lynch had represented Fianna Fáil policy as he explained it at the United Nations a few days previously. He said there was a fundamental difference in policy but it would take too long to elaborate. 'I think those that were responsible for this debacle have no alternative but to take the honourable course that is open to them.' He replied when asked to explain: 'I think it is pretty evident.'

Haughey refused to speculate on the question of party leadership. He said that he had been mentioned in the past as a candidate for Taoiseach, and 'I am not ruling out anything.'[311]

Lynch heard the news of the acquittals in New York, where, the day before the verdict, he had addressed the General Assembly of the United Nations. At a press conference he said he would meet any challenge to his leadership with confidence. He had received a mandate in the general election in 1969. He had the unanimous or near-unanimous backing of the recent ard-fheis. He said he would not take Haughey back into the Government. The ministers had been sacked because he, Lynch, could not fully rely upon them.

While he was not questioning the acquittal, there had been an attempt to import arms illegally. There was, he said, a legal method of importing arms, as was well known. His former colleagues had not kept him informed, and there was, therefore, a lack of mutual trust and confidence.[312] When asked to define republicanism, he said: 'Republicanism doesn't mean guns. It doesn't mean using guns. It is the state of a nation.'[313]

Blaney was in open revolt. An *Irish Times* editorial quoted him as having said on British television that had he been Taoiseach he would have sent the army into the North.[314] He told RTE that there was an honourable course open to Lynch and that he, like Haughey, would expect him to take it. He did not think that the party would tolerate the continuation in office of Lynch, Colley and Gibbons. As far as Blaney was concerned, any new leader of the party would have to be a traditional republican, 'otherwise he would not be my cup of tea.' He would support Haughey for Taoiseach. If the majority of the party wanted it, he said he would be prepared to become Taoiseach.[315]

Lynch returned to Dublin, via Shannon Airport, on 26 October. He was greeted at Shannon by a large number of party workers and activists from Cos. Clare and Limerick, including the Minister for Justice, Desmond O'Malley. He told journalists: 'I'm ready to meet any challenge that comes up, I assure you. I am, of course, taking it seriously.'[316] In Dublin he was met at the airport by the entire Government, with two exceptions, who were out of the country on official business, and some fifty TDs and senators. The political correspondent of the *Irish Times,* Michael McInerney, wrote that the Taoiseach was also 'surrounded at the airport by the 1916–1923 Republican Old Guard of Mr Frank Aiken, Mr Seán MacEntee, Mr Paddy Smith and Mr Mick Hilliard, the solid hard-core of the foundation Establishment.' He wrote that many saw the complete traditional republican blessing given to Lynch by the presence of the representative of President de Valera, Máirtín Ó Flaitheartaigh. McInerney concluded that

if anyone, after that display, wishes to say that they are better Republicans than Mr Lynch in Fianna Fáil, then they have a formidable task . . . It was the Republic *par excellence.*[317]

Lynch was uncompromising at the press conference. There would be no new policy statement, he said.

We have our party policy stated. I went before the electorate a year and a half ago on an agreed policy and my party and I got a very enthusiastic vote from the people and endorsement of our policy and programme, and I have no new proposals to put to the party as far as policy is concerned.

Writing that evening to Máirín in Majorca, he began:

Darling, The plane arrived in about 10.45 am and of course had the press conference—this time much bigger than usual because of the acquittal in the arms conspiracy case. I will not say much in this letter in case it does not reach you in time. Great demonstrations after the acquittal verdict last Friday and challenges about the leadership.

He continued:

Political scene very lively and somewhat intense but support seems as strong as ever. I was busy right up to the end . . . No let up since I came over—this week and the following are going to be tough. But in the mean-time you enjoy yourself and come back replenished and reinvigorated. We will need all our strength and RESISTANCE TOGETHER [double underlining]. My regards to Marion.[318]

If Lynch had an unmerited reputation for weakness, over the following days he showed that his critics and enemies were mistaken. He exhibited a determination reminiscent of a number of his predecessors in that post, from both sides, during the Civil War or the Second World War. That night, the 27th, he won a vote of confidence from the parliamentary party, by 70 votes to 3. He held a meeting of the Government the following day. At a press conference afterwards he said he was reserving his position on the issue of a general election and would decide after the no-confidence vote in the Dáil in two weeks' time. He said there had been no discussion on the expulsion of the three dissident ministers.

On 28 October the Taoiseach survived a vote in the Dáil by 75 to 67. Kevin Boland, unable to vote with the Government, stepped down. The Fianna Fáil TD and Dublin footballer Des Foley resigned his seat on 4 November. On 10 November, Blaney and Brennan voted with the opposition in a vote of no confidence in Jim Gibbons. Both were expelled from the parliamentary party a week later. Only Haughey remained. He was there for the long haul. Tom MacIntyre wrote:

Few Governments would have survived the tumultuous aftermath of the trial—but, in Dublin, the Party, long in power, kept power ... Oh, Cabbage Republic, 'tis of thee we sing.[319]

KEEPING A DIGNIFIED SILENCE

In the controversies that swirled around in the following years, why did Lynch rarely choose to defend himself from the attacks on his veracity? On one occasion in the Dáil he denied that any money had been used for the purpose of purchasing arms for distribution in Northern Ireland. In May 1970 he said:

I do not think the house could expect nor could I give any more inform-ation about the disposal of Secret Service funds. However, I want to add that I made specific inquiries as to whether any moneys could have been voted or could have been paid for out of Exchequer funds or out of any public funds in respect of a consignment of arms of the size we have been dealing with and I am assured that there was not nor could not have been.[320]

It is now evident that Lynch had made that statement in good faith. He had received the information from two excellent sources. The secretary of the Department of Finance, Charles Murray, wrote a minute on 4 November 1970 regarding the debate on Northern Ireland Relief and on the assurance Lynch had given the Dáil.

> In the Dáil yesterday Deputy FitzGerald referred to the assurance given by the Taoiseach that the money for the arms purchase had not come from any Government fund. He went on to state (as reported in the *Irish Times* today):— 'All the Taoiseach had to do was to ask the appropriate officials in the Department of Finance and they would have told him where that money had gone. But he had not gone that far . . .'

Murray went on to explain his own role in the framing of this statement:

> The Taoiseach's statement was based on information which I gave him, at his request. My information, in turn, was based on a very hurried reading of the papers relating to the Northern Ireland Grant-in-Aid. As is clear from the report which I subsequently prepared at greater leisure (on 9 October, 1970) these papers make no reference to the use of the funds for the purchase of arms. They show various small payments to certain— apparently reputable—individuals, and the bulk of the expenditure going to the Red Cross which, in turn, paid most of it to a Belfast fund for the relief of distress. On the information available early in May last (and without the benefit of hindsight) it was not possible to deduce from the official papers that these payments had been used to finance the purchase of arms, legally or otherwise.[321]

The secretary of the Department of the Taoiseach, Nicholas Nolan, wrote a minute to the Taoiseach on 4 November 1970, asking:

> Why would you not read out the text of the manuscript note which I passed over to you during the course of the Dáil debate last May? It seems to me to be grossly unfair that you should be attacked for statements made by you in this house on the basis of information conveyed to you in all good faith, of course, *and on the basis of the information then available*— by the Secretary to the Government and by the Secretary of the Department of Finance, the head of the Civil Service.[322]

Lynch, who had once been a civil servant, would have had to shift responsibility for his error to the two most senior civil servants in the country. Both had given him information—wrong, as it turned out—based on their reading of the documents on file. Lynch had an old-fashioned respect for both civil servants, Nolan and Murray, who served the state with such loyalty and professionalism.

Documents compiled in the autumn of 1970 by an investigation carried out under Chief Superintendent Fleming explained in great detail how the fund was used.

AN GARDA SÍOCHÁNA   METROPOLITAN AREA
3C/437/70 SECRET
Deputy Commissioner,
DMA.
Arms Conspiracy Trial: question of misuse of Public Monies.
(John P. Fleming)
CHIEF SUPERINTENDENT.

Reference to minute from the Secretary, Dept. of Justice of the 27th inst. and further to my report of the 1st August to the Commissioner and to the Chief State Solicitor of the 24th September, in connection with the above, I give hereunder a report on the up-to-date position of the investigation:—

On the 16/8/1969, the Government decided, inter alia, that : 'A sum of money—the amount and channel of disbursement of which would be determined by the Minister for Finance—should be made available from the Exchequer to provide aid for the victims of the current unrest in the Six Counties.' On the same date—16/8/69—the Government Information Bureau announced that: 'The Minister for Finance will make funds available for the relief of victims of the disturbances in the Six Counties and he will have an early consultation with the Chairman of the Irish Red Cross.'

Investigations show that £100,000 was made available by the Government and that the Minister for Finance at that time—Charles J. Haughey, TD.—would appear to have been responsible for its administration. This fund was know as the: 'Northern Ireland Relief Expenditure (Grant in Aid)' and was administered by Mr Anthony J. Fagan, Principal Officer in the Dept. of Finance, on Mr. Haughey's instructions.

As a result of investigations into the alleged conspiracy to import arms and ammunition illegally into the State, it was strongly suspected that monies from this fund were used to purchase the arms and ammunition. Orders under the Bankers Books Evidence (Amendment) Act, 1959, were obtained after the accused had been arrested on a conspiracy charge. It was established that an account had been opened at the Clones branch of the Bank of Ireland on the 9/10/1969 under the title—'The Belfast Committee for the relief of Distressed'[323] in the names of Patrick Kennedy, 200 Upper Newtownards Road, Belfast; Patrick McGrory, 1, Old Cavehill Road, Belfast and Patrick Joseph Devlin, 39, Greenan, Shaw's Road, Belfast. The total amount paid into this account was £15,000. The first £5000 was paid in by the Red Cross from Red Cross funds on the 9/10/1969 and the remaining £10,000 (ten thousand pounds) was paid from the 'Northern Ireland Relief Expenditure (Grant in Aid)' through the Irish Red Cross (No. 2 Account), Bank of Ireland, College Green, Dublin 2, as follows: £5000 on the 17th October, 1969 per Payable Order No. 02 13029 07 and £5000 on the 4th November, 1969 per Payable Order No. 02 13068 08. Bank Records show that, at present, there is a credit balance of £48. 11. 8. in this account in the Clones branch of the Bank of Ireland.

Endorsements on cheques drawn on the above account show that on the 10th October 1969 a Sean Mateer drew out the sum of £2000; on the 17th October, 1969 Patrick Kennedy drew out the sum of £2000; on the 24th October, 1969 a Seán Mateer again drew the sum of £2000 and on the 5th November, 1969 a John Kelly drew the sum of £2000. Two further cheques drawn on the account have not been endorsed and there is nothing to indicate who drew the cash on them. One cheque is for the sum of £2500 and is dated the 10th November, 1969 while the second cheque is for the sum of £4450 and is dated the 18th November, 1969.

Patrick Kennedy and Patrick Joseph Devlin referred to above are both Members of Parliament in Northern Ireland and Patrick McGrory is a Solicitor at the address given and is believed to be associated with the Belfast Citizens' Defence Committee. The person signing himself 'Seán Mateer' is unknown and the signature 'John Kelly' may be that of one of the accused, John Kelly 12 Adela Street, Belfast, who is Chairman of the Belfast Citizens' Defence Committee.

It appears from our enquiries that Captain James J. Kelly was acting as a liaison between the holders of the account and Mr. Haughey and Mr. Anthony J. Fagan in the Department of Finance. In November 1969 Captain James J. Kelly had a discussion with Anthony J. Fagan, Department of Finance, in the course of which he said that having the account in Clones was too inconvenient and that he wished to have it transferred to Dublin. Fagan then contacted Mr. William Walsh, Deputy Manager of the Munster and Leinster Bank, 2 Lower Baggot Street, by telephone, and told Mr. Walsh that a Mr. J. Kelly would be calling on him, that he was known to Mr. Fagan, and that he (Kelly) wished to transfer an account concerning the aid to Northern Ireland to the Baggot Street bank. Anthony J. Fagan due to his position in the Department of Finance was well known to Mr. Walsh and the Management of the Munster and

Leinster Bank, 2 Lower Baggot Street. Fagan at all times understood that Kelly was transferring the account from Clones and that this account would be identical with the Clones account as regards title and names.

Enquiries show that on the 11th November, 1969 a fresh account was opened in the Munster and Leinster Bank, 2 Lower Baggot Street under the title 'Relief Committee of Belfast Fund for the Relief of Distress' in the names of: 'John White, John Loughran and Roger Murphy' all of Cook Street, Belfast. It has not yet been established who opened this account. Enquiries have revealed, however, that the names: 'John White, John Loughran and Roger Murphy' are fictitious and that no persons by those names reside at Cook Street, Belfast. The Ledger Card relating to the account: 'Relief Committee of Belfast Fund for the Relief of Distress' has the following instruction typed on the top right-hand corner: 'Do not send out statement, no correspondence to be sent out, all enquiries to A. J. Fagan.' Mr. Fagan, however, insists that he never heard of: 'John White' 'John Loughran' or 'Roger Murphy' and that he did not authorise either Captain Kelly, the Munster and Leinster Bank or anybody else to have enquiries relating to this account addressed to him. He never received any such enquiries, bank statements, returned cheques or information of any kind concerning this account from the Bank.

The Ledger Card relating to this account shows that a total of £59,000 was paid into this account by the Irish Red Cross Society. In a statement of the 26th June, 1970, Anthony J. Fagan states that this £59,000 was paid in small amounts from the 'Northern Ireland Relief Expenditure (Grant in Aid)' into the No. 2 Account of the Irish Red Cross Society, Bank of Ireland, College Green, Dublin on the written directions of Mr. Charles J. Haughey who, at that time, was Minister for Finance. Mr. Fagan clarifies the position further by giving the dates on which those payments were made, the amount paid on each of the dates mentioned, and the number of the Payable Order issued by the Department of Finance in respect of each transaction.

The withdrawals from the 'Belfast Fund for Relief of Distress' account, as above, according to the Ledger Card, were all cash transactions with the exception of five (5). The exceptions are as follows:

On 5th December, 1969 the sum of £2,000 was paid to J. J. Kelly when he cashed cheque No. 354054;
On 6th January, 1970 the sum of £13,000 was paid to a 'George Dixon' when he cashed cheque No. 354058;
On 20th February, 1970 the sum of £12,000 was again paid to 'George Dixon' when he cashed cheque No. 354064;

On 13th March, 1970 the sum of £4,000 was again paid to 'George Dixon' when he cashed cheque No. 354065;

On 25th March, 1970 the sum of £4,000 was again paid to 'George Dixon' when he cashed cheque No. 354066.

A note of the Ledger Card for this account shows that the returned cheques were collected from the Bank on the 22nd January, 1970 and again on the 16th March, 1970. The Bank staff are unable to give any information as to who collected those cheques but Mr. Anthony Fagan emphatically denies having received them. When the account was inspected by Detective Inspectors Edward J. O'Dea and Patrick Doocey on the 4th June, 1970 there were only three returned cheques available as follows:—

Cheque No. 354066 for the sum of £4,000 marked 'Pay Cash.' This cheque was signed by 'John Loughran' and 'Roger Murphy' and was dated the 25th March, 1970.

Cheque No. 354068 for the sum of £1,000 marked 'Pay Cash' signed by 'John Loughran' and 'Roger Murphy' dated the 3rd April, 1970.

Cheque No. 354070 for the sum of £1,000 marked 'Pay Cash' signed by 'John Loughran' and 'Roger Murphy' and dated the 17th April, 1970.

The last entry in the Ledger Card for this account was on the 28th April, 1970 and shows a Credit Balance of £2,842. 17. 6.

On the 24th June, 1970, as a result of information received, I obtained further Orders under the Bankers Books Evidence (Amendment) Act, 1959 relating to the accounts of a 'George Dixon' and 'Ann O'Brien' at the Munster and Leinster Bank, 2 Lower Baggot Street. On the 25th June, 1970, accompanied by Detective Inspector O'Dea, I carried out an inspection of both those accounts. The Ledger Card relating to the 'George Dixon' account showed that this account had been opened on the 14th November, 1969 and that a lodgement of £11,450 had been made on the same date. No Lodgement Docket was available for this transaction.

On the 6th January, 1970 the sum of £13,000 was lodged by a 'J. Clarke' to this account.

On the 20th February, 1970 the sum of £13,000 was lodged to this account. The name of the person who made this lodgement cannot be deciphered from the document in my possession.

On the 13th March, 1970 the sum of £4,000 was lodged by 'J. J. Kelly.'

On the 25th March, 1970 the sum of £1,000 was lodged by 'P. Kennedy.'

It will be noted that: on the 6th January 1970 the sum of £13,000 was paid to 'George Dixon' out of the 'Belfast Fund for the Relief of Distress' account and on the same date this amount (£13,000) was lodged to the 'George Dixon' account.

On the 20th February, 1970 the sum of £12,000 was paid to 'George Dixon' out of the 'Belfast Fund for Relief of Distress' account and on the same date a similar amount was lodged to the 'George Dixon' account.

On the 13th March, 1970 the sum of £4,000 was paid to 'George Dixon' out of the 'Belfast Fund for Relief of Distress' and on the same date a similar amount was lodged to the 'George Dixon' account.

On the 25th March, 1970 the sum of £4,000 was again paid into the [crossed out] to 'George Dixon' out of the 'Belfast Fund for the Relief of Distress' account and on the same date the sum of £1,000 was lodged to the 'George Dixon' account.

In all, a total of £41,450 was lodged to the 'George Dixon' account. The last cheque drawn on this account was on the 17th April, 1970 and the Ledger card for that date shows a credit balance of £200 in the account. A note on this Ledger Card shows that the returned cheques were collected from the Bank on the 22nd January, 1970 and again on the 16th March, 1970. Those are also the dates on which the returned cheques relating to the 'Belfast Fund for the Relief of Distress' account were collected.

When I inspected the 'George Dixon' account on the 25th June, 1970 there were only three returned cheques available as follows:

Cheque No. M. 925392 for the sum of £200, marked 'Pay Cash', signed 'G. Dixon' and dated the 13th March, 1970.

Cheque No. M. 925393 for the sum of £200, marked 'Pay Cash', signed 'G. Dixon' and dated the 25th March, 1970.

Cheque No. M. 925394 for the sum of £600, marked 'Pay to Cash', signed 'G. Dixon' and dated the 17th April, 1970.

The Ledger Card in respect of this Account had the following heading:-

'Dixon George, c/o 2 Lower Baggot Street, Dublin 2; Business Man; No correspondence whatever. All enquiries to A. J. Fagan c/a.'

The Ledger Card relating to the 'Ann O'Brien' account shows that this account had also been opened on the 14th November, 1969 and that a lodgement of £2,500 had been made on that date. The Lodgement Docket for this transaction shows that this amount was lodged by: 'A. O'Brien, Stephen's Green.' Other Lodgement Dockets relating to this account show the following lodgements:—

11th December 1969   £1,000 lodged by 'George Dixon';
22nd December, 1969   £1,000 transferred from the 'George Dixon' account;
12 February 1970   £1,000 transferred from the 'George Dixon' account;
25th March, 1970   £1,000 lodged by 'P. Kennedy.'

In all, a total of £6,500 was lodged to this account.

A note on the Ledger Card shows that the returned cheques for this account were also collected on the 16th March, 1970.

When I inspected this account on the 25th June, 1970 there were only two returned cheques available as follows:—

Cheque No. M. 925411 for the sum of £500, marked 'Pay Cash', signed 'Ann O'Brien' and dated the 31st March 1970.

Cheque No. M. 925414 for the sum of £900, marked 'Pay to Cash', signed 'Ann O'Brien' and dated the 17th April, 1970.

This was the last cheque drawn on the 'Ann O'Brien' account and the Ledger Card for that date—17th April, 1970—shows a Credit Balance of £49. 13. 9.

The Ledger Card for this account also shows that a 'Mr. S. Brady' cashed three cheques drawn on this account as follows:

On the 11th December, 1969 cheque No. 925401 for the sum of £800;

On the 2nd January, 1970 cheque No. 925405 for the sum of £500;

On the 16th January, 1970 cheque No. 925407 for the sum of £600.

There is nothing on the Ledger Card to indicate who else drew money from this account as the remaining withdrawals are marked 'Pay Cash.' This Ledger Card bears the following heading:

'O'Brien, Ann, St. Stephen's Green, Dublin 2; Spinster; Clerk. Introduced by A. J. Fagan; Care—no correspondence.'

In a statement of the 26th June, 1970 Mr. Anthony J. Fagan emphatically denied having ever heard of either 'George Dixon' or 'Ann O'Brien' or of Bank Accounts in those two names at the Baggot Street branch of the Munster and Leinster Bank. He also stated that he never received any enquiries, Bank Statements, returned cheques or information of any kind concerning those two accounts and was not aware that they were in existence.

On the 1st July, 1970, accompanied by Detective Inspector Edward J. O'Dea, I interviewed Mr. William Walsh who had been Deputy Manager of the Munster and Leinster Bank, 2 Lower Baggot Street, Dublin, from September, 1968 to December, 1969. He made a statement in writing, a copy of which is attached. He stated that on or about the 11th November, 1969, he received a telephone call from Mr. A. J. Fagan concerning the opening of an account in his Bank for the relief of distress in Northern Ireland and that this account was subsequently opened in the names of 'White', 'Loughran' and 'Murphy.' He was unable to state what member of the bank staff dealt with the person who opened this account and he never met either 'White', 'Loughran' or 'Murphy.' He also stated that he received a second telephone call from Mr. A. J. Fagan intimating that he wished to open two other separate accounts and that a Mr. J. Kelly would call to see him and make the necessary arrangements. He further stated that later on the same date Captain James Kelly called to the bank and arranged with him to open two separate accounts; that he handed two signature cards to Kelly who subsequently returned them in the names of 'George Dixon' and 'Ann O'Brien.' He never met either 'George Dixon' or 'Ann O'Brien.' Walsh also said that he understood from his telephone conversation with A. J. Fagan that the accounts opened in the names of 'George Dixon' and 'Ann O'Brien' were subsidiary accounts and would be funded from the joint account in the names 'White', 'Loughran' and 'Murphy' which, in turn, would be funded through the Irish Red Cross Society. He confirmed that he had, on a few occasions, been involved in cashing cheques for Captain James Kelly drawn on the accounts of 'George Dixon' and 'Ann O'Brien' and that, on at least one of those occasions, Kelly asked him for English currency.

Thomas D. Moore, Head Ledger-Keeper at the Munster and Leinster Bank, 2 Lower Baggot Street was also interviewed on the 1st July, 1970 and a statement in writing obtained from him. He was unable to give much assistance beyond the fact that Paddy Kennedy, Republican-Labour M.P., had, on occasions, cashed cheques in the bank and that Captain James Kelly had cashed cheques drawn on the 'George Dixon' and 'Ann O'Brien' accounts. The 'S. Brady' referred to as having cashed cheques drawn on the 'Ann O'Brien' account is identical with Seamus Brady, former Editor of the 'Voice of the North' publication.

On the 18th September, 1970 I interviewed Mr. B. Deacon, Manager of the Munster and Leinster Bank, 2 Lower Baggot Street. He was unable to assist me in any way and said he had no dealings with the various accounts referred to herein. He declined to make a written statement.

On the 21st July, 1970, accompanied by Detective Inspector Doocey, I interviewed Mrs. Leslie Bean de Barra, Chairman of the Irish Red Cross Society, and Miss Mary B. Murphy, Secretary of the Society. Both ladies refused to answer any questions or to make written statements. Mrs. de Barra stated, however, that they would be more than willing to co-operate if they were given in writing a list of the questions to which we required answers. Later that day—21st July, 1970—I handed questionnaires to Mrs. De Barra and Miss Murphy, on the understanding that their answers would be given to me on the following day. I received their replies to the various questions on the 18th September 1970. Photocopy of the questions and answers received is attached.

It will be seen from the foregoing report that the money from the 'Northern Ireland Relief Expenditure (Grant in Aid)' was first paid into the No. 2 account of the Irish Red Cross Society, Bank of Ireland, College Green, from which £15000 was transferred to the Kennedy, Devlin and McGrory account, Bank of Ireland, Clones, and £59000 was transferred into the 'White, Loughran and Murphy' account in the Munster and Leinster Bank, 2 Lower Baggot Street, Dublin 4. From the latter account money was transferred into the 'George Dixon' and 'Ann O'Brien' accounts which were being operated by Captain James Kelly. No approach has been made to Captain James Kelly or any of the others involved regarding the operation of the accounts.

Investigations are continuing and I have requested the Law Agent for the Munster and Leinster Bank Ltd., 2 Lower Baggot Street not to release any documents relating to the 'Relief of Distress Account' or the subsidiary accounts in the names of 'George Dixon' and 'Ann O'Brien' to any person before being made available for scrutiny by me. He has promised his full co-operation in the matter.[324]

(John P. Fleming)

CHIEF SUPERINTENDENT.

The Committee of Public Accounts, under an order of Dáil Éireann dated 1 December 1970, conducted a detailed inquiry into the circumstances surrounding the spending of the money referred to in the report by Chief Superintendent Fleming. The first sittings were in January 1971 and it sat for almost a year. This was one of the most outstanding exercises conducted since the foundation of the state. The committee examined in minute detail the money trail, interviewing senior civil servants and all major actors in the complex web of events surrounding the attempt to import arms in 1970 and subjecting them to the most exacting interrogation. A detailed examination of the outstanding work of that committee, which is outside the scope of this book, ought to be the subject of a major historical study.

'YOU CAN HAVE BOLAND BUT YOU CANNOT HAVE FIANNA FAIL': THE 1971 ARD-FHEIS

It is now time to return to the first weeks of January 1971. Lynch was correct to anticipate an even more difficult ard-fheis than that of 1970. I do not know who drafted his speech on this occasion: it may have been Ken Whitaker, and Martin O'Donoghue may also have been involved. But the speech— strong, determined and courageous as it was—was overshadowed by the extraordinary events of that weekend.

The *Irish Times* published a front-page story on the opening day of the ard-fheis, 20 February 1971, reporting that 4,500 delegates were coming to the RDS hall in Ballsbridge. One unnamed minister had told the paper the previous night: 'They are coming to Dublin from under the stones, from the high roads and by-roads, from every village to demonstrate for Jack and they will not tolerate anything that makes for disunity.' The article also spoke of the dangers

of division over the events of the past year and the question of partition.[325]
John Healy of the *Irish Times* described 1970 as 'one glorious bloody year' for
Jack Lynch: 'The proof of it is there this morning—a greater rallying than ever
before in the history of Fianna Fáil, and not a wan of them with warts on the
palm of his hands the way they couldn't clap enthusiastically.'[326]

The political correspondent of the *Irish Independent*, Chris Glennon, set
the scene for one of the greatest tests of Lynch's leadership skills. Could he
keep the party from splitting? Writing on 20 February 1971, Glennon reported
that Lynch's support 'throughout the cumainn seems quite likely to succeed
. . . [and] there is unlikely to be any real controversy.' According to party
supporters, Lynch was 'so firmly in control, that any dissident elements will
await a better time to launch an assault on his policies or his leadership.'[327]

A motion signed by twenty-nine cumainn, comhairlí dáilcheantair
(constituency councils) and comhairlí ceantair (district councils) recorded
confidence in the Taoiseach and the Government and pledged unwavering
support in their efforts to end partition by peaceful means, in accordance with
the traditional policy of the party. While Glennon felt that there remained the
possibility of some demonstrations, or a walk-out, 'the nearer the approach of
the Ard Fheis the less likely this has seemed.' He did expect that the debate on
the Border before the party leader's speech would be quite difficult.[328]

In another article, Glennon wrote about the demanding role of the chairman of the ard-fheis and of the limits being imposed on speaking. He stated
that Kevin Boland, who had been known to speak for six hours and more in
the Dáil, might find it difficult to restrict himself to five minutes on the
Northern question. He felt that the same applied to Neil Blaney—'another
noted for his ability to put a fantastic number of words, into a speech even a
relatively short one (for him) of 10–15 minutes.'[329] What will happen, Glennon
asked, if he decided to speak? Either of the two would get 'rapt attention,' he
thought. There might be an opportunity to launch an attack on the party
leadership. Asking a Government minister if he was looking forward to the
weekend, Glennon received the reply: 'I'm looking forward to a very interesting weekend.' Concluding his article, Glennon wrote: 'A sentiment that may in
the end of the year review, rank as the political understatement of the year.'[330]

Lynch presided over what turned out to be an uproarious gathering of
'some 5,000 delegates,' according to the *Irish Times* on 22 February 1971.
Declaring the ard-fheis open, he was given a standing ovation by delegates.

Events got off to a stormy start when the standing orders proposed by
the chairman, Paddy Smith, were challenged. Smith intervened to say that
delegates were being confined to three minutes.[331] When the first delegate,
Maurice Downey, was invited to speak, another delegate, Joan Buckley, took to
the rostrum to protest against the shortening of the speaking time. There was

chaos for fifteen minutes. Amid the din, the remark 'We will continue under the leadership of our Taoiseach, Jack Lynch' merited a standing ovation. Buckley finally left the platform and was escorted back to the floor of the hall. Two delegates then spoke against the adoption of the secretary's report.

The atmosphere of the weekend was captured in the following episode. When the Minister for Agriculture, Jim Gibbons, rose to speak he could scarcely be heard as a group of delegates shouted 'Judas,' 'perjurer' and 'traitor.' One group of delegates shouted 'We want Jim,' while others chanted 'Out, out, out!'[332]

What is most remembered, however, is the ferocity and determination with which a usually mild-mannered Patrick Hillery held the floor, in spite of terrible verbal and physical intimidation. When Hillery was called to the podium, Kevin Boland appeared on the platform as if to speak. Uproar continued for several minutes amid cheers and jeers and shouts of 'Free speech' and 'We want Jack.' Fist-fights broke out below the podium. Lynch appealed for calm. Amid the din, Hillery said that the Lynch policy was that of de Valera and Lemass. Those who were causing disturbances would not be allowed to prevent the ard-fheis from deciding policy, he said. They would continue the party policy despite the bully-boys in the organisation. He asked the ard-fheis to make up its mind. They were dealing with the enemies of the party.

> We can no longer stay silent. We have been silent since last May. We have been silent for the sake of the country. If people want a reply, they will have it. They can no longer claim to be members of Fianna Fáil.[333]

Boland, with curled index finger, baited Hillery, inviting him to 'come on, come on.' The rostrum was toppled over as the ex-minister was led down to the floor of the hall amid scuffles and exchanges of punches between rival delegates.[334] Nell McCafferty, an *Irish Times* reporter, wrote: 'The crowd came to blows, and a woman pushed past me, advising me to get out of the arena.'[335] It was a fist-fight reminiscent of a Wild West saloon. On the podium, Erskine Childers sat with his head in his hands. Amid the din and the uproar Hillery continued:

> If you succeed in getting rid of one of us, there will be more of us. Fianna Fáil will survive. You can have Boland, but you cannot have Fianna Fáil.

At that point the treasurer's report was adopted. There were charges that delegates were being allowed to jump the queue, and this led to disorder near the rostrum.

An appeal for calm and unity came from an unlikely source. Neil Blaney, joint treasurer of the party, made a conciliatory speech.[336]

John Healy reported that by the late Saturday afternoon 'you were either for Jack or against him. There was no middle ground.' He said that the ten 'dissenting minutes of Saturday morning swelled on Saturday night, to three hours of sustained dissent and counter-dissent.' It would go into the files, he wrote, as the three most difficult hours a Fianna Fáil president ever had to endure in public. The atmosphere was like what it must have been at Madison Square Garden when Tunney and Dempsey met, as the anti-platform claque lined up in solid block to the left of the Taoiseach as he faced them.

Lynch supporters were three times as solid on the right of the platform. The tea recess did not dislodge the five hundred delegates who were seated and standing in front of the platform. As the clock ticked down to 8:45, the time at which Lynch was to address the delegates, Boland was still back in the queue of speakers yet to be called. At 8:23 Paddy Smith called him to the rostrum. Boland refused to speak out of turn and left the platform in disgust. That was the signal to invite the veteran Seán MacEntee to speak. He began amid boos and chants of 'Boland, Boland.' It was 'an astonishingly sad moment,' Healy wrote, as he witnessed 'men half his age' standing and brandishing their fists at him, 'and while he was still fighting to make his case, the platform ambushed him from the wing by gonging him for time.' MacEntee continued to try to speak above the din. The platform then disconnected the amplification, and 'with the place in an uproar he went flailing on, unheard and becoming more and more excited.' Joe Groome, a party official, escorted him from the platform. On the podium, 'only then did Erskine Childers lift his shamed head off the table.'337

Lynch moved to the podium. The veteran reporter Healy believed that there had never been a presidential address like it in the history of the party. As Lynch began to speak, Kevin Boland was carried shoulder-high in a lap of honour around part of the hall. He was then carried to the back and outside, where Neil Blaney was to be found smoking his pipe. Half way through the speech Boland returned and took a seat at the back of the hall. There were scuffles and a fist-fight in which blows were landed, according to Healy. There were also scuffles in the body of the hall.

> Mr Lynch, amidst boos and cheers continued on. He never saw it: it wasn't happening. Not a worded eyelid did he bat . . . In the end, if Mr Lynch had to say that God was dead, the crowd was ready and willing to cheer it, with two hands in the air.338

The drama of the occasion may have detracted from closer scrutiny of the content of the speech.339 When Lynch began his address he was greeted with bursts of applause but also with slow hand-claps and shouts of 'Union Jack.'340 He made a number of indirect references to the events of the previous year and to his own role as leader of Fianna Fáil. 'He is not worthy to be a leader who avoids and evades whatever problems arise and fails to face up to decisions and actions however unpalatable,' he said. He emphasised that he was not afraid to give an account of his stewardship over the recent period

> to any man, and I totally reject any allegation—no matter where it comes from, be it from within or without—that I have ever by word or by deed reneged on the trust reposed in me by this party or by the people as a whole in the last general election.

He said challengingly that each member of Fianna Fáil was free to express his or her own views, but 'then must accept as party policy whatever the party decides.'[341]

On Northern Ireland he said, departing from his script, that he had never acknowledged that any section of the community that happened to be a majority in any part of the country had the right to opt out of the nation. But his Government wished to 'extend an olive branch to the North.' If that meant that they 'must grasp some nettles which might sting our pride then we will readily do so if the result be a just and last peace throughout Ireland, throughout a united Ireland.'[342]

Delegates gave him a standing ovation for what has been estimated at between two and three minutes. When the motions were put following the speech, each one was cheered through. Lynch, John Healy wrote, 'has come out of the speech with an endorsement and that is as much as any leader can hope for in such circumstances.'[343]

In his concluding remarks, Lynch surprisingly described the party gathering as 'the most successful ard-fheis that Fianna Fáil has ever had.' He said that when the chips were down and the going got rough, that was when Fianna Fáil came forward. Formed in adversity, it had made the republican ideal more virile. He denied that there had been any shift in republican policy within Fianna Fáil. The heart of the party was sound, 'and the future of Ireland is safe in your hands.' He said it was inevitable that pent-up feelings that had been gathering in the party over the past year would find expression during the ard-fheis. Even if such feelings were more pent-up than anticipated, a little letting off of steam did everybody good, he said. At the close of proceedings for another year, Jack Lynch was accorded a standing ovation.[344]

Editorial coverage was very critical of the weekend's events, if offering Lynch's personal stance qualified praise. The *Irish Independent* asked in the heading on its editorial, 'Is this politics?' The ard-fheis was described as a 'shoving and shouting match' that had solved nothing. Although Lynch had received a vote of confidence, his description of the weekend events as a letting off of steam was criticised. The editorial argued that Fianna Fáil had been 'attacked by a cancer which will respond only to surgery.' Lynch was the man to carry out the operation, but he 'obviously fears the effect such action would have on the general health of his party.' The question was posed whether the internal crisis in Fianna Fáil had not sapped the strength of the Government. Was it the case that the men at the top would be more concerned with the future of Fianna Fáil than with the future of the country? The editorial concluded that the ard-fheis had left a lasting impression in the country that would be remembered at the next general election.[345]

An editorial in the *Irish Times* on 22 February said that the 'weekend certainly was not only a personal triumph for the Taoiseach but the burial of some part of Fianna Fáil.' It described his speech as brave, and Lynch as refusing to evade 'his responsibilities of pressing home some of the implications of his policy on the North.' But he also left room for manoeuvre, the editorial continued, and he was agile enough to advance a little or withdraw a little as events moved him. But the editorial did not see as helpful his proclamation of the policy of unity as being the same as that of de Valera and Lemass. Neither of the two former leaders of Fianna Fáil had to deal with the practicalities of closer co-operation, it said. 'Invocations of the desire for that unity may now be over.' The brawling at the ard-fheis put an end to the patter that the party 'was united as never before.' That line, it argued, was 'contemptuous of the intelligence of the people,' and it had not yet been force-fed to viewers and readers. However, Lynch's 'cheery reference at the end of the proceedings to a little letting off of steam' prompted the leader-writer to comment that the brawling at the ard-fheis 'was a symptom of the schizophrenia that has afflicted Fianna Fáil for a long time.'[346]

Over that stormy weekend Lynch had, on balance, seen off the immediate challenge to his leadership. He had managed to retain party unity, if only because the Blaney-Boland-Haughey trinity was in disarray. Moreover, he secured the election of his strongest supporters to important posts in the party. By an overwhelming majority, Patrick Hillery and Joseph Groome were elected, in place of Boland, joint honorary secretaries. George Colley won a runaway victory for the post of joint treasurer; Anthony Hederman obtained the other position, ahead of Blaney, who ran him a close race.[347] The outcome of the ard-fheis, according to Stephen Collins, 'cemented Lynch's authority and for the moment put to rest doubts about his continued leadership.' Gerard Collins, from Limerick, was given the job of trying to get control of the party organisation for him. Des Hanafin continued in charge of party fund-raising.

Lynch also set about reforming the senior ranks of the army and the Gardaí.[348]

The outcome of the ard-fheis was only a lull in hostilities. But the dissidents chose very different ways and tactics to express their opposition. Boland believed that the first aim of Fianna Fáil had been replaced 'by the entirely new policy that Partition was to be solved only by the effluxion of time and without any help from them.' He resigned from Fianna Fáil on 1 May 1971. On 19 September he founded Aontacht Éireann as 'an instrument by which the people could keep faith without coming into conflict with the established institutions of the state.' Captain James Kelly was a vice-president. The new party staggered on until 1976, when Boland was forced to state that the people 'didn't want a Republican Party.'[349] But residual dissent within Fianna Fáil sometimes came to the surface. A Co. Mayo TD, Joe Leneghan, voted against the Government and was expelled from the party. Des Foley of Dublin and Timothy O'Connor of Kerry abstained in a vote in April 1971.

Blaney, in contrast, kept faith with Fianna Fáil even if it had left him. He was 'externally associated' with the party. Haughey, on the other hand, boxed clever and played a waiting game; at the ard-fheis of 1972 he was elected one of five honorary vice-presidents of Fianna Fáil.[350] Patience, discipline and hard work made his return to political respectability virtually unstoppable. Lynch, as will be argued later, showed bad judgement in permitting the return of the prodigal.

Seán Lemass, former Taoiseach and Haughey's father-in-law, died on 11 May 1971. He was acknowledged as the architect of modern Ireland, and tributes were received from all sides in Irish politics. His passing was a cause for genuine national mourning. The national press agreed on the verdict that he had been a 'man of reality'. According to the *Irish Times,* he was 'a mould-breaker and a mould-maker.'[351] Lynch said that Lemass was 'not only a great man but was a giant amongst men.' He had devoted himself to the service of his country and his people with a sincerity of purpose and spirit of selfless dedication that few could ever equal and none could surpass, Lynch said, and there was scarcely any sphere of the country's economic and social progress to which one could point without recalling his intimate involvement with it. The country owed Lemass 'a debt of gratitude which can never be repaid.'[352]

On 12 May 1971 schools were closed and civil servants were given time off to attend the funeral. Citizens lined the streets of the capital as the coffin, draped in a Tricolour, was taken on a gun carriage from the Mater Nursing Home, where two thousand people had gathered on the street outside to pay their respects.[353] Members of the public were six deep along O'Connell Street. The Dublin Brigade of the Old IRA provided a guard of honour, while another contingent marched behind the coffin with members of Cumann na mBan. The cortège passed in front of the GPO, where President Éamon de Valera, the Taoiseach and Government, leaders of the opposition and the diplomatic corps were present. Lemass's son-in-law, Charles Haughey, was among the mourners, as were Neil Blaney, Kevin Boland and Mícheál Ó Móráin. They travelled in official cars and joined other Government ministers at the church, where the remains were received by the Archbishop of Dublin, John Charles McQuaid.

On 13 May, after 11 o'clock requiem Mass at the Church of the Good Shepherd, Churchtown, Dublin, a bearer party of ten NCOs carried the coffin to the gun carriage for the journey to Dean's Grange Cemetery. Eight staff officers from Army Headquarters flanked the coffin. A firing party presented arms and then rested on arms reversed, the ceremonial posture of respect for the dead. The Army No. 1 Band marched ahead of the procession. At Dean's Grange, Lynch gave the graveside oration before a large gathering, including President Éamon de Valera and a full muster of the leadership of Fianna Fáil. If Lynch had been fighting a few months before at the ard-fheis to maintain the unity of the party, he was on that sad day the leader of the Irish Government and was perceived to be the rightful and hand-picked inheritor of the legacy of Seán Lemass.

Between August 1969 and May 1971 Lynch had lived in a twilight world where deception was, for a number of his party opponents, the norm and dis-simulation a commonplace. The Minister for External Affairs, Patrick Hillery, in conversation with President de Valera in Áras an Uachtaráin in late 1969, asked him to compare contemporary Irish politics with what it had been like when he was Taoiseach. The difference between then and now, de Valera said, was that 'there was no intrigue in the party in my day.'[354] Perhaps that remark may tend to romanticise old Fianna Fáil; but the former Taoiseach had been able to contain dissent and keep personality and policy conflict 'in lodge'. Lynch lived in a very different era. He had been a sporting hero and not a survivor of the 1916 Rising. But in 1969–70 Lynch did the state some service. He successfully stood out against physical-force nationalism. He mobilised the institutions of the state to fight the subversion of a reconstituted IRA. Support for subversion and violence extended to within his very Government. His singular stance has been underestimated. During the crisis in May 1970 he provided decisive leadership. His choice of the new Minister for Justice, Desmond O'Malley, was as prudent as his selection of his predecessor had been ill-judged. With the help of many of his ministerial colleagues, civil servants and gardaí, such as Chief Superintendents John Fleming and Phil McMahon, and members of the army he led the Irish state through its worst crisis since the Civil War.

The novelist Leonardo Sciascia described the Italian state at the time of the Aldo Moro kidnapping crisis in 1978 as follows:

It's as if a dying man had risen from his bed, leapt into the air to swing from the chandelier like Tarzan from the liana, then rushed to the window and vaulted out to land, hale and hearty, in the street. The Italian State has revived. The Italian state is alive and strong, safe and sound.[355]

Largely thanks to Jack Lynch and his close party supporters, the post-Arms Trial Irish state was 'alive and strong, safe and sound.' Lynch deserves special recognition and respect for that alone. The Blaney-Haughey alternative may not merely have provided a change of leadership: it might have been a case of regime change, with bloody consequences for Northern Ireland.

Chapter 8

IRELAND AND EUROPE: NEGOTIATING MEMBERSHIP OF THE EEC

While the focus of Government attention was on the growing crisis in Northern Ireland, Lynch and his colleagues had also to keep the routine business of government going. Parallel to what was unfolding in the North, the Lynch Government conducted successful negotiations to bring Ireland into the EEC. The negotiations required close co-operation with London precisely at a time when Anglo-Irish relations were going through a transformative process. Despite the deterioration of the situation across the border, both Dublin and London succeeded in maintaining a close and good working relationship during the EEC negotiations. That was a tribute to both sides. Neither sought in Brussels to link progress in Northern Ireland to the entry talks.

The enlargement of the EEC was given a new lease of life by the dramatic turn of political events in Paris in the early months of 1969.[1] After an unprecedented defeat in a referendum in France on his proposals for regional and Senate reforms, President Charles de Gaulle resigned suddenly on 28 April. His successor, Georges Pompidou, had previously served as prime minister. Jacques Chaban-Delmas became Prime Minister. The government remained substantially Gaullist; but among those appointed to senior ministerial positions were two convinced 'Europeans', Maurice Schumann as Minister for Foreign Affairs and Valéry Giscard d'Estaing as Minister for Finance and the Economy.

Before the new French policy on enlargement had become clear, the Irish Government continued to fear most that the British Government would secure a community of six-plus-one,[2] the original six plus Britain.

The general election on 18 June 1969 had returned Jack Lynch to power. Dr Patrick Hillery, his new Minister for External Affairs,[3] was an experienced and energetic politician.[4] Hillery was close to Lynch, and the two men worked well together in the pursuit of Irish membership of the EEC. In Dublin the new

Government and its senior civil servants began to allow themselves to believe that enlargement might be possible. By coincidence, Charles de Gaulle was visiting Ireland at about the time of the election. He had spent most of his holidays in Caherdaniel, Co. Kerry. On election day he was staying with the President of Ireland, Éamon de Valera, in Áras an Uachtaráin. De Gaulle was in retirement, and it was the first time since the Liberation that he was not in France for the anniversary of his call for resistance on 18 June 1940.[5]

However, de Gaulle's negative impact on the integration process had conditioned many of the people sitting on the Interdepartmental Committee of Secretaries to feel pessimistic. All had experienced rejection in 1963 and again in 1967. When they met on 4 July 1969 to review developments, Charles Murray had replaced T. K. Whitaker as secretary of the Department of Finance.

The new Minister for External Affairs, Patrick Hillery, gave priority to meeting the senior members of the European Commission. Hugh McCann, Dónal O'Sullivan and Seán Morrissey accompanied him.[6] Hillery stressed the importance of the Irish application on 14 July 1969 during discussions with the president of the Commission, Jean Rey. He also emphasised how important it was to Ireland that it not be left out if Britain were to succeed in its bid for EEC membership. Rey recognised Ireland's belief in the political ends of the Community.

The idea of Britain adhering alone was largely a personal opinion held by Jean Monnet but not shared by the Community. The Commissioner for External Affairs, Edoardo Martino, re-emphasised this point, stating that he favoured the 'ten' rather than the 'seven' approach. Hillery spoke of the air of optimism in Europe since de Gaulle's retirement and asked whether the recent change in the French government would speed up the process of enlargement. Rey did not want to predict but reminded his visitor that the Council had not met since the formation of the new French government. But even if the French government had not changed its views, Rey was convinced that the issue of enlargement would have to come up again before the end of the year. He could not make any guarantees that Ireland would automatically enter with Britain. However, he acknowledged the delicate position Ireland might find itself in economically if such a situation arose. Norway had also emphasised to Rey the importance of simultaneous adhesion.

Rey stated that in his opinion the Six were ready to resolve the question about financing the Common Agricultural Policy and would then concentrate on enlargement. Hillery enquired how long the negotiations were likely to last. This was difficult to predict, but Rey estimated that they would last at least one year.[7] Later that day Hillery also met the Belgian Minister for Foreign Affairs, Pierre Harmel. That meeting covered familiar ground. In the evening of 14 July 1969 he met the British Foreign Secretary, Michael Stewart, who was 'cautious about the prospects for expansion of membership. But the outlook was better than it had been before.' He agreed with Hillery that there would be a decision by the end of the year on whether negotiations would go ahead or not. The 'seven' versus 'ten' issue was raised, and Hillery said there was support in Europe for the Irish position.[8]

Discussions took place in London on 15 July 1969 with Dr Joseph Luns, the Netherlands Minister for Foreign Affairs and then chairman of the EEC Council. The Irish delegation was somewhat alarmed to find that Luns tended to favour the idea of first negotiating with the British. Luns agreed to see 'that our interests were taken care of.'[9] On 16 July 1969 Hillery was in Bonn for a meeting with Dr Gerhard Jahn, State Secretary to the Foreign Minister. He felt it better not to raise public expectations at that stage: better a policy of 'cautious optimism.'[10] Lynch read the reports and initialled them on 25 July 1969.

On 26 June, Chaban-Delmas outlined a new French policy to the National Assembly, stating that the French government was 'prepared to go as quickly and as far as our partners themselves are prepared to go, quickly and far towards a Europe aware of her own destiny.'[11] Pompidou provided more detail at a press conference on 10 July. He stated that France would be open to discussion with the Six on enlargement. However, the Irish ambassador, T. V. (Thomas) Commins, urged caution in his report from Paris on 22 July:

> You will see, from what both Chaban-Delmas and Pompidou said, that, while there was a change in style and the introduction of an element of tractability in the attitude of the French Government in the matter of the Common Market . . . There is really little change of substance which would justify the assumption that the way is now open for Britain and the other applicants to enter the Community in the immediately foreseeable future.[12]

But, he warned, 'a basic classical element' remained of established French policy: before negotiations with applicants, extensive discussions should take place within the Community.[13] In Brussels the Council took Pompidou at his word. A series of discussions were set up to discuss enlargement,[14] leading to the summit meeting of the Six in the Hague on 1 and 2 December 1969.

A meeting between Hillery and the French Foreign Minister, Maurice Schumann, took place at the French permanent mission to the United Nations in New York on 20 September 1969. Hillery was accompanied by Hugh McCann and the permanent representative at the United Nations, Con Cremin; Schumann by the director-general for political affairs in the French Foreign Ministry, M. Beaumarchais, and the French permanent representative to the United Nations, Jean Bérard. In response to a question from Hillery,

Schumann said that the Six would be meeting in November to decide on the issue of enlargement. He gave it as his personal hope that the decision would be a positive one. Schumann also assured Hillery that any talk of a Six-plus-Britain expansion 'had now been killed. France, for one, would not consider dealing with one applicant, however important, in advance of the other three.' The British were also aware of this. Schumann said that when the British Foreign Secretary, Michael Stewart, had been with him that morning he had made it clear that there would be no question of a British application being dealt with before the others.[15]

Amidst wide-ranging speculation,[16] the summit conference on 1 and 2 December 1969 in the Hague favoured enlargement under article 237 of the Treaty of Rome. The news was gratefully received by the Irish Government, and Jack Lynch in a press statement congratulated the EEC on the outcome. It had become a matter of urgency for Dublin to get agreement with London on the negotiating strategy of simultaneous entry for both countries. Lynch also wanted the two governments to work as closely as possible on the negotiation process.

On 10 December, Dr Hillery travelled to London with the Minister for Finance, Charles Haughey, to meet the Chancellor of the Duchy of Lancaster (minister without portfolio), George Thomson, and the senior civil servant co-ordinating the British application, Sir Con O'Neill. In anticipation of the meeting, British and Irish officials had met in London the previous day. Thomson led the British negotiating team. Hillery stressed the need for the closest possible contact between London and Dublin both before and during the negotiations. He believed that such consultation was of vital importance because of the 'interdependence of the two economies and of the existence of the Anglo-Irish Free Trade Area Agreement.' The Irish minute recorded:

> Mr Thomson agreed it was important that both sides should keep in close touch and referred to the discussions which officials had had on this question the previous day. He said that contact should be maintained at diplomat level and mutual efforts should be made to ensure that they were fruitful. He welcomed the suggestion that positive steps should be taken to achieve greater liaison in Brussels including the idea that there should be regular meetings there at Counsellor level. He would also be happy to go along with the idea that there should be discussions between officials in London and Dublin, on the understanding that these discussions would take place when there was something worthwhile to talk about.[17]

Hillery stressed that it would be essential during the actual negotiations for Ireland to be kept fully informed on matters relating to its vital interests likely to arise during the British negotiations. Thomson agreed that this was the intention of his government, but he warned that 'problems might arise.' However, he said, 'subject to the inhibitions of negotiations, they would be prepared to deal frankly with us during the negotiations.'[18] Hillery met Thomson again in February 1970, leaving London with the assurance that contacts would continue through the embassies in Dublin and London.[19] Two meetings of British and Irish officials on aspects of entry into the EEC took place in December 1969.[20]

However, the Government went through a number of anxious moments before that outcome had been secured. At the beginning of 1970 Hillery did a tour of a number of the European capitals, accompanied by Hugh McCann. Following talks in Bonn he wrote to Lynch on 6 February that his reception at all levels by the German government could not have been warmer, as was also its support for Irish membership. The Chancellor (head of government), Willy Brandt, having returned directly from a meeting in Paris with Pompidou, seemed convinced of the sincerity of the French on the question of the expansion of membership. There was a general expectation in Bonn that negotiations would open that summer. There was some feeling, however, that the negotiations might take a little longer than expected. The Germans considered that the accession of new members should not take place before suitable arrangements had also been worked out for Sweden, Switzerland and Austria. Brandt readily accepted Hillery's proposition that it was important that Irish negotiations begin and finish at the same time as the British negotiations, that accession should take place at the same time, and that there should be consultations on matters arising in other negotiations of direct interest to Ireland. Hillery concluded that the discussions in Bonn seemed to confirm the suspicion Irish officials had from their meetings with Sir Con O'Neill that the British had not abandoned the hope of getting going first and also, perhaps, of securing different transitional periods for agriculture and industry. Hillery suggested an early meeting of the Government sub-committee to discuss this question of the transitional period.[21]

Hillery met the French Foreign Minister, Maurice Schumann, in Paris on 10 April 1970 and was told by his counterpart that negotiations should start together, and that the member-countries of the European Free Trade Association (EFTA) also needed to be considered. Asked about Sweden, 'Schumann expressed the view that having a policy of neutrality would not be, to his mind, incompatible with membership of the Common Market.' He agreed that Ireland should be consulted about British negotiations that would have a bearing on it. A French official present, M. Brunet, said that because of the complexities governing the links between the two economies the same transitional period for agriculture and industry would be the likely solution.

He said the French position tended to favour a 'shortish' period. The French were not prepared to give assurances that the Anglo-Irish Free Trade Area Agreement could be maintained during that transitional period. On the topic of defence, Hillery mentioned that the Western European Union would not be suitable for Ireland as a forum for political co-operation.

In conclusion, Hillery 'made it clear that we had no reservations about making progress in the political field. In fact, from Ireland's point of view, the political and cultural attractions of being a part of the new Europe would perhaps be greater than the purely economic.'[22] That was very much Lynch's line of thought on the matter. But the time of having to enter into political union was a long way off.[23]

That policy formulation succinctly summarised the position taken by the Government throughout public debate on EEC membership, leading up to the referendum in May 1972.

The Government, however, had to accomplish a pressing foreign policy objective: to quarantine the deteriorating situation in Northern Ireland and not to allow that aspect of Anglo-Irish relations to adversely influence co-operation and good will between Ireland and Britain on their common goal of achieving membership of the EEC. The authorities in Brussels were well informed about increasing problems in Northern Ireland. Johannes Linthorst Homan, reporting from the delegation of the European Communities in London to the president of the European Commission on 8 April 1970, referred to Northern Ireland by saying 'Le volcan est là, et reste actif [The volcano is there, and remains active].'[24]

Hillery met the president of the Commission, Jean Rey, in Brussels on 28 April 1970, when he again emphasised Ireland's political as well as economic reasons for seeking membership. He stressed again that negotiations should begin at the same time as those with Britain and that there should be simultaneous accession. He also urged that consultation with Dublin should take place before decisions were made on matters of mutual interest. He pointed out that the British had agreed to full consultation. Rey replied that he could not say what the negotiating procedure would be, as the Six had not yet come to an arrangement. That would be decided at the May meeting of the Council. The opinion of the Commission was that there should be the same transition period for all countries covering agriculture and industry.[25] British and Irish officials, meeting in London on 21 May 1970, further advanced the level of co-operation between the two countries.[26]

Despite increasing violence in Northern Ireland (discussed in the next two chapters), Anglo-Irish relations in the area of the EEC maintained an air of 'business as usual'. Sir Con O'Neill, in his published report on the negotiating process, confirmed the anxiety of the Irish to 'keep extremely close' to the

British. He speculated that Dublin probably felt 'at the time a little remote from Community developments.' The Irish made no secret of the fact, he recorded, that they wanted to continue to sell into the British market but at the higher EEC prices. O'Neill noted that the Irish 'did not [feel], and fortunately for them, the Community did not feel either, any difficulties or scruples arising from their neutral status.' In his notes of a conversation with the Irish ambassador in March 1970, O'Neill recorded that the defence implications of membership presented the Irish Government with no difficulty.

> Changes in the Irish Government—especially the departure of Mr. Aiken, who had been a great man for neutrality—had altered the Irish attitude and the present Irish Government saw no difficulty about accepting defence commitments in Europe, even if it were to mean—and he hardly thought it would—membership of NATO.[27]

He commented further:

> The general attitude of the Community seems to have been that though the Irish Republic was neutral, it was less neutral than others; and the question of the compatibility of neutrality with membership of the community, which caused the Swedes such nightmares, never troubled the Irish.[28]

O'Neill concluded that Ireland was 'condemned to tag along behind us,' recalling that within a few months of the opening of the formal negotiations a member of the Irish delegation replied to a question about how they were getting on, 'Oh, we're riding along on the back of the British.'[29] Whatever about the accuracy of this comment by the unnamed and highly imprudent Irish diplomat, co-operation between Dublin and London on the strategy for EEC membership withstood the terrible pressures between the two countries over Northern Ireland. It even withstood the change of government in Britain on 19 June 1970 that brought the Conservatives and Edward Heath to power. The new government immediately proclaimed its readiness to open negotiations. Sir Alec Douglas-Home was appointed Foreign Secretary. Responsibility for the negotiations was placed in the hands of Anthony Barber, Chancellor of the Duchy of Lancaster (minister without portfolio). Geoffrey Rippon succeeded him in September as leader of the British delegation.[30]

The president of the Council of the Communities, Pierre Harmel, Belgian Foreign Minister, wrote on 9 June 1970 to the four applicant countries—Britain, Ireland, Denmark and Norway—inviting them to a meeting in Luxembourg on 30 June for the formal opening of negotiations.[31] Jack Lynch, in anticipation of the decision, announced on 27 May that Dr Hillery would lead the Irish negotiating team.[32] Hillery returned to Brussels on 19 June for talks with Harmel in preparation for the Council meeting that would take the formal decision to open negotiations.

The discussion again focused on the issue of transition, which provided the main difficulties for Ireland.[33] Later, Hillery told the Council that he was willing to 'participate fully in this very important work, confident that it will be aimed at achieving a harmonious and steady economic growth in all parts of the enlarged Community.' He referred to transitional arrangements for agriculture and industry and for fisheries and to the importance of continuing the economic trading relationship between Ireland and Britain.[34] His British counterpart, Anthony Barber, outlined his country's difficulties in the forthcoming negotiations as relating to agricultural policy, the contribution to the community budget, Commonwealth sugar exports, New Zealand's special problems and certain other Commonwealth questions.

At home Lynch had led the debate in Dáil Éireann that had begun on 23 June 1970 with the motion that the Dáil 'takes note of the White Paper entitled *Membership of the European Economic Communities: Implications for Ireland.*' The leader of Fine Gael, Liam Cosgrave, spoke strongly in favour of full membership. The Labour Party, led by Brendan Corish, favoured associate membership. Corish argued that full membership would lead to a loss of 'our sovereign independence' and that Ireland would be forced 'to abandon our traditional role of neutrality.' The EEC institutions were undemocratic, he said, and as a full member Ireland's influence would be 'marginal if not minimal.' It was evident that there was a substantial majority in the Dáil in favour of Lynch's motion. The debate adjourned on 9 July and was resumed on 10 March 1971.

Outside the Oireachtas, various groups aligned against membership, among them the Common Market Defence Campaign and the Common Market Study Group. The Irish Congress of Trade Unions opposed membership, as did both wings of Sinn Féin, Cumann Cearta Sibhialta na Gaeltachta (Gaeltacht Civil Rights Association) and a number of other radical political groups.[35]

Ireland had two ministerial negotiation meetings, on 21 September and 14 December 1970. There were also two meetings at deputy level on 20 October and 27 November. On 21 September, Hillery laid out the Irish case in great detail. D. J. Maher, who was a member of the Irish negotiating team, explains the process in *The Tortuous Path.*[36] The pace of progress by the end of December 1970 was slow but steady. At the turn of the year the different delegations set their sights on the completion of the task by the autumn of 1971.

Stress needs to be laid on the fact that the negotiations were conducted against a background of unprecedented turmoil in the ruling Fianna Fáil

party. The ard-fheis on 20 February 1971 was noted for the disorder that characterised its deliberations. Lynch devoted a small section of his presidential
speech to the benefits of EEC membership. He predicted membership by
January 1973 on the basis of a five-year period during which industrial tariffs
against the other member-states would be removed. Foreign investment
would continue to grow, he argued. He was confident that Ireland could negotiate terms acceptable and beneficial to the country and to the EEC.[37]

The Department of External Affairs reported to Lynch on 14 May 1971 a
comparative lull in the negotiations over the previous few months. It concluded that it was reasonable to think 'that solutions on all the major British
problems may be agreed before the end of July.' It was felt that a package
might therefore be agreed before the summer recess involving the major
issues, leaving the relatively minor items for discussion in the autumn.

> We have just received a most promising indication of a successful outcome
> to the negotiations in the form of remarks made to the Ambassador in
> Paris by a high ranking Foreign Ministry official to the effect that, after this
> week's meeting between the Community and Britain, President Pompidou
> has decided to open the door to British membership at his meeting with
> Mr Heath next week. He added that 'Ireland is now in the Community—
> congratulations!' We can therefore expect that events will move very rap-
> idly in the coming weeks. For this reason it is important that we be fully
> prepared for early and substantive negotiations on our major problems.

Although Lynch did not participate in the direct negotiations, he remained
close to the process. He chaired meetings of the sub-committee on EEC
membership and was briefed daily. He presided over a meeting on 17 May in
the Department of the Taoiseach to review the recent progress regarding
Ireland's application.[38] He held another meeting on the EEC application on 27
May 1971. The next meeting was fixed for 10 June, and Lynch again presided.
A further meeting was provisionally fixed for the morning of 24 June. And so
it continued. Space does not permit a detailed reproduction of the reports of
the meetings of the same status; but by the end of the year, negotiations had
been successfully completed. With the exception of the fisheries industry, the
deal won was very favourable to Ireland. Lynch and Hillery signed the instru-
ments of accession in Brussels on 22 January 1972. The Taoiseach moved a
motion on 21 March that Dáil Éireann take note of the white paper *The
Accession of Ireland to the European Communities* and the supplement thereto.
He told the Dáil that the country stood

at a most important crossroads in our history. The road we take will determine not only the future of our country for generations to come, but also the contribution we make to the creation of a Europe that will measure up to the ideals of the founders of the Community.[39]

Fine Gael supported the motion and the Labour Party opposed—a number of deputies, such as Conor Cruise O'Brien, somewhat half-heartedly. The Dáil and Seanad had passed the Third Amendment of the Constitution Bill by 24 February 1972. That provided for an addition to article 29.4 of a new sub-section.

The public debate leading up to the referendum on 10 May 1972 witnessed the two major political parties, the major farming organisation, the organs of industry and all the national daily papers in favour of a Yes vote. The outcome was decisive, with 1,253,781 (83 per cent) in favour and 211,891 against. The Third Amendment of the Constitution Act became law on 8 June 1972. The European Communities Bill, giving effect to the provisions of the treaties of the three communities and of the acts adopted by those institutions, also authorised the making of ministerial orders. This became law on 6 December 1972.[40] Three of the four applicant countries—Ireland, Britain and Denmark—successfully completed all the entry requirements. Norway's electorate voted against membership. At a summit meeting of the Nine in Paris on 19 and 20 October 1972 Lynch urged the strengthening and deepening of the EEC. The new member-states became full members on 1 January 1973.

Lynch and Hillery had a strong reason to be satisfied about the outcome of more than ten years of hard diplomacy. They had secured Ireland's primary foreign policy goal: full membership of the EEC. But parallel to the years of negotiations with Brussels the Government faced the repercussions of a breakdown of the Northern Ireland polity and an unprecedented challenge to democratic government from within the Irish state itself.

Chapter 9 ∿

CONSTITUTIONAL POLITICS AND REVOLUTIONARY CHALLENGE, 1971–3

The British Prime Minister, Edward Heath, wrote in his memoirs regarding Northern Ireland that once returned to power in the general election of 18 June 1970 he 'was determined to find a lasting political settlement which would unite moderate opinion across the religious divide. I never underestimated the challenge.'

> Those who have never visited the province cannot appreciate the bitter, tribal loathing between the hard-line elements in the two communities, springing from an atavism which most of Europe discarded long ago. This chasm in Northern Ireland inspired the Protestant majority to discriminate shamelessly against their fellow citizens for almost half a century. Denied adequate housing, jobs and social services, and poorly represented as a result of gerrymandering, the Catholic minority in the north had eventually formed a Civil Rights Association in 1968 . . .[1]

Heath was not alone among British politicians in expressing surprise about the 'atavism' and 'tribal loathing' found in Northern Ireland. It was a part of the United Kingdom for which the British Government had responsibility. But Heath and his contemporaries behaved in 1970 as if they were Christopher Columbus discovering America. Northern Ireland was *terra incognita* for Conservatives and Labour alike.

Yet since the foundation of Northern Ireland in the 1920s successive British Governments allowed a double standard to obtain in the United Kingdom. This resulted in the emergence of a two-tier democracy in which the rights of nationalists in Northern Ireland were not protected. The Stormont Government tolerated, if it did not cultivate, sectarian practices that would be impermissible under English law. Despite the beginnings of pressure for reform from London in 1968, those efforts were too little and too late and did not prevent the breakdown of civil society in the summer of 1969.

Although part of the United Kingdom, Northern Ireland was not an issue that senior Tory party members relished. After Stormont had been prorogued and the post of Secretary of State for Northern Ireland was created, even the Conservative Party, which historically had close ties with Unionism, would come to regard this posting as the 'short straw'.

Heath made Reginald Maudling his Home Secretary. After his first visit to Belfast, on 1 July 1970, Maudling sat in the office of a senior British officer and said: 'Oh, these bloody people! How are you going to deal with them.' On his way back on the plane to London he is believed to have said: 'For God's sake bring me a large Scotch. What a bloody awful country!'[2] He remained responsible for that 'bloody awful country' between 1970 and 1972. The phrase is very revealing: Northern Ireland was not England, Wales or Scotland.[3]

The new Prime Minister wrote loftily in his memoirs that he had built his Northern Ireland policy on the twin pillars of security and reform. 'It was not enough for them [Catholics] to be protected from discrimination': they 'had also to be given a positive role in governing the country in which they lived, at both local and national level.'[4] Such an approach, he wrote, would be successful only if moderates remained in power.

His solution to the problems of Northern Ireland involved a tripartite approach made up of the Governments of Northern Ireland, Ireland and the United Kingdom. No Irish nationalist would have disagreed with such an analysis. But those words, written in retirement in the mid-1990s, were mild-mannered and reductionist in tone. It was a fair summary of what his policy became in the latter part of his time in office. But that was before the enlightenment dawned that military and counter-terror measures were not enough, and Heath's Government made egregious mistakes that resulted in glacial relations between Dublin and London. Despite the tensions between them, the personal relationship between Heath and Lynch remained professional and, for the most part, cordial. Heath wrote that Lynch was a 'charming man, who was trying hard, in the face of much conservative opposition from within his own Fianna Fail party, to refashion Irish nationalism.' Reflecting on his relationship with Lynch, Heath wrote: 'He and I were not always in agreement, but the likeliest replacement for him was a government led by the likes of Charles Haughey.' Alec Douglas-Home advised Heath 'that "Mr Lynch is the best Irish Prime Minister we are likely to have." I never came to doubt Alec's judgement.'[5]

The Northern Prime Minister, James Chichester-Clark, faced a radical decline in the situation in Northern Ireland in early 1971. His government sat in semi-permanent session. On Sunday 14 March he told his colleagues that he was going to London to request the British to provide more security back-up. He travelled on the 15th, and he received a promise of 1,300 troops. According to Brian Faulkner, he returned to Belfast 'virtually empty handed.'[6]

Heath sent a personal letter to Lynch on 17 March through the British embassy in Washington. Lynch, who was at the White House for St Patrick's Day, was told that Chichester-Clark's early resignation was a real possibility. Heath said that moderate supporters of Unionism were being driven into the extremist camp. In order to survive, Chichester-Clark needed results against the physical-force nationalists. Heath asked Lynch to

> take early and effective action against the IRA. Could you actively harass the IRA training camps? Could gunmen wanted by the British be told that they could not expect to avoid surrender to the UK authorities by pleading a political motive? Could you encourage, however obliquely, the public to help the police against the IRA?

He further asked if the Taoiseach could do anything to patrol the border area more effectively. Lynch was also asked if he, together with the Old IRA, would condemn the IRA and deter headstrong youths from going north in the 'foolish belief [that] they were thereby serving Ireland's cause.' Heath assured Lynch that 'we shall not go back on our commitment to reform.'[7]

There was no necessity to remind Lynch of his duties in the area of security. Under the determined direction of the Minister for Justice, Desmond O'Malley, significant state resources had been employed to defeat the IRA and other republican physical-force organisations. The Government did not require any promptings from Heath to do its duty in that area. It was fully aware of the gravity of the situation and of the challenge it confronted. The British Government harboured unrealistic expectations of what a Taoiseach could do to stem the activities of subversives.

But an increase in violence in Northern Ireland intensified Heath's concern to secure some magical breakthrough by Dublin in its war against the IRA. Belfast pressed for an increase in the deployment of troops to meet the deteriorating situation. On 20 March 1971 the Defence Secretary, Lord Carrington, and the chief of the general staff visited Belfast and told the Northern Government that the number of soldiers being asked for was not possible. Chichester-Clark resigned in protest. In the contest for the leadership, Brian Faulkner defeated his extremist colleague William Craig. He was Prime Minister until the abolition of Stormont in March 1972.

The new Northern Prime Minister made overtures to the SDLP, offering members a place on Stormont committees. Had such an offer been made some months earlier the outcome might have been different. But political events circumscribed the freedom of action of Gerry Fitt, John Hume and others. The Irish Government was solidly in support of the SDLP.

Eamonn Gallagher, whose reports were very influential on Government policy, quickly formed a poor opinion of Faulkner. In January 1972 he wrote that

> the accession of Mr. Faulkner to the Office of Prime Minister in March, accompanied by statements by Mr. Heath to the effect that this represented no change of policy, represented the end of a useful dialogue as, despite what Mr Heath had said, by the end of May it was becoming apparent that Mr Faulkner would dominate Stormont/Whitehall discussions rather than the reverse.

It was Gallagher's judgement that as Prime Minister, Faulkner had reverted to

> old-style unionism disguised in a modern-dress vocabulary. His actions spoke even more loudly than his words of his intention to restore unionism but with some reduction in obvious discrimination.

Gallagher referred to how the Irish Government had continually 'harped on the need for radical reform to be brought in fast and continued to do so until May 1971.' Conversations at the official level with British and Irish civil servants had broken down at that point on the question of stopping the 'creation of ex-B-Special gun-clubs and the issue of thousands of gun licences by Stormont.' Irish efforts to change that policy came to naught when officials were told that the voluntary surrender of weapons was the method chosen by the Northern Ireland Government to deal with the matter; 'and that, inferentially, was that.'[8]

Violence against nationalist communities was evident daily in the summer of 1971. It was too late for Faulkner's half-hearted efforts to win over the SDLP. On 8 July 1971, 28-year-old Séamus Cusack was shot dead by British soldiers in disputed circumstances during a demonstration near Old Bogside Road in Derry. He was unarmed. The same day nineteen-year-old Desmond Beattie was also shot dead by British soldiers. On 9 July the SDLP walked out of Stormont in protest at the presence of hard-line Unionists in the Government and over the killing of the two unarmed Catholic men in Derry.

Eamonn Gallagher, continuing his travels in Northern Ireland, reported on 26 July 1971:

> We may take it for granted that a thorough revision of the Northern institutions is a necessary precondition to bringing the opposition back to Stormont in due course.

He added:

> The present apparent policy of outright repression and total support for
> the restoration of Unionism can hardly be maintained by the British
> Government for very long provided the Opposition in the North play their
> cards carefully.[9]

On Saturday 10 July, President de Valera unveiled a plaque at the Mansion
House in Dublin commemorating the ending of hostilities between Irish and
British forces, arranged on 8 July 1921 and with effect from the 11th. The ceremony was attended by ninety-year-old Robert Barton, one of the Irish team
who had negotiated the Anglo-Irish Treaty on 6 December 1921. The following day the President attended Mass in the Church of the Holy Trinity, Dublin
Castle. He was received by an Old IRA guard of honour; afterwards he went to
the Garden of Remembrance, where he dedicated a monument representing
the Children of Lir by Oisín Kelly, dedicated to all who had died for Ireland.
He laid a wreath on behalf of the people of Ireland. The Last Post was sounded
as the national flag was hoisted to full mast.

Lynch used the historic occasion to make a major policy speech on Northern
Ireland. He said that the Ireland Act (1949) had encouraged physical, cultural
and geographical separation that could not and would not solve the kind of
problem that then existed. There were not two separate Irelands, he argued.
Dwelling on the question of Irish identity, he said there were many kinds of
Irishmen, and he asked that the national majority 'examine their consciences'
regarding the national minority.

> Have our political concepts been sufficiently wide to include them? Have
> we been considerate enough about the things they believe in as passion-
> ately as we might believe otherwise? Do we agree that as John Hewitt
> writes: they 'have rights drawn from the soil and sky' which are as good as
> any title held by any previous migration into Ireland?

Lynch did not believe that the notion of being Irish was the prerogative of
sectional interests; it was not a private possession. 'To make it so is further to
divide,' he said. He said that the division of Ireland had been compounded by
thoughtless misrepresentations on all sides. The resorting to casual violence,
and the deaths of many people, were frightening realities. 'Let us today rededicate ourselves to reconciliation among Irishmen, North and South,' he
concluded.[10] Lynch's emphasis on Irish unity eclipsed his very positive
comments about the diversity of Irish identity and the insensitivity of the
majority towards minority rights.

Criticism came from three very different sources. The political correspondent of the *Irish Times,* Michael McInerney, commented that the speech 'raised in its sharpest form since 1969 the view that the supreme issue in Northern Ireland today is a United Ireland.' Government policy had emphasised up to then that the main issue had been peace, to be won by reforms and equal citizenship, he wrote.[11] The Northern Prime Minister, Brian Faulkner, described Lynch's speech as 'unhelpful and ill-considered.' He said it could only help terrorists north and south of the border.[12]

Ken Whitaker wrote to Lynch commending him for making a speech that 'put it up to the British to be more positive.' However, he was worried about its effects on

N.I. Protestants (and many Catholics!) if they were misled into believing that you want to see their agricultural, social welfare etc supports from Westminster withdrawn.

He suggested to Lynch that

it would be well to take an early opportunity of re-assuring them on this score—that it would continue to be the responsibility of the U.K. Govt. to provide similar standards in N.I. to those available in Gt. Britain until the terms of unification were agreed: by then, economic and social harmonisation in the EEC context as between North and South could be expected to have largely disposed of the problem.[13]

Whitaker was always frank and forthright in his advice to Lynch on Northern Ireland. The Taoiseach valued counsel from that source, even if, as seems likely, the Department of the Taoiseach and Department of External Affairs may not have been quite so appreciative. However, Lynch did not discourage Whitaker's private communications. He was a valuable point of reference for the Taoiseach with senior civil servants and leading members of the professions in Northern Ireland.

There was a good example of such an initiative shortly before Lynch delivered his speech. In a note marked 'secret' and dated 12 July 1971, Whitaker wrote to Lynch about a meeting with the Governor of Northern Ireland, Lord Grey. A New Zealander, Grey had served in the British colonial service in Nigeria and Guyana (then British Guiana). Their meeting had taken place at a dinner party in the home of a friend called O'Driscoll near Belfast. Grey had expressed to their host 'a wish to meet some "reasonable" person from the South.'[14] O'Driscoll chose Whitaker. The latter described Grey as 'urbane, dispassionate, [and] a shrewd judge of people and their motives.' Whitaker said

'he was cautiously frank in his criticism of various individuals and, at times, of the Govt. of N.I. (e.g. in relation to appointments on Housing Executive).'
Whitaker outlined his views on Northern Ireland. Grey's response was

> to express a weariness with extremism and emotionalism, a wish that people in the whole of Ireland would be more realistic and get back to working for their progress and not be always seeking excuses for not doing so, a belief that the Orangemen were incorrigible, that the present rigidities on both sides were irreconcilable and outmoded, and that the only hope lay in an evolution which the E.E.C. should hasten.[15]

Whitaker kept stressing the need for the light of political change in Ireland at the end of the tunnel, agreeing that the EEC should shorten the tunnel. When he was leaving, Grey told O'Driscoll that the talk 'had been useful and that the time seemed to be ripe for starting a quiet, unofficial dialogue between the Governments on the political question.'[16]

This correspondence was followed on the 14th by a short note to Lynch in which Whitaker explained:

> Lord Grey in a letter of thanks to M. R. O'D. following the dinner party says: 'Do we perhaps talk too much about Ireland's woes? One ought not to let talk be a substitute for action—if action is open to one.'[17]

The action of the British Government that followed was of a kind that neither Grey, Whitaker nor Lynch wanted.

INTERNMENT

Confronted by the growing unrest in August, Faulkner urged the British Government to introduce internment without trial. The Cabinet Committee on Northern Ireland had already discussed the issue on 15 March. That was before the resignation of Chichester-Clark. On 22 July 1971 Heath obtained a Cabinet decision to give him power to take whatever steps he felt necessary to halt the violence in Northern Ireland. He discussed the idea of introducing internment with Maudling, Carrington and Douglas-Home before bringing it to the Cabinet on 5 August.[18]

Maudling was made aware on 2 August that Faulkner and the Northern Ireland Government were about to make a formal request to London to introduce internment. He wrote in his memoirs:

> I was myself deeply worried about this whole question. In particular I feared any retaliation that the Provisional I.R.A. might embark upon, for

example, a campaign of kidnapping innocent people, possibly even children. There were very few signs of any limit to the barbarity of the tactics that they might adopt. But I was persuaded, as was Ted Heath, that of all the courses open to us in an exceedingly dangerous situation this seemed the least disadvantageous. Accordingly, we went ahead . . .[19]

Some months later it was reported to Eamonn Gallagher that Maudling had referred privately to Faulkner

as a 'slimy little beast' and has said that he has seriously misled the British Government on three occasions . . . It would be reasonable to assume . . . that one of them has to do with internment.[20]

Heath admitted in his memoirs to disquiet about a policy of internment, fearing that Stormont would use it 'disproportionately as a weapon against Republicans.' But as violence had increased, containment was required before peace could be established, he believed. Heath and his Government acquiesced.[21]

After a Cabinet meeting at which a decision to send more soldiers to Northern Ireland had also been taken, Faulkner met Heath, Carrington, Maudling, the chief of the general staff, Sir Michael Carver, and the commander of British forces in Northern Ireland, Lieutenant-General Harry Tuzo. Aware that the IRA knew of the imminence of internment, they agreed to move it forward by a day, to 9 August.[22]

Ironically, there had been a debate in the House of Commons on Northern Ireland the day the Cabinet took the fateful decision. The shadow Home Secretary, James Callaghan, called for the establishment of a Council of Ireland. He also urged immediate tripartite talks between Dublin, London and Belfast. Those policy ideas would form part of the basis of the future Sunningdale Agreement.

In Dublin on 5 August the Taoiseach told the Dáil that this was a 'historic phase' in the nation's development and that the outcome of the situation in Northern Ireland was crucial to the country's future. He said it was the will of the Government and of the majority of the Irish people to bring about a future in which the country would be united and peaceful. That was not to be achieved through violence but through friendship, good will, respect and understanding among Irishmen of all traditions. It could not be achieved through an instant or imposed solution.[23] The Taoiseach informed the Dáil about impending talks at Chequers, the official country residence of the British Prime Minister.

Some forty-eight hours before the implementation of one of the British Government's most catastrophic policy decisions regarding Northern Ireland,

John Healy, the *Irish Times* political commentator, wrote on 6 August that 'we are but a short remove from a full-blooded civil war which, when it flares, will be fanned by the most evil winds you can fear: religious hatred.'[24] Heath, wishing to maintain a sense of normality, departed to take part in the Fastnet yacht race. On 7 August, Healy presciently warned him:

> By now you'll have learned that there's a particularly strong tide-rip off the Antrim coast and indeed the contrary winds blow up equally when you least expect them . . . Just now there's a really dirty bit of weather in this area, with wind running against tide and several dirty undercurrents all converging.[25]

On 6 August, London instructed the British ambassador to find out where Lynch was likely to be at the weekend. As it was Horse Show Week, the Taoiseach was remaining in Dublin. Peck called on him to enquire whether, if internment without trial were introduced in the North, the Government would introduce it in the South. Lynch gave Peck the 'most solemn warning that the consequences in the North would be catastrophic; for every man put behind the wire a hundred would volunteer.' Peck reported Lynch's gloomy warning to his superiors. In his memoirs he wrote that those who considered internment at the time to be 'an appalling error' were 'absolutely right.'[26]

Shortly after 4 a.m. on 9 August 1971 thousands of British soldiers, accompanied by RUC Special Branch detectives, set out in squads throughout Northern Ireland to raid designated houses and to arrest identified individuals. As news of the operation spread, women banged dustbin lids and blew whistles to warn of the danger. When the operation ended, at 7.30 a.m., 342 men had been snatched, taken to police stations and rearrested, and then brought to holding centres at Belfast, Magilligan (Co. Derry) and Ballykinler (Co. Down). Within two days, 104 had been released; the remainder were jailed in Crumlin Road Prison, Belfast, or on a prison ship, the *Maidstone*, in Belfast Dock.[27]

The historian Jonathan Bardon wrote:

> Internment was entirely one-sided. No attempt was made to arrest loyalist suspects despite the UVF's record of violence. A very few Protestants were arrested . . . There was not a single person on the army's list of 452 names who was not an anti-partitionist.

He also argued that the action was a 'major blunder if only because it failed to bring about the seizure of the leading members of the Provisional IRA.'[28]

Lynch had read the situation correctly. The policy was as ill-conceived as it had been poorly executed.

After the round-up the Irish ambassador in London, Dónal O'Sullivan, reported that he had been called to the Foreign Office and told that internment was being introduced as they spoke. He was informed that it was still London's intention to go on with the reform in the North. O'Sullivan immediately reported the content of the conversation to Seán Ronan in the Department of External Affairs.[29] In Dublin the British ambassador delivered a 'secret and personal' letter from the British Prime Minister to the Taoiseach in which Heath explained that the Northern Ireland Government, after consultation with London, had decided to activate its powers of internment. He wrote that

> the Security Forces are accordingly arresting and detaining people suspected of responsibility for committing or abetting acts of terrorism and other breaches of the peace designed to lead to a breakdown of law and order in Northern Ireland.

He further told Lynch that Faulkner would announce at the same time that all marches and parades were banned until further notice. That would initially be for six months but it would be made clear that consideration would be given to the need to extend the ban. There would be a separate announcement that all outstanding applications to start rifle clubs were being refused, and that no new applications would be considered.

Heath wrote that he thought Lynch would understand that it was impossible to give notice of a decision to introduce internment before the operation to give effect to it. He explained that Faulkner, in talks in London the previous week, had explained that in his judgement the consequences of the containment of the IRA by military means over the long haul would 'be worse than the consequences of what is now proposed.' Heath had laid down the condition that the British would lend support only if there was a complete ban on marches and parades of all kinds, which would need to remain in force for more than six months. Heath was aware that such decisions carried their dangers as well as their advantages, 'and I am well aware of their implications and dangers for you.' He felt that 'the effectiveness of internment in Northern Ireland could have been increased if you had felt able to take similar measures on your side of the border.' But Peck's reports made it clear that there was no chance of that.[30] Heath emphasised 'our view that the measures taken should not discriminate as between the different sections of the community, except as the facts of the situation make inevitable.' He said the marches in Derry on 12 August and in Belfast would not take place. An advisory committee was being set up to which anyone who was interned had the right to make representation. Regarding the measures being introduced, he hoped that Lynch would 'be able to react to them with understanding, even if with regret.' He expressed the view that 'a reminder from you that violence serves no purpose, and that internment is aimed against particular individuals who are avowedly working for a breakdown of law and order, would be invaluable.'

Heath viewed internment as 'strictly temporary' and claimed it would not prejudice the task of building more harmonious inter-community relations. Above all, he hoped that

> this will not be allowed to affect the good relationship which you and I have established, and the close relations between our two countries on so many matters of importance to us both: and particularly on entry into the European Union.[31]

There was little in the letter with which Lynch could agree, except the last line. Peck was left to pick up the pieces in Dublin. He wrote in his memoirs: 'The slope down which we were all slithering in the dust of the Northern Ireland Government was getting steeper and bloodier every minute.'[32]

On 9 August the Government Information Bureau quickly had the text of a statement for issue to the press on behalf of the Taoiseach. It said that the introduction of internment without trial was deplorable evidence of 'the poverty of the policies' that had been pursued there for some time.

> The sympathies of the Government and of the vast majority of the Irish people North and South go to the Nationalist minority in the North who are again victimised by an attempt to maintain a regime which has long since shown itself incapable of just Government and contemptuous of the norms of the British democracy to which they pretend allegiance.[33]

There was little Lynch could do except watch the tragedy unfold.

Faulkner made a public statement at 11:15 p.m. the same day stating that his Government was 'quite simply at war with terrorism.' Between the ending of the round-up and the time he issued his statement, smoke rose over Belfast amid gun battles that had broken out in several districts. By the end of the day two British soldiers and eight civilians were dead. Protestant families had fled the Ardoyne district in Belfast, some setting fire to their abandoned houses. Off the Crumlin Road, Catholic families fled their homes in the face of sectarian attacks. The violence also spread to Derry, Armagh and Newry.

Had the round-up netted the most prominent members of the Provisional IRA? The organisation held a press conference at which 'some of their best-known leaders' were present.[34]

As the relationship between Dublin and London dipped below freezing point, David Blatherwick, later ambassador to Ireland, phoned from the

British embassy to ask Eamonn Gallagher whether Lynch's statement had been prepared before the Faulkner broadcast. Gallagher said he presumed so, in the light of the reference to the banning of parades. Blatherwick wondered whether the Taoiseach was going to make another statement in relation to Faulkner's banning of parades and of rifle clubs. Gallagher enquired whether the ban also applied to existing rifle clubs. He was not aware of what the Taoiseach had in mind regarding another statement. Blatherwick then volunteered the view that 'banning parades was the other side of the bargain.' Gallagher replied that he did not know of such a bargain. Blatherwick then used the term 'package deal', to which Gallagher replied that he was not aware of any deal and he could not 'in conscience accept any implication that Stormont could threaten parades and then set them off against further moves to repress the minority.'[35]

Writing in January 1972, Gallagher reported on the result of his wide travelling in Northern Ireland.

Internment has been a political disaster; it has led to repression of the ghettos in the hope of catching the IRA; it has confirmed virtually the whole minority in extreme anti-unionist attitudes, and the clock cannot be turned back on this. This polarisation in the North has put in question any possibility of reorganising the state at all. It has certainly ensured that its reorganisation on unionist lines can be prevented.

He concluded that the Taoiseach had raised the question of Irish unity in his speech on 11 July 1971 and 'Mr Faulkner ensured on August 9th that it would not go away.' What was the path open to the minority?

If reform had therefore become unlikely if participation had become a chimera there was only one way forward for the minority i.e. to break down the state utterly. Historically, there could be only one tactic for doing this—to oppose Orange nationalism with an extended Irish nationalism.[36]

While diplomacy took its course, the Northern opposition parties met on 9 August at Dungannon, Co. Tyrone. The combined meeting of SDLP, Nationalist and Republican Labour parties expressed great concern at the direction events were taking and called for the withholding of all rents and rates.[37] They entered into discussions with the Irish Government, conveying a sense of urgency and gloom about the unfolding events. The *Irish Times* headline on 10 August was '12 die on first day of North's internment.' Fighting intensified in Belfast. Many houses in mixed Catholic and Protestant areas were abandoned and set alight so as not to allow them fall into the hands of a family from the 'other side'.[38] The paper's editorial commented sardonically: 'Heath, meanwhile, sailed on. Like his opposite number in Stormont, he was heading into a storm which may yet sink him.'[39]

The Government met on 10 August in the wake of the spread of violence and civil unrest in Northern Ireland. Lynch issued a statement afterwards that was

> solely intended to try to bring present unrest to an end and to begin again the promotion of economic, social and political progress for all the people of Ireland and the ensuring of peace and harmony among them.

Lynch had hoped for an acceptance of his offer 'to participate in discussions among all those concerned to find an amicable solution to the problems in Northern Ireland.'

While Heath believed that internment was a necessary prelude to the restoring of greater peace and harmony between the communities in Northern Ireland, Lynch believed 'on the contrary that these operations are driving them further apart.' He stated that many thousands of refugee women and children had fled across the border over the previous few days. He referred to mass resignations from public office in Northern Ireland.

Lynch sent Hillery to London on 11 August to discuss the crisis with Maudling. It was the first time the two men had met. While Maudling believed that the fighting was dying down, Hillery replied that the British were pursuing a policy 'which could lead to war in Ireland as a whole,' adding that London's Northern policies had 'created the IRA.' He was not seeking a 'warlike solution,' as history had proved that a policy based on force 'is a failure.' Such a policy 'destroys relations between us and runs the risk of creating sectarian strife throughout the whole island.' Internment at that time was wrong, he said. The consequence of interning political leaders was to foment sectarianism. The British Government had been backing Unionism 'against the principles of their democracy.' The Stormont Government, he said, had always regarded anybody with aspirations to the unification of Ireland as being subversive. The emphasis ought to be on trying to find a political solution in Northern Ireland.

Maudling described the situation as being 'a uniquely unhappy one.' He could not accept that the Orange Order was running the North. The people being interned were the leaders of the IRA. He felt it was important that London and Dublin should concentrate more on making known what had been achieved in Northern Ireland.[40]

Hillery intervened to observe that Faulkner had at one stage said that the forces would shoot on sight, and John Taylor had promised a reign of terror.

He stressed that the position had now been reached where people would cease to listen to the Taoiseach. There had been a growing feeling that his policy was one of allowing things to drift along. The only way to remove the IRA was to establish political leadership and not through one-sided internment. He reported that Catholics had been told by the British forces that they could not in all cases be protected from sectarian attack. He spoke about the withdrawal of the opposition from Stormont. 'The truth is that Stormont is finished and that the British are using vast resources to keep it alive. The obvious thing is to let Stormont die.' He said that both London and Dublin should ask where Faulkner went for his orders: 'Half his cabinet goes to the Orange Order.' He asked Maudling if he regarded Orangism as normal, to which Maudling replied that in fact he hated it.[41]

Hillery reported that there were more than two thousand refugees in the South, who had fled because of a lack of security. He said that internment would build up the IRA south of the border. He said there was no solution in a policy aimed at bashing the Catholics, and the Taoiseach could not be seen as appearing to support Unionism. He also said that the SDLP could not return to Stormont. He urged the setting up of a commission in which the two communities might participate.

At that point Maudling sought to terminate the discussion. Hillery continued that if the British Government wanted co-operation from the Irish Government they must be prepared to talk about a united Ireland. Maudling rejected the idea of a commission as being disastrous for Northern Ireland. Any change in the constitution at that point would lead to a catastrophe. He did not regard Stormont as having been a great success. He hoped the two leaders would contact each other before a statement was issued, and he said he would report the content of their conversation to Heath.[42]

As Hillery was talking on 11 August to Maudling in London, Lynch met members of the Northern nationalist opposition. Charles Haughey, now a backbencher, issued a statement seeking a recall of the Dáil and requesting the sending of a UN peace-keeping force to Northern Ireland. He described the introduction of internment as a 'historically tragic decision,' which had 'brought the North beyond the point of no return.' It had brought a new dimension of terror into the situation and unleashed a hail of deaths and destruction in Protestant and Catholic areas. Haughey said that the British army was no longer a peace-keeping force. It had lost the confidence of the people, and its actions had increased popular hatred of them. He said the agony of the North was the agony of all Irish people. Even if the emotions of some were not involved, their self-interest was threatened.[43] This was a very emotive statement, riddled with ambiguity and certainly not designed to help Lynch and his Government handle the matter calmly.

On the night of 11 August, Heath returned to London after leading the British team to victory in the Fastnet race.[44] Hillery flew back to Dublin on 12 August to brief the Government. The *Irish Times* for the same morning quoted an army source to the effect that 4,339 people from the North were taking refuge in the South. A special train had brought women and children from Belfast to Dublin.

In the midst of this chaos Lynch issued a statement in which he called for the abolition of the Stormont regime and its replacement with an administration that had equal representation from the two communities. This would take precedence over the achievement of a united Ireland. He told questioners that he was not contemplating internment at present and implied that his Government had been under pressure from the British to do so.[45] Lynch told Heath that his Government had urged patience and had sought to get people to accept the intention of the British Government to honour the Downing Street Declaration of August 1969. He said that Dublin had repeatedly urged the minority 'to reject the use of violence because not only would violence preclude the achievement of their civil rights but it would perpetuate the divisions among the Irish people.' He said that 'we have acted with responsibility and restraint throughout all the difficulties of the past two years.' But there had been a deliberate decision by the Stormont Government to 'attempt the outright repression of the minority.' The main victims of the violence were 'the people in areas that have been consistently victimised by the Stormont system.'[46]

Lynch argued that there existed in Northern Ireland 'a Government whose main concern appears to be to meet the wishes and demands of the most extreme elements within the unionist community.' The implementation of the Downing Street Declaration had been 'delayed and distorted' by Stormont. He stated that his Government had been in discussions with elected leaders of the Northern minority in the previous few days. 'We are united with them in our determination to ensure that the misgovernment to which the North has been subjected for so long shall end.' He urged that 'the Stormont regime, which has consistently repressed the non-unionist population and bears responsibility for recurring violence in the Northern community, must be brought to an end.' It needed to be replaced with an administration in which 'power and decision-making will be equally shared between unionists and non-unionists.'[47]

Lynch had worked on the draft himself and edited out a number of emotive passages, such as 'It is a government unfit to govern. It has brought about instead increasing tragedy.' The following sentence was also excised from the draft: 'There is now no possibility that such a Government can expect the co-operation of the general population, nor can it, with blood on its hands, attract the respect of the Irish government.' Despite being toned down, the text stood out as one of Lynch's strongest speeches on the North during those early years of the troubles.[48]

Eamonn Gallagher, who was in close touch with the elected leaders of the Northern minority, may have drafted the statement. Lynch's language was direct if not robust. It was a reflection of the temper of even moderate nationalists at the time as they watched helplessly as the initiative slipped to the extremists and the exponents of physical force. One-sided internment was a recruiting boon to the IRA.[49]

The *Irish Times* in an editorial addressed the topic of 'Mr Lynch's new language'. It observed that his recent statement showed 'a big break from past attitudes on the question of the North and of Irish unity; also in its manner of approach to Britain.' It noted that it was without precedent in the past fifty years for the head of the Government to make a 'full frontal attack on the elected representatives of the Northern State.' There was also a shift in policy from national unity to an agreed administration in the North. The editorial also commented that the speech represented a 'frontal attack on the British Government's attitude.' It concluded that the speech was not Lynch's normal style and, 'arguably, represents a concession to his more expressive followers and a hoped-for containment of them.' It was an endorsement of the SDLP position.[50]

Faulkner quickly rejected Lynch's call for the abolition of Stormont, claiming that Dublin was seeking to do by political means what the IRA was seeking to achieve through violence. This led to a war of words. On 13 August the Minister for Justice, Desmond O'Malley, rejected Faulkner's claims, saying that the Government was doing everything possible to contain subversion in the South.[51]

On 15 August opposition MPs in Northern Ireland officially launched a campaign of civil disobedience. At one point in their 2½-hour meeting British soldiers surrounded the hotel where the MPs were gathered, and they were also searched at a check-point when driving away. On 18 August, John Hume and Ivan Cooper were arrested by British soldiers in Derry following a sit-down protest by hundreds of people, using the technique of passive resistance.[52]

In Dublin, Lynch met the leaders of the opposition, Liam Cosgrave of Fine Gael and Brendan Corish of the Labour Party, to discuss the question of constitutional reform. However, the crisis in Northern Ireland dominated the agenda.

The reason for Lynch's radical shift is simply understood against the backdrop of what was happening in Northern Ireland in the three weeks following internment. According to Jonathan Bardon, in that period

more than one in every hundred families in Belfast were forced to move— intimidation, fear of intimidation, and the destruction of homes were the reasons given for moving. Other families left to get away from constant street gun battles and an uncounted number of families had burned or wrecked their homes as they left to prevent 'the other side' moving in. About 2 per cent of the 45,000 Catholic households in Belfast and 0.5 of 135,000 Protestant households were displaced. Altogether 60 per cent of the movements were made by Catholic families and 40 per cent by Protestant families. In short, this was the biggest enforced movement of population in Europe since 1945.[53]

Faulkner was summoned to Chequers on Wednesday 18 August to meet Heath, who also asked the Foreign Secretary, Sir Alec Douglas-Home, and the Defence Secretary, Lord Carrington, to join the talks. Exasperated by what had unfolded, Lynch sent a telegram to the meeting.

It must be obvious to you that solutions require to be found through political means and should be based on the principle of immediate and full equality of treatment for everybody in Northern Ireland irrespective of political views or religion.

In the event of the continuation of British policies of attempting military solutions, Lynch said, 'I intend to support the policy of passive resistance now being pursued by the non-Unionist population.' In the event of agreement to a policy of finding solutions by political means,

I am prepared to come to a meeting of all the interested parties designed to find ways and means of promoting the economic, social and political wellbeing of all the Irish people, North and South, without prejudice to the aspiration of the great majority of the Irish people to the re-unification of Ireland.

For a reason yet to be explained, this telegram was sent by the normal route and did not get to Heath until after Faulkner had left for Belfast. Lynch made the text public.

According to the British ambassador, John Peck, 'understandably Mr Heath and Mr Maudling were not amused.'[54] While the ambassador was relaxing at his official residence in Leopardstown, Co. Dublin, at about 9 p.m. on 19 August he received a phone call from Heath's private secretary, Robert Armstrong. He wanted Peck to take down a statement and to deliver it to Lynch before 10 p.m., when Heath was going to go on television. In non-diplomatic language, the ambassador described what he took down as 'a fair stinker.' Escorted by a detective, Peck made his way to Lynch's home in Rathgar and delivered the poorly typed text. It read:

(1) Your telegram of today is unjustified in its contents, unacceptable in its attempt to interfere in the affairs of the United Kingdom and can in no way contribute to the solution of the problems of Northern Ireland.

(2) You should know that the principle of equality of treatment for everyone in Northern Ireland irrespective of political views or religion is the accepted policy of the governments of the United Kingdom and of Northern Ireland and is being fully implemented. By seeking to obscure this fact you do no service to any of the people of Northern Ireland.

(3) The military operations to which you refer are designed solely for the defence of the people against armed terrorists whose activities, many of which originate in or are supported from the Republic, I hope you would deplore and join me in suppressing. These operations are thus a necessary prelude to the restoration of greater harmony between the communities in Northern Ireland.

(4) While I naturally welcome contacts with you as the head of a friendly government, and while Mr. Faulkner and I have often made clear our desire to see greater cooperation between all governments concerned in promoting the mutual prosperity and well-being of peoples of Northern Ireland and the Republic, I cannot accept that anyone outside the United Kingdom can participate in meetings designed to promote the political developments of any part of the United Kingdom.

(5) I find your reference to supporting the policy of passive resistance now being pursued by certain elements in Northern Ireland calculated to do maximum damage to the cooperation between the communities in Northern Ireland which it is our purpose, and I would hope would be your purpose, to achieve.

(6) I deeply regret the fact that, when a meeting has already been arranged between us to discuss the whole range of matters of common interest to our two countries, you should have publicly taken up a position so calculated not only to increase the tension in Northern Ireland but also to impair our effort to maintain good relations between the United Kingdom and the Irish Republic.

(7) Since the text of your telegram was given to the Irish press before it was received here, I am also releasing the text of this message to the Press. Edward Heath[55]

The tone of the telegram was not what usually characterises discourse between the leaders of friendly sovereign powers. Lynch received a right royal dressing-down, or six of the best, in public-school argot. Not even Winston Churchill had attempted to speak to Éamon de Valera during the tense years of the Second World War in such a condescending tone.

In fact Lynch's political position was very difficult. He had been the recipient of continuing criticism from his backbenchers.[56] The chief of staff of the Official IRA, Cathal Goulding, had sent a statement to Government Buildings on 19 August demanding that the Government 'immediately use the Irish Army to defend the persecuted people of the Six Counties.' He also called on Lynch to seek a meeting of the UN Security Council and the General Assembly. Goulding wanted the Irish diplomatic delegation at the UN to talk for a change about Ireland 'after years of talk about Tibet and Peru.'[57]

The Northern opposition, having withdrawn from Stormont, were in discussion about the establishment of an alternative assembly. The leader of the Nationalist Party, Eddie McAteer, was seeking a meeting with Lynch and Hillery to discuss the form that initiative might take.

In such a climate, Lynch replied on 20 August to Heath's public criticism. He regretted that Heath had not accepted his offer to participate in discussions among all those concerned to find an amicable solution to the present unrest and to begin the promotion of economic, social and political progress for all the people of Ireland and the ensuring of peace and harmony among them. He said that no more than a handful of the hundreds arrested in Northern Ireland over the past few years were from the South. He felt that the military operations in the North were driving the communities further apart. He instanced the mass resignation of people from public offices in which they had given remarkable service. Contrary to Heath's claim that the military operations were solely for the defence of the people against armed terrorists, many thousands of refugees had flooded south in the previous twelve days, mainly from the Catholic ghettos in Belfast. Lynch stated that all would be happy that the principle of equality of treatment for everyone was being respected in Northern Ireland, irrespective of political views or religion. The fact that internment without trial, he argued, was 'so patently directed at the non-Unionist community only does not encourage this belief.'

Lynch said that the record spoke for itself on the impairing of good relations between Ireland and Britain. He did not accept Heath's view that what was happening in Northern Ireland was no concern of the Taoiseach. The division of Ireland had never been acceptable to the great majority of the Irish people. No generation of Irishmen, he said, had ever willingly acquiesced in that division. Lynch felt that the time had come for all those who could contribute to a peaceful solution of current problems in Northern Ireland to come together to discuss constructively how that could be achieved.

The British ambassador, Sir John Peck, wrote in his memoirs: 'It is hard to imagine the heads of government of any two other states brawling publicly in this fashion.'[58] He believed that the recent spat was in need of immediate closure. At his own request, Peck went on 23 August to see the secretary of the

Department of External Affairs, Hugh McCann. He explained the circumstances of his going to the Taoiseach's home the previous Thursday. McCann commented that he was personally very disappointed upon reading Heath's telegram, not alone because of its possible effects on the relations between the two Governments but also because of its effect on public opinion. He stressed that Heath's Government had publicly supported the Downing Street Declaration. However, earlier suspicions about Heath and Northern Ireland were resurfacing. In reply, Peck stressed that Heath had been incensed by the fact that the telegram had not reached him before it had appeared in the press. McCann minuted that the ambassador 'appeared to agree that Mr Heath's telegram . . . was unfortunate.' Asked whether the telegram was an aberration on Heath's part, Peck 'discreetly agreed and said that it was so regarded generally in Whitehall.' Peck said that if he personally could have stopped the publication of the message he would have done so but there had been no time. He had been in touch with London on Friday and Saturday and 'was aware that they were trying to undo the harm caused.' He had received a message on Saturday indicating that Heath would see Lynch sooner than the October meeting if desired. He wanted to get that message to the Taoiseach before he met his ministers and the elected representatives from the North. That was his explanation for trying to see the Taoiseach at his home the previous day.[59]

McCann, who had interrupted his holidays to return to work, took a particularly hard line. He could not understand how Heath could suggest that the Taoiseach had no right to be heard on the problems of the North, Patrick Hillery having established that right with the previous Labour government after the sad experiences of the summer of 1969. McCann wanted the dialogue to continue between the two governments, and the ambassador agreed, stating that there was no desire on the part of the British to terminate that dialogue. He volunteered the view that Hillery and Lynch were right about the effects of interment in the North. McCann reminded the ambassador that they had also been right in 1969 and 1970 and that it was about time that London should start listening to himself (McCann) rather than to the 'spurious guidance they must be receiving from Belfast.'[60]

Peck returned to the message that Heath would be prepared to meet Lynch sooner, if desired, and that he would be prepared to discuss all questions of mutual interest. (That was taken as including the North.) He thought there could be an early meeting, provided the realities were recognised on both sides. That meant that Lynch could not expect the end of Stormont, nor Heath that all IRA suspects would be locked up in the South. McCann said that if Lynch agreed to an early meeting he could not come away empty-handed. Peck said that Lynch should be fully aware of Heath's willingness to have an early meeting before the Taoiseach took decisions in support of passive resistance in the North.[61]

As Peck was meeting McCann on 23 August, Lynch held a meeting with sixteen Stormont SDLP and Nationalist Party representatives. He was accompanied by the Minister for External Affairs, Patrick Hillery, the Minister for Finance, George Colley, the Minister for Labour and Social Welfare, Joseph Brennan, and the Minister for Education, Pádraig Faulkner. Also present were the leader of Fine Gael, Liam Cosgrave, and the secretary of the Labour Party, Roddy Connolly.

The situation in Northern Ireland had grown progressively worse; but the war of words between Lynch and Heath abated swiftly.[62] Behind the scenes, both Dublin and London sought to patch up the relationship. Lynch was invited to Chequers for talks on 6 and 7 September 1971. He accepted the invitation to talks but turned down the invitation to stay, preferring to be lodged at the Irish embassy in London.

In his memoirs Heath wrote that the first day was constructive but that Lynch grew restless towards the evening and 'at ten to six he got up, followed by his private secretary, and said that they would come back at six o'clock and tell me whether or not he was prepared to go on with the meeting.' Looking across at the Irish ambassador, Heath heard that Lynch had gone out to have a glass of Paddy. While Lynch was out of the room Heath secured a bottle of Paddy from the housekeeper and offered a glass on his return. He did the same the following morning at about eleven o'clock.

The talks were a success, but it would be incorrect to give Irish whiskey the credit. According to Garret FitzGerald, 'the meeting marked a significant advance on the British side since it recognised the Irish Government's legitimate interest in a situation threatening the security of both parts of the island.'[63] Lynch agreed to tripartite talks between Faulkner, Heath and himself. Faulkner and Lynch met face to face at Chequers on 27 and 28 September. Heath wrote: 'This was one of the historic events of my premiership, and I expected it to be very tense indeed.' The meeting was the first between the three prime ministers in seventy years. Heath was delighted to see how well the two men got on together and 'that they were not so very different after all.' Although unintentionally patronising, Heath's comments reflected the reality.[64]

Having made a dreadful mistake by allowing the introduction of internment, Heath began to speak firmly in public to the Northern Unionists. In November he said: 'They could not expect to have an absolute veto over any political progress.' On 15 November he told the annual Lord Mayor's Dinner in London that Britain had 'no selfish interest in Northern Ireland and that, should the people of Northern Ireland ever wish to join the Republic, they would be free to do so.'[65]

Lynch met Heath in London on 6 December in his office in the House of Commons. The talks lasted twenty-five minutes. Lynch stressed that because of the effect of internment Dublin was losing influence over the situation and that more recent developments in the North, such as the cratering of roads, had proved to be counter-productive. He said it was regrettable and dangerous that British forces should come as far as the indeterminate border, and that there should be incidents of firing into the territory of the Republic.[66]

Heath told Lynch that some of those engaged in violence were taking refuge in the South, and he wondered whether there was any possibility of extraditing some of those people. Lynch replied that extradition was a matter for the courts, and he stressed that the influence of his Government on the Northern situation was waning. He mentioned the pressure to which he had been subjected, following the publication in August of the Compton Report on allegations of physical brutality and the receipt of other information, to seek recourse to the European Commission on Human Rights in Strasbourg.[67] Heath replied: 'You resisted as long as you could.' Lynch urged the need for an urgent initiative to start talks between the parties in the North. Heath replied that any mention of an initiative brought a fresh outbreak of IRA violence. He did not see anything substantial happening before Christmas.[68]

Lynch pressed the question of reunification. He urged that if the British people could be encouraged to think that reunification was the only ultimate solution and this was supported by the British Government, 'then the Unionists in the North might tend to fall into line.' If the grip of the Unionists could be loosened, he argued, 'then the Dublin Government might find it easier to move in their direction.' Heath referred to his speech at the Lord Mayor's Dinner, in which he had made it clear that 'reunification is a rightful aspiration to hold.' Where the Irish Government was unrealistic, he said, was 'in thinking that one million Unionists want a united Ireland.' Lynch said that there were indications that Paisley was prepared to think in terms of a united Ireland. Heath replied: 'You know my views on Paisley.'

Lynch stressed again the need for an early breakthrough in the North, or else the situation 'will go from bad to worse.' Heath said he fully appreciated the seriousness of the situation and concluded that it was important that 'talks between them should continue.'[69]

Just before Christmas, Heath made his first trip to Northern Ireland. He flew to Derry and viewed the city from the walls. Flying back to Belfast, he was driven through the streets in an armoured car and saw the damage and an enormous security fence, on the other side of which 'were screaming women, banging the pavement with bin lids.' Despite the violence in the North, Heath wrote in his memoirs that he was 'much more optimistic than I had been a year previously.'[70]

There was little to be optimistic about. At the end of 1971 the death toll was 180, of whom 94 were civilians. Some 44 British soldiers, 11 members of the RUC and five UDR men had been killed. Three loyalist paramilitaries and twenty-three republicans were also dead in the violence. By December 1971 a total of 1,500 people had been arrested, but nearly a thousand had been released without charge. Persistent charges of brutality were levelled against the authorities. Internees had been beaten with batons, were forced to run over broken glass, were hooded and, in some cases, dropped from a helicopter that—unknown to the victim—hovered just above the ground.

The year ended in Belfast with the bombing of McGurk's Bar, in which fifteen people died. On the Protestant Shankill Road a bomb caused the death of four people, including a seven-month-old baby. Worse was to follow.

INTERVENTION BY MAIRIN LYNCH

A growing number of episodes of murder and brutality were carried out by the IRA in the ghettos of Belfast and Derry. Máirín Lynch found herself the subject of public attention towards the end of 1971. On a visit to Monaghan her husband invited her to read out a letter she had written to the press protesting about recent incidents in the Bogside of tarring and feathering and of shaving women's heads. She also made reference to the 'young boys of the British army.' About that time she may have been referring to nineteen-year-old Stephen McGuire, a Catholic member of the British army who was shot in Belfast on 4 November, to eighteen-year-old Paul Genge, shot by the IRA in Lurgan, or to 23-year-old Ian Curtis, shot by the IRA in Derry on 9 November. Fifty-year-old Dermot Hurley, a Catholic member of the RUC, was also shot by the IRA on 11 November in north Belfast.

The Derry Women's Action Committee reacted strongly to Máirín Lynch's condemnations.[71] Many people came to her defence. The poet and former diplomat Máire Cruise O'Brien wrote on 4 December 1971:

I and my family—including Conor—were deeply moved. May success attend your efforts and may we live to see this nightmare lifted from all our lives. Please give my warm personal regards to the Taoiseach—I always remember him as the most considerate of Ministers to work for . . .

Bride Mullins wrote from 6 Haddington Terrace, Dún Laoghaire, on 17 November 1971:

It took the bravery and the courage of Joan of Arc to act as you did last Saturday. You were inspired as she was and what matters if the reaction is indifferent, someone—the Taoiseach's wife has spoken out in civilized,

Christian feminine way and has appealed for sanity for all our suffering humanity. That is on the record now for all time.

Isobel J. Ruby of 1 Vernon Grove, Rathgar, Dublin, wrote on 15 November 1971:

I have been asked by some friends to thank you on behalf of the 'silent majority' for your wonderful words of compassion in connection with the sad happenings in the north.

The painter Frances Kelly (wife of the diplomat Freddie Boland) wrote on 27 November 1971:

Your letter moved me to tears. As long as we have Jack for Taoiseach there is some hope for us. He is a man who is true to his country and his high ideals, and good to his own people, and I know that the people love and respect him as we do.

Father John Feighery, writing on 16 November 1971, summed up the thinking of many people in the country at the time.

I think that Ireland has been blessed at this time in having in your husband a man who seems to deeply understand the depth of insanity and suffering which physical violence represents. It is not a realisation which pervades the Irish consciousness, spared as we have been from two world wars. In many ways people, North and south, are now being pursued by the political failures and selfishness of the past—but your husband's insistence on a peaceful solution is the only way to a united Ireland worth having. In honesty, I must state (as a person of no strong political affiliations) that I don't think the Fianna Fáil government deserves to continue in office but I can see no other taoiseach at the moment holding the country together peacefully—which, as he sees, is the supreme priority.[72]

Máirín Lynch took the unusual step of writing to the press to defend herself against accusations of being a supporter of the British army. On 3 December 1971 she sent the following to the *Irish Press*:

I have been accused of standing over the inhuman treatment meted out by some personnel of the British army to the Catholic minority in the North. Because I have only once spoken out in regard to the current troubles in the north—the tarring of the Derry girl—I have been accused of this bias. The reason is simple; I find it very difficult to express my feelings in public because I am too nervous to speak in public. I wish to make my position clear. My desire is a united Ireland obtained by peaceful means. I condemn all acts of violence which bring suffering and tragedy to the Catholic minority in the north, and I abhor the excessive acts of violence of some of the British soldiers. I also abhor all acts of violence done in the cause of Irish unity. People are people the world over, with the same aspirations, feelings, loves and hurts.[73]

Máirín Lynch provided an example from among the recent killings. Robert Benner, aged twenty-five, had been born in Dundalk. He was a member of the British army, with a family address in Leicestershire. Posted to Northern Ireland, he visited his fiancée, Lucy Connolly, in Dundalk to make preparations with the parish priest for their wedding. On 28 November 1971 his body was found lying on the road a hundred yards from the border near Crossmaglen, Co. Armagh. The Official IRA had shot him.[74]

In this context, I wish to express my heartfelt sympathy to Lucy Connolly because of the unbelievable sorrow and bewilderment she must now be feeling as a result of the brutal killing of her fiancée Robert Benner. What right have these so called arbiters of justice to wreck the lives of these young people? To what sympathy or understanding are they entitled in support of the cause they serve? To me this cause is suspect and is certainly neither Christian nor wholesome.[75]

While the Taoiseach could not give expression in such a personal way to sentiments of that kind, Máirín Lynch articulated values shared with her husband about the use of violence.

SUNDAY, BLOODY SUNDAY

A number of Eamonn Gallagher's reports are to be found among Jack Lynch's personal papers. One, written on 19 January 1972 and quoted in part earlier, argued in favour of a continuation of the Taoiseach's more radical policy line on Northern Ireland adopted in July 1971. Gallagher posed two questions, based on the assumption that existing British policy in Northern Ireland would not be allowed to continue indefinitely: (1) whether Heath's policy was to maintain the Northern state as part of the United Kingdom as long as Britain could do so, and (2) whether the present British military policies could reduce the level of violence to one readily compatible with the first question.

Gallagher again expressed his disagreement with the policy of internment and the follow-up tactics used by Lieutenant-General Tuzo in the Catholic ghettos. He argued that the military tactics might have been 'probably effective in dis-organising the IRA and sufficient to force them into random bombing and random assassination and away from major operations,' but they ran counter to the principles of counter-insurgency published by Brigadier Frank Kitson, and Tuzo must have known that. It appeared not unreasonable to Gallagher to suggest that, as a matter of military conduct, Tuzo had decided to achieve the objective set for him in the simplest way, i.e. eliminate the gunmen. His real and proper objective should have been—as it was before internment was introduced—to separate the gunmen from the people; instead he imposed the gunmen on the ghettos. His military success must therefore be a political failure. Gallagher concluded that if Tuzo was the political general he was reputed to be, and had been opposed to internment in the first instance, then he may have given Faulkner the 'wrong victory'.[76]

Most of Gallagher's contacts in the North believed that the IRA could not be beaten, but one had to be careful to understand what 'victory' meant in those circumstances. 'I believe that the British body politic can take a certain level of endemic violence in the North more or less indefinitely.' He argued that if IRA activities could be reduced 'to such a bearable level of violence then, of course, the IRA would be "beaten" in a sense at least for the time being.' He held that it was possible for the British army to achieve that main objective while its government could maintain the current levels of expenditure in the North for as long as they wished. A military policy of that kind 'is, therefore, sustainable by the British Government. I think it would be dangerous to have illusions about this.'[77]

Gallagher argued that Faulkner's assessment of the situation was 'almost entirely wrong.' He and his most important official adviser, William Stout, had been instrumental in the defeat of the IRA in the 1956–62 campaign.

> Essentially they have attempted to use the tactics which succeeded then in a situation which was massively different. This must represent a failure of political sensitivity.

He argued that it stood out

> in any analysis of the present situation that Faulkner sold whatever chance he had of becoming Prime Minister of all the people for the consolidation of his own position in the Unionist Party. In doing so he is likely to find that he has become the servant of the right-wing, including the Orange Order, and not its master.

Gallagher concluded that Faulkner, whom he considered to be a 'political lightweight,' had 'rarely shown any evidence of understanding the minority.'

He believed that Faulkner's position in London would become more difficult if the IRA was to be weakened and the minority remained steadfast in their refusal to accept Unionist government. In that context, he reported that London 'would be forced to act in radical ways.'[78] Gallagher believed that the main lines of policy on the North should be retained, particularly the maintenance of a tough attitude against 'current British repression of the minority.' That included refusal to be intimidated by British propaganda about such things as the 'gelignite trail'. The Government should 'overtly encourage the minority to resist, by passive means, the restoration of unionist control.' The Northern situation should be internationalised at every reasonable opportunity—with particular reference to the US and European government opinion. The British Labour Party should be encouraged to break with the bipartisan policy. Events might encourage the Irish Government to interpret the Northern problem as a colonial one. That had the advantage of supporting the thesis that the majority of the Irish people were entitled to decide the issue. The corollary was that the Northern majority was a colonial occupation. 'We should, also, therefore, have an open policy of encouraging Protestant opinion to consider unity, on terms, as a reasonable and valid alternative to supporting what is in fact a police state.'[79]

In January 1972 Jack Lynch and Patrick Hillery went to Brussels to sign the Treaty of Accession to the European Communities. At Heath's request, he and Lynch met on Sunday 23 January in the house of the British ambassador in Brussels. Lynch began by saying that he had recently called in the British ambassador 'as he [Lynch] was genuinely worried about the trend of events in relation to the North.' He referred to the setting up of the new internment camp 'in a provocative situation near Derry.' There was, he said, the question of rising unemployment in both jurisdictions, leaving many young people on the streets; and their frustration with the present policies might lead them into dangerous paths. He thought the time had come to reappraise the whole situation. There could not continue to be a confrontation on the old stands, he said. He was anxious to work out with the Prime Minister a peaceful solution. Even if the IRA were beaten by the 'present efforts at securing a military solution,' that would not be the end of it. 'The kids on the street,' he said, 'who are already involved in the conflict, will be 18 and 19 years of age before too long and trouble will inevitably break out again if there is no political solution.' Lynch went on to say that 'Stormont will never be accepted again as it has been up to now.' He wondered whether it would be possible to persuade Brian Faulkner to take action. He wanted to avoid in any future talks the restating of hard-line positions.[80]

Heath replied that he was prepared to talk at any time. It was important to keep the temperature down, and he referred to what he described as the unfortunate remarks recently made by the Minister for Justice, Desmond O'Malley, at Strasbourg. O'Malley had drawn attention to the passive support for the IRA that seemed to be increasingly evident in the South. Peck had made a particular plea that he not make a provocative speech.

Lynch defended O'Malley and what he had said. O'Malley was typical of 'the bright young people in Ireland today and what he had said, supplementing his script, reflected the concern and frustration the young people felt about present policies in relation to the North.' Heath said that the matter might come up again in Strasbourg, and he had told his people to keep the temperature as low as possible.[81]

Heath expressed his frustration with the SDLP, who had refused to participate in talks. He thought that 'there was not much point in trying to talk' to that party. He asked who represented the Catholics in Northern Ireland, feeling that the SDLP did so less and less, and that 'one must take account of the limits within which one can operate in order to get a political solution.' Faulkner was prepared to enter into talks, provided there was no question of a change to the border. Heath felt that 'the IRA are certainly taking hard knocks now. At some stage they may give up violence and look at the situation in another way.'

In reply, Lynch said that he saw Heath's difficulty about the IRA:

If one seemed to be giving in to the Provisionals it could be said one was giving in to violence. On the other hand, merely putting down violence is no solution as then the Unionists would say they had won and there would be no give on their part towards arriving at a political solution. Now that the IRA are still active might be the opportune moment for loosening the Unionist grip. There are some indications that the IRA are talking about a political solution.

Referring to internment, Lynch said that while it was there now, and no doubt many of those interned would carry guns, there were also a lot of people interned who would never touch a gun. He urged an early move to political talks in conjunction with some concession on internment. That might get the IRA off the streets, and the 40 per cent minority community might move away from supporting the IRA, he said. In such circumstances the SDLP might enter talks. He felt that that party was there and could not be written off. There were also the old-style Nationalist Party, who were not as rigid as the SDLP. As in industrial disputes, Lynch argued, there was the problem that neither could accept less than the other.

Lynch re-emphasised the point that the ending of internment could prove to be a significant move forward. He said that the IRA realised now that they

could not achieve a united Ireland at one fell swoop, and they were realistic
enough to see a slow movement towards that goal. He said he was prepared to
talk to all the people in Ireland, urging them to get together and try to stop
the present deteriorating situation. He was prepared to tell the people in the
South that they could not be expected to hang on to everything to suit themselves and that they must change in order to secure progress. He would hope
thereby to give encouragement to moderate Protestant opinion in the North.[82]

Heath asked a series of questions on what the minority wanted in the
North, and he wanted to know what was meant by stating that Stormont was
finished. Lynch replied that there should be community government in the
North, involving both Unionists and Nationalists, based on a system of proportional representation. He noted that Faulkner had refused to have anyone
in his cabinet with aspirations for a united Ireland. Lynch predicted that
Paisley might move in and take over. Heath said that it was not even clear
what was meant when one talked about a change in the constitutional
position. If that meant a united Ireland, neither Faulkner nor himself nor the
British parliament would agree to a change. If, however, it meant constitutional change within the North, then Heath and Faulkner could discuss it in
all its aspects. Lynch replied that if the minority could have some real share of
responsibility—some seats in the cabinet—that might go some distance to
satisfying them.[83]

On the question of detention, Heath reported that some thirty internees
had been released. But in the course of a review he said there was little doubt
but that those who were interned were those who were carrying on the battle.
Lynch said that for every single person interned ten more replaced them outside. He complained about the construction of an internment camp at
Magilligan, near Derry. That was both 'dangerous and provocative.' He said
that Ivan Cooper intended leading a march to that camp. It was a great pity
that the retrograde step of a second internment camp had been taken and,
worse still, that it should have been sited where it was. Heath said that the
second camp was designed to provide better standards of accommodation
and ease of access for visitors. If it had been situated out in the wilds they
would have been criticised for its inhumane location.[84]

Lynch raised the question of the spread of violence. Cardinal Conway
believed that the crust of peace in the South was very thin, 'and violence could
spread south.' He said if there was not political progress the trouble could
spread and could be carried across the channel into Britain. Then there would
be the awful situation such as the 1939 bombing campaign in Britain.
Violence, said Lynch, could spread in both islands. He hoped that he had got
across to Heath 'that the current policy in relation to the North would
provide no solution.'[85]

In London on 26 January, Lynch had follow-up talks with the secretary of the Cabinet, Sir Burke Trend, and the deputy under-secretary at the Foreign Office, Sir Stewart Crawford. He was accompanied by McCann and the Irish ambassador, Dónal O'Sullivan. Lynch said there was little he could add to what he had already told the Prime Minister. He had hoped for a political initiative in Northern Ireland; but after two visits to Chequers there had been the recent development of the issuing of new instructions to the British army and the setting up of a new internment camp. All this had created a growing impatience that nothing helpful was happening. There was increasing concern about the deteriorating situation in Northern Ireland. He said he intended to make a major policy speech about February and he was prepared to give Peck sight of the text in advance. He said that he and his colleagues were increasingly disappointed by the fact that Faulkner seemed to be dictating policy to the British Government. There needed to be an urgent advance in London on the attitude towards reunification.[86]

On the question of talks, Sir Burke Trend asked whether the SDLP would be regarded as acceptable spokesmen in talks by the minority. Lynch replied that the alternative to them was the IRA. He said there had been incidents of unnecessarily rough treatment of youngsters apprehended by the British army. Those youngsters would be the IRA heroes five or six years hence. If the IRA were beaten now, the Unionists would become more intransigent. The present was the time to tell Faulkner to move away from the stand he was taking. Trend enquired why the present was the right moment. Lynch replied that if there was not a very early initiative he might lose public support for his policy of moderation. He pointed out that he did not have a majority in the Dáil, as a result of which he could not completely control the situation. He said that ministers with constituencies in border areas were bringing him reports of growing unrest.[87]

Trend then asked, In the event that talks were to get going, what would they be about? Lynch replied that representation in government for the minority would be an absolute essential. There was a follow-up question on the size of the representation, to which Lynch replied that it would be a matter for discussion and negotiation. Crawford enquired whether Lynch in his intended policy speech wanted to evoke a response from Faulkner. He said he wanted it recognised that his government must go some way in trying to remove misgivings in the minds of the Northern majority.

On the question of security, Crawford remarked that there 'should be some new turning of the wheel,' and he asked the Taoiseach whether he envisaged 'more activity on the IRA on the Border.' Lynch replied that the British army did not agree with the cratering of roads and that such cratering was not done for security but 'principally to embarrass him.' He said that he had

brought home as many Irish soldiers from Cyprus as he could. He stressed
that, short of internment, he could do no more than he was doing at present
in relation to the IRA. He pointed out that there had been quite a few convictions lately for politically motivated offences, for example the robbing of
banks. Crawford said it would be helpful if Lynch could do something more
on the security front in order to encourage the right response from Faulkner.
Lynch repeated that there was nothing more he could realistically do on
security. The discussion ended there.[88]

Earlier the Taoiseach had met the leader of the British opposition, Harold
Wilson, on 25 January 1972 at the Irish embassy in London. Wilson felt that
Tory attitudes were hardening in relation to Northern Ireland in recent weeks.
He had advocated inter-party talks, but the Conservatives were arguing that,
as the SDLP would not enter into talks, the whole operation was pointless and
should be abandoned. He would not accept that such talks should be on Privy
Councillor terms, which precluded disclosure. He took the opposite viewpoint. He wanted the blame for any veto used to fall in the right quarters,
namely on Faulkner. Besides Gerry Fitt, Wilson wanted either John Hume or
Austin Currie to be included in any SDLP delegation. He would have talks first
in London with the Liberal Party, and then he hoped the SDLP would join in.
If Faulkner was not prepared to participate he would go ahead with as many
other Northern parties as were prepared to join in. The third stage would
bring in the Dublin parties. Lynch would have to consider whether his party
would participate in talks without the presence of either the Conservatives or
the Faulkner Unionists. There was also the question of gaining approval from
those in Long Kesh internment camp. Wilson intended to involve his friend
Cardinal Heenan in the process in order to persuade those imprisoned.

The Dublin side speculated that Wilson had himself in mind for the role
of chairman of the talks. Wilson said he had ruled out the idea of Ireland's re-
entry into the Commonwealth and proposed instead the concept of dual
nationality. There was a brief discussion on the role of James Callaghan.
Wilson said they had not been seeing entirely eye to eye but he was now 100
per cent with him 'out of fear that Mr Roy Jenkins might try to take over the
Labour Party.' Callaghan had been ill. Wilson had handled matters on
Northern Ireland himself in view of the urgency of the question. He fully
shared the Taoiseach's concern about moving forward rapidly.[89]

The situation in Northern Ireland had grown more serious in the days
that Lynch was in Brussels and London. But nobody predicted quite how disastrous the last days of January 1972 would prove to be. On 18 January,
Faulkner had banned all parades and marches until the end of the year. But
an anti-internment rally was held on 22 January at Magilligan Strand, outside
the new internment camp. There were clashes between demonstrators and the

British army, in which the army fired rubber bullets and cs gas into the crowd. On 28 January the Northern Ireland Civil Rights Association sought to ensure that there would be a peaceful, incident-free day on 30 January for a march planned in Derry.

By the end of January 1971 the British Ambassador, John Peck, was

> tortured officially by doubts about the policy of the government I was serving as the Queen's representative; tortured, personally, by doubts about the impact of the reports, analyses, opinions that I and my Embassy were sending to the Foreign Office; tortured by doubts whether it might be too late for anyone involved in Northern Ireland, whether from London, Dublin or Westminster, to make any dent at all in the monolith which had established itself in Stormont fifty years earlier. Was there to be no flexibility anywhere?[90]

He had given his personal view that unless some drastic initiative was taken the situation in Ireland as a whole could only get worse. He asked in exasperation whether there was any point in carrying on in his post. His despatch was a 'pretty gloomy document,' as he had to describe the mounting tension and uncertainty and 'the fear of an extension into the Republic of the steadily worsening security situation in the North.' He 'ventured the opinion that to take no decision was itself a decision whose consequences could be more tragic with every day that passed (or words to that effect).' The ambassador felt that 1971 had been a bad year for Jack Lynch's 'peaceful approach' and working through the British policy. 'And I said so.' He knew that that would not be welcome, 'and it wasn't.'[91]

In defiance of a ban, a large civil rights march was planned for Derry on Sunday 30 January. The organisers were pleased with the turn-out. Some fifteen thousand people walked past the Bogside en route to the Guildhall, when they were stopped by the British army at William Street. Changing their plans, the organisers sought to lead the protest to Free Derry Corner, amid rioting and stone-throwing. Contrary to the view of Inspector Frank Lagan, one of the most senior Catholics in the RUC, the commander of land forces in Northern Ireland, Major-General Robert Ford, ordered the Parachute Regiment to go in. Jonathan Bardon wrote:

> Then the killing began. People on the march were certain the first shots were fired by the army; troops, on the other hand, said they came under fire as they moved forward to make arrests. Whatever the truth of the matter, there is no doubt that men of the Parachute Regiment continued shooting, firing 108 rounds, injuring thirteen, including one woman, and killing thirteen men, seven of them under nineteen years of age.[92]

Father Edward Daly, a priest from the Bogside and later Bishop of Derry, was an eyewitness to the slaughter. A seventeen-year-old youth running beside him was killed by a bullet.

When the dead were counted, the Derry city coroner, Major Hubert O'Neill, noted that many had been shot in the back. 'It strikes me that the Army ran amok that day and shot without thinking. They were shooting innocent people . . . I say it without reservation—it was sheer, unadulterated murder.'[93] That was certainly my reaction when I heard the news while at work on the sub-editors' desk of the *Irish Press*.

Bad weather kept the British ambassador in his residence on the weekend of 29/30 January 1972. On the night of the killings he received a phone call from the Chancery Office in London.

'Head of Chancery here. Have you heard the news?'
'No, what?'
'There was trouble at the civil rights march in Derry. The paratroops have killed thirteen Catholics.'
'Anything more come through? Well, thank you very much. Goodnight.'

Lynch, according to the account in Heath's memoirs, phoned him that night 'in a very emotional state.' A transcript of that phone conversation states in part:

Lynch: I am told that, according to reports I received and checked on the spot, the British troops reacted rather beyond what a disciplined force might be expected to . . . but when the funerals take place on either Tuesday or Wednesday I hate to think of what could happen . . .
Heath: . . . it is very difficult to accept a condemnation of Stormont for doing something which you yourself have requested, you have constantly requested. You spoke to me last summer that marches should be banned.
Lynch: . . . I will say that I have asked you to take very firm political steps to the point of taking over security and making some alternative arrangement as far as Stormont is concerned.
Heath: Well you can tell me how taking over security and changing Stormont is going to make people obey that law and not challenge with marches.
Lynch: Well I think it will certainly avoid situations like this arising again . . . the repercussions South of the Border, as I see myself, are going to be so serious that we will both have a much more difficult situation on hand as a result of this unless Westminster does take firm action at this stage.

Heath: Well perhaps if you had condemned people beforehand who were going to challenge the law the march might not have taken place.

Lynch: I do not believe that would have happened anyway. Words would come easily from me but people are not going to obey or accord to what I think might be done in certain circumstances . . . I cannot tell people not to support them . . .

Heath: . . . you could deal very toughly with those who are using the South as their refuge and I have always told you this for many months.

Lynch: I know you have . . . But on the other hand within the limits of our own law—

Heath: If you had dealt with them this would have been over long ago.

Lynch: I do not believe it would. No I say it would have been much worse. We know what happened as a result of internment in the North and in fact the suggestion you have been making that we should intern them in the South would have been far worse . . .

'This was hardly a time for small talk,' Heath recorded breezily in his memoirs.[94]

In the circumstances, Lynch had spoken in measured tones. Heath hectored him, though less aggressively than in the wake of the introduction of internment. The facts spoke for themselves. 'Alienation is pretty total,' John Hume said on RTE.[95] In such an inflamed atmosphere Lynch was challenged to react with control and decisiveness. Describing the shootings as 'unbelievably savage and inhuman,' he took the unprecedented step of recalling the Irish ambassador from London as the strongest possible gesture of his Government's displeasure with the actions of the British Government. He declared 2 February 1972 a national day of mourning.

In the coming days the Department of the Taoiseach and Lynch's house in Rathgar were gathering-points for prominent visitors from Derry, many of them giving first-hand accounts of what they had seen happening before their eyes. Father Edward Daly was among those visitors. Later Lynch asked him to go to the United States to give his account of those terrible events. Following Lynch's death in 1999, Bishop Daly in his retirement recalled those events and his trip to America in a letter to Máirín Lynch. (See chapter 11.)

On 2 February the trade union movement planned a rally and protest march. Crowds later gathered outside the British embassy in Merrion Square, near Holles Street Hospital. Only a railed basement area stood between the gathering crowds and the building itself. A few gardaí stood on the pavement and on the steps outside the door. It was virtually an impossible building to defend.

The Minister for Justice, Desmond O'Malley, in an interview in the television documentary 'Seven Ages', described the policy options open to the

Government. Force would have had to be used to defend the building, he said. That would have meant having to deploy the army. 'They were not prepared to go in with lead,' he explained. 'Militarily they were right.' The political decision hinged, therefore, on whether it was more important to protect lives or property. 'The sacrifice was made,' said Mr O'Malley, and 'the burning took place. The emotions of the time spent themselves in the flames of that building.'[96] Such a reading of the events reflects the pragmatism of the Government and its determination not to have a massacre on the streets of Dublin.

What happened that day was much more sinister than the irrational actions of people driven by blind emotion—some thirty thousand, according to Jonathan Bardon.[97] Trade unionists turned out in their thousands to protest against the indiscriminate killings in Derry. The march ended in a rally and speeches. The formalities over, many thousands of people were left leaderless in the environs of the embassy. I found myself in the garden of Merrion Square, directly in front of the embassy—a fine, newly restored Georgian building. Suddenly an instruction was given to knock down the railings by a man standing next to me. As I looked incredulously at him, a mob began to follow his lead and shake the railings in unison. Within seconds more than fifty yards of railing had been knocked down and people surged forward onto the street in front of the embassy. The small Garda force on duty was powerless to protect the building. What happened next had been planned. Two men, one with a lump hammer, scaled the area to a window ledge and smashed the glass. Molotov cocktails were lobbed at the building, one smashing against the wall; but others were on target. The building quickly caught fire, to an atavistic chant of 'Burn, burn, burn.' Later I saw members of the Provisional IRA in uniform taking over 'crowd control'. It was a profoundly sad moment for Irish democracy.

David Blatherwick, a future British ambassador to Ireland, was the last person to leave the burning building. As the embassy caught fire he went over the garden wall at the back and left through a laneway, possibly bringing code books with him.

Lynch was at home, meeting a delegation from Derry, when he was told that that the embassy was in flames. Máirín Lynch recalled that feelings were running high in the room. All the visitors apparently left the house when the Taoiseach returned to his office by car. (The Department of the Taoiseach was then on the opposite side of Merrion Square to the burning embassy, adjacent to the Natural History Museum.) When Máirín went inside to the living-room she found a priest who wished to remain until the Taoiseach returned home. He wanted guns for the North, she told me.

Fear drove many to think in an irrational manner at that time. There was again a clamour for guns. John Hume was not among that chorus. If any episode had shown the futility of the use of force it had been that Bloody Sunday. Lynch absorbed the pressure, and his Government refused to yield. He called for an international inquiry.

In the wake of the burning the Gardaí intensified their campaign to curb the activities of the IRA. The force had been humiliated by the destruction of the embassy. An incident of that kind had never been allowed to happen in the history of the state. The Minister for Justice, Desmond O'Malley, was decisive in his leadership against all subversive organisations. (The Provisional IRA paid him the ultimate compliment, as will be seen below.) Heath and the British Government persistently chided the Irish authorities for not taking sufficiently strong action against the IRA. London was consistently wrongheaded in its criticism. The Irish state had battled successfully against the IRA and other subversive organisations since its foundation. The files in the Department of Justice show, and will continue to show, the measure of Special Branch success.

The British Government named the Lord Chief Justice, Lord Widgery, chairman of an inquiry into the Derry shootings. His findings, which were published in April, did not satisfy the Irish Government or the families of the victims. In the House of Commons on 19 April, Heath deeply regretted that there had been casualties, whatever the individual circumstances. He wanted a return to legality, reconciliation and reason in Northern Ireland. There was no reason to believe that soldiers would have opened fire, he said, if they had not been fired upon first. The opposition, although critical, broadly supported the Government.[98]

Bloody Sunday 1972 remains one of the most controversial and divisive events to occur during the cycle of violence that enveloped Northern Ireland between 1969 and the mid-1990s. The Saville Tribunal, established in 1998, continued in 2007 to inquire into the controversial events of that day.

Despite the terrible events of Bloody Sunday, there appeared to be little appetite for compromise in Northern Ireland. The Stormont Government showed itself to be even more incompetent. Unionism was hopelessly split. On 12 February, William Craig held the first rally of his Ulster Vanguard at Lisburn, Co. Antrim. On 22 February the Official IRA exploded a bomb in the officers' mess of the 16th (Parachute) Brigade at Aldershot in Hampshire, killing seven people: a Catholic chaplain, a gardener, and five women who worked in the canteen.

On 24 February the House of Commons passed the Northern Ireland Act (1972), conferring retrospective powers on the Northern Ireland Government. On 25 February the radical Unionist John Taylor was shot by the Official IRA but survived the assassination attempt. On 2 March, Heath announced that hooding, wall-standing, subjection to white noise and deprivation of sleep or food would no longer be used in Northern Ireland. On 4 March the Provisional IRA planted a bomb in the Abercorn restaurant in Belfast, killing two people and injuring 136. There was no warning. Among those who survived, four people lost both legs, one of whom also lost an arm.

The Provisional IRA called a 72-hour truce on 10 March 1972. They demanded a British withdrawal, the release of IRA prisoners and the end of Stormont. According to Garda intelligence, the Army Council of the Provisional IRA held that the purpose of the three-day truce was to 'demonstrate to [the] Stormont and Westminster Governments how well disciplined and controlled their members were and to give an indication that, in the event of a suitable settlement being proposed by Heath, the IRA could control its members and call off the violence if they so wished.' As regards the three-point plan for peace, they stated that they knew well that their full terms would not be met but they wanted to show Heath the only type of conditions that would satisfy them and hoped that he might include them in his proposed political initiative.[99]

The leader of the opposition in Britain, Harold Wilson, flew to Dublin and met the leaders of the Provisional IRA on 13 March 1972 in the home of a Labour Party TD, Dr John O'Connell, in Inchicore, Dublin. Present were Dáithí Ó Conaill, Joe Cahill, John Kelly and Séamus Twomey. This maverick act angered and embarrassed Lynch and his Government. Wilson had ostensibly come over for talks with the Taoiseach and had used that as a pretext for meeting the leadership of the IRA. According to Garda intelligence, the Provisional IRA decided to 'time their first explosion a half an hour after [the] termination of the truce period and to continue with explosions and shootings as before.'[100]

That campaign restarted with a new ferocity. On 20 March a bomb planted by the IRA exploded in Donegall Street, Belfast, killing two policemen and four civilians. Out of more than a hundred people injured, nineteen received serious injuries. The IRA mounted an ever greater threat. Faulkner did not appear to be in a position to retain control of Unionism. On 18 March, according to the *Irish Times*, about sixty thousand people had attended a Vanguard rally at Ormeau Park, Belfast, to express their frustration at the drift of events.

In this situation, the British Government's patience ran out, and Faulkner's Government was in danger of being suspended. Heath, fearing that Northern Ireland was on the 'threshold of complete anarchy,' favoured proroguing Stormont, but he found it difficult to get Cabinet unity on this recommendation. Alec Douglas-Home and Reginald Maudling were reluctant to accept the move. The former was in despair of finding a solution and felt that 'we should start to push the people of Northern Ireland towards a united Ireland, rather than trying to get them more closely into the United Kingdom.'[101] Heath claimed in his memoirs that he was working for a lasting, cross-community settlement and that only direct rule would offer the breathing space necessary for building it. In the end he got a unanimous Cabinet decision in favour of proroguing Stormont.[102]

Faulkner was invited to London on 22 March, where he was confronted with the British Government's change of policy, which proposed the phasing out of internment and the holding of a plebiscite on the border issue, with London to assume direct control of security. Back in London the following day, Faulkner remained intransigent. On 24 March, Heath announced the suspension of Stormont for one year after Faulkner had refused to cede control of law and order to London. The last sitting of the Northern Ireland Parliament was held on 28 March 1972. William Whitelaw, who had been to Northern Ireland only twice in his life, was appointed Secretary of State. He flew to Belfast and on 30 March took over at Stormont Castle, faced with the task of running 'a community in a state of utmost turbulence.'[103] He began with the gradual release of internees. On 27 April he lifted the ban on marches and demonstrations. By 26 May the SDLP had ended its members' boycott of public office. The Official IRA suspended all military operations.

On 14 April, Lynch made a speech on Northern Ireland. The introduction of direct rule was a policy success for the Government; but Lynch was not inclined to give in to the emotion of saying to Heath, 'I told you so.' Anglo-Irish relations had moved to another level, where the British Government acknowledged a place for the Irish Government in the resolution of the problems of Northern Ireland. Heath replied by letter to Lynch on 24 April 1972, stating that while the prospects for peace had improved 'we still have a long way to go.' He acknowledged that 'many of the minority have spoken up for peace, and that the IRA are in some disarray, but violence continues.' Heath stated that their policy of reconciliation, reflected in the release of internees and the closure of the prison ship *Maidstone*, 'threatens their standing with the minority of the North.' The IRA saw the continuance of violence as 'necessary to preserve their position.' Heath felt that the 'next few weeks will be of critical importance,' as 'on our success in re-establishing law and order stand the chances of creating in the longer term a stable and prosperous society in Northern Ireland with peace and justice for all.' The failure to bring 'terrorism to an end despite the political initiative we have embarked upon' would have 'incalculable' consequences 'for the whole of Ireland.'[104]

Because of the 'vital importance of this for both our Governments,' Heath told Lynch he wanted 'to take you into my confidence as our thinking develops.' He could not lay out in detail 'our future policy . . . but I thought you might welcome some indication of our thoughts as matters stand.' He told Lynch that Whitelaw would continue to administer Northern Ireland on the lines laid down, while at the same time trying to bring together for talks all parties in Northern Ireland committed to peaceful policies in order to evolve a new and acceptable form of administration.

He defended the idea of holding plebiscites as 'an essential element in a balanced package.' They would act as a 'continuing reaffirmation by HMG [Her Majesty's Government] to the Catholics of the ultimate possibility of unification (which remains a legitimate political aspiration, peacefully expressed), and as such should be a positive ingredient in the solution of the present problem.' On the other hand, the plebiscite system would 'be a necessary reassurance to the Protestants that the view of the majority of the people will decide.' There were risks involved, but he felt that most people would accept that the ballot box was preferable to the bullet and the bomb.

Heath also addressed the question of the 'Economic Council for Ireland', which Lynch had raised. He believed that 'both North and South could benefit, economically and politically, from the proposal.' However, it would be risky to revive the idea 'before Protestant fears have calmed.' Membership of the EEC would offer opportunities in which such a council could play a useful role.[105]

Heath then returned to an old theme. 'Our hopes will crumble into dust if the IRA's sterile policies of violence are allowed to carry the day.' It was his earnest hope that Lynch would now feel freer to act 'vigorously against their units operating or sustained from the Republic.' In response to the arguments from Dublin that there would be no progress in Northern Ireland without a political initiative, his Government had 'taken considerable risks.' But, he continued,

> if this spring is indeed to be a turning point for Ireland, the IRA must be hit hard, and hit now: it is fair to ask that there should be a response from you, in the form of effective measures against the IRA, including not only action to prevent them exporting violence to the North, but also measures to hinder leading figures from visiting Londonderry, Belfast and other places where they seek to rally the IRA militants and to frustrate the efforts of the majority of Catholics to find a peaceful way forward.

Heath suggested that there was value in a 'closer and officially recognised working co-operation between the Garda and the Security Forces along the Border.' Unofficial contacts were quite good in some areas but were notably lacking elsewhere: 'You will find us very ready to respond to developments on your side of the Border.' There was a reference to the cratering of roads, which could not be stopped while IRA active service units continued their operations. He made reference to the IRA group operating in the Lifford-Strabane area. 'If they were to be cleared out, terrorist activity in the Strabane/Castlederg area to cease, and the Border thereabouts effectively policed on your side, the roads in the area cold be progressively restored.' He would like to see that practical measure being adopted along every mile of the border as 'a symbol of improved relations between North and South.' He asked: 'In the wake of the political initiative, would not local opinion rally to a vigorous lead from you, and support a Garda campaign against the IRA units?' He hoped that Lynch would examine the question sympathetically and urgently 'and give Sir John Peck the opportunity to discuss it privately with those responsible on your side with the purpose of taking action on both sides.'[106]

Earlier in the letter Heath had ruled out the possibility of an early meeting between the two heads of government, as it 'would be misinterpreted in Protestant circles and would complicate rather than ease Mr Whitelaw's task.' But they should keep in touch through diplomatic channels 'until the right time comes, and there will no doubt be opportunities for contacts between your people and Mr Whitelaw and his officials.' As the 'situation changes almost daily . . . I hope therefore we can keep in close touch,' he concluded.[107]

By degrees, Heath seemed to be moving away from a purely military solution in the North. Lynch did not support the idea of a plebiscite. But Anglo-Irish relations were entering a more constructive phase.

THE IRA DISCUSSES ASSASSINATING THE MINISTER FOR JUSTICE

The Special Branch provided the Government with a very good profile of IRA activity for March 1972. The gravity of its findings underlines the hostility felt by Lynch and his Government colleagues towards the Wilson-IRA meeting in Dublin. The Commissioner, Michael Wymes, sent Lynch a 61-page report. It was stamped 9 May 1972 but the report related to activities in March. It estimated that the combined strength of the IRA in that month was 1,740, made up of 684 for the Goulding group, 967 for the Ó Brádaigh group and 89 for splinter groups. The report alarmingly revealed that the activities of the Minister for Justice, Desmond O'Malley, and the enforcement of the Offences against the State Act, which had led to many arrests, were discussed at length at a recent meeting of the Army Council of the Provisional IRA.

The assassination of the Minister was discussed and some of those present at the meeting were in favour of it. Three members, however, did not favour it and any further action against the Minister was deferred until a later date.

The matter is to be discussed again in the near future, and, because of recent activities of the Gárdaí, who, the IRA say, are acting on the instructions of the Minister for Justice, these activities will be condemned by all members of the Army Council and they will blame the Minister for directing them.[108]

Wilson had met a number of the IRA leaders who would have been present at the meeting of the Army Council at which the assassination of the Minister for Justice had been discussed. Lynch had given O'Malley clear instructions to ensure that subversion should be curtailed. O'Malley was as tough as nails. The IRA leadership may not have been aware that the minister's grandfather had been shot in a hotel in Limerick by the Black and Tans during the War of Independence. O'Malley, who was personally close to Lynch, had a young family, who already had to cope with heavy security on the most routine movements, such as going to school. His wife was also quite seasoned. She was from Enniskillen and was not intimidated by the security measures or the unwelcome attention the family received. But members of the IRA had shot Kevin O'Higgins, one of O'Malley's predecessors, on 10 July 1927. The Government took no chances and doubled his personal protection and that of his family.[109]

O'Malley pressed for the introduction of an effective legal response to the threat of subversion. There was widespread intimidation of jurors. On 26 May 1972 the Government brought section V of the Offences against the State Act (1939) into operation. This established the Special Criminal Court, consisting of three judges sitting without a jury. This was the first time that this instrument had been used since 1961. The court sat for the first time on 8 June 1972.

As the Offences against the State Act came back into operation, the fight against the IRA was stepped up. On 26 June, Neil Blaney, who had remained defiant in his opposition to Lynch, was expelled from Fianna Fáil by an overwhelming majority of the National Executive for 'conduct unbecoming a member of the organisation.' Ironically, there was an acceleration of the crackdown on the IRA just at a time when the leadership of that organisation were discussing the idea of a ceasefire. The background to that initiative has yet to be explained in detail.

WHITAKER OPENS LINES OF COMMUNICATION WITH UNIONISM
In a biography of Jack Lynch it is important to lay emphasis on his indirect and private initiatives to bring about a breakthrough in Northern Ireland. While he continued to conduct Anglo-Irish relations through orthodox diplomatic channels, he encouraged his close friend Ken Whitaker to open up lines of communication with Unionism. For example, Whitaker may have been indirectly involved in encouraging the former Prime Minister of Northern Ireland, Terence O'Neill, to meet President de Valera. Lynch responded favourably to that request. On 21 April 1972 Whitaker accompanied the former Prime Minister of Northern Ireland to Áras an Uachtaráin. Twice in the interview de Valera said that it was one of his dearest dreams fulfilled as President of a united Ireland to have an O'Neill sit with him. The latter said

that he had a special interest in visiting the Áras. His mother, a daughter of Lord Houghton, later Marquis of Crewe, had played in the Viceregal Lodge (now Áras an Uachtaráin) as a child. Lord Houghton, a liberal home-ruler, had been sent to Ireland as Lord Lieutenant in 1892. Irate Protestants had pelted him with mud as he drove in from Kingstown (Dún Laoghaire)—a fate similar to that suffered by his grandson in the latter days of his premiership of Northern Ireland.[110]

Both men then talked about the Government of Ireland Act (1920) and the beginnings of Northern Ireland. De Valera maintained that Churchill had tricked Collins into virtual acceptance of the position intended for 'Southern Ireland' under the act. He himself had been given to understand that no oath of allegiance would be required. He said he had not understood the depths of the religious antagonism of Northern Protestants to Irish unity, but Erskine Childers had. De Valera admitted that he had completely underestimated the feelings and prejudices of the men of the Shankill Road. He thought Edward Carson was no more than a political opportunist.

O'Neill confirmed that Carson was a disappointed opportunist. He had been thwarted in his ambition of becoming Lord Chancellor of England. But O'Neill also confirmed that the fears of working-class Northern Protestants concerning home rule were powerful and primitive and could still be played upon by the present-day successors to Carson: the Paisleys, Craigs and Billy Hulls.[111]

O'Neill asked de Valera whether Irish neutrality during the Second World War would have been maintained even if the Americans had promised to persuade the British to concede a united Ireland in return for the entry of the South into the war on America's (as distinct from Britain's) side. It would have been very difficult for the British Government to say no. De Valera replied that even such an offer by the Americans, had it been made, would not have deflected him from his policy of neutrality at the time. He had seen the suffering and death caused among his friends and neighbours by the dreadful carnage of the First World War. He wanted to save the people from a repetition of that.

He would not be drawn on the Heath initiative except to express the hope that it would bring about peace.[112] There the meeting ended.

The meeting was of no great political significance. Symbolically, however, it demonstrated that normal relations between North and South could and should continue, notwithstanding the violent conflict.

Whitaker was involved in another 'peace' initiative. On 12 May 1972 he sent a letter of congratulation to the Taoiseach over his victory in the EEC referendum.[113] In it he mentioned that he had had a talk on the phone with the under-secretary at the Northern Ireland Office, Kenneth Bloomfield (who had previously served as deputy secretary to the Northern Ireland cabinet

from 1963 until the proroguing of Stormont in 1972). In his memoirs
Bloomfield described Lynch as 'an agreeable, soft-spoken, pipe-smoking Cork
man, who bore with humorous equanimity the absurd experience of being
pelted with snowballs by Paisley and his friends as his car turned around the
grandiose statue of Lord Carson at the head of Stormont's processional
drive.'[114] That was when he had gone to meet Terence O'Neill in 1966.

Whitaker stated in his letter that he was prepared to meet a group of
Northern Protestants and Catholics, together with the Governor, Lord Grey,
about 25 May. He enclosed a copy of a letter from Dr G. B. Newe, a Catholic,
founder and secretary of the Northern Ireland Council of Social Services.
Newe did not know to what extent it would be possible to resume the discussions 'we had when I was in office.' He mentioned that

> K.P.B. [Ken Bloomfield] is keen, but feels that he should make soundings.
> Shea is quite keen. Unfortunately, Dugdale has had a heart attack and, while
> I am glad to say, he is making a good recovery and come out of hospital
> today, it will be, I imagine, some time before he can be really active again.

What Newe felt was most urgent was getting through to 'your Boss Man' what
well-informed Catholics and Protestants were thinking. He did not feel that
Dublin was properly informed 'about the real position here.' They did not
appreciate the depth and strength of the fears of the Protestant community—
and some sections of the Catholic community too—

> that your men and the men in London are engaged in, or may become
> engaged in, some sort of 'deal' involving unity. There is also an immense
> fear of the IRA.

If those fears and suspicions were not allayed in some positive and open way,
the North could well be facing 'a pretty serious situation.'

> Unity may come, probably must come, in some form, in the long run, but
> it will have to be brought about by the sensible, honest and open efforts of
> Irish men, North and South.

He felt that at the moment, party politicians were wasting time playing inter-
party 'games.' He wanted 'a strictly private meeting' with 'that someone'
(Whitaker) who could hear the views of five or six highly responsible
Catholics and Protestants, evaluate them and convey them to the 'Boss Man'.
The group included a priest, a Presbyterian minister, possibly a Church of
Ireland cleric, a doctor and a couple of businessmen, who were described as

being 'men of great discretion and who are not politically involved in a party sense.' Newe said that Whitaker might stay with 'our civil service friends.' He also said that Lord Grey was anxious to meet him privately and in confidence.

The tragedy was that Grey did not include Newe informally and privately long ago. Grey had served in other posts where he had encountered similar situations. Newe was going into hospital, but he could make all necessary arrangements if Whitaker came up.[115]

Whitaker sent the Taoiseach a letter on 19 May with an enclosure, requesting that Lynch look at it when he returned to Dublin. The enclosure is not in the file;[116] but included is what is probably a draft for a speech, dated 18/5/72, initialled by Whitaker and endorsed 'for Mr O'Dowd as arranged.' The handwritten excerpt reads:

Much of the bombing and shooting which still most regrettably continues is not only senseless but seems intended to serve the most sinister and inhuman purposes—that of arousing sectarian passions and provoking a civil war. It is utterly to be condemned and no one with any decent instincts will give it any form of support. The excuse of defence has no relevance whatever to these activities. We, for our part, are determined that private armies will not be allowed to use our territory in any way to impose their will on the people of Northern Ireland, indeed, the people of this state itself. For the same reason the British Government must not allow private armies of any sort to operate in Northern Ireland.[117]

When Whitaker returned from Northern Ireland he wrote a report on 29 May to the Taoiseach in which he first outlined his discussions with Lord Grey. He found Grey to be

dispassionate, equally out of sympathy with Protestant extremists as with the IRA. His hope was that enough mutual confidence could be built between moderates, North and South, to keep civil war at bay and take all parties forward into an EEC which would eventually make Partition irrelevant.[118]

Whitaker heard a Protestant view expressed by Rev. John Young, a liberal Presbyterian minister. He said that he had never voted Unionist. Terence Duncan, a Belfast businessman with interests in Dublin, also presented a Protestant viewpoint. Catholic views were given by Dr Newe and by Father Desmond Wilson and his brother, Dr Kevin Wilson. Both Young and Dr Wilson spoke about the frightening extent to which the professional classes were deserting Northern Ireland. 'Jobs for doctors, which hitherto would have been regarded as "plums" had recently to be filled by Indians and Pakistanis.'

Fifty families had left in Young's own middle-class parish. Duncan said that many businessmen and industrialists 'had also had enough.'[119]

The main findings of the discussion were summarised as follows:

(1) Protestants in the North were 'terrified that London will do a deal with Dublin behind their backs, propelling them willy-nilly into a united Ireland.' Faulkner had convinced even Protestants who disliked him that he had been betrayed by Heath. They had no faith in the Conservatives and less in a Labour government. 'Though it may not sound over-complimentary,' wrote Whitaker, 'Lynch would be trusted far more than Heath.'

(2) Allied to that fear was a tendency to regard a united Ireland as an *imminent* possibility. That would cost the North dearly in economic terms. Surely the Republic, they said, should admit that it was not ready for unity yet.

(3) Constitutional change in the Republic would have only a minor influence on the attitude of Northern Protestants. The effective administration of the law was far more important to them. Therefore, they could not understand why both wings of the IRA had the freedom to direct from Dublin their campaign in the North. Neither could they understand why the South could be used by the IRA as a training base and a source for the smuggling of arms into Northern Ireland. They found 'most repugnant of all the unfettered policy-direction of the campaign from Dublin.' Protestants could

not stomach the fact that Ruairí Ó Brádaigh and Tomás Mac Giolla are regarded as legitimate political parties and given disproportionate publicity on RTE; and that Mac Stiofáin and Goulding move around freely under the eyes of the police; and that juries and jurors are so soft on IRA members.

(4) It was emphasised that the Ulster Defence Association was dangerous, well armed and organised 'and intent on causing serious trouble unless the IRA campaign is brought to an end within a few weeks.' They feared that civil war was a real and immediate risk, 'particularly with so many "decent" Protestants in their present confused state of mind.'

(5) RTE's reporting was slanted, not only in the undue prominence given to Sinn Féin and the IRA but in its coverage of events in the North and its constant use of offensive terms such as 'Six Counties'.[120]

Whitaker concluded that, in the light of these views, it was necessary to reassure moderate Protestants, particularly on the point that their agreement to enter a new Ireland would be required. They should be assured that they would have a full voice about the kind of Ireland it would be. Further, they needed reassurance that the Republic desired that there would be a phased movement towards any such development, without any reduction in standards or opportunities for the people of Northern Ireland. What had been done about the Special Criminal Court was a step towards meeting their views, he concluded.[121]

Whitaker wrote to Lynch on 14 June, enclosing a letter from Newe dated 10 June. Newe said that the position had deteriorated 'very considerably since we met.' He referred to a BBC programme on the UDA. Its import 'has been frightening,' and 'we may be in the middle of a very vicious and destructive sectarian war within a week to ten days.' While many Protestants did not want the sort of 'war' that seemed about to break out, 'they may have just as little choice as Catholics have had when intimidated by the IRA.'

The fear was very real that London and Dublin might do a deal of some kind. Newe wanted Lynch to make a statement that, while not disavowing unity, his Government would not be party to any 'back door' deal with the British to secure such a goal. He wanted the three principal parties in the Republic to make such a statement. He felt that the Irish Government ought to 'twist the arms' of the SDLP 'to the end that they engage in talks at once.' They would have to review their present stance that they would not engage in talks while internment lasted. If they did not move now, other Catholic leaders might have to take over and bypass them and just ignore them. 'Else there will be only death and destruction on a massive scale to talk about,' he wrote.

Newe did not think that Faulkner was showing the best leadership: he was 'trying to ride the two horses, an exercise which rarely ever pays good dividends.' In conclusion, he said that 'Ken Bloomfield had a bad spell, too; we were all under great strain. He is coming along ok and I am glad you are keeping in touch.'[122]

Whitaker, in his note to Lynch, said that the views of all the people of Northern Ireland would have to be taken into account in any approach to the peaceful settlement that the Government and all parties here want to see, and want to see quickly. He felt that discussions between political representatives were an urgent necessity.[123]

In line with the urgency of providing new thinking on Northern Ireland, Lynch prepared an article for the prestigious American journal *Foreign Affairs*. Drafted by a young civil servant in the Department of External Affairs, Noel Dorr, it appeared in the July issue.[124] Lynch stated that after fifty years it was evident 'that Lloyd George's solution was not the right one. Partition shelved, but did not solve, the "the Irish Question".'[125] He wrote: 'I consider that the only solution in Ireland is an Ireland united by agreement, in independence; an Ireland in a friendly relationship with Britain; an Ireland which will be a member with Britain of the enlarged European Community.'[126] Lynch stressed that 'a united Ireland will not be an Ireland in which the present state in the "South" takes over the "North" and assimilates it into its existing structures.'[127] He felt that 'the 1937 Constitution as it stands is not suitable for a new Ireland.' The new Ireland, he wrote, should be regarded as 'an entirely new political entity which should work out and enact for itself its own constitution.' The constitution of the new Ireland 'would have to be a written one with firm and explicit guarantees for the rights and liberties of all who live under it.' He proposed that 'Ireland as a whole should assert a new and more comprehensive identity.'[128]

Whitaker, who was given sight of the text before publication but had not been invited to make any suggestions, wrote to Lynch on 21 June about the 'admirable statement of your views in *Foreign Affairs.*' But he favoured a slightly different ordering of the priorities. Firstly, he felt that there was an urgency to stress the immediate need for a form of regional administration that would enable the whole community to live and work together in peace, while leaving the door open to an approach, by majority consent and possibly gradually, to the 'new Ireland' concept. Secondly, there was a need—however regretfully—to state that the aim of a united Ireland might take many years to achieve, 'though that is no reason for not starting on the path without further delay.' Thirdly, he felt that the 'phasing out over a period of years' of British subsidies might be misunderstood.

> Ought these subsidies not be maintained *in full* until the final stage when N.I. leaves the UK and joins an independent 'new Ireland'? At that point, if necessary, one might envisage a 'phasing out' rather than an abrupt cessation.[129]

While such ideas were very much for a distant future, Whitaker had, with the support of his friends in Northern Ireland, contributed to the opening up of a peace initiative in the early summer of 1972.

SUMMER PEACE OVERTURES END IN FAILURE

On 13 June, William Whitelaw rejected an invitation from the Provisional IRA to discuss a three-point programme. On 15 June he met the leadership of the SDLP in London. This coincided with a hunger strike by members of the Provisional IRA in Crumlin Road Jail, Belfast; there was also a hunger strike in Mountjoy Prison, Dublin. The SDLP felt that they could not continue the talks unless some concession was made. On 16 June, Whitaker wrote to Lynch to tell him that 'W.W.' (Whitelaw) had asked him to

> beg of you to let him know in advance if you should decide to do anything about Mountjoy hunger-strikers—I gather he would feel obliged to follow suit. It was clear, however, that he wd. prefer to stick it out and not give in to them.[130]

Lynch did not give in to the IRA hunger-strikers. On 19 June, Whitelaw told Lynch through the British embassy in Dublin that while he was having discussions with the SDLP 'it was proposed to him that he should personally meet representatives of the Provisional IRA.' He was further told that the Provisional IRA wanted to raise two matters with him. Firstly, they wanted an assurance that if they declared a ceasefire it would not be made the opportunity for harassment and the picking up of people the authorities had hitherto not been able to lay their hands on. Secondly, there was the wish that prisoners be given the status of 'political prisoners'.[131]

Whitelaw told the SDLP that he would not meet the IRA himself but he would nominate 'persons who would be instructed to explain to the Provisional IRA what his position was in relation to matters that it had been reported to him they were concerned about.' He made it clear that his representatives were 'not engaged in any kind of negotiation whatsoever, but are solely authorised to explain the position which he takes up.' He would have no difficulty in saying that if a ceasefire was declared there would not be a major 'lift'. As far as the claim for the recognition of political prisoners was concerned, he was

> prepared to look sympathetically at any specific request for treatment within the prison rules, e.g. about clothes, visits etc., but is not prepared to create a new category, i.e. political prisoners. Any concessions about treatment would need to be extended to all prisoners.[132]

In the end, Whitelaw agreed to grant a 'special category' status, which allowed more visits and the use of civilian clothes by eight IRA and forty loyalist prisoners. On 20 June the hunger strike was called off.[133]

A Special Branch report casts an interesting light on events behind the scenes about that time. Superintendent M. Fitzgerald made a report for the attention of the Commissioner in July 1972 that provided intelligence background to that decision. Special Branch sources revealed that the Provisionals' Army Council had held numerous meetings, finally agreeing to allow John Kelly and his Peace Group to negotiate. The report had earlier identified Kelly as being 'now a member of the Army Council.' The document pointed out that the Governor of Northern Ireland, Lord Grey, had a meeting with members of the SDLP and subsequently with representatives of the IRA. After reporting the outcome of the meeting to Whitelaw, Grey sent Lord Windlesham to meet the four IRA representatives, including John Kelly and Ruairí Ó Brádaigh. Seán Mac Stiofáin, Dáithí Ó Conaill and the Belfast group were among those on the Army Council opposing that path to peace. However, the Special Branch reported that 'Kelly succeeded in wining over the majority of the

Belfast group to support the peace plan.' Ó Brádaigh finally supported him in that initiative.

John Hume was a go-between with the IRA. He had met Provisional leaders in the Creggan, Derry, and in a pub in Co. Donegal. This paved the way for the meeting that followed. A meeting with Lord Windlesham took place at Stormont Castle, probably on 20 June. Having heard an opening statement from the 'peace delegation', he stated 'that this was putting him in an intolerable position as he understood the general purpose of the meeting was considered to be on a conciliatory basis.' The question of a united Ireland and the withdrawal of the British army met with a similar reply. Windlesham said that if the violence would stop he would promise 'immediate new initiatives.' When pressed again on the subject 'he included the release of internees.' That release, he said, could take place within the next few weeks, 'but they also had to pacify the Vanguard Movement.'

The peace talks were abandoned because of the arrest and imprisonment of Ruairí Ó Brádaigh. Many IRA leaders from the South had gone on the run to Derry. When Ó Brádaigh was released, the peace talks resumed and a temporary truce was called.[134]

The Provisional representatives also had a meeting with the Unionist radical William Craig, but he had adopted a 'no surrender' policy and threatened civil war in the event of a united Ireland. The Garda reported concluded: 'Neither Mr Craig nor Mr Faulkner want peace in the North at present—they want the Whitelaw initiative to fail.'[135]

Garda intelligence also reported that a breakaway group from the Provisional IRA was not in favour of the truce. This group was planning to continue the campaign of violence. The same source estimated that they were in a possession of 'a fair supply of arms, ammunition and explosives, including a number of armalite automatic rifles.' This weapon was described as being of high velocity, with a Bakelite stock on a hinge, which made it very light and easy to conceal. It fired a 5.56-mm armour-piercing bullet. One of the rifles had the serial number S.11462. The weapons had been smuggled in from the United States. Another group, called 'Freedom Fighters', was also operating in Belfast. Composed of members of Saor Éire, the Officials and the Provisionals, it was opposed to the truce. They were 'mainly criminals' and would 'undoubtedly continue their campaign of looting, robbing etc.'[136]

On 24 June 1972 the Provisional IRA announced a ceasefire, to come into effect on midnight on the 26th. The violence was intensified in the days leading up to the cessation, three British soldiers being killed on the 24th.

In London, Whitelaw responded positively to the outcome of the complex and multi-stranded contacts that had brought such a successful result. Whitaker wrote to Lynch on 29 June, enclosing a copy of a letter he had received from G. B. Newe in which the latter spoke about the fact that

> things have taken a dramatic turn and we are now face-to-face with the most testing time of all. Decent Protestants are half-pleased but still worried and anxious.

It was a time for cool heads among the party men, both North and South. But he felt that Faulkner was not 'behaving well—although he is under great pressure.' He felt that Hume

> should have much more sense than B. [Faulkner] as he is an educated man, but he is a political amateur; and Paddy Devlin is regarded by many Catholics as a liability.

Newe wanted the Taoiseach to stress that he was not against a Stormont of some sort. He should continue to make it clear that 'we have a place in a United Ireland when we are ready to seek it.' He should not 'let up on the IRA even if he has to do it more quietly.' Neither should Lynch say who should be at the conference table. Newe felt that the peace was indeed fragile, 'and the next few weeks would test us.'[137]

On the streets of Belfast members of the UDA mustered on one occasion as many as eight thousand, demanding the creation of 'no-go areas', which they would patrol. An agreement was reached that the British army and the police together with unarmed members of the UDA would patrol the areas.

On 7 July 1972 Whitelaw and other ministers met the leadership of the IRA at the London home of the Minister of State for Northern Ireland, Paul Channon. The meeting took place with the permission of the Prime Minister. Whitelaw said in his memoirs that the IRA made impossible demands, 'which I told them the British Government would never concede.'[138] Talking proved futile. Two days later the ceasefire ended, and ten people died that weekend, including a thirteen-year-old girl and a Catholic priest.[139]

The IRA issued a statement revealing that its leadership had talked to Whitelaw. Whitelaw's first reaction was to offer to resign. However, he flew to Belfast, where he had talks with Lord Grey, and he received strong support and encouragement to stay on. Both men flew back to London, where Whitelaw went to Downing Street to see Heath and to face the House of Commons. The Prime Minister was very supportive. In the House of Commons he faced criticism, but there was general sympathy for his actions.[140] Wilson, after all, had met the IRA leadership in Dublin a few months before.

There followed one of the most ferocious days in the entire IRA campaign. The killing began shortly after midnight. A 21-year-old Catholic was shot at his doorstep in a sectarian attack on 21 July. In the twenty-three hours that followed the IRA mounted a ferocious attack on Belfast, setting off twenty-six bombs within sixty-five minutes, killing eleven people and injuring 130. There were three large explosions in Derry and thirty-nine altogether in Northern Ireland on what became known as 'Bloody Friday'. It was a day of infamy.[141] The leading Southern newspapers echoed the revulsion felt by people about the events of a day that had helped remove feelings of ambivalence about the IRA campaign.

It was a good opportunity for Heath to conduct what Jonathan Bardon has described as 'the biggest British military operation since Suez.'[142] On 31 July the British army launched 'Operation Motorman' to put an end to the 'no-go areas' in the Bogside and the Creggan, Derry. Using twenty-six companies, the British army had overrun the barricades by first light and were in control of the areas. Two youths were killed in gun battles. Barricades in Derry's Protestant areas were also removed. In Belfast sixteen army posts were assembled in Andersonstown and in the surrounding areas.

The British ambassador, John Peck, called by appointment on Hugh McCann at the Department of External Affairs at 6:30 p.m. on 1 August and was handed a copy of the note that the Irish ambassador in London was to deliver later that night to the British Prime Minister. Lynch, in his note, thanked Heath for his message of 30 July. He regretted the two fatal casualties in Derry but added 'that the military activity taken throughout the North yesterday resulted in so few casualties, is a considerable relief.' He re-emphasised what Patrick Hillery had told Whitelaw on 21 July, that 'my colleagues give no countenance to the Provisional IRA as a matter of decided Government policy. We quite agree that political progress is seriously disaffected by their existence.' He told Heath that Northern Ireland had been discussed 'searchingly among ourselves,' and, referring to his recent article in *Foreign Affairs,* he said the principal underlying view was 'that the door to Irish unity, by agreement, must be unlocked'—a view shared by the minority. The Government was fully prepared, he said, to play a constructive role in finding ways and means to end violence and provide a long-term solution to Northern Ireland.

Lynch was anxious that the previous day's military actions would be followed by political actions and decisions designed to restore confidence among the minority. That meant they had to be assured 'unequivocally that there is no question whatever of their being returned to the control of a sectarian administration or of the RUC as at present constituted.' The question of the policing of minority areas was now a matter appropriate to political discussion. Having demonstrated the determination and military capacity 'in regard to extremists on one side, there is no reason for not facing up to extremists, such as the Ulster Defence Association, on the other,' he wrote.

That included taking up licensed as well as unlicensed weapons, especially in Belfast, where about thirty cases of sectarian assassination had occurred in July.

In his discussions with Peck, McCann raised the issue of closing Long Kesh, the need for impartial action against militants, no return to the former political structures of Stormont, and the unfortunate and ill-advised action of the British military in occupying Casement Park, the GAA stadium in Belfast. Above all, he stressed the necessity for Irish involvement, if not in 'first instance' talks then in later talks once possible solutions were being considered.

Dónal O'Sullivan met Heath at 10:30 p.m. on 1 August. He delivered Lynch's letter and developed a number of points: (1) There could be no solution without the Irish Government playing an adequate role—not necessarily with full publicity. (2) The time had arrived to disarm the North completely. (3) There could be no question of the minority being returned to the control of a sectarian administration. Members of the Government were meeting the SDLP that night. (4) Long Kesh should be emptied right away as a gesture of good intentions.

Heath assured the ambassador that the position in the North would never be the same again, and that all would be treated equally; 'no extreme element would be treated better than another.' The ambassador said Heath was 'extremely gracious and could not have been more friendly personally.' Heath would not commit himself on the question of consultation, 'and the ambassador came back to the point again and again.' Finally Heath yielded a little, saying: 'I know Jack Lynch is a good friend; leave it with me and I will think about it.' On escorting the ambassador to the door, Heath said: 'There is something in this and I will see what I can do.'

Heath had talked freely about eventual reunification, and he saw the EEC as an important factor in that context. O'Sullivan urged him to face the question of the majority squarely. Heath asked that his regards be conveyed to Lynch, 'with an indication that he wished him luck in today's by-election' (which was being held in Cork and was won by Fianna Fáil).

Meanwhile, G. B. Newe wrote on 1 August to Ken Whitaker, saying that

the events of the last 48 hours have been dramatic, and on the whole, amazing in the outcome—so far. While Catholics will not shout it from the house-tops I should say that 90 per cent are pleased. It now depends upon the way the Army handles it plus the speed at which the politicians can talk.

But he warned Whitaker:

Mr Lynch will have to be careful about what he says and does and he must not appear to be 'the Catholic Prime Minister of a Catholic people.' A united Ireland may be a self-evident desideratum for him but for the majority of people here it is not such, as yet. A breathing space has been gained and talks must proceed with a readiness to give and take and a concern for people—all people.[143]

Newe had written to the leader of the SDLP, Gerry Fitt, on 1 August, congratulating him on the decision to take part in talks with the Secretary of State and with the other political parties. He implored Fitt not to close any doors.[144]

On 3 August 1972 Newe wrote to Whitaker, expressing his satisfaction at the pressure being put on the SDLP by the Irish Government. He also commended the Government for the restrained and sensible statement on the taking over of the 'no-go areas'. He said that the SDLP might protest and engage

> in infantile posturings but, when all is said and done, what is the alternative? As a Party and as individuals, they seem so unsure of themselves as to appear to want to attempt to ride two, if not three(!) horses at the same time.

He said there had been growing disenchantment at what somebody had called the 'windy posturings' of the SDLP folk,

> especially Hume and Devlin. Although Fitt is the Parliamentary leader of the Party, it is such a loosely knit group of amateur politicians that we have to suffer stupid efforts on the part of individual members to talk with a loud and not always sensible voice so as to 'hit the headlines' at every opportunity.

Newe felt that

> it is but good sense and logical that the Taoiseach should have a part in the discussions, but the fact that he should inevitably raises the hackles of some Unionists. So, while he must 'do his thing' and say his piece as leader of a political party, as well as leader of the Government, he will have to be careful of what he does say. We have a tough job ahead. I am doing my best to keep Gerry encouraged and, at the same time, trying to persuade Brian F. that his side will have 'to give' in respect of some of the things he regards as principles.

He mentioned the method of choosing a government in the Netherlands and felt that the difficulty of having Faulkner and Fitt in a government together might be overcome if that were to be adopted. He was off to Belfast the following day and would have lunch with Faulkner.[145]

On 5 August 1972 Whitaker wrote to Lynch, congratulating him on

> trying to knock sense into the SDLP. With Whitelaw's referendum looming up in the late autumn, I would like: (1) to renew the suggestion I made to you on the 'phone on 19th July that, if some counter-gesture has to be made here, it should take the form of a motion expressing the desire of the people of this state for unity by agreement which all parties would pass in the Dáil (referendum here, we agreed, would simply give a field-day for emotive campaigning on the IRA); and (2), to put in your mind the thought that we here should define as clearly as possible in advance of the N.I. referendum what in our view is the alternative available to N.I. people as against staying permanently in the U.K. If we don't, the question in the N.I. referendum will be interpreted there as 'do you want to be taken over by the Republic, or not?' Could there be inter-party agreement on this and could a pamphlet be circulated in good time to all the N.I. voters? I hope some of the points in my notes to you on the gradual approach to unity (including the idea of a new Agreement between ourselves and Britain) would be helpful in this context.[146]

Meanwhile Hillery went to London on 4 August 1972 to meet William Whitelaw. Hugh McCann and the Irish ambassador, Dónal O'Sullivan, accompanied him. Whitelaw said he was glad of the opportunity for a talk. He spoke of the intensification of the military operation and said that after 'Bloody Friday there was great emotional feeling in the North.' The British army, he said, had to move. Every effort was made to avoid bloodshed in the Bogside and Creggan. People did not lie down in front of the army vehicles, and 'the reaction of the minority since the start of the military operation has on the whole been encouraging.' Whitelaw gave Hillery an assurance that extreme elements on both sides were equally dealt with and the British were 'picking up unlicensed weapons on the basis of fairly accurate intelligence information.' But he did admit that RUC intelligence was likely to be more detailed for minority areas. 'The RUC are, to some extent, a problem,' he said. Special machinery had been set up to investigate complaints against the army, he said, and 'some of these complaints are, no doubt, justified.' He said there was a lack of co-ordination within the army, but he was 'hopeful of being able to overcome this quickly.'[147]

Hillery said the Government had recently met the SDLP and the Nationalist Party. The emptying of Long Kesh was a precondition for entry into political talks. Whitelaw felt that he could not do that, because of the impact it would have on the morale of the police and the army. But when pressed he said he was prepared to consider some arrangements for the ending of internment, provided certain conditions were met. But he could not undermine his standing with the majority and with the backbenchers in his own party. He defended the stance of his Government on the plebiscite. He did not think the IRA would cease their activities after the recent actions of the British army. They would fan out into the countryside and conduct new attacks.

Whitelaw paid 'warm tribute to the efforts made in the South to deal with the IRA and said that any further assistance we could give in increasing our security would be greatly welcomed.' He felt he had to move with considerable caution. He and the British Government 'could not be more firmly convinced that the solution for the North has to be a political one.' The British Government were convinced that the solution would have to be found quickly. He acknowledged a number of times during the meeting the need for close contact with Dublin on developments. He repeated this again at the conclusion of the talks.[148]

On 10 August 1972 Heath replied to Lynch that the military steps recently taken 'should quickly be followed by political measures. We have always emphasised that the problem will not be solved by military means alone.' He stated that Whitelaw's meetings with the SDLP were to resume on Friday. He hoped they would participate in the conference planned for the near future. 'We think that the political parties in Northern Ireland should be given the opportunity of working out their own solution of the long-term problem.' The conference would be limited to the parties in Northern Ireland.

> This, however, should not prevent us from keeping in the closest touch on all these matters. I very much hope that by one means and another we shall be able to maintain contact over all these problems as the solutions develop, as is our hope, over the next few months.

He stressed that 'these contacts should be confidential (though they need not necessarily be secretive) between your Government and ours.'[149] Heath said that he fully recognised that Lynch had 'a contribution to make in the search for a solution and I should be anxious that your viewpoint should be in the minds of those attending the conference.' He added:

> As I said in a speech last November, if the majority of the people in the North want Northern Ireland to become part of a United Ireland, I do not believe that any United Kingdom Government is going to want to stand in their way. The door is certainly not locked and we do not want to lock it: but it must be for the people of Northern Ireland to decide whether and when they want to come through it.

Heath expressed his gratitude 'to you and your colleagues for your actions against the Provisional IRA.' He also said that it was the firm intention of the British Government 'that there should be no discrimination as between the communities when it comes to measures to keep violence in check.'

The military measures that have been taken were 'designed to help the minority to get the IRA off their backs.'[150]

Another statement from the British Government, probably delivered to the Taoiseach by the British ambassador, Sir John Peck, asked him to consider the Irish Government's position on continuing with the case lodged on 15 December 1971 with the European Commission in Strasbourg. Heath acknowledged the pressure to which the Irish Government had been subjected at the time. He was also aware that it was under considerable pressure from its backbenchers to continue with the application. But 'the Irish Government's real quarrel was with the Unionist regime.' The cases were brought at a time when Dublin felt that

> this regime would continue indefinitely. But it is a matter of historical record that the situation has now changed. It is surely true to say that our aims, those of the Irish and British Governments, are now the same. The prosecution of these cases can only do harm to these aims and give encouragement to extremists.

Heath concluded that the choice was therefore 'between a sterile and continuing conflict raking over past discontents; and the prospect of progress towards our common aim of peace and justice for all in Northern Ireland.'

On 15 August, Dónal O'Sullivan reported that he had seen the deputy secretary of the Foreign and Commonwealth Office, Sir Stewart Crawford, the previous day, at his request. He urged the dropping of the cases in Strasbourg at a time when political progress could be made. Otherwise 'each side would have some nasty things to say to and about the other.' He felt that a 'slanging match in Strasbourg would undoubtedly be damaging to our bilateral relations.'

O'Sullivan pressed the Irish case but said that the position of Dublin 'might be softened if something worthwhile and saleable as a *quid pro quo* were forthcoming from London.' It might be helpful 'if there were to be a public acknowledgement by the Government here of our right to be involved in the settlement of the Northern problem and a declaration of intention to consult us fully.' Stewart said he thought the recent message from the Prime Minister to the Taoiseach 'represented a considerable advance on their previous attitude to our involvement in the findings of a settlement for the North.' The Prime Minister had been 'unusually forthcoming' in that message, as had Mr Whitelaw in his discussions with Dr Hillery.[151]

McCann wrote to Lynch on 16 August, arguing against the abandonment of the case at Strasbourg. That might only be contemplated in a situation 'where we had a firm promise from Mr Heath of working towards a solution of the Northern problem in a manner acceptable to us (with some public commitment also).' Heath had been very careful 'to avoid giving us any such promise.' McCann made reference to the unhelpful decision to go ahead with the plebiscite. He did note, however, that Heath's recent message to Lynch 'represents some advance on their previous attitude to our involvement in the finding of a settlement for the North.' It was not clear whether the message could be interpreted as inviting Lynch's views on a solution before the forth-coming conference. It was not obvious whether those views would be known to the Northern participants or to Heath. But McCann felt that, 'if you wish, I think that you could interpret it as an invitation to express your viewpoint to Mr Heath.' But that did not provide grounds for the dropping of the cases in Strasbourg.[152]

On 31 August the secretary of the Department of External Affairs, Hugh McCann, made the following suggestion to Lynch for his meeting in Munich with Heath on 4 September 1972: (1) Urge a new kind of administration in the North, involving built-in safeguards for the minority so that discrimination could not continue. (2) Incorporate a North-South link. (3) Encourage post-ponement of the plebiscite, or, if that did not prove possible, minimise the damage it could cause. (4) Set up firm arrangements for future consultation between London and Dublin. (5) Withstand pressure to drop the Strasbourg case. McCann ended: 'If one could be convinced that he would work with you towards the right solution, one could go further in cooperation to bring about a solution.'[153]

WHITAKER AND THE PARALLEL TRACK TO THE UNIONISTS AND THE BRITISH

Behind the scenes throughout August, Ken Whitaker had continued a dia-logue with his various Conservative, Unionist and academic contacts willing to discuss the future of Northern Ireland. He wrote to Lynch on 8 August, enclosing his correspondence with Newe and with the Conservative MP David James. The two men had been speaking on the phone earlier in the afternoon. He also enclosed a letter he had sent to Professor Norman Gibson in Derry. As regards the pamphlet he had mentioned in a letter on 5 August he felt it ought to deal with pertinent economic points as well as with political issues:

(1) comparing like with like, the virtual equality of income per head in the Six Cos. and in Leinster; (2) The closeness of social welfare payments; (3) agricultural supports will be the same under EEC conditions; (4) our

population is rising (pace *Unionist Review* of July 1972); (5) The attractive quotas and other aids which have given us an industrial grown rate of 8% p.a. for many years; (6) The identity of interests N and S in EEC regional development politics.

He said he had mentioned those points—and their context—to Martin O'Donoghue and that he would be glad to help in fleshing out the draft pamphlet, which would need contributions from various streams, including the Inter-Party Constitutional Committee. He signed off: 'Have a good holiday.'[154]

Whitaker wrote on 8 August 1972 to Professor Norman Gibson. He agreed with his analysis made at the Irish Association, and he laid before him his own ideas for reform in Northern Ireland. The outline is given again in a letter from Whitaker to David James MP,[155] a copy of which he sent to the Taoiseach.

Whitaker wrote that, to clear away present ambiguities and causes of dissension and start with a cleaner sheet, there would be merit in a new treaty or agreement between the two sovereign states, governing the relationship of each to Northern Ireland and confirming whatever provisions were made for regional administration there, assuming that those left an opening for movement by agreement towards a united Ireland. A new agreement would be more meaningful and acceptable than other links, such as rejoining the Commonwealth or joining NATO. The agreement would be founded on the fact that the two countries shared an urgent concern that conditions should be established enabling 'all the people of Northern Ireland to work together in peace and justice for their social and economic progress.' Membership of the EEC rendered that co-operation not only desirable but essential. Both Governments would absolutely abjure the use of force as a means of effecting political change in Northern Ireland or of preventing change decided upon democratically. They would affirm their intention of preventing any illegal organisation or private individual from using either country as a base from which to carry out acts of violence, intimidation or other measures to effect political change by force. Stringent regulations would apply in both jurisdictions on the right to hold firearms. All unofficial armies should be illegal in both countries. There would be a withdrawal of all existing firearm licences. The British and Irish Governments would consult one another and the elected representatives in Northern Ireland about the kind of police force or forces best suited to Northern Ireland. Security would remain the responsibility of London for at least ten years. There would be joint commitment to non-discriminatory and socially progressive policies in the two countries. A Bill of Rights would guarantee civil and religious rights to all people. A desire to change the status of Northern Ireland would be regarded as a legitimate field of political action. Aggrieved residents would have a right of appeal to an international court, whose decisions would be binding on the Northern authorities.

While Northern Ireland would remain part of the United Kingdom as long as a majority there wished it to be so, the United Kingdom would in no way impede any arrangements that looked towards the participation of Northern Ireland in a united Ireland. The United Kingdom would guarantee financial provisions for a transition.

For regional administration in Northern Ireland there would be one representative for every 15,000 people. Membership of the assembly would be renewed every five years. There would be commissions of not more than five people responsible to the assembly. Members of the commissions would meet representatives of the two Governments once a year. The chairpersons of the commissions would meet as an executive. He also favoured the establishment of an Irish Co-operative Council.[156]

James replied on 15 August that he had no objections to Whitaker sending the Taoiseach a copy of his letter. If a special treaty relationship were to be set up it must be 'underpinned by special arrangements for cross-fertilisation of ideas by a two-way traffic in visiting MPs and TDs.' That point was important if 'you assure me that it would be politically impossible for Ireland to rejoin the commonwealth, or join N.A.T.O.,' as both the main sources of inter-parliamentary visits were from those sources. He liked the idea of a special treaty, 'the more particularly since the only viable alternative would be a re-partition of the north of Ireland, mass movements of the civilian population, both ways across the border, and the erection of some form of Iron Curtain.' At a moment when the frontiers of Europe were 'opening up,' he felt that that would be a 'disastrously retrograde step.'

He wanted to feed Whitaker's thoughts in at every possible point to, in the first instance, William Whitelaw. He wanted to send the letter to Bill Deedes, an MP who wielded 'enormous influence on the Tory back benches and to Peter MacLachlan of our research department,' and to David Wood of the *Times*. He wanted Whitaker to publish an amended version of his letter as a signed article in the *Times*.[157]

Whitaker, who went on holidays to Co. Mayo, where the 'weather is too good for fishing,' did not receive James's letter of the 15th until a few days before the 28th. As he was still in the public service, Whitaker could not, without express Government approval, publish anything in the press on a current political issue. He told James that it might be better 'that I should go about things as unobtrusively as possible.' If James was in Dublin from 16 to 18 October, Whitaker felt he could arrange a meeting with the Taoiseach.[158]

On 28 August 1972 Whitaker wrote to Lynch, enclosing the letters from James. Meanwhile he had sent his blueprint to G. B. Newe, who prepared a document for submission to William Whitelaw. Whitaker was pleased generally with the thrust of the document. He said he preferred 'a gradualist approach which avoids major confrontations but allows, by way of Parliamentary (or Assembly) decision, cumulative progress in the transfer of appropriate all-Ireland functions to a Council of Ireland.'

On 8 September, Newe sent Whitaker a copy of his final text, which he had sent to Whitelaw. Lynch received copies of all this correspondence.

On 19 December, Whitaker sent the Taoiseach a copy of his ideas for a new system of administration in Northern Ireland.[159] Lynch had relied on Whitaker at critical points since 1969, and in the late summer and autumn of 1972 he was able to feed those ideas into the policy-making system. It is important to note that Whitaker was also influencing opinion in Northern Ireland and in London. This was at the behest of Lynch, who was kept informed and copied all relevant correspondence.

In September 1971 G. B. Newe, one of Whitaker's friends in Northern Ireland, had become the first and the only Catholic to serve in the Northern Ireland Government since the passing of the Government of Ireland Act (1920). Although he was never a member of the Unionist Party, Faulkner gave him the post of minister of state in the Prime Minister's Office, and he served between late 1971 and the proroguing of Stormont in March 1972. It was a controversial appointment, and Newe was criticised widely by nationalists and members of the SDLP, who were boycotting that institution at the time. Brian Faulkner praised him for behaving in a 'statesmanlike' way while in office.[160]

Whitaker wrote to Lynch on 2 September, wishing him 'all the best in Munich.' The previous night he had had a conversation with 'the Cardinal' (William Conway) about 'personal views' put forward by the British Lord Chancellor, Lord Hailsham. Briefly, the Hailsham approach was to constitute under a new treaty between three 'sovereign states' (Northern Ireland presumably being the third) a set of tripartite bodies: one judicial, to guarantee rights in all three states on the model of the European Convention for Human Rights, the second ministerial, to co-ordinate economic and political polices in matters of common interest, and the third a parliamentary tier. Whitaker summed up:

> The idea of a sovereign NI and of something approaching a British Isles Federation seems to underly [sic] these thoughts, which are probably not fully developed. The cardinal raised a question whether Hailsham carries a lot of weight in the British Cabinet.[161]

Whitaker had kept the lines of communication open with diverse personalities throughout the summer. Lynch certainly realised the value of being able to float ideas in Unionist and British circles without going through official channels. Heath and Whitelaw may also have appreciated and encouraged similar private activities on their side.

ANGLO-IRISH RELATIONS IN THE AUTUMN OF 1972

In the context of imminent entry into the EEC, Lynch had a series of meetings with Heath in the autumn of 1972. The first meeting, on 4 September, took place at the British consulate-general during the Olympic Games in Munich. Stressing that the meeting was confidential, Lynch said he had not had the opportunity to reply to Heath's last letter, of 10 August, because of the holiday period and the expectation that a meeting might be arranged. He stated that he had publicly commended Heath's initiative of March in the suspension of Stormont. He knew it had not been an easy decision. There was 'tremendous goodwill for Mr Whitelaw's efforts and recognition of the difficulty of his task.' He had accepted publicly the stated intentions of 'Operation Motorman', but he noted that there was an apprehension that the British army was 'concentrating on minority ghettos and there was little apparent Army activity in ghettos of the majority.' He added: 'Such one-sided action against Catholic areas tended to encourage support for the Provisionals.' Lynch did not wish to disparage Whitelaw's efforts. There was also a feeling that the partiality of the RUC had not been eradicated. Lynch, for his part, was anxious that a peaceful solution should be pursued by political initiatives. He had spoken to the SDLP and was keen that the conference should proceed and succeed in working out an agreement.

Lynch felt in a stronger position now to influence policies after the referendum and the by-election in Cork. He wanted to know the thinking of the British Government on the North.[162]

Heath found the Taoiseach's statement interesting. A great deal had happened since they had last met. He said he was keen on talks with Lynch, 'and those who were critical of such talks in Northern Ireland would have to lump it.' He admitted that the 'take-over of Stormont had been very difficult for his government.' He was convinced that they were right and hoped they had shown firmness when confronted with Protestant interests. 'Operation Motorman' had been a grave decision, as there was the danger of loss of life and a fear that the Provisionals would stand and fight, or go to ground. He felt that the army had dealt with the situation well, and there had been very few complaints. The army had left all schools except three in Belfast, where other arrangements had been made for the children.

Heath then turned to outline his political ideas. The British army could leave only if there was an effective police force, and 'it was a continuing problem of how to build up a police force there the same as in the rest of the UK.'

London would drive ahead with the Whitelaw conference. He said the SDLP had had a good talk with Whitelaw and he would see them the following week. He said 'it was for the people of N.I. to sort out what they wanted.' But the suspension of Stormont was not satisfactory as a permanent solution. He favoured securing a parliamentary structure for the North, and he would explain his position to the SDLP.[163]

Heath then assured Lynch that he was prepared 'to make special arrangements through the Foreign Office to keep the Taoiseach informed, in which it would be open to the Taoiseach to inject his views or make proposals.' He felt it would be helpful if Lynch made a speech to support the conference. In spite of the many changes in the North, 'people would say that nothing had been got back from the republic.' He wanted more action from Lynch on border security, mentioning that there had been twenty-eight raids across the border since 'Operation Motorman'. As Seán Mac Stiofáin was 'at the heart of this and should be arrested,' Heath asked why the Taoiseach did not have him arrested and brought before the courts. All this was very difficult for Heath. From his standpoint there appeared to have been very little North-South co-operation in Faulkner's time; now Britain was prepared to go further with this in the context of the conference, and they had a list worked out, but it would be difficult to go ahead unless the Republic finally cracked down on the IRA.

Heath then raised the problems his Government was having with Ugandan refugees. They were putting a strain on housing and other resources.

> This connected up with the Irish in Britain. If the Uganda refugee position were not sorted out soon, it could raise the whole citizenship question for other troubled spots like Hong Kong, and the Irish could be included too. As he saw it, the situation was an explosive mixture.[164]

Heath raised the question of the human rights case in Strasbourg. The timing of the hearing was the same as the Whitelaw conference. If it went ahead they would fight it. But 'it all happened before direct rule so the argument would be about the past.' He felt that the lawyers 'should get together and work out a way of dropping it.' On the question of the plebiscite, he knew that Lynch did not like it, but it was 'part of the package for the Protestants' and a 'genuine attempt to restore normal life in N.I.'

Lynch replied that he hoped the plebiscite idea would be postponed further, if not dropped, as it was not proving anything. The minority would boycott it, the two communities would be further polarised and it would be a platform for the Provisional IRA from which to launch demonstrations and more violence. As regards the Strasbourg case, Lynch felt that it would be difficult for him to withdraw it at that stage, especially while internment continued. Heath pressed Lynch not to proceed with the case; if it went to the European Court it 'would be a vendetta for which his government was not responsible.'[165]

Lynch argued that Unionist domination in Northern Ireland must not emerge again, and prospects must be opened for ultimate reunification. He was apprehensive about the possibility of citizenship legislation in Britain. He understood British feelings about the IRA, 'but short of interment everything possible was being done within the law to curb them.' As regards Mac Stiofáin, he was on the run and could not be found. 'We had been after him for a long time but it was very difficult to get evidence against him that would stand up in Court.' His house had been searched on one occasion and 'the only thing found was a bullet.' He had been fined, and somebody had paid the fine on his behalf.

Lynch returned to Mac Stiofáin later in the talks and said that there was the problem of adequate evidence and proving a case in court, for example the substance of public utterance in relation to membership of the IRA. 'We were continuing to bring charges against the IRA, and sixty convictions had been obtained,' he said.[166]

Lynch sought the removal of the British army from the Casement Park GAA grounds in Belfast. Heath replied that the park was of military importance in the area.

> He said *with some emphasis* that the GAA should be told that the sooner they kicked the gunmen from the area the quicker a sensible solution would be possible and their park returned to them. He was worried about the younger generation of the minority and had heard from the Cardinal and priests that they were not amenable to reasonable controls.

Lynch replied that if a bold decision were to be taken to release all internees it might yield good results, but he appreciated what had already been done. Heath said he had taken the risk of releasing the regular IRA internees, and it worked. With the hard-core Provisionals it was, he said, a matter for judgement whether internment was responsible for the violence or whether they believed in going on with the shooting. Lynch said he would 'crack down on the IRA to the utmost possible extent, and he had not neglected to do so within the law and the Constitution.' The Government had strengthened the law in several respects and would, if necessary, strengthen it further to deal with IRA activities. He said that there was always the problem of conforming to their written constitution.[167]

The SDLP published a document on 20 September entitled *Towards a New Ireland,* which proposed that Britain and Ireland have joint sovereignty over

Northern Ireland. The British were asked to agree to ultimate unity. There was to be a Northern Ireland assembly with increased powers and an all-Ireland senate.

On 27 September the British convened a conference at Darlington for all the parties in Northern Ireland. The SDLP, the Nationalist Party and Ian Paisley's Democratic Unionist Party stayed away; but the Unionist Party, the Alliance Party and the Northern Ireland Labour Party attended. While the outcome was inconclusive, it showed that movement of a kind was possible. It helped Whitelaw test his ideas before issuing his green paper.

In Dublin, meanwhile, measures against Sinn Féin were stepped up. Newspapers regularly received IRA statements signed 'P. O'Neill' from the Provisional Sinn Féin head office in Kevin Street, Dublin. On 6 October 1972 the Gardaí closed the offices down. This provoked strong protests and vitriolic criticism of the Taoiseach. On 21 October, Heath and Lynch met again briefly in Paris.

On 28 October a bomb exploded at Connolly Station, Dublin, and four hotels in the city were fire-bombed. The perpetrators were most probably loyalist paramilitaries. On 30 October 1972 Whitelaw published a green paper entitled *The Future of Northern Ireland: A Paper for Discussion*. A section on the 'Irish dimension' declared that for many years no British Government had wished to impede the realisation of Irish unity arrived at by genuine consent.

Sir Kenneth Bloomfield wrote immediately to Ken Whitaker, stating that he did not believe 'it contains anything which would be incompatible with what we have discussed, or with the scheme in your letter to Norman Gibson.' He stated that many people in the North were 'disturbed by the "Irish dimension"—a sensitive, generous and courageous response from your side could have—in the longer term at last—significant consequences.' He felt that a constitutional revision in the South to make unity a cherished aspiration rather than a claim would 'be of tremendous psychological effect; and in saying this, I don't underestimate the political difficulties on your side.' He felt that the new institutions in Northern Ireland 'must be recognised and accepted as legitimate throughout Ireland' if they were to be capable of forceful evolution and change. He hoped that Whitaker might find an opportunity to come to the North soon.[168]

Whitaker replied on 2 November 1972, acknowledging receipt of the green paper and congratulating Bloomfield 'on so fair and comprehensive a document . . . every reasonable person must regard it as balanced and progressive.' He expected that the Government should be able to respond to it positively. It was logical that new institutions in the North that provided for effective co-operation in matters of interest to the whole of Ireland and that put no limit to the powers and functions that might, by agreement on both sides, be entrusted to an all-Ireland council should be recognised and accepted by the Republic as legitimate. Whitaker's own view was that it might be easier to do that with a new treaty than by direct amendment of the Constitution of Ireland. He could not muster any enthusiasm for the plebiscite. He was going to hand on Bloomfield's letter to the Taoiseach.[169]

Although it was only a green paper (proposals for possible legislation, issued for public comment), the ideas presented demonstrated the distance travelled by British policy-makers since the times when Heath was scolding Lynch for his interference in Northern affairs. Credit must go to Whitaker for his quiet and unobtrusive role in helping to influence the emergence of a new way of seeing the triangular relationship between Dublin, Belfast and London. The British ambassador, John Peck, also played an important role in keeping channels open, even during the most difficult times over the previous two years. It was now important for Lynch to seize the initiative.

On 2 November, Peck sent Lynch a 'strictly personal and confidential' letter. He was writing on his own initiative and not disclosing the existence of his note to anyone.

I am seriously concerned about an attitude of mind in London which main- tains that the Republic is very happy to leave all the dirty work to us and that all the South need do is to go on demanding reunification without making any constructive suggestions as to how this can come about. My own belief—and I am speaking solely for myself—is that the desire to see the Irish problem settled through reunification is far more widespread than you might think, and that when HMG [Her Majesty's Government] say that should a majority of people in the North opt for reunification we would put no obstacle in their way, this is in fact an understatement—as Mr Maudling intimated pretty clearly in the House of Commons just a year ago. A great many people are no longer asking themselves whether but how and when.[170]

Those who were asking 'how' would probably settle for encouraging both parts of Ireland to work very discreetly and apolitically to strengthen and add to the links that were never severed by partition. In immediate practical terms that meant working on regional development, an embryonic Council of Ireland capable of growth, and closer contacts between North and South, whether on the ministerial, official or non-governmental level. To be seen to be encouraging this too obviously would be political dynamite in the present mood of the Northern Protestants. The presence, he concluded, of

the remarkable passage on 'The Irish Dimension' in the Green Paper does provide a golden opportunity for you to set these fears at rest by spelling out in more concrete form the sort of steps by which you envisage the 'new Ireland' coming about.[171]

On 22 November, in anticipation of the Lynch-Heath meeting on 24 November in London, Peck called on Hugh McCann to have a chat about what might take place at the meeting. McCann stressed the importance of the meeting being serious and constructive. Peck mentioned that the white paper on Northern Ireland was being finalised. It would be Lynch's last chance of a serious discussion before its publication. McCann regretted that Whitelaw would not be in a position to meet the Taoiseach; the plea of constituency business was not a very strong reason for not being available. He wondered whether there was any divergence of opinion between Whitelaw and Heath on Northern Ireland.

Peck replied that he had some indirect evidence that that might be so. He wanted the Taoiseach to draw Heath out, using statements that Whitelaw had made in the House of Commons, such as 'Any new arrangements for Northern Ireland should, while meeting the wishes of Northern Ireland and Great Britain, be so far as possible acceptable to and accepted by the Republic of Ireland.'[172] Peck related a personal experience he had with Heath when the latter expressed strong irritation with him, saying that he had just been reading the ambassador's annual round-up report on the Irish situation, in which Peck had reported the Irish Government's dissatisfaction about the lack of a meaningful and constructive dialogue on the North. Peck was so upset that he bluntly asked Heath whether he wished the ambassador to report objectively on the situation in Northern Ireland as he saw it or report what he thought Heath would like to hear. Heath smiled and said, 'You are quite right.'[173]

Peck told McCann that Heath, with Alec Douglas-Home, might launch into the importance of taking further steps to deal with the IRA. The Taoiseach should arm himself with a catalogue of all that had been done and put that bluntly to the Prime Minister. There was also some discussion on the question of the Council of Ireland. McCann expressed the view that it should be a North-South body.[174]

In the days leading up to his meeting with Heath, Lynch faced a crisis in his relationship with RTE over broadcasting policy and the IRA. On 1 October 1971 the Taoiseach had issued the first directive under section 31 of the Broadcasting Authority Act (1960), prohibiting the station from broadcasting anything that could be interpreted as supporting the aims or activities of organisations that 'engage in, promote, encourage or advocate the attainment of any political objective by violent means.' On 19 November 1972 Kevin O'Kelly, one of the most widely respected journalists in the country, interviewed the leader of the Provisional IRA, Seán Mac Stiofáin. The Gardaí, keeping such activities under close surveillance, arrested Mac Stiofáin and took him to the Bridewell Garda Station in Dublin, where he immediately went on a hunger and thirst strike. The Government gave an ultimatum to the RTE Authority to accept its interpretation of the Broadcasting Act and to halt any broadcasting of interviews with leading members of the IRA. A programme based on the interview was broadcast.

Mac Stiofáin's trial began on 24 November. O'Kelly, called as a witness, refused to identify the accused as the subject of the interview, and he was given three months' imprisonment for contempt of court. The nine-member RTE Authority failed to furnish the required assurance to the Government, and it was sacked and quickly replaced. This was a very serious decision but one that showed Lynch's determination to ensure that RTE operated within the parameters set down by the Government.

Mac Stiofáin was convicted and sentenced to prison. He stayed on his hunger and thirst strike, vowing to continue the fast until death. In response, Sinn Féin organised a rally at the GPO and invited the crowd to keep vigil outside the Mater Hospital, where the prisoner was detained. IRA men dressed as priests made an unsuccessful attempt to rescue him, during which a shoot-out ensued with the Special Branch. Mac Stiofáin was transferred by air to the Curragh military prison, where he was persuaded on 16 January to give up his thirst strike after fifty-seven days. Throughout the crisis Lynch displayed a strong resolve, refusing to yield to pressure from various groups.[175]

Amid that crisis, Heath and Lynch had a working dinner in London on 24 November 1972. The Foreign Secretary, Sir Alec Douglas-Home, the secretary of the Cabinet, Sir Burke Trend, the principal private secretary, Robert Armstrong, and the Irish ambassador, Dónal O'Sullivan, were also present. The Taoiseach expressed satisfaction with the line taken in the green paper, noting that a return to Stormont was not contemplated. He welcomed the concept of the 'Irish dimension', which needed to be given meaningful expression. He also welcomed the idea of a Council of Ireland, which should be strong and should have evolutionary responsibilities. He was greatly encouraged by the statement in the green paper that any solution reached for the North must be acceptable to and accepted by the Republic. He stressed the need to set up an assembly with a multi-party executive. He objected to the plebiscite and to the stark nature of the two questions proposed. He mentioned the pressure that existed for the holding of a simultaneous plebiscite in the South.[176]

Turning to domestic matters, Lynch told Heath that the arrest of Mac Stiofáin would provoke a strong reaction at home. The sacking of the RTE Authority, he said, would bring serious attacks on his Government. He also explained about the introduction of new legislation to facilitate the apprehension of members of the IRA. That legislation, if approved, would place the

Driving in for the captain's prize
at Muskerry Golf Club in 1971.
(*Irish Examiner*)

Máirín in later years. (*Máirín
Lynch Papers*, NLI)

With members of the Government and the Northern Ireland nationalist opposition in Dublin, 1971. (*PA Photos/Topfoto*)

With other EEC leaders, including Willy Brandt, Chancellor of Germany (*fifth from left*), Georges Pompidou, President of France (*fourth from right*), Edward Heath, Prime Minister of Great Britain (*third from right*) and Giulio Andreotti, Prime Minister of Italy (*second from right*), 8 November 1972. (*Hulton Archive/Getty Images*)

Dr Patrick Hillery, later to be President of Ireland, at a bitterly divided Fianna Fáil ard-fheis in 1971. (*Colman Doyle/NLI*)

With Patrick Hillery, Minister for Foreign Affairs, signing Ireland's accession to the European Economic Community in 1972. (*Topfoto*)

With Margaret Thatcher while she was leader of the opposition. Behind them stand Airey Neave (*left*), later assassinated by the INLA, and Michael O'Kennedy, Irish Minister for Foreign Affairs. (*Popperfoto/Getty Images*)

At the Palazzo Chigi in Rome with the Italian Foreign Minister, Amintore Fanfani (*left*), and the Prime Minister, Aldo Moro, who was later assassinated. (*Topfoto*)

In many ways Lynch was one of the last of the old-style campaigners. This photograph was taken in Ennis, Co. Clare, during his general election campaign in 1977. He was famously described by the leader of the opposition, Liam Cosgrave, as the most popular politician in Ireland since Daniel O'Connell. (*Colman Doyle/NLI*)

Máirín and Father Brian D'Arcy accompany Lynch's coffin from Mount Argus church, Dublin. (PA *Photos/Topfoto*)

A panoramic shot of Lynch's funeral as the cortège passed over St Patrick's Bridge and into Patrick Street in Cork city centre. (*Irish Examiner*)

Probably the finest of all portrait photographs of Lynch. (*Colman Doyle/NLI*)

onus of proving their innocence on the accused, and this would give rise to an outcry on the grounds that it was uncharacteristic of democratic legislation, and it might be challenged as unconstitutional. But Lynch firmly underlined his determination not be 'deflected from his resolve to deal with the IRA because of the trouble he is likely to face from these developments.' In the Special Court, he said, there had been 130 cases and 103 convictions. They had difficulty finding accommodation for all the prisoners. He raised the allegations made by a large number of priests in Belfast that people in the Catholic ghettos were subject to continued harassment and brutality by the armed forces.[177]

Heath replied that he was glad to see that there was a considerable meeting of minds between them on many of the issues to be faced. The British Government wanted to move ahead but they had yet to clear their minds on the precise content and timing of the white paper. They were already firmly committed to holding the plebiscite as soon as the legislative and other procedures permitted. Lynch interjected that the white paper should come first. Heath felt that the Council of Ireland could have an important role in the economic and social spheres in the context of the Common Market. He could not agree to 'negotiations' on the Council of Ireland, but there could be 'consultation, discussion and contact.'

Later in the discussion he agreed to a significant advance on that position. Lynch expressed disappointment that the Prime Minister could not agree to negotiations about the scope and functions of the Council of Ireland. He asked Heath whether there could not be agreement to early meetings between officials on both sides in order to contribute towards a suitable proposal. The Prime Minister agreed to that proposal.[178]

Heath expressed appreciation of the efforts being made by the Taoiseach to deal with the IRA. Lynch said he was disturbed by the tendency of the British to continue to blame him for not doing more about the IRA, and the 'Prime Minister indicated understanding.' Referring to RTE, Heath admitted that he had his problems too and would 'wish at times to be able to take the same forthright action against the BBC.' On the issue of the complaints by the Belfast priests, Heath said that he had investigated the matter but that the 'complaints are greatly exaggerated.' He would investigate the matter further.

Lynch again urged the need for an assembly in the North with a multi-party executive. Discrimination must be finally outlawed so that the two communities could learn to live and work together. Reunification would continue to be the ideal of the overwhelming majority of the Irish people. It was an ideal for which there had to be full scope for legitimate expression by the minority in the North.[179]

According to the minute written by Dónal O'Sullivan, Lynch in his con-cluding statement spoke with 'great candour and considerable force.' He wanted to avoid the mistakes of the past. If correct and courageous decisions were not taken now, trouble would erupt again. He regarded it as essential that the minority have a voice in the running of the area and have a place in the executive. It was no less important that the Council of Ireland should be a strong one and should have built into it the possibility of evolution. If the right structures were put in place he would be prepared to accept and support them.

Lynch said also that 'he was prepared to consider the possibility of han-dling the security problem on an all Ireland basis.' Heath said he was always ready to talk to the Taoiseach. He welcomed the very frank statement made by Lynch and said he would take note of what was said and repeated that there was a good deal of common ground between them.[180]

Dónal O'Sullivan followed up on 12 December with a meeting with Sir Stewart Crawford, Philip Woodfield, deputy secretary in charge of the Northern Ireland Office, and Kelvin White, head of the Republic of Ireland Department of the Foreign and Commonwealth Office. There was agreement to start talks between British and Irish officials on New Year's Day, 1973, at the Foreign and Commonwealth Office. The talks would be as frank and produc-tive as possible.[181]

On his return to Dublin, Lynch dealt with the RTE question and began to prepare the introduction of the Offences against the State (Amendment) Bill. This permitted the conviction of a suspect on the word of a senior Garda officer that he believed the accused to be a member of an illegal organisation. This was in response to the growing violence perpetrated by the two wings of the IRA within and outside the jurisdiction. The bill divided the Dáil, with Fine Gael and the Labour Party vigorously opposing it. Patrick Cooney, a future Minister for Justice in the National Coalition (1973–7), said that its likes could be found only on 'the statute books of South Africa.'

As the debate headed into its final stages on 1 December it looked as if the Government faced defeat, by 70 to 71. News began to reach the Dáil that two bombs had gone off in the centre of Dublin, killing two people and injuring 127.[182] The attack provoked a *volte face*. Fine Gael withdrew its amendments and decided to abstain. Lynch, despite a mini-revolt within his own party, won the vote, by 69 to 22. The Seanad voted through the bill the following day, and President de Valera signed it into law the same evening.

The legislation gave the Gardaí wide powers in their battle against the IRA. There was an immediate security sweep in the days that followed, and 120 people were arrested.[183]

In a further response to the new British thinking on Northern Ireland, Lynch held a referendum on 7 December 1972, covering two amendments to the Constitution. In the mid-1960s a report by a constitutional review committee recommended the amendment of article 44, which recognised the 'special position' of the Catholic Church. Lynch and his Government had grown to accept the need to revise that article, particularly in the light of impending developments in North-South relations. The proposed fifth amendment to the Constitution would delete this section. It was carried by 721,003 votes to 133,430. Lynch saw the outcome as an important step towards the development of more inclusive policies in the South, as outlined by him in his speech at the Garden of Remembrance.

The other proposition before the electorate was the fourth amendment to the Constitution, which would lower the voting age from twenty-one to eighteen. This also was carried, with 724,839 in favour and 131,514 against.

As 1972 drew to a close, Lynch had greater cause for optimism about the state of Anglo-Irish relations than a year earlier. The Provisional IRA called a Christmas ceasefire, which lasted from 22 December until the 25th. But then it was business as usual.

On 28 December loyalists carried out a bomb attack in Belturbet, Co. Cavan, in which a teenage boy and a girl were killed. Loyalists also shot dead a young engaged couple in Co. Donegal on 30 December.

The violence in Northern Ireland had reached terrifying proportions during 1972: 103 British soldiers and 41 RUC and UDR men had been killed, as well as 323 civilians, 121 of these being classified as sectarian murders.[184] Both loyalist and IRA paramilitaries were growing in determination and desperation. While the British interned a number of loyalists in February 1973, the Irish Government had stepped up its activities against the IRA. The president of Provisional Sinn Féin, Ruairí Ó Brádaigh, was arrested on 29 December and on 11 January was jailed for six months for membership of the IRA. The same fate befell many of the 120 caught in the Garda swoop earlier in the month.[185] By the time Lynch left office, in March 1973, his Government had gone a good distance towards establishing the principles on which the Sunningdale Agreement was drafted and implemented.

Chapter 10

OPPOSITION AND RETURN TO POWER, 1973–9

In 1973 Lynch was obliged to confront the troubling fact that he was now the leader of a *de facto* minority Government. Defections from his party made his position precarious, as leader of Government and of the party. Yet he had a year and a half to run on his 1969 mandate.

There were strong tactical reasons why he might have gone to the country in January; but the idea of fighting an election in high winter held little appeal for politicians. Moreover, Lynch had reason to expect an electoral bounce from the country becoming a member of the EEC on 1 January. Britain and Ireland were equal members of an evolving community of states, membership of which would have the most profound impact upon the future prosperity of both countries. Northern Ireland was now an integral part of a community of states that had helped bring about the normalisation of relations in the post-war world between Germany and the once-occupied states of France, Denmark, Belgium and the Netherlands. EEC membership was a milestone in Irish history and one, Lynch hoped, that the electorate might remember on polling day.[1]

But the benefits of membership were still very remote from the electorate in the winter of 1973. Fianna Fáil had been in power since 1957. Lynch knew that his party was losing popularity. Party discipline also remained a problem. Industrial relations remained troublesome. In 1972 a national wage agreement granted a 21 per cent increase to trade unions; but eaten bread is soon forgotten.

There was no good time to go to the polls. On 5 February 1973 Lynch called a general election. Polling day was the 28th. In 1969 the opposition had been hopelessly divided, and the Labour Party was ideologically opposed to coalition government *per se*. However, the day after the announcement of the election Fine Gael and the Labour Party agreed to a fourteen-point electoral pact with, in the words of Joe Lee, attractive promises for 'virtually everyone'.[2] Auction politics were in vogue. The leaders of Fine Gael and the Labour Party, Liam Cosgrave and Brendan Corish, respectively, appeared united in their determination to get Fianna Fáil out.

AIKEN RESIGNS OVER HAUGHEY NOMINATION

The 1973 general election was the first since the Arms Crisis, and at least one founder-member of Fianna Fáil was concerned that the 'wrong sort of people were gaining ground.' That was Frank Aiken's view, as recorded by his son, Frank junior. The 'wrong sort', he explained, were 'people who my father would not have admired as being representative of the men who set up Fianna Fáil.'[3]

The evening following the dissolution, Tuesday 6 February, there was a dinner in Leinster House to commemorate Jack Lynch's twenty-five years in Dáil Éireann. The Taoiseach was flanked by the 'two fifty-year men: Frank Aiken on his right and Paddy Smith on his left.' Frank Aiken junior wrote: 'My father told Mr Lynch during the dinner that there were people who shouldn't be ratified by the Fianna Fáil party. He specifically mentioned Mr Haughey.' He also told Lynch 'that if Charles Haughey was ratified as a candidate by Fianna Fáil, he would resign from the party. He would also write a letter to the papers for publication explaining the reasons why he would be resigning from politics.'[4]

Conventions were held throughout the country on Thursday night, the 8th, and in Dublin on Sunday the 11th.[5] On 7 February 1973, the day after speaking to Lynch, Aiken wrote to the Fianna Fáil director of elections, setting down the condition on which he would allow his name to go forward for selection:

In view of the shortness of time before Nomination Day I wish to give you due warning, as quickly as possible, that after much consideration I finally decided this morning that if I am selected as a candidate and that Charles Haughey is selected and ratified by the National Executive I shall withdraw my agreement to stand as a Fianna Fáil candidate.[6]

Aiken did not make his reservations known when he was nominated on 8 February at the convention in Co. Louth. According to his son's account, his first words were: 'I'm very happy for Pádraig [Faulkner] but I'm not so sure myself . . .'[7] On that occasion Aiken did not take either Faulkner or his election agent and close friend, Senator Joe Farrell, into his confidence. After his nomination he failed to turn up in Co. Louth over the weekend to meetings about election arrangements. Faulkner and Farrell sensed that there was something wrong but had no idea of the gravity of the situation.

On Saturday 10 February, the day before the Dublin conventions, Lynch asked President de Valera to ask Aiken to go to Áras an Uachtaráin. There was a rugby match on that day between Ireland and England, which the President wished to attend, in view of the fact that the Scottish and Welsh teams had refused to come to Lansdowne Road in 1972 because of the Northern violence.

De Valera told the Taoiseach: 'You ring Mr Aiken and tell him I'd like to see him this evening after the match.' Aiken used to visit the Áras frequently, for reasons of business or friendship. As neither Aiken nor de Valera trusted the phone system, all matters of a confidential nature were discussed person-to-person.[8]

De Valera, who wished Aiken to succeed him as President, told him that the publication of a letter giving his reasons for not standing in the general election would damage his presidential chances. Aiken, who did not wish to stand for the presidency, was not swayed by this argument. He intended to resign. On Sunday 11 February, President de Valera's secretary, Máire Ní Cheallaigh, phoned Frank junior's home in Greenore, Co. Louth, to get the family to persuade their father not to publish his reasons for resigning from Fianna Fáil during the election campaign.[9]

On Monday 12 February, when Aiken learnt that Haughey had been ratified, he withdrew his nomination and told Lynch he intended giving his reasons to the press. In an effort to win support for his position he had written to Paddy Smith, looking for support for his stance against Haughey. On 12 February, Smith sent him a handwritten letter:

> I understand now what is in your mind. It is at least two years too late in my view. This man for better or worse, has been functioning in the party ever since he made that speech after the trial. He has voted and worked with the party and is Chairman of one of its committees. At the last Ard Fheis of the party while I was in the Chair he was proposed as one of our Vice Presidents and was approved with acclaim by all the delegates.

Smith continued:

> I did not arrange all this nor did you but neither of us tried to stop it. He has attended party meetings, he has attended the Dáil and voted with us on all issues. He is now selected by the Reps. of the Cumann in his own constituency and is up like others to be vetted and approved or rejected. I do not see with that history I have inadequately set out in great haste can be side-stepped by us when this matter is before us. I have no brief for the man, I am not trying to be his case maker but I know I have no course open to me but to do the only logical thing left to me, and you are just as guilty as I am and every other member of the party is.

Smith ended:

> The time to take action or propose the taking of such action was before this history I have so crudely outlined here. It is the truth Frank and it does not change the story to attempt to shy away from it. I think it is worth

trying to lead before taking such a foolish course. The proposal for a Currie or Hume walk over I regard as far too childish. I hope you are well and all belonging to you. I am sorry I could not see you but maybe this rough record of my thoughts is best.[10]

In stepping down, Aiken had thought that either John Hume or Austin Currie should be invited to stand in his place as independents in Co. Louth.

Jack Lynch, Paddy Smith, Seán MacEntee and George Colley met on the night of 12 February to discuss the crisis in Co. Louth. All agreed that Joe Farrell, in the words of Aiken's son, 'was the man nearest to my father.' Paddy Smith warned his colleagues: 'Joe will probably agree with Frank.'[11] Later that night George Colley phoned a 'flabbergasted' Pádraig Faulkner to tell him that Aiken was not standing. Faulkner and Farrell, director of elections in the constituency, were summoned to Dublin to meet the Taoiseach. Faulkner went to Farrell's home that night. As one of Aiken's closest friends, Farrell was 'dumbfounded' on hearing the news.[12]

The following morning, Farrell went to Dublin to meet the Taoiseach. Lynch came out of a Government meeting to meet him, saying:

> Joe, I don't know what I'm going to do. Frank Aiken has pulled out. He thinks I should not have ratified Charles Haughey. He is going to write to the press and tell the people why.

Lynch said that it was bad enough having Aiken pull out, but if he went to the papers during the election the opposition would be able to say that Fianna Fáil was split. Lynch asked Farrell to go and have a chat with him. Aiken was in Colley's office. As Farrell left the room, Lynch said: 'When he wouldn't do it for Mr de Valera, I don't believe that anyone can stop him now.'

'Are you the last?' Aiken greeted Farrell, who replied: 'It doesn't matter whether I am the first or the last. I know you too long and too well to try and twist your arm. What I'm sorry to say is that I disagree with your timing.'[13]

Farrell explained that the party would be split from top to bottom if Lynch had done what Aiken wanted him to do. Aiken replied that he did not want to split the party but merely to help Fianna Fáil.

> The reason I didn't do it sooner is that I thought I would not have to do it, that somebody else would. But, when nobody else did it, I believe that I owe it to the men who went before me in this party. I'm convinced of that.

Farrell agreed with Aiken's objective and said that if it had been six months earlier he would have been with him; there would have been a lot of other people with him. 'Look now, Frank,' Farrell continued. 'You made your protest from the highest motives. In the light of the fact that Jack couldn't very well do what you want at this stage, don't go ahead now. Nobody knows anything but five or six people.'

Aiken replied: 'Look, Joe. I have a conscience, and I have to live with it.'

Farrell countered:

If you go to the press with a letter you will be remembered as the man who split the Fianna Fáil party. I know the things you did down the years. You did say it to me many years ago that you always believed you had your life's work done when the Fianna Fáil party was founded. The work you did when Fianna Fáil came into government, the setting up of Bord na Móna and, in particular, the work in Foreign Affairs, all of that will be forgotten if you go to the press. I'm going to ask you for something, Frank.

Aiken responded: 'You never asked me for anything before.'

Farrell then said: 'It is not for myself. I am asking your permission that when I go back to Mr Lynch that I can tell him that you are standing down on doctors' orders.'

Aiken stared at Farrell across the table for a long time. Then he said: 'All right. Go ahead.'

Farrell reported back to Lynch, who said: 'Joe, I didn't think that when you went out that door that you would come back with this. I can never tell you what this means to me because I didn't know what to do if it appeared in the papers.'[14]

Aiken stepped down on the morning after Haughey's ratification. But the drama was not yet over. Aiken arranged a meeting at noon on Tuesday 13 February with John Hume in Austin Currie's home in Dungannon. He wanted him to stand as an independent candidate in Co. Louth. Austin Currie phoned Joe Farrell that evening to say that Hume would not stand.

That night, 13 February 1973, Lynch announced in the Town Hall, Dundalk, on the occasion of Aiken's seventy-fifth birthday, that he had learnt with great regret that the former Tánaiste and Minister for External Affairs was retiring from politics, on doctors' orders.[15] Joe Farrell would stand in his stead, with Pádraig Faulkner.

Aiken kept his word: he did not reveal to the electorate his reasons for refusing to stand. On 17 February 1973 he asked the voters of Co. Louth to support the two Fianna Fáil candidates, as they had been to the forefront 'in helping the Taoiseach to maintain the national and international policy based on peace, democracy, justice and co-operation . . . laid down by the founder of Fianna Fáil.'[16] His son concluded this account: 'My father tried to change the course of Fianna Fáil in 1973. After that, he never attended another Ard Fheis nor took any part in Fianna Fáil affairs.'[17]

VICTORY FOR THE NATIONAL COALITION

Fine Gael and the Labour Party fielded a number of attractive and well-known candidates, including Garret FitzGerald, Conor Cruise O'Brien and Justin Keating. An editorial in the *Irish Times* acknowledged that Fianna Fáil had 'in Mr Lynch the most successful vote getter in its history.' But against that, it warned, 'may be its very arrogance in claiming that there is no alternative. Whether Lynch or Cosgrave were to become the next Taoiseach, 'leading the mob from behind is not on for 1973.'[18]

The *Irish Times* the following day argued that it was not enough for

Fianna Fáil to ask the people to give Mr Lynch a mandate. The question must be—a mandate for what? Nor is it enough to say that Mr Lynch should be given backing to finish the job. What job? The same applies to the other parties.[19]

On 8 February the *Irish Times* attacked the Fianna Fáil line on coalition.

The idea that the Republic can produce only one team of men capable of manning a Cabinet is an insult to every voter. The progress of the Coalition parties in building up their case will be a welcome sight to the people of the Republic.[20]

John Healy, in his 'Backbencher' column on 10 February, referred to the professionalism of Lynch and of Fianna Fáil.

He is, frankly, the hottest professional in these islands today. I see nothing in Europe to touch him since de Gaulle left the scene. He is bigger than de Valera ever was as a vote-getter. Attacking Jack Lynch is about as profitable as pissing against the wind, most of it comes back on top of you . . . The more Jack Lynch is heckled and booed and called "Union Jack," the more he'll love it.

However, Healy concluded his column by saying that Lynch needed time in opposition to work out his ideas on the new Ireland: 'He needs a sabbatical. I favour giving it to him.'[21]

Healy identified one theme in the very professional campaign against a coalition Government. It was the 'politics of fear'. The divisions between the two coalition parties would make them weak on the central issue of 'law and order', and between them they would wreck the economy. After a week of campaigning, Healy felt that Fianna Fáil professionalism had come to the fore, and coalition was the issue.[22] Lynch, during the second week of the campaign, told a rally in Athlone and Mullingar that a defining characteristic of coalition government was 'their total inability to make firm and final decisions on policy of any kind.' Fianna Fáil, he said, was 'the only political organisation in the state capable of applying sound, long-term policies based on fundamental principles.'[23]

By 22 February it was evident that the Fianna Fáil message was not getting across. The party changed direction and began to offer increased social welfare and children's allowances, the abolition of rates on private dwellings by 1 April 1974, and a pound of butter for 8d monthly to every family on social welfare. The *Irish Times* in an editorial viewed the *volte face* as panic measures and claimed that the calibre of the Lynch Government was 'now mercilessly exposed to the television cameras.'[24]

In view of Aiken's hostility to Haughey's candidature, how did the battle develop in the Dublin North-East constituency? Reduced from a five-seat to a four-seat constituency, it saw Haughey again facing Conor Cruise O'Brien for the Labour Party. Theirs had been a bruising encounter in the general election of 1969, when Cruise O'Brien won a Dáil seat for the first time. In 1973 he was relatively safe, as he was receiving Fine Gael second preferences under the pre-election agreement.

It was a dour battle. Cruise O'Brien, according to his biographer, Donald Akenson,

> ran hard, especially against Haughey, a man whom he believed to be deeply evil. Conor called particular attention to reports of Haughey's assuring IRA sympathizers in Dublin North-East of his sympathy with them, using the words, 'deep down I feel exactly as you do, and if I am returned to office, I will see things are done our way.'[25]

Haughey headed the poll, with 12,901 first preferences. Cruise O'Brien received 7,774. In Dublin County South, Kevin Boland, standing for his new party, Aontacht Éireann, got 2,142 votes and lost his seat. (In 1969 he had got 5,441 and had taken the third seat.) Boland learnt the hard way. Outside Fianna Fáil, votes were hard to get. In 1973 the leading Fianna Fáil candidate in Dublin County South, Ruairí Brugha, got 6,381. In three other Dublin constituencies Boland's new party failed to register a serious vote. It fared equally badly in country constituencies.

Another dissident from 1970, Neil Blaney, headed the poll in Donegal North-East, obtaining 8,368 votes—a drop of only 338 from 1969. In Donegal-

Leitrim, Joseph Brennan's vote was down by nearly four thousand, to 10,240.

In Cork City, Jack Lynch swept back with 12,427 first-preference votes, bringing in Seán French on his massive surplus. Yet despite outstanding individual performances, the arithmetic did not favour Fianna Fáil. The party had 69 seats and the coalition parties 73. There were two independents, Neil Blaney and Joseph Sheridan. Fianna Fáil had actually increased its share of the first-preference vote, from 45.7 to 46.2 per cent. Fine Gael also improved, from 34.1 to 35.1 per cent, while the Labour Party dropped from 17 to 13.7 per cent. But the PR system favours vote management.

The National Coalition came into power on 14 March. Liam Cosgrave was Taoiseach and Brendan Corish was Tánaiste. The new Minister for Foreign Affairs was Garret FitzGerald. The Minister for Posts and Telegraphs, Conor Cruise O'Brien, was the Labour Party's spokesman on Northern Ireland. Meanwhile Lynch, after being in Government since 1957, had to get used to being in opposition.

LYNCH, THE NATIONAL COALITION AND SUNNINGDALE, 1973

Sir John Peck retired as British ambassador during the general election. It was his last posting. He had served with distinction. In his memoirs he wrote of Jack Lynch that 'all those concerned with, and committed to, peace with justice in the North owe a very great deal to his courage and tenacity in pursuing what he believed to be the right policy.' Between 1969 and 1973 Lynch held Fianna Fáil together and maintained popular support for his 'peaceful approach' in the face of 'fearful pressures from all quarters.' Peck felt that Lynch never wavered from his conviction that 'he was right to put his trust in the British government.' But Peck felt that Lynch never succeeded after Bloody Sunday 'in convincing British politicians of how much we owed him at that stage, or what the consequences would have been if he had lost his head.'[26]

Assessing his relationship with Heath, Peck characterised it as 'accident-prone'. He did not think it was quite 'a dialogue of the deaf, but caught in the middle as I was, I sometimes felt that a pair of powerful hearing aids would come in handy.'[27]

Life moved on in the wake of the election, and Peck settled down to retirement in Dún Laoghaire. The new ambassador, Sir Arthur Galsworthy, called on Hugh McCann on 5 March 1973. The British timetable for reform in Northern Ireland was very tight. The new Dáil was not scheduled to meet until 14 March. Heath would be happy to meet the Taoiseach and the Taoiseach-designate, Liam Cosgrave, or Cosgrave alone, if that was preferred, and had kept 12 March entirely free for such a meeting. He would 'be very happy to fall in with what was considered right at this end.' He wanted to give a general outline of the forthcoming British white paper on Northern Ireland and to discuss in particular the Irish dimension. He felt that a visit by Cosgrave and Lynch might bring in an element of bipartisan policy on the Irish side. There was urgency on the British side. Direct rule had to be renewed. Heath was having growing difficulties with some elements in the right wing of his party.[28]

On 8 March 1973 a referendum was held in Northern Ireland on the question of remaining in the United Kingdom. The SDLP and other nationalist parties discouraged voting. There was a turn-out of 59 per cent, of whom 591,820 voted for and 6,463 against. Two car bombs exploded in London, killing one person and injuring 243. Cosgrave and Corish went to London on 8 March for talks with Heath, which lasted four hours. Heath wrote in his memoirs that he found the new Taoiseach to be still exhausted after his election campaign, but he found it 'still useful to become acquainted with him.'[29] This was the beginning of a productive relationship.

Much of the preliminary work for the setting up of a new agreement to establish a power-sharing Executive had been laid down during the period of the Lynch Government. The framework for such talks at the level of officials, ministers and heads of government had also been established.

On 20 March the British Government published the long-awaited white paper, *Northern Ireland Constitutional Proposals.* This proposed a unicameral eighty-seat assembly, to be elected by proportional representation. There would be a nominated Executive, which was to include members of the nationalist community.

On 20 May there were elections in Northern Ireland to newly formed district councils. The Official Unionists won 201, DUP and VUUP (Vanguard) 74, Alliance 59 and the SDLP 76.

The Northern Ireland Assembly Act (1973) had been passed on 3 May, establishing a 78-member Assembly to be elected under proportional representation, using the British House of Commons constituencies. On 28 June there was a general election for the new Assembly. The Unionists were divided, official Unionists getting 23 seats, unofficial Unionists 10, DUP 8, VUUP (Vanguard) 7 and West Belfast Loyalist Coalition 2. The Northern Ireland Labour Party got 1 seat, Alliance 8 and the SDLP 19.

This proved a very successful venture, if on occasions tempers got out of hand. On 31 July the first meeting of the Assembly ended in disorder after twenty-six loyalist members refused to accept the presiding officer's ruling that the Assembly adjourn. On 5 December members of the DUP and Vanguard assaulted unionist supporters of Brian Faulkner.

On 28 July the Northern Ireland Constitution (Amendment) Act (1973) was passed. This abolished the Northern Ireland Parliament and the office of

Governor. It provided for an Executive of not more than twelve members (increased to fourteen in December), to be appointed by the Secretary of State for Northern Ireland when he considered it likely to be widely accepted. Replacing the declaration in the Ireland Act (1949), there was a new declaration that Northern Ireland would not cease to be part of the United Kingdom without the consent (in a referendum) of the majority of the people.

Heath visited Northern Ireland at the end of August and warned local politicians that London 'could not wait for ever.' The terms of the new power-sharing Executive needed to be agreed for the new Assembly to take on its powers.[30]

At the annual conference of the Conservative Party, Heath warned against moving too swiftly towards making concessions on the question of partition. His words provoked a strong reaction from the SDLP, a party, as we have seen, close to Fianna Fáil. One section of the SDLP, led by John Hume, pressed for greater movement on Northern Ireland. The Irish Government was also radicalised and pressed for a wider role for the Council of Ireland. The Northern Secretary, William Whitelaw, was inclined to accommodate that view.

On 17 September 1973 Edward Heath became the first British Prime Minister to make an official visit to Ireland since the foundation of the state. He met Cosgrave and members of the Government at Baldonnel Aerodrome, Co. Dublin, for nine hours, where they discussed the Council of Ireland. In his memoirs, Heath stated that Cosgrave, however much he might have liked to do so personally, would not agree to a commitment to remove articles 2 and 3 of the Constitution of Ireland.[31] Garret FitzGerald, in his memoirs, stressed the failure to get agreement on the timing of setting up the Executive. Heath wanted to do so before a conference on Northern Ireland. The Irish Government position was to hold out until after the meeting.[32] Progress was made at the level of officials over the following weeks. Whitelaw, meanwhile, convened a meeting at Stormont on 5 October of Northern political leaders, made up of six Unionists, six SDLP and three Alliance. The discussions continued to the verge of collapse on 21 November 1973, when agreement was finally reached. Whitelaw proposed an eleven-member core Executive, made up of six Unionists, four SDLP and one Alliance, with four non-voting members: SDLP (two), Unionist (one) and Alliance (one).[33] This was the breakthrough required. But Whitelaw was not given the opportunity to see things through to the end of an important phase.

A conference was held at Sunningdale, Berkshire, on 6–9 December, between the representatives of the British and Irish Governments and the Northern Ireland Executive-designate. The Irish Government 'fully accepted and solemnly declared that there could be no change in the status of Northern Ireland until a majority of the people of Northern Ireland desired a change in

that status.' The British Government declared support for the wishes of the
majority of the people of Northern Ireland. Both declarations were registered
with the United Nations.

There was agreement to set up a Council of Ireland. That body was
confined to representatives of both parts of Ireland (seven each from the
Irish Government and the Northern Executive, with a consultative assembly),
with safeguards for British interests. There was agreement that persons com-
mitting crimes of violence in any part of Ireland should be brought to trial,
irrespective of the part of Ireland in which they were domiciled, and there
would be an Anglo-Irish Law Commission, which would seek to deal with
fugitive offenders.

Described by Cosgrave as 'the road to peace', the agreement was attacked
by both the Provisional IRA and radical unionists. There was violence on the
streets. In the midst of this tension Heath replaced Whitelaw with Francis
Pym as Secretary of State for Northern Ireland at the end of November 1973.
Fortunately, Pym was well versed in the politics of Northern Ireland. His first
task was a daunting one.

What had come into existence was based on the hard work of many
people in Ireland and in London. However, many of the ideas put forward
by Ken Whitaker and by Jack Lynch's Government had been transformed
into new political-administrative structures and enshrined in law. It was a
brave experiment, but it lasted only until the Ulster Workers' Council 'strike'
in May 1974, when the Labour Government of Harold Wilson, which had
come into power, buckled under pressure from the mob on the streets of
Northern Ireland.

LIFE IN OPPOSITION

Following his defeat in the general election, Jack Lynch could only watch as
many of the ideas on Northern Ireland developed during his term in government were put into practice. Life in opposition gave him the time to set about
the task of reorganising and rebuilding Fianna Fáil. He chaired a meeting of
the 'shadow cabinet' at the end of March 1973. Until he had an opportunity to
reshuffle his front bench, all former ministers were appointed as spokesmen
for their former portfolios.

The line-up by September was: David Andrews, Justice; Sylvester Barrett,
Transport and Power; Joe Brennan, Industry and Commerce; Ruairí Brugha,
Posts and Telegraphs; George Colley, Finance; Gerry Collins, Agriculture;
Pádraig Faulkner, Social Welfare; Robert Molloy, Local Government; Desmond
O'Malley, Health; John Wilson, Education and the Arts; Ray MacSharry, Office
of Public Works; Liam Cunningham, Lands; Joseph Dowling, Labour; Brian
Lenihan, party leader in the Seanad (he had been a short-lived Minister for

Foreign Affairs but had unexpectedly lost his seat in the election); Thomas Meaney, Defence; Michael O'Kennedy, Foreign Affairs; Jim Tunney, Gaeltacht; Paddy Lalor, chief whip; Seán Browne, assistant whip; William Kenneally, Fisheries; Noel Lemass, Physical Planning and the Environment; Pearse Wyse, Youth and Community Care.[34]

The same meeting also discussed the reorganisation of Fianna Fáil head office and plans for the approaching Seanad elections. The whip was instructed to provide each member of the front bench with direct telephone lines, filing-cabinets and dictating machines.[35] Despite having been in power for sixteen consecutive years, or more probably because of it, Fianna Fáil had failed to modernise its party structure. Its head office infrastructure remained under-developed for a national organisation of such numbers and complexity. Lynch, therefore, sought to address the issues of the day while conducting long-term structural reform.

On 4 May 1973 the shadow cabinet met to discuss the issue of Seanad candidates. There was also a discussion on party policy towards the vacant office of President of Ireland. Éamon de Valera was stepping down after serving two terms. He attended a ceremony on 24 June at Boland's Mills in Dublin to mark his retirement from the post and from public life. T. Ryle Dwyer speculates that Jack Lynch could have had the party nomination.[36] It was evident, however, from the aftermath of the Arms Crisis in May 1970 that Lynch was committed to retaining his position as leader of Fianna Fáil. At no time did he hint in public or in private that he wanted to go to the Phoenix Park. Opposition did not change his determination to remain on as party leader.

Lynch favoured the candidacy of Erskine Childers, former Tánaiste and one of his rock-like supporters in the difficult days following the ministerial sackings of May 1970. The son of the executed anti-Treatyite, Childers had always shown himself to be a dignified presence and a moderate voice in Irish politics. His tragic family history motivated him to act as a reconciler in a parliamentary system in which the wounds of the Civil War ran deep and the bitterness lasted for generations. Childers stood against the politics of bitter-ness and recrimination. In his entire public life he never made reference to the execution of his father. Courteous and gentlemanly, he remained one of Lynch's most loyal and courageous allies on Northern Ireland.

The shadow front bench gave Childers time to make a decision on whether he was prepared to run. A special meeting of the parliamentary party was called for 6 April to select a candidate. The unanimous choice was Childers.[37] He was a member of the Church of Ireland, and his selection was an important signal to the majority in Northern Ireland and to the religious minority in the South. His opponent, Tom O'Higgins, was a scion of a Free State family.

People went to the polls on 30 May 1973 and elected the Fianna Fáil candidate by 635,162 votes to 587,577. It was an outstanding personal performance. The election victory was also seen as a personal victory for Lynch, giving him a much-needed boost after the debacle of the general election.

Childers became the first of the modern presidents. He threw himself into developing the office, becoming more active than his three predecessors and travelling throughout the country and making himself available to various groups and charities. He set himself a punishing pace.

Meanwhile the shadow cabinet continued to rebuild the party and prepare for a return to power. On 23 May 1973 it agreed that there were to be no official pairings with members of the Government except in the case of necessary attendance abroad. It was also decided that the salary of head office employees should be absorbed by the party leader's allowance.[38] On 12 June 1973 Lynch presided over a meeting at which it was decided that the appointment of two new members of the staff was to be raised with the secretarial committee. There was a discussion on Fianna Fáil's alignment in the European Parliament. The shadow cabinet decided to send two emissaries to Brussels and that the Fianna Fáil group would form a new grouping. There were also discussions on landing rights at Shannon and Dublin Airports and on a by-election in Co. Monaghan resulting from the election of Childers to the presidency.[39] (Fine Gael took the seat on 27 November 1973.)

Lynch and his closest supporters began in the summer of 1973 to lay down the strategy for a Fianna Fáil comeback. Lynch's economic adviser, Dr Martin O'Donoghue of Trinity College, retained this role. In the shadow cabinet minutes for 19 June 1973 there is a reference to the setting up of a Party Advisory Group, with a preliminary meeting having taken place in Lynch's home.[40] This is the first mention of the group that ultimately produced the controversial general election manifesto for 1977.

It is evident from the shadow cabinet minutes that great efforts were being made to tighten discipline within the party, to force members of the front bench to have speeches cleared before delivery and to ensure that there was the tightest control over any statement made by Fianna Fáil on Northern Ireland. Lynch took firm control of his front bench. His inner circle, listed in part above, formed a phalanx around him. The narrative that follows, based on minutes of the shadow cabinet, illustrates these points.

On 26 June 1973 the shadow cabinet discussed the successful conclusion of the agreement that resulted in the establishment of a new alignment with the Gaullists in the European Parliament, known as the European Progressive Democrats. There was also discussion on the establishment of an all-party committee on unity and on Jack Lynch's speech on 22 June on the Six Counties.[41] On 3 July 1973 the shadow cabinet discussed the terms of reference of an inter-party committee on unity.[42] On 10 July it named four deputies to that committee. Among those selected to serve were Michael O'Kennedy and Vivion de Valera.

Northern Ireland figured on the agenda of the shadow cabinet on 17 July 1973. There was a discussion on an IRA press conference on 13 July. The question of pairing also arose. It was decided that Fianna Fáil members of the Dáil attending the European Parliament were to be paired only with coalition Dáil members of the European Parliament.[43]

Leaving the worries of opposition and party reconstruction behind him, Jack and Máirín Lynch travelled to their cottage in west Cork to spend the month of August away from national politics. But a statement issued when he was in a relaxed mood and away from it all nearly forced him into premature retirement.

THE LITTLEJOHN AFFAIR: 'STINKING TO HIGH HEAVEN'

Garret FitzGerald identified several sources of tension between Dublin and London during the term of office of the National Coalition: the Littlejohn affair, the Strasbourg case, 'and the (to say the least) uneven behaviour of the British army in Northern Ireland.'[44]

The 'Littlejohn affair', as it came to be called, revealed a serious breach of trust in the relationship between Dublin and London, involving 'black operations' by British intelligence agencies in Ireland. However, a by-product of this sordid affair revealed a fundamentally decent side to Irish politics. When Lynch was vulnerable and in deep trouble, FitzGerald chose to help him find a way out of a dilemma that might have resulted in his premature resignation as leader of Fianna Fáil.

In August 1973 Kenneth and Keith Littlejohn were on trial for bank robbery in Dublin while Lynch was on holidays in Co. Cork. In their defence during extradition proceedings in London in January of that year, the two brothers claimed they had been requested by British intelligence to carry out a bank robbery in Dublin, for which they had subsequently been charged. Both claimed that the robbery had been part of a plan to goad the Irish Government into introducing internment.

The secretary of the Department of External Affairs, Hugh McCann, showed the following report submitted by the Irish ambassador in London, Dónal O'Sullivan, to the then Taoiseach, Jack Lynch.

17 Grosvenor Place
SW1X 7HR
SECRET

January 3rd 1973

Dear Secretary,

As I mentioned to you on the telephone I was asked by Sir Stewart Crawford to come and see him this morning. He said he had some information to communicate to me which he was most anxious should be brought to the Taoiseach's personal attention before the Taoiseach leaves for the U.S.A.

When I saw Sir Stewart at mid-day he had with him Mr. Hetherington from the Law Office. Sir Stewart spoke to me from a document of which he said he regretted he could not give me a copy to take away. I made very full notes of what he had to say and the succeeding paragraphs summarise the situation. Sir Stewart's request to me to call on him was related to the case of Mr. Kenneth Brian Littlejohn (alias Kenneth Austin) who is sought by us for his part in a bank robbery in Dublin on the 13th October last. Littlejohn is Scottish and was born in Argyll on the 19th October, 1941. Littlejohn was arrested at our request on the 19th October, 1972 and he indicated in court that he would resist extradition on the grounds that the offence for which he was required was political and that British national security interests would be involved in his being tried in Ireland.

The extradition proceedings are being heard on the 11th January and Littlejohn's lawyers have asked that the case be heard in camera. There is no certainty that this request will be acceded to.

By way of background, Sir Stewart told me that in November 1971 Littlejohn offered himself to British Intelligence as an informant on the IRA. He claimed that he had joined the Provisionals, that he was inspired by lofty motives, namely, a concern about the risk of the spread of communism in Ireland, and that he was in a position to give information about IRA intentions to buy Czech arms.

Littlejohn's offer was accepted but the Intelligence Service here subsequently discovered that he had connections with the IRA in the area of illegal fund raising. (Sir Stewart observed at this point that I knew, no doubt, what was meant by 'illegal fund raising'—presumably bank robberies). Because of these connections which Littlejohn had, the Intelligence Service concluded that there was obviously a serious risk of his being involved in these fund-raising activities. They, therefore, made it clear to him that if he were to become so involved he would be doing so without any authority from them. If he were to get into trouble with the police in Ireland there was nothing the British could do, or would do, to help him. Incidentally it emerged from general conversation later that Littlejohn has had quite a long criminal record in this country mainly, I gathered, in connection with bank and other robberies.

Arising out of a letter which the Authorities here have now received from the defending solicitors it appears that a lot of IRA connections could come out in the trial and that there is a strong possibility that the political argument could be used against extradition. Sir Stewart then told me that the Director of Public Prosecutions here usually acts for our Attorney General in extradition cases. The British are most anxious that the Littlejohn case should be handled with the least embarrassment and they want him sent back to us. Under the reciprocal extradition arrangements which the British have with us there is provision that the man arrested here must be brought before a Magistrate's court. If there is any danger that on his return to us he could be tried for a political offence then the Magistrates would be very likely to refuse extradition. Littlejohn as a member of the Provisional IRA could conceivably be charged under our new Offences Against the State legislation. In order to ensure his return to us the Director of Public Prosecutions would need to be fortified with an Affidavit, presumably from our Attorney General, in which there would be a specific undertaking that Littlejohn on return would not be charged with any offences other than the bank robbery charge for which we require him. The upshot of all this was that Sir Stewart asked if it would be agreeable to us to have the Director of Public Prosecutions (Sir Norman Skelhorn) go to Dublin on Friday to settle the necessary Affidavit with the Attorney General. I told Sir Stewart that the story which he unfolded to me was clearly one which I would have to convey to Dublin by special courier particularly in view of his request that this be brought personally to the Taoiseach's attention. It was not a matter which I could mention on the telephone or on the teleprinter. From a political angle the case seemed to me to stink to high Heaven. I could offer no view as to what the reaction in Dublin would be. I queried Mr. Hetherington on the likelihood of our Affidavit becoming public knowledge here. His reply was that if the case were heard in camera only those in court would know about it. The position would, of course, be quite different if the case were heard otherwise. I then enquired whether the possibility might not exist of an appeal by Littlejohn to a higher court where the proceedings would be held in public. Mr. Hetherington thought this a possibility. He also agreed that the Affidavit would in any event appear in due course in the court records. I told them both that I was glad to have this additional information as the provision of an Affidavit by us seemed to me to open up the possibility of serious political embarrassment.

As I have told you on the telephone I am sending a colleague to Dublin this evening with the story.

There were a few references at the end of our conversation to the Wyman case. Sir Stewart told me that they are a little worried about some aspects of the preparations for the hearing of this case. According to his latest information the book of evidence has not yet been made available to Mr. Wyman's lawyers. Sir Stewart went on to say that Wyman appears to be having difficulty in getting access in private to his legal advisers. There is, apparently, a tendency for some of the jail staff to be within earshot.

Finally Sir Stewart asked if I could be telephoned tomorrow if possible with an indication as to whether the Attorney General will be prepared to see the Director of Public Prosecutions on Friday.[45]

The Stewart Crawford mentioned in the report was the permanent under-secretary at the Foreign Office and chairperson of the Joint Intelligence Committee.

The reference in the final paragraph to the 'Wyman case' also relates to the last months of the Lynch Government and requires further explanation. On 21 December 1972 the Minister for External Affairs, Dr Patrick Hillery, called in the British ambassador, Sir John Peck—a formal process of censure. He told him that, following deliberations at a Government meeting that morning, he had been requested to inform the ambassador that 'they were satisfied that an attempt has been made to suborn and subvert a member of the Garda Síochána by one or more people working for the British Department of Defence.' Hillery was instructed to 'protest to the ambassador about that activity.' At the same time 'the Taoiseach had asked him to convey to the Ambassador the Taoiseach's personal disappointment insofar as this activity betrays a lack of confidence in the relations that should exist between two friendly Governments.'[46]

Peck 'expressed surprise and denied any knowledge of the activity.' He undertook to report the protest immediately to his government, but in the absence of any knowledge of the subject matter he personally could not accept the protest or otherwise. He said he would share the Taoiseach's concern if the allegations should prove to be true and suggested that the minister might convey to the Taoiseach the ambassador's personal concern in the whole matter. He emphasised his denial of any knowledge of the operation, stating that 'his only knowledge was what he learned from the media about the Court case now pending.'

At this point in the document there is a handwritten minute in the margin: *'This reference could be to Littlejohn but is more likely to be to Wyman who was arrested c.20/12/72.'*

The memorandum continued: 'If a British subject should be involved in the Court case one should consider the question of his safety if he were lodged in jail with members of the IRA.' Hillery stated that he had no doubt the Minister for Justice would be conscious of this aspect. The minister then mentioned to Peck *en passant* that it was noticeable that information received from the British about the IRA had substantially improved in quality. Peck commented that that in itself was not proof of the allegations made. While agreeing that it was not proof in itself, Hillery said that the fact that it had improved following the activity complained of was significant. The ambassador then withdrew in order to report the matter immediately to his government. Hugh McCann was present throughout the interview.

There is a further note that makes reference to Wyman, in connection with two telephone calls from 'C3' (the Security and Intelligence Branch of the Garda Síochána). On 15 December 1972 a flat was raided in Decies Road, Ballyfermot, Dublin, owned by thirty-year-old Alex Fursey. The search recovered seven hundred rounds of .22 and .303 ammunition, a smoke bomb, half a stone of a white powdery substance and two walkie-talkies. Fursey, who was English, owned a shop in Ballyfermot and 'had come under notice recently—believed to be sympathetic to the IRA.' He was taken into custody.

Fursey informed the Gardaí that he had an appointment to meet a certain person on 18 December. The Gardaí kept the appointment open, and a John Wyman, a resident of London, turned up. He was detained under section 31 of the Offences against the State Act. The Garda note stated that he had been born in Bulu, Cameroon, in 1937 and that he was attached to 'Bateman's Investigations, London.'

> The Gardaí suspect that he is an MI5 Agent and that Fursey has been feeding information to him about the IRA. He had booked a room at the Burlington Hotel, Dublin, and hired a car. Wyman has asked to meet the Deputy Commissioner.[47]

On 3 January, McCann showed the ambassador's report, quoted above, to the Taoiseach. (The envelope containing a number of copies of the note of that date quoted above may have been given to the Taoiseach for circulation to relevant members of the Government on the same day, though that is only a surmise on my part.) Lynch asked McCann to give a copy of the report to the Minister for Justice, Desmond O'Malley.

Lynch left on 4 January on an IDA trade mission to the United States. In the

Taoiseach's absence, the British Director of Public Prosecutions, Norman Skelhorn, visited the Attorney-General, Colm Condon, with regard to the affidavit. O'Malley sat in on the meeting. Condon agreed to the affidavit on a number of conditions. (1) As the Wyman case was pending, an assurance was sought that neither of the Littlejohn brothers had been employed by the British Government to suborn any member of the Irish police or military. (2) Neither of the Littlejohns had passed to the British Government information obtained from the Irish police or military. (3) The British Government would not seek to use the fact that the Irish Attorney-General was prepared 'to give an indemnity' to Littlejohn in respect of possible political offences as an argument against the prosecution of Wyman for offences under the Official Secrets Act. (4) There was no connection between the Littlejohn case and the Wyman case.

The British Government may have amended the original Irish wording of the affidavit. There were further communications from the British Government on 6 and 10 January.[48] A slightly different version of these conditions appeared in the press in August 1973.[49]

On 10 January 1973 Dónal O'Sullivan reported to McCann that Sir Stewart Crawford had visited him, accompanied by Mr Hetherington of the Attorney-General's office. Crawford said that the British Government was 'able to give the required assurance on each of the four points.' If the Irish Government should have any second thoughts about the use by them of the affidavit, it was essential that they be informed that afternoon, as their intention was to use the affidavit at the court hearing the following day. He assumed it would be all right for them to go ahead.

Crawford thought he should mention one point, as it might come up in the court hearing. 'When Littlejohn first contacted the authorities here to offer his services he asked to be seen by a Minister. Lord Carrington agreed to this request and Littlejohn was, in fact, seen very briefly by Mr Geoffrey Johnson Smith, and then passed down the line.'[50] Here was official confirmation that Littlejohn had official contact with the British authorities and with British Intelligence.

The extraditions went forward. On 3 August 1973 the Special Criminal Court in Dublin sentenced Kenneth and Keith Littlejohn to twenty and fifteen years' imprisonment, respectively, for their part in a bank robbery in Grafton Street, Dublin, on 12 October 1972. The Littlejohns claimed they had been acting under instructions from the British Ministry of Defence.

The Government issued a statement on 10 August, stating that it had informed the British Government of its deep concern over British activities such as the Littlejohn affair. Instead of keeping quiet until he could check the facts, Lynch claimed in a statement that the first contact the Government had with the British Government about its involvement with the Littlejohn affair was the request for an affidavit to be sworn by the Attorney-General, Colm

Condon, in connection with the extradition proceedings. Lynch's mistake was that he had completely forgotten the fact that Hugh McCann had given him documentary evidence on the matter on 3 January 1973.

The Minister for Foreign Affairs, Garret FitzGerald, asked Hugh McCann to remind Lynch of the contents of the correspondence he had received. Lynch immediately made good his mistake, holding a press conference in Skibbereen, Co. Cork, where he apologised for his memory lapse, adding that he would have to consider whether he should continue as leader of the opposition. So shaken was he by the error that he seriously contemplated standing down. Family, friends and political colleagues successfully prevailed upon him to stay on.

In his memoirs, Garret FitzGerald explained the lapse as being due to Lynch's visit to the United States and to the pressure of fighting a general election, which he had lost. 'Under the pressure of events, everybody involved had forgotten what had happened, apart from the vigilant Hugh McCann,' wrote FitzGerald, who graciously acknowledged that he too had forgotten having been shown the same set of papers in May 1973 by an ever-vigilant secretary of the Department of Foreign Affairs.[51]

The thesis that Lynch had self-servingly forgotten embarrassing facts both in late 1969 and early 1970 has been rejected in the previous chapter. He made a mistake in August 1973, for which he apologised. In retrospect, it is clear that Lynch would have been better advised to allow the former Minister for Justice, Desmond O'Malley, to make the necessary statement. But he too was on holidays.

As a postscript, when the Wyman case came to trial the Government had evidence that Detective-Garda Patrick Crinnion of the Special Branch had been leaking detailed information about the IRA to Wyman. That material found its way to the Secret Intelligence Service (commonly known by its earlier name, MI6). A protracted trial would have been embarrassing and damaging to both Dublin and London, and the state entered a *nolle prosequi*. Released from custody, Crinnion was driven to Dublin Airport by his solicitor, together with Wyman. En route, the disgraced garda asked the solicitor to stop the car in the Dublin suburb of Whitehall. He got out, and disappeared. Wyman presumably returned to his handlers in London.[52]

REVIVING FIANNA FÁIL

Lynch caused a panic inside the party on his return from holidays at the end of the summer of 1973. He had abandoned any self-doubt about continuing as party leader. Having earlier faced a personal crisis of confidence following the Littlejohn affair, he threw himself into the work of reforming the structures at Fianna Fáil head office.

The long-serving general secretary, Tommy Mullins, retired but remained active and was still working in head office when the party was returned to power in 1977. He was replaced by Séamus Brennan, a young Galway activist with an outstanding organisational brain and a gift for working the PR system to the best advantage. On 25 September 1973, at a meeting of the shadow cabinet, Lynch announced that he had appointed Esmond Smyth to co-ordinate the support services for the party and to set up a library at head office. Concern was repeated at the meeting over the need to provide better public relations for the parliamentary party. It was agreed that a part-time press publicity man should be found. 'The whip was instructed to seek facilities for monitoring Radio and T.V. and to seek a photo-copying machine for the Party as separate from the House facility.' A decision was also taken to occupy the fourth floor committee room for party purposes. A case was also successfully made for increased secretarial services, and the whip was instructed to raise the matter with the secretarial committee.[53]

The minutes reveal the underdeveloped nature of structures at Fianna Fáil head office at that time. But there was steady movement forward. At a meeting on 2 October 1973 the shadow cabinet agreed to appoint two new typists, to give a pay increase of three pounds per week to full-time staff members, and to increase the allowance to the chief whip and assistant whip to eighty pounds and fifty pounds per month, respectively. There was also a discussion on the Monaghan by-election and on the Government's refusal to participate in the RTE 'Politicians' programme.[54]

On 30 October 1973 a sub-committee comprising Ruairí Brugha, Brian Lenihan, Paddy Lalor and Hugh O'Flaherty was appointed to make recommendations regarding the appointment of a press officer.[55] On 31 October 1973 the front bench met in the party leader's rooms in Leinster House at 8 p.m. to discuss the escape of three 'political prisoners [Séamus Twomey, J. B. O'Hagan and Kevin Mallon] by helicopter from Mountjoy jail earlier in the day.' Twomey had been sentenced to three years' imprisonment on 8 October. A statement was prepared and issued to the media.[56]

On 10 December 1973 Lynch called a special meeting to discuss the communiqué that would follow the ending of the tripartite talks over the future of Northern Ireland.

The Party leader who said that he would be going on radio at lunchtime and television on 7 Days programme said it would be as well to have no other comment to the media from members until the full document was processed. He would endeavour to make early arrangements for this processing and would make urgent use of the back-up service.[57]

On 11 December 1973 Lynch convened a meeting of the shadow cabinet in room 356 in Leinster House to discuss the Sunningdale communiqué. He 'promoted a full discussion.' There was general agreement with the line he had already taken on radio and television interviews, and he got the meeting's full support for a continuation of the same line of action at the forthcoming debate in the Dáil.[58]

On 18 December 1973 the front bench discussed the Health (Family Planning) Bill. Members were asked what the attitude of the party should be if section 17 of the bill was declared unconstitutional by the Supreme Court.

> It was decided that there should be no immediate re-action from us as it will be up to the Government to take appropriate steps in the event of a finding of unconstitutionality. The Party leader said that in such an event he would also be seeking the observations of the appropriate back-up group.[59]

Lynch also urged each member to endeavour to recruit additional experts for their groups, where required, 'but to check with him before actual selection of personnel.'[60]

The front bench returned on 8 January 1974 to a discussion of the bill arising out of the Supreme Court decision on section 17 of the Criminal Law (Amendment) Act (1935).

> It was felt that the government might sit tight and not introduce amending legislation for the present. It was felt that a party decision on Miss Robinson's Bill in the Senate should not be taken until the Seanad is about to discuss it at Second Stage.[61]

There was also discussion about a letter from Terry Doyle asking the leader and front bench to add their voice to the demand to have the Price sisters transferred to serve their sentences in a prison in the Six Counties. (Marian and Dolours Price had been jailed for their part in a bombing attack in London in March 1973 and later went on hunger strike.) The whip was instructed to reply that Lynch had already taken the matter up with the appropriate minister.[62]

There had been dramatic developments in Northern Ireland since the Sunningdale Agreement had been signed. On 1 January the Northern Ireland Executive took office under the leadership of Brian Faulkner. Amid protests, the Ulster Unionist Council met and rejected the agreement after five hours of bitter debate. Faulkner resigned as leader of the Unionist Party but remained in the Northern Ireland Assembly. He now led the pledged Unionists, or those who supported the agreement.

On 16 January, Faulkner and Cosgrave met at Baldonnel Aerodrome, Co. Dublin. They met again on 1 February 1973 at Hillsborough, Co. Down, together with seven members of the Irish Government and seven members of the Northern Executive. On 15 January 1974 the Fianna Fáil front bench discussed Sunningdale, and Lynch also raised the matter of various legal submissions regarding the process.[63]

The shadow cabinet also discussed preparations for the forthcoming ard-fheis. Lynch told his colleagues that the motions would be available at the following meeting of the front bench. Shadow ministers, he said, would have a strong indication of what they were going to have to confront and they should prepare accordingly.[64] At the meeting on 22 January the motions were distributed and discussed. Lynch told the meeting of his 35-minute talk with the Taoiseach, Liam Cosgrave, and of his meeting the Northern Ireland Prime Minister, Brian Faulkner.[65]

On 29 January 1974 the front bench had a long discussion on ard-fheis procedure. There was further discussion on the appointment of a press officer.[66] On 5 February 1974 the front bench agreed to advertise the post in the four national papers. Lynch reported on a meeting he had had with John Hume and Paddy Devlin. 'The summary of it was that he had got very little information to add to what already was public knowledge.'[67]

On 12 February the front bench agreed to raise the matter of the second stage of the Health (Family Planning) Bill at the meeting of the parliamentary party the following day.[68]

It is clear from a review of the deliberations of the Fianna Fáil front bench in 1973 and early 1974 that Lynch had taken a firm hand in the running of the party. Speeches by shadow ministers at public gatherings had to be cleared. The level of discipline was strong and there was no stepping out of line. In response to a motion on Northern Ireland by Neil Blaney in the Dáil, the front bench agreed to add by way of addendum the present Government amendment, with the exception of the final paragraph of that amendment, which would be deleted and the following inserted:

Re-affirming the inalienable right of the people of Ireland to a united Ireland, reaffirming their aspirations to achieve this by peaceful means, and accepts that for practical purposes this involves the agreement of the people of Northern Ireland.[69]

In the midst of grave disturbances in Northern Ireland, Edward Heath called a general election for 28 February 1974. In Northern Ireland, not surprisingly, it was turned into a referendum on Sunningdale and on the concept of the Council of Ireland. The anti-agreement United Ulster Unionist Council won eleven seats in the British House of Commons. The leader of the SDLP, Gerry Fitt, held his seat. The Faulkner Unionists did not win a single seat.

In Britain the Conservative Party was decisively defeated. The new Prime Minister, Harold Wilson, appointed Merlyn Rees as Northern Secretary. It was not a happy situation. The Labour Party's narrow majority forced Rees to remain in London much of the time. He did not give the Executive the support it needed to survive. The Council of Ireland remained a cause of great division.

On 5 March 1974 the Fianna Fáil front bench discussed Sunningdale and the outcome of the British general election. It was again agreed that 'the Party Leader was the only one to officially comment' on the affairs of Northern Ireland.[70] Lynch was missing from the front bench meeting on 12 March, and George Colley was cleared to respond to the Taoiseach's statement on Sunningdale. A copy of Cosgrave's comments would be requested by the party to enable Colley to prepare his text. There was a brief reference to the Littlejohn case: 'D. Andrews said he would allay [sic] raising the question of the Littlejohn escape for the present.'[71]

On 11 March, the day before the meeting, Kenneth Littlejohn escaped from Mountjoy Prison. His younger brother, Keith, was recaptured within minutes of scaling the wall.

The Fianna Fáil front bench spent a good deal of time on domestic issues. On 23 April, Lynch made reference to the 'Late Late Show' on 20 April when tapes of conversations with himself 'had been abused.' This reference is to the superimposing of laughter on an interview he had done on the Littlejohn affair. This was to demonstrate how it was possible to manipulate and distort a serious news item. Lynch explained that the director-general of RTE, Tom Hardiman, had phoned him to apologise and 'apart from his having made observations to Mr Hardiman on having such tapes available he felt that nothing further [should] be done about it.'[72]

On 30 April 1974 Lynch introduced the new press officer, Frank Dunlop, to the members of the front bench. He was on a three-year contract but was unable to begin until he had been released from his RTE appointment after 1 June.[73] Lynch later introduced him at a meeting of the parliamentary party. News of his appointment was greeted with silence. When Lynch asked for questions, the veteran Paddy Smith asked: 'What is it exactly you will be doing for us, young fella?'

Writing more than twenty-five years later, Dunlop said that on taking up his new post he found the party 'in a time warp'. The front bench was old, the only fresh blood being John Wilson. He registered 'shock at the disarray, shock at the ignorance of prominent members as to the workings of the media, shock at the blatant and naked antipathy that existed amongst former senior ministers towards named journalists.' He observed that for a number of front-benchers politics took second place to professional work. He felt that men who had been ministers for a decade or more found it difficult to live on the salary of a TD. He stated that George Colley and Desmond O'Malley had resumed their practice as solicitors; David Andrews and Michael O'Kennedy were at the bar. Jim Gibbons and Brian Lenihan were appointed to the European Parliament. Dunlop found the parliamentary party 'at sea,' 'rudder-less' and 'totally lost.' 'Whatever the country was expecting, to say nothing of the hopes of Fianna Fáil supporters around the country, the front bench line-up didn't augur well for revolutionary new ideas or policies.'[74]

Making allowances for an understandable desire to build up his own role in the turnaround of the party's fortunes by the general election of 1977, Dunlop had objective grounds for his initial despondency. The front-bench minutes between 1973 and 1976 do not exactly portray a thrusting, dynamic, energetic party. Fianna Fáil had a serious problem in trying to relate to RTE and the mass media in general. In contrast, the new press secretary had come from the RTE news room. He knew how the station worked. His contribution at that level was highly significant.

But the situation was not as bad as he had painted it. Lynch had already appointed both Esmond Smyth and Séamus Brennan to help run the head office. Dunlop was fortunate in the timing of his appointment. Major reforms were in train.

As Fianna Fáil reorganised, the situation in Northern Ireland was sliding towards revolution. On 14 May 1974 Lynch reported to his shadow cabinet that he had met the Northern Secretary, Merlyn Rees, and the British ambassador, Arthur Galsworthy, that morning for half an hour. Rees spoke of Faulkner's attendance at Sunningdale and also discussed the report of the Law Enforcement Commission. Lynch said he had stressed a preference for an all-Ireland court and also for the early establishment of the Council of Ireland.[75] Events in Northern Ireland were running out of control, in large measure because of the weakness of the Wilson Government. The Ulster Workers' Council called what has been termed erroneously a general strike on 14 May in protest against the Sunningdale agreement, the power-sharing Executive and the proposed Council of Ireland. The British Government buckled under the pressure.

On 17 May a loyalist group planted bombs in Dublin and Monaghan that killed twenty-two people and injured more than a hundred. It was the worst outrage in the South during the entire period of the 'troubles'. On 21 May 1974 the shadow cabinet decided to postpone the party meeting the following day to allow deputies and senators attend the Mass for the victims at 11 o'clock in the Pro-Cathedral. There was a long discussion on the Northern situation, with particular reference to the Law Enforcement Commission, whose report was due to be published within the coming days. Lynch gave his views on it and said he had sought the advice of his legal experts. The question of an all-Ireland court had been speedily dismissed. There was a preference for an extra-territorial jurisdiction system; that could be objected to on the grounds that it was not in keeping with articles 2, 3 or 28 of the Constitution. Lynch said he had already expressed his doubts to the Taoiseach on the 15th and had stated that 'he could not be expected to speedily go along with the report, and subsequent legislation.'[76]

On 22 May 1974 Lynch told his front bench that the British ambassador had called on him and given him a copy of Faulkner's statement in which, among other things,

> he had said that there would now only be a council of 7 ministers from each side as a Council of Ireland, with no separate secretariat and no assembly and that the second tier section was being postponed until after an election in 1977/78.[77]

On 28 May, Lynch gave his front bench an account of his meeting the previous night with Ivan Cooper and Paddy Devlin of the SDLP. They had called to his home to emphasise 'how important it was to the SDLP that they should be seen to have the support and goodwill of Fianna Fáil.' Cosgrave had phoned him that morning to brief him, but he learnt no more from that source than he had heard from the SDLP. A general discussion followed, and the meeting felt it should express its support for the SDLP in its determination to sustain the power-sharing Executive.[78]

It was decided to send a telegram to the British Prime Minister:

> Fianna Fáil calls on the British Government to discharge fully their responsibility, by using all their resources to maintain the authority of the elected Representatives in Northern Ireland as expressed through the Power Sharing Executive, to safeguard the basic right of all the people of Northern Ireland and to ensure that the campaign of intimidation and violence will not succeed.[79]

The British Government, having caved in and allowed the 'strike' to continue for fourteen days, witnessed the collapse of the Executive on 28 May and the resignation of its members. The shadow cabinet met at 5:30 that afternoon to consider the latest position, in 'that the Northern Executive has now collapsed following the resignation from it of B. Faulkner and his unionists. The Party Leader cleared a statement he proposed to make in the house [Dáil Éireann] at 7 p.m.'[80]

In the aftermath of the collapse, Lynch instructed a number of his ministers to remain in close contact with members of the SDLP. In London, meanwhile, Bernard Donoughue, head of the policy unit of the Prime Minister's Office, recorded in his diary for the 29th:

> Merlyn Rees, the Northern Ireland Secretary, came in at noon and told us that the Protestant workers' strike was over. The Protestants have won. They have succeeded in destroying the experiment with Catholic partici-pation in the power-sharing Executive. His position is that he is *pleased* the new power-sharing Executive established after Sunningdale has resigned, because it frees his hands to take direct action. And he thinks the Protestants have become very fascistic.[81]

Wilson's weakness had guaranteed the collapse of a brave and imaginative constitutional experiment. As his speech was being prepared for Parliament, which had been recalled to discuss the crisis in Northern Ireland, Donoughue recorded in his diary on 3 June:

> . . . and studied the PM's very secret memo on a scenario for withdrawal from Ireland and giving Ulster Dominion status, which I had originally suggested to him. It was personal to Robert Armstrong . . .

On 4 June, Donoughue continued working on Wilson's speech:

> Spent the morning working on HW's speech. The civil servants made a massive attack to force him to leave out a sentence saying N. Ireland could 'go it alone.' Joe and I resisted—lost the words but kept the idea fairly clearly . . . At last it is a day when Irish policy has been pushed a little nearer to sanity.[82]

Wilson's pragmatism on Northern Ireland had moved closer towards the idea of withdrawal. It is little wonder that opportunists and hawks in Fianna Fáil took the opportunity a year later to press the British Government to declare its intention to withdraw from the North.

At a meeting on 11 June 1974, George Colley and Ruairí Brugha gave a 'run down of the meeting with SDLP men, Currie, Devlin and O'Hanlon.'[83] The same meeting was also concerned about the hunger strike of IRA men and women in London, protesting at having been refused a transfer to Northern Ireland. Michael Gaughan died on 3 June 1974 in Parkhurst Prison, Isle of Wight, after sixty-five days on hunger strike. He was buried in Ballina, Co. Mayo, where an IRA guard of honour accompanied the remains and shots were fired over the grave.[84] The Fianna Fáil meeting on 11 June discussed the Northern situation, and David Andrews was 'instructed to raise a question [in the Dáil] about the lack of action by the authorities in relation to the Gaughan funeral on Sunday last where subversives had blatantly paraded and fired volleys.'[85]

When the front bench met on 3 July 1974 it had 'a full and comprehensive discussion on the Contraceptive Bill [*sic*] and arrangements were made for alternative suggestions to be made.' It was agreed 'that as a party we should oppose the Bill.'[86] On 16 July the Taoiseach, Liam Cosgrave, led six Fine Gael deputies into the opposition lobby to defeat his own Government's Health (Family Planning) Bill. The margin was 77 to 61.

Michael O'Kennedy, at a meeting of the front bench on 9 July, raised the question of the possibility that the All-Party Committee might have proposed to it the deletion of articles 2 and 3 of the Constitution of Ireland. 'It was decided that we could not accept this.' A statement was cleared for issue on the British white paper on the Northern Ireland constitution. There was also a reference to the 'present controversy on land deeds,' with reference to planning and zoning in the Dublin area. It was decided to conduct 'our own investigation internally within the party into this question to ascertain the facts in so far as they can be.' Deputies Molloy and Cunningham were asked to conduct that investigation.[87] The present writer has not discovered a copy of that report.

On 13 November, Seán Brosnan held a seat for Fianna Fáil in the Cork North-East by-election. But Lynch soon faced an unexpected election.

On 19 November the shadow cabinet adjourned as a mark of respect to the memory of President Erskine Childers, who had died on Sunday 17 November. He had suffered a heart attack after delivering a speech at the College of Surgeons in Dublin. He was survived by his wife, Rita, and their six children. As speculation mounted in the press about the possibilities facing the Government regarding his successor, Rita Childers made an unexpected entry into the political arena. She made a public statement deploring the speculation over a successor and the cat-and-mouse game between the parties. She said she had decided to intervene and to expose 'the political cynicism that was gripping Leinster House' and not to allow 'such corrosive, destructive cynicism about politics to contaminate that high office.' The Government was attracted by the prospect of naming Rita Childers as an agreed candidate.

On 22 November, Lynch led a discussion at the shadow cabinet on the filling of the presidential vacancy either by an agreed candidate or by the party nominating a candidate.[88] The question was again taken up at a meeting of the shadow cabinet on the morning of 26 November. A decision was taken to adjourn to enable David Andrews and Michael O'Kennedy to call 'to see Mrs

Childers with a view to expressing to her our feelings on her candidature which was a question which had emerged since we had last met on Tuesday 22nd.' The deputies reported back that afternoon to the resumed meeting that they had not seen Mrs Childers and 'had instead encountered her step-son Erskine B., who having heard their purpose in calling, conveyed to them after checking with Mrs Childers that she saw no point in their meeting.' The meeting adjourned until the following morning, when it was decided to recommend to the parliamentary party that 'we should adjourn till later in the week.'[89]

In the intervening days there was speculation that Lynch himself might stand; but he quickly ruled out such a possibility. The name of Dr Kenneth Whitaker may also have been mentioned at that time in regard to the vacancy. Lynch, in conversation with the EEC Commissioner, Dr Patrick Hillery, asked him to approach the former Chief Justice Cearbhall Ó Dálaigh, then a judge in the European Court of Justice in Luxembourg, to determine if he would be interested in principle in going forward. Hillery received a positive response.

On 28 November, Lynch presided over a meeting of the shadow cabinet. As Mrs Childers had offered herself as a non-party candidate, he recommended that the parliamentary party meet at 12:30 that day 'to authorise the Party Leader to submit the name of Chief Justice Cearbhall Ó Dálaigh to the Government leader as an agreed candidate.'[90] On 4 December 1974 the shadow cabinet noted that Ó Dálaigh had become president-elect.[91] On the 19th, Dáil Éireann assembled for the election of nominees for the office of President of Ireland. Ó Dálaigh was proposed and elected unanimously. He would be in office for one year and five months.[92]

The crisis over the presidency was certainly the main reason for the postponement of Lynch's planned summer reshuffle of his front bench. Now the burning question within the party was whether or not he would bring Haughey back to the front bench. The latter had behaved in a restrained manner since the heady days of his dismissal in May 1970. He had painstakingly attempted to rebuild his tarnished reputation throughout the country. A campaign was being run to rehabilitate him. The pressure intensified in the latter part of 1974, and Lynch was the recipient of many representations. One journalist reported that the weight of opinion held by influential members of the party was in favour of giving Haughey a position 'that would be relatively important yet remote from the sensitive area of Northern policy.'[93] George Colley forcefully opposed any such act of clemency. Seán MacEntee, a party elder, also remained hostile to his rehabilitation.

Lynch and Colley were more than political allies: they were close personal friends. On this occasion Lynch decided not to heed the advice of his friend. On 30 January 1975 Jim Gibbons accepted Agriculture, and Charles Haughey returned as shadow spokesman on Health.[94] Colley and Lynch did not fall out, but it was a low point in the close relationship between the two men.[95]

Haughey, on the day of his return to the opposition front bench, engaged in a delightful piece of revisionism. He denied ever calling in 1970 for Lynch's resignation. 'That was an interpretation put on these events at the time which was in fact never intended by me.' He said that he never mentioned Lynch's name at the time. He always supported Fianna Fáil policy; 'I do now and I hope I always will.'[96] Lynch might have taken a strong warning from the facility with which Haughey could engage in radical revisionism. If Lynch calculated that he could keep him under greater control, however, he was very much mistaken.

On 4 February 1975 Lynch told members of the new front bench 'to dedicate themselves to the task in hand.' He stressed that 'we should be prepared at any time for any eventuality.'[97] In the shadow cabinet minutes for 11 February, 'Charles Haughey raised the question of the line to be followed in relation to the ard-fheis motion on Family Planning. This led to a comprehensive discussion on the contraception issue. It was finally agreed that the matter should be discussed further.'[98] Haughey was back, and determined to make his mark. On an underperforming front bench his ability, his work rate and his presidential-style politics made him stand out. The gift of prophecy was not needed to realise that his ambition was unlimited.

The political correspondent of the *Irish Independent*, Chris Glennon, pointed out that the Lynch reshuffle had displeased some in the party.[99] John Healy of the *Irish Times* commented that the reshuffle had produced a 'mountainous mouse'.[100] Gene Fitzgerald from Cork had been given Labour. There were also changes in the shadow portfolios of Fisheries (Denis Gallagher), Planning and Environment (John O'Leary) and Public Health (Tom Fitzpatrick). Lynch needed to shake up his underperforming colleagues and was under pressure to rekindle party morale at the approaching ard-fheis.

The central message before the ard-fheis, when it began on 14 February 1975, was to prepare for an election to oust the National Coalition. 'We did it in 1957. We can do it in 1975' was on a poster seen by Dick Walsh of the *Irish Times*.[101] As Sinn Féin protested outside the RDS hall in support of hungerstrikers in Port Laoise prison, Brian Lenihan told delegates that there was a substantial difference between the coalition Government of Fine Gael and the Labour Party on the one hand and Fianna Fáil on Northern Ireland: 'We stand for unity and we stand for unity of all our people.'[102] When Lynch spoke he received a three-minute standing ovation. 'We have the people, we have the policies, we await the opportunity.' Much play was made of the fact that 101,725 people were unemployed. Haughey pledged to bring in a bill on contraception once Fianna Fáil had been returned to power.[103] However, the *Irish Times* in an editorial referred to the proceedings of the ard-fheis as being 'imbued . . . with dullness and complacency.' By way of Northern Ireland policy, 'nothing was offered but childish bromides.' The editorial complained that Fianna Fáil had not yet come to terms with opposition: 'It regards itself as a kind of Government in exile,' waiting for the tide to turn again, as it did in 1951 and 1957, and 'wash it back into office.' The editorial concluded: 'To be a way of life is not enough; Fianna Fáil must be a political party as well.'[104] The editorial in the *Irish Independent* stated that that Fianna Fáil was still in search of policies.[105]

Haughey knew how to fill that vacuum. On 5 March 1975 there is the following reference in the minutes: 'The whip was instructed to submit a motion regarding Energy which he received some time ago from C. Haughey.'[106] At a meeting on 11 March, Lynch wanted his shadow cabinet to be

> more resolute and constructive in our opposition from here on and indicated that each front bench spokesman to endeavour to propose at least one motion for consideration and to be submitted to the House [Dáil Éireann] as a private members motion. Charles Haughey undertook to submit a motion on Health later in the week.[107]

In 1974 Lynch had appointed Ruairí Brugha,[108] the son of Cathal Brugha, to a newly created post on the front bench as spokesman on Northern Ireland. Brugha was a strong supporter of the Taoiseach and very much in sympathy with his line on Northern Ireland. Lynch relied upon him to act as a liaison with the SDLP and to develop links with moderate unionist politicians. Brugha had an unrivalled knowledge of Northern politics, garnered through study and frequent visits across the border.

Brugha's wife, Máire MacSwiney, records in her memoirs that 'debates in the Dáil between Ruairí and Dr Cruise O'Brien were amicable, because that is the way Ruairí always behaved.' According to the same source, 'he reshaped Fianna Fáil policy on Northern Ireland, basing it on reconciliation between the peoples of different traditions on the island. He also focused political attention on getting Britain to face up to its responsibilities in the area, and to working jointly with the Irish government.' He went to the British-Irish Association at Oxford, and John Hume introduced him to David Trimble, who refused to shake hands with the 'son of a murderer.' Hume took umbrage, 'but Ruairí intervened—he was ever a man to pour oil on troubled waters and to prevent conflict.'[109]

The Lynch-Brugha line on Northern Ireland was official opposition policy. Brugha stood between Lynch and a number of revivalist nationalists who sensed the British Labour Government's complete lack of commitment to remaining in Northern Ireland. Tension grew in the party during the latter part of 1975 over existing Fianna Fáil policy. But that test was postponed for a few months.

On 29 April 1975 Haughey was again mentioned in the minutes, in relation to a letter written by Ruairí Brugha to the *News Letter* (Belfast). He was showing his appetite for hard work. At the same meeting, Lynch mentioned that 'Gay Byrne had been chasing him to appear on the Late Late Show and he had agreed subject to being confronted with the Taoiseach.' The meeting favoured the idea of George Colley going on the programme.[110]

At the meeting on 6 May 1975 the Brugha letter was discussed at length. Lynch agreed to 'clear up the matter with a statement to the parliamentary party meeting the following day. There can be no further question of changing our constitution to appease the Loyalists,' the minutes read. There was also a discussion 'on the possibility of an early general election and it was agreed that we need to generate optimism in relation to the Tully carve-up and that the Dublin situation needs urgent attending to.'[111] The 'carve-up' is a reference to the handiwork of the Minister for Local Government, Jim Tully, a member of the Labour Party. He had been responsible for a radical reform of electoral boundaries, carried out with the same partisan intention with which Kevin Boland had once performed the same task. Tully had substituted three-seat for four-seat constituencies in Dublin, where Fianna Fáil was thought to be vulnerable. In the countryside he increased the number of four-seat and five-seat constituencies where Fianna Fáil was known to be strong. The logic behind his strategy was as simple as it was transparent. A swing against the Government was inevitable, and it was expected that the Tullymander (a name it earned as a Southern version of the gerrymander in Northern Ireland) would work in favour of the coalition.[112] Ironically, the much-maligned Fianna Fáil manifesto of 1977 contained a pledge never to repeat the Tully experience. It called for an all-party committee to conduct the redrawing of constituencies. Senator Neville Keery, a member of the Fianna Fáil planning group, had a clause to that effect inserted without any fuss or opposition in the 1977 manifesto.[113]

Evidence of a strong Haughey comeback was reflected in the minutes of the shadow cabinet in mid-1975. On 13 May, Haughey presented a policy document on health, agreeing to discuss it later that week.[114] On the 15th the meeting discussed the document fully and placed it on the agenda for the following meeting for final approval. On 20 May the meeting cleared the health document for circulation to the party and to branches throughout the country.[115]

Haughey did not confine himself to his portfolio. As a former Minister for Finance he had much to say about the National Coalition's handling of an ever-deteriorating economy. It was a bad time to be in office. Since coming to power in 1973, the year of an international oil crisis, the coalition had floundered. The unemployment figure had risen in January 1975 above 100,000 for the first time since 1942. Inflation was running at nearly 25 per cent, the national debt was mounting and the Government appeared to be out of ideas.[116]

The Fianna Fáil electoral machine had performed quite well since its loss in the 1973 general election. Erskine Childers, the Fianna Fáil candidate, had won the presidential election in May 1973. The party had lost a Monaghan by-election on 27 November 1974 to Fine Gael but had won a by-election in Cork North-East on 13 November 1974. In 1975 Fianna Fáil won two out of three by-elections: on 4 March it took Galway West and Galway North-East. Máire Geoghegan-Quinn won the latter. On 12 November, Enda Kenny took a seat in Mayo West for Fine Gael that had been held by his late father.

Éamon de Valera, the founder of Fianna Fáil, died on 29 August 1975. He was given a state funeral and was buried on 2 September in a modest grave in Glasnevin Cemetery, Dublin, beside his wife, Sinéad, who had died in January. Lynch took the opportunity to emphasise both that de Valera rejected the violence of the Provisional IRA and that no section had the right to vote itself out of a nation. He was saddened, he said, by the events in the North, particularly by sectarian violence. After he had retired as president, Lynch said, de Valera spoke more freely and endorsed completely his (Lynch's) approach as Taoiseach.

> He absolutely rejected violence. He stressed often, as far back as the end of the Civil War that further violence was not in the national interest. When Fianna Fáil was founded, he said force was not the way. I think you can say specifically that he rejected the violence of the Provisionals.

Lynch said that de Valera did not want an oration or eulogy over his grave. He was a humble and simple man essentially, he said. Lynch concluded: 'The monument we can erect is to perfect our desire for peace, unity and reconciliation, as he desired it up to his death.'[117]

There may have been no correlation between those remarks and the fact that there was growing unrest in Fianna Fáil over Lynch's policy on Northern Ireland. There were those in the party who wanted to exploit the ambivalence of the British Prime Minister on Northern Ireland. In the autumn of 1975 Lynch temporarily lost control of his Northern policy, and he and Ruairí Brugha, his spokesman on Northern Ireland, suffered a humiliating set-back. Michael O'Kennedy, front-bench spokesman on foreign policy, had developed the habit of straying beyond his brief. On 28 September 1975 he asserted that the majority in Northern Ireland did not have the right to determine the direction of the relationship of Northern Ireland with the Irish state. Two weeks later he was quoted as requesting the British to make a declaration of intent to leave. Lynch responded that the speech represented a 'conflict of expression rather than of policy.'[118] That was not the case: there was more than a mere difference of emphasis on the front bench. The *Irish Times* reported further that the party confronted three choices: (1) call for a declaration of intent; (2) reaffirm the Lynch line; (3) attempt a compromise.[119] An editorial entitled 'Shattered consensus' asked why O'Kennedy had chosen that time to add his voice to those calling for a British declaration of intent to withdraw from Northern Ireland. The most obvious explanation, it replied, was that 'he has taken the temperature of his party and found that there is a majority in favour of demanding a declaration of intent—and thereby posing a renewed challenge to Mr Lynch's policies and leadership.'[120]

In an effort to retrieve the situation, Lynch invited Michael O'Kennedy, John Hume and Austin Currie to dinner at his home to discuss Northern policy. According to Currie, 'it did not take us long to realise that the purpose of the get-together was to talk sense to O'Kennedy. But it was also clear to us that O'Kennedy was voicing' a view that 'was becoming increasingly common within Fianna Fáil, and one which Lynch would find it difficult to stem.' When O'Kennedy left the dinner party early, probably not convinced by their arguments, according to Currie, he was in 'no doubt about the views of his leader and the SDLP.'[121] The party followed O'Kennedy. On 30 October 1975 the *Irish Times* called it a 'bad day's work' for the opposition party to adopt as policy that the British Government should 'declare Britain's commitment to implement an ordered withdrawal from her involvement in the six counties of Northern Ireland.'[122]

In February 1976 Fianna Fáil's forty-fifth ard-fheis was hailed as significant or, as Dick Walsh opined, 'the most influential' for the party since the Arms Crisis of 1970.[123] Falling in the fiftieth anniversary year of the party, it would be the first without Dev alive. The prospect of a divisive or disruptive motion on readmitting Neil Blaney hung uneasily over many delegates' heads. That did not materialise. On the opening night Charles Haughey made a strong appeal for party unity. Standing to the right of Lynch, he declared: 'There is no leadership crisis in Fianna Fáil. We are not casting around for a leader. We have a leader, democratically chosen and as such commanding the support and allegiance of the party.' Dick Walsh commented that Lynch nodded, but was it 'in agreement or in perplexity?'[124]

Lynch's address concentrated on the coalition's record in amassing £2 billion in debt, and on a host of alternative proposals from Fianna Fáil. He attacked the coalition's abolition of house-buyers' grants and reiterated the established Fianna Fáil line on rates on private property. 'I wish to repeat at this point our firm commitment to remove rates from homes as further evidence of our support for home ownership.'[125] An *Irish Times* editorial commented that the 'scent of office' pervaded Fianna Fáil during the ard-fheis.[126] However, Lynch's return to office was not inevitable. Fianna Fáil suffered two by-election defeats in June 1976, in Donegal North-East and Dublin South-West. But the party continued to prepare with care for a general election.

Meanwhile the National Coalition faced a critical challenge in the economic and security areas. Industrial unrest disrupted the life of the country. Workers in the banks went on strike on 28 June and did not return until 6 September. The 'Ulster Freedom Fighters' claimed responsibility for setting off bombs on 3 July in hotels in Dublin, Killarney, Limerick and Rosslare. On 15 July explosions in the Special Criminal Court in Dublin resulted in the escape of four prisoners (three of whom were captured almost immediately). On 21 July 1976 the British ambassador to Ireland, Sir Christopher Ewart-Biggs, and a civil servant in the Northern Ireland Office, Judith Cooke, were killed by a landmine, planted by the Provisional IRA, as they drove near the ambassador's residence at Sandyford, Co. Dublin. The murdered ambassador had presented his credentials to President Ó Dálaigh only two weeks before. The Government responded to the crisis in a decisive manner. On 1 September the Oireachtas declared that 'a national emergency exists affecting the vital interests of the state.' On 26 October, President Ó Dálaigh signed the Criminal Justice Bill. After consulting the Council of State, he referred the Emergency Powers Bill—a new measure to allow detention without charge for seven days for the preservation of the state at 'a time of armed conflict'—to the Supreme Court to test its constitutionality. On 15 October the Supreme Court declared the bill not repugnant to the Constitution. (It is important to stress that the Supreme Court also noted that the bill did not provide the basis for the abnegation of the rights of an accused person to communication, legal and medical assistance and access to the courts.)

On 18 October 1976 the Minister for Agriculture, Patrick Donegan, described President Ó Dálaigh as a 'thundering bollocks' while speaking at a function in Columb Barracks, Mullingar.[127] Under the Constitution the 'supreme command of the Defence Forces' is vested in the President. On 21 October the Dáil voted by five votes against a demand that the minister resign. Although a written apology was sent to the President, Ó Dálaigh felt obliged to resign in order to protect the integrity of the office, and he did so on the 23rd. His was a noble and distinctive act in a culture where resignation was not, nor would it become, the norm. Ó Dálaigh died on 27 March 1978.

Cosgrave, seeking to contain the damage done by the resignation, approached Lynch to find an agreed candidate as rapidly as possible. Dr Patrick Hillery, then fifty-three, was about to retire as an EEC Commissioner. When approached about becoming President he felt obliged to take on the job, although he had no ambitions in that direction. Dr Hillery became

President on 3 December 1976, and, having served two terms, retired in 1990 and died in 2008.

THE ROAD BACK TO POWER

Fianna Fáil had been preparing for a general election since 1974. Within its Support and Information Services, Lynch had assembled at various times a formidable 'Rapporteurs Committee'. Informally known as the 'Saturday Group', this 'think tank' was first chaired by Anthony (Tony) Hederman. Its members included Dónal Barrington, Hugh O'Flaherty, John McKenna, Dr Michael Woods, Esmond Smyth, Martin O'Donoghue, Brian Hillery, Eoin Kenny, Noel Mulcahy, J. O'Connor, Nicholas Kearns, Barry Early and Neville Keery. (This list may not be comprehensive.)[128]

By early 1974 many of the essential elements of the 1977 manifesto had already been discussed, researched and formulated. Dr Martin O'Donoghue, a Trinity College economist, had already formulated some of the more imaginative financial elements of that document. At a Support and Information seminar on 5 January 1974 he presented a paper on finance in which he reiterated policy on eliminating rates on dwelling-houses, addressed the questions of farmers' tax and the removal of subsidies, suggested the introduction of an accruals tax to cover capital, sought modifications to inheritance tax, and mooted a proposal entitled 'industrial democracy' that envisaged a prices and incomes policy, the former to be influenced by Common Market channels, the latter through national wage agreements.[129] Those proposals were duly adopted—or adapted—by the party.

Emphasis and of course timing always play a crucial role in determining how ideas move from the formation to the policy stage. Nothing illustrated this better than the subtle editing that fudged the cost issue in relation to rates in the 1977 manifesto. An advance draft of that publication stated: 'The full cost of removing the rates could be met by a 5% increase in indirect taxation for example the 20% rate of VAT could be increased to 21%, but extra taxation on this scale will not be necessary.'[130] This was excised from the final published document. While I cannot analyse the whole of the manifesto in detail, an examination of the general economic proposals and the rates issue is useful, given the controversial nature of both.

Fianna Fáil's analysis of the economic policy options was intriguing. In September 1976 the Press and Information Service, under the directorship of Frank Dunlop, issued the party's proposals, entitled 'The Economic Emergency'.[131] The document surmised three options facing the economy:

(1)   A continuation of present policies
(2)   Spending our way out of the depression
(3)   The belt-tightening option.

Each option was examined in detail, and three-year projections were fac-
tored in for inflation, growth, employment and balance of payments deficit,
but 'the outcome in each case is found to be unacceptable particularly in
regard to unemployment.' The preferred option then was a combination of the
better elements of spending and belt-tightening—simultaneously! Fianna Fáil
dismissed the coalition's policy as Micawberish, attempting to maintain living
standards by matching inflation with pay and welfare increases and trying to
eliminate the current budget deficit of £327 million by 1979. The latter could
only be achieved, Fianna Fáil maintained, at the cost of unemployment rising
to 150,000 by 1979 and no improved living standards for those with jobs.[132]
Increased Government spending alone was ruled out as an option.[133] Such a
policy was dismissed as 'a recipe for long term disaster.' The belt-tightening
option seemed, on paper at least, the most promising, as it predicted a rise in
the growth rate to a 'respectable level of 5%' by 1978 and lesser tax increases to
eliminate the budget deficit. But improvement in employment would not be
'on the scale needed to make a worthwhile breakthrough.'

Some of the underlying assumptions of this option seemed unlikely to
produce any worthwhile electoral breakthrough either: the main plank
assumed that a pay freeze in 1977 would reduce inflation to 9 per cent but
reduce living standards by 3–4 per cent.[134]

Nevertheless, Fianna Fáil proposed a combination of belt-tightening and
spending as the recipe for 'rapid and sustained growth'. The major components
of the 'Economic Emergency' document—which would underpin the 1977
election manifesto—were:

- increased Government spending of £100 million in 1977, providing
  twenty thousand immediate jobs
- tax reductions of £100 million in 1977 (20 per cent cut in income tax,
  and employers' social welfare contribution reduced to parity with that
  of employees)
- agreement by trade unions and employers to substitute tax cuts for pay
  rises, with pay rises limited to maintain living standards for 1977/78,
  followed by a modest rise in real wage rates in 1979—the improvement
  in living standard arising from lower prices
- an intensified campaign to use Irish products, with a target of switch-
  ing 3 pence in the pound from imports to domestic goods.

Additional action areas included the implementation of Fianna Fáil's commitment to remove rates from private dwellings in 1978, minor alterations in
VAT, export credit and insurance, subsidising interest on farm development, and
some creative use of EEC regional funds. And, given its dismissal of Government

policy, the document promised, almost tongue in cheek, that social welfare benefits 'will as a minimum be increased in line with the cost of living.'[135]

Many of the components were considered 'interdependent'. While the initial job creation would immediately affect unemployment, there would eventually be problems to be faced on the imports front as well as high Government borrowing, though these might be offset by tax cuts pushing up exports and a renewed 'Buy Irish' campaign. Combined with the pay freeze, this was the recipe for the stimulus to the economy. And this was September 1976. The timing, at that stage, was indeed propitious for a kick-start to the economy.

But some of the means Fianna Fáil proposed were already suspect. For example, the creation of twenty thousand jobs in 1977, at the cost of borrowing £100 million, contained the seeds of mangled Keynesian principles. It may have been good sense to allocate £30 million to generating five thousand jobs in the construction industry, but the other allocations—£50 million for ten thousand more teachers, gardaí and health workers—was simply undisguised non-productive borrowing for current (or recurrent) spending, whatever about allocating £20 million to absorbing five thousand young people in community projects.[136]

Fianna Fáil would not indulge in economic analysis of its policies when it could easily attack the Government for its performance in this field. In his address to the ard-fheis in February 1976 Lynch lambasted the Government over increased borrowing, rising prices and rising unemployment. He correctly identified the jobs crisis—or looming crisis—as a serious concern. He mooted the community employment scheme then, without elaborating on the details. 'Take our young people leaving school and college. Why should they bear the brunt of the economic crisis and be demoralised by the lack of job opportunities?'[137] His message was unmistakable: 'We will concentrate on getting people back to work.' Against that background it was hardly surprising that Fianna Fáil should unveil the 'Economic Emergency' document seven months later.

The proposal to abolish rates on private dwellings was already established Fianna Fáil policy before its inclusion in the 1977 manifesto. In his presidential address to the party at the previous year's ard-fheis, and in the context of the coalition's abolition of house-buyers' grants, Lynch reiterated the line: 'I wish to repeat at this point our firm commitment to remove rates from homes as further evidence of our support for home ownership.'[138]

There were deep-rooted concerns relating to the rates issue at the policy formation level in Fianna Fáil. Responding to the 1972 white paper on Local Finance and Taxation, Neville Keery made a number of salient observations. He argued:

It is claimed that the White Paper will reform the rating system so as to
eliminate its undoubted defects. Its two main defects—namely, the fact
that it hits people regardless of their ability to pay and that the rates must
carry the health charges burden—both remain untouched by the White
Paper proposals.[139]

What was worse, in Keery's view, was the fact that 'the White Paper does not
deal adequately with alternatives to the rating system.' The main changes he
surmised were 'purely administrative'. And while he welcomed some proposals
for charges for local services—such as a user-pays basis—he felt that those
proposed in the white paper

> (with the exception of the planning fees proposal) are disturbing, as they
> appear to hit services which are either essential or of most benefit to the
> less-well-off.

Against such a background, Fianna Fáil research services advanced a radical
position on the rates issue. It argued in 1972 that

> rates as a tax are not related to people's current capacity to pay. Thus a
> family owning a rapidly appreciating house find their *wealth* increasing
> but their current income may be rising, constant or even falling. During
> periods of rapid inflation rates can rise rapidly—in the 4 years 1968/69 to
> 1972/73 they rose by over 80%. Some anomalies in rates can be removed by
> a general revaluation—at present older properties are on average under-
> valued in relation to new—this would ensure similar treatment of similar
> property. The differential treatment of business firms—who can deduct
> rates as an expense against other taxes—while individuals cannot, is
> another serious anomaly. The FF proposal is to remove rates from
> dwellings. This would cost about £35 millions in 1972/73 rates bills—about
> 50% of the total. This would make house ownership cheaper. If some of
> the cost is to be recovered from owners one step, which would also
> simplify the tax structure—would be to disallow mortgage interest as a
> deduction for income tax. Local authorities could also charge more realistic
> amounts for services—e.g., library fees, planning permissions, sanitary
> services. These or other changes in the nature and structure of local
> financing should be related to changes in the number, nature and func-
> tions of local authorities—i.e., should take account of any reforms.[140]

From this rudimentary position Fianna Fáil would refine and polish its
stance on the rates issue, weaving it into an overall financial proposal. The

result was an election-winner. It put money in people's pockets. Fianna Fáil promised a radical decline in unemployment, and it appealed to an electorate battered by four years of coalition Government at a time of international crisis.

Liam Cosgrave called a general election on 25 May 1977. Polling day was 16 June, nine months earlier than was legally necessary. Fine Gael and the Labour Party took the decision in confident mood. Many respected political commentators, including Michael Mills and Dick Walsh, continued to believe right up to the end that the coalition would win. 'Coalition set to take election,' read the headline in the *Irish Times* on election day, over a report by Dick Walsh, the paper's highly experienced political correspondent. Michael Mills, his counterpart in the *Irish Press*, was slightly more qualified in his prediction, but he did tip the coalition to win.

Fianna Fáil got away to a flying start. It published its election manifesto on 26 May, the day after the election was called. During the campaign Lynch said:

The first public presentation of [the manifesto] . . . was not just the opening of a carefully prepared election campaign. It was the culmination of four years of research and political reappraisal, sure in its purpose and unassailable in its costing and coherence. Received as such by you, the Press, it has stood up equally well to the critical scrutiny of economic commentators and the business community . . . We know . . . [the manifesto] is an election winner.[141]

Lynch was correct: the manifesto was an election-winner. It was the product of four years of thought, although promises such as the removal of car tax on vehicles of less than 1,600 horsepower appeared to have been thrown in towards the end, adding sugar to an already sweet cake. Lynch, still the party's major electoral asset, was the cornerstone of the campaign. The manifesto also played a major part. It put money in the pocket of every member of the electorate. Lynch helped deliver that message and give credibility to the extravagant promises of Fianna Fáil. He expended great energy, touring different parts of the country to get out the vote. His style was presidential and he left no sector uncanvassed. He was accused of visiting almost every convent in the country on the campaign trail.

The combination of Lynch's leadership, the manifesto and a strong, well-organised electoral campaign turned trends around and confounded the opinion polls. No matter how numerous nuns were in the country, they could not account for such a decisive swing to Lynch and his party. The coalition was badly damaged by the resignation of President Ó Dálaigh, and the efforts at a gerrymander backfired badly. In one of the less-noticed clauses of the

Fianna Fáil manifesto there was a pledge that Neville Keery had inserted to ensure that future constituency reorganisation would be undertaken by an all-party committee of the Oireachtas.[142]

Fine Gael fell from 53 to 43 seats and the Labour Party from 20 to 17. The National Coalition had run a complacent campaign. Back came Fianna Fáil with an unassailable 84 TDs—a twenty-seat majority. Whatever Lynch did, it worked; he himself polled 20,079 in Cork City. (In 1973 he had received 12,427 votes in the Cork City North-West constituency.)

Due recognition for his part in the victory had to be given to Charles Haughey. He played a prominent role in delivering votes for Fianna Fáil, being one of the major architects of the party's campaign strategy. His own personal vote remained very high, despite the redrawing of the constituency boundaries for Dublin (Artane). He headed the poll with 11,041 votes and helped bring in another Fianna Fáil candidate. His party arch-rival, George Colley, got a highly creditable 8,768 votes in the neighbouring Dublin (Clontarf) constituency.

FIANNA FAIL RETURNS TO POWER

Back in power with an unassailable majority, Lynch rewarded three members of the party's election committee: he appointed Séamus Brennan, Michael Yeats and Noel Mulcahy to the Seanad. He also nominated two friends and unofficial advisers over the years: Dr T. K. Whitaker and Gordon Lambert, the latter a prominent industrialist and a patron of the arts. Other supporters appointed to the Seanad were a former Lord Mayor of Cork, R. Valentine Jago, and Bernard McGlinchey from Co. Donegal. Lynch fulfilled his pledge to appoint women to the Seanad, choosing Lady Valerie Goulding, director of the Central Remedial Clinic, Dublin, and Eileen Cassidy, a widow and mother of five children. Mary Harney, a young TCD graduate in her early twenties, was also put into the Seanad. She had failed to get elected but had polled 1,588 votes in the Dublin South-East constituency. Prof. Brian Hillery, a first cousin of the President and a personal friend of Jack and Máirín Lynch, was another appointment.

The new Government held only a few surprises. George Colley was named Tánaiste and Minister for Finance. Desmond O'Malley was made Minister for Industry, Commerce and Energy. Pádraig Faulkner was given Tourism and Transport and also Posts and Telegraphs. Brian Lenihan, who had regained his seat, was appointed to Fisheries. Gerard Collins was given Justice. John Wilson was made Minister for Education. Robert Molloy was given Defence. Denis Gallagher took over the Gaeltacht portfolio, and Sylvester Barrett got Environment. Gene Fitzgerald was appointed to Labour. Anthony Hederman was made Attorney-General. Lynch put Michael O'Kennedy in Foreign Affairs. But for the vagaries of PR his decision might have favoured Ruairí Brugha, who had lost his seat through internal constituency rivalry.

Jim Gibbons returned to the Government as Minister for Agriculture. Charles Haughey was made Minister for Health and Social Welfare. A new Department of Economic Planning and Development was given to Dr Martin O'Donoghue; the removal of certain areas of competence from the Department of Finance was controversial in the extreme. In general, the choice showed yet again that Lynch was insufficiently ruthless in defence of his own personal position within the party. He needed to deepen the roots of personal allegiance among the younger generations of TDs. He did not do so, and within two years his wing of the party paid a very high price.

The election defeat brought about inevitable changes in the leadership of Fine Gael and the Labour Party. Dr Garret FitzGerald replaced Liam Cosgrave, and Frank Cluskey took over from Brendan Corish. Both men, very different in style from their immediate predecessors, led a strong and constructive opposition in the Dáil.

Despite the weak economic situation in the country, with 106,000 people unemployed in 1977, the new Government began its term in a spirit of optimism. There was a determination to improve national finances, reduce the high unemployment figure and direct the country towards the creation of full employment. Economic expansionism was the philosophy in vogue; the hair-shirt days of the National Coalition were at an end. Lynch, advised by O'Donoghue, gambled on growth. On 12 January 1978 a white paper, *National Development, 1977–1980*, was published. Another white paper, *Programme for National Development, 1979–1981*, was issued on 6 January 1979. It was a courageous but, some might say, foolhardy venture. The strategy, according to its main creator, was based on the German 'social market economy': 'use as much competition as possible and as much planning as necessary.' And it did change things.[143]

The package of tax cuts and reforms was introduced in the 1978 budget, with the abolition of rates on housing, abolition of the wealth tax, and a reform of social welfare to be based on pay-related contributions. The first steps were taken to equalise 'the income treatment of married couples by making the tax-free allowance double that of a single person.' Action was take to increase employment by voting additional funds for construction and for youth employment schemes. New schemes for industrial development were established.

A national wage agreement had been agreed in 1978, granting increases of up to 8 per cent. A 'national understanding' was negotiated by the spring of 1979, based on the idea of a social contract. Martin O'Donoghue points to the fact that the number of people at work in April 1980 had risen by eighty thousand over the April 1977 level. 'Inflation did fall from the 18 per cent of 1976 and 15 per cent of the first half of 1977 to 7.5 per cent in 1978,' he wrote.

Government spending also fell.[144] That is one committed view of the impact of the 1977 manifesto on Irish society. The opposition argued that the Lynch Government had undermined recovery and accentuated the downward spiral of the economy, which went into free fall by the early 1980s after two-and-a-half years of Fianna Fáil being back in power.

Moving away from the two diametrically opposed views, what, it might be asked, would have been the impact of the Lynch Government's reforms in general if it did not have to redeem costly election promises, such as the abolition of rates, car tax and other non-productive give-aways? Part of the answer may be that the 1977 election was a breakthrough in what later came to be known as auction politics. This helped to fuel a growing sectionalism in society and an unfounded fear in Irish politics that it was necessary to 'buy off' sections of the electorate in order to be returned to power. That perception has eclipsed a careful analysis of the years between 1977 and 1979 and of the longer-term strategies implemented by that Government.

However, international economic trends and continued labour unrest were a serious obstacle to the plans of the new Government. The oil crisis of 1979 was a crippling blow to a small economy completely dependent for its competitiveness on the erroneous doctrine of low fuel prices. After the emotional high of the election victory in 1977, Lynch at sixty faced demanding challenges. Not least was the growing dissent within the party in 1978 and a restiveness to find a new and more 'modern' leader.

Improving the national economy was the principal objective of the new Government. No matter how demanding the domestic political situation, Lynch was obliged to keep Northern Ireland high on his personal policy agenda. He was at a distinct disadvantage. He had lost Ruairí Brugha, his main adviser on Northern Ireland, from the front bench. In October 1975 his party had adopted in opposition a policy line that demanded that Britain make a 'commitment to implement an ordered withdrawal' from Northern Ireland. In office, such a demand was an embarrassment. Soon after the election the British ambassador, Robin Haydon, met Lynch and reported that the new Taoiseach was 'out of touch with trends and personalities in Northern Ireland' and that this 'could be advantageous in that we should be able to feed our own thoughts and ideas into the new government.' London was reassured that Lynch was unlikely to renege on security commitments, such as 'photo reconnaissance overflights' along the border. The British Labour Government, however, held firmly to the view that there should be no admission of a willingness to work with the Irish Government to find a political settlement.[145]

Ironically, despite the false perceptions of the British Government, the Irish Government, on 25 July, had considered and approved the recommendations in a memorandum entitled 'Overflights by foreign military aircraft,' brought to the Government by Michael O'Kennedy. It reviewed in detail the existing provisions that the Cosgrave Government had agreed in June 1976 after the murder of the British ambassador, Christopher Ewart-Biggs. O'Kennedy recommended that 'the present arrangements in respect of overflights be continued and, in particular, that no alterations be made in the conditions under which existing permissions to overfly were granted.' The Government agreed.[146] In the autumn of 1979 that issue would be used by his critics inside the party to discredit Lynch. Haughey was among those who would have received a copy of the memorandum in his papers for the Government meeting of 25 July 1977. Government colleagues, who knew otherwise, were deafeningly silent when Lynch ultimately faced a backbencher revolt in 1979.

James Callaghan had taken over as British Prime Minister in April 1976. His Government had been defeated in the House of Commons in February 1977. The opposition tabled a vote of no confidence on 18 March, and Callaghan's Government faced defeat on the 23rd. The Labour Party survived by making a deal with the Liberal Party and the Ulster Unionists. The manoeuvre is best known for the emergence of the Liberal-Labour pact. But Northern Unionists, led by James Molyneaux and Enoch Powell, won an unconditional offer from Callaghan to refer demands for equal representation for constituencies in Northern Ireland in the House of Commons to an all-party committee chaired by the Speaker.[147] They had an unlikely supporter in Michael Foot, who, within the Cabinet, had urged an increase 'because the average number of electors for each seat was much higher than in Britain.'[148] That quotation, from the memoirs of James Callaghan, reveals the consistent subconscious position of British leaders of both major parties. There was 'Britain' and there was 'Northern Ireland.' In fairness, however, it must be said that Callaghan did not concede two other demands: the return of local government and of devolved government. Three unionists, including Powell, abstained on 23 March. Molyneaux and his other Unionist colleagues voted against the Government.[149] In the end, Northern representation was raised from 12 to 17, and this became operational in the 1983 general election. But in the years left to Callaghan in power, his Government was constantly under threat from Unionist MPs. That was not an environment in which it was easy to contemplate a breakthrough on Northern Ireland.

Notwithstanding the position of the British Government, Lynch and Callaghan maintained personal contact. They met regularly at European Council meetings. In September 1977 they met at Callaghan's invitation in London for talks. Dermot Nally, secretary of the Department of the Taoiseach, was among those who accompanied Lynch to the meeting. He was very experienced, and Lynch was fortunate to have such an able civil servant at his disposal. Bernard Donoughue, adviser to Harold Wilson, wrote in his memoirs for 5 March 1976 of a visit by the Taoiseach, Liam Cosgrave, to Chequers: 'Lunch with the Irish, which was very friendly. I sat next to Dermot Nally, from the Taoiseach's office. It is clear that their operation is very simple and primitive. But Nally is very good.'[150] I am sure Mr Nally would have been very reassured by the entry. More importantly, Lynch held the same opinion of him.

Regarding Lynch, Callaghan records in his memoirs that,

> although our discussions were cordial, I was not satisfied that he was taking sufficiently seriously the vital need for close border cooperation if the IRA threat was to be contained, and I employed the argument that this threat was potentially as grave for the Republic as for the North.

Several weeks later, Callaghan recorded, the Irish Government

> took steps to stiffen the penalties for conviction on charges of armed robbery, of which there had been a spate, and whose proceeds we suspected went to swell the coffers of the IRA, but even so more police cooperation was needed.[151]

Whether the Labour Party or Conservative Party was in power, the perennial London complaint against successive Irish Governments was a lack of resolve in dealing with the IRA and a tardiness in co-operating with the police and British army in the North.

At the end of the meeting the British and Irish Governments stood very far apart on Northern Ireland. The final text of the press communiqué excluded Lynch's suggestion of including a reference to nationalist aspirations. The Taoiseach also wanted to include the Sunningdale promise that if in the future a majority of those in Northern Ireland demonstrated a wish for unity, the British Government would support that wish. Callaghan accepted that that was still British policy but declined to include it, on grounds of expediency.

The vulnerability of the minority Labour Government ruled out any bold initiative on Northern Ireland for the duration. Callaghan admits as much in his memoirs.

> I gave both Secretaries of State encouragement to put forward ideas and proposals, and they produced a stream of assessments, analyses, minutes, progress reports, meetings which, interspersed with my spasmodic and fleeting visits to the Province, gave me a snapshot picture of the community's difficulties and of the wretched conditions under which police and Army were working.

But 'we never seemed in sight of an agreement (much less a settlement),' he wrote. 'At no time did I feel we were doing more than breasting the tide.'[152] In essence, the Northern Secretary, Roy Mason, was interested in defeating the paramilitary forces and in creating jobs.

The Irish Government, on the advice of the ambassador in London, Paul Keating, set out to establish a good working relationship with the leader of the Conservative Party, Margaret Thatcher, and her spokesman on Northern Ireland, Airey Neave. Lynch met both on 29 September after his meeting with Callaghan. The Irish party found Thatcher 'much more open' to the need for political initiatives than Labour ministers had shown themselves to be. When discussing Callaghan's sensitivity about continuing to use the word 'power-sharing,' she interjected to ask, Was not power-sharing 'our' initiative?[153]

But while the Labour Party was in a precarious position in Parliament, there was no possibility of a breakthrough in Northern Ireland. It took Lynch some time to restore nuance to his Northern policy, a policy that sought to prepare the Irish state for a post-partition Ireland and for the creation of a more just and tolerant society in the 26 Counties. But in that 'waiting for Godot' world between 1977 and 1979, Lynch sought to find a new lever for change in Washington.

During the National Coalition's time in office the Minister for Foreign Affairs, Garret FitzGerald, had placed great emphasis on gaining the active support of leading Irish-Americans to underpin a peace process in Northern Ireland. Supported by John Hume of the SDLP, the 'Four Horsemen'—the governor of New York, Hugh Carey, Senator Daniel Patrick Moynihan, Senator Edward Kennedy, and the speaker of the House of Representatives, T. P. 'Tip' O'Neill—emerged as a strong united voice for American engagement in Northern Ireland. The Irish ambassador in Washington, Seán Donlon, together with his associate Michael Lillis, helped co-ordinate the process.

The four issued a joint statement for St Patrick's Day, 1977, appealing for an end to the campaign of violence and further appealing to all Irish-Americans to embrace the goal of peace and renounce any action that promoted violence or provided support or encouragement to organisations engaged in violence. That statement received wide coverage and support. There was a parallel development. Through the State Department, President Jimmy Carter had requested the preparation of a draft statement pledging $100 million in aid if a political solution were reached in Northern Ireland. The document was shown to both the Irish and the British Governments. The latter was not very supportive of the proposition. The change of Government in Ireland provided the State Department with an opportunity to recommend the 'parking' of the initiative; but O'Neill pressed on. As the British wanted to gain landing rights for Concorde in Washington and New York, both O'Neill and Carey were in a strong position to link landing permission to the release of the Carter statement.

On 30 August 1977 the presidential statement was published. Although it made no mention of pledging a specific sum of money, it did commit the US government to securing private investment and 'to see how additional job-creating investment could be encouraged.'[154] The statement also recognised that the Irish Government had a role to play in any settlement; Carter pledged his administration's support for a system of government achieved by peaceful means that would be acceptable to both sections of the community in the North. That was a policy victory for the staff of the Irish embassy in Washington.

On 8 January 1978 Lynch called for a British declaration of its intention to withdraw from Northern Ireland. He hinted that he might offer an amnesty to IRA prisoners in the South. The Archbishop of Armagh, Tomás Ó Fiaich, agreed in public with the Taoiseach that the British should withdraw. The British Labour Government, headed by James Callaghan, remained unmoved. On 18 January 1978 the European Court of Human Rights in Strasbourg found, after six years, that the British were guilty of 'inhuman and degrading treatment.' The Irish Government had brought the case, and the European Commission of Human Rights had made a ruling in 1976. The court rejected the commission's original ruling. The Four Horsemen continued to criticise British policy in Northern Ireland throughout early 1978.

On St Patrick's Day fourteen prominent American politicians—including the Four Horsemen—issued a joint statement sharply criticising British policy in the wake of the European court pronouncements on 'inhuman and degrading treatment'. The Taoiseach visited the White House for St Patrick's Day. He then went to New York, where on 25 May he addressed the United Nations conference on disarmament. On both visits he urged Carter and the White House to continue an active policy interest in Northern Ireland. Meanwhile both O'Neill and Kennedy issued statements in early 1978 criticising the Callaghan Government for its failure to take the initiative in Northern Ireland.

In the summer of 1978 Amnesty International sent an inquiry team to Northern Ireland. It found evidence of seventy-eight cases in which suspects suffered serious physical injury while in the custody of the RUC in its use of 'in-depth' interrogation techniques on fourteen internees at Holywood, Co. Down, in 1971. The case had been taken by the Irish Government.[155] Moynihan visited London in December 1978 to assess the situation and came away with the view that 'there was no political will to settle.' The Northern Secretary, Roy Mason, was determined to allow British troops to remain there.[156] Labour Party policy lacked imagination and the determination to press on towards finding a *modus vivendi*.

The year 1979 began badly for the Lynch Government. The price of milk and butter rose as the Government began to phase out consumer subsidies. On 8 January an explosion on Whiddy Island in Bantry Bay, Co. Cork, destroyed the French oil tanker *Betelgeuse* and killed fifty men. A national bus strike was declared on 5 January, and the country remained without transport until the 19th. The first national postal strike began on 19 February and ended on 25 June. On 27 February thousands of farmers protested in Port Laoise against a levy of 2 per cent on farm produce, forcing the Government to back down and to discontinue the levy at the end of the year.

On 2 March 1979 Lynch experienced a great and unexpected personal loss. On his way into Cork he stopped his car on the Brian Bórú Bridge to buy an *Evening Echo*. The newspaper boy told him of the death of Christy Ring. 'Oh, no, it can't be true,' he said. Christy Ring, considered by many the greatest hurler of all time, had collapsed near the School of Commerce at about 3:30 p.m. and was taken to the South Infirmary, where he was pronounced dead on admission. He was fifty-nine. The two men had been close as players on Cork and Munster sides from the late 1930s and throughout the 1940s and remained friends in retirement. In the late 1950s Lynch had intervened to try to make Christy Ring's job (as a driver with Irish Shell) more secure. He even encouraged him to stand for Fianna Fáil, but the offer had been declined.

During his sporting career, which lasted from 1937 until 1963, Ring had won more honours than any other player. These included eighteen Railway Cup medals with Munster, eight all-Ireland senior hurling medals and thirteen senior hurling championship medals with Glen Rovers.[157] In a poem by Bryan MacMahon, Ring's sporting prowess is commemorated:

How oft I've watched him from the hill move here and there in grace,
In Cork, Killarney, Thurles town or by the Shannon Race;
'Now Cork is bet; the hay is saved!' the thousands wildly sing—
They speak too soon, my sweet garsún, for here comes Christy Ring.[158]

Lynch, paying tribute to his friend that evening at a function in the Metropole Hotel, said he had first hurled with him on the Cork team in 1939. His greatest memory of Ring was of playing against Limerick in a Munster final. Cork were being well beaten, he said. 'Ringie had been quiet but he came alive and unleashed three of the greatest goals I have ever seen in a long career. He literally turned defeat into victory. He literally had that quality.'[159]

The funeral was one of the largest seen in Cork since the deaths of the lord mayors Tomás Mac Curtáin and Terence MacSwiney in 1920 and of Michael Collins in 1922; the likes were not seen in Cork again until Jack Lynch's own funeral twenty years later. A long line of people filed by the remains at Forde's funeral home. Mourners filled thirty books of condolence. Father Charlie Lynch, parish priest of Ballinlough and brother of Jack, received Christy Ring's remains at the Church of Our Lady of Lourdes. The Bishop of Cork, Cornelius Lucey, presided at the Mass. In a sermon he praised Ring's sporting achievements and also his unassuming character and his role as a father and a role model for the young. The lessons were read by the president of the GAA, Con Murphy, and the chairman of Glen Rovers, Dr Jim Young. There were thousands outside the crowded church wishing to pay their last respects, and it took the funeral more than three hours to reach Cloyne. There the Bishop of Cloyne, John Ahern, recited the prayers for the dead. Jack Lynch delivered a memorable oration.

> Before we leave this hallowed spot let us bide just a few moments longer and cast our thoughts back over the years through which so many of us had the honour to know, to play with or against Christy Ring. What more can be said of him, of his prowess, of his competitiveness, that has not been said already? . . .
>
> As long as the red jerseys of Cork, the blue of Munster and the green, black and gold of Glen Rovers, colours that Christy wore with distinction, as long as we see these colours in manly combat, the memories of Christy's genius and prowess will come tumbling back in profusion. We will relish and savour them, for we will hardly see their likes again. And men who are fathers and grandfathers now will tell their children and grandchildren with pride that they saw Christy Ring play. The story will pass from generation to generation and so it will live. Even before half of his playing days were over, his feats and his skills were legendary . . .
>
> As a hurler he had no peer. As a friend he was intensely loyal. As a man he was vibrant, intelligent and purposeful. As a husband and a father he was loving, concerned and tender. This I know.[160]

Lynch faced the emotional devastation caused by such an unexpected death. He was sixty-two and had been in national politics since 1948. But the untimely death of his friend did not convince him to retire. He was undecided before that about his immediate future; but it compelled him to reflect more actively on his options and on thinking of a life beyond politics, a choice that would be popular with his wife.

Meanwhile he returned to Dublin to face the grim reality of economic and industrial life. The year 1979 was one of radical industrial unrest, with disruptions in various industries, including transport, construction, the post office, and banks. On 20 March 1979 about 200,000 PAYE taxpayers marched in all the cities and big towns to demand tax reform. The national debt rose from £4,220 million in 1977 to £6,540 million in 1979. The Government's popularity had not been helped by George Colley's hair-shirt budget and the fact that a national postal strike was in its fifth month.

In those troubled times Lynch faced the electorate on 7 June. Local government elections and the first direct elections to the European Parliament were held on the same day. Neither set of results provided any consolation for Lynch or for Fianna Fáil. The salad days of June 1977 were now long forgotten by an electorate many of whom faced unemployment or having to raise a family at a time of high inflation and job uncertainty. Apathy was reflected in the poor turn-out: out of an electorate of 2,188,798 only 1,392,285, or 64 per cent, voted.[161] Lynch's party received only 35 per cent of the vote, and Fianna Fáil backbenchers were quick to realise that a similar performance in a general election would result in the end of many political careers. Fianna Fáil had five members of the European Parliament, Fine Gael four and the Labour Party four. There were two independents: T. J. Maher, a farmers' candidate, won a seat for Munster, and Neil Blaney took a seat for Connacht-Ulster, sending shock waves through the parliamentary party.

Lynch could take some comfort in the result of two referendums held on 5 July, on adoption and on university representation in the Seanad. Both were successfully carried; but the turn-out was less than 28 per cent. Ireland was also burdened in the summer of 1979 with taking over the rotating presidency of the European Communities for a six-month period. That placed new responsibilities on the shoulders of the Taoiseach, further deflecting his attention from party and national politics.

In contrast, the Minister for Health and Social Welfare, Charles Haughey, hit the ground running after his return to ministerial office. His portfolio gave him wide public exposure. His handling of the Health (Family Planning) Bill, passed on 17 July 1979, showed his adroitness in finding a way out of a legislative cul de sac that had confounded the National Coalition. Haughey found growing favour among the '1977 generation' of principally first-time TDs anxious to hold their seats in the next general election. He had an opportunity to play on the growing anxieties within Fianna Fáil, and he worked hard to extend his influence in the party. As ever, his public relations team was slick and professional.

Lynch should have listened to Colley. Haughey was a 'Trojan horse' within the Government, and he simply bided his time. His opponents—including Lynch—were complacent, believing that he could be contained all the better from 'inside the tent.' There was also a mistaken view that the unthinkable could not happen: that the once-disgraced minister could achieve the leadership of the party and the position of Taoiseach.

Meanwhile, Lynch busied himself with affairs of the state. The EEC, Anglo-Irish relations and Northern Ireland took up much of his time. In Washington the Irish ambassador, Seán Donlon, had worked hard to persuade the US government to move away from its traditional pragmatic stance on Northern Ireland, namely that it remained a matter exclusively for the British Government. The speaker of the US Congress, T. P. O'Neill, led a delegation of fourteen members of the Democratic and Republican Parties to Ireland in the spring of 1979. Their findings resulted in further criticism of British policy in the North, particularly a potential Labour Party deal with Unionism.

On 30 March 1979 the Conservative Party spokesman on Northern Ireland, Airey Neave, was killed in the car park of the House of Commons in London when a bomb planted by the INLA, a republican breakaway group, exploded under his car. A close ally of Margaret Thatcher, who had ousted Heath as party leader in February 1975, Neave had helped craft that victory,[162] after which he would have become Secretary of State for Northern Ireland.

It looked as if the Irish Government's efforts over the past decade had achieved little towards a peaceful settlement in Northern Ireland. In the British Parliament there were signs that the bipartisan approach to Northern Ireland was breaking down. The Prime Minister, James Callaghan, announced that representation from Northern Ireland in the House of Commons would be increased. But that did not save the Labour Government. It was defeated by 311 to 310, with Gerry Fitt—a most reliable supporter—voting against, angered by the decision to increase the representation of Northern Ireland.

Callaghan admitted in his memoirs that by January 1969, when he was Home Secretary, he had reached the conclusion that 'the cardinal aim of our policy must be to influence Northern Ireland to solve its own problems.' That was still his view as, out of office, he wrote his memoirs in 1987. 'It is still my view that there will be a settlement only when both communities in the Province desire it, work in cooperation to rid themselves of their extremists, and of their own free will produce terms that are acceptable to both, with Britain at hand to urge and nudge them forward.' Callaghan made this explicit in a speech in the House of Commons on 2 July 1981. In effect, his message was that 'Britain was incapable of ever offering a settlement that would satisfy both sides.' In his memoirs he said he envisaged the emergence of an independent state of Northern Ireland, with dual citizenship for those who wished it. He concluded that Britain would continue to meet its financial responsibilities and help the new state become a member of various multilateral organisations, such as the EEC, NATO, GATT and the International Monetary Fund. He encouraged the British Government to find a solution; 'but if no one can produce anything that is acceptable, then the time will come when Britain and Northern Ireland must begin to think the unthinkable.'[163]

In the 1990s a future Labour Secretary for Northern Ireland, Mo Mowlam, would show more determination to find a solution, as would also, in the interim, the Conservative Prime Minister, Margaret Thatcher, who swept into office in April 1979, and her successor, John Major, Prime Minister from 1990 to 1996. Thatcher visited Northern Ireland and promised that a Conservative Government would establish regional councils, in line with Unionist wishes. She showed signs of renewed toughness, and her style forecast a return to the more militarist policies of the early 1970s in the North. She appointed Humphrey Atkins as Northern Secretary. In May, Lynch held talks with Thatcher in London and expressed his support for a new political initiative.

The Four Horsemen, meanwhile, intensified their campaign to persuade the British Government to initiate a change in policy. This led to a bitter war of words between the former National Coalition minister Conor Cruise O'Brien and Senator Moynihan. The introduction of a ban on the supply of American guns to the RUC caused great controversy. Unionist opinion was outraged at what was perceived as a boost by the Carter administration for those who used violence against the RUC. Despite the smouldering resentment over the arms ban, at a meeting in London the governor of New York, Hugh Carey, pressed the Northern Secretary, Humphrey Atkins, to attend discussions with the Irish Government in New York. However, because of intransigence on the part of Thatcher, the British informed Carey on 23 August that they would not be represented at any talks.

Thatcher was steeled by a tragedy in the summer of 1979. Lord Louis Mountbatten, a cousin of the Queen of England and an uncle of the Duke of Edinburgh, was murdered by the IRA on 27 August when a bomb destroyed his light fishing-boat off Mullaghmore, Co. Sligo. His fifteen-year-old grandson and a fifteen-year-old boy who was the pilot of the boat were also killed instantaneously. Lord and Lady Brabourne, their son and the mother of Lord Brabourne were seriously injured in the blast. The same day the IRA killed eighteen soldiers in an explosion on the Newry–Warrenpoint Road. Mountbatten was an annual summer visitor to Ireland from the early 1970s and was assigned a bodyguard that numbered twenty-eight in 1974. His visits were no secret. The boat in which the party went out most days was left unguarded for long periods. That provided the cowardly IRA with an opportunity to plant the fatal bomb that killed the 79-year-old Mountbatten and other innocent victims.[164]

Jack Lynch, on holidays in Portugal, issued a statement expressing his outrage and praising Lord Mountbatten as 'a man of great courage' with a 'remarkable record of service to mankind.' He described the perpetrators as 'relentlessly and invidiously proving to be the real enemies of Ireland.' He said that 'all true Irish people utterly renounce and condemn the IRA campaign of violence and destruction,' which had brought 'shame to all Irish people at home, and abroad, who wish to see Ireland progress politically and economically and in harmonious relationship with Britain.' He pledged that no effort would be spared to bring the criminals to justice. He also sent a telegram of condolence to the British Prime Minister, Margaret Thatcher.[165]

In Lynch's absence the Tánaiste, George Colley, and the Minister for Justice, Gerard Collins, took charge of the investigation. However, Lynch's failure to return immediately to Dublin was the source of considerable criticism. 'It is a duff Government,' concluded an editorial in the *Irish Times* on 30 August, arguing that the Taoiseach 'sojourned on' after 'one of the most distinguished Europeans is done to death in our territorial area; the honour of the head of that State which is our neighbour is affected.' While acknowledging that every senior politician deserved holidays, the paper concluded that in the circumstances the Taoiseach had 'let Ireland down. His Government failed in not having him back earlier. Belatedly, the executive jet plane went out for him yesterday afternoon.'[166]

What the editorial failed to point out was that Lynch invariably spent his summer holidays in west Cork. Appearances can be cruelly deceptive. Lynch wanted to return immediately on hearing the news of Mountbatten's murder but was persuaded to delay his departure until all arrangements had been made for the ceremonial return of the bodies to London.[167] In taking the advice of senior civil servants Lynch exercised poor judgement.

The *Irish Times* editorial went on to inflict further damage on Lynch's leadership by referring to Ireland's presidency of the EEC. Lynch was praised as being the local politician *par excellence*. 'His Corkonian aphorisms, his love of Cork sport, Cork whisky, everything Cork, is an aid to vote-getting, and not only in his own area, for people like a man who respects his origins.' But the editorial claimed that the 'local-lad role' could be overplayed, as it obscured the real role of the deputy or minister, which was 'to legislate, to lead, above all to inspire.' The Irish presidency was not seen as providing leadership in the EEC. 'Must we be mealy-mouthed?' the editorial asked; and it concluded: 'Must we act as if Dublin was still subservient to Westminster? Must we trail so obviously? Must we, in MacNeice's words, slough around the world? Must the Provos make the headlines for Ireland?'[168]

Lynch was lacerated by the *Irish Times* for his failure of leadership, of which the decision to postpone his return to Dublin from Portugal was a symptom. Why, if Margaret Thatcher could fly to Belfast, could Lynch not return to Dublin?

Such criticism brought joy to those in Fianna Fáil gathering to oust Lynch. An *Irish Times* editorial on 28 August put the delicacy of the situation starkly. Mountbatten 'met his death within the territory of the Republic. The world will hold responsible for his death our people and, in particular, the Government . . . Where has it been decided that the Irish people must go down in ignominy?'[169]

The political correspondent of the *Irish Times,* Dick Walsh, wrote on 1 September of Anglo-Irish relations deteriorating in the aftermath of the murder of Mountbatten to a level reached only with the burning of the British embassy in 1972. He reported that Lynch was being 'called to London next week to answer for the Republic's culpability not only for the Mountbatten murders but for the handling of security generally.' There was a sense in Dublin that Thatcher had 'summoned' the Taoiseach; for that reason Dublin sought to convey the impression that the talks following the funeral would concentrate on the political dimension of the Northern 'troubles'. Lynch wished to emphasise that progress would not be achieved by military means alone. The Government wanted a long-term political solution in order to wrest the reins from the proponents of violence.[170]

The *Irish Times* editorial on 1 September 1979 took Lynch to task for not having been the first to request a meeting with Thatcher. She 'got in first. She wants to talk primarily about security, and the Taoiseach is once again on the defensive.' Thatcher's action was 'marked by an astuteness, sadly lacking in Dublin,' wrote the editorial writer.[171] The same day John Healy wrote a damaging column about the central place of violence in Irish history.

> We have glorified the gun, and we have glorified and honoured the men, in word, in song, and in history . . . The Fianna Fáil cabinet, which let a mob burn down the British Embassy, may regret that today, and will stoutly maintain that the IRA has no mandate from the people of Ireland, but it has an historically approved mandate; from the mythologisers and historians, and that's good enough for 'the lads,' and the 'sneaking regarders.'[172]

Máirín Lynch reacted vigorously to that taunt. On 3 September the *Irish Times* published her reply to Healy. 'What a provocative, untrue, irresponsible and dangerous statement—as well he knows,' she wrote of Healy's charge that the Government 'let a mob burn down the British embassy' in 1972. It was sad, she said, that Mr Healy's utter dislike for Jack Lynch and the Government would allow him 'to use his pen in a way that could be harmful to his government.' She argued that Ireland was living through a particularly sensitive and crucial time in its history and needed moderation and 'fair comment from our own news media.' Tragically, she felt, Irish history had shown that the economic and political progress of the country had been 'impeded many times by the uncaring, insensitive and deliberate acts and statements of her own people.' How pleased, she concluded, the extreme Unionist John Taylor must have been 'that he had found in John Healy a supporter for his gospel of incitement.'[173]

On 3 September an editorial in the *Irish Times* described Lynch as 'enduring one of the most stressful and dispiriting mental storms to have hit this island for a long time. Out-gunned, numerically, in the propaganda war, he has much ground to make up in the eyes of the British public.'¹⁷⁴ On 5 September another editorial advised that there was 'too much of "the politics of the last atrocity" about the summit.' But it was a time for 'counting friends and exploring the areas of common interest, not for scratching wounds and allowing them to fester.'¹⁷⁵

Lynch travelled to London and attended the Mountbatten funeral on 5 September. At the Anglo-Irish summit meeting that followed he was accompanied by the Tánaiste and Minister for Finance, George Colley, and the Minister for Foreign Affairs, Michael O'Kennedy. The British delegation was made up of Margaret Thatcher, the Foreign Secretary, Lord Carrington, and the Secretary of State for Northern Ireland, Humphrey Atkins. Following a working lunch, talks were held on Anglo-Irish relations, the EEC and international developments.

The report in the *Irish Times* concluded that if the summit produced 'neither dramatic results nor evidence of a meeting of minds, it was generally considered that much had been done to help still the passions which Earl Mountbatten's murder had raised, fed, Mr Lynch pointed out, not by the British Government, but by its popular press.' Lynch had emphasised forcibly that 'one cannot exclude a political initiative from the solution of other problems, that getting at the cause of the problems was more important than dealing with their effects, horrifying though they may be.'¹⁷⁶

Behind the rhetoric Lynch had entered the talks shamed by the failure of Irish security to protect Mountbatten. Thatcher and her officials were primarily concerned with matters of immediate security interest. It was important to review all levels of security co-operation between Dublin and London, and Lynch was asked to make practical concessions for improving security. While the details of such agreements remained secret, the meeting led to a heightened level of co-operation between security agencies. Thatcher had been very forceful. The details of the overflight agreement with the British, dating from the time of the National Coalition and renewed by the Fianna Fáil Government in the summer of 1977, was reviewed and modified. Although it did not make sense to give the public details of enhanced cross-border security arrangements, in retrospect it can be seen that Lynch made a mistake in not making a clear statement of principle relating to the overflight arrangements. Leaks were inevitable, and disquiet grew within the parliamentary party.

There was concern in Fianna Fáil about Lynch at a number of levels. The party's poor showing in the elections to the European Parliament underlined its potential vulnerability. The 'generation of 77' was growing nervous and restive.

As it was known that Lynch was probably going to step down in early 1980 following the ending of the Irish presidency of the European Communities, the jockeying for position and preferment had begun in a most unseemly fashion. There were TDS hungry for office, which they believed could be obtained by a change of leadership. For many in the younger generation that did not mean the election of George Colley. Charles Haughey opened the way for preferment, and he was the boy to make extravagant promises to all and sundry. He had an ability to play on the insecurities of his fellow-TDS. He was a combination of Santa Claus and Torquemada. He could be as charming as he was sometimes menacing and aggressive. He had an effective personal publicity team, which was now acting as a leadership election committee.

Although much had happened behind the scenes, the first public challenge in a new round of heaves against Lynch came on 9 September 1979. Síle de Valera, a granddaughter of Éamon de Valera, delivered the graveside oration at the commemoration in Fermoy of Liam Lynch, the military leader of the anti-Treatyite forces, shot in action during the last weeks of the Civil War in 1923. She had not cleared the content of the speech with the party whip before circulating the text to the press. Lynch called her in. Reading the text in her presence, he told her that it was 'contrary to Government policy, wrong, unhelpful and untimely.' She left Government Buildings fully aware that her speech was not acceptable.[177]

But she did not amend her text. She referred to devolution and a Council of Ireland as half-measures that could only serve to exacerbate and fester the problem. Only a naïve politician would attempt to look for a political framework acceptable to the North in isolation.[178] She made links between the IRA of the Civil War and those who had taken up arms in Northern Ireland in the 1970s. She encouraged Lynch to provide republican leadership and to refuse to co-operate against those who were striving to end partition: 'They [the British Government] have the effrontery to ask our permission for their army to operate a mile or so over the border.' She opposed any form of integrated cross-border approach to the combating of subversion.[179]

Lynch, unable to stop de Valera giving the speech, prepared his own text, which was published on the same day as the report of the commemoration. He reproduced a number of paragraphs from the de Valera text, stating that her words were open to misinterpretation. He stated that the atrocities of the Provisional IRA would have been as abhorrent to Pearse, de Valera and Lemass as they were now 'to all of us.' He stressed that it was Government policy to support the setting up of a form of devolved government. He said he regretted the tone and tenor of her remarks.[180]

De Valera issued a terse statement. With matters unresolved, she left for the United States. She told the American correspondent of the *Irish Times* in New

York that the cause of violence in Ireland was the existence of the border. There would be no true peace till partition was abolished, she said. She felt that her speech in Fermoy expressed the views not only of the rank and file of Fianna Fáil but of Irish people generally.[181] Her comments widened the gulf between herself and the Taoiseach and caused more embarrassment to the Government.[182]

The letter columns of the national papers reflected the intensity of the debate. De Valera went to the meeting of the parliamentary party on 28 September ready to press strongly her challenge to Lynch on Northern policy and republicanism. Lynch planned to meet the challenge head on, in keeping with his stance since the deputy spoke at Fermoy. There was a full attendance of more than a hundred TDs and senators at the meeting. In her unrepentant reply, de Valera told TDs that the Taoiseach had not been so strong in his objections on the Friday they had met in his office, before the weekend on which the speech was delivered. Lynch explained how co-operation with the British had resulted in the Sunningdale agreement. He also argued that lasting peace would come only through accommodation and the recognition of the richness of both traditions.[183] He reiterated the requirement that all speeches or papers on the North be submitted to the chief whip before delivery or publication.

A motion supporting party policy as expressed by the Taoiseach was unanimously adopted. According to Dick Walsh's report, de Valera withdrew any criticism of party policy on Northern Ireland or of the leadership, expressed or implied. She emerged from the meeting with a different view. 'There is no question of my backing down, no question of that at all. I am happy with the outcome of the meeting. I am indeed.' Her support was for Fianna Fáil policy as articulated in 1975, which included a demand for a British declaration of intention to withdraw from the North.[184] Lynch had a very different conception. On 18 October he was reported as urging his party towards acceptance of an internal settlement in the North, without first seeking a British declaration. It was obvious that he had always been uncomfortable with the 1975 formulation. He did not say so; but he did emphasise that it was party policy to seek devolution and power-sharing but not, before that, a commitment by Britain to withdraw from the North.[185]

While disagreement with the party's Northern policy was one reason for changing the leader, there were other factors that propelled the dynamic for change. Powerful economic forces were at work to secure the position of Taoiseach for Haughey. He was already in debt and beholden to his financial backers. He had a life-style that required large infusions of capital to remain afloat. The mystery of the financing of that life-style has been partially answered by the facts uncovered by different tribunals in the latter part of the twentieth century and the early years of the twenty-first. Haughey was a strong supporter of the principle of 'Government Light,' a man who would roll back the frontiers of the state and deflect Fianna Fáil in power away from neo-corporatism and the welfare-state model. The neo-liberal model of development was the preferred philosophy. In power, he would continue to need infusions of money, as a hopeless drunk required alcohol. Haughey would not be asked for favours in any crude sense. Fingerprints would not be left on decisions; there would be no paper trail leading to the taking of decisions favourable to his backers. Instead he would keep government off the backs of his backers. That was not too much to expect in return for un-declared, clandestine, tax-free financial support!

Reviewing his situation in the autumn of 1979, Haughey had one major tactical advantage: his victory in a leadership race was unthinkable to his opponents. The Haughey camp believed they had a strong chance of capturing the leadership. His backers were on the campaign trail; in contrast, the Lynch-Colley camp was naïve. They could not conceive of a campaign in which there would be no rules, no boundaries, no depths to which their opponents would not sink to secure victory for their candidate. In the autumn of 1979 Irish politics entered a dark and murky phase. A less idealistic leader would have concentrated his energies on rallying the loyalty of his backbenchers. Instead Lynch was attending to affairs of state. Ireland held the presidency of the European Communities for the final six months of 1979. That placed a significant burden upon the Taoiseach, many of his ministers and senior civil servants.[186]

Lynch was also heavily involved in the preparations for the first papal visit to Ireland. Pope John Paul II was due to arrive in Dublin on 29 September 1979 and to remain until 1 October. It was a state visit with a difference. Besides the formal dinners and receptions, the Pope had a punishing schedule, taking him to different parts of the country. In the wake of the Mountbatten murder there was considerable disquiet about the Pope's safety, particularly if he were to cross the border and take part in an open-air ecumenical celebration of reconcili-ation in Armagh. Very late in the planning of the trip the Vatican reluctantly took the decision not to include the event in Northern Ireland in the schedule.[187]

Pope John Paul II was received with great ceremony by Irish people, who flocked in tens of thousands to the different venues around the country to hear his homilies. Jack Lynch was heavily committed to host and to attend many events during the visit. The Pope said Mass in the Phoenix Park before more than a million people and at Drogheda delivered a strong appeal to the IRA on bended knee to lay down their arms and take the path of peace. On 30 September he went to Clonmacnoise, to Galway and to Knock. On 1 October he travelled to St Patrick's College, Maynooth, and to Limerick before leaving for a tour of the United States.

No sooner was the Pope safely on his way to Boston than Lynch confronted one of the most bizarre episodes in a long career in public life. Rumours
had been circulating during the papal visit about the state of President Patrick
Hillery's marriage, and more besides. On one evening, when many journalists
expected Dr Hillery to resign, an RTE studio was on stand-by to do a special
programme covering the constitutional crisis. Was this a 'black operation' by
elements within Fianna Fáil? I believe it was.

When reports of the rumours reached him, Hillery phoned the Taoiseach to
seek his advice about whether he should go public and issue a denial. He was
discouraged from the idea of holding a press conference; instead he invited
the editors of the three national daily papers and RTE to Áras an Uachtaráin.
They suggested that their political correspondents should go in their stead;
these were accordingly called to the Áras to take part in a press briefing that
offered a denial to a rumour whose existence most people in the country had
not even been aware of.[188] There were those who remained convinced that the
attack on the President was of a piece with the efforts to get rid of Lynch.
Frank Dunlop, the Government press officer, wrote about that period: 'It was
obvious that a destabilization campaign of a very personal nature, which both
of us had discussed and dismissed previously, was under way.'[189]

In the context of rising tension within the party and rumours about co-
operation with British forces, Lynch confronted the challenge of two by-
elections in Co. Cork—one in his own constituency of Cork City and a
second in Cork North-East. According to one source, the selection process did
not go entirely as Lynch would have wished. Máirín Quill, a young teacher
from Co. Kerry living and working in Cork, was Jack Lynch's preferred choice.
She had stood in the 1977 election and polled strongly. Speaking twenty-five
years later, she would not say that she would have won the seat in 1979, but she
was convinced that she would have made a strong showing. A Fianna Fáil
caucus, meeting in the Winning Post pub on Western Road, opted for an
alternative to the Lynch candidate.

Jack Lynch was present at the convention in the Metropole Hotel on 10
October 1979, and he addressed the meeting. Quill was defeated, by 39 votes
to 16, and John Dennehy, a welder in Irish steel, was selected instead. The
Minister for Labour, Gene Fitzgerald, was director of elections. Pearse Wyse
and Seán French, who were elected in 1977, were to direct the canvassing.

In Cork North-East, Fianna Fáil picked John Brosnan, a solicitor, whose
father's death had caused the vacancy. Fine Gael chose the experienced Liam
Bourke for the city and a 22-year-old primary teacher, Myra Barry, in Cork
North-East. The Labour Party ran Toddy O'Sullivan in the city.

On the face of it, Cork City was one of the safest Fianna Fáil seats in the
country. The bookies were opting for a Fianna Fáil double, with the odds in

Cork City running at 1:6 on Dennehy. Fine Gael was 3:1 and the Labour Party 10:1. In the general election in 1977 Fianna Fáil in Cork polled 30,162 first-preference votes, or 59 per cent, to Fine Gael's 12,655 first preferences, or 25 per cent. The Labour Party received 5,254 first preferences, or 10 per cent. It was noted at the time that in the local elections in June 1979 the Fianna Fáil voted had dropped to 40 per cent in Cork and the Fine Gael vote was up to 36 per cent, with the Labour Party getting 15 per cent.

Every effort was being made by Fianna Fáil to get the loyal Jack Lynch vote out.[190] The question was whether it would be possible for Fianna Fáil to rekindle the spirit of 1977. Lynch left nothing to chance. He campaigned vigorously, travelling to Cork on four consecutive weekends to lend his support to the party effort. His message extolled the Government's record of successful job creation, improving living standards, helping to radically slow down emigration and achieving a high economic growth rate.

As a party, Fianna Fáil appeared apathetic and sluggish. Head office sent down a number of prominent campaigners. Ray Burke, a strong Haughey supporter, arrived in the city constituency and was assigned to canvassing with Máirín Quill. After knocking on a number of doors he quickly concluded that they were wasting their time. The candidate had no name recognition. He simply gave up and returned to Dublin.[191]

As the campaign was progressing, Lynch confronted growing unrest within the parliamentary party. On 24 October he arrived late for a meeting at which Tom McEllistrim, a close friend of Neil Blaney, had put down a question. Had the Taoiseach given permission to the British to overfly the border? If the answer was yes, he moved that the permission be rescinded. The chief whip, Dr Michael Woods, failed in an attempt to have McEllistrim withdraw the motion. Lynch is quoted as having replied: 'As of now, the British have not permission to overfly the border.' He also assured the meeting that 'the British army will not be allowed across the border.'[192] He left the meeting without convincing TDs that that was the full story. This issue soon returned to haunt him.

Lynch did a party political broadcast on RTE television before returning to Co. Cork to participate in the final rallies, speaking in Cork, Cóbh and Midleton. The political correspondent of the *Irish Press,* Michael Mills, watched his final election rally in the city. A strong admirer of Lynch, he was surprised by what he saw. 'Gone was the old enthusiasm of the crowds; in its place was a dull apathy which, I suggested to some of my colleagues, did not bode well for Fianna Fáil's prospects in the by-elections.'[193] On 7 November 1979 an editorial in the *Irish Times* stated: 'By-elections do matter and would matter even if the Government had a hundred seats.' But it did acknowledge that by-elections were not a particularly good test of anything. It was rather 'something of an essay on the personal TAM [television audience measure-ment] ratings of Jack Lynch, a gauge of the applause meter for Cork's own Taoiseach.'[194]

Because of the political unrest within the party, the outcome of the by-elections mattered greatly to Lynch. Before the results were known he left for the United States on 7 November to pay an official visit in his capacity as pres-ident of the European Communities. T. P. O'Neill, Edward Kennedy and other prominent Irish-American politicians had worked hard to ensure that the visit would be a success. The Irish party also included the Minister for Foreign Affairs, Michael O'Kennedy, together with members of the Irish press corps.

The timing of the visit was unfortunate. President Jimmy Carter was having to deal with the occupation of the US embassy in Tehran and the seizure of more than sixty American hostages. One of Lynch's first calls, on 8 November, was on President Carter in the White House. Despite being in the throes of the hostage crisis, Carter had mastered his brief on Northern Ireland, and he asked very specific questions regarding recent developments. Lynch was ill prepared for a discussion of such a technical nature and had to be rescued by his officials. The report on the meeting did little to please O'Neill.[195]

The television networks covered the Carter-Lynch press conference. Both men committed themselves to defeating terrorism in Iran and in Ireland. There was a formal dinner that evening in the White House. Unfortunately, the defeat of Fianna Fáil in both Cork by-elections was the lead story in the press on 9 November. Lynch learnt of the setback amid a round of heavy engagements at the White House, at the State Department and with T. P. O'Neill.

The Government had suffered a double defeat in the by-elections, in which Fianna Fáil lost the Cork City seat with a drop of a 'staggering 22 per cent' in its vote and a drop of 12 per cent in Cork North-East.[196] The result made no material difference to the strength of the Government: it still had eighty-three seats. But it was a personal and psychological blow to Lynch. Voters in his own constituency had come out against Fianna Fáil in a way that had not been seen since he entered national politics in 1948.

In reply to questions in Washington, Lynch said: 'We will treat it as a serious mid-term reminder to the Government to tackle the outstanding problems facing our people.'[197] He interpreted the outcome as indicating that people wanted quick solutions to problems. The electorate was much more volatile than before. They used the vote to express the fact that they wanted things done in a different way. But Lynch was clear that by-elections were not a reliable guide to what was likely to happen in a general election.[198]

Frank McDonald in the *Irish Times* speculated that the defeats were bound to raise questions about Lynch's continuing leadership of the party.[199] In

Washington, Lynch insisted that the results had not changed his leadership plans in the slightest, 'noting with some asperity that at almost every press conference since his accession to the leadership, 13 years ago, such questions had been raised.' He said: 'My position is still the same,' but added: 'Naturally one always has to look at one's past and one's future as a result of by-elections and general elections.' He said there would be a Government reshuffle early in the new year, which had nothing to do with the by-election losses.[200] The editorial in the *Irish Times* commented that the reshuffle might prove to be more of a convulsion. It added starkly:

> When Cork says to Jack Lynch: 'In the name of God, go' every Fianna Fáil TD may well shiver in his boots . . . It is clear that Jack Lynch's own personality and repute were being put forward as the major Government argument. What a mighty fall.[201]

Worse was to follow. On 9 November, Lynch gave an interview to the 'Today Show' on NBC television. He also gave interviews to *us News and World Report*, *Time* and the *New York Times* and spoke at the National Press Club in Washington. Seán Cronin, the correspondent of the *Irish Times*, asked about security arrangements between Britain and Ireland. Lynch stressed that it was important to keep secret the security arrangements that had been made. He made reference to the military aircraft overflight agreement of 1952. 'We have decided to improve this situation very, very slightly. There is no question of a free corridor.' He added: 'We have not given the British Government the right of invading our sovereign territory.'[202] 'Oh, Jesus,' Dermot Nally, secretary of the Department of the Taoiseach, is alleged to have said. Michael Mills, who was present, wrote a report that confirmed his original story published in the *Irish Press* a few weeks earlier, which had been officially denied.[203] Dick Walsh of the *Irish Times* wrote that the problem was all the more grave because Lynch had refused to confirm or deny the change in security arrangements when questioned in the Dáil by both Garret FitzGerald, leader of Fine Gael, and Frank Cluskey, leader of the Labour Party.[204]

Damage limitation was needed. Lynch put O'Kennedy in charge of regulating any overflights by British military aircraft in border areas. That policy would operate under the Air Navigation (Foreign Military Aircraft) Order (1952).[205] The fudging and equivocation further exacerbated tensions inside Fianna Fáil.

John Healy, who was a declared admirer of Charles Haughey, wrote in the *Irish Times* on 10 November: 'It is a whole new ball game, and on the latest showing it is taking all of Jack Lynch's ability to stay in the ball-park, never mind the ball game.' He noted that the party professionals had always concluded that Lynch's face on the election posters would do the trick. 'It was the great comforting certainty in the uncertain world of politics.' But that was no longer the case, despite the great effort Lynch had put into getting out the vote in the two Co. Cork constituencies, he wrote. He felt that Lynch had allowed dissatisfaction to fester over the previous months. With a new leader, he continued, Fianna Fáil could make up the lost ground. 'All it needs is today's men with today's politics, a man with vision of where Ireland should be going in the 80s and a team around him to take the country there.'[206] This was all happening while Lynch was in the United States on official business.

Lynch was being depicted as yesterday's man. In the party, the Cork defeats were the final proof needed that a change in leadership was necessary. The economy had slid downwards. Industrial unrest was widespread. The mood in the country was restive. The Taoiseach's duties under the Irish presidency of the EEC were onerous. Lynch was perceived to have grown remote from the backbenchers. The names of Pádraig Flynn (Mayo West) and Mark Killilea (Galway East) were now openly identified with criticism of the leadership.[207]

Meanwhile the Minister for Health, Charles Haughey, announced on 9 November that every national-school child in the country would receive a free toothbrush as part of National Dental Health Week. That weekend he openly laid down his challenge to Lynch. At a dinner organised by Cumann Bhean an Phiarsaigh in Dublin he stated that partition was 'totally inconceivable' to Pearse. He regarded Pearse as a democrat, believing that he had recourse to the use of arms because no other way was open to him. He also said that Pearse regarded Ireland, by its history, as being emotionally, spiritually, intellectually and politically one indissoluble nation.[208]

Lynch, in New Orleans, faced down the Haughey challenge. He added a passage to a prepared speech:

> We are not concerned now with the legitimacy of nationhood, for we are fully accepted in the brotherhood of nations throughout the world. The sacrifice of past generations has guaranteed that. But we are concerned with the moral, cultural and material well-being of the Irish people; and that can be advanced not by killing, not by death or hatred or destruction, but by life. The paradox of Pearse's message for the Irish nation today is that we must work and live for Ireland, not die, and most certainly not kill for it.[209]

According to the *Irish Times* political journalist Denis Coughlan, the Taoiseach's comments were interpreted by his listeners as 'a rebuke to the Minister and a response to his criticism, both overt and covert, from within the party.'[210]

The Lynch wing of the Government mounted a strong defence over the same weekend of 11 and 12 November. The Minister for Industry, Commerce and Energy, Desmond O'Malley, said on RTE radio that it was wrong and unfair to blame Lynch for the by-election failures. He hoped that Lynch would lead the party into the next general election and beyond.[211] The weekend dissent within the governing party did not escape the attention of the Fine Gael frontbencher John Kelly. He commented that Haughey saw in his party's recent defeat 'a new chance for his own pathological ambitions.'[212]

There were further disturbing developments. Michael Mills wrote in the *Irish Press* that Deputy Bill Loughnane, who had asked a question about British overflights when the *Irish Press* story was first published, now allegedly called Jack Lynch a liar. Lynch was furious. The group of Irish journalists travelling with him on his American trip were 'practically frozen out as he wrestled with the internal partly problems threatening to undermine his leadership.' Mills wrote that even Máirín Lynch found it difficult to give the customary good morning to the journalists as they boarded the plane.[213]

The Irish party travelled from Washington to New Orleans and Houston via Chicago. By the time they had arrived in Houston, Lynch had decided to ask the Tánaiste, George Colley, to put down a motion at the next meeting of the parliamentary party to remove the whip from Loughnane. Lynch phoned Colley while attending a rodeo at a ranch outside Houston. Mills recorded that when Lynch was about to phone Dublin he was 'clearly in a bad mood. I greeted him but he barely nodded in reply.'[214]

The by-election defeats were discussed at a meeting of the National Executive on 12 November. The following day, the eve of the meeting of the parliamentary party, Loughnane said he would withdraw nothing, 'but I didn't say that Jack Lynch told lies.' He had asked the chief whip to point out to the newspaper concerned that he had not used the word 'lie': he claimed that Lynch had 'hid the thing from us.' At the meeting of the parliamentary party, Lynch had said there was going to be no infringement of Irish sovereignty. Loughnane claimed that he had asked, 'Do you mean that the British army will not be permitted by our government to cross the border?' Lynch's reply was that they would not. 'Now there is a relaxation and the British army can fly over. It's one thing or it's another thing. You tell the truth some place and lie in the other place.' If the party wanted to take the whip from him 'there will be trouble.' Loughnane claimed he could get '14,000 to 20,000 votes in the West of Ireland, whip or no whip. We don't want fellows in khaki uniform across the Border here.'[215]

Síle de Valera had earlier revealed her opposition to Government policy on Northern Ireland. She now announced that she was going to raise the Lynch leadership and the implications of the by-election defeats at a meeting of the parliamentary party on Wednesday 14 November. At this meeting Colley confronted the intransigent Loughnane. His motion to remove the whip did not succeed, particularly after the deputy denied that he had called the Taoiseach a liar. Vivion de Valera (a son of Éamon de Valera and uncle of Síle de Valera) opposed the motion, saying that Lynch had not provided a proper answer to Loughnane's original question about cross-border overflights. Several other TDs voiced opposition to giving the British increased access to the territory of the Republic. Loughnane withdrew those statements in which he allegedly called Lynch a liar.[216]

The meeting lasted for the full day. It was bad-tempered, and it ended in humiliating defeat for the leadership.

In New York, Lynch's final press conference was dominated by his vigorous rejection of the reports that he had revealed details of Anglo-Irish security arrangements while in Washington. He had simply confirmed that the Government was co-operating with the British on the basis of the 1952 agreement, entered into by his predecessor, Éamon de Valera. He stated that his eight-day trip to the United States had been a success, both in attracting investment and in making political leaders in the United States aware of the threat posed by terrorists.[217]

The Taoiseach returned on 16 November to Shannon Airport, where he was greeted by local TDs. At Dublin Airport he was welcomed by the Tánaiste, George Colley, by ministers and by about forty TDs and senators. Haughey was not among the reception party, though his home was close to the airport. Later that day the Government Press Office quoted Haughey as saying that he had a 'previous family engagement.' Olivia O'Leary wrote in the *Irish Times* that the reason for his not being there was 'left pointedly vague.'[218] Trying to put a brave face on the situation, Michael Woods, the chief whip, said there was no 'whip' on TDs to be at the airport. Dick Walsh, noting that Lynch had proved to be resilient in 1970, 1973 and 1977, observed that on this occasion the size of the welcoming party at the airport was 'a signal of distress rather than a triumphal celebration.'[219]

Lynch faced questions in the Dáil on 20 November on the overflights controversy. He failed to satisfy the leaders of Fine Gael and the Labour Party, Garret FitzGerald and Frank Cluskey. FitzGerald had stated that the 'variation' agreed by Lynch to the 1952 agreement had been rejected by the coalition Government in 1976.

As Lynch faced the parliamentary party on 21 November, Dick Walsh reflected on the damage done by the Cork by-election defeats and the poor showing in the European Parliament and local elections. He argued that Lynch's leadership had been undermined gradually but perceptibly over the previous few months by his failing to confront head-on the challenge to his authority by Jim Gibbons's refusal to vote for the Health (Family Planning) Bill and by Síle de Valera's insistence that she held 'the key to Northern policy.' Walsh asked on the day of the parliamentary party meeting, 21 November: Has Lynch the resolve to see things through on this occasion?[220]

Lynch reported in detail on his visit to the United States. A list of dissidents around Tom McEllistrim had signed a petition requesting him to step down; but the predicted confrontation did not take place. The challenge was postponed rather than dissipated. Lynch received support from the former leader of the SDLP, Gerry Fitt.

> There have been occasions when I have abused the present Taoiseach in the Republic. I am fully in support of his attitude now when he says that we must begin by trying to unite the people of Northern Ireland before you can unite the people of Ireland.[221]

But Neil Blaney, speaking at the fifty-ninth anniversary of the Kilmichael ambush in Co. Cork, said: 'It has come to the stage where now the very dogs in the street know that the British must go. It is the only realistic initiative left to them.'[222]

The same weekend, Lynch denied that the 'Irish dimension' had been abandoned in his policy on Northern Ireland. He rejected criticism on that point coming from members of the SDLP. John Hume, the acting SDLP leader, accepted that when Lynch spoke of devolved government as a priority he did not rule out an Irish dimension.[223]

In the last week of November the country was in the grip of a cold spell, and unofficial disputes at the Dublin depot of Coal Distributors and of Calor Kosangas threatened the supply of bottled gas and fuel to the capital. Dublin Castle was turned into a virtual fortress as the army and Gardaí mounted a large security operation to protect the visiting heads of government attending the European Summit. The presence of the British Prime Minister, Margaret Thatcher, was a matter of particular concern.

The event involved the active participation and leadership of many of the Government. Lynch chaired what turned out to be a difficult summit meeting, at which Thatcher threatened the unity of the EEC. There was an inconclusive outcome.[224] Lynch received little praise within his party or from the public for his role in the event. Reflecting on the events of the previous weeks, the *Irish Times* wrote: 'Jack Lynch emerges from all this as standing head and shoulders above them all. There is no contest. It is the Sham Fight of Scarva all over again, and, like King William, Jack Lynch always wins.'[225]

With the departure of the European leaders there was a return to domestic party politics with a vengeance. It had been commonly accepted that Lynch had planned to resign following the conclusion of the Irish presidency of the EEC at the end of December. The calculation had been that there would be a leadership contest in January or early February. In fact Lynch had discussed the matter with his wife in the summer of 1979, and his decision was to quit at the end of the Irish presidency. He told President Hillery of his intention. In anticipation, Haughey had conducted a formidable campaign for the leadership for months, if not years, beforehand. He was more prepared for a snap contest than the anticipated Lynch-backed rival, George Colley. Alarmed at Haughey's popularity and growing support within the party, Lynch received a small delegation to discuss the timing of a leadership contest. He was persuaded, against his better judgement, to retire early, on the grounds that he had received assurances that Colley had the numbers to defeat Haughey. In retrospect, it can be seen that an early contest suited Haughey more than it did Colley. The latter was not prepared. Convinced that Haughey was not suitable as a party leader, some close supporters of Colley made the mistake of considering him to be unelectable. While members of the pro-Lynch wing were sleep-walking, Haughey and his followers were campaigning and counting heads.

Geraldine Kennedy reported in the *Irish Times* on 5 December, the day of the resignation announcement, that Lynch would tell his party colleagues of his decision before Christmas. A number of her sources believed that an announcement was 'imminent,' she wrote. She also reported that her sources placed Haughey ahead in a two-horse race, Colley being the other candidate. The winner needed to get 42 votes, and her sources told her that Haughey would get 38 votes and Colley 36, with 8 deputies undeclared. A three-man race, her sources maintained, would throw the contest wide open. Desmond O'Malley and Michael O'Kennedy were regarded as being the compromise candidates.

Amid the rumours and speculation, Lynch stunned many of his parliamentary party colleagues at a meeting on 5 December when he announced that he was stepping down as Taoiseach and leader of Fianna Fáil. While Lynch refused to endorse any of the potential candidates, Colley knew that he had given him 'the nod'. His daughter, Anne Colley, said: 'They were very close and there was great trust.'[226] In fact Lynch had accommodated Colley and his supporters, who thought that a short, sharp campaign would give them the advantage. The reality was otherwise. One Dublin bookie first made Colley the even favourite, with Haughey at 6:4 against. Both men were soon 5:4 against. No bets were being laid on Colley.[227]

It was to be a 48-hour campaign, voting to take place on 7 December. On the surface, Colley had the full Government behind him, or so he thought. He had strong backers in Séamus Brennan, Martin O'Donoghue,

Desmond O'Malley and Bobby Molloy. Controversially, Michael O'Kennedy changed sides. Many TDs had personally assured Colley of their support. Retrospectively, supporters of Colley stated that his high standards would not permit him to make promises to TDs and to ministers. Colley would not offer inducements or 'sweeteners' or engage in auction politics. No such reticence was to be found in the opposition camp. Haughey was promiscuous with his promises. He mounted a strong and aggressive final campaign, which continued to the very day of the vote.

TDs were placed under pressure in their hotels and lodgings in Dublin the night before the election. Canvassing continued into the morning of 7 December as TDs were cajoled, bullied and intimidated into submission. In contrast, Colley was too high-minded to make extravagant promises or to glad-hand TDs.[228] As it turned out, he was naïve to take too much on trust. Whatever the outcome, an editorial in the *Irish Times* on the day of the election stated: 'We have long ceased to expect a Moses who will lead us into the Promised Land.'[229] The political correspondent of the *Irish Press*, Michael Mills, recalls being shown a list of Colley supporters. He recognised a number of names he knew to be in the Haughey camp.

The vote took place on 7 December in a climate of fear. TDs, concerned about their future, were mistrustful of the confidentiality of the 'secret ballot'. According to Garret FitzGerald, 'some deputies claimed that they had been told that unless as they walked back [from the booths at each end of the party room] to deposit their votes in the box they showed them to members of the Haughey camp they would be assumed to have voted for Colley and would subsequently be treated accordingly.'[230] Haughey won by 44 votes to 38.

Predictably, the reaction among Colley supporters was one of shock and disbelief. Anne Colley was in her kitchen when she heard the leadership result announced on the radio. 'I could not believe it. I was shattered,' she said. She remembered going to her parents' home, where, throughout the day, many people came to sympathise with her father and mother.[231]

In the days that followed there was a danger of a split in Fianna Fáil. But Colley gave conditional loyalty to Haughey, agreeing to serve in the new Government on condition that he have a veto over the appointments to Defence and Justice. That extraordinary agreement revealed a level of lingering mistrust and suspicion between the two wings, with echoes of the events of 1969–70. However, Fianna Fáil was ever good at invisible mending.

Lynch made only one request to the new Taoiseach. He asked Haughey to nominate Dr Martin O'Donoghue for the post of EEC Commissioner due to become vacant in January 1981. 'I sincerely regret that while he was well disposed,' Lynch told the press, 'the Taoiseach said he was unable to accede to my request.'[232] The Irish nomination ultimately went to Michael O'Kennedy.

Lynch, meanwhile, took a seat on the back benches on 12 December, in time to witness the debate on the ratification of Haughey. The opposition, sensing that there might be a split in Fianna Fáil, mounted a merciless attack. The independent TD Noël Browne described Haughey as a 'dreadful cross between Richard Milhous Nixon and Dr Salazar [former dictator of Portugal].' The leader of Fine Gael, Garret FitzGerald, said that Haughey came with a 'flawed pedigree'.[233] He said that people in his own party saw him as a man of over-weening ambition, with a wish not so much to serve as to dominate and to own the state.[234] The leader of the Labour Party, Frank Cluskey, said that Haughey had played a big part in bringing about the unjust society in Ireland today. He belonged to a breed of people dominated by the principle that the end justified the means. They set out to acquire personal wealth, influence and political power and were responsible for land speculation and jerry-built houses.

Haughey's nomination received the necessary majority. He announced his new Government on 11 December. George Colley remained Tánaiste but took the portfolio of Tourism and Transport. Desmond O'Malley got Justice and Pádraig Faulkner was given Defence. Michael O'Kennedy, who had switched from the Colley to the Haughey side in the leadership contest, was given Finance. Haughey dropped four senior ministers: James Gibbons (Agriculture), Martin O'Donoghue (Economic Planning and Development), Denis Gallagher (Gaeltacht) and Bobby Molloy (Defence). There were five new ministers: Máire Geoghegan-Quinn (Gaeltacht), Michael Woods (Health and Social Welfare), Ray MacSharry (Agriculture), Albert Reynolds (Posts and Telegraphs), and Paddy Power (Fisheries and Forestry).

In the same debate on 12 December the Dáil heard many glowing tributes to Lynch. Garret FitzGerald expressed his sincere regret at his departure. Lynch had served well as deputy, minister and Taoiseach and had earned the respect of all sides. Small, ambitious men had brought him down, he said. History would give a more definite judgement of his contribution to public life. Frank Cluskey praised Lynch's integrity and said he was a man totally lacking in personal ambition or concern for personal advancement. He felt that Lynch had been Taoiseach during the most difficult time since the foundation of the state. Both men were as generous and genuine in their praise of Lynch as they were implicitly critical of his successor.

Lynch replied that this praise was better deserved by his wife, because of the way she had helped him throughout his political career. The time of his going had been of his own choosing. Stating that Haughey was taking over in difficult times, he wished him well. He felt that the new Taoiseach had the ability, the capacity and the will to overcome the problems.[235] But had he got the judgement to govern wisely? Lynch kept his silence for the rest of his life on that controversial topic.

Chapter 11

'HAPPY IS THE MAN WHO FINDS WISDOM': RETIREMENT AND FINAL YEARS, 1980–99

Having given notice of his intention to step down from public life, Jack Lynch told Dáil Éireann on 16 May 1980: 'For some time before I resigned as Taoiseach I had made up my mind on this course. I have decided to announce my decision now, for two main reasons.' He felt that he owed it to his fellow party members in Cork to advise them early of his intention to stand down, and he also believed that a younger man should represent the city in Dáil Éireann.[1] He had served as a TD for thirty-two consecutive years.

There was all-party support in Cork Corporation (City Council) for bestowing on Lynch his native city's highest honour, and on 19 December 1980 he was awarded the freedom of the city.[2] The lord mayor and Labour Party TD, Toddy O'Sullivan, praised Lynch's careers in sport and in politics, saying that in public life he had 'always shown concern for his fellow-countrymen, and despite the high offices which he has held, he has never lost the common touch, always remaining one of "our own".' He had always acted in those offices, O'Sullivan said, 'with dignified restraint, firmness and, most essential, with humour and humility.'[3] Other honours followed. In July 1981 the Prime Minister of Luxembourg, Pierre Werner, presented Lynch with the Gold Medal of European Merit in recognition of the work done to advance European integration.[4]

During Lynch's retirement the couple continued to live at 21 Garville Avenue, Rathgar, Dublin, where they had lived since the 1950s. As a former Taoiseach he had an official car with an assigned driver and 24-hour Garda protection.

Lynch remained active in the business and sporting worlds. He served as chairman of Galway Crystal, as acting chairman of Irish Distillers and as a director of the Smurfit Corporation, New Ireland Assurance and the Algemene Bank of the Netherlands. He was also a member of the board of Irish National Ballet, a project with which both he and his wife had been associated for many years.[5] Very much in demand, at annual general meetings the former Taoiseach remained popular with shareholders as he moved with ease around the meeting room, greeting people and shaking hands. His old charm continued to work on his new constituencies.[6] Given his popularity, Lynch could have taken on more directorships; but he had never belonged to the new acquisitive culture, with its emphasis on acquiring the trappings of personal wealth. He was too secure in himself to need such external validation.

Lynch remained president of his old GAA club, Glen Rovers, and was a frequent visitor to local fixtures on his visits to Cork.[7] The couple's great retreat was their holiday home at Roaringwater Bay, near Ballydehob, in west Cork. There they enjoyed the company of friends, neighbours and visitors to the area, including Dr Garret FitzGerald, Peter Sutherland, and Jim O'Keeffe and his wife, Meadhbh. Dr Tony O'Reilly, who had a house nearby, was also a good friend and a visitor. In Dublin they frequently had close friends over for drinks or dinner, among them Senator Eoin Ryan, Brendan Smith and his wife, Beryl, Dr Ken Whitaker and Dr Brian Hillery of UCD. George Colley and his wife were often invited, together with their children. The Lynches visited the Colley household and were friendly with their children, in particular Anne, who was a TD for the Progressive Democrats from 1987 to 1989. In Cork or Dublin, those invited transcended party-political divisions.

Although staying out of the public eye, Jack and Máirín Lynch were in no sense reclusive. They shared a love of the arts, of opera and of ballet and went quite often to the theatre and to concerts. Bernadette Greevy was one of the former Taoiseach's favourite singers.[8] On Sundays, Jack and Máirín Lynch usually attended ten o'clock Mass at Mount Argus in Harold's Cross, which was often celebrated by Father Herman Nolan.[9] The then parish priest, Father Ralph Egan, knew the couple well. He was struck by their informality and approachability. After Mass they used to chat freely with friends and well-wishers; afterwards Máirín would go shopping in a local supermarket.[10] On holidays abroad they visited Russia, Turkey and China. Italy was among their favourite destinations.[11] *In fine*, Lynch and his wife led a quiet life, with none of the trappings usually associated with a retired head of government.

STAYING OUT OF POLITICS

In the early years of his retirement Lynch's decision to step back from national politics was made easy by the new party leadership. Michael Mills, a critical admirer of the former Taoiseach, wrote:

Under Haughey, a Stalin-like purge began to erase Jack Lynch's name from the records. His name was not mentioned at the party Ardfheis and his picture was not published in the annual Clár. Many leading members of the party of whom more might have been expected, allowed this shameful behaviour to pass unchallenged.[12]

Osip Mandelshtam's famous lines about Stalin come to mind:

And around him a riff-raff of scraggy-necked chiefs;
He plays with the lackeydoms of half-men
Who warble, or miaow, or whimper
He alone prods and probes . . .[13]

Lynch may not have been declared a non-person, but he was just as thoroughly expunged from history as one of the 'fallen' in Russia, according to Mills. The criticism is not applicable to all who served in Haughey's first Government. George Colley, Desmond O'Malley, Mary Harney and Séamus Brennan were among those who showed courage amid the emerging culture of 'lackeydom'. While the ruthlessness of the purge in Fianna Fáil must have rankled at the personal level, Lynch allowed speculation and controversy about his actions in public life to be judged by historians. (With one exception: following the publication in *Magill* of articles on the Arms Trial, Lynch put his position on the record in Dáil Éireann.) Finbarr Lynch once asked his brother why he remained silent in the face of so much provocation. 'I couldn't be bothered,' Lynch characteristically replied.[14] But that did not mean he was indifferent to what was happening in public life. He found the antics within Fianna Fáil to be unedifying. He kept a disciplined reserve, as befits a national political leader in retirement.

Charles Haughey's first general election as leader of the party, on 11 June 1981, ended in disaster. He lost power to a short-lived coalition of Fine Gael and the Labour Party headed by Garret FitzGerald. Within nine months that Government had collapsed. A new election was held on 18 February 1982, and Haughey was returned to power with the slenderest of majorities, having to rely upon the support of a few independents and members of the Workers' Party. In the wake of that election Desmond O'Malley challenged Haughey for the leadership, but he withdrew on 25 February, the day of the party meeting. Martin O'Donoghue and Séamus Brennan were the chief forces behind the anti-Haughey move. Stephen Collins has chronicled the events leading up to the failure of that 'heave'. Heavy-handed tactics were used to deliver a majority, and the Haughey side canvassed in characteristically robust style.[15]

Pádraig Faulkner, who had been a TD for twenty-five years and Ceann Comhairle up to the election of 1982, returned to Dáil Éireann to discover that things had changed radically. 'A culture totally alien to the culture permeating the Fianna Fáil party I had known, and of which I was justly proud, now pervaded the party.'[16] George Colley and Bobby Molloy canvassed Faulkner's support for O'Malley. Faulkner had been told of an unwarranted threat from a member of the Government to his future as a TD. He was sent for by Haughey, but he refused to reveal to him how he was going to vote.

The occasion of the leadership challenge was one of the very few times in his retirement when Lynch made a public comment about the contemporary political situation. He was quoted as saying that O'Malley had been correct to allow his name to go forward, in the light of the numerous requests from members of the party following the failure to get an overall majority in the general election. Lynch said that he had always regarded O'Malley as one of the most able members of Dáil Éireann and of Fianna Fáil Governments. He was certain he would be a future leader of that party and a future Taoiseach. Lynch was further reported as saying: 'My hope now is that we will have on March 9 a government of stability that can tackle courageously the many problems, economic, social and political that face the country.'[17] His failure to mention that it would be a Fianna Fáil Government was seen as a deliberate snub to Haughey. Sources close to the party considered the comments 'unhelpful'.[18] The party's spokesman on Finance, Ray MacSharry, and on Justice, Seán Doherty, refused to accept that Lynch had not been involved in the heave. Doherty considered it strange that Lynch's former press secretary was acting for O'Malley.[19]

At the meeting of the parliamentary party, Faulkner spoke in favour of unity and asked O'Malley to withdraw, on condition that Haughey give a commitment to enter into dialogue and consult the dissidents.[20] To the surprise of many TDs, Martin O'Donoghue reversed his position as leading supporter of the dissidents and also advocated a show of unity. The O'Malley leadership attempt was a lost cause.[21] Left with little alternative, O'Malley withdrew his nomination, and Haughey was unanimously selected for nomination as Taoiseach. He won the Dáil vote, with the support of independents and members of the Workers' Party.

Despite his commitment to consult and to enter into dialogue with his critics, Haughey did not offer the olive branch to the dissidents. George Colley was offered a place in the new Government but he would not be reappointed Tánaiste. He declined to serve. The Haughey activist Ray MacSharry became Tánaiste and Minister for Finance.

The 1982 Government was noted for its 'grotesque, unbelievable, bizarre and unprecedented' goings-on, for which Conor Cruise O'Brien memorably made up the acronym GUBU, capturing the rich, murky tapestry that ultimately led to the ignominious collapse of truly the most bizarre Government in the history of the Irish state.[22] That Government fell on 4 November 1982, and on the 24th Fianna Fáil was defeated. On 14 December, Garret FitzGerald again became Taoiseach and leader of a coalition of Fine Gael and the Labour Party.

Immediately, Haughey found himself in the eye of a political storm. The new Minister for Justice, Michael Noonan, investigated a report in the *Irish Times* that his predecessor, Seán Doherty, had ordered the tapping of the phones of two journalists, Geraldine Kennedy and Bruce Arnold. Both were friendly with George Colley. On 20 January 1983 Noonan confirmed the accuracy of the newspaper reports, and he further revealed that Ray MacSharry had used Garda equipment to record clandestinely a conversation in his office with a fellow-minister, Martin O'Donoghue. The finger of suspicion pointed to Haughey. Amid renewed resignation rumours, Haughey denied any knowledge of the actions of his Minister for Justice. At the time, Doherty took the blame for everything. In 1992, however, he confirmed that in 1982 he had informed Haughey of the phone-tapping.

On Sunday 23 January a special meeting of the parliamentary party was held. At that meeting Faulkner put it on record that he could not condone the recording of a ministerial colleague's conversation without his being aware of it. A committee was set up to investigate the allegations. It did not yield fruitful results. As the Dáil resumed on 27 January, rumours of Haughey's resignation persisted. But it was not to be. Faulkner has written of the climate in the party, in which 'any open and frank debate on issues was viewed as being disloyal to the leader.' He concluded that 'it was no longer the party I had joined so enthusiastically over 40 years earlier.'[23]

A further meeting of the parliamentary party took place on 2 February 1983. The previous day the Donegal Fianna Fáil TD Clem Coughlan had been killed in a car crash. Haughey paid a tribute to the dead man; this was followed by a minute's silence. At that point the chairman, Jim Tunney, abruptly adjourned the meeting. Immediately, forty-one deputies signed a petition demanding a meeting. In the intervening days Haughey mounted a strong personal campaign to retain the leadership. His direct appeal to the grass roots caused even greater anger within the parliamentary party. Ben Briscoe, who had previously supported Haughey, handed in a motion requesting his immediate resignation.

At this point the disunity in the anti-Haughey camp over an agreed candidate worked to the advantage of the incumbent. Haughey's supporters turned the episode into an attack on the party itself at the hands of disloyal elements. Members of the Haughey camp professed their loyalty to the leader in an emotional manner. It was similar to a profession of faith.[24]

On 7 February the parliamentary party met. The bugging issue was the first item on the agenda. The report, presented by Bertie Ahern, came down on the side of Haughey and his ministers, and the leader was cleared of any knowledge of the phone-tapping. David Andrews, a member of the committee, wrote a minority report. The debate on that first item on the agenda lasted until 8 p.m. Haughey asked the meeting to remove the whip from Martin O'Donoghue and Seán Doherty. Both men resigned after the meeting.

The proceedings then turned to the vote on the leadership. In a secret ballot, Haughey won by 40 votes to 33. His leadership was again secure; but for how long?[25]

What was Lynch's reaction to the bugging scandal? The evidence is sketchy. Denis Reading and Val Dorgan, writing in the *Cork Examiner* on 27 January 1983, stated that Lynch was 'known to be deeply concerned about the events of the last week, which have left party members all over the country shocked and even ashamed to be associated with the present FF regime.' They wrote that Lynch had refused to do interviews for RTE, the BBC, and all the Irish newspapers. Quoting sources close to Lynch, they wrote that 'one of the reasons he has deliberately refrained from being involved is because of his previous experience in the O'Malley leadership challenge.'[26]

But there were indirect ways of showing dissent. Historically, the graveside oration frequently served such a purpose. Within a year, three leading members of Fianna Fáil had died: Frank Aiken on 18 May 1983, George Colley on 17 September 1983 and Seán MacEntee on 12 January 1984. All three funerals exemplified in different but subtle ways the anti-Haughey sentiments within Fianna Fáil.

Frank Aiken, who died at the age of eighty-five, had been a Dáil deputy for fifty years and a Government minister for thirty-five of those years. A close friend of Éamon de Valera, he had refused to contest a seat in the 1973 general election because of his antipathy to the rehabilitation of Haughey. Haughey was quoted in the *Irish Times* on 19 May as saying that the country had lost a distinguished public man; his integrity and selfless dedication to his political ideals, and his devotion to the Irish language, had won him the admiration and respect of all sides.[27] Jack Lynch described Aiken as a patriot in the true traditional mould and a man intensely loyal to his ideals—republican and cultural.[28] An editorial in the *Irish Times* said that 'the nation has lost, in the phrase of another generation, a very gallant gentleman.'[29]

After Mass at St Mary's Church, Sandyford, Co. Dublin, Aiken's coffin, draped in the Tricolour, was met by an army guard of honour and hundreds of mourners. The remains were taken across the border to his native Camlough, Co. Armagh, for burial in a graveyard that lay in the long shadow of Slieve Gullion. George Colley gave the graveside oration, describing Aiken's rock-like integrity and his refusal to be swayed by self-interest. 'He was one of the many men and women whose nationalist faith was grounded in true republicanism, devoted not to self-seeking but to the advancement of the interests of the Irish people.' He said that his 'basic republican principles enabled him to serve the interests of the Irish people without fear or favour, courteously but firmly resisting pressure from any church or any state.'[30] The oration was an implicit criticism of the new order in the party. Cardinal Tomas Ó Fiaich said the prayers as the coffin was lowered into the grave.

Less than four months later George Colley too was dead, at the age of fifty-seven. Admitted for treatment for a heart complaint to Guy's Hospital, London, he died unexpectedly on 17 September 1983 a week after undergoing surgery. His remains were flown back to Dublin, accompanied by his family and by Jack Lynch, Desmond O'Malley and the chief executive of Aer Lingus, David Kennedy. In a tribute, Lynch said that Colley had been 'forthright, loyal and true. His likes do not come often.' He exemplified 'everything that was good and honourable in Irish political life during the last three decades.'[31] The *Irish Times,* in an editorial, went even further.

> Many believe that the conscience of Fianna Fáil will be buried with George Colley; the conscience of the Fianna Fáil party that was . . . He is a great loss to his own party and to public life in general, for honesty, and a streak of stubbornness or persistence.

Colley represented

> the old separatist ideal of a pluralist Ireland, an approach which charac-terised the earlier Fianna Fáil . . . his vision of the future of this state and of Ireland was sound as a bell. He is a big loss to us all.[32]

Senator Eoin Ryan, in the oration at the graveside in Templeogue, Co. Dublin, said that Colley was

> a man of integrity . . . A man of integrity is a man who has a set of stan-dards, a philosophy, a conviction as to how he should order his life—and who lives in accordance with these principles. His actions are an integral part of this pattern, and they have a consistency and a perspective in which the wider implications, and long-term effects are never ignored. Into the hands of such a man one can safely entrust one's welfare.

He said that Colley was

in the tradition of the men who founded Fianna Fáil—of de Valera and Aiken, and all those mighty men who achieved what appeared at one time to be impossible.

He had played an honourable and outstanding part in carrying on that tradition. He would be best remembered by 'living up to the ideals, and by endeavouring to realise the vision, of George Colley.'[33] There were few people at the graveyard that day who could not but read into those words a sharp rebuke to the Haughey leadership.

When Seán MacEntee died on 12 January 1984 his daughter, Máire Cruise O'Brien, invited Lynch to give the graveside oration. He agreed to do so but added the warning: 'Tell no-one, not even the undertaker.'[34] It poured rain the day of the funeral, and in the freezing cold old constituency workers lined up outside MacEntee's home in Booterstown, Co. Dublin. At Glasnevin Cemetery the Taoiseach, Garret FitzGerald, walked to the graveside behind the coffin of his godfather and the friend of his father, Desmond Fitzgerald.[35] Haughey, the leader of the opposition, together with members of his shadow cabinet, came behind the Government ministers and family. At the appointed time, Máire Cruise O'Brien wrote:

> Like the hurler that he was, coming out of the sun, the 'real Taoiseach' appeared out of nowhere and began to speak. He spoke beautifully, remembering also my mother and my uncle Paddy, who were buried in the grave where we had laid my father.[36]

Lynch's encomium extolled the virtues of a great patriot and a statesman, an accomplished parliamentarian, a superb orator, an able administrator, a man of the highest integrity, a tenacious debater, a formidable adversary and a republican in the fullest sense of the word. A veteran of the 1916 Rising and the War of Independence, the deceased had many disappointments in public life, the chief among those being the lack of progress towards the reunification of the Irish people.

> He totally abhorred the violent and inhuman activities of the Provisional IRA and the so-called Irish National Liberation Army, and rejected their audacious presumption that they are the heirs of those who, with him, Seán MacEntee, fought the good and honourable fight to attain Irish freedom.

Lynch stressed the deceased's hatred of violence.

> Each brutal action, each sectarian killing, divides more and more the communities and sets further and further back the attainment of the unity

dreamed of by those brave and highly motivated men and women almost seven decades ago.

The final tribute to MacEntee would be the coming together of all the Irish people in peace.

> We must continue to encourage the two communities in the North along this course, an essential prerequisite to a final political solution to be agreed between the two sovereign governments of Ireland and Britain.[37]

Earlier in his oration Lynch referred to MacEntee's speech during the Treaty debate in 1921, when he had set the standards that informed his public and private life for the remaining sixty-two years. On that occasion MacEntee had said: 'Every man must be a conscience unto himself and every man must act true to the truth as he sees it; when honour and expediency conflict, let honour triumph.'[38] Those words had a contemporary political resonance.

It is telling but not surprising that the leader of Fianna Fáil had not been invited to give the oration at the funeral of any of the three distinguished members of his party. All were known to be in the anti-Haughey wing and had remained stern critics of the leadership style that had provoked the frat-ricidal strife besetting a party once characterised by its ability to keep disputes private. In 1984 Haughey and the leadership of Fianna Fáil were in sorry need of being reminded of the high standards and ideals of Aiken, MacEntee, Lemass, de Valera and Colley. All was not well in Fianna Fáil.

Proof of Jack Lynch's enduring popularity was further displayed on the occasion of the centenary all-Ireland hurling final on 2 September 1984. Before a crowd of sixty thousand people at Semple Stadium in Thurles, Cork beat Offaly to win the county's twenty-fifth championship. On that occasion members of what had been termed the 'hurling team of the century' were pre-sented to the crowd. 'By far the loudest and most sustained cheer from the crowd . . . was for Jack Lynch. As a hurler and a politician he drew a more enthusiastic response . . . than anyone else,' wrote Séamus Martin in the *Irish Times*.[39] Frankie Walsh, the legendary Waterford hurler, said the crowd 'tore the place down' at the moment when Lynch was presented.[40]

On 20 February 1985 Desmond O'Malley supported the Government's Health (Family Planning) Bill. He was expelled from Fianna Fáil on 26 February. Amidst the political turmoil, Lynch kept his counsel. However, he did make a speech on 4 November regarding probity in public life. Speaking at the Adult Education Centre in Loreto Abbey, Gorey, he said that a vociferous presentation or over-exaggeration of a cause 'can be and usually is counter-productive.' He warned: 'Do not over-do the making of it.' He argued that governments and politicians would always be the subject of criticism: 'But criticism there must be and politicians will have to accept it. When criticism is genuine and concerned they even welcome it.' He pointed out that the majority of politicians at the local or national level were there by sheer dedication and genuine motivation, ideological or otherwise, to serve the public. It could be said with reasonable conviction that with few exceptions there was a high standard of behaviour among people in public life in Ireland—a standard that could compare favourably with any in the modern democratic world. He believed that the standard of integrity particularly in the Irish civil service was as high as anywhere on the globe.[41]

O'Malley, having been expelled from Fianna Fáil, founded the Progressive Democrats on 21 December 1985. This was a new departure in Irish politics, and it attracted three talented Fianna Fáil TDS: Mary Harney, who had been appointed by Jack Lynch to the Seanad in 1977, Bobby Molloy from Galway, and Pearse Wyse from Cork. In a general election in 1987 that saw the return of Haughey's Fianna Fáil to power, the PDS became the third-largest party in the Dáil, with fourteen seats. Despite its drop to six seats following the 1989 general election, Haughey was forced to break with tradition and enter into coalition with his erstwhile party colleagues. Des O'Malley was named Minister for Industry and Commerce. Bobby Molloy was given the Energy portfolio and Mary Harney was made Minister of State at the Department of the Environment and Local Government. She became leader of the Progressive Democrats in 1993 but stepped down in 2006. She was succeeded by Michael McDowell, though she briefly resumed the position again after McDowell lost his Dáil seat and resigned the leadership in 2007. Harney had negotiated the PDS' entry into coalition in 1997 and 2002. She served as Minister for Enterprise, Employment and Trade. In 1994 she took over the Health portfolio, and she remained in that position in 2008.

Máirín Quill was another distinguished founder-member of the PDS. Formerly a member of Fianna Fáil, she has served as a TD, a senator and a long-standing member of Cork City Council.

Lynch lived to see the sad political demise of Charles Haughey in 1992. Replaced by a former staunch supporter, Albert Reynolds, the most contro-versial figure in twentieth-century Irish politics was brought down by a number of factors, not least the revelations about the bugging scandal that had taken place a decade earlier. A former Minister for Justice, Seán Doherty, finally broke his silence on a late-night television programme, 'Night Hawks', stating quite emphatically that Haughey knew at the time about the bugging.

There was now no alternative. He had to go, and go he did, claiming modestly that he had 'done the state some service.' Long before he died, on 13 June 2006, his reputation as a politician was in tatters. He lived out the latter days of his life in the northern suburbs of Dublin in a house designed by Gandon, a small man lost among his considerable art collection and deserted by many of his erstwhile friends and hangers-on. After his death a devastating judgement was delivered on 19 December 2006 by the first report of the Moriarty Tribunal, which found that during his political career his actions had devalued the quality of a modern democracy.[42]

Haughey had been sculpted many times. He was also painted in hunting gear on horseback. Another painting in his considerable collection is Robert Ballagh's study of Haughey receiving the adulation of his followers at the end of an ard-fheis. On the surface it is a flattering portrait, but its comparison with David's *Crowning of Napoleon* is striking. Haughey's life-style was an affront to many of the old guard of Fianna Fáil, such as Aiken, Lemass, MacEntee and Colley.[43] There was never any mystery about the source of their earnings or income. Lynch also hid nothing and had nothing to hide.

DEATH AND FUNERAL

Jack Lynch's health had been generally quite good in his early retirement. He continued to suffer from damage done to his leg in a fall near his holiday home in the mid-1970s. He smoked his beloved pipe, a feature of his public image through his years in public life; but smoking had a cumulative and damaging impact on his health. On 2 November 1993 he suffered the first of a series of strokes at his home, and he was taken to St Vincent's Private Hospital.[44] After Christmas he had made sufficient progress to be transferred to the Royal Hospital, Donnybrook, where he was said to be making 'substantial progress'. Máirín felt that while he was responding very well to the excellent therapy and nursing it would be 'some time before he is allowed home.'[45] He battled on against poor health for six more years.

In November 1995 Lynch was well enough to attend a ceremony at the University of Limerick, where an honorary doctorate was conferred on him.[46] In failing health and almost blind, he stayed at Milford House in Castletroy, Limerick, where he was looked after by the 'Blue Nuns'. After the ceremony he and Máirín attended a dinner in their honour at Plassey House, University of Limerick. He made a short speech in which he said that the achievement of peace and harmony on the island of Ireland had been the most important goal in his public life. This inevitably meant that 'we in the South would have to alter some of our attitudes and customs for the greater good.' He regretted all the years of the GAA ban and its negative impact on participation in sport. He felt that the fewer barriers created in bringing different traditions together the better. Stephanie Walsh, daughter of his Fine Gael constituency rival, legal colleague and personal friend Stephen Barrett, was present with her husband, Edward Walsh, president of the university. She remembered that Lynch then regaled the audience with stories of sport and politics. As he sat down she could sense 'the satisfaction of the master politician who knew he could still keep an audience in the palm of his hand.' It was one of his last public appearances.[47]

A few months later Lynch was back in the Royal Hospital, where, on 10 August 1996, he celebrated his golden wedding anniversary. In a rather shaky hand he wrote a card to his wife with the following message: 'I thank God for giving you to me and I thank you for giving me fifty years of love and happiness.' She wrote in a card to him: 'You have been a wonderful husband and a great friend, you gave my life happiness and contentment, and, without you, it would have been less fulfilled. Thank you. Máirín.' There is another fragment of correspondence surviving from his time in hospital. Lynch wrote: 'I am only disappointed it is now 15 minutes since "physio" ended and I have not yet had the pleasure of your company. I will need a detailed encyclopaedia for you to explain your wanton neglect. Yours encouragingly, Jack.' An envelope survives with the following words written in his own hand at a more critical stage in his life: 'To my darling wife Máirín—Tell her, I love her too, I have more reason than she has.' By the time he wrote those words his health had been seriously compromised and he was blind.

Discharged from hospital, he lived at home for another few months. The former ombudsman and political correspondent of the *Irish Press*, Michael Mills, recalled the occasion of Lynch's eightieth birthday, 15 August 1997. At Mass in Mount Argus the celebrant, probably Father Herman Nolan, wished the former Taoiseach well, and 'the entire congregation spontaneously broke into applause . . . The image of a man with rare charm and almost unbelievable humility remained in their hearts.'[48] Members of the same congregation would have remembered, as did Father Nolan, often seeing Lynch—the legendary sportsman now completely blind—saying the Rosary, sitting in front of the Sacred Heart side altar in the same church. He suffered further strokes, which left his speech severely impaired.

There was a distressing episode in early 1999 when reports circulated that Allied Irish Banks had cancelled the debts of the former Taoiseach, Charles Haughey. This turned out to be true; the figure was several hundred thousand pounds. Three former Taoisigh—John Bruton, Albert Reynolds and Liam Cosgrave—insisted that no bank had ever given them preferential treatment. Lynch, too ill to issue his own statement, allowed Máirín to ask the bank to review his account. AIB wrote to her on 18 February 1999: 'We wish to advise you that we have inspected our records. We now confirm that all accounts held in the name of your husband, the former Taoiseach Mr. Jack Lynch, have at all times operated subject to the Bank's normal terms and conditions. In addition, we confirm that no loans in your husband's name were ever foregone.'[49] Máirín then told the press that, following a detailed review of her husband's banking activity, she could state categorically on his behalf that 'he never sought, nor was given, any favourable treatment in his bank dealings and never had any debts written off by his bank while in politics or at any other time.'[50] His record was clear and clean.

In May 1999 the press reported that Lynch was not well enough to attend the opening of the road tunnel under the River Lee. Still capable of making a joke, however, he said on learning that the tunnel was to be named after him: 'They want to bury me while I am still alive.' He was represented at the ceremony by his sisters, Rena Dunne and Eva Harvey, and by his surviving brother, Finbarr. Plaques bearing his image were unveiled on each side of the entrance to the 610-metre tunnel.[51]

Lynch spent his last months back in the Royal Hospital, Donnybrook. Father Ralph Egan, parish priest of Mount Argus, a regular visitor, was struck by the width of the dying man's shoulders. Another visitor, Dr Patrick Hillery, remarked on how illness had wasted a man of such great physical strength. Those who knew him and nursed him in his final weeks were struck by his good humour, his composure and his sense of calm. His nurse, Marcella Murrin, recalled that she found him to be the most gentle and courteous of patients. Despite his illness, she said he remained cheerful and very self-controlled. Only once did she witness him momentarily losing his composure. On 12 September 1999 Cork played their traditional rivals Kilkenny in the all-Ireland hurling final. Listening to the radio commentary, Lynch heard the band play 'The Banks of My Own Lovely Lee'. At that point the nurse saw tears come to his eyes. But the outcome pleased him. It was not a repeat of the famous 1939 'thunder and lightning' final, when Lynch captained the losing Cork side, being defeated by Kilkenny by a single point. Fittingly, in 1999 the Cork hurlers won by thirteen points to twelve—ironically and historically, victory by a single point. It was Jack Lynch's last all-Ireland. He died on 20 October.

Immediately, private and public messages of sympathy reached Máirín Lynch. On 24 October 1999 Sister Patricia Somers of the Religious Sisters of Charity wrote to her on behalf of the staff of the hospital:

> From meeting you some years ago when your husband first became ill, I know that you have been at his side throughout these difficult years and letting him go is possibly more difficult following such a protracted illness than if he had died without these years of special devotion to his every need. I am happy that Dr Keating and all concerned in the care of Jack did all they could to help him but I know that you were really his 'special' nurse.[52]

The doctors in question were Denis Keating and John Buckley.

The Archbishop of Armagh, Cardinal Cahal Daly, wrote to Máirín on 26 October, recalling meeting Jack Lynch at St Vincent's Hospital, Dublin:

I was struck by the fact that Jack remained so cheerful in spite of his stroke and his difficulty in speaking. It proved a long and trying illness after that, but I am sure that he never lost his cheerfulness and still could manage that inimitable smile which he had. You will miss him sorely. You were the perfect couple, so happy together and so devoted to one another.

He concluded:

Jack was exactly the same age as myself and I have always felt that to be a special bond. I greatly admired his total integrity, his lack of pomposity or self-importance, his qualities of leadership, his great human qualities. He brought honour to politics and to his country.[53]

The President of Ireland, Mary McAleese, paid tribute to the late Taoiseach: 'He was a gentleman, a complete gentleman, in absolutely everything he did, in every aspect of his life.'[54] The Taoiseach, Bertie Ahern, described him as one of Ireland's greatest statesmen and sportsmen, 'forever in so many Irish minds the real Taoiseach.' The Tánaiste and leader of the Progressive Democrats, Mary Harney, said that Lynch's life proved that a very ordinary person in politics could make an extraordinary contribution.[55] Albert Reynolds, a former Fianna Fáil Taoiseach, said Lynch had 'an easy style of leadership but when toughness was demanded, he showed it.'[56] A former Taoiseach and leader of Fine Gael, Liam Cosgrave, said: 'Jack Lynch was a gentleman. At one time he was the most popular politician in Ireland since O'Connell. Ar dheis Dé go raibh a anam.' Another former Fine Gael Taoiseach, Dr Garret FitzGerald, said: 'He was genial, warm and good fun. He won affection from everybody he came into contact with. He was a difficult politician to oppose, because if you opposed him you damaged yourself.'

Charles Haughey, with considerable generosity, said that Lynch possessed tremendous inner strength, which enabled him to carry the country through very difficult times.[57] He said that Lynch had 'the most wonderful capacity to reassure the public and to sort of persuade them that everything was in good hands, no matter what the difficulties were.' He said he more than admired Lynch: he was 'personally very fond of him and worked very closely with him for years.' He admired his unrivalled popularity 'and of course his wonderful personal qualities, like his unfailing courtesy and great personal charm and likeability.'[58]

The leader of Fine Gael, John Bruton, viewed Lynch as epitomising 'politics as the service of the public. He was a servant of the people in the truest sense of the word. He had a great sense of patriotism and a belief that the nation was greater than the individual.' The Labour Party leader, Ruairí Quinn, stressed the mutual courage of Lynch and Seán Lemass in pursuing membership of the European Union, viewing it as 'a major step in history.'[59] A former President of Ireland and one of his closest friends and strongest supporters in Government, Dr Patrick Hillery, spoke about him in the context of the outbreak of violence in Northern Ireland: 'We were lucky we had him there. His head was clear about what he should do and regardless of any consequences to himself politically.' He was convinced that Lynch had 'suffered terribly' during 1969–70.[60]

Senator Des Hanafin, who managed the fund-raising for Fianna Fáil throughout the 1970s, said that Lynch would insist on sending back donations that he considered suspect. 'It would go back straight away. I would show him the list as funds came in and, if he didn't like any name or if there was a hint of a scandal or a hint of anything that wasn't right, that subscription had to go back.'[61] Jack McGowan-Smyth, a former clerk of the Seanad and retired deputy director-general of the European Parliament, wrote to Máirín Lynch on 22 October 1999: 'Jack was indeed a statesman, a man of great integrity and charisma and one who has earned a proud place in the history of Ireland as a great ambassador for our country in the difficult times as well as the good ones.'[62]

The former ombudsman and political correspondent of the *Irish Press,* Michael Mills, wrote that

historians in the future will assess his place in the calendar of 20th century Irish leaders, but on the question of popular leadership, his place has long been decided. He was unequalled. Not only Fianna Fáil supporters but thousands of people who never voted Fianna Fáil voted Jack Lynch.

Mills felt that 'the Cork people would have loved an opportunity to make it up to him for the loss of those two by-elections [in 1979].'[63]

They found the opportunity to do so at his funeral. Lynch's journey to his final resting place in Cork was memorable. Máirín Lynch asked the Department of the Taoiseach to respect her wishes in the following: Firstly, the coffin was not to be taken on a gun carriage, and there was to be no volley of shots over the grave. Secondly, as Jack Lynch had left no instruction about who was to give the graveside oration, it was her wish that Desmond O'Malley should do so. These wishes were honoured in every respect.[64] She also wanted O'Malley to sit with the immediate family and relatives during the funeral service, though he was to find that there was no space there and instead sat with members of the Council of State.

During Lynch's final illness, arrangements had been made for the Dublin and Cork parts of the funeral services. The lying in state ought to have taken place in the Church of the Three Patrons, Rathgar, as Jack Lynch was a member of that parish. Two issues determined that the service be held elsewhere. Firstly, the church in Rathgar did not have adequate parking facilities. Secondly, the parish priest, Father Pat Dowling, knew that Máirín and Jack Lynch went regularly to Mount Argus in Harold's Cross to hear Mass in Irish. He suggested that Máirín approach Father Ralph Egan, parish priest of Mount Argus, to use that church for the state occasion. That was agreed, and it was further decided that Father Dowling would officiate.[65]

Jack Lynch's body was removed after a brief service from the Royal Hospital, Donnybrook, on Thursday 21 October. His remains were taken to Mount Argus Church, arriving at 7 o'clock. There was a short service for receiving the remains. An inter-denominational service was held the following day, after which the coffin was flown at 5:15 to Cork Airport, where it arrived at 6 p.m. The cortège left for the North Cathedral at 6:15, where Bishop John Buckley received the remains. On Saturday 23 October, Requiem Mass was celebrated at noon and the burial took place at St Finbarr's Cemetery, Glasheen, Cork. The individual services will now be described in greater detail.

First there was a private ceremony at the Royal Hospital, Donnybrook, which was attended by President McAleese. Draped in a Tricolour, the coffin was then borne by a bearer party of military police and placed in the hearse. The cortège was escorted by eighteen motorcyclists from the 2nd Cavalry Squadron to the Church of St Paul of the Cross, Mount Argus, Harold's Cross, where dignitaries of church and state had already assembled.[66] It was another homecoming. There was a short service, involving hymns, prayers and readings from the New Testament. The actor Niall Tóibín, who had been a neighbour of Jack Lynch growing up in Cork, read from the Epistle to the Romans. The Auxiliary Bishop of Dublin, Bishop Éamonn Walsh, said that Máirín Lynch had lost 'a loving, wonderful and honourable husband.' It was difficult for the family in recent years to see illness ebb away and drain the life of one so noble and great. Describing Lynch as honest and trustworthy, the bishop said he had been given 'a wonderful hand by life, and he played it one hundred fold.'[67] The coffin, draped in the Tricolour and with a single wreath of white lilies and red and white roses on top, remained overnight in the church.

The following day, Friday 22 October, an inter-denominational service was held. That was Máirín Lynch's idea, as she felt it best reflected her late husband's personal wishes.[68] Sister Aideen Kinlen told Máirín in a letter how she failed to reach the church for the service:

I'm sure you were heartened and supported by the nationwide mourning for 'the real Taoiseach' and by the many public tributes to him and indeed to yourself. However, your bereavement is a huge one and, knowing that, I feel very deeply for you. I tried to get to Mount Argus last Friday morning. I never met such traffic jams. Eventually I had to give up but my Mass that day was offered for Jack. Life is such a mystery. But, with your support he lived it generously and honourably, an inspiration badly needed. The response in the psalm of today's liturgy is 'our God is a God who Saves.'[69]

In a church filled to overflowing, the congregation included President McAleese, the Taoiseach, Bertie Ahern, and members of the Government and the Oireachtas. Lynch's only surviving brother, Finbarr, his two sisters, Rena Dunne and Eva Harvey, were present, as were the former President Patrick Hillery and the former Taoisigh Liam Cosgrave and Garret FitzGerald. Desmond O'Malley and Martin O'Donoghue were also among the mourners. Jack Lynch's administrator in the Department of the Taoiseach, Kathleen Gannon, was also in the congregation. Present were leading members of the judiciary and of the diplomatic corps, including the Papal Nuncio, Archbishop Luciano Storero. The Chief Rabbi, Dr Gavin Broder, was in the congregation.[70] Judge Hubert Wine represented the Jewish Representative Council.[71] Other religious groups in Rathgar were represented by their pastors. Rev. Mary Hunter of the Presbyterian Church, Rev. Nigel Mackey of the Methodist Church and Rev. Wilbert Gourlay of the Church of Ireland read the lessons and the gospel.[72]

The Auxiliary Bishop of Dublin, Bishop Fiachra Ó Ceallaigh, paid a tribute to Jack Lynch. He recalled his sporting greatness and told the congregation that he had witnessed one of his goals in hurling, which he described as a 'masterpiece'. His own father, Seán, who was a Fianna Fáil TD for Co. Clare, had been one of a group of deputies who had approached Jack Lynch in 1966 to urge him to run for the leadership of the party. The bishop compared Lynch to the heroes of Irish mythology. He concluded by praising Máirín Lynch for the 'unstinting support she has given Jack down the years but particularly over the last six years since he became ill.'[73]

Christopher Moriarty, on behalf of Máirín Lynch, paid tribute to the doctors and nurses who looked after the former Taoiseach and to the gardaí who took charge of his security. Garda John O'Dea had been with Jack Lynch for thirty-three years and the late Garda Tom O'Loughlin for twenty-five years. Dr Denis Keating and Dr John Buckley were remembered, as was Nurse Marcella Murrin.

The mourners followed the military police pall-bearers out of the church to the strains of 'Going Home', from the second movement of Dvořák's New

World Symphony.[74] In the chapel grounds members of the Government formed a guard of honour.

The cortège then left the church for Casement Aerodrome, Baldonnel. Sixty members of the Air Corps lined the route as the remains arrived. The cold weather forced Máirín to watch from a car. When the hearse reached the runway the bearer party removed the Tricolour from the coffin before placing it on their shoulders and marching towards the aircraft. Members of the Government were present, together with Finbarr Lynch, Eva Harvey and Captain Dan Harvey, a nephew of Jack Lynch. Also present was the officer commanding the Air Corps, Brigadier-General Patrick Cranfield. An army chaplain, Father Tony O'Keefe, blessed the coffin. At 5:30 p.m. the plane carrying the remains took off. The chief mourners followed in an Aer Lingus jet.[75]

When the plane landed in Cork, an army motorcycle escort accompanied the hearse from the airport. As a mark of respect, the cortège paused in the Jack Lynch Tunnel under the River Lee. It then moved slowly towards the city and to the North Cathedral, or North Chapel, as Jack Lynch would have called it as a boy. Bishop John Buckley was there to receive the remains.

The following morning, 23 October, the cathedral was filled to capacity for the Requiem Mass at noon. It was unable to take the numbers who turned up, however, and thousands gathered outside to pay their respects. Máirín Lynch took her place in the front seats with family and friends. There was one slip-up in protocol. Máirín had expressly invited Desmond O'Malley to sit with the family. Not finding any room there, he was ushered over to where members of the Council of State were seated. He chose instead to go where there was more room, only to find Charles Haughey sitting beside him. It was incorrectly reported that the two men refused to shake hands at the 'sign of peace' during the Mass. In fact they shook hands twice, once when they found themselves seated together and also at the sign of peace.[76]

The Mass was concelebrated by the Archbishop of Cashel and Emly, Bishop Dermot Clifford, the Bishop of Cloyne, Bishop John Magee, Bishop John Buckley of Cork, the Auxiliary Bishop of Dublin, Bishop Fiachra Ó Ceallaigh, and a first cousin of the deceased, Father Michael O'Reilly. The music chosen for the occasion was Seán Ó Riada's Requiem Mass. The first reading was from the Book of Ecclesiastes.

> There is a time for everything, a time for every occupation under heaven,
> A time for giving birth,
> A time for dying,
> A time for planting,
> A time for uprooting what has been planted.
> . . .

A time for keeping silent,
A time for speaking
A time for loving,
A time for hating;
A time for war,
A time for peace.

The second reading, from the Epistle of St Paul to the Romans, began: 'The life and death of each of us has its influence on others; if we live, we live for the Lord; and if we die, we die for the Lord, so that alive or dead we belong to the Lord.' The gospel was taken from John. It began: 'Do not let your hearts be troubled . . . Jesus said: I am the Way, the Truth and the Life. No one comes to the Father except through me.'[77]

In his sermon Bishop Buckley said he would leave it to historians to make an assessment of the former Taoiseach's commitment and contribution to the national life of the country. On this occasion he preferred to reflect on the private person behind the public persona. The bishop, who grew up in Inchigeelagh in west Cork, knew Jack Lynch personally from his regular visits to the area when Lynch's brother Charlie was the parish priest. He quoted Jack Lynch's words at the graveside of the legendary hurler Christy Ring: 'As long as young people swing their camán for the sheer thrill of the tingle in their fingers of the impact of ash on leather, the story of Christy Ring will be told, and that will be for ever.' Those words, he said, were equally applicable to Jack Lynch. Describing him as a 'man of peace', he said: 'No person worked harder to promote peace in our country. It is our prayer today that this peace which Jack longed for will soon become a reality—a peace that was not made at the conference table but in the hearts of men.'[78]

At the offertory procession Jack Lynch's brother Finbarr brought the scales of justice to the altar as a reminder of his life as a barrister. Liam Ó Tuama, chairman of Glen Rovers, carried offerings of hurling and football jerseys. Schoolchildren from Blackrock brought a pair of doves in a cage.[79] Finbarr, Rena and Eva also participated in the offertory procession.[80]

The Mass ended with the solo 'A Rí an Domhnaigh' sung by Fiona O'Reilly. The choir sang 'Ecce Panis Angelorum'.[81] At that point Máirín Lynch moved towards the back of the church, where a seat had been provided for her. She had insisted that space be reserved for people of Blackpool and Shandon. 'It's what Jack would have wanted,' she said.[82] The President of Ireland, Mary McAleese, made mention of this fact in a handwritten card to Máirín Lynch on 26 October.

My heart soared when I heard you were going to spend a few minutes at the end of Mass, with the people of Shandon and Blackpool. It was the right thing to do and no-one begrudged a second of it so please do not apologise for it. From start to finish Jack's funeral was a beautiful celebration of his life and gifts and the things he loved. The people of Cork showed their love for him so graciously and gently that it was necessary to find a way round all the formality, to show them how loved they were too. So well done—you got it absolutely right. May I also compliment you on the serenity and composure you displayed throughout those difficult days. I don't know where your stamina came from after all you have been through and especially given Jack's absence but [you] radiated such certainty of his spiritual presence that it was [a] privilege to be there and to be part of that special goodbye.[83]

About five thousand people had gathered outside the cathedral during Mass.[84] They stood in silence as the cortège left the cathedral grounds and made its way through Blackpool. An estimated fifty thousand people lined the route through the city.[85] The coffin was carried by members of the 3rd Garrison Military Police Company along narrow streets lined on each side by silent onlookers who had come to pay their last respects. Men tipped their caps in respect and stood with their hands clasped behind their backs. Others made the sign of the cross as the cortège passed. The Shandon Steeple, in whose shadow Lynch had been born and reared, towered over the mourners. The cathedral bells rang out as the funeral moved along Roman Street and on to Pope's Quay. Boys in the Glen Rovers colours formed a guard of honour before the Christy Ring Bridge. As the Band of the Southern Brigade played 'The Banks of My Own Lovely Lee' the silence turned to applause, which grew in intensity along Camden Quay, Patrick's Bridge and then along Patrick Street.

The applause changed momentarily to boos as the official car carrying the former Taoiseach Charles Haughey passed down the main thoroughfare of the city.[86] 'Bastard!' shouted one man, and another: 'Are you selling any shirts today, Charlie?' amid booing and humourless laughter.[87] Too much ought not be made of that minor incident on a day of great dignity and solemnity. But it was an unfortunate lapse in decorum and a departure from Lynch's own high standards in public life.

Timothy Horgan's letter to Máirín Lynch on 20 January 2000 summed up what the funeral meant to many tens of thousand of Cork people of all political faiths and none.

I made a point of standing at the Christy Ring bridge—could anything be more appropriate? And it was particularly moving when the cortege came down the hill with the band playing 'The Banks.' Very hard to suppress the tears.

What really impressed Timothy Horgan was the large number of young people, teenagers and children who were there to honour

> a legendary hurler who had brought so much glory to Cork long before they were even born. They really wanted to pay their respects, as I know from teaching in Farranferris where the youngsters held Jack Lynch in awe when they heard so much about him.

He concluded:

> I think RTE did a wonderful job of the funeral service—celebration would be a more appropriate term—and I cherish my video copy of it. Finally, I'd like to express my admiration for the great dignity you maintained, Mrs Lynch, throughout what must have been a very difficult time. Also, I'd like to comment on the truly touching service in the North Chapel, as Jack would have known the Cathedral, and your part in arranging it.[88]

Apart from those who had lined the main route, thousands of people made their way to St Finbarr's Cemetery, awaiting silently in the rain the arrival of the hearse. The cortège passed through the main gate and drove to the right to the Republican Plot, where many political activists of previous generations are buried. The skies were dark and overcast. Rain fell.

O'MALLEY'S GRAVESIDE ORATION

The grave, in a distant part of the cemetery, was surrounded by a large crowd. President McAleese and the chief mourners took their place. Máirín Lynch stood beside Desmond O'Malley and President McAleese. O'Malley's voice carried to the very back of the crowd, where I stood.

Jack Lynch, he said, was a 'man who exuded warmth, affection and a sense of fun that usually were matched equally by strength, determination and courage.' That combination of qualities was unusual, if not unique, and unmatched by anyone else he knew in public life. He said that the Irish people held Lynch in unparalleled affection, something that he had experienced at first hand. That affection, he said, would not easily pass from the hearts of the Irish people and least easily from those in Cork. Praising Lynch's grace and dignity as a sportsman, O'Malley said: 'On the hurling and football fields he made difficult things seem easy and that elegance and simplicity of manner in the political field made it appear at times as if he were scarcely trying.' His style reminded him of the lines of Yeats: 'The best lack all endeavour and the worst are fuelled with passionate intensity.' He said Lynch was unique in twentieth-century Ireland because he could evoke support and even enthusiasm from the supporters of other parties and from the followers of other leaders. 'When you campaigned with him, you felt you could not lose, and he lost only once. Looking back, it was a miracle he ever lost.' He noted that out of thirty-three years in Dáil Éireann twenty of those were spent in Government. Making a fleeting reference to the post-Lynch era, he said: 'After him came a deluge of volatility, among other things.'[89] The well-chosen phrase spoke volumes.

Northern Ireland was Lynch's greatest challenge, O'Malley said; 'for the safe existence of this democratic state in which we live today is very much Jack Lynch's political legacy.' He continued:

Thirty years ago as a nation, we were faced with a stark choice. We could have caved in to sinister elements and put our country at mortal risk. Jack Lynch chose not to. When he came to the crossroads of history thirty years ago he knew which turn to take. Confronted with some of the most difficult decisions to face any Taoiseach of the modern era, he took determined and resolute action to defend democracy and to uphold the rule of law. Upon such foundations are freedom and prosperity built. Had this country taken the wrong turn thirty years ago, I fear to think what might have befallen us. We didn't, and for that alone Jack Lynch deserves his place in history.[90]

O'Malley pointed out that Lynch had been the first leader of the post-independence generation. The old certainties and the inherited prejudices began to disappear, he said, and Lynch was a bridge to the new Ireland, to Europe and beyond, presiding over a transition that was not always popular but necessary in order to expand the national economy.

Concluding, O'Malley said that Lynch represented Ireland with 'a gracious dignity and with unerring modesty, simplicity and good taste.' His grace and elegance, his integrity and dedication to duty were always mirrored by his wife, Máirín. He added a final wish that the life and career of Jack Lynch would inspire younger people to seek to follow his example 'and to be publicly generous of themselves at a time when the commitment of integrity is so badly needed.'[91]

Following the final prayers, the Tricolour was removed from the coffin and handed to Lynch's nephew, Captain Harvey, who passed it to Máirín. Trumpeters played the last post as the coffin was lowered into the ground. Máirín Lynch was comforted by President McAleese. A long queue quickly formed as people sought to offer her their personal condolences. 'It was a very fitting tribute, because Jack loved his Cork,' Máirín later said in gratitude to the people of the city and county.[92]

IN APPRECIATION OF A PUBLIC LIFE

In the days and weeks following the funeral there was a flow of tributes from Jack Lynch's friends and admirers. Canon Salter of 66 Wellington Row, Cork, wrote on 24 October:

> The funeral service was a wonderful tribute to Jack—in which you obviously played your part. We felt that a sense of 'peace' and 'fulfilment' emanated from the funeral mass and we thank you for that and for the life of Jack and his witness in high office to our beloved country.[93]

Sister Alice, a member of the Sisters of Charity who taught in St Vincent's Convent School, St Mary's Road, Cork, wrote on 26 October:

> As you know Jack was a past pupil of St Vincent's convent school, and we are justly proud of him! We had Mass in the convent chapel on the morning of his funeral attended by the sisters. And the ladies who are in residence in our centre—one of these Bridie Lynch, who is a relation of Jack's was v. pleased to bring up a photograph of him at the offertory procession. The funeral mass and burial was a real spiritual experience for all of us—thank you for planning it so beautifully.[94]

Maeve Binchy wrote to Máirín:

> You were great. You gave your husband such a wonderful funeral. He was always so obviously proud of you and loved you so much. I spend my time watching people and I could see that he just enjoyed talking to you—he relied on you to remind him who people were—you'd get the feeling he was always eager to share things with you. You have always been so strong for him, just know that your many friends and admirers were as proud of you today as he would have been.[95]

Within days of the funeral, Máirín sent a letter of thanks to the Taoiseach, Bertie Ahern, asking him to pass on her warm wishes and gratitude to the Gardaí, the army and the staff of the different Government departments, including the personnel in the Department of the Taoiseach. He replied on 27 October 1999:

> I know that their efforts were considerably assisted by the wonderful co-operation they received from many different organisations such as the Royal Hospital Donnybrook, the community and staff at Mount Argus and the clergy and staff at the North Cathedral.

Speaking for many people, he added:

> I think all of us will have a lasting sense of gratitude that we were privileged who signed the Books of Condolences, who called to pay their respects at Mount Argus Church and the North Cathedral on Thursday and Friday nights, who lined the routes of the processions and who attended the different services, all attest to the great love and affection in which Jack was held by the people of Ireland. It was very generous of you to share Jack with us at such a difficult time. Personally and on behalf of the Government I thank you for your unfailing patience and courtesy throughout. You have no idea how much they meant to us.[96]

Máirín received many letters of condolence from foreign politicians and diplomats. The former British Prime Minister Edward Heath wrote on 20 October 1999:

> I was deeply saddened to hear of the death of your husband Jack. He was a valued and trusted colleague with whom it was a privilege to work when I was Prime Minister. I particularly recall our close co-operation during the preparation for the entry of our two countries to the European Community. Please accept my deepest sympathy.[97]

A former British ambassador to Ireland, Robin Haydon, wrote:

> I send you my deepest and genuine sympathy on the death of Jack. I was British Ambassador when Jack was Prime Minister of Ireland. I have the fondest memories of his kindness to me and to my darling Elizabeth who died 12 years ago. I shall always remember how he arranged for us to go to a clinic in his constituency in Cork and to Croke Park—both firsts for a British Ambassador! It was so good to be dealing with someone I trusted completely and I think and hope he trusted me. A thousand memories of a fine man and a great athlete. I send you my affectionate wishes for the future.[98]

The serving British ambassador, Ivor Roberts, wrote on 20 October 1999:

> Although I never had the privilege of meeting your husband, he had been a figure of the greatest stature for the whole of my life in the public service. He had to wrestle with problems of great difficulty and sensitivity in relations between our two countries and did so in ways which preserved much which could otherwise have been lost.[99]

Bishop Edward Daly, retired Bishop of Derry, had strong personal reasons to record his thanks for the work of Jack Lynch on behalf of Catholics in Northern Ireland. He wrote on 25 October:

> Jack was one of my childhood heroes, whilst I was growing up in Fermanagh, for his exploits in hurling and football. A quarter of a century later, I was a curate in the Bogside in Derry in the 1960s and early 1970s. I listened to his famous, and often misquoted broadcast in August 1969 with hundreds of others, standing on a wracked and riot-torn street in the heart of the Bogside.

They met in person for the first time two years later, on the evening of Monday 31 January 1972.

> It was the day after Bloody Sunday. I had travelled from Derry to take part in a Seven Days programme on RTE. Jack was in RTE making a television address to the nation at that time of sadness and darkness. He asked to see me and we had a lengthy conversation. He asked me if I would be prepared to go to the USA to contradict the false propaganda there about events of the previous day. I agreed to go. It was a visit that was well worthwhile.

Bishop Daly said that he met Jack in Government Buildings on the day he returned,

> and he graciously thanked me for what I had done and I was glad to thank him for the opportunity he afforded me to tell Americans the true story of what had happened.
>
> Jack deserves all the many generous tributes that he has received in recent days. He brought great credit to himself and to his country. He was a good, wise, decent and honourable man. I retired some yeas ago after two strokes. Thank God, I have made a good recovery and I am reasonably well.[100]

The former Northern Ireland Ombudsman, Maurice Hayes, wrote on 25 October 1999 that Jack Lynch

> was one of my youthful heroes as a hurler and I have admired him since in everything he did. He had so much grace and dignity, class and style. Living where I do in the North I am, along with tens of thousands of others, grateful to him for his wisdom and good judgement and his courage thirty yeas ago when he stopped a conflagration in which we might all have been consumed on the bonfire of somebody else's patriotic rhetoric.[101]

The former EU Commissioner and Attorney-General Peter Sutherland sent a handwritten note on 22 November:

> He was such a fine man that I would have wished to record one person's loss, shared by so many others, at his passing. It is of course impossible for me to even imagine how you must feel. I have never suffered the loss of any close relative let alone someone as close as Jack was to you. I hope that you can take some consolation from the full and important life that he led and the immense love which he so obviously felt for you. Above all you will be consoled by knowing that he is enjoying his reward for eternity.[102]

The businessman Dr Tony O'Reilly wrote on 20 December about his long association with Jack Lynch.

> I first met Jack in the Board Room of the Munster and Leinster Bank in South Mall, Cork, in 1960, under the flinty gaze of one Tom Casey, the bank manager. I had just gone to live in Cork and to teach at UCC. Cork then was a city of the Crosbys, the Murphys, the Dwyers and the Sullivans, and the Board Room of the M and L were full of these worthy souls, which Jack and I viewed with a certain suspicion. We shook hands and looked across the divide of the Gaelic world and the world of rugby, and we instantly liked each other. We were athletic friends in the Hall of Mammon.[103]

Recalling that Lynch had asked him to become chief executive officer of the Irish Sugar Company and later of An Bord Bainne, Dr O'Reilly was struck by 'how directly he looked at me, and how totally without side he appeared to be.' He was later told by a friend that Jack Lynch and Stephen Barrett had tossed a coin to decide which party they would represent, and the coin 'came down for Jack and Fianna Fáil.' He added that he could never be sure with his friend 'what is myth and what is reality, but it seems such a good story and it captured Jack's Irishness and lack of partisanship.' In summing up Lynch's life, Dr O'Reilly wrote that during the 1970s and 1980s

> he was a great beacon of dignity and decency in Ireland, and I held your friendship with great price and the feeling that as long as Jack was there, decency and common sense would prevail.

He concluded by saying that 'death comes to us all,' and in the end the simple question posed to each and every one is, 'Did you make a difference?' Answering that question in the final sentences of his letter, he wrote:

Jack and you can answer that question very simply. Yes, you did—to your country, to our friends and I might say, when crossed, to his enemies. You will sense from all of this that there was no better man in this century than Jack Lynch.[104]

Throughout his public life Jack Lynch had enjoyed a particularly close relationship with the Irish Jewish community. The Chief Rabbi, Dr Gavin Broder, writing on 21 October, described Lynch as

a man of great stature and dignity both in Politics and Sport and will always be remembered by the people of Ireland as one who truly gave of himself.[105]

The honorary secretary of the Jewish Representative Council of Ireland, Howard M. Gross, wrote on 26 October:

Ireland has lost one of its finest leaders, and we in the Jewish Community have lost a good friend. We hope that the Almighty will comfort you at this time and spare you from any grief for many years to come.[106]

Leading members of the Protestant churches also sent messages of condolence. The Church of Ireland Archbishop of Dublin, Walton Empey, wrote on 8 November 1999:

While your husband served this state magnificently it always seemed to me that you were ever at his side and in your own way made a vital contribution to his success. Both my wife, Louie, and I always considered you as a pair rather than individually and I think that would be in the hearts and minds of many others. His loss will be a great gap in your life but you can be assured of the prayers of many people including mine own.[107]

The retired Church of Ireland Archbishop of Dublin, Donald Caird, wrote from 3 Crofton Avenue, Dún Laoghaire:

As a bishop and archbishop for thirty years I had the privilege of meeting him in his public capacity on many occasions and discovering all that he did for the good of all the people of Ireland. He was a great Taoiseach and an incomparably good man. We were privileged to have known him.[108]

Rev. Terence McCaughey, academic and Presbyterian minister, wrote from Trinity College, Dublin, recalling that

on several occasions at the beginning of the northern troubles, I wrote to
your husband and how he did me the honour of replying.

He added:

He had that blend of strength, courtesy and integrity which is so badly
needed in public life. You will be comforted, I'm sure, to find during these
days how widely he was honoured and respected.[109]

A large number of letters were sent by Catholic priests who had been
friendly with Jack and Máirín Lynch. Father Michael Hurley, a Jesuit who
had devoted much of his life to promoting inter-faith dialogue, wrote on
21 October:

I shall be offering mass this evening for Jack and yourself. May he rest in
Peace. Like so many others I am greatly indebted to him. He was very kind
and sympathetic and helpful especially in connection with the publication
in 1970 of *Irish Anglicanism* and with the beginnings of the Irish School of
Ecumenics. Please accept my deepest sympathy.[110]

Jack Lynch had quietly helped many causes and institutions during his
life. This side of his life was reflected in a letter of 2 November from the
provincial head of the Irish Christian Brothers, Brother J. K. Mullan:

We are aware of Jack's close association with the Brothers from his earliest
days in school in the North Monastery, Cork. I make particular mention
of his genuine interest in the work of the Artane School of Music in the
late 1980s and well into the mid 1990s. I was privileged to meet yourself
and Jack at many of the enjoyable ceremonies held in Artane and the
Christian Brothers are very grateful for the support and encouragement he
offered to young musicians in their formative years.[111]

Another religious, Father Dave Sullivan of the White Fathers, wrote from
Lublin, Poland, recalling the kindness of Jack Lynch to his mother, Sheila
Sullivan, of 22 Garville Avenue, a next-door neighbour.

In our family we remember him not just as politician but also as a neighbour. We still remember how, when he was Taoiseach, on more than one
occasion he gave my mother a lift into town in the official car. That sort of
simple kindness and courtesy makes a lasting impression and testifies to
the greatness of the man; being in charge of the whole country he still had
time for the neighbour across the road.[112]

Andrew Nugent of the Benedictine Monastery of Ewu Ishan in Edo State, Nigeria, wrote:

> Even in this outpost of the African bush—Jack will never be forgotten. He was a great and thoroughly decent man. God will welcome him as his own. I think of happy days on Heir [Hare] Island with Don and Mary [O'Connor]—and chez Lynch on the mainland.[113]

Father Hugh O'Byrne, Parochial House, Blackwater, Enniscorthy, Co. Wexford, wrote on 28 October:

> I will always remember the ovation he received in Thurles in September 1984 when he was presented to the spectators. He was certainly the uncrowned King of Ireland or should I say Rí na hÉireann.[114]

There were many other letters of condolence and of appreciation. Máirín Lynch answered all in her own hand.

After Jack Lynch's death, Máirín lived on quietly in the family home. Her eyesight deteriorated, as did her general health. I visited her on a number of occasions, at her request. Our conversations were always quite general and, except for one occasion, there was a third party present. She was very helpful but never wished to do an interview. I encouraged her to speak about her own background and her mother.

Máirín Lynch wrote to me a number of times in the years that followed. She also phoned a number of times, and on one of those occasions she told me that she had commissioned the sculptor Ken Thompson of Ballytrasna, Co. Cork, to carve Jack Lynch's monument. His letter to her read:

> Here at last is a drawing of what I propose for your husband's (and our great Cork Taoiseach) memorial stone in St. Finbarr's cemetery. My quarry tells me that they will be able (with some difficulty) to locate the Cork limestone which I suggest. It is much whiter than the Kilkenny and with deeply cut letters picked out in a terracotta colour it will I think look rather fine (and of course red and white are the Cork colours) The HEAD (should it face the other way?) I propose to carve in Portuguese Limestone which is more suitable for detail carving and will go well with our limestone being a creamy colour. You will note that the stone I suggest is a very substantive 9" thick and that the base takes up the whole width of the grave. The head will be very slightly smaller than life size.[115]

Máirín Lynch paid for the work on 11 December 2000. She asked Val O'Connor to seek permission from Cork City Council for the erection of the stone. There is a further draft note in her handwriting to Ken Thompson, stating:

> I intend to be cremated and wish my little urn to be put into Jack's grave beside him. In which case I presume my name—Máirín Lynch—will be put on the headstone.

It is not clear that that letter was ever sent.[116] But her wishes ought to be honoured.

With the help of friends, she set about sorting her husband's belongings. Before his death Jack Lynch had generously disposed of many valuable medals and mementos from his sporting career and from his life in public office. Máirín made a gift of various pieces of sculpture and other items to the museum in Fitzgerald's Park, Cork. She also gave paintings and other items to friends of the family.

In October 2000 Máirín Lynch was unable to attend the unveiling of a bust of Jack Lynch at City Hall, Cork. The Tánaiste, Mary Harney, attended, and she described Lynch as a

> beacon of integrity . . . In these difficult times in our country, with scandal in public life, and integrity being questioned, we should never forget the examples in leadership and inspiration that he gave us.[117]

One of Máirín Lynch's last public appearances was in 2002 at the handing over of the EEC accession papers to the National Archives. The Taoiseach, Bertie Ahern, said: 'Generations owe a debt of gratitude to Jack for his leadership and his vision in seeing that Ireland's future lay in being part of the great project of a union of European states.' In reply, Máirín Lynch expressed her gratitude for the invitation and singled out a number of people in her talk. Her speaking notes record that she spoke graciously about Dr Patrick Hillery and others. She said of the former leader of Fine Gael:

> Dr Garret—I am delighted that you are here tonight. Jack always thought very highly of you, and I knew that you were good friends, but I do not think quite as good on the floor of the house.

Referring to Dr Tony O'Reilly, she made reference to their friendship and to the good times they had together in west Cork. She recalled that he was unkind to 'our little boat—the yellow bird—when it misbehaved bringing you over to Heir Island to visit our mutual friends Don and Mary O'Connor.'[118]

On 15 July 2002 Máirín Lynch travelled to Cork to unveil a statue of her husband. The west Cork sculptor James MacCarthy chose as his subject Jack Lynch seated on a bench, reading the front page of the *Cork Examiner*. The sculpture now graces the Blackpool Shopping Centre. 'It is wonderful to be back in Blackpool, where Jack is now,' she told the large crowd who had turned out for the occasion.[119]

The media respected Máirín's privacy. However, 'An Irishman's Diary' by Wesley Boyd in the *Irish Times* on 16 August 2003 disturbed her. That was certainly not the intention of the writer; but its contents proved to be an unwelcome intrusion on her privacy. The article contrasted Bertie Ahern's refusal to be manipulated by 'marketing gurus' during the wedding of his daughter, which had been covered by the 'celebrity' magazine *Hello,* with Jack Lynch's alleged naïveté in 1968 when he and his wife were the guests of Gulf Oil on a trip to Japan, where Máirín had been invited to launch the super-tanker *Universe Ireland* in Yokohama. The invitation had come from Bill Finnegan, public relations officer for the company in Ireland, where Gulf Oil had a major interest in Whiddy Island in Bantry Bay. On that occasion, Boyd wrote, the 'multinational Gulf Oil put up the cash and tried to run the show for its own benefit.' The single event of the launch of the oil tanker 'mysteri-ously started to blossom into a grand tour,' financed by Gulf Oil, according to the article. The Taoiseach would make official visits to Lebanon, India, Thailand, Hongkong and Japan. The official party consisted of Mr and Mrs Lynch and a senior official from the Department of Foreign Affairs. Gulf Oil, according to the implication in the article, was paying for their expenses, while Bill Finnegan and his wife also went along. The press corps, represent-ing three newspapers and RTE, were in steerage. 'We were all being paid for by our various organisations,' he wrote.

The article then quoted sources claiming that Gulf Oil executives had gained privileged access to the Indian minister by being attached to the official visit being made by Lynch. The same occurred in Hongkong and Thailand, while Japan was the exception: only the senior official from External Affairs was allowed to accompany Lynch to meet the emperor. Boyd recorded that Mrs Lynch 'graciously performed the launching ceremony.' The party then moved to Honolulu and then to the United States. While they were in Hawaii, Soviet tanks invaded Prague, and the Irish journalists sought a state-ment from Lynch. Bill Finnegan refused to disturb the Taoiseach. The journalists were obliged to work through the official from the Department of Foreign Affairs (which they ought to have done in the first instance). 'Mr Lynch appeared almost immediately in his pyjamas and, courteous as always, made a statement condemning the invasion.'[120]

On reading this article, Seán MacHale, of Westminster Road, Foxrock, Co. Dublin, wrote to Máirín Lynch on 4 September 2003 to state that he had been greatly upset by Wesley Boyd's article. He felt that she was owed a wholesome apology for 'this offensive and unfeeling article and I will pursue Boyd for same.' He concluded: 'I trust you are keeping well. Memories of Jack frequently come to my mind and always with great pleasure.'

His reply to Boyd was enclosed. It read in part: 'In my opinion Mr Jack Lynch represented the best interests of Ireland politically, commercially and personally on the world stage as our Taoiseach and throughout his career.' He rejected Boyd's comparison with contemporary Irish politics, stating that Jack Lynch made good use of the occasion.[121] He was uncertain as to what point Boyd was trying to make when he said that Gulf Oil 'tried to run the show for its own benefit.'[122]

> Jack and Máirín Lynch were never compromised by the courtesy shown to them by Gulf Oil or their very large retinue of international business friends and contacts, world leaders or their friends in Europe and Ireland.

He concluded:

> You were privileged to have been with the party in Japan and as a consequence should show respect to his wife Máirín and the late Jack Lynch by avoiding ludicrous comparisons in the national media that bear no relationship to Jack Lynch being an outstanding businessman as well as a politician.[123]

In earlier years Máirín Lynch would have rushed to the defence of her late husband's reputation. On this occasion she left it to others to respond on her behalf.

DEATH OF MAIRIN LYNCH

In her final two years Máirín Lynch travelled privately to visit her husband's grave and took the opportunity to meet old friends in Cork. However, in the last few months of her life a combination of frailty and illness prevented her from making the journey. She continued to have fresh flowers regularly put on her husband's grave.

I continued to hear from her on the phone until late 2003. The last letter I received from her was dated 11 March 2003. It read:

> Dear Dermot,
>   I hope these books will not tire you too much, but I have great respect, admiration and amazement for the Trojan work done by this lady, who compiled all the paper cuttings, and photographs, for these three books. I know Jack would have been surprised and embarrassed on being singled out, but who could not have been flattered! I could prefer not to have been mentioned, but nevertheless pleased that I was remembered. We were not

very political people, but had great admiration for Éamon de Valera, and [were] deeply committed to God's will and to each other.[124]

Her health deteriorated in 2004 and she was removed to hospital. Nurse Marcella Murrin, who was with her husband through his final illness, took care of her. On 13 May 2004 President McAleese wrote to her:

We are all sorry to hear that you have been so ill lately. I hope the joy of the lovely month of May will be able to penetrate through the pain and discomfort. I know you have a formidable spirit and love of life—enough I hope to see you through these harder times. We will keep you in our prayers and thoughts. Please God all will be well and soon. Le grá . . .[125]

Máirín Lynch died in St Vincent's Private Hospital, Dublin, in mid-June 2004. Her will left a large sum of money to 'Goal'—most probably the proceeds of the sale of the family home. Her funeral was at the Church of the Three Patrons, Rathgar, at which Desmond O'Malley spoke of her 'happy, ful-filled, and very lovely life,' which could be summed up in six words—warmth, energy, punctiliousness, consideration, dignity and loyalty.[126] In accordance with her wishes she was cremated and the ashes taken to Cork. On 17 June 2004 a funeral service took place in the North Cathedral. At the end of the Mass, Dr Ken Whitaker said in a tribute that Máirín Lynch was friendly, kind and quick to acknowledge and appreciate help and advice. He said that 'Jack's modesty coupled with Máirín's happiness of spirit won the respect and admiration of everyone who knew them.' He recalled that after Jack's death she had replied in her own hand to countless people who had written to her.[127]

After the Mass a Garda escort led the hearse to St Finbarr's Cemetery, along virtually the same route taken by her husband's funeral. Máirín's ashes were buried in the same plot. The inscription, in terracotta lettering on white Cork limestone, reads:

In loving memory of
Jack Lynch
15 August 1917–20 October 1999
Iar-Thaoiseach
Happy is the man who finds wisdom

Chapter 12

JACK LYNCH'S PLACE IN IRISH HISTORY

This book has analysed the life and times of Jack Lynch, setting him in his family, social, sporting, professional and political contexts. Biography is a difficult medium for a historian. In using a personality as the prism through which to review the past, one is in constant danger of distortion, of exaggeration and of either canonisation or demonisation. Professional over-identification with a subject of investigation leads to hagiography in the more extreme cases. The opposite reaction is to develop a sense of antipathy, contempt even, for a person with whose life and times one has become familiar over a period of years of research.

Every biographer confronts a unique challenge. By any standard, Jack Lynch was a difficult subject to study. He did not leave a large personal archive. There is no corpus of writings and correspondence. I have not found any rich seam of archival material in a private collection. His wife did not preserve a large collection of personal papers. One challenge posed was in relying upon material in the National Archives of Ireland and other holdings of official papers, in the National Archives in London and the us National Archives in Maryland. It was important to seek out personal collections of papers, conduct interviews and find other mechanisms to fill in the gaps in the life of this intensely private man who spent his working life in the public eye and in pursuit of the commonweal. An editorial in the *Irish Times* on 21 October 1999 called him 'a far-seeing patriot.' But not everyone would, or will, accept such a benign judgement of his political legacy.

Jack Lynch played many different roles in his lifetime. Dick Walsh, in a tribute in the *Irish Times*, stated that on two occasions he and Lynch were in adjoining rooms in St Vincent's Hospital. They spoke about Blackpool and not about politics. As a boy, Walsh recalled seeing Jack Lynch for the first time on the playing-field.

Taut as a coiled spring in a red jersey as he shot a point for Cork which set the crowd in Limerick's Gaelic Grounds reeling with admiration. The best of it was that as he crouched by the sideline 40 yards out, he knew he could depend on wrist and eye; he wasn't going to miss. 'There you are,' said my father, 'and he's a TD and a barrister to boot.' 'Or not to boot,' said the cool Corkman beside us. 'Didn't he throw the boots away at half time.' You could tell the story about many another player-turned-politician—if they were good enough—but only in Lynch's case is it close to being the whole truth. His wife Máirín, his native Cork, politics and hurling were his life.

And a good life it was.[1]

Walsh has gone a long way to sum up the self-contained world of Jack Lynch. He was a man shaped in his formative years by his family background, his social surroundings, his education and his engagement with sport at the highest level.

Lynch grew up surrounded by rank poverty in the laneways and tenements on the north side of Cork. He was not from a poor family but he was a witness to the social inequality that characterised his native city and that blighted the lives of those who lived in the neighbourhood. Social stratification prevented 'upward mobility' in a city where snobbery was rampant and an impediment to economic development. Emigration was a harsh fact of the daily lives of many poor Cork families.

Daniel Lynch had a political influence on his youngest son. He was a tailor and a trade-union activist, a social reformer with a strong interest in labour politics. He had supported William O'Brien's All-for-Ireland League. There was an anti-Treaty wing in the extended Lynch family. But the Lynch household was not divided against itself. Daniel Lynch was not doctrinaire, and certainly not a doctrinaire republican. As a trade-unionist he may have voted for the Labour Party candidates who were known to the family; but it is probable that by the late 1920s he favoured Éamon de Valera's Fianna Fáil, whose social policy was not very far removed from the Labour Party's position.

Jack was five when civil war broke out. He was sixteen in 1933 when he carried a burning sod in a torchlight procession to welcome de Valera to Blackpool during the general election. But that admiration was not translated into political action until his election to Dáil Éireann in 1948, after which the newly elected deputy became a close friend of 'the Chief'.

Educated in the North Monastery Christian Brothers' School, Jack Lynch was one of the very few fortunate enough to earn a corporation (city council) scholarship in open competition. He was in the A class in the North Monastery, receiving a solid education among bright and ambitious youngsters in that stream. Poverty and high unemployment meant that teaching, the civil service, the corporation and state-sponsored companies were the careers open to boys of Lynch's generation and class.

Jack Lynch joined the civil service and went to work in Dublin in the mid-1930s. By that time he was becoming a national sporting hero in football and in hurling, playing for club, county and province. His sporting prowess greatly facilitated a transfer back to Cork, where he worked as a court clerk and studied law at University College. Having met his future wife in 1943, he returned to work in the civil service in Dublin in the Department of Justice and to study for the bar. His experience as a civil servant helped to shape his ideas in a way that would have a significant bearing on his future behaviour as a politician.

Jack and Máirín married in 1946 and lived in Cork, where Lynch began to practise as a barrister. That lifelong relationship had certainly the most enduring influence on Jack Lynch's outlook. Máirín is deserving of a biography. This book has sought to describe her background and her ideas. Her relationship with Lynch helped strengthen his greater openness to different political and religious trends.

Máirín Lynch worked as a civil servant in the Department of Industry and Commerce for most of the 1930s until the end of the Second World War, when she was forced to resign because of the marriage bar. She also inherited from her mother a strong commitment to 'buying Irish' and building up the national economy. That was partly her motivation for making her own clothes and later wearing the Irish-made clothes of young Irish designers. Her mother was very close to the couple, living with them in Dublin in the 1960s during the last years of her life. The ethos of the civil service permeated their mutual approach to politics and public life. Both understood the workings of the civil service and knew personally many of the officials who came to serve at a senior level.

The couple had no children. Both took a lifelong interest in the issue of adoption and of legislative reform in that area. Jack and Máirín were also much committed to improving the lot of widows in society. They were a very united couple, sharing cultural and musical interests. Jack Lynch tried to return home to lunch most days, even when serving as Taoiseach. He travelled everywhere with his wife. In many ways they were an 'old-fashioned' couple by the standards of the flash and fast 1960s. She wore Irish tweeds and distinctive hats. Lynch was photographed with a pipe, and a cap or hat purchased from his Cork supplier. They might have belonged to the de Valera era. However, they had a strong sense of public service and a commitment to maintaining the highest standards in high places. Máirín Lynch was highly political but not in a partisan sense. She shared, and helped shape, her husband's political convictions. On occasions she felt compelled to enter the public arena. They were both far-seeing patriots.

An *Irish Times* editorial of 21 October 1999 recorded that Jack Lynch did not come from a conventional political background 'and he was sometimes tempted to see this as a handicap in a party and a country where tradition counted for so much.' His strengths, the editorial said, were rooted in his time and place and, without having to work at it, he never forgot either the city of his youth or how it was in the 1930s. True, Jack Lynch was not a scion of a 'great' republican family. That proved to be both an advantage and a disadvantage in his later political life, particularly when having to deal with Northern Ireland in the late 1960s and 70s. His political pluralism, seen as heresy by some, was a strength, as it enabled him to form friendships across the floor of Dáil Éireann. One of his closest friends from the time he entered politics in 1948 was the Fine Gael TD Stephen Barrett. His political openness also enabled him, at a time of national crisis in the late 1960s and early 70s, to stand out against the forces of atavism that risked returning the country to a state of war and mayhem.

In this context Lynch's professional formation as a civil servant in the Department of Justice in the mid-1940s must be added to his unconventional political background. However, his implicit confidence in the ability of the civil service system to function was not always well founded. He developed a close personal friendship with a small number of civil servants, in particular with Dr Kenneth Whitaker.

Lynch grew up close to the rank poverty on the north side of Cork. He came from a family with progressive social ideas. His concerns about social inequality were reinforced by his experiences as a court clerk and later while working as a barrister. From the time he entered politics he demonstrated his commitment to advancing educational reform and industrial development. As a backbencher and junior minister he was noted as a reformer and a good constituency worker. As Minister for Education, from 1957 to 1959, he had an opportunity to make a start on the reform of a moribund and arthritic primary school system by reintroducing married women into the classrooms. This may not appear to have been a major advance; but, given the conservatism at the highest level in that department, his contribution was significant. He was also fortunate to have served in that position at a time when new, younger members of the department pressed for change. His short tenure made the path to reform by his successor, Dr Patrick Hillery, considerably easier.

The choice of Lynch by Seán Lemass in 1959 for the post of Minister for Industry and Commerce gave him responsibility for a portfolio that was vast in dimension. Lynch had primary responsibility for leading the Department of Industry and Commerce—a bastion of economic protectionism since 1932—to embrace a new philosophy of free trade, open markets and membership of the European Economic Community. The new minister was an unapologetic supporter of the new economic strategy of freer trade. It would lead to economic dislocation and undermine weak industries working in the womb of protectionism but it would provide a springboard to massive new job creation, higher educational standards and economic and agricultural development. Having experienced the disappointment of failing to achieve membership of the EEC in 1961–3 he continued to work towards that goal as Minister for Industry and Commerce, as Minister for Finance and then, finally, as Taoiseach. He had the distinction of signing Ireland up as a full member of the EEC in 1972. That single initiative was one of the most profound political, economic and social achievements of the Irish state since its establishment in 1922, or possibly since the signing of the Treaty with Britain in December 1921.

Lemass, impressed by Lynch's record in Industry and Commerce, secured Lynch's election as leader in 1966. The *Irish Times* editorial mentions that it was often said that he was a reluctant leader of Fianna Fáil, 'but many who watched him closely were convinced that the reluctance was often attributed to him by those who nurtured ambitions of their own and would have been happier if he had never succeeded Éamon de Valera and Seán Lemass.' The editorial argued that 'he fitted naturally into the line of succession which passed logically from de Valera to Lemass.' There is no sense in which Lynch might justifiably be described as a 'reluctant' Taoiseach. Family circumstances, in particular the serious illness of his mother-in-law, obliged him to take some time before he accepted the invitation from Lemass. Lynch had to be respectful of his wife's feelings at the time. Being an only child, she was preoccupied with the deteriorating state of her mother's health. If such sensitivity for his wife's feelings is perceived as being a character defect in the world of macho politics, then Irish society has evolved in the wrong direction.

Lynch was a modern leader and a moderniser. The editorial argues that some of his successors 'reverted to a style of leadership more appropriate to the 1930s than to the last quarter of the century.'[2]

It is appropriate for the historian to evaluate Lynch in the context of his predecessors. He was the first Taoiseach not to have been part of the revolutionary generation that had helped set up the state. Lynch remained unapologetically antagonistic to the shibboleths of an era that cultivated ambivalence and ambiguity towards the use of violence. There was continuity in his philosophical thinking. He was part of a line of parliamentary nationalists from O'Connell to the Irish Party and William T. Cosgrave's Cumann na nGaedheal. He joined Fianna Fáil when it had long ceased to celebrate its 'slightly constitutional' character.

Much to the annoyance of more traditional elements in Fianna Fáil, Lynch as Taoiseach was not a doctrinaire nationalist. He did not cultivate or condone any ambivalence towards the employment of violence to achieve a united Ireland. Born in 1917, he was either two or five years older than the state (depending on whether 1919 or 1922 is taken as the date of its foundation). During almost ninety years of existence it has enjoyed a period of stable parliamentary democracy, unbroken by *coup d'état* or foreign occupation. There are few European countries that have enjoyed a more tranquil and irenic time. Yet the new Irish state had, at its very origins, to confront the outbreak of a civil war in 1922 and to secure victory in 1923. The state has also had to confront the existence of the IRA, in different factions and manifestations, since its origins.

The presence of an unofficial army—or armies—necessitated permanent vigilance on the part of the Government authorities and a strong resolve to confront subversive organisations, of whatever political orientation. That threat was not uniform: it dipped and grew in intensity. Perhaps the greatest danger arose during the Second World War, when the IRA collaborated with Nazi Germany in preparation for a possible invasion. Their actions inside the Irish state helped to provoke large-scale internment, while the courts in some cases handed down death sentences for capital crime, which were, for the most part, carried out. Without exception, successive heads of government up to the 1960s—William T. Cosgrave (president of the Executive Council), Éamon de Valera, John A. Costello and Seán Lemass—handled the internal IRA security problem with a firm hand.

When Jack Lynch came to power at the end of 1966 he found within two years that he confronted a major political threat from a resurgent IRA—ironically at its weakest militarily since the 1920s. The confrontations provoked by the civil rights movement in Northern Ireland in 1968 and 1969 acted as a flashpoint. The virtual disintegration of that state created a situation in which Catholics in many nationalist areas in Northern Ireland felt exposed and subject to attack by loyalist paramilitary forces, by B Specials and, in some instances, by members of the Royal Ulster Constabulary itself. The Irish Government predicted the cataclysm in Northern Ireland and had repeatedly warned the British Government of the unravelling of Unionist rule.

Despite anticipating the Northern crisis, Lynch did not prepare sufficiently. The Irish army was under-resourced and lacking in necessary equipment and transport. Military Intelligence was understaffed and poorly led. The decision to put so few operatives into the field showed very poor professional judgement. The Government had not established a reliable network of informants to report on the unfolding events in Northern Ireland. The diplomatic service had no Northern Ireland division in 1969, though it reacted quickly in deploying a diplomat north of the border who acted as a liaison with Dublin. Insufficient attention had been paid to the press and propaganda side of handling the crisis in diplomatic missions abroad. Only the Garda Special Branch, small in numbers but with remarkably good sources within the IRA, was performing to the highest possible standard in the autumn of 1969. Lynch was far too slow to monitor the performance of his ministers, and to sack those who were underperforming.

Altogether, despite the clear evidence of an impending crisis in 1969, Lynch and his Government did not adopt sufficient contingency plans to deal with predictable eventualities.

When the membrane that held civic society together was finally breached in Northern Ireland in the late summer and autumn of 1969, Lynch was obliged to handle the situation in a state of crisis, seeking to put together the different components necessary for responding cohesively to that multifaceted problem. That led to fragmented decision-making. Actions were taken sometimes without an awareness of how they might affect the general situation. The presence of public relations personnel from Government departments and state-sponsored organisations was often resented by the professional diplomats, who felt that the people concerned were naïve and amateurish. Members of the diplomatic service had cause for concern. Mistrust was running very deep at the time.

Poor decisions were also taken on a strategy for the international distribution of the message from the Irish Government. The press officers seconded to embassies had to be recalled, though not fast enough to prevent collateral damage. The employment of the public relations agency Markpress was a waste of taxpayers' money. The partial funding of *The Voice of the North* only helped to confuse the irenic message of the Government with the belligerent policy of the IRA.

Yet despite the failure to make remote preparations for the handling of the Northern crisis, Lynch acted with decisiveness in his unwavering commitment to the preservation of democratic institutions. When he had proof that two members of his Government had abandoned any notion of collective responsibility, he acted with determination over the plot to import arms for distribution in Northern Ireland. That resulted in the sacking of Haughey, Blaney and, in effect, Ó Móráin too.

Whatever the criticisms might be, Lynch acted with determination and removed three senior ministers—two of whom were powerful both nationally and within the Fianna Fáil party. He foiled a plot from within the Government to import arms for distribution in Northern Ireland while at the same time taking on two of the most powerful figures in national politics.

It is difficult to realise after more than twenty-five years just how strong Neil Blaney was in the party in 1969. The crisis in Northern Ireland had elevated the profile of the Minister for Agriculture, who, of course, represented part of a county contiguous to Northern Ireland. Blaney was a potential successor to Lynch, as was Haughey. Both saw themselves as being more deserving leaders of Fianna Fáil than Lynch. Their sacking in the dead of night was one of the most dramatic acts—if not the most dramatic—in Irish politics since the foundation of the state. Lynch's reassertion of control of both his Government and the party in the wake of the sackings was a major political contribution, and in retrospect, its significance grows in historical importance.

The *Examiner*, in an editorial on 21 October 1999, praised the fact that when the Northern crisis erupted 'he kept his head at a time when factions within Fianna Fáil wanted the Army to cross the border.' It recalled that Lynch always held that had he acceded to such pressure 'nothing less than a bloodbath would have resulted. History has borne him out in this regard.' Yet, the editorial stated, he acted decisively when the Catholic community in Northern Ireland came under direct attack. In face-to-face meetings he pressed the British Prime Minister, Harold Wilson, to redraw gerrymandered boundaries and to end discrimination in housing allocation and in schooling.

The *Examiner* also argued that he made the correct decisions when faced with division inside his party. 'Unflinching as Taoiseach, Jack Lynch made the difficult decision to sack two Ministers—C. J. Haughey and Neil Blaney—leading to the Arms Trail which remains among the most controversial events in modern Irish history.'[3] In its editorial on 21 October 1999 the paper described Lynch as follows: 'Deceptively tough, he brought to politics the quality of steel forged in the heat of the hurling and football arenas where he had won six consecutive All-Ireland senior medals.'[4] That may be true; but it detracts from the fact that Lynch was a conviction politician. He held to a set of fundamental values during that difficult period, and he won through, remaining as leader of Fianna Fáil until 1979.

The same editorial described Lynch as 'a charismatic leader, political icon, and statesman, [who] was quintessentially a man of the people.' He inspired affection and admiration. It said that he brought a remarkable sense of ordinariness and a total lack of pretension to leadership and government. That contrasted with the remote style of Éamon de Valera and Seán Lemass. 'In the unforgiving world of politics, Mr Lynch earned a well-deserved reputation for integrity in an era of growing cynicism.'[5]

Dick Walsh rejected the thesis that Lynch was a 'soft touch'. Using the words of the Labour Party TD Justin Keating, he wrote: 'History will be kind to Jack Lynch.'[6] An article in the *Examiner* was of the same opinion: 'History will be kind to Jack Lynch. Even his critics agree that had he not remained steadfast when the North erupted there was every likelihood of a civil conflict which could have engulfed the entire island.'[7]

The phrase 'history will be kind to Jack Lynch' is unintentionally patronising. Historians, not History, are required to make judgements. Whether he exercised good judgement when he returned Charles Haughey to the front bench and then gave him a ministry will remain a matter for debate. There is no doubt that George Colley's opposition to the initial rehabilitation showed wisdom and far-sightedness that were lacking in his leader.

Finally, Lynch led his party into the 1977 general election on a platform that set a trend for future elections and for auction politics. Fianna Fáil was returned to power with a landslide victory. Lynch must take responsibility for the adoption of the economic strategy behind the general election campaign of 1977. Arguably, with Lynch as leader Fianna Fáil would have won without having to promise so much. It was one of his best personal performances, and the party's electoral strategy was built around his charisma and popularity. However, he was encouraged to adopt the 'give-away' election manifesto by a strong consensus within his own party.

The Northern tsunami helped shape the Lynch legacy. There has been a strong emphasis on the role he played in the suppression of the arms conspiracy of 1969–70. That is merited. It is part of his most enduring and most contentious legacy, but the emphasis on this has tended to overshadow, if not eclipse, Lynch's role in the country's transition from protectionism to free trade. He helped negotiate Ireland's membership of the EEC and presided over the second Irish presidency of the EEC in 1979. An important question may be formulated thus: How would Lynch's leadership be evaluated had there been no conflict in Northern Ireland? Such counterfactual speculation is useful if only to point out the extent to which the question of Northern Ireland dominated his time as Taoiseach. At a time when the Lynch generation should have been concentrating exclusively on the modernisation of Irish society, considerable energy and resources had to be deflected into dealing with the corollaries of the Northern crisis, both nationally and internationally. Government ministers appeared to spend a disproportionate amount of time fixating on Northern Ireland. That detracted from the precious time that might otherwise have been spent building stronger economic foundations for an economic take-off. Moreover, the sacking of Haughey in May 1970 removed a very able minister from the Government. The ensuing civil war inside the governing party had consequences yet to be calculated.

Northern Ireland and the attendant issues of security consumed him. After the Arms Crisis he felt compelled to take personal control of all aspects of Northern policy, sharing the burden with his close confidant Ruairí Brugha in the mid-1970s. After 1969 Lynch's main focus was rarely on economic recovery. There were four years of unprecedented bloodshed. Lynch's Government had to confront a growing threat from internal subversion and the spawning of revolutionary organisations. There were spates of bank robberies that resulted in the deaths of two unarmed gardaí. Ironically, he lost power in 1973 to the

National Coalition, which deprived him of the opportunity to implement reforming ideas in the context of full membership of the EEC.

The burden of leadership weighed heavily on Lynch, for three inter-related reasons. Firstly, there was the hierarchical nature of Irish government. Secondly, there was the persistent and consistent underperformance of various ministers. Thirdly, there was the pre-modern nature of Fianna Fáil. Lynch could do little in the short term with the first. He took over from Seán Lemass in 1966, only seven years after Éamon de Valera had stepped down. The latter had developed a strong *caudillo*-style system of government. Lemass was less caught up in the idea of the projection of his own personality. Lynch, by temperament and by training as a civil servant, was more disposed to follow the Lemass model of managerial politics; yet he was required by his party to play the charismatic persona. That proved burdensome. Lynch had also inherited a Government decision-making system that relied heavily on the Taoiseach or 'chief'. As a former civil servant he sought to allow ministers greater autonomy in pursuing their duties without undue interference from above. But without the development of a system of necessary checks and balances, latitude led to licence, as witnessed in the autumn of 1969 and spring of 1970.

Secondly, Lynch did not have a great pool of talent from which to draw in the selection of his ministers. He was far too reluctant to sack those who did not perform or those who deviated from Government policy on matters of policy substance. He stood by ministers who should have been sacked. He repeated his errors of judgement even in the selection of members of his 1977 Government. According to Napoléon Bonaparte, a leader has to be lucky in his generals. But Lynch sometimes made his own bad luck. He was, on the other hand, fortunate in having promoted Desmond O'Malley to the Department of Justice in 1970. However, for every good appointment he made many other poor choices. Unlike Charles de Gaulle, Lynch did not believe in the Nietzschean concept of the state as a *monstre froid* or cold monster. That approach to statecraft required a cold-blooded analysis of the interests of the state divorced from personal considerations. It did not leave any room for sentiment or regard for the personal circumstances of ministers. He who best served the interests of the *monstre froid* continued to be allowed to hold office. Those who did not were sacked. Lynch was far more humanistic. He made allowances for human failings. That was at once a strength and a weakness.

Thirdly, Lynch inherited a Fianna Fáil party machine that was a formidable force at election time; but it was not a modern political party. It was only during his time in opposition, from 1973 to 1977, that he had the opportunity to try to develop a head office staff, employ a full-time public relations officer and set up policy committees. The burden of the work for the modernisation of the party fell on the shoulders of Séamus Brennan who died in 2008. The changing of the party image was entrusted to Frank Dunlop, a young reporter recruited from RTE who took up his job in the mid-1970s. By the time of the general election in 1977, Fianna Fáil had moved decisively in the direction of modernising its structures.

Since he took over as Minister for Industry and Commerce in 1959, Lynch had worked under great pressure. The call on his reserves had continued up to the general election of 1977, when, at the age of sixty, he displayed a youthful exuberance for the campaign trail. But he was tired, and both he and his wife hoped for a quieter life. The final two years of his public life proved very difficult. The spectre of Northern Ireland and the spillover south of the border again preoccupied him. He could have chosen to step down from the leadership soon after the general election, but he was propelled along by events. Máirín was keen to see him step down. The decision was taken that he would do so after the papal visit and after the end of the Irish presidency of the EEC in December 1979.

However, during his last months in office he proved to be more accident-prone. Against his better judgement he allowed himself to be persuaded that if he resigned in December 1979 the *dauphin*, George Colley, would be elected his successor. It was in the bag. A proponent of the *monstre froid* philosophy would not have been so easily persuaded. The proposition would have been tested, tried and proved true or false. Based on a calculation that Charles Haughey had a good possibility of winning, nothing should have been left to chance. The *dauphin* should have been sent to Dauphiné until the time was more opportune. But sentiment, rather than calculation, predominated, and Lynch listened to those who believed that Haughey's election as leader, being unthinkable, made him unelectable.

Lynch, Colley and Colley's supporters were up against a practitioner of the philosophy of the *monstre froid*. Haughey was ruthless in the manner by which he came to power. Prompted by his absolutist behaviour, his opponents would quote the phrase of Louis XIV '*L'état c'est moi.*' More appropriately, one might quote in that context the remark allegedly pronounced by a polished Medici Renaissance prince, or 'a devious double-tongued politician and an inveterate nepotist,'[8] upon receiving news of his election as Pope Leo X: 'Now that God has given us the Papacy, let us enjoy it.' Only in the late 1980s and 1990s were the Irish public made aware of how appropriate it was to apply that phrase to Haughey.

A national political leader sometimes has the good fortune to be succeeded by somebody whose career is so controversial and destructive that comparison always favours the earlier generation. Contrasting Lynch's leadership style with that of Charles Haughey, an *Examiner* editorial argued that Lynch's style was the antithesis 'of the corrosive system moulded' by his immediate successor. That inculcated 'a sense of political fear and fostered the patronage of wealthy businessmen.'[9]

Fintan O'Toole, appraising Lynch in contrast to his successor, Charles Haughey, concluded:

How bitterly Fianna Fáil must now regret the wider shift in its culture that happened when Charles Haughey replaced Jack Lynch. That change was not merely a matter of style or personality, though the contrast between Lynch's genuine courtesy and charm and Haughey's abrasive self-aggrandisement could hardly be greater. It was also about what does or does not remain at the end of a public life. In Lynch's case, what remains is the legacy of a State that stepped back from civil war. In Haughey's, it is a series of buried landmines and hidden time bombs. One man's life is an open book, the other's a heap of lapsed memories, missing files and shredded diaries.[10]

The *Irish Times* editorial on 21 October 1999 stated that

Jack Lynch led his party and this State, through some of their most difficult years and lost neither his dignity nor his decency in the struggle. He was naturally diffident, which sometimes led critics to suspect that he lacked confidence and an appetite for hard work. But it took a cool head and a core of steel to surmount the challenge he met.

It was no exaggeration to say, it added, that respect and affection for Jack Lynch

transcended party boundaries to a degree unique among political leaders in the history of the State. In the many tributes which have been paid, the voices of ordinary people who knew him as a friend have been most eloquent. He was a committed, far-seeing and practical patriot. And he was a warm, honourable and generous man.[11]

Lynch was all of the above and more besides. He was a gentleman, a man of integrity and a politician of the highest probity. When confronted with having to make the major political decisions likely to shape the future development of Ireland, he was guided by a *sense de l'état*. That *sense de l'état* was taken for granted during the early decades of the history of the state. Whichever party, or combination of parties, came to power, defence of the national interest was guaranteed. Lynch—together with his predecessors, William Cosgrave, John A. Costello, Éamon de Valera and Seán Lemass— worked in the national interest. Lynch was, as the editorial quoted above stated, a 'far-seeing and practical patriot.'

NOTES

Preface
1. Bruce Arnold, *Jack Lynch,* and T. Ryle Dwyer, *Nice Fellow.*

Chapter 1 (P. 1–25)
1. Despite her private misgivings about a life in politics for her husband, she told me, she could see that he was happy, and that was what finally swayed her. Conversation with Máirín Lynch in her home in Rathgar, Dublin, November 2000. I never sought to interview Mrs Lynch, but I did have a number of extended conversations with her between 2000 and 2002. We also spoke on the telephone and she sent me a number of letters.
2. In the early years of his political career, Dáil Éireann debates record his name as John Lynch. But as a sportsman, as a barrister on the Munster Circuit, on election literature, to his constituents and to Irish people generally he was known as Jack Lynch.
3. My colleague Dr Andrew McCarthy prepared the following short section on public health in Cork in the period from 1916 until the early 1930s. The city engineer, J. F. Delany, drew heavily on a report prepared in 1916 by Dr Denis Donovan, medical officer of health for Cork County Borough (city) and professor of hygiene in University College, Cork.
4. J. F. Delany, *Report of the City Engineer on the Housing Problem in Cork,* p. 9.
5. J. F. Delany, *Report of the City Engineer on the Housing Problem in Cork,* p. 11.
6. J. F. Delany, *Report of the City Engineer on the Housing Problem in Cork,* p. 14.
7. J. F. Delany, *Housing Report of City Engineer on the Local Government Circular of 23 December 1918,* p. 5.
8. For an excellent overview of developments relating to public health in this period see Ruth Barrington, *Health, Medicine and Politics in Ireland,* chap. 5, especially p. 90–6.
9. Ruth Barrington, *Health, Medicine and Politics in Ireland,* chap. 5, especially p. 104.
10. Cork Child Welfare League minute book, 12 February 1918 (Cork Archives Institute). Although the meeting was 'largely attended,' the mayor was not present; his wife deputised for him and thereafter played the active role in the league.
11. The Bishops of Cork and Ross served as patrons, the lady mayoress as president, with four vice-presidents, including Lady Windle, wife of the president of University College, Cork, Sir Bertram Windle. The honorary treasurers were the prominent citizen A. F. Sharman Crawford and a local banker, H. A. Pelly. By the end of the month 'nearly all the charitable and other institutions had appointed

representatives.' Cork Child Welfare League minute book, 19 February 1918 (Cork Archives Institute).

12. Cork Child Welfare League minute book, 28 March 1918 (Cork Archives Institute).

13. See Ruth Barrington, *Health, Medicine and Politics in Ireland,* chap. 5, especially p. 102–, for general details on the restructuring and background to the introduction of the County Medical Officer of Health system.

14. *Annual Report of the Medical Officer of Health, County Borough of Cork, 1930,* p. 34.

15. *Annual Report of the Medical Officer of Health, County Borough of Cork, 1930,* table 16, p. 31.

16. *Annual Report of the Medical Officer of Health, County Borough of Cork, 1930,* p. 4.

17. *Annual Report of the Medical Officer of Health, County Borough of Cork, 1930,* table II.

18. *Annual Report of the Medical Officer of Health, County Borough of Cork, 1930,* table 5.

19. *Annual Report of the Medical Officer of Health, County Borough of Cork, 1930,* table 10.

20. An analysis of the 1930 data suggests that the incidence of the disease fell most heavily in the 1–5 and 5–10 age groups, more so in the latter. The number of secondary cases (within the same household) was small and it was spread through missed cases or 'carriers', mainly through the schools. *Annual Report of the Medical Officer of Health, County Borough of Cork, 1930* (tables 10, 11, 13 and 14) shows that in 1930, 59 of the 64 deaths occurred in children under the age of ten.

21. *Annual Report of the Medical Officer of Health, County Borough of Cork, 1930,* p. 23 and tables 10 and 15.

22. *Annual Report of the Medical Officer of Health, County Borough of Cork, 1930,* p. 48–49. It might actually have been alarming had they known that this survey was undertaken only on a 'voluntary' basis through the good offices of Dr W. J. O'Donovan of the Bacteriology Department in University College, Cork.

23. Ruth Barrington, *Health, Medicine and Politics in Ireland,* p. 103.

24. Cork County Borough Council, Public Health Committee, minutes of meeting of 26 September 1916 (Cork Archives Institute).

25. Cork County Borough, School Medical Service Report, 1927, Hickey and Byrne, Cork, 1928, CP 121, p. 10–13 (Cork Archives Institute).

26. In the absence of a Lynch family archive, the reconstruction that follows is based largely on a range of printed sources and on conversations and interviews with Jack Lynch's wife, Máirín, his family, friends, relatives and contemporaries.

27. Interview with Finbarr Lynch, 23 August 2002.

28. See Tim Cramer, "'Neath Shandon Bells,' in Liam Ó Tuama, *Jack Lynch,* p. 1.

29. The details about the marriages of Rena and Eva Lynch are to be found in T. P. O'Mahony, *Jack Lynch,* p. 29.

30. Interview with Rena Lynch by Eileen Compagno, January 2002.

31. T. Ryle Dwyer, *Nice Fellow,* p. 13.

32. Jack Lynch, 'My life and times,' *Magill,* November 1979, p. 34.

33. Jack Lynch, 'My life and times,' *Magill*, November 1979, p. 34.

34. Jim Cronin, *Making Connections*, p. 323–.

35. Interview with Jim Crockett by Eileen Compagno, February 2002.

36. Interview with Finbarr Lynch, 23 August 2002.

37. Finbarr Lynch also remembers that his father was a good all-round sportsman. Austere and somewhat introspective, he did not talk much to his children about his sporting career, but they overheard some details when their father's close friend and best man, Dave Mahony, visited the family home. The latter was a meal merchant from Bantry, and the men got together a few times a year. On those occasions the austere and temperate Daniel might be tempted to take an extra drink. On such occasions Finbarr recalls his father saying that there were two long-jumpers from Bantry; the other was dead, leaving him the best long-jumper alive. He also said that he was a fine bowl-player. (Interview with Finbarr Lynch, 23 August 2002.)

38. T. Ryle Dwyer, *Nice Fellow*, p. 14.

39. There may be an element of confusion over where Daniel Lynch worked in Co. Cork. I have listed all the places named above. I place most reliance on the account given by Tim Cramer, ''Neath Shandon Bells,' in Liam Ó Tuama, *Jack Lynch*, p. 1.

40. Tim Cramer, ''Neath Shandon Bells,' in Liam Ó Tuama, *Jack Lynch*, p. 2.

41. Nora O'Donoghue, Jack Lynch's mother, was born on a farm in Glaunthaune. Her father was a publican who owned the Cork Arms in what is now MacCurtain Street. He was also a 'broker' at the Cork Corn Exchange.

42. Marriage certificate of Daniel Lynch and Norah O'Donoughue (this is the spelling on the certificate), no. 239, 30 September 1909. Daniel's profession is given as 'tailor'; Nora has no trade listed. Daniel's father, Timothy Lynch, was a farmer. Nora's father, James O'Donoghue, was a corn-broker. The presiding priest was Patrick Tracy and the witnesses were David O'Mahony and Katty McCarthy.

43. The house belonged to 'old' Mrs O'Donoghue, who lived with the young couple. She died in 1929. (Interview with Jim Crockett by Eileen Compagno, February 2002.)

44. Quoted by T. P. O'Mahony in *Jack Lynch*, p. 28.

45. Interview with Finbarr Lynch by Eileen Compagno, February 2002.

46. Quoted by T. P. O'Mahony in *Jack Lynch*, p. 31.

47. Interview with Finbarr Lynch, 23 August 2002.

48. This is quoted from T. P. O'Mahony, *Jack Lynch*, p. 27.

49. Finbarr Lynch stressed to me that his mother worked for Daniels' directly. She may have helped her husband at home with some work; but she was employed independently in her home by the firm where she had formerly worked full time. (Interview with Finbarr Lynch, 1 March 2003.)

50. Quoted by T. P. O'Mahony in *Jack Lynch*, p. 28.

51. It would be a mistake to read this as a sign of conspicuous wealth. Home help of that kind was not uncommon in those social circumstances. The family went on an annual holiday to the popular seaside resort of Myrtleville, some thirteen

miles from the city, where the extended family rented a large house; this also should not be read as a sign of conspicuous consumption.

52. Interview with Finbarr Lynch, 23 August 2002.
53. Interview with Jim Crockett by Eileen Compagno, February 2002.
54. Jack Lynch, 'My life and times,' *Magill*, November 1979, p. 34.
55. T. Ryle Dwyer, *Nice Fellow*, p. 14.
56. Nora went with a near neighbour and close friend, Hanna Riordan, whose husband, Tadhg, had a drapery shop in Patrick Street. They lived in Eason's Place. That family had a pony and trap, in which the Lynch family were often invited to go for a spin. Two of their sons became priests. (Interview with Finbarr Lynch, 23 August 2002.)
57. Fred had been in the British civil service and had been posted for a number of years to Malta. Jim Crockett, son of Elizabeth and Fred, recalled that Daniel was known to all the children as 'Pappy'. (Interview with Jim Crockett by Eileen Compagno, February 2002.)
58. Interview with Finbarr Lynch, 23 August 2002.
59. Interview with Finbarr Lynch, 23 August 2002.
60. I am grateful to Angela Devlin O'Donnell for the following information. Stephen Skiddy was born in Cork and worked most of his life in London as a vintner. He left money in trust in 1584 to be distributed at the rate of £24 annually for the upkeep of Catholic and Protestant poor in Cork, which was administered by the Vintners' Society in London. Skiddy's charity joined with Bretridge's Trust in 1696. Bretridge was a Cromwellian soldier who had established an almshouse in Shandon Street. A new almshouse was built for both charities in 1718 in Bob and Joan's Walk. The almshouse functioned as an old people's home. The charity had premises in Cornmarket Street and also held the ground of the first almshouse at North Gate. The residents received a small weekly allowance.
61. Interview with Finbarr Lynch by Eileen Compagno, February 2002.
62. The almshouse was acquired by the North Infirmary, and it was planned to have it demolished to build a residence for nurses. Up to the sale it had been the oldest inhabited public building in Cork and one of the oldest in the country. There was strong local opposition, led by Dr J. B. Kearney and other prominent citizens. Fortuitously, Jack Lynch was then Taoiseach. He took a keen personal interest in the preservation of the building, which was already due for demolition. The parliamentary secretary to the Minister for Finance, Jim Gibbons, was asked to investigate the matter. He held a number of hearings in Cork and reported back to the Taoiseach. The Office of Public Works placed a permanent preservation order on the building. The Cork Preservation Society bought the building and it was fully renovated to mark European Architectural Heritage Year, 1975. As Taoiseach, Jack Lynch formally opened the reconstructed Skiddy's almshouse on 22 October 1978, praising the combined organisations that had helped preserve the building and convert it into twelve flats. Press cuttings kindly supplied by Angela Devlin O'Donnell: *Cork Examiner*, 14 September 1967, 18 September 1967, 27 September 1967, 23 October 1967 and 23 October 1978; *Irish Times*, 19 September 1967 and 23 September 1967.

63. Interview with Finbarr Lynch by Eileen Compagno, February 2002.

64. Jack Lynch, 'My life and times,' *Magill*, November 1979, p. 32–3.

65. *Official Record: Dáil Éireann: Minutes of Proceedings of the First Parliament of the Republic of Ireland, 1919–21*, Dublin: n.d., p. 22–3.

66. In the 1920s both the Lynch parents may have voted for the Labour candidate, Gerry Hurley. That allegiance was mostly due to a personal family connection. The eldest Lynch son, Theo, used to teach in Blackpool with the TD's brother. (Interview with Finbarr Lynch, 23 August 2002.)

67. Finbarr provided an interesting pen picture of life during the War of Independence. In the summer of 1920 Theo, Charlie and Finbarr went to Bantry. Finbarr stayed with his grandmother and remembers being stranded there by the war. But as the school year was about to begin, Daniel Lynch took passage on a pig boat from Cork to Bantry. There was no other safe or sure way of getting there. Arriving in Bantry, he hired a taxi to take his three sons back to the city. It was an eventful return journey. British soldiers stopped them at Dunmanway; when they found that the road was impassable their driver simply took the direct route across the fields. They made it safely back to Cork. (Interview with Finbarr Lynch, 23 August 2002.)

68. T. Ryle Dwyer, *Nice Fellow*, p. 14.

69. Interview with Finbarr Lynch, 1 March 2003.

70. I am grateful to Eileen Compagno for providing me with this information, based on the tapes she listened to from the Northside Oral History Project, Cork. Mary Forde's address was 40 Orrery Road.

71. *Sunday Independent*, 12 March 1978.

72. T. Ryle Dwyer, *Nice Fellow*, p. 14.

73. Theo Lynch, 'My young brother, the Taoiseach, by teacher Theo Lynch,' *Sunday Independent*, 12 March 1978.

74. Interview with Rena Lynch by Eileen Compagno, January 2002.

75. Charlie Mulqueen, 'Lynch: A power in the land,' *Cork Examiner*, 26 April 1983.

76. Tim Horgan, 'Jack Lynch: Six-in-a-row senior all Irelander,' part 4 of 'Cork hurlers of yesteryear,' *Evening Echo*, 15 January 1975.

77. Denis Owens, a friend of Jack Lynch, explained that 'blockie' was derived from the 'block' on which the hats used to be shaped in the factory.

78. For details of Lynch's youth see the fine essay by his brother Finbarr, 'Scoring goal at the Butter Market,' in Liam Ó Tuama, *Jack Lynch*, p. 7–12.

79. *Irish Press*, 12 February 1932. The report was incorrect in one respect: tar barrels were not used on that or other occasions. The barrels used came from the Dowdall factory, which made margarine.

80. *Irish Press*, 12 February 1932.

81. *Irish Press*, 12 February 1932.

82. Interview with Rena Lynch by Eileen Compagno, January 2002.

83. Interview with Finbarr Lynch by Eileen Compagno, February 2002.

84. T. Ryle Dwyer, *Nice Fellow*, p. 15.

85. *Cork Examiner*, 6 October 1932.

86. Interview with Jim Crockett by Eileen Compagno, December 2001.

87. Interview with Rena Lynch by Eileen Compagno; T. Ryle Dwyer, *Nice Fellow*, p. 15.

88. T. P. O'Mahony, *Jack Lynch*, p. 32.

89. His brother Theo had won the same scholarship, coming third in his year in the competition. Finbarr had failed to win a scholarship, coming fourteenth, though this was a high achievement in itself.

90. T. Ryle Dwyer, *Nice Fellow*, p. 15.

91. Copy of relevant roll-book pages for A class, 1935/6, North Monastery. I am grateful to Mr Tony Duggan, Gaelcholáiste Mhuire (North Monastery), for providing me with access to this source and for giving me photographs and contacts.

92. The latter's family had a bacon shop in Shandon Street. He went to University College, Cork, and later got a job there in the administration. He became registrar, and died in 1952.

93. Interview with Finbarr Lynch, August 2002.

94. Founded in 1901, it was named after the Catholic Church of St Nicholas, which was where the Church of the Annunciation stands today. The early history of the club was marked by strong political divisions and by schism. Division between supporters of John Redmond and the followers of William O'Brien resulted in a split and the founding of a breakaway O'Brien's Football Club. There was a reconciling and a resolution of differences in 1912. A new clubhouse was opened in Wherland's Lane. (Liam Ó Tuama et al., *The Nicks of Time*, p. 9–13.)

95. M. B. Céitinn, 'Long na Laoch,' p. 115–116. Drawings of the two men by Seán Keating, presented by the late Gerald Goldberg, hang in the Glen Rovers committee room.

96. Founded in 1916, it had a clubhouse on Bird's Quay.

97. Tim Horgan, 'Jack Lynch: Six-in-a-row senior all Irelander,' part 4 of 'Cork hurlers of yesteryear,' *Evening Echo*, 15 January 1975.

98. Tim Horgan, 'Jack Lynch: Six-in-a-row senior all Irelander,' part 4 of 'Cork hurlers of yesteryear,' *Evening Echo*, 15 January 1975.

99. Charlie Mulqueen, 'Lynch: A power in the land,' *Cork Examiner*, 26 April 1983.

100. Charlie Mulqueen, 'Lynch: A power in the land,' *Cork Examiner*, 26 April 1983.

101. Jack Lynch, 'Reminiscences,' p. 110.

102. See Liam Ó Tuama et al., *The Spirit of the Glen*; also Liam Ó Tuama et al., *The Nicks of Time*. See also Jim Cronin, *Making Connections*. I am grateful to Mr Denis Owens for lending me two of those precious books and for giving me an interview and a tour of Glen Rovers' clubhouse and grounds.

103. Tim Horgan, 'Jack Lynch: Six-in-a-row senior all Irelander,' part 4 of 'Cork hurlers of yesteryear,' *Evening Echo*, 15 January 1975.

104. It is quite a lengthy exercise to review Jack Lynch's sporting achievements in the years before he left school; Liam Ó Tuama has successfully carried out that task, and his findings are as follows. In 1929 he won the North Parish under-16 football championship. The following year he won the North Parish under-16 championship, city division, and a minor football championship. In 1931 he was again on the winning team for the North Parish under-16 championship. In 1932

he was on the Cork county minor football championship team. In 1933 he was on both the Cork football and hurling county minor championship teams. In 1934 he was on the Cork county senior hurling championship team, was captain of the Cork county minor hurling championship team, and was also on the Harty Cup colleges senior hurling championship team. In 1935 he was on the Cork county senior hurling championship team, the Harty Cup colleges senior hurling championship team, the Munster colleges senior football team, the inter-provincial colleges senior hurling championship team, the city division minor hurling championship team (as captain) and the city division minor football championship team. In his Leaving Certificate year, 1936, he was on the Cork county senior team, the senior hurling championship team, the Harty Cup colleges senior hurling championship team (as captain), the Munster colleges senior football championship team and the inter-provincial colleges senior hurling championship team (as captain). (Jack Lynch, 'Reminiscences,' in Liam Ó Tuama et al., *The Spirit of the Glen*, p. 110.) Lynch used to suffer from cramps in his early playing career. He was recommended a cure: rubbing his own urine into his legs. (Interview with Denis Owens, July 2005.)

105. Charlie Mulqueen, 'Lynch: A power in the land,' *Cork Examiner*, 26 April 1983.

106. The government had set that body up, under the Milk (Regulation of Supply and Price) Act (1936), following a strike.

107. Jack Lynch, 'My life and times,' *Magill*, November 1979, p. 35–6.

108. Jimmy Donoghue was also in the flat. They shared with four others who were also interested in hurling and football: Donie Riordan (who played hurling for Dublin), Paddy Kennedy (who also played hurling for Dublin), Maurice Prenderville (who played minor for Cork) and Jim Young (who starred with Jack Lynch). (Interview with Finbarr Lynch, 23 August 2002.)

109. Interview with Finbarr Lynch by Eileen Compagno, February 2002.

110. Jack Lynch worked with Alice Breen, whose sister was married to Dermot Twohig, a member of the Civil Service Commission. The latter knew Jack Lynch well and knew also about his desire to get a transfer to Cork. (Interview with Finbarr Lynch, 23 August 2002.)

111. Jack Lynch, 'My life and times,' *Magill*, November 1979, p. 36–7.

112. The details of Lynch's sporting career are taken from the outstanding book by Liam Ó Tuama, *Jack Lynch: Where He Sported and Played*. For the quotation about Lynch and the 1942 final see p. 86; for the quotation on his childhood hero, p. 193–8.

113. *Cork Examiner*, 28 November 1938. I am grateful to David Hennessy for finding this report for me.

114. Mr Edward O'Driscoll, solicitor, Bandon, is my source for this version of events. He was present at the match and witnessed the events. Other versions of the story have Jack Lynch diving headlong into the swollen river. Mr O'Driscoll assured me that he simply jumped in and waded out to catch the ball as it passed. (Meeting with Edward O'Driscoll, Bantry, November 2002.)

115. Liam Ó Tuama, *Jack Lynch*, p. 202.

116. Liam Ó Tuama, *Jack Lynch*, p. 202.

117. Interview with Jack Lynch by Mick Dunne, 27 September 1982, reproduced by Liam Ó Tuama, *Jack Lynch*, p. 173–4.

118. Interview with Con Murphy, 9 November 2002.

119. The night before the 1945 football all-Ireland final against Cavan, Lynch stayed in his digs in Terenure, Dublin. He told Jim Hurley, one of the selectors, that he would catch the number 16 bus to Croke Park; but he found a large queue at Kenilworth Square, and three buses passed full with crowds going to the game. Breaking the queue, he was about to be put off by the conductor when he said, 'Look, I'm playing in the all-Ireland today.' The conductor replied: 'Oh, that's about the best one I ever heard! Stay on.' He got to the dressing-room at the last minute and the door was opened by Jim Hurley. 'Hello, Jack. You were great to come,' was the greeting. (Interview with Jack Lynch by Mick Dunne, 27 September 1982, reproduced by Liam Ó Tuama in *Jack Lynch*, p. 183–4.)

120. Brendan Fullam, *Captains of the Ash*, p. 117–18.

121. Liam Ó Tuama, *Jack Lynch*, p. 86.

122. Dick Walsh, 'An appreciation of Jack Lynch,' *Irish Times*, 21 October 1999.

123. Tim Horgan, 'Jack Lynch: Six-in-a-row senior all Irelander,' part 4 of 'Cork hurlers of yesteryear,' *Evening Echo*, 15 January 1975.

124. David Marcus recalled that he had seen him working as the judge's clerk in the District Court when he had gone there to observe and get practical experience of the law. He also reminisced that 'even if I didn't recognise him by sight, I should have known him from his picture in the newspapers—for he was already an established national hero, famous for his prowess both in hurling and Gaelic football.' Those games had never held the slightest interest for Marcus; nevertheless Lynch and Marcus from the beginning 'got on excellently.'

125. David Marcus, *Oughtobiography*, p. 13–.

126. David Marcus to Dermot Keogh, 22 February 2002.

127. David Marcus, *Oughtobiography*, p. 13–.

128. David Marcus, *Oughtobiography*, p. 13–.

129. Marcus went to London and then to a career in literary journalism in the *Irish Press*, Lynch to a life in national politics. Although they did not maintain close contact, Marcus records that at a critical juncture in 1970 Lynch, who was then Taoiseach, phoned him out of the blue to ask him to write for him one of the most important political speeches of his political career. (David Marcus, *Oughtobiography*, p. 213–5.)

130. Interview with Máirín Lynch by Ida Grehan, *Irish Times*, 31 January 1972.

131. She was also accepted for the Department of External Affairs but chose the former, for reasons that will be explained later. (Conversation with Máirín Lynch.)

132. Bruce Arnold, *Jack Lynch*, p. 19. Their bicycles and cases did not arrive with them on the train and they were without luggage for a day. (Conversation with Máirín Lynch, 2001.)

133. Interview with Finbarr Lynch, 23 August 2002.

134. Discussion with Máirín Lynch, December 2000.

135. Bruce Arnold, *Jack Lynch*, p. 21. The other information concerning this holiday was kindly provided by Máirín Lynch.

136. Conversation with Máirín Lynch, December 2000. I am grateful to Dr Niall Keogh for the following information. There is only one Arthur O'Connor recorded in the list of Irish war dead. He is listed as a captain (temporary promotion) in the Norfolk Regiment. He was killed in action on 27 July 1916, during the attack on Thiepval, which began on 1 July 1916 at the beginning of the Battle of the Somme, some three weeks before Máirín was born. It is not certain that this is a reference to Máirín's father.

137. The Irish Industrial Development Association was founded in 1905 to further the interests of Irish manufacture. Within a few years about seven hundred firms had been issued with a licence permitting them to use the IIDA 'Déanta in Éirinn' trade mark. See E. J. Riordan, *Modern Irish Trade and Industry*.

138. The National Agricultural and Industrial Development Association was merged with the Federation of Irish Industries in February 1938 and changed its name to the Federation of Irish Manufacturers. See Mary E. Daly, *Industrial Development and Irish National Identity*, p. 22, 23, 30, 43, 53, 54, 56 and 129–30.

139. Interview with Máirín Lynch by Ida Grehan, *Irish Times*, 31 January 1972.

140. Conversation with Máirín Lynch, December 2000.

141. Mary MacGrois, 'I'm not power behind the throne,' *Irish Independent*, 23 February 1973.

142. Muckross Park convent kindly supplied me with this information. (Unsigned and undated note, March 2002.)

143. Conversations with Máirín Lynch, December 2000 and January 2001.

144. Muckross Park convent kindly supplied me with this information. (Unsigned and undated note, March 2002.)

145. Letter to the author, April 2002.

146. Interview with Gordon Lambert, *Sunday Press*, 25 November 1979. 'My personal friendship with the Lynches started with Máirín's mother Mrs Margaret O'Connor who spear-headed the Buy Irish promotion (the NAIDA) during the '50s and 60s and who later influenced me to become its president. Mrs O'Connor lived with them until she had to go to hospital—Jack was then Minister for Industry and Commerce.' Lambert, son of a vet, Bob Lambert (who was captain of the Irish cricket team and made a hundred centuries), was a graduate of Trinity College, Dublin, a chartered accountant and an inter-provincial badminton player. Referring to Jack Lynch, he said: 'As for the Taoiseach I am a contemporary of his and I am convinced that his leadership has been grossly underestimated. People are inclined to forget how he has coped with the various crises that have arisen through the years. I have been observing him for over 29 years now and admire his aims and principles.'

147. Orla McKeown and Hilary McDonagh, *The Lilac Years*, p. 71.

148. This cup was named after the president of the Irish Ladies' Hockey Association between 1905 and 1914. It was usually played at Easter. I am grateful to Dr Bernadette Whelan, University of Limerick, and Joan Morgan, executive secretary of the Irish Hockey Association, for this information.

149. My mother, Maureen O'Sullivan, worked in the Department of Justice from 1932 until 1944. She once told me that Lynch was very polite and courteous. Berry, she said, used to try to impress the female members of the staff by reading from the Bible in order to demonstrate that many Biblical events were scientifically impossible.

150. When growing up on the south side of Dublin, Máirín recalls that she had a number of close friends who were Protestants, among them Gerty Greig. J. B. Aiken was also a close friend of the family; he was 'a very wonderful person.' On her birthday and other special occasions she recalls that he would give her 3 shillings and 6 pence to enable her to buy the classics. She attended musical evenings frequently in the Aiken home in Glasnevin, Dublin. He 'educated my mind,' she said. He also taught her to drive.

151. Liam Ó Tuama, *Jack Lynch*, p. 95.

152. Jack Lynch to Jim Hurley, 5 July 1945. (Jim Hurley papers, in family possession, Cork.)

153. Minute in Hurley's hand. Jack Lynch to Jim Hurley, 7 July 1945. (Jim Hurley papers, in family possession, Cork.)

154. Liam Ó Tuama, *Jack Lynch*, p. 95.

155. Jack Lynch, 'My life and times,' *Magill*, November 1979, p. 36.

156. Con Murphy, from Innishannon, came to the North Monastery in 1937; during the war years he used to cycle the thirty-mile round trip daily to school. He first met Jack Lynch when the latter came to the school to present medals after the North Monastery team had won the Harty Cup. (There is an undated photograph of the occasion in *Cork GAA: A History*, p. 284.) His recollection was that it was the spring of 1939. (Interview with Con Murphy, 9 November 2002.)

157. Interview with Con Murphy, 9 November 2002.

158. In a handwritten letter, dated 20 September 1951, he politely but firmly declined. He admitted that the offer of putting on the Glen jersey and giving 'an hour of the best that's in me' tempted him 'not a little'; but the best he could do would not justify his place on any team, 'not to mention the Glen.' He confessed that 'I am almost 16 stone weight' and 'literally have not caught a hurley since last year's final just 12 months ago.' He would not 'have a chance to catch one or even run one round of a field between then and Sunday.' He wrote that he knew his limitations 'only too well' and 'it would be pure defeatism' to ask anyone like him to come back at that stage, particularly in a club that had won the minor and junior championships the previous year. 'No Seán,' he wrote, 'I am not looking for bouquets.' On principle he felt it would be most unfair to 'the new lads coming on if they, having played in this or that tournament or league match all the year, were dropped now for the semi-final to give way to a "has been".' That would be to 'throw our hats at our life-long policy of fostering our minors.' While he appreciated the 'high compliment' of being asked to play, he declined. (Facsimile of letter reproduced by Liam Ó Tuama in *Jack Lynch*, p. 37.)

159. Interview with Jack Lynch by Mick Dunne, RTE, 27 September 1982; transcript reprinted by Liam Ó Tuama in *Jack Lynch*, p. 188.

160. Liam Ó Tuama, *Jack Lynch*, p. 79.
161. Con Murphy recalled that on that occasion Máirín poured out whiskey for the group, giving Jack a small amount of his favourite Paddy. Lifting the glass, he said in an aside to Con Murphy, 'Who poured this out?' knowing that it had been Máirín. 'Oh, Jesus, fill it up,' he said to his old team-mate. He was then blind and in declining health.
162. David Hannigan, *Giants of Cork Sport*.
163. Interview with Con Murphy, 9 November 2002.   See also Maurice Gubbins, 'Lynch donates all Ireland medals to GAA museum,' *Cork Examiner,* 3 February 1996.

Chapter 2 (P. 26–48)

1. As a barrister, as a TD, as a minister and later as Taoiseach he always tried to get home for his lunch. That was particularly so when they lived at 21 Garville Avenue, Rathgar. From his earliest years in politics Máirín made a practice of not initiating a discussion with him on 'matters of state.' What she knew about politics was usually learnt from the daily papers, she said candidly. However, there were times when he confided in her, and that was certainly done at the most critical junctures during his long career in public life.
2. A profile written by a US embassy source in Dublin as a briefing note for an official visit to the United States in 1979 stated: 'According to the media, Mrs. Lynch is an energetic, well-organised and unassuming woman whose ability as a conversationalist has made her an asset to her husband's political career.' A good conversationalist, Máirín Lynch mixed with apparent effortlessness at formal receptions and was a lively dinner guest, with an ability to put people at their ease. When Lynch held ministerial rank she was popular among senior civil servants. They found that she represented her husband with discretion and professionalism.
3. Conversation with Máirín Lynch, November 2002.
4. Information kindly supplied by Stephanie Walsh, 8 November 2006.
5. I am grateful to Stephanie Walsh for this information.
6. Conversation with Máirín Lynch, November 2002.
7. 'Profile of Máirín Lynch, Ireland, prepared on occasion of visit by Taoiseach Jack Lynch to the United States, Autumn 1979' (John J. Burns Library, Boston College, Boston, Kirk O'Donnell Files, Tip O'Neill Papers, box 22, folder 'Ireland—Embassy of Ireland file, 1975,' 79, 80.
8. Interview with Rena Lynch by Eileen Compagno, February 2002.
9. The Delaney brothers were from Dublin Hill, Cork, and had been killed during the Civil War.
10. Jack Lynch, 'My life and times,' *Magill,* November 1979, p. 37.
11. T. Ryle Dwyer, *Nice Fellow,* p. 25–6.
12. 'Minister attacks Fine Gael policy,' *Cork Examiner,* 12 June 1946. The Minister for Finance, Frank Aiken, said: 'I did not come to Cork to tell you either that we have made the Twenty Six counties a heaven on earth, or that we are going to make them so, if you elect our candidate. We are going to pursue in the future our policy of steady progress towards a higher standard of life for our people.'

13. *Cork Examiner*, 12 June 1946.

14. Michael O'Driscoll, a barrister, stood for Fine Gael in the by-election. Lynch 'knew him well as I worked with him.' The two remaining candidates were the veteran republican Tom Barry and Michael O'Riordan of the Communist Party of Ireland. Lynch had gone to school with the latter. The surprise of the election was that O'Riordan attracted more votes than Barry: 3,184 to 2,574.

15. T. Ryle Dwyer (*Nice Fellow*, p. 27) writes that the invitation to stand for Clann na Poblachta came from a friend, a butcher named Paddy Murphy. Lynch told me he had been canvassed to stand for Clann na Poblachta while he was in the Teachers' Club in Dublin after a match. (Interview with Jack Lynch.) See Dermot Keogh, 'Jack Lynch' in Seán Dunne (ed.), *A Cork Anthology*, p. 336.

16. Interview with Finbarr Lynch, Cóbh, 2002.

17. Interview with Con Murphy, 9 November 2002.

18. Interview with Judge Tony Murphy, Cork, 24 October 2002.

19. Interview with Judge Tony Murphy, Cork, 24 October 2002.

20. Interview with Con Murphy, 9 November 2002.

21. My source is Commandant Dan Harvey (7 July 2006), who got the information from his mother.

22. See David McCullagh, *A Makeshift Majority*, p. 26.

23. *Evening Echo*, 20 January 1948.

24. *Cork Examiner*, 9 January 1948.

25. *Cork Examiner*, 9 January 1948.

26. *Evening Echo*, 20 January 1948.

27. Jack Lynch, 'My life and times,' *Magill*, November 1979, p. 37–8.

28. *Cork Examiner*, 9 January 1948.

29. *Cork Examiner*, 12 January 1948.

30. Interview with Máirín Lynch, *Irish Times*, 31 January 1972.

31. This is reflected in the tapes of reminiscences from the area. One north-side resident said that Jack Lynch was 'an ordinary fellow at the end of it all.' Another said that he had it all: looks, athletic prowess and intelligence. Yet another said: 'He respected his people—he never forgot his people.' I am grateful to Eileen Compagno for listening to the tapes of the Northside Project and providing me with these quotations.

32. Conversation with Dr Patrick Hillery, February 2006. Lynch had a good memory for people and for names and family connections. But as he was known to thousands of people, how could he be expected to remember all the individual names? When stuck he would usually wait until the person said to him: 'Do you not remember? I'm Matt Murphy.' He would then reply: 'Yes, of course, I knew that you were one of the Murphys, but which one I wasn't sure.' (Conversation with Máirín Lynch.)

33. *Cork Examiner*, 10 January 1948.

34. He added: 'The Government appears to pooh-pooh our anxiety concerning the annual emigration of 20,000 women and girls and the invasion of thousands of foreigners who, with their paper money, are buying up Irish homes and lands.'

O'Rahilly also attacked Fianna Fáil for its hostility to coalition government. He quoted the Tánaiste, Seán MacEntee, as saying that 'the objective of the forces hostile to our Christian democracy is the destruction of Fianna Fáil.' O'Rahilly was withering in his criticism of that statement and of the charge of communism against members of the opposition. Quoting Thomas Aquinas (in Latin), he argued that it was not a question of Manchesterism or communism, Adam Smith or Karl Marx, and he warned 'from out of the past a hostile critic might produce quotations to prove Mr de Valera an anarchist.' Those in glasshouses should not throw stones, he said. (*Cork Examiner,* 12 January 1948.)

35. *Cork Examiner,* 19 January 1848.
36. *Cork Examiner,* 21 January 1948.
37. *Evening Echo,* 4 February 1948.
38. *Cork Examiner,* 6 February 1948.
39. This table is taken from Brian M. Walker (ed.), *Parliamentary Election Results in Ireland.*
40. *Cork Examiner,* 7 February 1948.
41. *Cork Examiner,* 7 February 1948.
42. See David McCullagh, *A Makeshift Majority,* p. 7–71. See also Eithne MacDermott, *Clann na Poblachta,* p. 48–.
43. Ian McCabe, *A Diplomatic History of Ireland,* p. 26.
44. Patrick J. Lindsay, *Memories,* p. 152.
45. Jack Lynch, 'My life and times,' *Magill,* November 1979, p. 38.
46. *Parliamentary Debates: Dáil Éireann: Official Report,* vol. 110, col. 13 (May 1948).
47. *Parliamentary Debates: Dáil Éireann: Official Report,* vol. 113, col. 513–16, 25 November 1948.
48. *Parliamentary Debates: Dáil Éireann: Official Report,* vol. 113, col. 513–16, 25 November 1948.
49. *Parliamentary Debates: Dáil Éireann: Official Report,* vol. 113, col. 513–16, 25 November 1948.
50. *Parliamentary Debates: Dáil Éireann: Official Report,* vol. 113, col. 513–16, 25 November 1948.
51. *Parliamentary Debates: Dáil Éireann: Official Report,* vol. 119, col. 382–94, 21 February 1950.
52. *Parliamentary Debates: Dáil Éireann: Official Report,* vol. 119, col. 393, 21 February 1950.
53. *Parliamentary Debates: Dáil Éireann: Official Report,* vol. 120, col. 1047–58, 25 April 1950.
54. *Parliamentary Debates: Dáil Éireann: Official Report,* vol. 119, col. 1885–6, 15 March 1950.
55. On 7 April 1949 Lynch asked the Minister for Education whether he had received representations regarding the proposed closure of the national school at Rengaroga Island, Baltimore, Co. Cork. The minister, Richard Mulcahy, replied that the attendance had fallen to seven in 1947 and that it would be closed unless the enrolment rose to ten. The school was closed in June. A report was being

written on the situation. Lynch asked the minister on 30 November 1949 to bear in mind that the population of school-going children in the island was growing and asked him also if he would ask the investigator who would examine the situation to bear it in mind also.

56. *Parliamentary Debates: Dáil Éireann: Official Report,* vol. 118, col. 544, 3 November 1949.
57. *Parliamentary Debates: Dáil Éireann: Official Report,* vol. 118, col. 2241–62.
58. *Parliamentary Debates: Dáil Éireann: Official Report,* vol. 122, col. 1154–, 7 July 1950.
59. *Parliamentary Debates: Dáil Éireann: Official Report,* vol. 122, col. 1158, 7 July 1950.
60. *Parliamentary Debates: Dáil Éireann: Official Report,* vol. 122, col. 1150, 7 July 1950.
61. *Parliamentary Debates: Dáil Éireann: Official Report,* vol. 155, 11 May 1949.
62. Later in 1949 Lynch wanted to know the total increase in a twelve-month period, or such shorter period for which figures were available, in contributions under the Unemployment Insurance, National Health Insurance and Widows' and Orphans' Pensions Acts since the new rates imposed by the Social Welfare Act (1948) became operative. These were recurring preoccupations.
63. In a short exchange in the Dáil in 1950 Lynch rejected the three Government reasons for not building an airport at Farmer's Cross: lack of meteorological findings, the existence of an air agreement between Ireland and Great Britain dating from 1946 and the opposition of Aer Lingus itself. He said: 'We all learned in our school days of the British attitude towards military treaties. Thomas Davis referred to one as a treaty which was broken ere the ink with which it was signed was dry.' He was not advocating a disregard for international treaties, he said, but he wanted that one renegotiated and further stressed the economic, transport, tourist and defence advantages. He argued that Cork was the second industrial centre after Dublin. He also said it would save businessmen time in travel. (*Parliamentary Debates: Dáil Éireann: Official Report,* vol. 121, col. 839.)
64. *Parliamentary Debates: Dáil Éireann: Official Report,* 11 May 1949.
65. *Parliamentary Debates: Dáil Éireann: Official Report,* vol. 121, col. 1641, 14 June 1950.
66. *Parliamentary Debates: Dáil Éireann: Official Report,* vol. 119, col. 2247, 22 March 1950.
67. *Parliamentary Debates: Dáil Éireann: Official Report,* vol. 119, col. 1628–9, 9 March 1950.
68. *Cork Examiner,* 26 May 1951.
69. *Evening Echo,* 14 May 1951.
70. *Evening Echo,* 15 May 1951.
71. *Evening Echo,* 29 May 1951.
72. *Evening Echo,* 30 May 1951.
73. *Evening Echo,* 26 May 1951.
74. *Cork Examiner,* 28 May 1951.
75. Interview with Finbarr Lynch, August 2002.
76. *Cork Examiner,* 29 May 1951.

77. *Cork Examiner,* 29 May 1951.
78. *Cork Examiner,* 29 May 1951.
79. *Cork Examiner,* 29 May 1951.
80. *Cork Examiner,* 30 May 1951.
81. *Cork Examiner,* 30 May 1951.
82. *Cork Examiner,* 30 May 1951.
83. *Cork Examiner,* 31 May 1951.
84. *Cork Examiner,* 2 June 1951.
85. This table is taken from Brian M. Walker (ed.), *Parliamentary Election Results in Ireland.*
86. Jack Lynch, 'My life and times,' *Magill,* November 1979, p. 38.
87. Jack Lynch, 'My life and times,' *Magill,* November 1979, p. 38.
88. Jack Lynch, 'My life and times,' *Magill,* November 1979, p. 38.
89. Jack Lynch, 'My life and times,' *Magill,* November 1979, p. 38.
90. Cork Archives Institute, CAI/C/C/A 19, 19 July 1951. Sometimes Lynch made interventions of a legal and technical nature, as may be seen in the following quotation from the minutes of the city council: 'Following report of the meeting of the committee of whole council which was held the previous Tuesday May 15, 1951 and circulated—Alderman Lynch referred to cases recently before the high court and circuit regarding liability of two permanent employees of the Corporation to make contribution under the Local Government (Superannuation) Act 1948. The Judge had held that the two employees were entitled to claim the benefit of exemption under Sec. 63 (5) of the Act. While the two men concerned in the case were now exempted from payment of contributions, contributions were still being deducted from the remainder of the permanent employees. He thought that, as the cases were in the nature of test cases and as the Corporation had not exercised its right to have the matter considered by the Supreme Court, the other permanent employees should have been given the benefit of the Judge's decision. It would appear, and he understood that similar claims were to be made by other employees. The manager said that the responsibility was his and that he was bound to follow the legal opinion, which he had obtained. Councillor O'Brien moved that the corporation express its deep dissatisfaction of the action taken by the manager.' Cork Archives Institute, CAI/CP/C/A 18, 22 May 1951; CP/C/A 19, July 1951 to 23 August 1955.
91. Cork Archives Institute, CAI/CP/C/A 19.
92. *Parliamentary Debates: Dáil Éireann: Official Report,* vol. 133, 11 July 1952, Committee on Finance—Vote 50—Industry and Commerce.
93. *Parliamentary Debates: Dáil Éireann: Official Report,* vol. 133, 11 July 1952. McGilligan continued: 'Deputy Jack Lynch, the Parliamentary Secretary, is a man now stuck in an office with £3,000 worth of expense between himself and his staff and with no capacity to do anything . . .This is the time for the seasonal descent on the West again and maybe the Parliamentary Secretary is going to lead a couple of more Parliamentary Secretaries down there in order to do further surveys. So far as I remember, there were 13 reports on the congested districts, as between

reports by the old Congested Districts Board, the Report of the Gaeltacht Commission and so on. In all, there were 13 reports, and Parliamentary Secretary Lynch had to go on another to get up to date. I should like to know what he has in his office, apart from furniture and possibly these 13 old reports. The first time he has any record of work done will he come and let us have a full-dress debate on his achievement?'

94. *Evening Echo*, 27 April 1954.
95. *Cork Examiner*, 10 May 1954.
96. *Cork Examiner*, 11 May 1954.
97. This table is taken from Brian M. Walker (ed.), *Parliamentary Election Results in Ireland*.
98. Interview with Judge Tony Murphy, 24 October 2002.
99. Interview with Judge Tony Murphy, 24 October 2002.
100. Interview with Judge Tony Murphy, 24 October 2002.
101. Interview with Judge Tony Murphy, 24 October 2002. Edward O'Driscoll, a Bantry solicitor, recalled to me that he had briefed Jack Lynch in a case in which a client was being sued for 15 shillings over rabbit-snaring.
102. Lynch always remembered fondly his time at the bar in Cork. In a speech to a law dinner in Cork he related one experience as a young defence counsel. His client received a jail sentence for theft. Lynch, feeling sorry for him, visited him in the holding cells, only to be told in no uncertain terms that he would not be paid. 'At that point I realised that crime did not pay.' (Interview with Jack Phelan, solicitor, Cork.) Judge Murphy recalls that, while he was Taoiseach, Lynch on one occasion visited the Cork Courthouse. He went into the barristers' room and, sweeping up a pile of briefs into his arms, said jokingly they could all go home as he would handle all the cases. (Interview with Judge Tony Murphy, 24 October 2002.)
103. Interview with Judge Tony Murphy, 24 October 2002.
104. 'Message from Mr. Jack Lynch, Former Taoiseach and Club President in 1970.' This text was kindly found for me by Mr Feidhlim Ó Súilleabháin, president of Muskerry Golf Club, in 2003.
105. Reply dated January 24, 1956. See Cork Archives Institute, CAI/C/CP/A 20.
106. Cork Archives Institute, CAI/C/CP/A.
107. Cork Archives Institute, CAI/C/CP/A20.

Chapter 3 (P. 49–68)

1. Patrick J. Lindsay, *Memories*, p. 195.
2. This table is taken from Brian M. Walker (ed.), *Parliamentary Election Results in Ireland*.
3. Jack Lynch, 'My life and times,' *Magill*, November 1979, p. 40.
4. Interview with Judge Tony Murphy, 24 October 2002. Jack Lynch was made Minister for Industry and Commerce in 1959. On many subsequent occasions Judge Murphy reminded Lynch of those prophetic remarks.
5. Jack Lynch, 'My life and times,' *Magill*, November 1979, p. 40.

6. Cork Archives Institute, CAI/C/CP/A20.
7. At the time of writing (summer 2007) the Department of Education and Science had yet to transfer the substantial body of its files to the National Archives.
8. Patrick J. Lindsay, *Memories,* p. 162.
9. Seán O'Connor, *A Troubled Sky,* p. 16.
10. Seán O'Connor, *A Troubled Sky,* p. 17.
11. Seán O'Connor, *A Troubled Sky,* p. 37–8.
12. Seán O'Connor, *A Troubled Sky,* p. 1.
13. Jack Lynch, 'My life and times,' *Magill,* November 1979, p. 40.
14. 'He was good enough to recommend me to his successor, Dr Patrick Hillery, with whom I also had a very happy relationship.' Jim Dukes to Dermot Keogh, autumn 2002.
15. Jim Dukes to Dermot Keogh, autumn 2002.
16. Jim Dukes to Dermot Keogh, autumn 2002.
17. O'Connor makes specific reference to three sources of criticism: Father Seán Ó Catháin, 'Secondary education in Ireland: A new plan,' *Studies,* vol. 46, p. 60–76, and by the same author, *Secondary Education in Ireland* (Dublin: Talbot Press, 1958); Prof. J. J. O'Meara, *Reform in Education* (Dublin: Mount Salus Press, 1958); and Prof. E. F. O'Doherty, 'Bilingual education: Educational aspects,' *Advancement of Science,* 56, 1958, p. 282–290. All cited by Seán O'Connor in *A Troubled Sky,* p. 38.
18. Seán O'Connor, *A Troubled Sky,* p. 16–17.
19. Seán O'Connor, *A Troubled Sky,* p. 18–19.
20. Seán O'Connor, *A Troubled Sky,* p. 38.
21. The figures quoted had been arrived at by dividing the state expenditure in each case, including expenditure on administration, inspection, capital projects etc., by the number of pupils enrolled.
22. Seán O'Connor, *A Troubled Sky,* p. 34.
23. *Parliamentary Debates: Dáil Éireann: Official Report,* vol. 165, 19 February 1958.
24. *Parliamentary Debates: Dáil Éireann: Official Report,* vol. 165, 19 February 1958.
25. *Parliamentary Debates: Dáil Éireann: Official Report,* vol. 165, 19 February 1958.
26. On 25 March 1958 Browne asked Lynch to state (1) the total number of (*a*) lay teachers and (*b*) teachers in religion teaching in the national schools and (2) the total number of principals of schools who were (*a*) lay and (*b*) members of religious orders. The reply was as follows: 'In the school-year ended 30th June, 1957, there were 10,506 lay teachers and 2,891 teachers in religion on the normal staffs of national schools; 4,279 of the lay persons and 576 religious were principal teachers in the schools.' (*Parliamentary Debates: Dáil Éireann: Official Report,* vol. 166, 25 March 1958.)
27. *Parliamentary Debates: Dáil Éireann: Official Report,* vol. 166, 20 March 1958.
28. 'Report of Committee to examine the existing educational system, primary, secondary, technical, vocational and the provision available for university education and to make recommendations as to what changes and reforms, if any, are necessary in order to raise the standard of education generally and to provide

greater educational facilities for our people.' See memorandum, Department of the Taoiseach (National Archives, file S12891).

29. Seán Farren, *The Politics of Irish Education*, p. 228–. The council had been set up by the Minister for Education, Richard Mulcahy, during the Inter-Party Government, 1948–51. Dr Farren argues that the report concentrated on curriculum development and was very limited in scope. It was based, he writes, on 'a very traditional Christian-Catholic concept of childhood,' and he added: 'The report argued that a child was born in a state of sin and must, therefore, be trained in the "right" way.'

30. Seán O'Connor, *A Troubled Sky*, p. 37.

31. The 1960 report, for example, set out the aims and objectives of secondary schools as follows: 'Our schools are the heirs of a great tradition and it is universally recognised that their purpose is, in short, to prepare pupils to be God-fearing and responsible citizens. The school itself is seen as a social instrument, of its very nature subsidiary and complementary to the family and the Church. In our educational theory a fundamental position is taken up on the spiritual nature and destiny of man. There is no controversy as to the sacredness, responsibility and ultimate worth of the individual person. The purpose of school education, then, is the organised development and equipment of all the powers of the individual persona—religious, moral, intellectual, physical—so that, by making the fullest use of his talents, he may responsibly discharge his duties to God and to his fellow man in society.' (*Report of the Council of Education*, Dublin: Department of Education, 1960, p. 88.)

32. Secretary of the Department of Education, S. Ó Néill, to Secretary to the Catholic Hierarchy, Thomas O'Doherty of Galway, 24 March 1932 (National Archives, file D/T S623C).

33. Department of Education memorandum, 28 April 1958 (National Archives, file D/T S623C).

34. Secretary of the Department of Education, S. Ó Néill, to Secretary to the Catholic Hierarchy, Thomas O'Doherty of Galway, 24 March 1932 (National Archives, file D/T S623C).

35. Secretary of the Department of Education, S. Ó Néill, to Secretary to the Catholic Hierarchy, Thomas O'Doherty of Galway, 24 March 1932 (National Archives, file D/T S623C).

36. Secretary of the Department of Education, S. Ó Néill, to Secretary to the Catholic Hierarchy, Thomas O'Doherty of Galway, 24 March 1932 (National Archives, file D/T S623C).

37. Secretary of the Department of Education, S. Ó Néill, to Secretary to the Catholic Hierarchy, Thomas O'Doherty of Galway, 24 March 1932 (National Archives, file D/T S623C).

38. Department of Finance Memorandum for Government on 'Retirement of women teachers on marriage,' 19 February 1953 (National Archives, file D/T S6369).

39. Department of Education Memorandum to Government, 28 April 1958 (National Archives, file D/T S623/C).

40. Department of Education Memorandum for the Government, 13 February 1953, Department of Taoiseach (National Archives, file S6369A).

41. Department of Education Memorandum for the Government, 13 February 1953, Department of Taoiseach (National Archives, file S6369A).

42. Department of Finance Memorandum for the Government, 1953, Department of Taoiseach (National Archives, file S6369A).

43. Department of Finance Memorandum, 1953 (National Archives, file D/T S6393A).

44. *Parliamentary Debates: Dáil Éireann: Official Report,* vol. 150, col. 1205–7, 11 May 1955.

45. Seán O'Connor (in *A Troubled Sky,* p. 31–3), quoted at length below.

46. Department of Education memorandum, 28 April 1958, appendix A. This is almost certainly the complete text of the recommendation of the six-man committee that the marriage bar in primary education be abrogated (National Archives, file D/T S623/C).

47. Department of Education memorandum, 28 April 1958, appendix A (National Archives, file D/T S623/C).

48. Department of Education memorandum, 28 April 1958, appendix A (National Archives, file D/T S623/C).

49. Department of Education memorandum, 28 April 1958, appendix A (National Archives, file D/T S623/C).

50. Department of Education memorandum, 28 April 1958, appendix A (National Archives, file D/T S623/C).

51. Department of Education memorandum, 28 April 1958, appendix A (National Archives, file D/T S623/C).

52. Department of Education memorandum, 28 April 1958 (National Archives, file D/T S623/C).

53. Department of Education memorandum, 28 April 1958 (National Archives, file D/T S623/C).

54. Department of Education memorandum, 28 April 1958 (National Archives, file D/T S623/C).

55. Seán O'Connor, *A Troubled Sky,* p. 28–29.

56. Jack Lynch, 'My life and times,' *Magill,* November 1979, p. 40.

57. Séamas Ó Buachalla, *Educational Policy in Twentieth Century Ireland,* p. 280.

58. Séamas Ó Buachalla, *Educational Policy in Twentieth Century Ireland,* p. 279.

59. Seán Farren, *The Politics of Irish Education,* p. 233. In answer to a query from Noël Browne, Lynch expressed himself in support of an orthodox view of corporal punishment: 'I am glad to note that not one Deputy agreed with the views expressed by Deputy Dr Browne. I know he is convinced of the justice of the point of view which he holds, but I think that some corporal punishment is necessary. I can never understand why this expression "corporal punishment" is used so often to-day. In less extravagant days, people called it slapping or "biffing". The rule, as Deputies know, is that children may be slapped on the open hand. When some questions were put down on this subject during the course of the last year, I looked up what material there was in the Department. I was

amused to come across a reference to the subject in the *Irish School Monthly* for March, 1955, entitled "Punishment in the Schools". It referred to a country which, beyond saying any more about it, is a friendly democracy, and where, it says, physical punishment in the schools is forbidden and as a result juvenile delinquency has practically disappeared, only to be replaced by adult delinquency by juveniles. It goes on to give some general examples of that adult delinquency, which I need not go into, and refers to it as having reached terrifying proportions. I might say, too, that in his Encyclical Letter—Divini Illius Magistri—on the Christian Education of Youth, Pope Pius XII said that disorderly inclinations amongst children must be corrected. That was a direct reference to methods of correction.

'Dr Browne: Does the Minister realise that the-re are thousands of schools in which corporal punishment is not used in other countries and in which they get good results?

'Mr. J. Lynch: I will not deny it. In many other countries, the teacher may not administer corporal punishment, but he refers the pupils to the headmaster of the school. Generally, I should like to say that I do not think Deputy Dr Browne will deny the parents' right to correct their children in a fair manner. The child, as we seek to establish in this country, is given into the custody of the school manager, and while the child is there, the manager is *in loco parentis* and, to a large extent, he carries all the powers and rights of the parent. Certainly, by implication, he carries the power of correction, whether or not it is delegated to the teacher. Irish teachers are not sadists and only in very rare instances do we get a case where a teacher might have gone beyond the limits, but, as Deputy Russell pointed out, there are remedies for that and they are readily availed of.

'Dr Browne: If it is shown to be unnecessary, why continue to use it?

'Mr. J. Lynch: I said on rare occasions some teachers might go beyond the limits.'

60. Seán O'Connor, *A Troubled Sky*, p. 37. O'Connor treats of the manner in which the old inspection system, in consultation with the Irish National Teachers' Organisation, was replaced with a less punitive and invasive approach. But he had heard the view expressed that there had been a gradual decline in the quality of the work done in national schools 'and that the decline began with the easing of inspection.' See p. 16–17.

Chapter 4 (P. 69–88)

1. Cormac Ó Gráda, *A Rocky Road*, p. 25.
2. J. J. Lee, *Ireland, 1912–1985*, p. 514–15.
3. World Development Report, 1985, cited by A. Williams in *The Western European Economy*, London: Hutchinson, 1987, p. 27.
4. See Desmond A. Gillmor, 'Changing Ireland,' *Irish Geography*, vol. 3, 1966, p. 470–77.
5. *Census of Population of Ireland*, 1971, note 3, table 1, p. ix.
6. *Ireland Trade and Shipping Statistics, 1959*, table 2, p. 5–10; *Ireland Trade and Shipping Statistics, 1965–66*, table 11, p. 15.

7. *Ireland Trade and Shipping Statistics, 1959*, tables 6–7, p. 16–18; *Ireland Trade and Shipping Statistics, 1959–65.*

8. *Irish Trade Journal and Statistical Bulletin*, vol. 25, no. 1, March 1960, p. 4–5.

9. *Census of Population of Ireland, 1971*, vol. 3, table 1, p. ix.

10. John Horgan, *Seán Lemass*, p. 185. I believe that the loyalty of both MacEntee and Aiken to de Valera prevented any overt challenge to the known wishes of 'the Chief'. Lemass was known to be the heir-apparent, even if there were tensions over the years between himself and MacEntee. Gerry Boland, who was no longer on the front bench, remained a critic of Lemass from within the Fianna Fáil organisation.

11. A referendum, held on the same day as de Valera's success at the polls, rejected a Government-sponsored constitutional amendment that would abolish proportional representation. T. W. Moody, F. X. Martin and F. J. Byrne (eds.), *A New History of Ireland*, vol. 8, p. 439.

12. John Horgan, *Seán Lemass*, p. 185.

13. See J. J. Lee's profile of Lemass in *Ireland, 1912–1985*, p. 371–408.

14. Bruce Arnold, *Jack Lynch*, p. 54.

15. Jack Lynch, 'My life and times,' *Magill*, November 1979, p. 41.

16. J. Lynch, Address at Inchicore, 18 July 1959 (National Archives, file GIS 1/234), and J. Lynch, Speech to Debating Society, Dublin, 11 November 1959 (National Archives, file GIS 1/234).

17. In July 1959 Transport and Power became a new department. The Department of Labour was created in July 1966.

18. Information on departmental structure gleaned from *Thom's Directory*, 1960.

19. Foras Tionscal, Accounts for year ended 31/3/59 (National Archives, file DI&C UDA 3/24). The employment estimate refers to the year ended 31 March 1958.

20. Progress Report of Foras Tionscal, January–February 1952 (National Archives, file DI&C UDA 3/9).

21. Industry and Commerce Memorandum, March 1961, accompanying Foras Tionscal accounts for 1960 (National Archives, file DI&C UDA 3/26).

22. The momentum was building. Between 1 April and 26 August 1959 the IDA received 27 applications, 2 of which were approved, 14 pending and the rest rejected. An Foras Tionscal in the same year received 75 applications under the Undeveloped Areas Acts, of which 18 were approved, 35 rejected and 22 pending. From August to March 1960, 93 applications were received (including 14 pending from the IDA), of which 10 were approved, 57 rejected and 26 pending.

23. Departmental Conference No. 581, 8 June 1959 (National Archives, file D/I&C 2000/13/20).

24. *Parliamentary Debates: Dáil Éireann: Official Report*, vol. 203, col. 13–, 22 May, 1963.

25. *Irish Press*, 3 November 1961.

26. Jack Lynch, 'My life and times,' *Magill*, November 1979, p. 41. Lynch also said that he was usually only in a position to go away for weekends at very short notice. In 1971 they bought a cottage overlooking Carberry's hundred islands in west Cork.

27. *Irish Statistical Bulletin,* 39, 1, March 1964; *Irish Statistical Bulletin,* March 1967; *Irish Statistical Bulletin,* March 1972.

28. Charles McCarthy, *The Decade of Upheaval,* p. 1–2; see also p. 21, where McCarthy reproduces an extract from *Trade Union Information* (bulletin of the Irish Congress of Trade Unions) that showed that between 1964 and 1970 twenty-nine strikes, or 4 per cent of all strikes in this period, accounted for 83 per cent of total work-days lost, mainly because of the protracted nature of the disputes.

29. Charles McCarthy, *The Decade of Upheaval,* p. 250.

30. Departmental Conference No. 599, 30 November 1959 (National Archives, file D/I&C 2000/13/21).

31. Charles McCarthy, *The Decade of Upheaval,* p. 250.

32. He was succeeded by Dr Patrick Hillery, who was moved in 1965 from Education to Industry and Commerce. Lemass later moved Hillery to the newly created Department of Labour on 13 July 1966. It was a decision that ought to have been taken a decade earlier.

33. *Parliamentary Debates: Dáil Éireann: Official Report,* vol. 176, col. 917, 9 July 1959.

34. *Parliamentary Debates: Dáil Éireann: Official Report,* vol. 176, col. 920, 9 July 1959.

35. *Parliamentary Debates: Dáil Éireann: Official Report,* vol. 190, col. 220–1, 14 June 1961.

36. Departmental Conference No. 595, 2 November 1959 (National Archives, file D/I&C 2000/13/21).

37. Departmental Conference No. 610, 22 February 1960 (National Archives, file D/I&C 2000/13/22).

38. The Government then took a direct interest in the project, holding that CIE, rather than Aer Rianta, should be involved in the consortium. The chairman and general manager of CIE, C. S. (Tod) Andrews, stated that CIE would not be keen to participate merely as investors of capital. If requested by the Government to do so, Andrews said, CIE would undertake hotel work if it was offered the same terms. Further difficulties emerged after closer scrutiny of the consortium's investment package.

39. Departmental Conference No. 611, 29 February 1960; No. 613, 14 March 1960 (National Archives, file D/I&C 2000/13/22).

40. Departmental Conference No. 614, 21 March 1960; No. 615, 28 March 1960 (National Archives, file D/I&C 2000/13/22).

41. Departmental Conference No. 618, 25 April 1960 (National Archives, file D/I&C 2000/13/22).

42. Departmental Conference No. 624, 20 June 1960; No. 625, 4 July 1960; No. 637, 24 October 1960; No. 639, 7 November 1960 (National Archives, file D/I&C 2000/13/22).

43. The transfer was tactical and was the result of a trade-off. Lynch would give Childers Tourism if the latter conceded the licensing function within the Shannon development region to Industry and Commerce, thereby placing manufacturing licensing under one department. As the departmental record of the horse-trading put it, 'It was recalled that it had been suggested that the Minister

for Industry and Commerce might be prepared to exchange tourism for this licensing function.' Departmental Conference No. 616, 4 April 1960 (National Archives, file D/I&C 2000/13/22).

44. Cited by T. Ryle Dwyer in *Nice Fellow,* p. 91.

45. Tobin, *The Best of Decades,* p. 55.

46. T. Ryle Dwyer, *Nice Fellow,* p. 96.

47. Departmental Conference No. 593, 19 October 1959 (National Archives, file D/I&C 2000/13/21).

48. Departmental Conference No. 595, 2 November 1959 (National Archives, file D/I&C 2000/13/21).

49. J. Lynch address at Whitegate, 22 September 1959 (National Archives, file GIS 1/234); Lynch address to Cork Chamber of Commerce, February 1960 (National Archives, file GIS 1/235).

50. Departmental Conference No. 597, 16 November 1959 (National Archives, file D/I&C 2000/13/21).

51. Departmental Conference No. 594, 26 October 1959; No. 600, 7 December 1959; No. 630, 15 August 1960 (National Archives, file D/I&C 2000/13/21–2).

52. Departmental Conference No. 594, 26 October 1959; No. 626, 18 July 1960 (National Archives, file D/I&C 2000/13/21–2).

53. *Parliamentary Debates: Dáil Éireann: Official Report,* vol. 184, col. 288, 27 October 1960.

54. *Parliamentary Debates: Dáil Éireann: Official Report,* vol. 184, col. 289–91, 27 October 1960.

55. Departmental Conference No. 591, 5 October 1959 (National Archives, file D/I&C 2000/13/21); Department Conference No. 733, 27 April 1963 (D/I&C 2000/13/24).

56. Departmental Conference No. 733, 22 April 1963 (National Archives, file D/I&C 2000/13/24).

57. Departmental Conference No. 593, 19 October 1959 (National Archives, file D/I&C 2000/13/21).

58. Departmental Conference No. 598, 23 November 1959 (National Archives, file D/I&C 2000/13/21).

59. Departmental Conference No. 595, 2 November 1959 (National Archives, file D/I&C 2000/13/21).

60. Departmental Conference No. 599, 30 November 1959 (National Archives, file D/I&C 2000/13/21).

61. Departmental Conference No. 601, 14 December 1959 (National Archives, file D/I&C 2000/13/21).

62. Departmental Conference No. 605, 18 January 1960 (National Archives, file D/I&C 2000/13/22).

63. Departmental Conference No. 613, 14 March 1960 (National Archives, file D/I&C 2000/13/22).

64. Departmental Conference No. 616, 4 April 1960 (National Archives, file D/I&C 2000/13/22).

65. Departmental Conference No. 634, 12 September 1960; No. 616, 4 April 1960

(National Archives, file D/I&C 2000/13/22).

66. Departmental Conference No. 620, 9 May 1960 (National Archives, file D/I&C 2000/13/22).

67. Departmental Conference No. 628, 3 August 1960 (National Archives, file D/I&C 2000/13/22).

68. Departmental Conference No. 744, 29 July 1963 (National Archives, file D/I&C 2001/13/24).

69. Departmental Conference No. 746, 15 August 1963; No. 747, 2 September 1963 (National Archives, file D/I&C 2001/13/24).

70. Departmental Conference No. 766, 3 February 1964 (National Archives, file D/I&C 2001/13/25).

71. Departmental Conference No. 769, 23 March 1964 (National Archives, file D/I&C 2001/13/25).

72. This table is taken from Brian M. Walker (ed.), *Parliamentary Election Results in Ireland.*

73. John Horgan, *Seán Lemass,* p. 201.

74. On 8 October 1964 he was moved to Agriculture, following the resignation of Paddy Smith. Brian Lenihan, the son of a Fianna Fáil TD and party elder, was made Minister for Justice. John Horgan, *Seán Lemass,* p. 197.

75. See national newspaper reports of Lynch's address to Trinity College Historical Society, 2 November 1961. In an address to Drogheda Chamber of Commerce three weeks later he presented the prospects for industry as having turned more positive, with the emphasis on the opportunities the larger market would present for manufacturers setting up within the EEC. See *Irish Press,* 21 November 1961.

76. *Irish Press,* 1 January 1962.

77. *Irish Independent,* 16 February 1962.

78. *Irish Press,* 27 March 1962.

79. *Irish Times,* 26 April 1962.

80. *Sunday Press,* 4 May 1962.

81. Department of Industry and Commerce, Review of Industrial Grants, Memo for Government, May 1962 (National Archives, file D/F 2001/3/436).

82. Department of Industry and Commerce, various correspondence, November 1962 to January 1963 (National Archives, file D/F 2001/3/436).

83. Department of Industry and Commerce, review of CIO Interim Report on Industrial Grants, January 1963.

84. N. Ó Nualláin [Nicholas Nolan] to J. C. B. MacCarthy, 26 April 1963 (National Archives, file D/ I&C 2000/12/1/AIT 1).

85. *Irish Independent,* 15 February 1963; *Irish Times,* 15 February 1963. See full text of Lynch's address to the Federation of Irish Industries on 14 February 1963 (National Archives, file GIS 1/237).

86. *Irish Times,* 23 October 1963. This concern was again emphasised in an address to the Irish Institute of Secretaries the following month; see *Irish Times,* 11 November 1963.

87. *Irish Independent,* 2 January 1964.

88. *Survey of Grant Aided Industry,* table 2.4.

89. *Survey of Grant Aided Industry,* p. 25.

90. *Survey of Grant Aided Industry,* p. 26.

91. *Survey of Grant Aided Industry,* p. 25.

Chapter 5 (P. 89–115)

1. See Terence O'Neill, *Ulster at the Crossroads,* p. 155–83.

2. Lemass set up an all-party committee on the Constitution in 1966, which report-ed in 1967 when he was still a TD but was no longer Taoiseach. It recommended recasting the definition of the national territory (articles 2 and 3) and reframing the article on religion (article 44).

3. Roy Foster, *Luck and the Irish,* p. 71.

4. 'Casement's remains in Pro-Cathedral,' *Irish Times,* 1 March 1965.

5. 'Casement's remains in Pro-Cathedral,' *Irish Times,* 1 March 1965.

6. Seamus Kelly, 'An Irishman ends his journey home,' *Irish Times,* 2 March 1965.

7. The by-election was caused by the death of the Labour Party TD Dan Desmond. His widow, Eileen Desmond, was standing for Labour. Between 1963 and 1965 Fianna Fáil had to contest five other by-elections. On 30 May 1963 Patrick Belton took the seat for Fine Gael. On 19 February 1964 two by-elections were held, one in Cork County Borough (city) and the other in Co. Kildare; Fianna Fáil won both. In Co. Roscommon on 8 July 1964 Joan T. Burke took the seat held by her late husband for Fine Gael. On 3 December 1964 John F. Donnellan won a seat for Fine Gael. Those five by-elections placed the life of the Lemass Government under threat; he survived with the support of independents.

8. 'Lemass threatens general election,' *Irish Times,* 6 March 1965.

9. 'Lemass call stirs Mid-Cork fight,' *Irish Times,* 8 March 1965.

10. 'Taoiseach announces a general election,' *Irish Times,* 12 March 1965.

11. 'Whether there be prophecies' (editorial), *Irish Times,* 12 March 1965.

12. *Irish Times,* 13 March 1965.

13. *Irish Times,* 22 March 1965.

14. Special correspondent [probably John Healy], 'Drastic changes in the corridors of power: Backroom boys are taking over,' *Irish Times,* 15 March 1965.

15. 'Fianna Fáil would go into opposition,' *Irish Times,* 25 March 1965.

16. *Irish Times,* 23 March 1965.

17. *Irish Times,* 23 March 1965.

18. Backbencher [John Healy], 'MacEntee on MacEntee,' *Irish Times,* 27 March 1965.

19. *Irish Times,* 17 March 1965.

20. John Horgan, *Seán Lemass,* p. 206–8.

21. Brian M. Walker (ed.), *Parliamentary Election Results in Ireland,* p. 206.

22. T. K. Whitaker, Note for Minister, 22 April 1965 (National Archives, file D/F F43/5/64, part I). I am grateful to my colleague Dr Andrew McCarthy, who researched and drafted much of this chapter. We are grateful to Tom Quinlan, National Archives of Ireland, and Pat Hickson, Department of Finance, for securing access to this file and others related to Jack Lynch's tenure in the Department of Finance.

23. T. K. Whitaker, Note for Minister, 22 April 1965 (National Archives, file D/F F43/5/64, part I).
24. Finance Memorandum for the Government: Budget position and Supply Services Estimate, 3 February 1965 (National Archives, file D/F F43/5/64, part 1).
25. Finance Memorandum for the Government: Budget position and Supply Services Estimate, 3 February 1965 (National Archives, file D/F F43/5/64, part 1).
26. See draft of memorandum, March 1965, in National Archives file D/F F43/5/64, part 1).
27. Department of Finance Memorandum on Capital Programmes 1964/65 and 1965/66, 12 April 1965 (National Archives, file D/F 2001/3/1072).
28. Letter of M. Moynihan, 12 March 1965 (National Archives, file D/F 2001/3/1072).
29. National Archives, file D/T S17564.
30. For Minister's Information Only, Note on revision of estimates for voted capital services, undated (National Archives, file D/F F43/5/64, part 1).
31. National Archives, file D/F F43/5/64, part 1.
32. Finance memorandum for the Government, 3 May 1965 (National Archives, file D/F F43/5/64, part 1).
33. *Second Programme for Economic Expansion, Part II*, p. 271.
34. S. Lemass, address to IMI, 29 April 1965 (National Archives, file D/F F39/1/65).
35. Undated draft sections of Financial Statement contained in 1965 Budget, 1: Economic Survey (National Archives, file D/F F39/1/65).
36. *Second Programme for Economic Expansion: Progress Report for 1965*, table 29, p. 124.
37. *Second Programme for Economic Expansion: Progress Report for 1965*, p. 18.
38. Tax changes: Double-taxation agreement with Britain to remain in effect until new British corporation tax came into operation in April 1966, with negotiations for new reliefs; exports tax relief, mining relief and double allowances for capital expenditure to have their period of operation extended; writing off capital expenditure on scientific research reduced from five years to one year; relief from stamp duty in cases of reconstruction or amalgamation of companies; in partnerships, each partner to be assessed separately for income tax; limited circumstances whereby the profits of a subsidiary company might be treated as the profits of the parent company repealed; a right of appeal to the High Court for taxpayers and the Revenue Commissioners; provisions to be enacted to ensure the proper taxing of builders' profits and speculative dealings; devices used to avoid liability to income tax of profits from letting buildings and land to be defeated by further enactments. *Turnover tax:* A farmer's retail sales in excess of £150 per month to be liable for tax; other persons selling goods to have the threshold for tax registration lowered from £250 to £150 per month. *Death duty:* On estates not exceeding £15,000 in value the estate duty on benefits to which the widow or children under the age of sixteen succeed to be abated at the rate of £150 for the widow and £100 for each child; legacy and succession duties abolished; provision relating to death duties on gifts made within three years of the donor's death extended to five years, but exemption increased from £100 to £500; gifts

made in consideration of marriage exempted.

39.　*Parliamentary Debates: Dáil Éireann: Official Report,* vol. 217, col. 1071.

40.　*Parliamentary Debates: Dáil Éireann: Official Report,* vol. 217, col. 1074.

41.　*Parliamentary Debates: Dáil Éireann: Official Report,* vol. 217, col. 1075–6.

42.　*Parliamentary Debates: Dáil Éireann: Official Report,* vol. 217, col. 1192.

43.　*Parliamentary Debates: Dáil Éireann: Official Report,* vol. 218, col. 1332–, 9 September 1965.

44.　*Parliamentary Debates: Dáil Éireann: Official Report,* vol. 218, col. 1350–.

45.　*Parliamentary Debates: Dáil Éireann: Official Report,* vol. 218, col. 1376.

46.　*Parliamentary Debates: Dáil Éireann: Official Report,* vol. 218, col. 1378–79.

47.　*Parliamentary Debates: Dáil Éireann: Official Report,* vol. 218, col. 1403.

48.　*Parliamentary Debates: Dáil Éireann: Official Report,* vol. 218, col. 1404.

49.　*Parliamentary Debates: Dáil Éireann: Official Report,* vol. 218, col. 1405.

50.　T. K. Whitaker to T. Ó Cearbhaill, 22 October 1965 (National Archives, file D/F F39/7/65).

51.　T. K. Whitaker to T. Ó Cearbhaill, 22 October 1965 (National Archives, file D/F F39/7/65).

52.　Finance Memorandum, 26 October 1965; Interdepartmental Committee Second Report, 26 October 1965 (National Archives, file D/T 97/6/557).

53.　Finance Memorandum, 26 October 1965; Interdepartmental Committee Second Report, 26 October 1965 (National Archives, file D/T 97/6/557); T. Ó Cearbhaill to Private Secretaries of Government Ministers, 2 November 1965 (National Archives, file GC 11/32).

54.　Finance Memorandum on Public Capital Programme, 29 November 1965 (National Archives, file D/F F43/11/65).

55.　Finance Memorandum on Public Capital Programme, 29 November 1965 (National Archives, file D/F F43/11/65), par. 12.

56.　Finance Memorandum on Public Capital Programme, 29 November 1965 (National Archives, file D/F F43/11/65), par. 15.

57.　Dept of Local Government, Notes on Capital Requirements, 29 November 1965 (National Archives, file D/T 97/6/428).

58.　J. Lynch to D. O'Malley, 3 November 1965 (National Archives, file D/T 96/6/407).

59.　J. Lynch to S. Lemass, 4 November 1965 (National Archives, file D/T 96/6/407).

60.　D. O'Malley to J. Lynch, 4 November 1965 (National Archives, file D/T 96/6/407).

61.　D. O'Malley to J. Lynch, 4 November 1965 (National Archives, file D/T 96/6/407)

62.　D. O'Malley to S. Lemass, 20 July 1965 (National Archives, file D/T 96/6/406).

63.　Department of Health Memorandum on Proposed White Paper, 30 November 1965 (National Archives, file D/T 96/6/407).

64.　Appendix to Health Memorandum, 30 November 1965 (National Archives, file D/T 96/6/407).

65.　Ruth Barrington, *Health, Medicine and Politics in Ireland,* p. 261.

66.　Ruth Barrington, *Health, Medicine and Politics in Ireland,* p. 263. See also p. 264–5 for later difficulties encountered in financing the proposed changes and promises in the 1966 White Paper.

67. N. S. Nolan to Private Secretary, Minister for Finance, 2 December 1965 (National Archives, file D/T 97/6/428).

68. Unsigned minute (most probably Whitaker's) for J. Lynch, December 1965 (National Archives, file D/F F39/7/65).

69. J. J. Lee, *Ireland, 1912–1985*, p. 353.

70. *Parliamentary Debates: Dáil Éireann: Official Report*, vol. 219, col. 1524, 6 January 1966.

71. Finance memorandum on PCP, 14 February 1966 (National Archives, file D/T 97/6/429).

72. Finance memorandum on Current Expenditure, 14 February 1966 (National Archives, file D/F F39/7/65).

73. The Financial Situation: Talk with the Taoiseach, 28 January 1966 (National Archives, file D/F F39/8/65).

74. T. K. Whitaker to S. Réamonn, 16 February 1966 (National Archives, file D/F F39/7/65).

75. T. K. Whitaker minute for J. Lynch, 28 February 1966 (National Archives, file D/F F39/7/65).

76. N. Blaney to J. Lynch, 24 February 1966 (National Archives, file D/F F39/7/65).

77. *Parliamentary Debates: Dáil Éireann: Official Report*, vol. 221, col. 1286–, 9 March 1966.

78. Finance memorandum on current Budget, 1966–67, 9 June 1966 (National Archives, file D/F F39/7/65).

79. T. K. Whitaker to S. Réamonn, 12 March 1965 (National Archives, file D/F F39/1/65).

80. Department of Finance, Draft memorandum for Government, April 1965 (National Archives, file D/F F39/1/65).

81. A Bird's-Eye View of Part VII, undated notes for Lynch for Committee Stage of 1965 Finance Bill (National Archives, file D/F F39/1/65, Continuation File).

82. This commemoration is most perceptively analysed by Rory O'Dwyer in Gabriel Doherty and Dermot Keogh (eds.), *1916: The Long Revolution*, p. 24–8.

83. Whitaker to Lemass, 12 September 1966 (National Archives, file D/T 96/6/35 and S12891F).

84. Quoted by Diarmaid Ferriter in *The Transformation of Ireland*, p. 597.

85. J. J. Lee, *Ireland, 1912–1985*, p. 362.

Chapter 6 (p. 116–162)

1. John Horgan, *Seán Lemass*, p. 326–. Horgan charts Lemass's history of poor health in a convincing manner.

2. After much research I am now in complete agreement with Michael Mills. In my book *Twentieth Century Ireland* I suggested that Patrick Hillery may have been his first choice; what I now believe is that Dr Hillery was a possible choice but not his first choice.

3. Dick Walsh, *The Party*, p. 89.

4. Jack Lynch, 'My life and times,' *Magill*, November 1979, p. 42.

5. Bruce Arnold, *Jack Lynch*, p. 67–68.

6. The economic situation was deteriorating, and serious cut-backs had been implemented, as has been shown in the last chapter. He found the atmosphere at meetings of the parliamentary party more fractious and rebellious. On 9 March 1966 Lemass had pressed, against backbench opposition, for the holding of local elections; two weeks later the parliamentary party voted 51 to 6 in favour of postponement, in open defiance of the Taoiseach's stated position. He had to accept the decision. John Horgan, *Seán Lemass*, p. 328–9.

7. Haughey won 12,415 first-preference votes in the 1965 election and Colley received 5,745. The two men knew each other since their school days in St Joseph's, Fairview, which Boland also attended. Haughey's father had joined the Free State army on its foundation. George Colley's father, Henry (Harry) Colley, had remained on the republican side in the Civil War and had been a founder-member of Fianna Fáil.

8. He had been parliamentary secretary to the Minister for Lands from 21 October 1964 until the general election in March 1965. Colley represented the same constituency as Charles Haughey. His father, Henry (Harry) Colley, had been a TD from 1944. Haughey, who entered the Dáil for the first time in 1957, took his seat. Haughey and Colley were politicians of two very different types. Colley set himself impossibly high standards in political life and endeavoured in a high-minded and idealistic way to live up to them.

9. Lemass could rely on the support of the party elders. The much-respected Dr Jim Ryan had retired in 1965. Seán MacEntee, on the backbenches in 1966, was seventy-seven. The Minister for External Affairs, Frank Aiken, was sixty-eight and had no intention of drawing his pension. He may have still entertained an unfulfilled ambition of taking over for a brief period; but Lemass knew that he could carry the day.

10. Two other members of the party enjoyed equal popularity in their constituencies. In the general election of 1965 Dr Patrick Hillery polled 14,372 first-preference votes in Co. Clare. Charles Haughey received 12,415 first-preference votes in Dublin North-East and Lemass 12,400 in Dublin South-Central.

11. Stephen Collins, *The Power Game*, p. 27.

12. Anon., 'From political tyro to cabinet minister: Charles J. Haughey' (2), *Irish Times*, 10 June 1969.

13. Anon., 'From political tyro to cabinet minister: Charles J. Haughey' (2), *Irish Times*, 10 June 1969.

14. 'Lynch gets assurance of election,' *Cork Examiner*, 3 November 1966.

15. John Horgan, *Seán Lemass*, p. 334.

16. Phone interview with Bishop Fiachra Ó Ceallaigh, 18 July 2005. His father had told him of the meeting. He had no memory of being told who attended. Patrick Hillery had told the bishop that he had not been present.

17. Dick Walsh, *The Party*.

18. 'Lynch gets assurance of election,' *Cork Examiner*, 3 November 1966.

19. Jack Lynch, 'My life and times,' *Magill*, November 1979, p. 42.

20. Máirín Lynch to news editor, *Cork Examiner*, 10 September 1973 (National Library of Ireland, Máirín Lynch Papers, acc. 6260, box 1). There is another version of this letter in the same file. The letter was timed to follow Lynch's announcement about his continued leadership of Fianna Fáil. Máirín admitted wishing 'for a quieter life' recently (September 1973); 'however, I am sure that this is the wish of many political wives but they still do an excellent job and enjoy doing it.' She said she was not a devotee of the women's liberation campaign, 'because I recognise the special position of man in this God-made world, but I do appreciate the frustration that, at times, motivates the members of that organisation.'

21. Máirín Lynch to news editor, *Cork Examiner*, 10 September 1973 (National Library of Ireland, Máirín Lynch Papers, acc. 6260, box 1).

22. Interview with Máirín Lynch by Ida Grehan, *Irish Times*, 31 January 1972.

23. Jack Lynch, 'My life and times,' *Magill*, November 1979, p. 42.

24. John Horgan, *Seán Lemass*, p. 336. This is based on Blaney's view of events.

25. John Horgan, *Seán Lemass*, p. 336. Horgan provides parallel texts of versions by Blaney, Boland and Haughey of what happened. There is a certain amount of overlapping, but the views are very distinctive.

26. 'Lynch looks certain to be Taoiseach,' *Cork Examiner*, 3 November 1966.

27. John Horgan, *Seán Lemass*, p. 336–7.

28. 'Lynch for Taoiseach,' *Irish Examiner*, 4 November 1966.

29. 'My greatest decision, says Lynch,' *Cork Examiner*, 5 November 1966.

30. The political correspondent of the *Irish Press*, Michael Mills, wrote a story on the imminent retirement of Lemass about a week before the formal announcement. Government sources vehemently denied it and sought the publication of a correction in the *Irish Press* of the wild and unsubstantiated rumour.

31. Bruce Arnold, *Jack Lynch*, p. 65.

32. John Horgan, *Seán Lemass*, p. 337–8.

33. Stephen Collins, *The Power Game*, p. 37.

34. John Horgan, *Seán Lemass*, p. 338.

35. 'Lynch sweeps in as new leader,' *Cork Examiner*, 10 November 1966.

36. 'Lynch sweeps in as new leader,' *Cork Examiner*, 10 November 1966.

37. John Horgan, *Seán Lemass*, p. 339.

38. 'Cork enthusiastic welcome for new Taoiseach,' *Cork Examiner*, 14 November 1966.

39. 'Cork enthusiastic welcome for new Taoiseach,' *Cork Examiner*, 14 November 1966.

40. 'Cork enthusiastic welcome for new Taoiseach,' *Cork Examiner*, 14 November 1966. The paper reported that 'last night' Lynch was in Killarney. It is not clear whether he was there on the Friday or the Sunday night; it is possible that he could have driven down to Killarney after the match. However, the people of Killarney gave Jack and Máirín Lynch a most warm reception. Recalling the sporting clashes against Kerry, he made nostalgic reference to a number of memorable games.

41. 'Cork enthusiastic welcome for new Taoiseach,' *Cork Examiner*, 14 November 1966.

42. 'I'll be vigorous,' says Taoiseach,' *Cork Examiner,* 17 November 1966.
43. 'I'll be vigorous,' says Taoiseach,' *Cork Examiner,* 17 November 1966.
44. 'I'll be vigorous,' says Taoiseach,' *Cork Examiner,* 17 November 1966.
45. 'I'll be vigorous,' says Taoiseach,' *Cork Examiner,* 17 November 1966.
46. Martin Mansergh (ed.), *The Spirit of the Nation,* p. 87–90.
47. After he became a TD in the late 1950s Haughey hired a consultant. Turned down by 'Terry O'Sullivan' (Tomás Ó Faoláin) of the *Evening Press,* he hired Tony Gray of the *Irish Times.* He also developed strong personal contacts in the media.
48. Stephen Collins, *The Power Game,* p. 41.
49. Bruce Arnold, *Haughey,* p. 61–2, and Stephen Collins, *The Power Game,* p. 39.
50. Martin Mansergh (ed.), *The Spirit of the Nation,* p. 92–4.
51. Dorothy Walker, *Michael Scott, Architect,* p. 215–16.
52. Martin Mansergh (ed.), *The Spirit of the Nation,* p. 86–7.
53. Anon., 'Horseman, pass by!: Charles J. Haughey' (3), *Irish Times,* 11 June 1969.
54. Ken Whitaker, *Interests,* p. 96–8.
55. Frank McDonald, *The Destruction of Dublin,* p. 18–. See also the same author's *Saving the City: How to Halt the Destruction of Dublin.*
56. Frank McDonald, *The Destruction of Dublin,* p. 165–.
57. Fergal Tobin, *The Best of Decades,* p. 159.
58. Anon., 'Horseman, pass By!: Charles J. Haughey' (3), *Irish Times,* 11 June 1969.
59. Anon., 'Horseman, pass by!: Charles J. Haughey' (3), *Irish Times,* 11 June 1969.
60. Charles McCarthy, *The Decade of Upheaval.*
61. Charles McCarthy, *The Decade of Upheaval,* p. 253.
62. Charles McCarthy, *The Decade of Upheaval,* p. 169. See also chapter 5, p. 150–83.
63. I am most grateful to Aoife Keogh, who put her research and knowledge of the archives in Dublin, London and Florence at my disposal for the writing of this section of the book. She is the author of a forthcoming study on Ireland and the EEC, 1966–1973. This will be part of an IRCHSS series on Ireland and the EEC undertaken by a team of scholars led by members of the UCC History Department.
64. D. J. Maher, *The Tortuous Path,* p. 199–201.
65. D. J. Maher, *The Tortuous Path,* p. 202–4.
66. D. J. Maher, *The Tortuous Path,* p. 208.
67. D. J. Maher, *The Tortuous Path,* p. 209.
68. Government Memorandum, National Archives, file D/T S18981B 98/8/856.
69. Department of External Affairs Memorandum, National Archives, file D/T S18981B 98/8/856.
70. Department of External Affairs memorandum, National Archives, file D/T S18981B 98/8/856.
71. Present at the meeting were T. K. Whitaker (Department of Finance), J. C. B. MacCarthy (Department of Industry and Commerce), J. C. Nagle (Department of Agriculture and Fisheries), H. J. McCann (Department of External Affairs), J. O'Mahony (Department of Agriculture and Fisheries), D. J. Maher (Department of Finance), T. Godfrey (Department of Industry and Commerce) and P. Carthy (Department of Finance) (National Archives, file D/T 98/8/856 S18981B).

72. D. J. Maher, *The Tortuous Path*, p. 192–5.

73. See D. J. Maher, *The Tortuous Path*, p. 129–32, and Maurice Fitzgerald, *From Protectionism to Liberalisation*, p. 128–9 and 154.

74. D. J. Maher, *The Tortuous Path*, p. 207–8.

75. The matter had been raised by the Irish side in the context of a meeting on 2 December 1966 during Anglo-Irish discussions. The British welcomed such discussions on technical matters but felt it was too early to establish machinery for that purpose. They proposed deferral until the results of the British exploratory talks were known. A memorandum prepared for the meeting of secretaries, entitled 'Liaison at official level with Britain on EEC matters,' confirmed further that there was continuous contact between the embassies in that area. There was also no obstacle to *ad hoc* meetings of experts on points of interest or concern. More regular contacts could be arranged when the need arose. Meeting of Secretaries (National Archives, file DT 98/8/856 S18981B).

76. Also in attendance were the secretary of the Department of Finance, Ken Whitaker, and the assistant secretary of the Department of External Affairs, Dr D. O'Sullivan, and on the British side the Commonwealth Secretary, Herbert Bowden, the Minister of State at the Foreign Office, F. Ulley, the joint parliamentary under-secretary at the Department of Economic Affairs, Peter Shore, the deputy under-secretary of the Commonwealth Relations Office, Sir Arthur Snelling, the deputy secretary of the Ministry of Agriculture, Fisheries and Food, R. Wall, a representative of the Cabinet Office, B. M. Thimont, and the private secretary in the Prime Minister's Office, D. H. Andrews. See National Archives, file DT 98/8/856 S18981B.

77. Government report on meeting with Wilson (National Archives, file DT 98/8/856 S18981B).

78. See J. W. Young, *Britain and European Unity*, and J. W. Young, *Britain, France and the Unity of Europe*, 1984).

79. Government report on meeting with Wilson (National Archives, file DT 98/8/856 S18981B).

80. D. J. Maher, *The Tortuous Path*, p. 211.

81. National Archives, file DT 98/8/856 S18981B.

82. Government report on meeting with Wilson (National Archives, file DT 98/8/856 S18981B).

83. These remarks took place in the context of a discussion on the harmonisation of industry. F. Mulley took the lead in the discussion at that point (National Archives, file DT 98/8/856 S18981B).

84. D. J. Maher, *The Tortuous Path*, p. 213.

85. National Archives, file DT 98/8F/856 S18981B.

86. Government report on meeting with Wilson (National Archives, file DT 98/8/856 S18981B).

87. See text of communiqué, 1 May 1967 (National Archives, file DT 98/8/856 S18981B).

88. Wilson's speech to the House of Commons is quoted extensively by D. J. Maher in *The Tortuous Path*, p. 211–13.

89. Lynch wrote to van Elslande, 10 May 1967 (National Archives, file DT 98/6/861 S8131E).

90. The Government had worked extremely hard in 1961 and 62 to convince the EEC to open negotiations for EEC adhesion. They did not want to have to repeat this process in 1967. Despite Britain's plans to make a completely new application, Ireland simply wanted to reactivate its 1961/2 application. See D. J. Maher, *The Tortuous Path*, p. 214.

91. Ireland had no nuclear power and would not benefit directly from membership of Euratom. The Government had considered this alternative energy source in the 1950s but had not adopted it, because of the cost of installing it.

92. The Government had learnt from its rushed and unsuccessful application in 1963 to proceed in 1967 with 'dignified calm.' Whitaker to Cremin, 1 March 1962 (National Archives, file DT S17246D).

93. Meeting of Committee of Secretaries, 23 May 1967 (National Archives, file 98/6/857 S18081C).

94. Meeting of Committee of Secretaries, 23 May 1967 (National Archives, file 98/6/857 S18081C).

95. Van Elslande wrote to Lynch on 6 June 1967 (National Archives, file DT 98/6/861 S8131E).

96. Britain had applied for membership of the EEC on 10 August 1961 and negotiations had opened on 8 November 1961. Denmark had submitted its application for membership on 10 August 1961 and negotiations had opened on 30 November 1961.Norway applied on 30 April 1962 and negotiations opened on 12 November 1962. Ireland was the first of the four to apply for membership of the EEC, on 31 July 1961. However, the European Council only confirmed that negotiations with Ireland could take place on 22 October 1962. The Council stated that the date for negotiations would be agreed later. Negotiations never opened and the enlargement debate ended in deadlock when the French vetoed the enlargement of the EEC in January 1963. Ireland was the only country of the four applicant members not to hold negotiations with the EEC in its first attempt at enlargement. D. J. Maher, *The Tortuous Path*, p. 138 and 160.

97. D. J. Maher, *The Tortuous Path*, p. 217.

98. The French only answered the Irish request to make a formal visit to France in August 1967. D. J. Maher, *The Tortuous Path*, p. 228.

99. For a detailed account of this process see Dermot Keogh and Aoife Keogh, 'Ireland and European Integration, p. 6–50.

100. D. J. Maher, *The Tortuous Path*, p. 237.

101. Maurice Fitzgerald, *From Protectionism to Liberalisation*, p. 237–91.

102. D. J. Maher, *The Tortuous Path*, p. 236.

103. Conclusion to Commission report on Ireland, Britain and Denmark's application to join the EEC (European Union Archives, Florence, Eduardo Marino Papers, 169.)

104. Department of Finance, Digest of Developments in the European Community and in Trading Groups—Quarter ended 31 March 1968 (National Archives, file DT 99/1/494 S18081N).

105. Whitaker to McCann, 23 May 1968, enclosing Department of Finance memorandum, signed E. J. Brennan, 24 May 1968 (National Archives, file DT 99/1/494 S18081N).

106. See Jean Lacouture, *De Gaulle: The Rebel*, and Jean Lacouture, *De Gaulle: The Ruler*.

107. Wilson introduced increased taxes, curtailment of credit and the application of an import deposit scheme principally to manufactured goods in order to correct the British adverse balance of payments. The import deposit scheme required importers to deposit half the value of their goods in Britain for six months. D. J. Maher, *The Tortuous Path*, p. 242–3.

108. D. J. Maher, *The Tortuous Path*, p. 242–4.

109. Robert McNamara, 'Irish perspectives on the Vietnam War,' p. 83.

110. Aiken to Rusk, 7 September 1967 (UCD Archives, Frank Aiken Papers, P104/7221); Memos, Katzenbach to Johnson, 7 April 1967; 'United States airline entry into Dublin,' 31 March 1967; Read to Rostow, 7 March 1967 (LBJ Library, Ireland, vol. 1, country file: Ireland, NSF, box 195).

111. Memorandum, Department of External Affairs to Government, 'The situation in Vietnam,' 1 February 1968 (UCD Archives, Frank Aiken Papers, P104/6906).

112. A letter from the US ambassador to Ireland, Raymond R. Guest, 6 November 1967, thanking Lynch for his statement on the need for the cessation of hostilities would appear to back up this point (National Archives, file DT 97/6/320). See also Robert McNamara, 'Irish perspectives,' p. 84. Despite considering a partial termination of the Civil Air Agreement to force Dublin into a more compromising position, the Department of State believed that such action would be unwise and continued on the path of negotiation by 1968 (LBJ Library, Report, Ireland: section 11, p. 4, chapter 3 (Europe): section D, Administrative History of the Department of State, box 1). This may have been because of the decision by the Johnson administration to consult Congress to gauge the feeling of Irish pressure groups before deciding on an appropriate course of action (LBJ Library, Memos, Bator to Johnson, 3 May 1967; Katzenbach to Johnson, 7 April 1967, Ireland, vol. 1, country file: Ireland, NSF, box 195).

113. Memorandum, Read to Rostow, 23 January 1968 (LBJ Library, Ireland, vol. 1, country file: Ireland, NSF, box 195). Similar sentiments were expressed in other memos contained in this file: Springsteen to Rusk, 8 June 1968; Rostow to Johnson, 24 January 1968; Bator to Johnson, 15 March 1967; Read to Rostow, 7 March 1967.

114. Memorandum, Read to Rostow, 24 January 1968 (LBJ Library, Ireland, vol. 1, country file: Ireland, NSF, box 195).

115. Memorandum, Rostow to Johnson, 24 January 1968 (LBJ Library, Ireland, vol. 1, country file: Ireland, NSF, box 195).

116. A memorandum on political broadcasting, prepared in January 1967, had suggested the need for the relationship between RTE and the Government to be re-examined and further stressed that extreme control could not be exercised over RTE's right to free opinion but that 'serious cause for complaints may be

referred to the Parliamentary Secretary' (UCD Archives, Frank Aiken Papers, P104/7135 (2), Memo, Transport, Energy, Posts and Telegraphs to Government, 'Political broadcasting,' 11 January 1967).

117. T. Ryle Dwyer, *Nice Fellow,* p. 146.

118. *Irish Times,* 15 April 1967; UCD Archives, Frank Aiken Papers, P104/7139 (2).

119. Memo, External Affairs to Government, 'The situation in Vietnam' (UCD Archives, Frank Aiken Papers, P104/6906, 1 February 1968).

120. 'Text of statement furnished to the President of the Union of Students in Ireland,' 16 November 1967 (UCD Archives, Frank Aiken Papers, P104/6903). The proposal was for a group of countries in the south-east Asian region 'to organise themselves into a neutral area of law and limited armaments. That area of peace should exclude all foreign military bases and should be guaranteed against aggression by the United Nations and by all the Great Powers, including China.'

121. On this point see Greg Spellman, 'Ireland at the United Nations,' p. 233.

122. Lynch to Briggs, 3 January 1968 (UCD Archives, Frank Aiken Papers, P104/6905).

123. Despite the 'generalised conversation', which was joined by Princess Grace of Monaco, Rusk privately expressed pessimism to Fay about the progress of peace talks with the North Vietnamese in Paris, stressing how they were just as 'intransigent' as the North Koreans (National Archives, file DT 99/1/567, Report, Fay to McCann, 20 June 1968).

124. Memorandum of conversation, 'Visit of Irish Prime Minister,' Johnson, Rostow, Duke, Abell, Springsteen, Goldstein, Lynch, Cosgrave, Corish, Fay, 6 June 1968 (LBJ Library, The White House, Ireland, vol. 1, country file: Ireland, NSF, box 195).

125. Report, Fay to McCann, 20 June 1968 (National Archives, file DT 99/1/567). Also quoted by McNamara in 'Irish perspectives,' p. 91.

126. On this point it is interesting to note Fay's comments on the American press notices about Lynch on his election to the office of Taoiseach, where the fact that many of the media, including CBS, referred to 'Jack Lynch' 'should be considered as gratifying evidence of his having already achieved an international name.' Report, Fay to McCann, 15 November 1966 (National Archives, file DFA 2001/43/193).

127. LBJ Library, Report, Ireland: section 11, p. 1, chapter 3 (Europe): Section D, Administrative History of the Department of State, box 1).

128. Terence O'Neill, *The Autobiography of Terence O'Neill,* p. 74.

129. Terence O'Neill, *The Autobiography of Terence O'Neil,* p. 74.

130. Lynch visit to Stormont, 11 December 1967 (note prepared by T. K. Whitaker) (National Archives, file D/T 98/6/435 S16272L).

131. Lynch visit to Stormont, 11 December 1967 (note prepared by T. K. Whitaker); Report, Fay to McCann, 15 November 1966 (National Archives, file D/T 98/6/435 S16272L).

132. Lynch visit to Stormont, 11 December 1967 (note prepared by T. K. Whitaker) (National Archives, file D/T 98/6/435 S16272L).

133. Lynch visit to Stormont, 11 December 1967 (note prepared by T. K. Whitaker) (National Archives, file D/T 98/6/435 S16272L).

134. Lynch to O'Neill, 15 December 1967 (National Archives, file D/T 98/6/435 S16272L).

135. National Archives, file D/T 99/1/283 S16272M.

136. National Archives, file D/T 99/1/283 S16272M.

137. Terence O'Neill, *The Autobiography of Terence O'Neill,* p. 74.

138. Whitaker to O'Neill, 19 January 1968 (UCD Archives, Dr Kenneth Whitaker Papers, P175).

139. Paul Bew and Gordon Gillespie, *Northern Ireland,* p. 3–6.

140. Michael Kennedy, *Division and Consensus.*

141. Paul Bew and Gordon Gillespie, *Northern Ireland,* p. 3–6.

142. Whitaker letter, draft O'Neill note and draft answer to parliamentary questions on Northern Ireland, 22 October 1968 (Jack Lynch Papers).

143. Dr John O'Connell (Labour Party), question to Taoiseach (*Parliamentary Debates: Dáil Éireann: Official Report,* vol. 236, 23 October 1968). The wording of the draft parliamentary reply told the Labour Party deputies Michael O'Leary and John O'Connell that no arrangements had been made for a meeting between O'Neill and the Taoiseach 'although I hope that the practice of periodic meetings initiated close on four years ago will be continued.' Whitaker's draft reply continued that Lynch had conveyed to O'Neill the Government's anxiety that the root [crossed out] social causes of demonstrations would be eliminated as quickly as possible. He would restate the views expressed at Kilkenny, repeating that, 'as my predecessor and I, myself, have stated many times, the view of the Government is that the solution of Partition is one to be reached by agreement in Ireland between Irishmen.' The draft answer then picked up the wording of the draft note to O'Neill about Dublin expecting a benevolent attitude from the British. (Draft O'Neill note and draft answer to parliamentary questions on Northern Ireland, 22 October 1968, Jack Lynch Papers).

144. Briefing notes prepared by Department of External Affairs for Taoiseach's meeting with the British Prime Minister on 30 October 1968.

145. T. K. Whitaker memorandum, 'A note on North-South policy,' 11 November 1968 (UCD Archives, Dr Kenneth Whitaker Papers, P175).

146. T. K. Whitaker memorandum, 'A note on North-South policy,' 11 November 1968 (UCD Archives, Dr Kenneth Whitaker Papers, P175).

147. T. K. Whitaker memorandum, 'A note on North-South policy,' 11 November 1968 (UCD Archives, Dr Kenneth Whitaker Papers, P175).

148. T. K. Whitaker memorandum, 'A note on North-South policy,' 11 November 1968 (UCD Archives, Dr Kenneth Whitaker Papers, P175).

149. T. K. Whitaker memorandum, 'A note on North-South policy,' 11 November 1968 (UCD Archives, Dr Kenneth Whitaker Papers, P175).

150. T. K. Whitaker memorandum, 'A note on North-South policy,' 11 November 1968 (UCD Archives, Dr Kenneth Whitaker Papers, P175).

151. T. K. Whitaker memorandum, 'A note on North-South policy,' 11 November 1968 (UCD Archives, Dr Kenneth Whitaker Papers, P175).

152. T. K. Whitaker memorandum, 'A note on North-South policy,' 11 November 1968 (UCD Archives, Dr Kenneth Whitaker Papers, P175).

153. T. K. Whitaker memorandum, 'A note on North-South policy,' 11 November 1968 (UCD Archives, Dr Kenneth Whitaker Papers, P175).

154. T. K. Whitaker memorandum, 'A note on North-South policy,' 11 November 1968 (UCD Archives, Dr Kenneth Whitaker Papers, P175).

155. Paul Bew and Gordon Gillespie, *Northern Ireland*, p. 7–8.

156. Paul Bew and Gordon Gillespie, *Northern Ireland*, p. 8.

157. Paul Bew and Gordon Gillespie, *Northern Ireland*, p. 9–10.

158. O'Neill to Whitaker, 18 December 1968 (UCD Archives, Dr Kenneth Whitaker Papers, P175).

159. Michael Kennedy, *Division and Consensus*, p. 320.

160. Paul Bew and Gordon Gillespie, *Northern Ireland*, p. 11–12.

161. 'Lynch's address to ard fheis delegates,' *Irish Times*, 29 January 1969.

162. 'Lynch's address to ard fheis delegates,' *Irish Times*, 29 January 1969.

163. 'Lynch's address to ard fheis delegates,' *Irish Times*, 29 January 1969.

164. 'Lynch's address to ard fheis delegates,' *Irish Times*, 29 January 1969.

165. I am not persuaded to accept Dr Michael Kennedy's conclusion that Lynch 'was siding with the hawks in his cabinet' (Michael Kennedy, *Division and Consensus*, p. 320). The Blaney speech at Letterkenny in December 1969 revealed the thinking of a hawk. Lynch never approached that level of nationalist extremism.

166. Michael Kennedy, *Division and Consensus*, p. 322.

167. Michael Kennedy, *Division and Consensus*.

168. Whitaker to Haughey, 21 April 1969 (UCD Archives, Dr Kenneth Whitaker Papers, P175).

169. Report of ambassador, J. G. Molloy, 7 May 1969 (National Archives, file 2000/6/657, S9361M.

170. Points for discussion with the British authorities, 29 July 1969 (National Archives, file 2000/8/38 and DFA 305/14/386).

171. Michael Kennedy, *Division and Consensus*, p. 326.

172. Michael Kennedy, *Division and Consensus*, p. 329.

173. Brian M. Walker (ed.), *Parliamentary Election Results in Ireland*, p. 211–12.

174. Dermot Keogh, *Twentieth Century Ireland*, p. 296.

175. Anon., 'Horseman, pass by!: Charles J. Haughey' (3), *Irish Times*, 11 June 1969.

176. Dermot Keogh, *Twentieth Century Ireland*, p. 294–5.

177. Fergal Tobin, *The Best of Decades*, p. 217. This point has been made by Tobin and by other writers.

178. Doland Harman Akenson, *Conor*, vol. 1, p. 335–6. See also, Conor Cruise O'Brien, *Memoir*, p. 317–.

179. As a student in UCD I was very much persuaded by the appeal of the radical policies of the Labour Party and was naïve enough to believe in a major advance for the cause of socialism in Ireland. It was a pipe-dream.

180. Conor Cruise O'Brien explained the logic behind Joe McCarthyism Irish-style as follows: 'But in fact "communism" is a technical term in the political vocabulary of the Catholic state. Formally, in the late 20th century, you can't be seen to go round demanding to know when your opponent was last at mass, confession or

holy communion. This would be sectarian behaviour: unmodern, uncivilized, resembling the goings-on in the North of Ireland. But if there is reason to believe your opponent may be vulnerable in this area, you could at that time hit him just as accurately by calling him a communist. This was a political charge, impeccably 20th century in character. (The fact that Senator Joe McCarthy was eventually discredited never made much impact on public opinion in Ireland.) But as well as being a political term, "communism" carried a "religious" message: communists are known to be atheists also. So the question of the opponent's religious faith, or lack of it, comes automatically into the zone of legitimate political discussion. A good Catholic, by definition, cannot be a communist. But a bad Catholic may well be one since he, also by definition, being bad, is capable of anything, so may very well be a communist. So, if you call someone a communist, and have no proof of this, you may discreetly adduce indications establishing a presumption of communism: educated at a Protestant school and university, first marriage ended in divorce. These proofs are not coercive in respect of communism, but communism is really beside the point. The point is to show that your opponent is a bad Catholic, so as to enlist the help of the church in eliminating him and his associates from public life, to the benefit of yourself and your associates.' Conor Cruise O'Brien, *Memoir*, p. 319–20.

181. Doland Harman Akenson, *Conor*, vol. 1, p. 337–8.
182. 'Lynch calls on Corish to define "New Republic", *Irish Times*, 16 July 1969.
183. 'Choice is reality or Cuban myth—Lynch,' *Irish Times*, 17 June 1969.
184. A former chairman of CIE, A. P. Reynolds, had owned the property. See Dorothy Walker, *Patrick Scott, Architect*, p. 119.
185. Stephen Collins, *The Power Game*, p. 45–6.
186. Editorial, 'Mr Haughey's House (2),' *Irish Times*, 13 June 1969.
187. Editorial, 'Mr Haughey's House (2),' *Irish Times*, 13 June 1969.
188. Quoted by Dick Walsh in *The Party*, p. 95.
189. James Doyle, 'Taoiseach's cabinet changes awaited,' *Cork Weekly Examiner*, 26 June 1969.
190. Kevin Boland to Lynch, 27 June 1969 (Jack Lynch Papers).
191. Kevin Boland to Lynch, 27 June 1969 (Jack Lynch Papers).
192. Kevin Boland to Lynch, 27 June 1969 (Jack Lynch Papers).
193. Kevin Boland to Lynch, 27 June 1969 (Jack Lynch Papers).
194. Other appointments as parliamentary secretary were Paudge Brennan (Local Government), John Geoghegan (Social Welfare), Noel Lemass (Finance), Jerry Cronin (Agriculture and Fisheries), Robert Molloy (Education) and Gerry Collins (Industry and Commerce and the Gaeltacht).
195. *Parliamentary Debates: Dáil Éireann: Official Report*, vol. 241, col. 44–5, 2 July 1969.
196. *Parliamentary Debates: Dáil Éireann: Official Report*, vol. 241, col. 52, 2 July 1969.
197. *Parliamentary Debates: Dáil Éireann: Official Report*, vol. 241, col. 119–22, 2 July 1969.
198. *Parliamentary Debates: Dáil Éireann: Official Report*, vol. 241, col. 147, 2 July 1969.

199. *Parliamentary Debates: Dáil Éireann: Official Report,* vol. 241, col. 148, 2 July 1969.

200. *Parliamentary Debates: Dáil Éireann: Official Report,* vol. 241, col. 144, 2 July 1969.

Chapter 7 (P. 163–287)

1. Paul Bew and Gordon Gillespie, *Northern Ireland,* p. 16–17.

2. David McKittrick et al., *Lost Lives,* p. 32.

3. In the early days of the 'troubles' a violent death was still newsworthy. On 19 April, Samuel Devenney, aged forty-two, the father of nine children, was beaten and badly injured by the police as he stood talking to a neighbour near the front door of his house in William Street, Derry. A group of RUC men charged a group of young people, some of whom escaped through the Devenney house. They broke down the front door and batoned the family. Mr Devenney received multiple injuries and a possible fractured skull and also had a heart attack. He was discharged from hospital after three days but readmitted the following day and kept there until 19 May. He died on 16 July from what the inquest described as 'natural causes.' Inside the RUC a conspiracy of silence prevented any charges ever being brought. Feelings among nationalists were inflamed by the death. David McKittrick et al., *Lost Lives,* p. 32.

4. Minute by CH [Con Howard?], 24 July 1969 (National Archives, file 2000/8/38 and DFA 305/14/386).

5. Minute by CH [Con Howard?], 24 July 1969 (National Archives, file 2000/8/38 and DFA 305/14/386).

6. Minute by Con Howard, 24 July 1969 (National Archives, file 2000/8/38 and DFA 305/14/386).

7. Minute by Con Howard, 24 July 1969 (National Archives, file 2000/8/38 and DFA 305/14/386).

8. Points for discussion with the British authorities, 29 July 1969 (National Archives, file 2000/8/38 and DFA 305/14/386).

9. Memorandum of meeting on 1 August 1969 between the Irish Minister for External Affairs, Dr Patrick Hillery and the Secretary of State for Foreign and Commonwealth Office, Michael Stewart (National Archives, file 2000/8/38 and DFA 305/14/386).

10. Memorandum of meeting on 1 August 1969 between the Irish Minister for External Affairs, Dr Patrick Hillery and the Secretary of State for Foreign and Commonwealth Office, Michael Stewart (National Archives, file 2000/8/38 and DFA 305/14/386).

11. Memorandum of meeting on 1 August 1969 between the Irish Minister for External Affairs, Dr Patrick Hillery and the Secretary of State for Foreign and Commonwealth Office, Michael Stewart (National Archives, file 2000/8/38 and DFA 305/14/386).

12. Dick Walsh, 'N.I. cabinet to meet over marches issue,' *Irish Times,* 11 August 1969.

13. 'Prayers for peace in Derry churches,' *Irish Times,* 11 August 1969.

14. Dennis Kennedy, 'Bogside barricades go up as tempers flare,' *Irish Times,* 12 August 1969.

15. Editorial, 'Derry', *Irish Times*, 12 August 1969.
16. Various reports, *Irish Times*, 13 August 1969.
17. McCann to Ó Nualláin [Nicholas Nolan], 13 August 1969 (National Archives, file 2000/6/657 S9361 M).
18. McCann to Ó Nualláin [Nicholas Nolan], 13 August 1969 (National Archives, file 2000/6/657 S9361 M). The texts read as follows:

DRAFT A

'Irishmen in every part of this island have made known their deep concern at the bitter fighting which took place yesterday in Derry and to a lesser extent in some other northern towns. Their concern is heightened by the realisation that the new spirit of reform and inter-communal cooperation, introduced so hopefully under the Government of Captain O'Neill is slowly but steadily being eroded and unhappily seems to be giving way to the forces of sectarianism and prejudice and many are now afraid that reform when it comes may come too late. All men of good will must feel sorry and disappointment at this seemingly backward turn of events and must be apprehensive as regards the future.

'The Government share fully these feelings and wish to repeat that they deplore sectarianism and intolerance wherever they occur north or south in this island and no matter who is responsible. On 1st August the Minister for External Affairs went to London specifically to express to the British Government our grave concern at the possibility of widespread disorder and bloodshed in Derry on 13 August and the danger that the situation might get out of control. We urged strongly that the Parade should be banned, or failing that the British Government should take all possible action in advance to ensure that violence would not occur. In addition we pressed the need for the acceleration of the existing programme of civil rights reform and the widening of the scope of that programme to include further reforms. We pointed to the evidence that inter-group relationships had already seriously deteriorated as was shown by the growing tension and division on sectarian lines which was already taking place in the major northern towns and cities.

'The Government have no wish to do anything which might heighten the tensions and the divisions which exist in the north. Our policy has been to continue to cooperate in a spirit of friendliness and good neighbourliness with the Stormont Government without any deviation from our political principles: this will remain the policy of the Government. However, we must point out that if matters continue to worsen and the forces of reaction progressively gain ground in the future, this Government will not be able to sit idly by while Irish people suffer. We have said in the past and we repeat that there can be no question that the concern voiced by Irishmen in every part of Ireland at this time is the concern of the whole people of Ireland, and that as a democratically elected Government we have the right to speak on behalf of those people. In view of the gravity of the current situation, the Government have decided to request further discussions at the earliest date with the British government at the highest level.'

DRAFT B

'It is with deep sadness that I, in common with all Irishmen of goodwill, have learned of the tragic events which took place yesterday in Derry and elsewhere in the North in recent days. Our sorrow is heightened by the realisation that the new spirit of reform and inter-community co-operation introduced so hopefully is slowly but steadily being eroded and unhappily seems to be giving way to the forces of sectarianism and prejudice. All must share the sorrow and disappointment at this seemingly backward turn of events and must be apprehensive as regards the future. We deplore sectarianism and intolerance wherever they occur and, most of all, in this island, North or South, no matter who may be responsible.

'The continuing strife and unrest in the North clearly reflects the need for the acceleration of the existing programme of civil rights reform and the widening of the scope of that programme to include remedies for all outstanding widely felt grievances. In the situation with such a tragic history as the North, where the rights of the minority have been so frequently disregarded by the majority, promises of reform are in themselves not enough. In order that these may receive credibility from the minority they must be as comprehensive as possible and implemented without any avoidable delay. Meanwhile, the authorities in their day-to-day actions, whether at the central, local or police level, must not alone act fairly and without discrimination but also be seen to so act. Lest reform, when it comes, may come too late, I would earnestly urge the authorities in the North to re-examine their programme of reform to see in what respects they can widen its scope and expedite its implementation.

'In the present very tense situation I do not want to do or say anything which might exacerbate the position. I shall not, therefore, say more at this time on this point. The British Government are already aware of our views as, at my request, the Minister for External Affairs went to London at the beginning of this month specifically to make known to the British Government our concern about the whole situation. We have said in the past, and we repeat, that there can be no question but that this situation is the concern of the people in all parts of Ireland and that, as a democratically elected Government we have the right—indeed the duty—to speak.

'As you are aware, we as a government and people, have been doing what we can to promote the cause of peace in the world and respect for fundamental human rights and freedoms everywhere. We have been active at the United Nations. Our troops have served in this cause in Africa, Asia and in the Middle East. We are justly proud of the contribution they have made. It is my ardent hope that all Irishmen, North or South, will be inspired by the same desire for peace in our own island and I make this plea to them this evening. I earnestly appeal for restraint on all sides even in the face of provocation. Let no one do anything to aggravate the situation. Let us all work for peace—not just peace—but peace with justice for the whole of Ireland.

19. Interview with Dr Patrick Hillery, Spanish Point, Co. Clare, 25 August 2005.
20. Minute, 13 August 1969, 4.00 p.m. (National Archives, file 2000/8/657 S9361N). A phone call was received at 4 p.m. in the Taoiseach's office from Liam

Cunningham, TD for Blaney's constituency of Donegal North-East, to the effect that there had been a lull in the conflict in Derry at that moment but that further trouble was expected later that night. He said: 'Tear gas is being used on an extensive scale by the RUC.' The Bishop of Derry, Bishop Neil Farren, was trying to arrange for the evacuation of women and children and had asked the parish priest of Buncrana, Father O'Brien, to prepare the local hall to receive them.

21. Stephen Collins, *The Power Game*, p. 38.
22. Rush to McCann, 14 August 1969 (National Archives, file 2000/8/38). See also file DFA 305/14/386.
23. Dick Walsh, *The Party*, p. 96.
24. Stephen Collins, *The Power Game*, p. 38.
25. Pádraig Faulkner, *As I Saw It*, p. 91–2.
26. Stephen Collins, *The Power Game*, p. 38.
27. I am grateful to Commandant Victor Lang, head of Military Archives, for providing this information (phone call to History Department, UCC, 2 February 2007).
28. Dick Walsh, *The Party*, p. 96.
29. Pádraig Faulkner, *As I Saw It*, p. 91–2.
30. Dick Walsh, *The Party*, p. 98.
31. Stephen Collins, *The Power Game*, p. 56.
32. Pádraig Faulkner, *As I Saw It*, p. 91–2.
33. Michael Kennedy, *Division and Consensus*, p. 336.
34. Interview with Des Hanafin, 12 August 2005.
35. Desmond Fisher, 'An Irishman's Diary,' *Irish Times*, 25 October 1999.
36. Interview with Des Hanafin, Thurles, Co. Tipperary, August 2005.
37. The Cork county senior hurling championship was down to Glen Rovers v. Blackrock and UCC v. Muskerry. *Cork Examiner*, 14 August 1969.
38. Desmond Fisher, 'An Irishman's Diary,' *Irish Times*, 25 October 1999.
39. Pádraig Faulkner, *As I Saw It*, p. 92.
40. *Cork Examiner*, 14 August 1969.
41. 'UN force in North sought by Lynch,' *Irish Times*, 14 August 19569.
42. Andrew Whitaker, 'Britain rebuts Lynch,' *Irish Times*, 14 August 1969.
43. Eamonn Gallagher, Report, 25 September 1969 (National Archives, file 2000/6/659 D/T S93610).
44. Various reports in the *Irish Times*, 14 August 1969.
45. 'Army sets up Border hospitals,' *Irish Times*, 14 August 1969.
46. Editorial: 'Even the Devil,' *Irish Times*, 15 August 1969.
47. Nolan to McCann, 14 August 1969 (National Archives, file 2000/5/12 DFA 305/14/192E).
48. Nolan to McCann, 15 August 1969 (National Archives, file 2000/5/12 DFA 305/14/192E).
49. Stephen Collins, *The Power Game*, p. 32.
50. Whitaker to Lynch (draft letter), 15 August 1969 (UCD Archives, Dr Kenneth Whitaker Papers, P175).

51. Whitaker to Lynch (draft letter), 15 August 1969 (UCD Archives, Dr Kenneth Whitaker Papers, P175).
52. Whitaker to Lynch (draft letter), 15 August 1969 (UCD Archives, Dr Kenneth Whitaker Papers, P175).
53. Whitaker to Lynch (draft letter), 15 August 1969 (UCD Archives, Dr Kenneth Whitaker Papers, P175).
54. Whitaker to Lynch (draft letter), 15 August 1969 (UCD Archives, Dr Kenneth Whitaker Papers, P175).
55. John Lynch, Irish Unity, Northern Ireland and Anglo-Irish Relations (August 1969–October 1971), Government Information Bureau, Dublin, 1971, p. 4.
56. David McKittrick et al., *Lost Lives*, p. 32–7.
57. David McKittrick et al., *Lost Lives*, p. 38–9.
58. See photograph, *Irish Times*, 16 August 1969.
59. Lynch minute, 16 August 1969 (National Archives, file 2000/6/657 S9361M).
60. Lynch minute, 16 August 1969 (National Archives, file 2000/6/657 S9361M).
61. Also in attendance on the British side were Mr Fayle, private secretary to Lord Chalfont, and Mr Pendleton, News Department, Foreign and Commonwealth Office.
62. Memorandum on discussion at the Foreign and Commonwealth Office, 15 August 1969, concerning Northern Ireland [n.d.] (National Archives, file 2000/8/38). See also file DFA 305/14/386.
63. Memorandum on discussion at the Foreign and Commonwealth Office, 15 August 1969, concerning Northern Ireland [n.d.] (National Archives, file 2000/8/38). See also file DFA 305/14/386.
64. Memorandum on discussion at the Foreign and Commonwealth Office, 15 August 1969, concerning Northern Ireland [n.d.] (National Archives, file 2000/8/38). See also file DFA 305/14/386.
65. Noel Dorr, '1969: A United Nations peacekeeping force for Northern Ireland?' in Michael Kennedy and Deirdre McMahon (eds.), *Obligations and Responsibilities*, p. 262–3.
66. *Irish Times*, 16 August 1969.
67. Editorial, 'Time and the North,' *Irish Times*, 16 August 1969.
68. 'Sinn Féin request arms at barracks,' *Irish Times*, 16 August 1969.
69. Nolan to McCann, 16 August 1969 (National Archives, file 2000/5/12 DFA 305/14/192E.
70. Michael Kennedy, *Division and Consensus*, p. 346.
71. Nicholas Nolan minute, 18 August 1969 (National Archives, file 2000/6/658 S9361N).
72. Nicholas Nolan minute, 18 August 1969 (National Archives, file 2000/6/658, S9361N).
73. 'Gardai use batons on demonstrators,' *Irish Times*, 18 August 1969.
74. Department of External Affairs minute (copied to Taoiseach's private secretary and to Secretary of the Department of Justice, Peter Berry), 18 August 1969 (National Archives, file 2000/6/658 S9361N).

75. 'O'Brien sees necessity for quick solution,' *Irish Times,* 18 August 1969.

76. Paul Bew and Gordon Gillespie, *Northern Ireland,* p. 20–21.

77. Paul Bew and Gordon Gillespie, *Northern Ireland,* p. 20–21.

78. Paul Bew and Gordon Gillespie, *Northern Ireland,* p. 18 and 21.

79. Government Decision, Item 1, 21 August 1969 (National Archives, file DT S9361N).

80. Pádraig Faulkner, *As I Saw It,* p. 93.

81. Stephen Collins, *The Power Game,* p. 57.

82. Undated Government Information Bureau memorandum, c. 16 August 1969 (Jack Lynch Papers).

83. Frank R. O'Connor, assistant director, RTE, 26 September 1969 (National Archives, file 2000/6/660 D/T S93621P).

84. Briefing note from the Department of External Affairs entitled 'Implementation of Government's decisions,' 18 August 1969 (National Archives, file 2000/5/12 DFA 305/14/192E).

85. Undated Government Information Bureau memorandum, c. 16 August 1969 (Jack Lynch Papers).

86. Bruce Arnold, *Jack Lynch,* p. 108. See also Stephen Collins, *The Power Game,* p. 57.

87. Undated Government Information Bureau memorandum, c. 16 August 1969 (Jack Lynch Papers).

88. Seamus Brady, 'Eyewitness report from Derry,' 19 August 1969 (National Archives, file 2000/6/658, S9361N).

89. T. Ryle Dwyer, *Nice Fellow,* p. 188.

90. Seamus Brady, *Arms and the Men,* p. 59–61.

91. Confidential source.

92. *Irish Times,* 18 August 1969.

93. Briefing note from Department of External Affairs entitled 'Implementation of Government's decisions,' 18 August 1969 (National Archives, file 2000/5/12 DFA 305/14/192E).

94. Briefing note from Department of External Affairs entitled 'Implementation of Government's decisions,' 18 August 1969 (National Archives, file 2000/5/12 DFA 305/14/192E).

95. Noel Dorr, '1969: A United Nations peacekeeping force for Northern Ireland?' in Michael Kennedy and Deirdre McMahon, *Obligations and Responsibilities,* p. 267–8.

96. Noel Dorr, '1969: A United Nations peacekeeping force for Northern Ireland?' in Michael Kennedy and Deirdre McMahon, *Obligations and Responsibilities,* p. 268.

97. Noel Dorr, '1969: A United Nations peacekeeping force for Northern Ireland?' in Michael Kennedy and Deirdre McMahon, *Obligations and Responsibilities,* p. 270.

98. Cremin report, 13 October 1969 (National Archives, file S9361N).

99. DFA minute, probably Hugh McCann, 21 August 1969 (National Archives, file DT S9361N).

100. Editorial, 'The day's work,' *Irish Times,* 21 January 1969.

101. Department of Foreign Affairs minute, probably Hugh McCann, 21 August 1969 (National Archives, file DT S9361N).

102. Noel Dorr, '1969: A United Nations peacekeeping force for Northern Ireland?' in Michael Kennedy and Deirdre McMahon, *Obligations and Responsibilities*, p. 272.

103. Noel Dorr, '1969: A United Nations peacekeeping force for Northern Ireland?' in Michael Kennedy and Deirdre McMahon, *Obligations and Responsibilities*, p. 276–7.

104. 'IRA has units in the North,' *Irish Times*, 19 August 1969.

105. John Lynch, Irish Unity, Northern Ireland and Anglo-Irish Relations (August 1969–October 1971), Government Information Bureau, Dublin, 1971, p. 5.

106. Minute by Hugh McCann, 20 August 1969 (National Archives, file S9361N).

107. Minute by Hugh McCann, 20 August 1969 (National Archives, file S9361N).

108. 'Reaction to IRA statement,' *Irish Times*, 20 August 1969.

109. Máirín and Jack Lynch were close to McMahon. Before they bought their house in Rathgar in the 1950s they had a flat in the house owned by the McMahons. See Bruce Arnold, *Jack Lynch*, p. 130.

110. 'The Peter Berry diaries,' 19 and 20 August 1969,' *Magill*, June 1980, p. 52.

111. 'The Peter Berry diaries,' 19 and 20 August 1969,' *Magill*, June 1980, p. 52.

112. 'The Peter Berry diaries,' 19 and 20 August 1969,' *Magill*, June 1980, p. 51–2.

113. 'The Peter Berry diaries,' 19 and 20 August 1969,' *Magill*, June 1980, p. 51–2.

114. See 'The Peter Berry diaries,' *Magill*, June 1980, p. 52, quoted by Bruce Arnold in *Jack Lynch*, p. 115.

115. Jack Lynch desk diary, Wednesday 27 August 1969 (Jack Lynch Papers).

116. He was also listed to meet a Japanese television crew in the afternoon and Pearse Wyse TD at 4:30. See desk diary, 1969 (Jack Lynch Papers).

117. John Lynch, Irish Unity, Northern Ireland and Anglo-Irish Relations (August 1969–October 1971), Government Information Bureau, Dublin, 1971, p. 6–8. The text of the speech is as follows:

'I am glad that the British Home Secretary has come to Ireland to see and hear for himself. It is of vital importance that present tensions are eased and solutions of the immediate problems be found. For one thing, the minority in the North cannot be expected to live with a police force which they distrust and even fear: therefore, no one will disagree with Mr. Callaghan's contention that a police force that is respected and accepted is an essential element of a democratic society. Even if the Six County police force is to be reorganised and even if there is to be a marked acceleration in the pace of reforms, these would be interim solutions only. Nothing must be left undone to avoid a recurrence of the present troubles, whether in five or fifty years, but to continue to ignore the need for fundamental constitutional change, so clearly necessary, could only have such a tragic result. The time has come when everybody concerned must face up to the urgent necessity of finding an acceptable long-term solution. Already the presence of British troops and the placing of the existing police forces under the command of the British GOC have wrought a fundamental change in the constitutional status of the Six Counties. There can be no return to the status quo. Distrust and fear must be banished and the barriers of suspicion and prejudice must be removed. That this is possible is illustrated by the fact that people of all religions can live as equals in peace and friendship with each other in this part of the country and that the religious minority have no fears whatsoever of any discrimination against them. I know that the ultimate solution that we seek will not easily or expeditiously come about but the Irish Government are prepared to explore every reasonable prospect. A solution along Federal lines has been more than once suggested. My Government are ready and willing to discuss this possibility with the British Government. If this could be achieved only through intermediate stages—and such possibilities could well emerge in the course of objective examination and constructive discussion of the over-all problem—we would be more than anxious to pursue them. I recognise that there are social and economic problems involved as well but my Government do not regard these as insurmountable. We want to see all Irishmen living in peace and harmony together as one community and as one nation.'

118. Erskine Childers memorandum, 26 August 1969 (National Archives, file 2000/6/659 D/T 9361O).

119. Erskine Childers memorandum, 26 August 1969 (National Archives, file 2000/6/659 D/T 9361O).

120. Erskine Childers memorandum, 26 August 1969 (National Archives, file 2000/6/659 D/T 9361O).

121. Personal views of Heads of Missions on the North of Ireland, 16 September 1969 (National Archives, file 2000/5/15 DFA 305/14/193/3).

122. Personal views of Heads of Missions on the North of Ireland, 16 September 1969 (National Archives, file 2000/5/15 DFA 305/14/193/3).

123. Personal views of Heads of Missions on the North of Ireland, 16 September 1969 (National Archives, file 2000/5/15 DFA 305/14/193/3).

124. Personal views of Heads of Missions on the North of Ireland, 16 September 1969 (National Archives, file 2000/5/15 DFA 305/14/193/3).

125. Personal views of Heads of Missions on the North of Ireland, 16 September 1969 (National Archives, file 2000/5/15 DFA 305/14/193/3).

126. Molloy to McCann, 12 September 1969 (National Archives, file 2000/5/15 DFA 305/14/193/3.

127. Molloy to McCann, 12 September 1969 (National Archives, file 2000/5/15 DFA 305/14/193/3).

128. Molloy to McCann, 12 September 1969 (National Archives, file 2000/5/15 DFA 305/14/193/3).

129. Molloy to McCann, 12 September 1969 (National Archives, file 2000/5/15 DFA 305/14/193/3). The chargé d'affaires in Washington, Seán Donlon, wrote on 16 September in reply to the same circular. He suggested that the British Government should set up a canton comprising Belfast, Co. Antrim and north Co. Down as an autonomous mini-state within the present Constitution of Ireland. This would excluded the four-and-a-half counties where there was a majority of nationalists in favour of unification with the South. The British Government would transfer its present powers in relation to taxation, defence and external affairs to the all-Ireland government in Dublin. An alternative was

to have Stormont discredited and abolished and all powers transferred to the British House of Commons, when it would be easier to deal with the Attlee Government's pledge in the Ireland Act (1949). The second phase would be reunification. The Donlon proposal favoured the continuity of a reformed Stormont and after ten years reunification. In relation to the intervention of the United Nations he felt this could be achieved through an Irish military intervention across the border. But he felt this would be a high-risk policy, as 'whether or not the British Army reacted, the B Specials, Buntings group and many other Unionists certainly would, if not against the "invading" Battalion certainly against the Nationalist civilians in the North. There would be bloodshed, deaths and lasting bitterness among Irishmen for which the Irish Government would rightly be held responsible.' Donlon felt that if the British army reacted it would certainly defeat the Irish force. He felt that 'the Irish government could be in the wrong before the world as aggressors,' and 'British Government goodwill would be lost.' He mentioned the idea of sending in the Irish army because it had been put forward by some Irish-American groups, which had 'not thought the matter through.' In conclusion, he stressed the relevance of the canton option.

130. Whitaker to Lynch, 13 September 1969 (UCD Archives, Dr Kenneth Whitaker Papers, P175).

131. 'I would like in clear and simple terms to set out the basis of our thinking and policy. I hope that this will help to reduce those tensions in the North which arise from misunderstandings or apprehensions about our attitude or intentions.

'The historical and natural unity of Ireland was also a political unity until this was artificially sundered by the Government of Ireland Act passed by the British Government in 1920. The Act, in effect, provided for the partitioning of Ireland and the creation of a Government of Northern Ireland subordinate to Westminster. Partition was not expected to be permanent even by the authors of this statute—the ultimate aim of "one Parliament and one Government for the whole of Ireland" appeared in the official summary of the Bill preceding this legislation and provision was made for a Council of Ireland which, according as powers were transferred to it by the two parts of Ireland, might develop into an All-Ireland Parliament.

'Mr. Asquith, former British Prime Minister, said: "Ireland is a nation; not two nations, but one nation. There are few cases in history, and as a student of history in a humble way, I myself know none, of a nationality at once so distinct, so persistent, and so assimilative as the Irish."

'Mr. Winston Churchill once said: "Whatever Ulster's right may be, she cannot stand in the way of the whole of the rest of Ireland. Half a province cannot impose a permanent veto on the nation. Half a province cannot obstruct forever the reconciliation between the British and the Irish democracies and deny all satisfaction to the united wishes of the British Empire."

'King George V, speaking in Belfast at the opening of the Northern Ireland Parliament in June 1921, hoped that the opening would be: "the prelude of the day in which the Irish people, North and South, under one Parliament or two, as those Parliaments may themselves decide, shall work together in common love for Ireland upon the sure foundation of mutual justice and respect."

'I need not explain or justify the fundamental desire of the overwhelming majority of the people of this island for the restoration in some form of its national unity. This desire is not confined to Irishmen of any particular creed or ancestry. I want to make it clear, however, once more, that we have no intention of using force to realise this desire. I said as recently as 28th August that it was and has been the Government's policy to seek the re-unification of the country by peaceful means.

'The unity we seek is not something forced but a free and genuine union of those living in Ireland based on mutual respect and tolerance and guaranteed by a form or forms of government authority in Ireland providing for—progressive improvement of social, economic and cultural life in a just and peaceful environment.

'Of its nature this policy—of seeking unity through agreement in Ireland between Irishmen—is a long-term one. It is no less, indeed it is even more, patriotic for that. Perseverance in winning the respect and confidence of those now opposed to unity must be sustained by goodwill, patience, understanding and, at times, forbearance.

'The terrible events of the past few months have made it evident to all that, apart from disrupting the unity of Ireland, the 1920 devolution of powers has not provided a system of government, acceptable as fair and just, to many of the people in Northern Ireland. I need not detail these events nor refer to recent objective appraisals of that system of government. But change there obviously must be. We are concerned that the grievances of so many of our fellow Irishmen and women be quickly remedied and their fears set at rest. We also have a legitimate concern regarding the disposition to be made by the British Government in relation to the future administration of Northern Ireland. Our views on how peace and justice can be assured in this small island are relevant and entitled to be heard.

'Let me make it clear, too, that in seeking re-unification, our aim is not to extend the domination of Dublin. We have many times down the years expressed our willingness to seek a solution on federal fines and in my most recent statement I envisaged the possibility of intermediate stages in an approach to a final agreed solution.

'Whatever the constitutional setting might be—and we are prepared to explore all the possibilities in constructive discussion—the united Ireland we desire is one in which there would be a scrupulously fair deal for all. The Protestants of the North need have no fear of any interference with their religious freedom or civil liberties and rights.

'Differences in political outlook or religious belief need not set people apart. They exist in most countries and are no barrier to effective and constructive co-operation of the various elements in the community in national development. Indeed, diversity of cultural background can exert a stimulating influence. The real barriers are those created by fear, suspicion and intolerance.

'Every responsible person must hope that early and adequate reforms will bring peace and security to the people of the North of Ireland so that they may live together in neighbourliness without fear, sharing fairly in improving social and economic conditions, and with fading memories of past dissensions.

'It will remain our most earnest aim and hope to win the consent of the majority of the people in the Six Counties to means by which North and South can come together in a re-united and sovereign Ireland earning international respect both for the fairness and efficiency with which it is administered and for its contribution to world peace and progress.

'Finally, a few words on recognition. It is quite unreasonable for any Unionist to expect my Government, or any future Government, to abandon the belief and hope that Ireland should be re-united. It is unnecessary to repeat that we seek re-unification by peaceful means. We are not seeking to overthrow by violence the Stormont Parliament or Government but rather to win the agreement of a sufficient number of people in the North to an acceptable form of re-unification. In any case the Stormont Government, being the executive instrument of a subordinate parliament, cannot receive formal international recognition.

'It is also, for similar reasons, unreasonable and unnecessary to expect those living in the Six Counties who share our desire for unity to renounce their deepest hopes. We and they have accepted as a practical matter the existence of a government in the North of Ireland exercising certain powers devolved on it by the British Parliament. We have had many fruitful contacts with that Government in matters of mutual concern. I hope that this co-operation between North and South will continue. May I conclude by referring to the words of Lord Craigavon, the first Prime Minister of Northern Ireland, when he said: "In this island, we cannot live always separated from one another. We are too small to be apart or for the Border to be there for all time."'

132. Whitaker to Lynch, 22 September 1969 (UCD Archives, Dr Kenneth Whitaker Papers, P175).

133. Whitaker to Lynch, 22 September 1969 (UCD Archives, Dr Kenneth Whitaker Papers, P175).

134. Eamonn Gallagher report, 22 September 1969 (National Archives, file 2000/6/660 D/T S9361P).

135. Whitaker to Lynch, 22 September 1969 (UCD Archives, Dr Kenneth Whitaker Papers, P175).

136. Whitaker to Lynch, 22 September 1969 (UCD Archives, Dr Kenneth Whitaker Papers, P175).

137. Whitaker to Lynch, 22 September 1969 (UCD Archives, Dr Kenneth Whitaker Papers, P175).

138. Haughey to Lynch, 25 September 1969 (National Archives, file 2000/6/660 D/T S9361P).

139. Haughey draft letter (National Archives, file 2000/6/660 D/T S9361P).

140. Whitaker to Lynch, 24 November 1969 (National Archives, file 2001/8/6 (1)).

141. Department of Finance Memorandum, 'The Constitution of Northern Ireland'

(National Archives, file 2001/8/6 (1)).

142. Department of Finance Memorandum, 'The Constitution of Northern Ireland' (National Archives, file 2001/8/6 (1)).

143. Department of Finance Memorandum, 'The Constitution of Northern Ireland' (National Archives, file 2001/8/6 (1)).

144. Whitaker memorandum, 18 October 1969 (Jack Lynch Papers).

145. *Parliamentary Debates: Dáil Éireann: Official Report*, 22 October 1969.

146. Memorandum, 'Northern situation: Publicity campaign: Supplementary estimates: Parliamentary programme (National Archives, file 2000/6/660 D/T S9361P).

147. T. Ryle Dwyer, *Nice Fellow*, p. 189.

148. Justin O'Brien, *The Arms Trial*, p. 68.

149. Interview with Paul Mackay.

150. Seamus Brady, *Arms and the Men*, p. 94–5.

151. Justin O'Brien, *The Arms Trial*, p. 75–6.

152. Seamus Brady, *Arms and the Men*, p. 95.

153. Justin O'Brien, *The Arms Trial*, p. 75–6.

154. Justin O'Brien, *The Arms Trial*, p. 75–6.

155. Justin O'Brien, *The Arms Trial*, p. 78–9.

156. Interview with Paul Mackay.

157. Interview with Paul Mackay, Dublin, 17 August 2005.

158. Born in Bonnettsrath, Co. Kilkenny, in August 1924, he attended St Kieran's College, Kilkenny, and University College, Dublin. He was a member of Kilkenny County Council from 1954 to 1976 and was elected to Dáil Éireann in 1957.

159. Interview with Dr Patrick Hillery, Spanish Point, Co. Clare, 25 August 2005.

160. Frank Kilfeather, 'Death of Lieut-General Seán Mac Eoin,' *Irish Times*, 12 February 2007.

161. Confidential military source, Cork, 12 February 2007.

162. 'The Peter Berry diaries,' *Magill*, June 1980, p. 52.

163. Obituary, 'An Irish Dreyfus who spent a life trying to clear his name,' *Irish Times*, 19 July 2003.

164. Dáil Éireann, Committee of Public Accounts, Wednesday 27 January 1971, p. 315–17.

165. Obituary, 'An Irish Dreyfus who spent a life trying to clear his name,' *Irish Times*, 19 July 2003.

166. It may be worth asking, at this stage, about the level of co-operation between Military Intelligence and the Special Branch in the autumn of 1969. Was there an unhealthy rivalry between the two agencies? The pace of events took most agencies by surprise and personnel were very overworked.

167. Vincent Browne, 'The Arms Crisis, 1970, part 1,' *Magill*, May 1980, p. 33.

168. 'The Peter Berry diaries,' *Magill*, June 1980, p. 52.

169. 'The Peter Berry diaries,' *Magill*, June 1980, p. 52.

170. Berry recorded that the arrival of the Minister for Finance, in time for afternoon tea, caused greater excitement among the nurses than an earlier visit by President de Valera. 'The Peter Berry diaries,' *Magill*, June 1980, p. 52.

171. 'The Peter Berry diaries,' *Magill*, June 1980, p. 53.

172. Michael Mills, *Hurler on the Ditch,* p. 166.

173. 'The Peter Berry diaries,' *Magill,* June 1980, p. 53.

174. Michael Mills, *Hurler on the Ditch,* p. 166.

175. 'The Peter Berry diaries,' *Magill,* June 1980, p. 53.

176. 'The Peter Berry diaries,' *Magill,* June 1980, p. 54.

177. 'The Peter Berry diaries,' *Magill,* June 1980, p. 54.

178. 'The Peter Berry diaries,' *Magill,* June 1980, p. 54.

179. 'The Peter Berry diaries,' *Magill,* June 1980, p. 54.

180. 'The Peter Berry diaries,' *Magill,* June 1980, p. 54.

181. Michael Mills, *Hurler on the Ditch,* p. 166.

182. Lynch continued: 'Recent incidents fully justify the steps taken by the Government in recent months towards that end. We have known for a long time that arms were being imported illegally into the North by the Ulster Volunteer Force. For what purpose? Is it to defend themselves against attack from the South, attack which we have forsworn? Major Chichester-Clark has said that he "did not believe that any responsible Government would contemplate such an act of madness." Is the real purpose then, to prevent the reforms that we believe the Northern Premier and his colleagues are sincere about implementing? Do they want to incite retaliation in the belief that this would help them in their evil purpose? I hope that nothing will be done that would prejudice the full and speedy implementation of reforms in the North or that would retard in any way the reconciliation between Irishmen that we all desire.'

183. 'Force against N.I. not ruled out by Government—Blaney,' *Irish Times,* 9 December 1969.

184. 'Force against N.I. not ruled out by Government—Blaney,' *Irish Times,* 9 December 1969.

185. *Irish Times,* 10 December 1969.

186. Fergus Pyle, 'Blaney embarrasses Stormont opposition,' *Irish Times,* 10 December 1969.

187. Ken Gray, 'Hume calls Blaney speech negative,' *Irish Times,* 10 December 1969.

188. *Irish Times,* 10 December 1969.

189. Department of External Affairs note on meeting between Dr Hillery and George Thompson, 10 December 1969. The Irish minister also had talks with the British Secretary of State for Foreign Affairs, Michael Stewart. Thompson was accompanied by Sir Andrew Gilchrist, British ambassador to Ireland, and by W. K. K. White of the Foreign and Commonwealth Office. Dr Hillery was accompanied by Hugh McCann and the Irish ambassador, J. G. Molloy (National Archives, file 2000/6/662 D/T S9361R).

190. National Archives, file 2000/6/662 D/T S9361R.

191. Department of External Affairs note on meeting between Dr Hillery and George Thompson, 10 December 1969 (National Archives, file 2000/6/662 D/T S9361R).

192. Department of External Affairs note on meeting between Dr Hillery and George Thompson, 10 December 1969 (National Archives, file 2000/6/662 D/T S9361R).

193. *Irish Times,* 12 December 1969.

194. *Irish Times,* 15 December 1969.

195. *Irish Times,* 17 December 1969.

196. Memorandum for the Information of the Government—Policy in relation to Northern Ireland, 28 November 1969 (National Archives, file 2000/6/662 D/T S9361R).

197. Memorandum for the Information of the Government—Policy in relation to Northern Ireland, 28 November 1969 (National Archives, file 2000/6/662 D/T S9361R).

198. Memorandum for the Information of the Government—Policy in relation to Northern Ireland, 28 November 1969 (National Archives, file 2000/6/662 D/T S9361R).

199. Comments on Department of External Affairs draft, 'Memorandum for the Information of the Government—Policy in relation to Northern Ireland,' probably by Eamonn Gallagher (National Archives, file 2000/6/662 D/T S9361R).

200. 'The Peter Berry diaries,' *Magill,* June 1980, p. 55–6.

201. This was based on a Marxist analysis that saw future development in three phases. In the first stage a normal, liberal parliamentary democracy would be created in the North, leading to a radicalised and united Catholic and Protestant working class. In stage 2 the working class in both the South and the North would work in solidarity to bring about the third and final phase, the workers' republic. Ed Moloney, *A Secret History of the* IRA, p. 57–.

202. J. Bowyer Bell, *The Secret Army,* p. 366–.

203. Ed Moloney, *A Secret History of the* IRA, p. 71.

204. J. Bowyer Bell, *The Secret Army,* p. 367.

205. David McKittrick et al., *Lost Lives,* p. 47–8.

206. David Marcus, *Oughtobiography,* p. 213–15.

207. Kevin Boland, *Up Dev!,* p. 31.

208. Kevin Boland, *Up Dev!,* p. 33.

209. Kevin Boland, *Up Dev!,* p. 35.

210. In his autobiography, David Marcus makes little of being called upon to write that critical speech. But there is no doubting the importance of choosing the right person to script the correct words at a time when words really mattered.

211. On 18 January 1970, the day following the delivery of the speech, David Marcus received the following note from the Taoiseach: 'Thank you for your great help. As you will have read the affair went off well—yours were the best lines. Yours sincerely, Jack.' David Marcus, *Oughtobiography,* p. 215.

212. Jack Lynch Papers.

213. Kevin Boland, *Up Dev!,* p. 33.

214. Austin Currie, *All Hell Will Break Loose,* p. 156–8.

215. Austin Currie, *All Hell Will Break Loose,* p. 157–8.

216. On 16 April 1970 Ian Paisley and his colleague William Beattie won by-elections to Stormont. That underlined the growing radical unionist dissatisfaction with the reform package of the Prime Minister, Chichester-Clerk. Constitutional unionism had buckled under the pressure and the strain.

217. Dick Walsh, *The Party*, p. 102-3.

218. Dick Walsh, *The Party*, p. 120.

219. Ironically, Boland was not part of that inner circle and, for all his bluster, may not have agreed with its alleged collective actions that resulted in a failed gun-running attempt. He wanted a British declaration of withdrawal. Not expecting that partition would be ended over night, Boland anticipated a period of transition of two parliaments in a federal Irish state. In reality he was very far from the Blaney line—and the supposed Haughey line—which expected immediate full unity following a British withdrawal. Boland was also worlds apart socially from Haughey. Although they had attended the same secondary school, and Haughey had been in an accountancy partnership with Kevin Boland's brother, in 1969 they moved in very different social milieus—Haughey in the world of fine living, high art and the young entrepreneurial movers and shakers. As Minister for Finance, Haughey had to discipline the spending propensities of his colleague. He did not respect Blaney very much and, according to Bruce Arnold, felt that Lynch ought to have got rid of him early on because of his divergent views on the North. But that view was expressed before the 1969 general election.

220. 'The Peter Berry diaries,' *Magill*, 1980, p. 54.

221. 'The Peter Berry diaries,' *Magill*, 1980, p. 54.

222. 'The Peter Berry diaries,' *Magill*, June, 1980, p. 58.

223. There is an account of this episode by Seamus Brady in *Arms and the Men*, p. 106.

224. Vincent Browne, 'The Arms Crisis, 1970,' *Magill*, May 1980, p. 48. The order was subsequently written down by the director of plans and operations at the direction of the chief of staff.

225. I am grateful to Commandant Victor Lange, head of Military Archives, Cathal Brugha Barracks, Dublin, for sending me this document, together with a transcript and other documents.

226. I am grateful to Commandant Victor Lange, head of Military Archives, Cathal Brugha Barracks, Dublin, for sending me this document.

227. I am grateful to Commandant Victor Lange, head of Military Archives, Cathal Brugha Barracks, Dublin, for sending me this document.

228. I am grateful to Commandant Victor Lange, head of Military Archives, Cathal Brugha Barracks, Dublin.

229. 'Army considered incursion into North in 1970, documents reveal,' *Irish Times*, 2 January 2001.

230. Michael Mills, *Hurler on the Ditch*, p. 60.

231. 'Army considered incursion into North in 1970, documents reveal,' *Irish Times*, 2 January 2001.

232. Paul Bew and Gordon Gillespie, *Northern Ireland*, p. 26.

233. Justin O'Brien, *The Arms Trial*, p. 115.

234. Michael Mills, *Hurler on the Ditch*, p. 60-61.

235. Pádraig Faulkner, *As I Saw It*, p. 95.

236. Document stamped 'Top secret' and headed: ARMS CONSPIRACY TRIAL, An Examination of some of the Evidence pertinent to and directly concerned with

the Army, by ARMY INTELLIGENCE (Jack Lynch Papers).

237. Sean Boyne, *Gunrunners*, p. 28.

238. So thorough was the Garda investigation that the force interviewed republicans who had been active and imprisoned during the Civil War. Con Ahern (then aged sixty-six), farm manager for the Vincentian Order at All Hallows College, Dublin, was questioned. He had been imprisoned for his anti-Treaty activities in Co. Cork during the Civil War and released in 1924. After his release he joined the Vincentian Order as a brother. When he left he continued to work on the farm and later became farm manager. His son, Bertie Ahern, was Taoiseach in 2007. Con Ahern was removed from the Special Branch list after that episode. See Sean Boyne, *Gunrunners*, p. 31.

239. In the murky world of arms dealing and so-called revolutionary politics in Ireland, connections had been made in early arms deals in the autumn of 1969 between Pádraig (Jock) Haughey and the chief of staff of the IRA, Cathal Goulding. The Blaney links with Saor Éire are investigated as part of a strong piece of forensic investigation by Sean Boyne in *Gunrunners*, p. 27–88.

240. Stephen Collins, *The Power Game*, p. 72.

241. 'The Peter Berry diaries,' *Magill*, June 1980, p. 59.

242. 'The Peter Berry diaries,' *Magill*, June 1980, p. 59–60.

243. 'The Peter Berry diaries,' *Magill*, June 1980, p. 59–60.

244. 'The Peter Berry diaries,' *Magill*, June 1980, p. 60.

245. 'The Peter Berry diaries,' *Magill*, June 1980, p. 60.

246. Document stamped 'Top secret' and headed: ARMS CONSPIRACY TRIAL, An Examination of some of the Evidence pertinent to and directly concerned with the Army, by ARMY INTELLIGENCE (Jack Lynch Papers).

247. Document stamped 'Top secret' and headed: ARMS CONSPIRACY TRIAL, An Examination of some of the Evidence pertinent to and directly concerned with the Army, by ARMY INTELLIGENCE (Jack Lynch Papers).

248. Document stamped 'Top secret' and headed: ARMS CONSPIRACY TRIAL, An Examination of some of the Evidence pertinent to and directly concerned with the Army, by ARMY INTELLIGENCE (Jack Lynch Papers).

249. Document stamped 'Top secret' and headed: ARMS CONSPIRACY TRIAL, An Examination of some of the Evidence pertinent to and directly concerned with the Army, by ARMY INTELLIGENCE (Jack Lynch Papers).

250. Document stamped 'Top secret' and headed: ARMS CONSPIRACY TRIAL, An Examination of some of the Evidence pertinent to and directly concerned with the Army, by ARMY INTELLIGENCE (Jack Lynch Papers).

251. Document stamped 'Top secret' and headed: ARMS CONSPIRACY TRIAL, An Examination of some of the Evidence pertinent to and directly concerned with the Army, by ARMY INTELLIGENCE (Jack Lynch Papers).

252. James Kelly, *The Thimble Riggers*, p. 33.

253. Vincent Browne, 'The Arms Crisis, 1970,' *Magill*, May 1980, p. 45.

254. James Kelly, *The Thimble Riggers*, p. 33.

255. James Kelly, *The Thimble Riggers*, p. 33.

256. James Kelly, *The Thimble Riggers*, p. 35.

257. James Kelly, *The Thimble Riggers*, p. 36.

258. Document stamped 'Top secret' and headed: ARMS CONSPIRACY TRIAL, An Examination of some of the Evidence pertinent to and directly concerned with the Army, by ARMY INTELLIGENCE (Jack Lynch Papers).

259. Document stamped 'Top secret' and headed: ARMS CONSPIRACY TRIAL, An Examination of some of the Evidence pertinent to and directly concerned with the Army, by ARMY INTELLIGENCE (Jack Lynch Papers).

260. 'The Peter Berry diaries,' *Magill*, June 1980, p. 60.

261. 'The Peter Berry diaries,' *Magill*, June 1980, p. 60.

262. Berry made 'cryptic notes' of that conversation with Haughey in his personal diary. (He made more extended notes of the conversation in the department on Monday the 20th.)

263. 'The Peter Berry diaries,' *Magill*, June 1980, p. 61.

264. 'The Peter Berry diaries,' *Magill*, June 1980, p. 61.

265. 'The Peter Berry diaries,' *Magill*, June 1980, p. 60–3.

266. 'The Peter Berry diaries,' *Magill*, June 1980, p. 62.

267. The editor of *Magill*, Vincent Browne, wrote to Lynch on 23 June 1980: 'You may have noticed that during your absence in China we published two issues of Magill which had articles on the 1970 Arms Crisis, which dealt in some detail with your role in the affair. I did speak to you about the October 17, 1969, meeting you had with Peter Berry in Mount Carmel and about your comment to the cabinet [Government] on May 1, 1970 re the allegations that had been made about the involvement of two ministers in the attempted importation of arms. You may recall that this conversation took place in your room in Leinster House on May 6 last.

'Following that conversation I came into possession of further information which involved you, primarily that Peter Berry had a further meeting with you on April 13, 1970 at which he informed you in some detail about the involvement of two ministers in the arms plot and also about the meeting with him on April 30 where you informed him that it was not your intention to dismiss Mr. Haughey. I wrote to you prior to your departure to China, seeking a further meeting with you but this was obviously not possible given your time-scale just then.

'In the event of your reading the articles, particularly the one by me, I hope you will note that I have not impugned your integrity and that I have made a point of stressing that you attained your true stature only after the Arms Crisis. I suspect that you yourself would agree with this latter judgement. I would now like to talk to you again about the affair as I am writing a concluding article in the series for the July issue of Magill. In particular I would like to ask you about the two bits of information I came into possession of only after my conversation with you on May 6.

'This further conversation with you can be either on an off-the-record basis or for direct attribution. If you feel you would like to talk freely about your part in the affair then of course you would have exactly the same rights over the copy as you did over the autobiographical piece you did for us in November 1979.

'I feel personally unhappy about being in a position of writing critically about you because of your very considerable generosity to me personally but I hope you appreciate that journalism cannot operate on the basis of personal feelings. Regretfully others involved in these articles do not agree with this attitude.'

Lynch replied on 26 June 1980: 'I regret that this will not be possible. Because of the very big volume of work that accumulated during my official visit to China and my visit to other Far Eastern countries, I am unable to give interviews for some time to come.'

268. *Parliamentary Debates: Dáil Éireann: Official Report,* 1980.

269. Lynch added: 'The June [1980] issue of *Magill* purported to reproduce Mr. Berry's diaries. Diaries, in the accepted sense of the word, are a day-to-day record of events as they happen. It must be clear to everyone who read the reproduction of these 'diaries' in *Magill* that they were not in many instances diaries in the accepted sense in that there were alleged entries for some dates of events that had not yet occurred. It is clear, therefore, that much of these diaries were written from *post hoc* recollections which I respectfully suggest were faulty in many material respects.' *Parliamentary Debates: Dáil Éireann: Official Report,* 1980.

270. *Parliamentary Debates: Dáil Éireann: Official Report,* vol. 324, col. 1195–8, 25 November 1980.

271. Lynch added: 'I may add that after the publication of this account in Magill of my meeting with Mr. Berry it was volunteered to me by qualified medical sources who read the account that, having regard to the drugged conditions in which Mr. Berry was for the purpose of the tests which he was undergoing, it would be impossible for him or anybody to recollect a conversation while in that condition. In fact, I have had myself tests of a similar nature in connection with a foot operation I had early in 1977. I received some injections and, to use the lay-man's term, I was 'put on the drip.' I did not, or could not, have any recollection of anything I said in that condition.' *Parliamentary Debates: Dáil Éireann: Official Report,* 1980.

272. *Parliamentary Debates: Dáil Éireann: Official Report,* 1980.

273. 'The Peter Berry diaries,' Magill, *June 1980*, p. 63. Berry was also in the line of fire. On 22 April he had received a phone call at 1 p.m. from the Garda commissioner to say that the Special Branch had been experiencing difficulties with the Revenue Commissioners, who were stalling in answering questions. Berry phoned the chairman of the Revenue Commissioners, who replied that he could not give any answers until he had consulted a relevant colleague. Berry replied that 'heads would roll,' as the Taoiseach had directed him personally to hold a full Garda inquiry. When Berry saw Lynch on 23 April, the Taoiseach told him that the head of the Revenue Commissioners had been in to see him and had told him of Berry's threat. Lynch told Berry that he had no right to say what he had said; neither had he any right to say that Lynch had ordered a Garda inquiry. Berry wrote: 'I was dumbfounded. I had expected to be praised, not blamed. All my doubts of earlier months that the Taoiseach could not have some knowledge of what was going on in the background came flooding back; his remarks and

attitude did not seem to fit a head of Government who was anxious to bring malefactors to justice.'

274. *Parliamentary Debates: Dáil Éireann: Official Report*, vol. 234, col. 1195–9, 25 November 1980.

275. Sean Boyne, *Gunrunners*, p. 74–5.

276. 'The Peter Berry diaries,' *Magill*, June 1980, p. 65.

277. 'The Peter Berry diaries,' *Magill*, June 1980, p. 64–5.

278. Pádraig Faulkner, *As I Saw It*, p. 96.

279. Pádraig Faulkner, *As I Saw It*, p. 96.

280. Interview with Dr Patrick Hillery, Spanish Point, Co. Clare, 25 August 2005.

281. John Horgan, *Seán Lemass*, p. 344.

282. Stephen Collins, *The Power Game*, p. 75.

283. Pádraig Faulkner, *As I Saw It*, p. 99.

284. *Parliamentary Debates: Dáil Éireann: Official Report*, vol. 246, col. 518–19, 5 May 1970.

285. Stephen Collins, *The Power Game*, p. 77.

286. Following his dismissal, Charles Haughey issued a statement on 8 May 1970. 'Since I became a minister I have endeavoured to the best of my ability to serve my country, Dáil Éireann and the Government. I have never at any time acted in breach of the trust reposed in me and I regret that I am now compelled to refer to the circumstances which brought to an end my membership of the Government. The Taoiseach informed the Dáil that he requested my resignation on the grounds that he was convinced that not even the slightest suspicion should attach to any member of the Government. I fully subscribe to that view ... So far as I have been able to gather the Taoiseach received information of a nature which, in his opinion, cast some suspicion on me. I have not had the opportunity to examine or test such information or the quality of its source or sources. In the meantime, however, I now categorically state that at no time have I taken part in any alleged importation or attempted importation of arms into this country. At present I do not propose to say anything further except that I have fully accepted the Taoiseach's decision as I believe that the unity of Fianna Fáil is of greater importance to the welfare of the nation than my political career.'

287. Stephen Collins, *The Power Game*, p. 78.

288. Quoted by Justin O'Brien in *The Arms Trial*, p. 127.

289. Pádraig Faulkner, *As I Saw It*, p. 99.

290. Interview with Dr Patrick Hillery, Spanish Point, Co. Clare, 25 August 2005.

291. Interview with Dr Patrick Hillery, Spanish Point, Co. Clare, 25 August 2005.

292. Pádraig Faulkner, *As I Saw It*, p. 99–100.

293. *Irish Times*, 9 May 1970.

294. 'How Jack bought time,' *Irish Times*, 9 May 1970.

295. Andrew Hamilton, 'Regrets, but not ashamed—Blaney,' *Irish Times*, 1970.

296. Donal Musgrave, 'Cork solidarity behind the Taoiseach,' *Irish Times*, 8 May 1970.

297. 'Election now a danger, Lynch warns,' *Irish Times*, 2 June 1970.

298. Michael McInerney, 'Boland expelled by 60 votes to 11,' *Irish Times*, 5 June 1970.

299. Dick Walsh, 'Boland leaves Fianna Fáil,' *Irish Times*, 23 June 1970.

300. *Irish Times*, 24 June 1970.

301. 'Blaney freed—evidence insufficient,' *Irish Times*, 3 July 1970.

302. 'Force no solution—says Taoiseach,' *Irish Times*, 13 July 1970.

303. Editorial, 'In the other's weal,' *Irish Times*, 13 July 1970.

304. John Healy, 'Boland adds edge to sharp debate,' *Irish Times*, 31 July 1970.

305. *Irish Times*, 13 August 1970.

306. Backbencher [John Healy], 'Fianna Fáil pulls through,' *Irish Times*, 15 August 1970.

307. 'Boland attacks Lynch over speech,' *Irish Times*, 16 September 1970.

308. 'Death of Dr James Ryan,' *Irish Times*, 26 September 1970.

309. 'Funeral tributes to Dr Ryan,' *Irish Times*, 29 September 1970.

310. Tom MacIntyre, *Through the Bridewell Gates*, p. 207–8.

311. *Irish Times*, 24 October 1970.

312. *Irish Times*, 26 October 1970.

313. Dermot Keogh, *Twentieth Century Ireland*, p. 321.

314. Editorial, 'Facing the future,' *Irish Times*, 26 October 1970.

315. *Irish Times*, 26 October 1970.

316. *Irish Times*, 27 October 1970.

317. Dermot Keogh, *Twentieth Century Ireland*, p. 321.

318. See National Library of Ireland, Máirín Lynch Papers.

319. Tom MacIntyre, *Through the Bridewell Gates*, p. 209.

320. Jack Lynch Papers.

321. Jack Lynch Papers.

322. Jack Lynch Papers.

323. The end of this word is underlined in pencil, with a question mark in the margin. The correct name should be 'Belfast Fund for the Relief of Distress,' which is the name used subsequently in this document.

324. The following text was added to the end of Fleming's statement:
'The following documents are attached:—
'1)	Statement of Mr. Anthony J. Fagan;
'2)	Statement of Mr. Thomas Moore;
'3)	Statement of Mr. William Walsh;
'4)	Questionaire and answers from Mrs. de Barra and Miss Murphy of the Irish Red Cross Society;
'5)	Photocopy of available documents relating to the "Belfast Committee for Relief of Distressed" in the Bank of Ireland, Clones, Co. Monaghan, in the names of Patrick Kennedy, Patrick Joseph Devlin and Patrick McGrory—endorsements on the back of the cheques are shown underneath the copy of each cheque;
'6)	Photocopy of available documents relating to the "Belfast Fund for Relief of Distress" in the Munster and Leinster Bank Ltd., 2 Lower Baggot Street, Dublin 2 in the names of "John White, John Loughran and Roger Murphy";
'7)	Photocopy of the available documents relating to the "George Dixon" account in the Munster and Leinster Bank Ltd., 2 Lower Baggot Street,

Dublin 2;

'8) Photocopy of available documents relating to the "Ann O'Brien" account in the Munster and Leinster Bank Ltd., 2 Lower Baggot Street, Dublin 2.' Jack Lynch Papers.

325. 'Lynch's style of leadership too suspect,' *Irish Times*, 20 February 1971.

326. *Irish Times*, 20 February 1971.

327. Chris Glennon, 'Largest ard fheis yet,' *Irish Independent*, 20 February 1971.

328. Chris Glennon, 'Largest ard fheis yet,' *Irish Independent*, 20 February 1971.

329. Chris Glennon, 'Political Diary,' *Irish Independent*, 20 February 1971.

330. Chris Glennon, 'Political Diary,' *Irish Independent*, 20 February 1971.

331. 'Uproar at opening of Fianna Fáil ard fheis,' *Irish Times*, 22 February 1971.

332. *Irish Times*, 22 February 1971.

333. 'Uproar at opening of Fianna Fáil ard fheis,' *Irish Times*, 22 February 1971.

334. 'Uproar at opening of Fianna Fáil ard fheis,' *Irish Times*, 22 February 1971.

335. Nell McCafferty, 'Fianna Fáil's Weekend of the Long Knives,' *Irish Times*, 22 February 1971.

336. *Irish Times*, 22 February 1971.

337. John Healy, 'Rowdy ard-fheis backs Lynch against disruptive group,' *Irish Times*, 22 February 1971.

338. John Healy, 'Rowdy ard-fheis backs Lynch against disruptive group,' *Irish Times*, 22 February 1971.

339. Bruce Arnold states that Ken Whitaker had worked with Lynch in the past on important speeches. On the occasion of the ard-fheis in 1971 he credits the drafting of the speech to Martin O'Donoghue. The latter argued that the Northern section ought to come first. Lynch preferred to keep that section to the end. See Bruce Arnold, *Jack Lynch*, p. 161.

340. Dick Walsh, 'Renewed offer by Lynch to North,' *Irish Times*, 22 February 1971.

341. Text of speech, *Irish Times*, 22 February 1971.

342. Text of speech, *Irish Times*, 22 February 1971.

343. John Healy, 'Rowdy ard-fheis backs Lynch against disruptive group,' *Irish Times*, 22 February 1971.

344. '"Letting off steam" strengthened FF ard fheis,' *Irish Independent*, 22 February 1971.

345. Editorial, 'Is this politics?' *Irish Independent*, 22 February 1971.

346. Editorial, 'Letting off steam,' *Irish Times*, 22 February 1971.

347. Dick Walsh, 'Renewed offer by Lynch to North,' *Irish Times*, 22 February 1971.

348. Stephen Collins, *The Power Game*, p. 90.

349. Kevin Boland, *Up Dev!*, p. 41.

350. Stephen Collins, *The Power Game*, p. 92.

351. Editorial, 'Seán Lemass,' *Irish Times*, 12 May 1971.

352. '"Man of reality" theme in tributes to former Taoiseach,' *Irish Times*, 12 May 1945.

353. 'Lemass funeral today,' *Irish Times*, 13 May 1971.

354. Interview with Dr Patrick Hillery, Spanish Point, Co. Clare, 25 August 2005.

355. Leonardo Sciascia, *The Moro Affair*, p. 49.

Chapter 8 (P. 288–297)

1. See the description of the resignation of Charles de Gaulle in April 1969 by Jean Lacouture in *De Gaulle: The Rebel* and *De Gaulle: The Ruler*.

2. The Minister for External Affairs, Frank Aiken, told Lynch on 6 June 1969 in a letter that recent visits to Dublin by the German Minister for Agriculture, Herman Hocherl, and by Maan Sassen of the Commission had given opportunities to stress the importance of preserving the idea of simultaneous entry for the four applicants. See related correspondence, including Aiken to Lynch, 6 June 1969 (National Archives, file D/T 200/6/386 S18981R).

3. The Department of External Affairs was renamed Department of Foreign Affairs in 1969.

4. Dr Hillery had served as Minister for Education since 1958. See Dermot Keogh, *Twentieth Century Ireland*, p. 245.

5. *Irish Times,* 18 June 1969.

6. Denis Corboy, director of the Irish Council of the European Movement, sent reports to the EEC of public opinion in Ireland. The newspapers reported Hillery's visit to the Commission in different ways. Ireland had twice applied unsuccessfully for membership, which may account for the *Irish Independent's* more cautious reportage (article in *Irish Independent,* 10 July 1969). This report is also interesting because it underlines a more realistic account of where the Irish application stood and an increasing consciousness in the media regarding the political aspects of EEC membership. Denis Corboy writes to the Six and to the Commission on 12 July 1969, Community Archives, EM 97.

7. Report on meeting with Jean Rey, president of the European Commission, 14 July 1969 (National Archives, file D/T 2000/6/388 S18081S).

8. Report of Hillery's meeting with the British foreign minister, Stewart, on 14 July 1969 (National Archives, file D/T 2000/6/388 S18081S).

9. Report of Hillery's meeting with the Dutch foreign minister, Dr Luns, on 15 July 1969 (National Archives, file D/T 2000/6/388 S18081S).

10. Report on Hillery's meeting with Gerhard Jahn, secretary of the German Ministry of Foreign Affairs, on 16 July 1969 (National Archives, file D/T 2000/6/388 S18081S).

11. D. J. Maher, *The Tortuous Path,* p. 244.

12. Commins to Dublin, 22 July 1969 (National Archives, file D/T 99/1/496 S18081P).

13. In the meantime the Irish Council of the European Movement was arranging a conference in Dublin in June 1969. Walter Hallstein, president of the European Movement, invited Edoardo Martino to a conference on the institutional problems of enlargement on 20 and 21 June 1969. Jack Lynch opened the talks with a speech urging the members not to be deflected from the ultimate goal on which they were all agreed. Any temporary difficulties of a technical nature could be solved, given the good will and resourcefulness that the EEC had already shown in solving many more serious and intractable problems. The conference made a number of proposals regarding the future structure of the EEC if enlargement took place.

14. The six agreed that if Britain gained entry then Norway, Denmark and Ireland should too, because of their economies being so closely inter-related. A ten-member community would require a strengthening of institutions. This needed to occur anyway. even in a six-member community, if progress were to be made on customs union. Decision-making must be applied along treaty lines, and the strengthening of institutions should not interfere with treaties but simply procedure. The EEC should have complete control over its own resources. The names of the nominees to the European Parliament should be submitted to the Community for agreement between governments. The European character of the administration should be reinforced. In practice some officials at high postings became the property of the state they represented; this should be changed, so that some senior posts should be kept for permanent officials of the communities. The European movement would organise a study group to decide on language requirements for posts within the EEC. Report on proceedings sent to Edoardo Martino. Community Archives, EM 97.

15. Report of meeting between Hillery and Schumann, 20 September 1969 (National Archives, file D/T 2000/6/390 S18081).

16. For a brief instant, ambiguity surrounded Ireland's accession to negotiations for membership of the EEC when Joseph Luns, the Dutch foreign minister, stated that the succession of the three other candidates might follow that of Britain. This statement was retracted and the Dutch agreed that negotiations with all four candidates would begin and finish at the same time. Report from Seán Morrissey regarding Dr Luns's statement (National Archives, file D/T 200/6/341 S18081W). 'The government have always attached the greatest importance to our negotiations starting and ending at the same time as those of Britain. They have recognised, however, that for practical reasons, it might be necessary to have some staggering of various phases of the negotiations provided always—as indeed the Commission recommends—that there is co-ordination and consultation on matters of common interest.' *Parliamentary Debates: Dáil Éireann: Official Report*, vol. 243, 3 December 1969.

17. Minute of Hillery's meeting with Thomson, 10 December 1969 (National Archives, file D/T 200/6/341 S18081W).

18. Minute of Hillery's meeting with Thomson, 10 December 1969 (National Archives, file D/T 200/6/341 S18081W).

19. D. J. Maher, *The Tortuous Path*, p. 256.

20. Irish and British delegations met in Dublin on 21 May 1970 and discussed in detail transition arrangements and a standstill period. See D. J. Maher, *The Tortuous Path*, p. 261–3.

21. National Archives, file D/T 2001/43/942. A copy of the letter was sent to the Ministers for Agriculture and Fisheries, Finance, and Industry and Commerce.

22. Summary of Report of Meeting between Dr Hillery and M. Schumann, French Foreign Minister at the Quai d'Orsay, 10 April 1970 (National Archives, file D/T 2001/43/930).

23. The Department of External Affairs also gave Lynch a briefing document on the political implications for Ireland of integration. Dated 17 September 1969, it

restated the position as outlined by that department on many previous occasions. It envisaged greater political union, with contingent defence obligations somewhere in the distant future. It advised as follows: 'It seems reasonable to conclude from the situation sketched above that Ireland's commitment to the Rome Treaty and its political implications is unlikely, for a considerable time to come, even assuming our admission to membership of the Communities, to result in any restrictions on our sovereignty, including the constitutional right of Dáil Éireann to pronounce on our involvement in any military alliance. Indeed, no conclusive evidence exists that such a situation is ever likely to come about. This is not to say that the Government, with the assent of Dáil Éireann, might not at some future date voluntarily undertake defence commitments with their European partners as a contribution which they might feel to be incumbent upon them as a result of their membership of a European Community moving towards political union.' See Department of External Affairs brief for the Taoiseach, marked confidential and entitled 'Political Implications of Membership of the EEC—Situation as of Autumn 1969' (National Archives, file D/T 2000/6/389 S18081).

24. Linthorst Homan reported on Bernadette Devlin's arrest for allegedly having rioted and having encouraged others to take part in riots in 1969. Later, when other evidence presented itself, she was acquitted. Homan explained that 'Northern Ireland is economically deprived and rioting has not helped. The English government has also commitments to help other regions and has tried to boost NI by giving industry tax incentives to build factories there. The political situation is complicated, and a lot depends on London or Dublin attitudes.' Linthorst Homan reported that for now the Lynch Government was calm. British papers and politicians wrote that there was no chance that the United Kingdom would give up Northern Ireland. J. Community Archives, Florence, EM 166.

25. National Archives, file D/T 2001/43/932.

26. See D. J. Maher, *The Tortuous Path*, p. 261–3.

27. Sir Con O'Neill, *Britain's Entry into the European Community*, p. 286.

28. Sir Con O'Neill, *Britain's Entry into the European Community*, p. 284–5.

29. Sir Con O'Neill, *Britain's Entry into the European Community*, p. 283.

30. D. J. Maher, *The Tortuous Path*, p. 266.

31. D. J. Maher, *The Tortuous Path*, p. 264.

32. Those named were Seán Morrissey, now assistant secretary of the Department of Foreign Affairs, J. O'Mahony, assistant secretary of the Department of Agriculture and Fisheries, D. Culligan, assistant secretary of the Department of Industry and Commerce, D. J. Maher, assistant secretary of the Department of Finance, and S. Kennan, head of the Irish mission to the European Communities. Senior officials from other departments would be called into negotiations in Brussels as required. *Parliamentary Debates: Dáil Éireann: Official Report*, vol. 247, 27 May 1970.

33. National Archives, file D/T 2001/43/927.

34. D. J. Maher, *The Tortuous Path*, p. 269–70.

35. D. J. Maher, *The Tortuous Path*, p. 349.

36. D. J. Maher, *The Tortuous Path*, p. 273–7.
37. *Irish Times*, 22 February 1971.
38. National Archives, file D/T 2002-8-407 S18523I EEC and EFTA, 1 April to 18 May 1971.
39. D. J. Maher, *The Tortuous Path*, p. 344.
40. D. J. Maher, *The Tortuous Path*, p. 342–.

Chapter 9 (P. 298–367)
1. Edward Heath, *The Course of My Life*, p. 421.
2. Jonathan Bardon, *A History of Ulster*, p. 679.
3. Those comments were 'enlightened' compared with the musings of another Tory, Alan Clark. Visiting Belfast on 30 January 1991, he wrote in his journal: 'Northern Ireland is unbelievably nasty. Grey, damp, cold. Big puddles just lying; blackthorn hedges; low standards of life . . . But the general atmosphere is bleak; overlaid with the oppression of terror; deep and perpetual feuds, suspicion and callousness. I am confirmed in my opinion that it is hopeless here. All we can do is arm the Orangemen—to the teeth—and get out. This would give also the not slight advantage that, at a stroke, Infantry "overstretch" is eliminated.' His day was brightened when he saw a 'pretty girl' in a crowd outside a building where a 200-lb bomb had allegedly been planted: 'She was jumping about excitedly, very nice legs.' Alan Clark, *Diaries*, p. 395. The index makes no other reference to Northern Ireland; but in a reference to Ireland in a conversation with Ian Gow on 13 August 1985 he wrote: 'Ireland is a ghastly subject. Intractable. Insoluble. For centuries it has blighted English domestic politics, wrecked the careers of good men . . . We agreed that the Foreign Office now exists solely to buy off foreign disapproval by dipping into the till marked British interests.' Alan Clark, *Diaries*, p. 117.
4. Edward Heath, *The Course of My Life*, p. 423.
5. Edward Heath, *The Course of My Life*, p. 424.
6. Brian Faulkner, *Memoirs of a Statesman*, p. 75.
7. Heath to Lynch, 17 March 1970 (Jack Lynch Papers).
8. Eamonn Gallagher report, 'Northern Ireland: The present situation,' 17 January 1972 (Jack Lynch Papers).
9. Minute by Eamonn Gallagher, 26 July 1971 (Jack Lynch Papers).
10. '"Unity by agreement" plea from Lynch,' *Irish Times*, 12 July 1971.
11. Michael McInerney, 'Lynch departure in policy emphasis,' *Irish Times*, 12 July 1971.
12. Henry Kelly, 'Timing of Lynch words attacked by Faulkner,' *Irish Times*, 12 July 1971.
13. Whitaker to Lynch, 12 July 1971 (Jack Lynch Papers).
14. Whitaker to Lynch, 12 July 1971, note marked 'Secret' (Jack Lynch Papers).
15. Whitaker to Lynch, 12 July 1971, note marked 'Secret' (Jack Lynch Papers).
16. Whitaker to Lynch, 12 July 1971, note marked 'Secret' (Jack Lynch Papers).
17. Whitaker to Lynch, 14 July 1971 (Jack Lynch Papers).
18. Edward Heath, *The Course of My Life*, p. 427.
19. Reginald Maudling, *Memoirs*, p. 1184.

20. Eamonn Gallagher, 'Northern Ireland: The present situation,' 17 January 1972 (Jack Lynch Papers). Gallagher, despite considering it unfruitful to speculate, surmised that it might have been a reference to the effect of cratering border roads or his 'possible supposition that the government here would actively "go for" the IRA and whatever assessment of the political situation that Faulkner may have given Whitehall from time to time.'

21. Edward Heath, *The Course of My Life*, p. 428.

22. Edward Heath, *The Course of My Life*, p. 428.

23. '"Historic phase" in nation's development,' *Irish Times*, 6 August 1971.

24. Backbencher [John Healy], 'Dear Mr. Heath,' *Irish Times*, 7 August 1971.

25. Backbencher [John Healy], 'Dear Mr. Heath,' *Irish Times*, 7 August 1971.

26. John Peck, *Dublin from Downing Street*, p. 127–8.

27. Jonathan Bardon, *A History of Ulster*, p. 681–2.

28. Jonathan Bardon, *A History of Ulster*, p. 682.

29. At the meeting, Stewart Crawford told O'Sullivan that the British ambassador would be in contact with the Taoiseach about the introduction of internment that morning and the banning of parades, including the Apprentice Boys' parade in Derry on 12 August. He was informed that Brian Faulkner had made an announcement to that effect during the morning without referring to the fact that all outstanding applications for rifle clubs would be refused. Crawford said an advisory committee had been set up to consider representations in connection with the justification of interning individuals. Internment would apply to both sides and would last until peace had been restored and until such time as some form of participation by the minority could be built up. Crawford hoped that the Taoiseach would 'do everything possible to dampen down the situation.' Seán Ronan minute, 9 August 1971 (Jack Lynch Papers).

30. Heath to Lynch, 9 August 1971 (Jack Lynch Papers).

31. Heath to Lynch, 9 August 1971 (Jack Lynch Papers).

32. John Peck, *Dublin from Downing Street*, p. 127–128.

33. Draft statement, 9 August 1971 (Jack Lynch Papers).

34. Jonathan Bardon, *A History of Ulster*, p. 682.

35. Eamonn Gallagher minute, 9 August 1971 (Jack Lynch Papers).

36. Eamonn Gallagher, 'Northern Ireland: The present situation,' 17 January 1972 (Jack Lynch Papers).

37. 'Dungannon calls for total opposition,' *Irish Times*, 10 August 1971.

38. '12 die on first day of North's internment,' *Irish Times*, 10 August 1971.

39. Editorial, 'Failure of brinkmanship,' *Irish Times*, 10 August 1971.

40. Unsigned memorandum on Dr Hillery's talks with Maudling, 11 August 1971 (Jack Lynch Papers).

41. Unsigned memorandum on Dr Hillery's talks with Maudling, 11 August 1971 (Jack Lynch Papers).

42. Unsigned memorandum on Dr Hillery's talks with Maudling, 11 August 1971 (Jack Lynch Papers).

43. 'Haughey wants UN force in North,' *Irish Times*, 12 August 1971.

44. See *Irish Times*, 12 August 1971.

45. 'Lynch wants Stormont regime abolished,' *Irish Times*, 13 August 1971.

46. Text of Irish Government statement, 12 August 1971 (Jack Lynch Papers).

47. Text of Irish Government statement, 12 August 1971 (Jack Lynch Papers).

48. Draft speech, 12 August 1971, with handwritten changes by Lynch (Jack Lynch Papers).

49. Text of Irish Government statement, 12 August 1971 (Jack Lynch Papers).

50. Editorial, 'Mr Lynch's new language,' *Irish Times*, 13 August 1971.

51. 'Taoiseach accused of cant and hypocrisy,' and 'Lynch N.I. speech may cause rift,' *Irish Times*, 14 August 1971.

52. They were convicted but acquitted on appeal on 23 February 1972. Jonathan Bardon, *A History of Ulster*, p. 680–2.

53. Jonathan Bardon, *A History of Ulster*, p. 683–4.

54. John Peck, *Dublin from Downing Street*, p. 130–1.

55. Original text of Heath statement (Jack Lynch Papers).

56. His backbenchers were looking for radical action from the Government. For example, on 20 August Deputy Patrick Power (Kildare) phoned the Taoiseach's office to talk about the feelings of frustration in his constituency at the lack of positive action being taken in regard to the North. The official who took the call asked Power whether he was suggesting that the Government should use force. 'He said he wasn't suggesting it but he wasn't ruling it out.' The suggestions being put to him were that the Government should withdraw Irish soldiers from Cyprus, that it should pay the salaries of the MPs who had withdrawn from Stormont, that a campaign should be started to ban English goods, and that factories should be set up near the border for border people. Power ended by saying that the general complaint was 'that enough isn't being done.' Taoiseach's Office minute, 18 August 1972 (Jack Lynch Papers).

57. Irish Republican Army statement, under name of Cathal Goulding, chief of staff (Jack Lynch Papers).

58. John Peck, *Dublin from Downing Street*, p. 134.

59. Hugh McCann minute, 23 August 1971 (Jack Lynch Papers).

60. Hugh McCann minute, 23 August 1971 (Jack Lynch Papers).

61. Hugh McCann minute, 23 August 1971 (Jack Lynch Papers).

62. In London, policy planners began to set out the policy options open to Heath in Northern Ireland. The Central Policy Review Staff (part of the Prime Minister's office), reported on 3 September that the British Government had three main routes to choose between at that time: (1) re-partition that would divide Northern Ireland into Protestant and Catholic areas, the latter to have the option to join the South, (2) a coalition or power-sharing executive, giving Catholics guaranteed rights, and (3) condominium or the joint governing of Northern Ireland by the British and Irish Governments. Heath favoured the second option and invited Lynch to England on 6–7 September 1971. The Taoiseach turned down an invitation to stay at Chequers, the official country residence of the Prime Minister, preferring the Irish embassy in London.

63. Garret FitzGerald, *All in a Life*, p. 99.

64. But Heath resorted to cliché by placing so much emphasis on the diplomacy of whiskey. He had Bushmills, Paddy and Scotch placed before the guests. Both chose Scotch.

65. Edward Heath, *The Course of My Life*, p. 430–2.

66. Ambassador Dónal O'Sullivan minute on meeting between Lynch and Heath, 6 December 1971 (minute dated 7 December 1971) (Jack Lynch Papers).

67. Sir Edmund Compton headed an inquiry that reported on 16 November 1971. But its findings were seen as a whitewashing of the authorities and were quickly discredited by enquiries carried out by the *Sunday Times* 'Insight' Team, BBC Television's '24 Hours' and Amnesty International.

68. Ambassador Dónal O'Sullivan minute on meeting between Lynch and Heath, 6 December 1971 (minute dated 7 December 1971) (Jack Lynch Papers).

69. Ambassador Dónal O'Sullivan minute on meeting between Lynch and Heath, 6 December 1971 (minute dated 7 December 1971) (Jack Lynch Papers).

70. Edward Heath, *The Course of My Life*, p. 433–4.

71. 'Mrs Lynch views on tarrings criticised,' *Irish Times* and *Irish Press*, 15 and 16 November 1971

72. National Library of Ireland, Máirín Lynch Papers, acc. 6260, box 3.

73. *Irish Press*, 4 December 1971.

74. David McKittrick et al., *Lost Lives*, p. 121.

75. *Irish Press*, 4 December 1971.

76. Eamonn Gallagher, Northern Ireland: The present situation, 17 January 1972 (Jack Lynch Papers).

77. Eamonn Gallagher, Northern Ireland: The present situation, 17 January 1972 (Jack Lynch Papers).

78. Eamonn Gallagher, Northern Ireland: The present situation, 17 January 1972 (Jack Lynch Papers).

79. Eamonn Gallagher, Northern Ireland: The present situation, 17 January 1972 (Jack Lynch Papers).

80. Hugh McCann minute of meeting between Taoiseach and the British Prime Minister on 23 January 1972 (date on minute is 26 January 1972) (Jack Lynch Papers).

81. Hugh McCann minute of meeting between Taoiseach and the British Prime Minister on 23 January 1972 (date on minute is 26 January 1972) (Jack Lynch Papers).

82. Hugh McCann minute of meeting between Taoiseach and the British Prime Minister on 23 January 1972 (date on minute is 26 January 1972) (Jack Lynch Papers).

83. Hugh McCann minute of meeting between Taoiseach and the British Prime Minister on 23 January 1972 (date on minute is 26 January 1972) (Jack Lynch Papers).

84. Hugh McCann minute of meeting between Taoiseach and the British Prime Minister on 23 January 1972 (date on minute is 26 January 1972) (Jack Lynch Papers).

85. Hugh McCann minute of meeting between Taoiseach and the British Prime Minister on 23 January 1972 (date on minute is 26 January 1972) (Jack Lynch Papers).

86. Dónal O'Sullivan minute of meeting with Sir Burke Trend and Sir Stewart Crawford, 26 January 1972 (Jack Lynch Papers).

87. Dónal O'Sullivan minute of meeting with Sir Burke Trend and Sir Stewart Crawford, 26 January 1972 (Jack Lynch Papers).

88. Dónal O'Sullivan minute of meeting with Sir Burke Trend and Sir Stewart Crawford, 26 January 1972 (Jack Lynch Papers).

89. Minute (dated 26 January 1972) of conversation between the Taoiseach and Harold Wilson on 25 January 1972 (Jack Lynch Papers).

90. John Peck, *Dublin from Downing Street*, p. 137–8.

91. John Peck, *Dublin from Downing Street*, p. 138.

92. Jonathan Bardon, *A History of Ulster*, p. 687.

93. Jonathan Bardon, *A History of Ulster*, p. 688.

94. Edward Heath, *The Course of My Life*, p. 434–5.

95. Jonathan Bardon, *A History of Ulster*, p. 688.

96. T. Ryle Dwyer, 'Bloody Sunday tapes record the debt we owe to Lynch,' *Irish Examiner*, 4 October 2000.

97. Jonathan Bardon, *A History of Ulster*, p. 688.

98. Edward Heath, *The Course of My Life*, p. 435.

99. Garda Commissioner, Michael Wymes, report, stamped 9 May 1972 (Jack Lynch Papers).

100. Garda Commissioner, Michael Wymes, report, stamped 9 May 1972 (Jack Lynch Papers).

101. Edward Heath, *The Course of My Life*, p. 436.

102. Edward Heath, *The Course of My Life*, p. 436.

103. William Whitelaw, *The Whitelaw Memoirs*, 89.

104. Heath to Lynch, 24 April 1972 (Jack Lynch Papers).

105. Heath to Lynch, 24 April 1972 (Jack Lynch Papers).

106. Heath to Lynch, 24 April 1972 (Jack Lynch Papers).

107. Heath to Lynch, 24 April 1972 (Jack Lynch Papers).

108. Garda Commissioner, Michael Wymes, report, stamped 9 May 1972 (Jack Lynch Papers).

109. However, the Gardaí had a very good intelligence system in operation and the report—and others like them—reflected the amount of time expended on the surveillance of members of subversive organisations. The report also detailed attendances at meetings under the headings 'Communism' and 'Other organisations.' For example, on 11 March 1972 a public meeting was held in Mallow to protest at the decision of the Minister for Health to refuse approval of the retention of the local hospital as a general hospital. The Minister for Defence, Jerry Cronin, attended as a member of the public. The Bishop of Cloyne, Bishop John Ahern, received an anonymous phone call saying that the minister would be assassinated at the meeting. When informed, the minister was 'afforded discreet attention by the Gardaí.' Garda Commissioner, Michael Wymes, report, stamped 9 May 1972 (Jack Lynch Papers).

110. Dr Whitaker minute, 21 April 1972, of discussion at private meeting between President de Valera and Terence O'Neill (Jack Lynch Papers).

111. Dr Whitaker minute, 21 April 1972, of discussion at private meeting between President de Valera and Terence O'Neill (Jack Lynch Papers).

112. Dr Whitaker minute, 21 April 1972, of discussion at private meeting between President de Valera and Terence O'Neill (Jack Lynch Papers).

113. Whitaker to Lynch, 12 May 1972 (Jack Lynch Papers).

114. Ken Bloomfield, *Stormont in Crisis*, p. 82–3.

115. G. B. Newe to Dr Ken Whitaker, no date, with covering note from Whitaker to Lynch, 12 May 1972 (Jack Lynch Papers).

116. Whitaker to Lynch, 19 May 1972 (Jack Lynch Papers).

117. Whitaker to Mr O'Dowd, 19 May 1972 (with the enclosed extract from a draft speech) (Jack Lynch Papers).

118. Whitaker to Lynch, 29 May 1972 (Jack Lynch Papers).

119. Whitaker to Lynch, 29 May 1972 (Jack Lynch Papers).

120. Whitaker to Lynch, 29 May 1972 (Jack Lynch Papers).

121. Whitaker to Lynch, 29 May 1972 (Jack Lynch Papers).

122. G. B. Newe to Dr Whitaker, 10 June 1972 (Jack Lynch Papers).

123. Whitaker to Lynch, 14 June, 1972 (Jack Lynch Papers).

124. John M. Lynch, 'The Anglo-Irish Problem,' Foreign Affairs, July, 1972, p. 615–616.

125. John M. Lynch, 'The Anglo-Irish problem,' *Foreign Affairs*, July 1972, p. 602.

126. John M. Lynch, 'The Anglo-Irish problem,' *Foreign Affairs*, July 1972, p. 613.

127. John M. Lynch, 'The Anglo-Irish problem,' *Foreign Affairs*, July 1972, p. 615.

128. John M. Lynch, 'The Anglo-Irish problem,' *Foreign Affairs*, July 1972, p. 615–16.

129. Whitaker to Lynch, 21 June 1972 (Jack Lynch Papers).

130. Whitaker to Lynch, 16 June 1972 (Jack Lynch Papers).

131. Jack Lynch Papers.

132. Jack Lynch Papers.

133. William Whitelaw, *The Whitelaw Memoirs*, p. 94.

134. Superintendent M. Fitzgerald report, stamped 4 July 1972, copy in file marked 'Taoiseach's meeting with Mr Heath, 4th September 1974' (Jack Lynch Papers).

135. Superintendent M. Fitzgerald report, stamped 4 July 1972, copy in file marked 'Taoiseach's meeting with Mr Heath, 4th September 1974' (Jack Lynch Papers).

136. Superintendent M. Fitzgerald report, stamped 4 July 1972, copy in file marked 'Taoiseach's meeting with Mr Heath, 4th September 1974' (Jack Lynch Papers).

137. Extract of letter from G. B. Newe to Dr Whitaker, 26 June 1972 (Jack Lynch Papers).

138. William Whitelaw, *The Whitelaw Memoirs*, p. 100–1.

139. Jonathan Bardon, *A History of Ulster*, p. 695.

140. William Whitelaw, *The Whitelaw Memoirs*, p. 100–1.

141. Jonathan Bardon, *A History of Ulster*, p. 695–8.

142. Jonathan Bardon, *A History of Ulster*, p. 698.

143. G. B. Newe to Dr Whitaker, 1 August 1972 (Jack Lynch Papers).

144. G. B. Newe to Dr Whitaker, 1 August 1972 (Jack Lynch Papers).

145. G. B. Newe to Dr Whitaker, 3 August 1972 (Jack Lynch Papers).

146. Whitaker to Lynch, 5 August 1972 (Jack Lynch Papers).

147. Dr Hillery's meeting with Whitelaw, memorandum, 4 August 1972, Department of External Affairs (Jack Lynch Papers).

148. Dr Hillery's meeting with Whitelaw, memorandum, 4 August 1972, Department of External Affairs (Jack Lynch Papers).

149. Heath to Lynch, 10 August 1972 (Jack Lynch Papers).

150. Heath to Lynch, 10 August 1972 (Jack Lynch Papers).

151. Ambassador Dónal O'Sullivan to Department of External Affairs, 15 August 1972 (Jack Lynch Papers).

152. Hugh McCann to Lynch, 16 August 1972 (Jack Lynch Papers).

153. Hugh McCann to Lynch, 31 August 1972 (Jack Lynch Papers).

154. Whitaker to Lynch, 8 August 1972 (Jack Lynch Papers).

155. Whitaker to Professor Norman Gibson, 8 August 1972 (Jack Lynch Papers).

156. Whitaker to David James, 10 August 1972 (Jack Lynch Papers).

157. David James to Dr Ken Whitaker, 15 August 1972 (Jack Lynch Papers).

158. Whitaker to David James, 28 August 1972 (Jack Lynch Papers).

159. Whitaker to Lynch, 19 December 1972 (Jack Lynch Papers).

160. Brian Faulkner, *Memoirs of a Statesman*, p. 131–2.

161. Whitaker to Lynch, 2 September 1972 (Jack Lynch Papers).

162. Minute of Lynch meeting with Heath, Munich, 4 September 1972 (Jack Lynch Papers).

163. Minute of Lynch meeting with Heath, Munich, 4 September 1972 (Jack Lynch Papers).

164. Minute of Lynch meeting with Heath, Munich, 4 September 1972 (Jack Lynch Papers).

165. Minute of Lynch meeting with Heath, Munich, 4 September 1972 (Jack Lynch Papers).

166. Minute of Lynch meeting with Heath, Munich, 4 September 1972 (Jack Lynch Papers).

167. Minute of Lynch meeting with Heath, Munich, 4 September 1972 (Jack Lynch Papers).

168. Bloomfield to Whitaker, c. 31 October 1972 (Jack Lynch Papers).

169. Whitaker to Bloomfield, 2 November 1972; the same day Dr Whitaker sent the material to Lynch, 'As arranged in our telephone conversation this morning' (Jack Lynch Papers).

170. Peck to Lynch, 2 November 1972 (Jack Lynch Papers).

171. Peck to Lynch, 2 November 1972 (Jack Lynch Papers).

172. Hugh McCann minute of conversation with Ambassador Peck, 21 November 1972.

173. Hugh McCann minute of conversation with Ambassador Peck, 21 November 1972.

174. Hugh McCann minute of conversation with Ambassador Peck, 21 November 1972.

175. He was visited in hospital by the retired Archbishop of Dublin, John Charles McQuaid, and by his successor, Archbishop Dermot Ryan.

176. Ambassador Dónal O'Sullivan minute, 27 November 1972, of talks between Heath and Lynch (Jack Lynch Papers).

177. Ambassador Dónal O'Sullivan minute, 27 November 1972, of talks between Heath and Lynch (Jack Lynch Papers).

178. Ambassador Dónal O'Sullivan minute, 27 November 1972, of talks between Heath and Lynch (Jack Lynch Papers).

179. Ambassador Dónal O'Sullivan minute, 27 November 1972, of talks between Heath and Lynch (Jack Lynch Papers).

180. Ambassador Dónal O'Sullivan minute, 27 November 1972, of talks between Heath and Lynch (Jack Lynch Papers).

181. Ambassador Dónal O'Sullivan to Assistant Secretary of the Department of Foreign Affairs, R. McDonagh, 12 December 1972 (Jack Lynch Papers).

182. On 26 November 1972 five people were injured in an explosion at Burgh Quay, Dublin.

183. The terms of the bill had caused a revolt on the Fianna Fáil backbenches. On 11 December, Paudge Brennan and Des Foley were expelled from the parliamentary party after voting against the Government on the Offences Against the State (Amendment) Bill.

184. Jonathan Bardon, *A History of Ulster,* p. 701.

185. Dermot Keogh, *Twentieth Century Ireland,* p. 317–18.

Chapter 10 (P. 368–436)

1. The referendum on membership had been held on 10 May 1972. Lynch won by a landslide, 1,041,890 for and 211,891 against.

2. J. J. Lee, *Ireland, 1912–1989,* p. 468.

3. Intended final draft of article on Frank Aiken, sent by Geraldine Kennedy, political correspondent of the *Sunday Press,* to Frank Aiken (Jr), 23 June 1983 (UCD Archives Department, Frank Aiken Papers, P104/2341). I am grateful to Mr Rory O'Dwyer for providing me with this reference.

4. Intended final draft of article on Frank Aiken, sent by Geraldine Kennedy, political correspondent of the *Sunday Press,* to Frank Aiken (Jr), 23 June 1983 (UCD Archives Department, Frank Aiken Papers, P104/2341). I am grateful to Mr Rory O'Dwyer for providing me with this reference.

5. Intended final draft of article on Frank Aiken, sent by Geraldine Kennedy, political correspondent of the *Sunday Press,* to Frank Aiken (Jr), 23 June 1983 (UCD Archives Department, Frank Aiken Papers, P104/2341). I am grateful to Mr Rory O'Dwyer for providing me with this reference.

6. Handwritten letter from Frank Aiken to director of elections, Fianna Fáil, 7 February 1973 (UCD Archives Department, Frank Aiken Papers, P104/2339 (2)). I am grateful to Mr Rory O'Dwyer for providing me with this reference.

7. Intended final draft of article on Frank Aiken, sent by Geraldine Kennedy, political correspondent of the *Sunday Press,* to Frank Aiken (Jr), 23 June 1983 (UCD Archives Department, Frank Aiken Papers, P104/2341).

8. Intended final draft of article on Frank Aiken, sent by Geraldine Kennedy, political correspondent of the *Sunday Press,* to Frank Aiken (Jr), 23 June 1983 (UCD Archives Department, Frank Aiken Papers, P104/2341).

9. Intended final draft of article on Frank Aiken, sent by Geraldine Kennedy, political correspondent of the *Sunday Press,* to Frank Aiken (Jr), 23 June 1983 (UCD Archives Department, Frank Aiken Papers, P104/2341).

10. Handwritten letter from Paddy Smith to Frank Aiken, 12 February 1973 (UCD Archives Department, Frank Aiken Papers, P104/2340).

11. Intended final draft of article on Frank Aiken, sent by Geraldine Kennedy, political correspondent of the *Sunday Press*, to Frank Aiken (Jr), 23 June 1983 (UCD Archives Department, Frank Aiken Papers, P104/2341).

12. Pádraig Faulkner, *As I Saw It*, p. 109–13.

13. Intended final draft of article on Frank Aiken, sent by Geraldine Kennedy, political correspondent of the *Sunday Press*, to Frank Aiken (Jr), 23 June 1983 (UCD Archives Department, Frank Aiken Papers, P104/2341).

14. Intended final draft of article on Frank Aiken, sent by Geraldine Kennedy, political correspondent of the *Sunday Press*, to Frank Aiken (Jr), 23 June 1983 (UCD Archives Department, Frank Aiken Papers, P104/2341).

15. Intended final draft of article on Frank Aiken, sent by Geraldine Kennedy, political correspondent of the *Sunday Press*, to Frank Aiken (Jr), 23 June 1983 (UCD Archives Department, Frank Aiken Papers, P104/2341).

16. Copy of a statement by Frank Aiken to the electors of Co. Louth, c. 17 February, withdrawing his candidature for re-election for Fianna Fáil (UCD Archives, Frank Aiken Papers, P104/2338). I am grateful to my colleague Rory O'Dwyer for generously providing me with the reference and necessary documents.

17. Frank Aiken (Jr) wrote: 'During my father's funeral I was very surprised at the number of people who were already aware of some events leading to his resignation. I decided that the circumstances of his resignation should be on the public record after his death. I want that record to be full and accurate for my father's sake and for historical purposes.' Intended final draft of article on Frank Aiken, sent by Geraldine Kennedy, political correspondent of the *Sunday Press*, to Frank Aiken (Jr), 23 June 1983 (UCD Archives Department, Frank Aiken Papers, P104/2341).

18. Editorial, 'Clarify the issues,' *Irish Times*, 6 February 1973.

19. Editorial, 'For real, or not?' *Irish Times*, 7 February 1973.

20. Editorial, 'The voter's gain,' *Irish Times*, 8 February 1973.

21. John Healy, 'Inside Politics,' *Irish Times*, 10 February 1973.

22. John Healy, 'Campaign Comment,' *Irish Times*, 12 February 1973.

23. 'N.I. dangers main Lynch theme,' *Irish Times*, 15 February 1973.

24. Dermot Keogh, *Twentieth Century Ireland*, p. 319–21.

25. Donald Harman Akenson, *Conor*, vol. 1, p. 386.

26. John Peck, *Dublin from Downing Street*, p. 142.

27. John Peck, *Dublin from Downing Street*, p. 112–13.

28. Hugh McCann minute, 5 March 1973 (Jack Lynch Papers).

29. Edward Heath, *The Course of My Life*, p. 441.

30. Edward Heath, *The Course of My Life*, p. 440.

31. Edward Heath, *The Course of My Life*, p. 443.

32. Garret FitzGerald, *All in a Life*, p. 205–6.

33. Edward Heath, *The Course of My Life*, p. 442–4. See also Brian Faulkner, *Memoirs of a Statesman*, p. 226–38, and William Whitelaw, *The Whitelaw Memoirs*, p. 120–.

34. Shadow cabinet minute book (Jack Lynch Papers).
35. Shadow cabinet minute book (Jack Lynch Papers).
36. T. Ryle Dwyer, *Nice Fellow,* p. 308.
37. Shadow cabinet minute book (Jack Lynch Papers).
38. Shadow cabinet minute book (Jack Lynch Papers).
39. Shadow cabinet minute book (Jack Lynch Papers).
40. Shadow cabinet minute book (Jack Lynch Papers).
41. Shadow cabinet minute book (Jack Lynch Papers).
42. Shadow cabinet minute book (Jack Lynch Papers).
43. Shadow cabinet minute book (Jack Lynch Papers).
44. Garret FitzGerald, *All in a Life,* p. 198.
45. See Hugh McCann minute, 3 January 1973, envelope marked 'Strictly Private, Jack Lynch esq. TD' (Jack Lynch Papers). There is another copy of the same report with one difference: this report is signed by the Irish ambassador in London, Dónal O'Sullivan. It is likely that McCann sent the report to Lynch over his own signature.
46. Hugh McCann minute, 21 December 1972, handwritten on top: 'The protest related to Wyman only.' Envelope marked 'Strictly Private, Jack Lynch esq. TD' (Jack Lynch Papers).
47. Note of phone message from 3C, signed *SmcC* and dated 15 December 1972; a second phone message from 3C, also signed *SmcC*, is dated 19 December 1972, envelope marked 'Strictly Private, Jack Lynch esq. TD' (Jack Lynch Papers).
48. Dónal O'Sullivan to Hugh McCann, 10 January 1973 (Jack Lynch Papers).
49. 'Former Taoiseach forgot about report,' *Irish Times,* 14 August 1973.
50. Dónal O'Sullivan to Hugh McCann, 10 January 1973 (Jack Lynch Papers).
51. Garret FitzGerald, *All in a Life,* p. 204.
52. Confidential source.
53. Shadow cabinet minute book (Jack Lynch Papers).
54. Shadow cabinet minute book (Jack Lynch Papers).
55. Shadow cabinet minute book (Jack Lynch Papers).
56. Shadow cabinet minute book (Jack Lynch Papers).
57. Shadow cabinet minute book (Jack Lynch Papers).
58. Shadow cabinet minute book (Jack Lynch Papers).
59. Shadow cabinet minute book (Jack Lynch Papers).
60. Shadow cabinet minute book (Jack Lynch Papers).
61. Shadow cabinet minute book (Jack Lynch Papers).
62. Shadow cabinet minute book (Jack Lynch Papers).
63. Shadow cabinet minute book (Jack Lynch Papers).
64. Shadow cabinet minute book (Jack Lynch Papers).
65. The case of the Price sisters was also discussed, arising from correspondence received (shadow cabinet minute book, Jack Lynch Papers).
66. Shadow cabinet minute book (Jack Lynch Papers).
67. Shadow cabinet minute book (Jack Lynch Papers).
68. Shadow cabinet minute book (Jack Lynch Papers).

69. Shadow cabinet minute book (Jack Lynch Papers).

70. Shadow cabinet minute book (Jack Lynch Papers).

71. Shadow cabinet minute book (Jack Lynch Papers).

72. Shadow cabinet minute book (Jack Lynch Papers); see also articles by Ken Gray and Dick Walsh, *Irish Times*, 24 and 25 April 1974.

73. Shadow cabinet minute book (Jack Lynch Papers).

74. Frank Dunlop, *Yes, Taoiseach*, p. 8–11.

75. Shadow cabinet minute book (Jack Lynch Papers).

76. Shadow cabinet minute book (Jack Lynch Papers).

77. Shadow cabinet minute book (Jack Lynch Papers).

78. Shadow cabinet minute book (Jack Lynch Papers).

79. Shadow cabinet minute book (Jack Lynch Papers).

80. Shadow cabinet minute book (Jack Lynch Papers).

81. Bernard Donoughue, *Downing Street Diary*, p. 129.

82. Bernard Donoughue, *Downing Street Diary*, p. 132.

83. Shadow cabinet minute book (Jack Lynch Papers).

84. J. Bowyer Bell, *The Irish Troubles*, p. 423–4 and p. 473.

85. Shadow cabinet minute book (Jack Lynch Papers).

86. Fianna Fáil front bench meeting, 3 July 1974, minute book (Jack Lynch Papers).

87. Fianna Fáil front bench meeting, 9 July 1974, minute book (Jack Lynch Papers).

88. Shadow cabinet minute book (Jack Lynch Papers).

89. Shadow cabinet minute book (Jack Lynch Papers).

90. Shadow cabinet minute book (Jack Lynch Papers).

91. Shadow cabinet minute book (Jack Lynch Papers).

92. T. Ryle Dwyer argues that Mrs Childers's nomination was appealing to the coalition Government. At a function in Iveagh House the Taoiseach, Liam Cosgrave, suggested to Lynch that Rita Childers might be a compromise candidate. Lynch agreed to take the matter back to his party for discussion. However, there were leaks in the press in the following days, stating that Rita Childers had become an agreed candidate for the presidency. Angered by the reports, Lynch turned his back on that course of action. This account may also be accurate, although the timing appears to be out of line with events. T. Ryle Dwyer, *Nice Fellow*, p. 311–12.

93. *Irish Times*, 25 January 1975.

94. Bruce Arnold, *Haughey*, p. 132.

95. Interview with confidential source, February 2006.

96. *Irish Times*, 31 January 1975.

97. Shadow cabinet minute book (Jack Lynch Papers).

98. Shadow cabinet minute book (Jack Lynch Papers).

99. Chris Glennon, 'Front bench reshuffle an indicator at ard fheis,' *Irish Independent*, 14 February 1976.

100. *Irish Times*, 31 January 1975.

101. Dick Walsh, 'Accord at FF debate on North,' *Irish Times*, 15 February 1975132.

102. Dick Walsh, 'Accord at FF debate on North,' *Irish Times*, 15 February 1975.

103. Main reports on ard-fheis, 15 February 1975.

104. Editorial, 'Not so much a party . . .' *Irish Times,* 17 February 1976.

105. Editorial, 'Policies needed,' *Irish Independent,* 17 February 1976.

106. Shadow cabinet minute book (Jack Lynch Papers).

107. Shadow cabinet minute book (Jack Lynch Papers).

108. Brugha had been elected Fianna Fáil TD for South County Dublin in 1973.

109. Máire MacSwiney Brugha, *History's Daughter,* p. 222–4.

110. Shadow cabinet minute book (Jack Lynch Papers).

111. Shadow cabinet minute book (Jack Lynch Papers).

112. J. J. Lee, *Ireland, 1912–1985,* p. 481.

113. Interview with Neville Keery, Cork.

114. Shadow cabinet minute book (Jack Lynch Papers).

115. Shadow cabinet minute book (Jack Lynch Papers).

116. Bruce Arnold, *Haughey,* p. 133–4.

117. *Irish Times,* 1 September 1975.

118. *Irish Times,* 15 October 1975.

119. *Irish Times,* 15 October 1975.

120. *Irish Times,* 15 October 1975.

121. Austin Currie, *All Hell Will Break Loose,* p. 302–3.

122. *Irish Times,* 30 October 1975.

123. *Irish Times,* 13 February 1976. The ard-fheis ran from 13 to 14 February 1976.

124. *Irish Times,* 14 February 1976.

125. Presidential address by Lynch to Fianna Fáil ard fheis, 14 February 1976 (UCC Archives Department, Neville Keery Papers, BL/P/K 45).

126. *Irish Times,* 16 February 1976.

127. Confidential military source.

128. The informal nature of the group's meetings was clear from Neville Keery's papers, and from comments by Senator Keery himself, in conversation with Andrew McCarthy and Dermot Keogh. Senator Keery recalled that his involvement was minimal, perhaps even attending only one meeting.

129. Neville Keery notes on O'Donoghue paper on Finance, Support and Information Seminar, 5 January 1974 (UCC Archives Department, Neville Keery Papers, BL/P/K 35).

130. Draft section on Local Government, 1977 Manifesto (UCC Archives Department, Neville Keery Papers, BL/P/K 45). It should be noted that Neville Keery stressed, in private conversations with Andrew McCarthy and Dermot Keogh, that while he played a major role in writing the final version of the 1977 manifesto he largely inherited the documents on which it was based and was not involved in formulating the policies of the manifesto.

131. Fianna Fáil Research and Support Services, 'The Economic Emergency,' 1976 (UCC Archives Department, Neville Keery Papers, BL/P/K 45).

132. Fianna Fáil Research and Support Services, 'The Economic Emergency,' 1976 (UCC Archives Department, Neville Keery Papers, BL/P/K 45, p. 3–4).

133. Fianna Fáil Research and Support Services, 'The Economic Emergency,' 1976 (UCC Archives Department, Neville Keery Papers BL/P/K 45, p. 7–8).

134. Fianna Fáil Research and Support Services, 'The Economic Emergency,' 1976 (UCC Archives Department, Neville Keery Papers BL/P/K 45, p. 10–12).

135. Fianna Fáil Research and Support Services, 'The Economic Emergency,' 1976 (UCC Archives Department, Neville Keery Papers BL/P/K 45, p. 13–14).

136. Fianna Fáil Research and Support Services, 'The Economic Emergency,' 1976 (UCC Archives Department, Neville Keery Papers BL/P/K 45, p. 16–17).

137. Presidential Address by Lynch to Fianna Fáil Ard Fheis, 14 February 1976 (UCC Archives Department, Neville Keery Papers, BL/P/K 45).

138. Presidential Address by Lynch to Fianna Fáil Ard Fheis, 14 February 1976 (UCC Archives Department, Neville Keery Papers, BL/P/K 45).

139. N. Keery, Comments on White Paper on Local Finance and Taxation, 19 October 1972 (UCC Archives Department, Neville Keery Papers, BL/P/K 35).

140. Draft note on Finance, undated [1972], unsigned (UCC Archives Department, Neville Keery Papers, BL/P/K 35).

141. Draft Press Conference address prepared by Neville Keery for Jack Lynch, 11 June 1977 (UCC Archives Department, Neville Keery Papers, BL/P/K 45).

142. Neville Keery was responsible for the inclusion of that pledge. Interview with Neville Keery.

143. Martin O'Donoghue, 'Irish economic policy, 1977–1979,' Studies, vol. 79, no. 315, autumn 1990, p. 313.

144. Martin O'Donoghue, 'Irish economic policy, 1977–1979,' Studies, vol. 79, no. 315, autumn 1990, p. 309–11.

145. John Bew, 'Power sharing on backburner but don't tell Dublin,' Irish Times, 28 December 2007.

146. Stephen Collins, 'Lynch allowed British military overflights,' Irish Times, 28 December 2007.

147. Robert Shepherd, Enoch Powell, p. 470–1.

148. James Callaghan, Time and Change, p. 454.

149. Robert Shepherd, Enoch Powell, p. 471.

150. Bernard Donoughue, Downing Street Diary, p. 685.

151. James Callaghan, Time and Change, p. 499.

152. James Callaghan, Time and Change, p. 499–500.

153. John Bowman, 'Dublin's tracking of North keen and informed,' Irish Times, 29 September 2007.

154. Andrew J. Wilson, Irish America and the Ulster Connection, p. 126–.

155. Andrew J. Wilson, Irish America and the Ulster Connection, p. 154–.

156. Cork Examiner, 5 March 1979.   This article was written by Val Dorgan, a journalist with the paper. See Val Dorgan, Christy Ring, p. 225–.

157. Andrew J. Wilson, Irish America and the Ulster Connection, p. 155.

158. Cork Examiner, 5 March 1979.

159. Val Dorgan, Christy Ring, p. 229–30. Paddy Downey of the Irish Times wrote in appreciation: 'He turned games upside down with wonderful scores. People who witnessed it still talk of the goal that beat Limerick in the replayed Munster final of 1944. A classical goal that turned the game against Kilkenny in the All-Ireland

final of 1946 and three goals and a point which beat Limerick in the last few minutes of the Munster final of 1956 are also part of the folklore of hurling.' Downey, in the same article, regarded Ring as 'incomparable'. See Paddy Downey, 'Supreme master of the art of hurling,' *Irish Times*, 10 March 1979.

160. *Cork Examiner*, 5 March 1979.
161. Dermot Keogh, *Ireland and Europe*, p. 261.
162. Hugo Young, *The Iron Lady*, p. 96–7.
163. James Callaghan, *Time and Chance*, p. 499–501.
164. Philip Ziegler, *Mountbatten*, p. 698–699.
165. See various articles in the *Irish Times*, 28 August 1976.
166. Editorial, 'Purpose,' *Irish Times*, 30 August 1976.
167. Confidential civil service source.
168. Editorial, 'Purpose,' *Irish Times*, 30 August 1979.
169. Editorial, *Irish Times*, 28 August 1979.
170. Dick Walsh, 'British put blame on Taoiseach for security failures,' *Irish Times*, 1 September 1979.
171. Editorial, 'London summit,' *Irish Times*, 1 September 1979.
172. John Healy, 'Sounding off,' *Irish Times*, 51 September 1979.
173. Máirín Lynch letter, *Irish Times*, 3 September 1979.
174. Editorial, *Irish Times*, 3 September 1979.
175. Editorial, 'Lynch in London,' *Irish Times*, 5 September 1979.
176. Lead story, *Irish Times*, 6 September 1979.
177. Dick Hogan, 'Lynch objected beforehand to speech by Miss de Valera,' *Irish Times*, 17 September 1979.
178. Dick Walsh, 'Prompt Lynch reply shows concern at de Valera speech,' *Irish Times*, 10 September 1979.
179. T. Ryle Dwyer, *Nice Fellow*, p. 361–4.
180. Dick Walsh, 'Prompt Lynch reply shows concern at de Valera speech,' *Irish Times*, 10 September 1979.
181. Seán Cronin, 'Miss de Valera blames border for violence,' *Irish Times*, 14 September 1979.
182. Dick Walsh, 'FF row grows as deputy returns,' *Irish Times*, 18 September 1979.
183. T. Ryle Dwyer, *Nice Fellow*, p. 361–4.
184. Dick Walsh, 'Party rejects challenge by Síle de Valera,' *Irish Times*, 29 September 1979.
185. Dick Walsh, 'Lynch says withdrawal of NI troops not a priority,' *Irish Times*, 18 December 1979.
186. Frank Dunlop, who was the Government press officer, writes in his memoirs that he noticed Lynch becoming 'testier by the day and, unlike in the year after the election,' he found it increasingly difficult 'to engage the Taoiseach in matters concerning the Government.' He further writes that as long as he had known and worked for Jack Lynch he had a tolerance for whiskey that had not interfered with his capacity to do his work. Whenever they travelled abroad, a bottle or two of Paddy was brought. The party would share a few drinks in the evenings, and Lynch

would say, 'Let's see if we can get below Thurles'—a reference to the map of Ireland on the bottle. Dunlop wrote about Lynch's new mood, which sometimes resulted in his acting out of character. In the absence of corroboration from other contemporaries, which I have not found, I believe that Dunlop's judgement must remain one person's interpretation. In my interviews with many of Lynch's contemporaries this view of Lynch has neither been mentioned nor substantiated. Frank Dunlop, *Yes, Taoiseach*, p. 109–11.

187. I was working as a journalist with RTE radio and television during those months and went to Rome with a team to report on the Papacy and preparations there for the coming visit. It was made very clear to me by officials in the Vatican that there was a strong desire for the Pope to cross the border into Northern Ireland.

188. Frank Dunlop, *Yes, Taoiseach*, p. 111–12; T. Ryle Dwyer, *Nice Fellow*, p. 364–5.

189. Frank Dunlop, *Yes, Taoiseach*, p. 109–11.

190. Dick Hogan, 'FF vote likely to fall from '77 peak', *Irish Times*, 4 November 1979.

191. Confidential source.

192. T. Ryle Dwyer, *Nice Fellow*, p. 369–70.

193. Michael Mills, *Hurler on the Ditch*, p. 124.

194. Editorial, 'Votes do count', *Irish Times*, 7 November 1979.

195. Confidential source.

196. Frank McDonald, 'Double defeat for FF in Cork by-election', *Irish Times*, 9 November 1979.

197. Frank McDonald, lead story, *Irish Times*, 9 November 1979.

198. Dick Walsh, 'Reshuffle of cabinet in new year, says Lynch', *Irish Times*, 9 November 1979.

199. Frank McDonald, lead story, *Irish Times*, 9 November 1979.

200. Dick Walsh, 'Reshuffle of cabinet in new year, says Lynch', *Irish Times*, 9 November 1979.

201. Editorial, 'More of a convulsion', *Irish Times*, 9 November 1979.

202. Dick Walsh, 'Lynch explains air corridor provision to American press', *Irish Times*, 10 November 1979.

203. Michael Mills, *Hurler on the Ditch*, p. 125.

204. Dick Walsh, 'Lynch explains air corridor provision to American press', *Irish Times*, 10 November 1979.

205. Denis Coughlan, 'O'Kennedy's overflight role', *Irish Times*, 13 November 1979.

206. John Healy, 'The bob-sled picks up speed', *Irish Times*, 10 November 1979.

207. Denis Coughlan, 'Lynch faces challenge to his leadership', *Irish Times*, 10 November 1979.

208. 'Partition "inconceivable to Pearse"', *Irish Times*, 12 November 1979.

209. Dick Walsh, 'Today's violence a slander on Pearse—Lynch', *Irish Times*, 12 November 1979.

210. Denis Coughlan, 'Election inquest to await Lynch's return', *Irish Times*, 13 November 1979.

211. 'Wrong to blame Taoiseach for election defeats, says O'Malley', *Irish Times*, 12 November 1979.

212. 'Haughey accused of "pathological ambitions",' *Irish Times*, 13 November 1979.

213. Michael Mills, *Hurler on the Ditch*, p. 125.

214. Michael Mills, *Hurler on the Ditch*, p. 126.

215. Dick Walsh and Olivia O'Leary, 'FF may expel Loughnane for attack on Lynch,' *Irish Times*, 14 November 1979.

216. Olivia O'Leary, 'FF man retracts remarks on Lynch,' *Irish Times*, 15 November 1979.

217. Dick Walsh, 'Lynch denies he revealed Border security details,' *Irish Times*, 16 November 1979.

218. Olivia O'Leary, 'Haughey misses Lynch reception,' *Irish Times*, 17 November 1979.

219. Dick Walsh, 'Taoiseach set for party showdown on leadership issue,' *Irish Times*, 21 November 1979.

220. Dick Walsh, 'Taoiseach set for party showdown on leadership issue,' *Irish Times*, 21 November 1979.

221. Martin Crowley, 'Fitt attacks "republican element" and proclaims support for Taoiseach,' *Irish Times*, 23 November 19979.

222. 'Lynch secure in "dog-eat-dog" leadership test, says Blaney,' *Irish Times*, 26 November 1979.

223. Dick Walsh, 'Irish dimension not abandoned, says Taoiseach,' *Irish Times*, 26 November 1979.

224. Dennis Kennedy, 'EEC rift with Britain as wide as ever after summit's first day,' *Irish Times*, 30 November 1979.

225. Editorial, 'Jack always wins,' *Irish Times*, 29 November 1979.

226. Interview with Anne Colley, Dublin, 31 January 2006.

227. Geraldine Kennedy, 'Successor will need 42 votes to win,' *Irish Times*, 6 December 1979.

228. Interview with Paul Mackay, summer, 2005.

229. Editorial, 'You never can tell,' *Irish Times*, 7 December 1979.

230. Garret FitzGerald, *All in a Life*, p. 339.

231. Interview with Anne Colley, Dublin, 31 January 2006.

232. Dick Walsh, 'Lynch request to give O'Donoghue Euro job,' *Irish Times*, 13 December 1979.

233. Garret FitzGerald, *All in a Life*, p. 340–1. Dr FitzGerald devotes considerable space in his autobiography to explaining his 'flawed pedigree' remark. The context was a comparison with Haughey's predecessors in the post of Taoiseach. He acknowledged as a professional politician the danger of using such a 'colourful phrase', which could be distorted and easily taken out of the context in which he had used it.

234. 'Dáil report,' *Irish Times*, 12 December 1979.

235. 'Dáil report,' *Irish Times*, 12 December 1979.

Chapter 11 (P. 437–469)

1. Dick Walsh, 'Lynch to retire at next election,' *Irish Times*, 16 May 1980.

2. The Bishop of Cork, Cornelius Lucey, was given the freedom of the city on the same occasion.

3. Denis Reading, 'City proudly honours two great citizens,' *Cork Examiner*, 20 December 1980.

4. 'Gold Medal of Merit for Lynch,' *Evening Echo*, 10 July 1981. He had received the Robert Schuman Gold Medal in 1973 for his contribution to the development of Ireland and European integration.

5. Michael Hand, 'Jack is no hurler on the ditch,' *Irish Independent*, 15 February 1986.

6. My wife's parents, Joe and Brigid Grainger, were shareholders in Irish Distillers. They often recalled how much they liked meeting Jack Lynch at an annual general meeting.

7. Lynch was also the recipient of many sports awards. In 1981 he received the Bank of Ireland All-Time Hurling Award and in 1983 was made a member of Jury's Hall of Fame. He was named on the Hurling Team of the Century in 1984 and inducted in the same year into the Texaco Hall of Fame. He was also named Hurling Captain of the Forties, a member of the Cork Millennium Team and a member of the Team of the Millennium. Liam Ó Tuama, *Jack Lynch*, p. 201.

8. Michael Hand, 'Jack is no hurler on the ditch,' *Irish Independent*, 15 February 1986.

9. Lynch went elsewhere when the time of the Mass was changed to 9:30, as he used to listen to the BBC radio programme 'Alistair Cooke's Letter from America.'

10. Telephone conversation with Father Ralph Egan, 30 June 2005.

11. Michael Hand, 'Jack is no hurler on the ditch,' *Irish Independent*, 15 February 1986.

12. Michael Mills, 'His rivals found out he was no soft touch,' *Examiner*, 21 October 1999. This passage is reproduced practically verbatim by Mills in *Hurler on the Ditch*, p. 128.

13. Osip Mandelshtam, 'We exist, without sensing our country beneath us,' *Selected Poems*, London: Penguin Books, 1988, p. 65.

14. Interview with Finbarr Lynch.

15. Stephen Collins, *The Power Game*, p. 142–5.

16. Pádraig Faulkner, *As I Saw It*, p. 163.

17. See article by Denis Reading and Val Dorgan, *Cork Examiner*, 27 January 1983.

18. See article by Denis Reading and Val Dorgan, *Cork Examiner*, 27 January 1983.

19. See article by Denis Reading and Val Dorgan, *Cork Examiner*, 27 January 1983.

20. Pádraig Faulkner, *As I Saw It*, p. 163–5.

21. With reference to the spirit of intimidation pervading Leinster House in the period before the vote, Stephen Collins gained first-hand experience of one aspect of Haughey's *modus operandi*. There had been reports that Haughey was going to announce his resignation. Collins was sent by his editor to ask Haughey to confirm or deny the report. With the help of an experienced cameraman, Pat Cashman, Collins made his way to Haughey's office. After a few photographs Collins asked him directly if he was going to resign that day. 'The reaction was one of instantaneous and overwhelming anger. '"Would you fuck off," he shouted, making a run at me. I backed against the wall with Haughey shouting in my face, "That's FUCK OFF" he roared, spelling out each letter for emphasis.' Cashman by that time had got between the two of them and was attempting to calm Haughey down. Regaining his composure, Haughey asked Collins to repeat his question,

and replied: 'That's complete nonsense. I have no intention of resigning,' and walked away calmly. Stephen Collins, *The Power Game*, p. 143.

22. There was a second heave against the Haughey leadership when a former Haughey stalwart, Charlie McCreevy, put down a motion of no confidence in the Taoiseach on 1 October 1982. Desmond O'Malley, who was on holiday in Spain when the news broke, rushed back to Dublin. Martin O'Donoghue also supported the move; but both men felt they would have to resign their Government posts, as they were going to vote against Haughey. The leadership refused a secret ballot, much to the disgust of the veteran Pádraig Faulkner and others. A roll-call vote was taken, and Haughey won by 51 votes to 27. Disgraceful scenes followed, as Jim Gibbons was punched and ushers in Leinster House had to escort both himself and Charlie McCreevy to their cars. They were surrounded by an angry mob, insults were thrown and fists slammed on the roofs of the departing cars. In late October, Jim Gibbons suffered a heart attack. Irish democracy had not witnessed such scenes of violence even during the Treaty debates in 1921–2. The death of Bill Loughnane cut Haughey's majority further. Stephen Collins, *The Power Game*, p. 146.

23. Pádraig Faulkner, *As I Saw It*, p. 148–51.

24. Stephen Collins, *The Power Game*.

25. Pádraig Faulkner, *As I Saw It*, p. 175–81.

26. *Cork Examiner*, 27 January 1983.

27. 'Party leaders praise Aiken's contribution,' *Irish Times*, 19 May 1983.

28. 'Patriot in true tradition—Lynch,' *Irish Times*, 19 May 1983.

29. Editorial, 'Frank Aiken,' *Irish Times*, 21 May 1983.

30. Colley recalled Aiken's strong support for him in his public life. 'To have a man of his stature and experience being helpful to one in those days was most heartening and encouraging,' he said. Dick Walsh, 'Colley tribute at grave,' *Irish Times*, 21 May 1983.

31. 'Warm tributes from political leaders,' *Irish Times*, 19 September 1983.

32. 'George Colley,' *Irish Times*, 19 September 1983.

33. 'George Colley praised for life of service,' *Irish Times*, 21 September 1983.

34. Máire Cruise O'Brien, *The Same Age as the State*, p. 311–12.

35. Although the Civil War had placed the two families on different sides of the political divide in 1922–3, friendship was never lost. Desmond Fitzgerald, Garret's father, had helped save Seán MacEntee's life during those dark days. Máire Cruise O'Brien, *The Same Age as the State*, p. 310–11.

36. Máire Cruise O'Brien, *The Same Age as the State*, p. 311–12.

37. 'Lynch pays tribute at MacEntee's grave,' *Irish Times*, 13 January 1984.

38. 'Lynch pays tribute at MacEntee's grave,' *Irish Times*, 13 January 1984.

39. *Irish Times*, 3 September 1984.

40. There was a double presentation in Thurles that day, as the 1959 Waterford all-Ireland winning team was celebrating its silver anniversary. All the all-Ireland winning captains were presented with a commemorative piece of Waterford crystal. Jack Lynch had been nominated to the board of Galway Crystal the week before,

and Frankie Walsh remarked to him: 'Jack, now you can show how it is done by real craftsmen.' Interview by Paul Loftus with Frankie Walsh, 29 February 2008.

41. 'Lynch critical of pressure groups,' *Cork Examiner*, 5 November 1985.

42. The 600-page report stated that Haughey was paid £50,000 by a Saudi sheikh to facilitate passport applications. It said he accepted cash from wealthy business-men over a period of seventeen years, including eight years as Taoiseach, living a life vastly beyond the scale of what he earned throughout the period 1979–96. During that period his sole apparent income was used for the purpose of paying bills. After 1979 his borrowings receded and sums were derived primarily from clandestine donations, including funds intended for the medical expenses of a party colleague, Brian Lenihan. In relation to the public donations to the Brian Lenihan liver transplant fund, the tribunal established that up to £265,000 may have been collected for that purpose but no more than £70,000 was applied to the costs and expenses of Lenihan's medical treatment in the United States. The tribunal said it was satisfied that a sizeable portion of the excess collected was misappropriated by Haughey for his own personal use. It found that Haughey personally misappropriated one particular donation of £20,000 for Lenihan's benefit and took a series of steps to conceal his actions. Judge Michael Moriarty rejected Haughey's claim that he knew nothing about his finances. Secret pay-ments had been handled by Haughey's accountant, using a bank in the Cayman Islands. The judge said Haughey's claim that he had never heard of the Cayman Islands was 'unbelievable'. 'Apart from the almost invariably secretive nature of payments from senior members of the business community, their very incidence and scale—particularly during difficult economic times nationally, and when governments led by Mr Haughey were championing austerity—can only be said to have devalued the quality of a modern democracy,' the report concluded. We now know how he could afford to live as he did. Haughey owned a Gandon man-sion, an estate and a stable of horses in north Co. Dublin, had a fine personal collection of contemporary Irish art and owned an impressive yacht and an island with a modernised house off the coast of Co. Kerry.

43. All lived in modest retirement in homes that were neither lavish nor ostentatious. I visited the homes of Lynch, Aiken and MacEntee on different occasions to inter-view the founding fathers about different aspects of their political career. None had the ostentatious life-style of Charles Haughey.

44. *Cork Examiner*, 3 November 1993.

45. *Cork Examiner*, 5 January 1994.

46. Tony Purcell, 'Lynch is honoured with law degree,' *Cork Examiner*, 30 November 1995.

47. Stephanie Walsh, 'Jack Lynch, 1917–1999,' *Newport News* (Nenagh, Co. Tipperary), December 1999.

48. Michael Mills, 'His rivals found out he was no soft touch,' *Examiner*, 21 October 1999.

49. National Library of Ireland, Máirín Lynch Papers, acc. 6260, AIB folder, box 3.

50. Dick Hogan, 'Jack owed no money,' *Irish Times*, 19 February 1999.

51. Aileen Mulhall, 'Sisters to act for Jack,' *Evening Echo,* 14 May 1999.

52. Written from the Provincialate, Mary Aikenhead House, Donnybrook, Dublin (National Library of Ireland, Máirín Lynch Papers, acc. 6260, letters of condolence to Máirín Lynch, box 1).

53. National Library of Ireland, Máirín Lynch Papers, acc. 6260, letters of condolence to Máirín Lynch, box 1.

54. Bruce Arnold, *Jack Lynch,* p. 226.

55. Liam O'Neill, 'Glowing tributes to statesman,' *Examiner,* 21 October 1999.

56. Liam O'Neill, 'Glowing tributes to statesman,' *Examiner,* 21 October 1999.

57. Liam O'Neill, 'Glowing tributes to statesman,' *Examiner,* 21 October 1999.

58. Rita O'Reilly, 'Haughey admired "man of charm",' *Irish Independent,* 21 October 1999.

59. Liam O'Neill, 'Glowing tributes to statesman,' *Examiner,* 21 October 1999.

60. Lorna Reid and Ralph Riegel, 'Tributes for a peacemaker,' *Irish Independent,* 21 October 1999.

61. Lorna Reid and Ralph Riegel, 'Tributes for a peacemaker,' *Irish Independent,* 21 October 1999.

62. National Library of Ireland, Máirín Lynch Papers, acc. 6260, letters of condolence to Máirín Lynch, box 1.

63. Michael Mills, 'A leader who never lost his way with the common folk,' *Irish Independent,* 21 October 1999.

64. Miriam Donohue, 'How Haughey came to be seated next to O'Malley,' *Irish Times,* 21 October 1999.

65. However, Father Dowling was in Palestine when Lynch's death occurred and there was not enough time for him to return to take the service. Father Ralph Egan to Dermot Keogh, no date [July 2005].

66. Jim Morahan, 'Jack Lynch praised for his faith and integrity,' *Examiner,* 22 October 1999.

67. Michael O'Regan and Marie O'Halloran, 'Church is filled to overflowing for the removal of "one so noble and great",' *Irish Times,* 22 October 1999.

68. Seán Mac Carthaigh, 'Jack leaves capital for final journey,' *Examiner,* 23 October 1999.

69. She was a religious of the Sacred Heart and she wrote from Ardvaarda, 13 the Hill, Monkstown, Co. Dublin, on 25 October (National Library of Ireland, Máirín Lynch Papers, acc. 6260, letters of condolence to Máirín Lynch, box 1).

70. Michael O'Regan and Marie O'Halloran, 'Church is filled to overflowing for the removal of "one so noble and great",' *Irish Times,* 22 October 1999.

71. Judge Hubert Wine, a good friend of the family, sent a handwritten note on 27 October, explaining that he was to attend Jack Lynch's funeral in a private capacity but was asked to represent the Jewish Representative Council. 'The Rev. Father Ralph Egan C.P.P.P. could not have been kinder, and, I was so honoured when he brought me down from the altar to greet you, and, on the way allowed me the Jew mourner to say a prayer for your dearest Jack or Jacoob (Yaacov) every morning, and, will continue to do so . . . I do sincerely hope that this note finds you well—

the last few years, and, particularly the last few days must have been an ordeal to say the least, and, although under great strain, and stress, your tremendous courage was an example to us all. Your Darling Beloved Jack G.R.H. dear soul in peace, would have been so proud.' Judge Wine concluded: 'I do know that you both had, and, have a wonderful rapport for our Jewish Community, and I assume, it is indeed mutual. He was the "People's Champion".' A footnote to the footnote: Father Ralph Egan recalls: 'A little aside: in the haste of contacting the other ministers I totally forgot about the Jewish community. I don't know how because one of our local TDs in Mount Argus at the time was Ben Briscoe with whom I was very friendly. On the morning of the service, imagine my embarrassment when Justice Wine arrived and said he was representing the Jewish community. I thought as quickly as I could and asked him to join us on the sanctuary even though it was too late to arrange that he read or speak.' Father Ralph Egan to Dermot Keogh, no date [July 2005] (National Library of Ireland, Máirín Lynch Papers, acc. 6260, letters of condolence to Máirín Lynch, box 1).

72. Marie O'Halloran, 'Lynch is likened to legendary folk heroes,' *Irish Times*, 23 October 1999.

73. Marie O'Halloran, 'Lynch is likened to legendary folk heroes,' *Irish Times*, 23 October 1999.

74. Marie O'Halloran, 'Lynch is likened to legendary folk heroes,' *Irish Times*, 23 October 1999.

75. Roddy O'Sullivan, 'Troops pay respects on last journey,' *Irish Times*, 23 October 1999.

76. Dick Hogan, 'Political foes fail to exchange signs of peace,' *Irish Times*, 25 October 1999. A correction to that story was published later by the *Irish Times*.

77. Jack Lynch funeral Mass leaflet, Cathedral of St Mary and St Anne, Cork, 23 October 1999. I am grateful to Mrs Gretta Drummond for supplying me with a copy.

78. Dick Hogan, 'Political foes fail to exchange signs of peace,' *Irish Times*, 25 October 1999.

79. Dick Hogan, 'Political foes fail to exchange signs of peace,' *Irish Times*, 25 October 1999.

80. Ralph Riegel, 'Widow Máirín takes comfort from Leesiders,' *Irish Independent*, 25 October 1999.

81. Jack Lynch funeral Mass leaflet, Cathedral of St Mary and St Anne, Cork, 23 October 1999.

82. Ralph Riegel, 'Widow Máirín takes comfort from Leesiders,' *Irish Independent*, 25 October 1999.

83. There is an undated card from Áras an Uachtaráin saying they had Mass said for Lynch on 24 October. The President acknowledged receipt of an orchid sent by Máirín Lynch on 12 November 1999. In a handwritten note she said: 'You have had a difficult six years—a slow parting from a much loved partner . . . You have wonderful friends and of course you have the love of the nation—poor substitute for Jack . . . but all just anxious to give you a helping hand through the lonely times'

(National Library of Ireland, Máirín Lynch Papers, acc. 6260, letters of condolence to Máirín Lynch, box 1).

84. Michael O'Regan and Marie O'Halloran, 'Church is filled to overflowing for the removal of "one so noble and great"', *Irish Times*, 22 October 1999.

85. Michael O'Regan and Marie O'Halloran, 'Church is filled to overflowing for the removal of "one so noble and great"', *Irish Times*, 22 October 1999.

86. Dick Hogan, 'Church [and] State represented as Cork bids emotional farewell to former Taoiseach,' *Irish Times*, 25 October 1999.

87. Dick Hogan, 'Political foes fail to exchange signs of peace,' *Irish Times*, 25 October 1999.

88. His address was 4 Cahergal Park, Dillon's Cross, and he enclosed an article he wrote for *Southern Cross*, a tribute to Jack Lynch (National Library of Ireland, Máirín Lynch Papers, acc. 6260, letters of condolence to Máirín Lynch, box 1).

89. 'O'Malley pays tribute to "wonderful confluence of qualities" in Lynch,' *Irish Times*, 25 October 1999.

90. 'O'Malley pays tribute to "wonderful confluence of qualities" in Lynch,' *Irish Times*, 25 October 1999.

91. 'O'Malley pays tribute to "wonderful confluence of qualities" in Lynch,' *Irish Times*, 25 October 1999.

92. *Evening Echo*, 25 October 1999.

93. National Library of Ireland, Máirín Lynch Papers, acc. 6260, letters of condolence to Máirín Lynch, box 1.

94. National Library of Ireland, Máirín Lynch Papers, acc. 6260, letters of condolence to Máirín Lynch, box 1.

95. National Library of Ireland, Máirín Lynch Papers, acc. 6260, letters of condolence to Máirín Lynch, box 1.

96. He enclosed an article he wrote for *Southern Cross*, a tribute to Jack Lynch (National Library of Ireland, Máirín Lynch Papers, acc. 6260, letters of condolence to Máirín Lynch, box 1).

97. National Library of Ireland, Máirín Lynch Papers, acc. 6260, letters of condolence to Máirín Lynch, box 3.

98. National Library of Ireland, Máirín Lynch Papers, acc. 6260, letters of condolence to Máirín Lynch, box 3.

99. National Library of Ireland, Máirín Lynch Papers, acc. 6260, letters of condolence to Máirín Lynch, box 3.

100. National Library of Ireland, Máirín Lynch Papers, acc. 6260, letters of condolence to Máirín Lynch, box 1.

101. National Library of Ireland, Máirín Lynch Papers, acc. 6260, letters of condolence to Máirín Lynch, box 1.

102. National Library of Ireland, Máirín Lynch Papers, acc. 6260, letters of condolence to Máirín Lynch, box 3.

103. National Library of Ireland, Máirín Lynch Papers, acc. 6260, letters of condolence to Máirín Lynch, box 3.

104. National Library of Ireland, Máirín Lynch Papers, acc. 6260, letters of condolence to Máirín Lynch, box 3.
105. National Library of Ireland, Máirín Lynch Papers, acc. 6260, letters of condolence to Máirín Lynch, box 1.
106. National Library of Ireland, Máirín Lynch Papers, acc. 6260, letters of condolence to Máirín Lynch, box 1.
107. National Library of Ireland, Máirín Lynch Papers, acc. 6260, letters of condolence to Máirín Lynch, box 1.
108. National Library of Ireland, Máirín Lynch Papers, acc. 6260, letters of condolence to Máirín Lynch, box 1.
109. National Library of Ireland, Máirín Lynch Papers, acc. 6260, letters of condolence to Máirín Lynch, box 1.
110. National Library of Ireland, Máirín Lynch Papers, acc. 6260, letters of condolence to Máirín Lynch, box 1. There was also a letter of condolence from the Bishop of Cork, Cloyne and Ross, Rev. Paul Colton.
111. National Library of Ireland, Máirín Lynch Papers, acc. 6260, letters of condolence to Máirín Lynch, box 1.
112. National Library of Ireland, Máirín Lynch Papers, acc. 6260, letters of condolence to Máirín Lynch, box 1. The letter also recorded that Jack and Máirín Lynch attended his first Mass.
113. National Library of Ireland, Máirín Lynch Papers, acc. 6260, letters of condolence to Máirín Lynch, box 1.
114. National Library of Ireland, Máirín Lynch Papers, acc. 6260, letters of condolence to Máirín Lynch, box 1.
115. National Library of Ireland, Máirín Lynch Papers, acc. 6260, box 1.
116. National Library of Ireland, Máirín Lynch Papers, acc. 6260, box 1.
117. John Carroll, 'Family and friends salute "real Taoiseach"', *Irish Examiner*, 21 October 2000.
118. National Library of Ireland, Máirín Lynch Papers, acc. 6260, box 1.
119. Nick Miller, 'Jack's back among people of Blackpool', *Evening Echo*, 16 July 2002.
120. Wesley Boyd, 'An Irishman's Diary', *Irish Times*, 16 May 2003.
121. 'The comparison, made by you, of the occasion when Mrs Máirín Lynch was invited by Gulf Oil to launch the super-tanker "Universe Ireland" in Japan, with a family occasion of the current Taoiseach, bears no comparison. The Gulf Oil invitation created an opportunity whereby her husband, an Taoiseach—by his own volition and intuition—was able to utilise the travel and expense involved to officially visit, on behalf of Ireland, Lebanon, India, Thailand, Hong Kong, culminating with an official meeting with the Emperor of Japan, accompanied by a Senior member of the Department of Foreign Affairs. By your own admission, local interested Irish parties in the countries visited "would have to be here for years before getting invited to a reception like this" and all accommodated simply, efficiently and at little cost to Ireland by Jack Lynch's capacity to see an opportunity to promote Ireland while at the same time accompanying his wife to launch a ship in Japan' (National Library of Ireland, Máirín Lynch Papers, acc. 6260, box 3).

122. He wrote: 'Gulf, by its investment policies, is and has been a good citizen of Ireland and as such has every right to request the Taoiseach's wife to honour them by launching a super tanker. Payment becomes irrelevant when, as a guest, all outgoings are looked after by the inviter, in this case Gulf Oil . . . Thank God good interpersonal manners and etiquette would dictate that spouses should be included and I feel sure An Taoiseach requested that a senior member of the External Affairs should accompany him as Head of State. Ireland is a small minnow in the sea of international inward investment today and in 1968 needed to have as many state and industrial doors opened in as many countries as possible. This was, I suggest, Jack Lynch's objective in going to Japan in the first place. Perhaps, FORFAS, IDA and Enterprise Ireland could take the example of the Lynch basics today.' National Library of Ireland, Máirín Lynch Papers, acc. 6260, box 3.

123. National Library of Ireland, Máirín Lynch Papers, acc. 6260, box 3.

124. Máirín Lynch to author, 11 March 2003.

125. National Library of Ireland, Máirín Lynch Papers, acc. 6260, box 1.

126. Patsy McGarry, 'Death of Máirín Lynch "marks end of an era"', Irish Times, 14 June 2004.

127. Vincent Power, 'Loving tributes paid to Cork's "perfect lady"', Evening Echo, 18 June 2004.

Chapter 12 (P. 470–482)

1. Dick Walsh, 'A soft-spoken man who was never an easy touch in politics', Irish Times, 21 October 1999.

2. Irish Times, 21 October 1999.

3. Editorial, Examiner, 21 October 1999.

4. Editorial, 'Jack Lynch will be remembered with affection', Examiner, 21 October 1999.

5. Editorial, 'Jack Lynch will be remembered with affection', Examiner, 21 October 1999.

6. Dick Walsh, 'A soft-spoken man who was never an easy touch in politics', Irish Times, 21 October 1999. Dick Walsh reviewed two biographies: Bruce Arnold, Jack Lynch, and T. Ryle Dwyer, Nice Fellow. See also 'Mister Nice Guy', Irish Times, 20 October 2001.

7. Editorial, 'Jack Lynch will be remembered with affection', Examiner, 21 October 1999.

8. J. N. D. Kelly, The Oxford Dictionary of Popes, Oxford: Oxford University Press, 1986, p. 257.

9. Editorial, 'Jack Lynch will be remembered with affection', Examiner, 21 October 1999.

10. Fintan O'Toole, Irish Times, 23 October 1999.

11. Irish Times, 21 October 1999.

BIBLIOGRAPHY

PRIMARY SOURCES
— Archives Department, University College (now National University of Ireland), Cork:
— Jack Lynch Papers (entrusted to the author by Máirín Lynch for the writing of the biography and deposited in Archives Department, University College, Cork)
— Neville Keery Papers
— Jim Hurley papers (in family possession)

PERSONAL POSSESSION
— Scrapbook of photographs and press cuttings on career of Jack Lynch

— **Cork City Archives**
— Cork Corporation (city council) minutes
— Records on health and disease in Cork

— **NFP Archives, Blackpool, Sunbeam Industrial Estate, Cork**
— Martin O'Mahony interview with Thomas Walsh: Subject: Jack Lynch

— **National Archives of Ireland**
— Department of Education
— Department of Finance
— Department of Foreign Affairs
— Department of Industry and Commerce
— Department of Justice
— Department of the Taoiseach

Sources on Máirín Lynch
— Máirín Lynch Papers
[See also letters from Máirín Lynch to myself, and interview with Máirín Lynch by Ida Grehan, *Irish Times*, 31 January 1972]
— Notes on conversations with Máirín Lynch in November 2000 and in 2001 at her home in Rathgar, Dublin.
— Notes on telephone calls made by Máirín Lynch to my home.

— **National Library of Ireland**
— Seán T. O'Kelly Papers

— **Military Archives, Dublin**
— Files relating to 1967–70

— **History and Archives Department, University College, Dublin**
— Frank Aiken Papers
— John A. Costello Papers
— Éamon de Valera Papers
— Seán MacEntee Papers
— Maurice Moynihan Papers
— James Ryan Papers
— Dr Kenneth Whitaker Papers

— **Dublin Archdiocesan Archives**
— John Charles McQuaid Papers

— **US National Archives, Maryland**
— National Security Council (documents on Ireland)
— Justice Department (Files on Ireland)
— State Department (Files on Ireland)

— **Lyndon Baines Johnson Library, University of Texas**
— Files on Ireland
— Walt Rostow Files

— **Jimmy Carter Center**
— Files on Ireland

— **John F. Kennedy Presidential Library**
— Files on John F. Kennedy's Irish visit, 1962
— Ball Papers

— **John J. Burns Library, Boston College, Boston**
— T. P. O'Neill Papers

— **British National Archives**
— Foreign Office Files

— **Public Record Office, Northern Ireland**
— Select files on 1960s and 1970s

NEWSPAPERS
— *Cork Examiner* (later *Examiner,* now *Irish Examiner*)
— *Guardian* (London)
— *Irish Independent*

— *Irish Press*
— *Irish Times*
— *Times* (London)

INTERVIEWS
— Anne Colley
— Jim Dukes
— Eamonn Gallagher
— Des Hanafin
— Dr Patrick Hillery
— Neville Keery
— Finbarr Lynch
— Máirín Lynch
— Con Murphy
— Edward O'Driscoll, solicitor, Bandon
— Denis Owens
— Máirín Quill
— Stephanie Walsh

INTERVIEWS BY EILEEN COMPAGNO
— Jim Crockett
— Finbarr Lynch
— Irene (Rena) Lynch

BOOKS AND ARTICLES
— Akenson, Donald Harman, *Conor: A Biography of Conor Cruise O'Brien*, Montréal and Kingston: McGill University Press, 1994.
— Akenson, Donald Harman, *The United States and Ireland*, Cambridge (Mass.): Harvard University Press, 1973.
— Aldcroft, Derek, *The European Economy, 1914–70*, London: Croom Helm, 1978.
— Aldous, Richard, and Lee, Sabine (eds.), *Harold Macmillan and Britain's World Role*, London: Macmillan, 1996.
— Allen, Kieran, *Fianna Fáil and Irish Labour: 1926 to the Present Day*, London: Pluto Press, 1997.
— Andrews, C. S., *Man of No Property: An Autobiography*, Cork and Dublin: Mercier Press, 1979, vol. 2.
— *Annual Report of the Medical Officer of Health, County Borough of Cork, 1930*, Cork: Eagle Printing, 1931.
— Anon., *Cork: Its Trade and Commerce* (first issue), Cork: Guy and Company, 1919.
— Anon., *Fianna Fáil: An Chéad Tréimhse / The Story of Fianna Fáil: First Phase*, Dublin: Dollard, 1960.
— Anon., *Peace and War: Speeches by Mr. de Valera on International Affairs*, Dublin: M. H. Gill, 1944.

— Anon., 'The day of the bagman: The British Secret Service in Ireland,' *Magill*, vol. 2, no. 9, 1978, p. 12–21.

— Arnold, Bruce, *Haughey: His Life and Unlucky Deeds*, London: Harper-Collins, 1993.

— Arnold, Bruce, *Jack Lynch: Hero in Crisis*, Dublin: Merlin, 2001.

— Arthur, Paul, *Special Relationships: Britain, Ireland and the Northern Ireland Problem*, Belfast: Blackstaff Press, 2000.

— Arthur, Paul, and Jeffery, Keith, *Northern Ireland since 1968*, Oxford: Basil Blackwell, 1988.

— Bardon, Jonathan, *A History of Ulster*, Belfast: Blackstaff Press, 2001.

— Barrington, Ruth, *Health, Medicine and Politics in Ireland, 1900–70*, Dublin: Institute of Public Administration, 1987.

— Bell, J. Bowyer, *The Irish Troubles: A Generation of Violence, 1967–1992*, Dublin: Gill & Macmillan, 1993.

— Bell, J. Bowyer, *The Secret Army: The IRA, 1916–1979*, Dublin: Poolbeg Press, 1989.

— Bew, Paul, *Ireland: The Politics of Enmity, 1789–2006*, Oxford: Oxford University Press, 2007.

— Bew, Paul, and Gillespie, Gordon, *Northern Ireland: A Chronology of the Troubles, 1968–1993*, Dublin: Gill & Macmillan, 1993.

— Bew, Paul, Hazelkorn, Ellen, and Patterson, Henry, *The Dynamics of Irish Politics*, London: Lawrence and Wishart, 1989.

— Bew, Paul, and Patterson, Henry, *Seán Lemass and the Making of Modern Ireland, 1945–66*, Dublin: Gill & Macmillan, 1982.

— Bew, Paul, and Patterson, Henry, *The British State and the Ulster Crisis: From Wilson to Thatcher*, London: Verso, 1985.

— Bielenberg, Andy (ed.), *The Irish Diaspora*, London: Longman, 2000.

— Bishop, Patrick, and Mallie, Eamonn, *The Provisional IRA*, London: Corgi Books, 1987.

— Bloomfield, Ken, *Stormont in Crisis: A Memoir*, Belfast: Blackstaff Press, 1994.

— Boland, Kevin, *Fine Gael: British or Irish?*, Cork and Dublin: Mercier Press, 1984.

— Boland, Kevin, *The Rise and Decline of Fianna Fáil*, Dublin and Cork: Mercier Press, 1982.

— Boland, Kevin, *Under Contract with the Enemy*, Dublin: Mercier Press, 1988.

— Boland, Kevin, *Up Dev!*, Dublin: published by the author, 1977.

— Bowman, John, *De Valera and the Ulster Question*, Oxford: Clarendon Press, 1982.

— Boyce, George, *Ireland, 1828–1923: From Ascendancy to Democracy*, Oxford: Basil Blackwell, 1992.

— Boyce, George, *Nationalism in Ireland*, London: Routledge, 1995.

— Boyce, George, *The Irish Question and British Politics, 1868–1996*, London: Palgrave-Macmillan, 1996.

— Boyce, George, and O'Day, Alan, *The Making of Modern Irish History*, London: Routledge 1996.

— Boyd, Wesley, 'An Irishman's Diary,' *Irish Times*, 16 May 2003.

— Boyne, Sean, *Gunrunners: The Covert Arms Trail to Ireland*, Dublin: O'Brien Press 2006.

— Brady, Seamus, *Arms and the Men: Ireland in Turmoil,* Bray: published by the author, 1971.

— Bromage, Mary C., *De Valera and the March of a Nation,* London: Hutchinson, 1956.

— Brown, Terence, *Ireland: A Social and Cultural History, 1922 to the Present,* Ithaca (NY) and London: Cornell University Press, 1981.

— Browne, Noël, *Against the Tide,* Dublin: Gill & Macmillan, 1986.

— Browne, Vincent, 'My life and times,' *Magill,* November 1979, p. 33–47.

— Browne, Vincent, 'The Arms Crisis, part 1: Arms Crisis: The inside story,' *Magill,* May 1980, p. 33–56.

— Browne, Vincent, 'The Arms Crisis, part 2: The Peter Berry diaries,' *Magill,* June 1980, p. 39–75.

— Browne, Vincent, 'The Arms Crisis, part 3: The misconduct of the Arms Trial,' *Magill,* July 1980, p. 17–28.

— Browne, Vincent (ed.), *The Magill Book of Irish Politics,* Dublin: Magill Publications, 1981.

— Bruce, Steve, *God Save Ulster: The Religion and Politics of Paisleyism,* Oxford: Oxford University Press, 1986.

— *Bunreacht na hÉireann / Constitution of Ireland,* Dublin: Stationery Office, 1938.

— Cain, P. J., and Hopkins, A. G., *British Imperialism, 1914–1990,* New York and London: Longman, 1995.

— Callaghan, James, *A House Divided: The Dilemma of Northern Ireland,* London: Collins, 1973.

— Callanan, Mark (ed.), *Foundations of an Ever Closer Union: An Irish Perspective on the Fifty Years since the Treaty of Rome,* Dublin: Institute of Public Administration, 2007.

— Carroll, John, 'Family and friends salute "real Taoiseach",' *Cork Examiner,* 21 October 2000

— Céitinn, M. B., 'Long na Laoch,' in Liam Ó Tuama et al. (eds.), *The Spirit of the Glen, 1916–1973,* Cork, 1973.

— Chubb, Basil, *The Government and Politics of Ireland,* Oxford: Oxford University Press, 1971.

— Clark, Alan, *Diaries,* London: Weidenfeld and Nicolson, 1993.

— Coakley, John, and Gallagher, Michael, *Politics in the Republic of Ireland,* Limerick: PSAI Press, 1996.

— Collins, Stephen, *The Haughey File: The Unprecedented Career and Last Years of the Boss,* Dublin: O'Brien Press, 1992.

— Collins, Stephen, *The Power Game: Fianna Fáil since Lemass,* Dublin: O'Brien Press, 2000.

— Coogan, Tim Pat, *De Valera: Long Fellow, Long Shadow,* London: Hutchinson, 1993.

— Coogan, Tim Pat, *Wherever Green Is Worn: The Story of the Irish Diaspora,* London: Hutchinson, 2000.

— Coolahan, John, *Irish Education: Its History and Structure,* Dublin: Institute of Public Administration, 1981.

— Cooney, John, *John Charles McQuaid,* Dublin: O'Brien Press, 1999.

— Cooney, John, *The Crozier and the Dáil,* Cork: Mercier Press, 1986.

— Corry, Eoghan, *Catch and Kick: Great Moments of Gaelic Football, 1880–1990,* Dublin: Poolbeg, 1989.

— Cramer, Tim, "Neath Shandon Bells,' in Liam Ó Tuama (ed.), *Jack Lynch: Where He Sported and Played,* Dublin: Blackwater Press, 2000, p. 1–6.

— Cronin, Jim, *An Chéad Chéad: A Rebel Hundred: Cork's 100 All Ireland Titles,* Cork: no publisher, n.d.

— Cronin, Jim, *Making Connections: A Cork GAA Miscellany,* Cork, 2005.

— Crossman, Richard, *The Diaries of a Cabinet Minister,* London: Hamilton Cape, 1976, vols. 2 and 3.

— Cruise O'Brien, Conor, *Memoir: My Life and Themes,* Dublin: Poolbeg, 1998.

— Cruise O'Brien, Conor, *To Katanga and Back,* London: Four Square Books, 1962.

— Cruise O'Brien, Máire, *The Same Age as the State,* Dublin: O'Brien Press, 2003.

— Cruise O'Brien, Máire, and Cruise O'Brien, Conor, *Ireland: A Concise History,* London: Thames and Hudson, 1994.

— Currie, Austin, *All Hell Will Break Loose,* Dublin: O'Brien Press, 2004.

— Daly, Mary E., *Industrial Development and Irish National Identity,* Dublin: Gill & Macmillan, 1992.

— Deasy, Paddy, 'Tar barrels blazed for the winners: The North Mon years,' in Liam Ó Tuama (ed.), *Jack Lynch: Where He Sported and Played,* Dublin: Blackwater Press, 2000, p. 139–44.

— Delaney, Enda, *Demography, State and Society: Irish Migration to Britain, 1921–1971,* Liverpool: Liverpool University Press, 2000.

— Delany, J. F., *Housing Report of City Engineer on the Local Government Circular of 23 December 1918,* Cork: Guy and Company, 1919.

— Delany, J. F., *Report of the City Engineer on the Housing Problem in Cork,* Cork: Guy and Company, 1918.

— Deutsch, Richard, *Mairead Corrigan and Betty Williams,* New York: Barron's-Woodbury, 1977.

— de Valera, Terry, *A Memoir,* Dublin: Currach Press, 2004.

— Devlin, Paddy, *The Fall of the Northern Ireland Executive,* Belfast: no publisher, 1975.

— Dillon, Martin, *God and the Gun: The Church and Irish Terrorism,* New York: Routledge, 1999.

— Donoughue, Bernard, *Downing Street Diary: With Harold Wilson in No. 10,* London: Jonathan Cape, 2005.

— Dorgan, Val, *Christy Ring,* Dublin: Ward River Press, 1980.

— Downey, James, *Lenihan: His Life and Loyalties,* Dublin: New Island Books, 1998.

— Dudley Edwards, Owen, *Conor Cruise O'Brien Introduces Ireland,* Cardiff: University of Wales, 1967.

— Dudley Edwards, Owen, *Éamon de Valera,* Cardiff: GPC Books, 1987.

— Duignan, Seán, *One Spin on the Merry-go-Round,* Dublin: Blackwater Press, 1995.

— Dunlop, Frank, *Yes, Taoiseach: Irish Politics from Behind Closed Doors,* London: Penguin, 2005.

— Dunne, Mick, 'Down through the years' (transcript of radio interview with Jack Lynch), in Liam Ó Tuama (ed.), *Jack Lynch: Where He Sported and Played*, Dublin: Blackwater Press, 2000.

— Dwyer, T. Ryle, *De Valera's Darkest Hour, 1919–1932*, Cork and Dublin: Mercier Press, 1982.

— Dwyer, T. Ryle, *De Valera's Finest Hour: In Search of National Independence, 1932–1959*, Cork: Mercier Press, 1982.

— Dwyer, T. Ryle, *De Valera: The Man and the Myth*, Dublin: Poolbeg, 1991.

— Dwyer, T. Ryle, *Haughey's Thirty Years of Controversy*, Cork and Dublin: Mercier Press, 1992.

— Dwyer, T. Ryle, *Nice Fellow: A Biography of Jack Lynch*, Cork and Dublin: Mercier Press, 2001.

— Dyer, Louise, *Machiavelli and the Modern State*, Boston, Ginn, 1904.

— Eden, Anthony, *Days for Decision*, London: Faber and Faber, 1949.

— Eden, Anthony, *Memoirs: Full Circle*, London: Cassell, 1960.

— Elliott, Marianne, *The Catholics of Ulster: A History*, London: Allen Lane, 2000.

— English, Richard, *Irish Freedom: The History of Nationalism in Ireland*, London: Macmillan, 2006.

— Fallon, Brian, *An Age of Innocence: Irish Culture, 1930–1960*, Dublin: Gill & Macmillan, 1998.

— Fanning, Ronan, *Independent Ireland*, Dublin: Helicon, 1983.

— Fanning, Ronan, *The Irish Department of Finance, 1922–58*, Dublin: Institute of Public Administration, 1978.

— Farragher, Seán P., *Dev and His Alma Mater: Éamon de Valera's Lifelong Association with Blackrock College, 1898–1975*, Dublin: Paraclete Press, 1984.

— Farrell, Brian, *Chairman or Chief?: The Role of Taoiseach in Irish Government*, Dublin: Gill & Macmillan, 1971.

— Farrell, Brian, *Seán Lemass*, Dublin: Gill & Macmillan, 1983.

— Farrell, Brian (ed.), *The Irish Parliamentary Tradition*, Dublin: Gill & Macmillan, 1973.

— Farrell, John A., *Tip O'Neill and the Democratic Century*, Boston: Little, Brown, 2001.

— Farrell, Michael, *The Orange State*, London: Pluto Press, 1990.

— Farren, Seán, *The Politics of Irish Education, 1920–1965*, Belfast: Institute of Irish Studies, Queen's University, 1995.

— Faulkner, Brian, *Memoirs of a Statesman*, London: Weidenfeld and Nicolson, 1978.

— Faulkner, Pádraig, *As I Saw It: Reviewing Over 30 Years of Fianna Fáil and Irish Politics*, Dublin: Wolfhound Press, 2005.

— Feehan, John M., *Operation Brogue: A Story of the Vilification of Charles J. Haughey*, Dublin and Cork: Mercier Press, 1984.

— Feehan, John M., *The Statesman: A Study of the Role of Charles J. Haughey in the Ireland of Tomorrow*, Cork and Dublin: Mercier Press, 1985.

— Feeney, Brian, *Sinn Féin: A Hundred Turbulent Years*, Dublin: O'Brien Press, 2002.

— Ferriter, Diarmaid, *Judging Dev: A Reassessment of the Life and Legacy of Éamon de Valera*, Dublin: Royal Irish Academy, 2007.
— Ferriter, Diarmaid, *The Transformation of Ireland, 1900–2000*, London: Profile Books, 2004.
— FitzGerald, Garret, *All in a Life: An Autobiography*, Dublin: Gill & Macmillan, 1991.
— Fitzgerald, Maurice, *Protectionism to Liberalisation: Ireland and the EEC, 1957–1966*, Aldershot: Ashgate, 2000.
— Fitzpatrick, David, *The Two Irelands, 1912–1939*, Oxford: Opus, 1998.
— Flanagan, Thomas, *They Love You: Writings of Irish American Literature and History*, New York: New York Review Books, 2004.
— Foster, Roy. F., *Luck and the Irish: A Brief History of Change, 1970–2000*, London: Allan Lane, 2007.
— Foster, Roy. F., *Modern Ireland*, London: Allen Lane, 1988.
— Foster, Roy. F., *The Oxford Illustrated History of Ireland*, New York: Oxford University Press, 1991.
— Fullam, Brendan, *Captains of the Ash*, Dublin: Wolfhound Press, 2002.
— Fullam, Brendan, *Hurling Giants*, Dublin: Wolfhound Press, 1998.
— Fullam, Brendan, *Off the Field and On: Triumphs and Trials of Gaelic Games*, Dublin: Wolfhound Press, 1999.
— Gaelic Athletic Association, *Cork GAA: A History, 1886–1986*, Cork: Gaelic Athletic Association, 1986.
— Gallagher, Frank, *The Indivisible Island*, London: Gollancz, 1956.
— Gallagher, Michael, *The Irish Labour Party in Transition, 1957–82*, Dublin: Gill & Macmillan, 1982.
— Garvin, Tom, *1922: The Birth of Irish Democracy*, Dublin: Gill & Macmillan, 1996.
— Garvin, Tom, *Preventing the Future: Why Was Ireland So Poor for So Long?*, Dublin: Gill & Macmillan, 2004.
— Gillman, Peter, 'The quiet man,' *Sunday Times Magazine* (London), 30 July 1972.
— Girvin, Brian, *Between Two Worlds: Politics and Economy in Independent Ireland*, Dublin: Gill & Macmillan, 1989.
— Girvin, Brian, *From Union to Union: Nationalism, Democracy and Religion in Ireland: Act of Union to EU*, Dublin: Gill & Macmillan, 2002.
— Girvin, Brian, and Murphy, Garry (eds.), *The Lemass Era: Politics and Society in the Ireland of Seán Lemass*, Dublin: UCD Press, 2005.
— Goldthorpe, J. H., and Whelan, C. T. (eds.), *The Development of Industrial Society in Ireland* (Proceedings of the British Academy, vol. 79), Oxford: Oxford University Press, for the British Academy, 1992.
— Government of Ireland, *Bloody Sunday and the Report of the Widgery Tribunal: The Irish Government's Assessment of the New Material*, Dublin: Government Publications, 1997.
— Grehan, Ida, 'Interview with Mrs Maureen [*sic*] Lynch,' *Irish Times*, 31 January 1972.
— Gwynn, Denis, *De Valera*, London: Jarrolds Publishers, 1933.
— Hanley, Brian, *The IRA, 1926–1936*, Dublin: Four Courts Press, 2002.
— Hannigan, David, *Giants of Cork Sport*, Cork: Evening Echo, 2005.

— Hannon, Philip, and Gallagher, Jackie (eds.), *Taking the Long View: 70 Years of Fianna Fáil*, Dublin: Blackwater Press, 1996.

— Harkness, David, *Ireland in the Twentieth Century: Divided Island*, London: Macmillan, 1996.

— Heath, Ted, *The Course of My Life: An Autobiography*, London: Hodder and Stoughton, 1996.

— Hederman O'Brien, Miriam, *The Road to Europe: Irish Attitudes, 1948–1961*, Dublin: Institute of Public Administration, 1983.

— Hennessey, Thomas, *Northern Ireland: The Origins of the Troubles*, Dublin: Gill & Macmillan, 2005.

— Hennessey, Thomas, *The Evolution of the Troubles, 1970–1972*, Dublin: Irish Academic Press, 2007.

— Hennessey, Thomas, *The Northern Ireland Peace Process: Ending the Troubles*, Dublin: Gill & Macmillan, 2000.

— Hill, Jackie (ed.), *A New History of Ireland*, vol. 7: *Ireland, 1921–1984*, Oxford: Oxford University Press, 2003.

— Holland, Jack, *Hope Against History: The Ulster Conflict*, London: Hodder and Stoughton, 1999.

— Holland, Jack, and McDonald, Henry, *INLA: Deadly Divisions: The Story of One of Ireland's Most Ruthless Terrorist Organisations*, Dublin: Torc, 1994.

— Hoppen, K. Theodore, *Ireland since 1800: Conflict and Conformity*, London and New York: Longman, 1989.

— Horgan, John, *Christy Ring: Hurling's Greatest*, Cork: Collins Press, 2007.

— Horgan, John, *Noël Browne: Passionate Outsider*, Dublin: Gill & Macmillan, 1997.

— Horgan, John, *Seán Lemass: The Enigmatic Patriot*, Dublin: Gill & Macmillan, 1997.

— Horne, Alistair, *Macmillan, vol. 1: 1894–1956*, London: Macmillan, 1998.

— Horne, Alistair, *Macmillan, vol. 2: 1957–1974*, London: Macmillan, 1988.

— Howe, Stephan, *Ireland and Empire*, Oxford: Oxford University Press, 2000.

— Humphries, Tom, *Green Fields: Gaelic Sport in Ireland*, London: Weidenfeld and Nicolson, 1996.

— Jackson, Alvin, *Ireland, 1798–1998*, Oxford: Basil Blackwell, 1999.

— Jacobsen, John Kurt, *Chasing Progress in the Irish Republic: Ideology, Democracy and Dependent Development*, Cambridge: Cambridge University Press, 1994.

— Joannon, Pierre, *De Gaulle and Ireland*, Dublin: Institute of Public Administration, 1991.

— Joyce, Joe, and Murtagh, Peter, *Blind Justice*, Dublin: Poolbeg Press, 1984.

— Joyce, Joe, and Murtagh, Peter, *The Boss: Charles J. Haughey in Government*, Dublin: Poolbeg Press, 1983.

— Keatinge, Patrick, *A Place Among the Nations: Issues of Irish Foreign Policy*, Dublin: Institute of Public Administration, 1978.

— Keatinge, Patrick, *The Formulation of Irish Foreign Policy*, Dublin: Institute of Public Administration, 1973.

— Kelly, James, *Orders for the Captain*, Dublin: published by the author, 1971.

— Kelly, James, *The Genesis of Revolution*, Dublin: published by the author, 1976.

— Kelly, James, *The Thimble Riggers: The Dublin Arms Trials of 1970*, Dublin: published by the author, 1999.

— Kenna, Colm, 'Man of means: The story behind Haughey's millions,' *Irish Times Magazine*, 22 September 2001.

— Kennedy, K. A., and Dowling, B. R., *Economic Growth in Ireland: The Experience since 1947*, Dublin: Gill & Macmillan, 1975.

— Kennedy, Michael, *Division and Consensus: The Politics of Cross-Border Relations in Ireland, 1925–1969*, Dublin: Institute of Public Administration, 2000.

— Kennedy, Michael, and McMahon, Deirdre (eds.), *Obligations and Responsibilities: Ireland and the United Nations, 1955–2005*, Dublin: Institute of Public Administration, 2005.

— Kenny, Shane, *Go Dance on Somebody Else's Grave: The Inside Story of the Haughey Coalition*, Dublin: Kildanore Press, 1990.

— Keogh, Dermot, 'An eye witness to history: Fr Alexander J. McCabe and the Spanish Civil War, 1936–39,' *Breifne: Journal of Cumann Seanchais Bhréifne*, 1994, p. 445–488.

— —'Argentina and the Falklands (Malvinas): The Irish connection,' in Alistair Hennessy and John King (eds.), *The Land that England Lost: Argentina and Britain, a Special Relationship*, London: British Academic Press, 1992, p. 123–42.

— —'Catholicism and the formation of the modern Irish State,' in *Irishness in a Changing Society* (edited by Princess Grace Irish Library), Totowa (NJ): Barnes and Noble, 1989, p. 152–77.

— —'Church and state in modern Ireland,' in Réamonn Ó Muirí (ed.), *Irish Church History Today* (proceedings of Cumann Seanchais Ard Mhacha seminar, 10 March 1990).

— —'Church, state and pressure groups,' in Bernard Treacy and Gerry Whyte (eds.), *Religion, Morality and Public Policy* (a *Doctrine and Life* special), Dublin: Dominican Publications, 1995, p. 42–61.

— —'Church, state and society,' in Brian Farrell (ed.), *De Valera's Constitution and Ours*, Dublin: Gill & Macmillan, 1988, p. 103–22.

— —'Citizenship and the Irish Freedom of Information Act,' in Dónal de Buitléir and Frances Ruane (eds.), *Governance and Policy in Ireland: Essays in Honour of Miriam Hederman O'Brien*, Dublin: Institute of Public Administration, 2003, p. 59–72.

— —'De Valera, the bishops and the red scare,' in J. O'Carroll and John A. Murphy (eds.), *De Valera and His Times*, Cork: Cork University Press, 1983, p. 134–59.

— —'Éamon de Valera and Hitler: An analysis of international reaction to the visit to the German minister, May 1945,' *Irish Studies in International Affairs*, vol. 3, no. 1 (autumn 1989), p. 69–92.

— —'Episcopal decision-making in Ireland,' in Maurice O'Connell (ed.), *Education, Church and State: Proceedings of the Second Daniel O'Connell School*, Dublin: Institute of Public Administration, 1992, p. 1–18.

— —'Federalism, the Irish state and the challenge of European integration,' in Franz Knipping (ed.), *Federal Conception in EU Member States: Traditions and Perspectives*, Baden-Baden: Nomos, 1994, p. 192–207.

— —'Introduction: The vanishing Irish,' in Dermot Keogh, Finbarr O'Shea and Carmel Quinlan, *The Lost Decade: Ireland in the 1950s*, Cork: Mercier Press, 2004, p. 11–20.

— —'Ireland, 1945–2001: Between hope and history,' in Kathleen Burke (ed.), *The British Isles since 1945*, Oxford: Oxford University Press, 2003.

— —'Ireland, 1972–84,' in J. R. Hill (ed.), *A New History of Ireland*, Oxford: Oxford University Press, 2004, p. 356–930.

— —'Ireland and "emergency" culture, 1922–1961,' in *Ireland: A Journal of History and Society*, summer 1995, p. 4–43.

— —'Ireland and the historiography of European integration,' in *Historians of Contemporary Europe Newsletter*, vol. 7, no. 1–2, June 1992, p. 37–62.

— —'Ireland and the Holocaust,' in David S. Wyman (ed.), *The World Reacts to the Holocaust*, Baltimore (Md): Johns Hopkins University Press, 1996, p. 642–69.

— —'Ireland and the Holy See: A multifaceted relationship of enduring value and importance,' in Albert McDonnell (ed.), *Reflections at an Anniversary: Celebrating 75 years of Diplomatic Relations between Ireland and the Holy See*, Rome: Embassy of Ireland to the Holy See and Pontifical Irish College, 2005.

— —'Ireland and the Single European Act,' in Clive Church and Dermot Keogh (eds.), *A Handbook on the EEC and the SEA*, Cork and Dublin: Hibernian University Press, 1990.

— —'Ireland, 1972–84,' in J. R. Hill (ed.), *A New History of Ireland*, Oxford: Oxford University Press, 2003, vol. 7.

— —'Ireland, de Gaulle and World War II,' in Pierre Joannon (ed.), *De Gaulle and Ireland*, Dublin: Institute of Public Administration, 1991, p. 23–52.

— —'Irish Department of Foreign Affairs,' in Zara Steiner (ed.), *The Times Survey of Foreign Ministries of the World*, London: Times Books, 1982, p. 276–96.

— —'Irish neutrality and the first application for membership of the EEC,' in Michael Kennedy and Joseph Morrison Skelly (eds.), *Irish Foreign Policy, 1916–1966: From Independence to Internationalism*, Dublin: Four Courts Press, 2000, p. 265–85.

— —'Irish refugee policy, anti-Semitism and Nazism at the approach of World War Two,' in Gisela Holfter (ed.), *German-Speaking Exiles in Ireland, 1933–1945*, Amsterdam and New York: Editions Rodopi, 2006, p. 37–73.

— —'Jack Lynch,' in Seán Dunne (ed.), *A Cork Anthology*, Cork: Cork University Press, 1993, p. 334–41.

— —'Jewish refugees and Irish Government policy in the 1930s and 1940s,' in *Remembering for the Future* (preprint of conference proceedings), Oxford: Pergamon Press, 1988, vol.1, p. 395–403.

— —'Leaving the Blaskets, 1953: Willing or enforced departures?' in Dermot Keogh, Finbarr O'Shea and Carmel Quinlan, *The Lost Decade: Ireland in the 1950s*, Cork: Mercier Press, 2004, p. 48–71.

— —'Liam Cosgrave,' in Brian H. Murphy (ed.), *Nos Autem: Castleknock College and Its Contribution*, Dublin: Gill & Macmillan, 1996, p. 157–70.

— —'Mannix, de Valera and Irish nationalism,' in John O'Brien and Pauric Travers (ed.), *The Irish Emigration in Australia*, Dublin: Poolbeg Press, 1991, p. 196–225.

— —'Profile of Joseph Walshe, secretary of the Department of Foreign Affairs, 1922–46,' in *Irish Studies in International Affairs*, vol. 3, no. 2, autumn 1990, p. 59–80.

— —'The Catholic Church and politics in Ireland,' in *Anglistik und Englischunterricht—Ireland: Literature, Culture, Politics*, vol. 52, 1994, p. 147–68.

— —'The Catholic Church and politics in Ireland,' in Maurice O'Connell (ed.), *People Power: Proceedings of the Third Daniel O'Connell School*, Dublin: Institute of Public Administration, 1993, p. 57–79.

— —'The Catholic Church and the modern Irish state,' in *Renaissance and Modern Studies*, vol. 36, 1993, p. 70–92.

— —'The Catholic Church in Ireland since the 1950s,' in Leslie Woodcock Tentler (ed.), *The Church Confronts Modernity: Catholicism since 1950 in the United States, Ireland and Quebec*, Washington: Catholic University Press of America, 2007, p. 93–149.

— —'The Catholic Church, the Holy See and the 1916 Rising,' in Gabriel Doherty and Dermot Keogh (eds.), *1916: The Long Revolution*, Cork: Mercier Press, 2007, p. 250–309.

— —'The diplomacy of "dignified calm": An analysis of Ireland's application for membership of the EEC, 1961–1963,' in *Journal of European Integration History*, vol. 3, no. 1, 1997, p. 81–101.

— —'The Irish constitutional revolution: An analysis of the making of the Constitution,' in *Administration*, vol. 35, no. 4, 1988, p. 4–84.

— —'The Irish Free State and the refugee crisis, 1933–1945,' in Paul Bartrop (ed.), *False Havens: The British Empire and the Holocaust*, New York: University Press of America, 1995, p. 211–38.

— —'The Jewish contribution to twentieth-century Ireland,' in Denis Carroll (ed.), *Religion in Ireland: Past, Present and Future*, Dublin: Columba Press, 1999.

— —'The resilience of Catholic devotionalism,' in E. Grollet, N. Keogh and E. Keogh (eds.), *Collective Memory in Ireland and Russia*, Moscow: All-Russia State Library for Foreign Literature, 2007, p. 56–83.

— —'The role of the Catholic Church in the Republic of Ireland, 1922–1995,' in *Building Trust in Ireland* (studies commissioned by the Forum for Peace and Reconciliation), Belfast: Blackstaff Press, 1996, p. 85–214.

— —*Ireland and Europe, 1919–1948*, Dublin: Gill and Macmillan, 1988, p. 256.

— —*Ireland and the Challenge of European Integration*, Cork and Dublin: Hibernian University Press, for Irish Association for Contemporary European Studies, 1989, p. 180.

— —*Ireland and the Vatican: The Politics and Diplomacy of Church and State, 1922–1960*, Cork: Cork University Press, 1995, p. 410.

— —*Jews in Twentieth Century Ireland: Refugees, Anti-Semitism and the Holocaust*, Cork: Cork University Press, 1998, p. 336.

— —'Making Aliya: Irish Jews, the Irish state and Israel,' in Dermot Keogh, Finbarr O'Shea and Carmel Quinlan, *The Lost Decade: Ireland in the 1950s*, Cork: Mercier Press, 2004, p. 252–72.

— —'The Jesuits and the 1937 Constitution,' in *Studies,* vol. 78, no. 309, spring 1989, p. 82–95.

— —*The Vatican, the Bishops and Irish Politics,* Cambridge: Cambridge University Press, 1986 (reissued 2005), p. 316.

— —*Twentieth Century Ireland: Nation and State,* Dublin: Gill & Macmillan, 1994, p. 504 (reissued in 2005 with an extra chapter covering the period from the 1980s to 2005).

— Keogh, Dermot, and Bardon, Jonathan, 'Introduction: Ireland, 1921–84,' in J. R. Hill (ed.), *A New History of Ireland,* Oxford: Oxford University Press, 2003, vol. 7.

— Keogh, Dermot, and Church, Clive H., *The Single European Act: A Transnational Study,* Cork: Canterbury Consortium, 1991.

— Keogh, Dermot, and Doherty, Gabriel, *De Valera's Irelands,* Cork: Mercier Press, 2003.

— Keogh, Dermot, and Doherty, Gabriel, *Michael Collins and the Making of the Irish State,* Cork: Mercier Press, 1998, p. 224.

— Keogh, Dermot, and Doherty, Gabriel (eds.), *1916: The Long Revolution,* Cork: Mercier Press, 2007.

— Keogh, Dermot, and Haltzel, Michael, *Northern Ireland and the Politics of Reconciliation,* Cambridge and New York: Cambridge University Press, 1993, p. 267.

— Keogh, Dermot, and Keogh, Aoife, 'Ireland and European integration: From the Treaty of Rome to membership,' in Mark Callanan (ed.), *Foundations of an Ever Closer Union: An Irish Perspective on the 50 Years since the Treaty of Rome,* Dublin: Institute of Public Administration, 2007, p. 6–50.

— Keogh, Dermot, and Keogh, Aoife, 'Ireland's application for membership of the European Economic Community,' in Ariane Landuyt and Daniele Pasquinucci (eds.), *Gli Allargamenti della CEE/UE, 1961–2004,* Bologna: Il Mulino, 2005.

— Keogh, Dermot, and McCarthy, Andrew, *Limerick Boycott, 1904: Anti-Semitism in Ireland,* Cork: Mercier Press, 2005.

— Keogh, Dermot, and McCarthy, Andrew, *The Making of the Irish Constitution, 1937,* Cork and Dublin: Mercier Press, 2007.

— Keogh, Dermot, and McCarthy, Andrew, *Twentieth Century Ireland: Revolution and State Building,* Dublin: Gill & Macmillan, 2005.

— Keogh, Dermot, and Mulholland, Joe, *Education in Ireland: For What and for Whom,* Cork and Dublin: Hibernian University Press, 1990.

— Keogh, Dermot, and Mulholland, Joe, *Emigration, Employment and Enterprise,* Cork and Dublin: Hibernian University Press, for Patrick MacGill Summer School, 1989, p. 190.

— Keogh, Dermot, and O'Driscoll, Finin, 'Ireland,' in Tom Buchanan and Martin Conway (eds.), *Popular Catholicism in Europe, 1918–1965,* Oxford: Clarendon Press, 1996, p. 270–300.

— Keogh, Dermot, and O'Driscoll, Mervyn, *Ireland in World War Two: Neutrality and Survival,* Cork: Mercier Press, 2004.

— Keogh, Dermot, O'Shea, Finbarr, and Quinlan, Carmel, *The Lost Decade: Ireland in the 1950s,* Cork: Mercier Press, 2004.

— Kiberd, Declan, *Inventing Ireland: The Literature of the Modern Nation*, London: Jonathan Cape, 1995.
— Lacouture, Jean, *De Gaulle*, London: Hutchinson, 1970.
— Lacouture, Jean, *De Gaulle: The Rebel, 1890–1944*, London: Collins Harville, 1991.
— Lacouture, Jean, *De Gaulle: The Ruler, 1945–1970*, London: Collins Harville, 1991.
— Lambert, Gordon, Interview, *Sunday Press*, 25 November 1979.
— Lee, J. J., *Ireland, 1912–1985: Politics and Society*, Dublin: Gill & Macmillan, 1979; Cambridge: Cambridge University Press, 1989.
— Lee, J. J., and Casey, Marion R., *Making the Irish American: History and Heritage of the Irish in the United States*, New York: New York University Press, 2006.
— Lee, Joseph, and Ó Tuathaigh, Gearóid (eds.), *The Age of de Valera*, Dublin: Ward River Press, 1982.
— Lindsay, Patrick J., *Memories*, Dublin: Blackwater Press, 1992.
— Longford, Lord, *Ulster*, London: Weidenfeld and Nicolson, 1981.
— Longford, Earl of, and O'Neill, T. P., *Eamon de Valera*, Boston: Houghton Mifflin, 1971.
— Lydon, James, *The Making of Ireland: From Ancient Times to the Present*, London and New York: Routledge, 1998.
— Lynch, Finbarr, 'Scoring goals at the Butter Market,' in Liam Ó Tuama, *Jack Lynch: Where He Sported and Played*, Dublin: Blackwater Press, 2000, p. 7–12.
— Lynch, Jack, 'My life and times,' *Magill*, November 1979.
— Lynch, Jack, 'Reminiscences,' in Liam Ó Tuama et al. (eds.), *The Spirit of the Glen, 1916–1973*, Cork, 1973.
— Lynch, Jack, 'Spirit of the Glen,' in Liam Ó Tuama, *Jack Lynch: Where He Sported and Played*, Dublin: Blackwater Press, 2000, p. 139–44.
— Lynch, J. M., 'The Anglo-Irish problem,' *Foreign Affairs*, vol. 50, no. 4, 1972, p. 601–17.
— Lynch, John [Jack], *Irish Unity, Northern Ireland and Anglo-Irish Relations*, Dublin: Government Information Bureau, 1971.
— Lynch, John [Jack], *Presidential address by John Lynch, 28 January 1969*, Dublin, 1969.
— Lynch, John [Jack], Transcript of speech on Ireland and European integration, 25 February 1993, Dublin: Institute of European Affairs, 1993.
— Lyons, F. S. L., *Culture and Anarchy in Ireland, 1890–1939*, Oxford: Oxford University Press, 1979.
— Lyons, F. S. L., *Ireland since the Famine*, London: Collins, 1971.
— Macardle, Dorothy, *The Irish Republic*, London: Corgi Books, 1968.
— McCabe, Ian, *A Diplomatic History of Ireland, 1948–49*, Dublin: Institute of Public Administration, 1991.
— McCann, Eamonn, *War and an Irish Town*, London: Penguin, 1974.
— McCarthy, Charles, *The Decade of Upheaval: Irish Trade Unions in the Nineteen Sixties*, Dublin: Institute of Public Administration, 1973.
— McCullagh, David, *A Makeshift Majority: The First Inter-Party Government, 1948–51*, Dublin: Institute of Public Administration, 1998.

— MacDermott, Eithne, *Clann na Poblachta*, Cork: Cork University Press, 1998.
— McDonagh, Patrick, 'The remarkable story of Jack Lynch,' *Business and Finance*, 20 August 1965.
— McDonald, Frank, *Saving the City: How to Halt the Destruction of Dublin*, Dublin: Tomar Publications, 1989.
— McDonald, Frank, *The Destruction of Dublin*, Dublin: Gill & Macmillan, 1985.
— Machiavelli, Niccolò (edited with an introduction by Bernard Crick), *The Discourses*, Harmondsworth (Middx): Penguin, 1970.
— Machiavelli, Niccolò, *The Prince*, London: Humphrey Milford, 1903.
— McInerney, Michael (ed.), *Eamon de Valera: A Survey by the Irish Times of the Life and Influence of a Famous Leader*, Dublin: Irish Times, 1976.
— MacIntyre, Tom, *Through the Bridewell Gates: A Diary of the Dublin Arms Trial*, London: Faber and Faber, 1971.
— McKeown, Jim, et al., 'Jack Lynch remembered,' in *Cork Review 2000*, autumn 2000, p. 2–6.
— McKeown, Orla, and McDonagh, Hilary, *The Lilac Years: A History of Maids of the Mountain Hockey Club from 1918 to 1999*, Dublin: no publisher, 2000.
— McKittrick, David, et al., *Lost Lives: The Stories of the Men, Women and Children Who Died as a Result of the Northern Ireland Troubles*, Edinburgh and London: Mainstream, 1999.
— MacManus, M. J., *Eamon de Valera: A Biography*, Dublin and Cork: Talbot Press, 1944.
— McNamara, Robert, 'Irish perspectives on the Vietnam war,' *Irish Studies in International Affairs*, vol. 14, 2003.
— MacSwiney Brugha, Máire, *History's Daughter: A Memoir from the Only Child of Terence MacSwiney*, Dublin: O'Brien Press, 2005.
— Maher, Denis J., *The Tortuous Path: The Course of Ireland's Entry into the EEC, 1948–73*, Dublin: Institute of Public Administration, 1986.
— Mair, Peter, *The Changing Irish Party System*, London: Pinter, 1987.
— Mansergh, Martin (ed.), *The Spirit of the Nation: The Speeches of Charles J. Haughey*, Cork and Dublin: Mercier Press, 1986.
— Marcus, David, *Oughtobiography: Leaves from the Diary of a Hyphenated Jew*, Dublin: Gill & Macmillan, 2001.
— Mason, Roy, *Paying the Price*, London: Robert Hale, 1999.
— Maudling, Reginald, *Memoirs*, London: Sidgwick and Jackson, 1978.
— Mills, Michael, *Hurler on the Ditch: Memoirs of a Journalist Who Became Ireland's first Ombudsman*, Dublin: Currach Press, 2005.
— Moloney, Ed, *A Secret History of the IRA*, London: Allen Lane, 2002.
— Moody, T. W., Martin, F. X., and Byrne, F. J. (eds.), *A New History of Ireland, vol. 8*, Oxford: Oxford University Press, 1982.
— Moreton, Cole, *Hungry for Home: Leaving the Blaskets: A Journey from the Edge of Ireland*, London: Viking, 2000.
— Morrison, Tom, *For the Record: A History of the National Football and Hurling League Finals*, Cork: Collins Press, 2002.

— Murphy, John A., *Ireland in the Twentieth Century*, Dublin: Gill & Macmillan, 1975.
— Nevin, Donal, *Trade Union Century*, Cork: Mercier Press, in association with Radio Telefís Éireann and the Irish Congress of Trade Unions, 1994.
— Noland, K. B., and Williams, T. Desmond (eds.), *Ireland in the War Years and After, 1939–1951*, Dublin: Gill & Macmillan, 1969.
— Novick, Peter, *The Holocaust and Collective Memory*, London: Bloomsbury, 1999.
— O'Brien, Justin, *Modern Prince: Charles J. Haughey and the Quest for Power*, Dublin: Merlin, 2002.
— O'Brien, Justin, *The Arms Trial*, Dublin: Gill & Macmillan, 2000.
— Ó Buachalla, Séamas, *Educational Policy in Twentieth Century Ireland*, Dublin: Wolfhound Press, 1988.
— O'Carroll, J. Patrick, and Murphy, John A., *De Valera and His Times*, Cork: Cork University Press, 1983.
— Ó Catháin, Seán, *Secondary Education in Ireland*, Dublin: Talbot Press, 1958.
— O'Connor, Fionnuala, *In Search of a State: Catholics in Northern Ireland*, Belfast: Blackstaff Press, Belfast, 1993.
— O'Connor, Kevin, *The Irish in Britain*, Dublin: Torc, 1974.
— O'Connor, Seán, *A Troubled Sky: Reflections on the Irish Educational Scene, 1957–1968*, Dublin: Iona Print, 1986.
— O'Connor, Ulick, *The Ulick O'Connor Diaries, 1970–1981*, London: John Murray, 2001.
— O'Doherty, E. F., 'Bilingual education: Educational aspects,' *Advancement of Science*, 56, 1958
— O'Faolain, Sean, *De Valera: A New Biography*, London: Penguin, 1939.
— Ó Faoláin, Seán, *The Life Story of Eamon de Valera*, Dublin and Cork: Talbot Press, 1933.
— Ó Fearghail, Seán Óg, *Law (?) and Orders: The Belfast 'Curfew' of 3–5 July 1970*, Belfast: Central Citizens' Defence Committee, 1970.
— Ó Gráda, Cormac, *A Rocky Road: The Irish Economy since the 1920s*, Manchester: Manchester University Press, 1997.
— O'Halloran, Clare, *Partition and the Limits of Irish Nationalism*, Dublin: Gill & Macmillan, 1987.
— O'Halloran, Marie, 'Lynch is likened to legendary folk heroes,' *Irish Times*, 23 October 1999
— O'Halpin, Eunan, *Defending Ireland: The Irish State and its Enemies since 1922*, Oxford: Oxford University Press, 1999.
— Ó hEithir, Breandán, *The Begrudger's Guide to Irish Politics*, Dublin: Poolbeg, 1987.
— O'Leary, Olivia, 'Haughey misses Lynch reception,' *Irish Times*, 17 November 1979.
— O'Mahony, T. P., *Jack Lynch: A Biography*, Dublin: Blackwater Press, 1991.
— O'Malley, E., 'Problems of industrialisation in Ireland,' in J. H. Goldthorpe and C. T. Whelan (eds.), *The Development of Industrial Society in Ireland* (Proceedings of the British Academy, vol. 79), Oxford: Oxford University Press, for the British Academy, 1992.
— O'Malley, Eoin, *Industry and Economic Development: The Challenge for the Latecomer*, Dublin: Gill & Macmillan, 1989.

— O'Malley, Padraig, *Biting at the Grave: The Irish Hunger Strikes and the Politics of Despair*, Boston: Beacon Press, 1990.

— O'Malley, Padraig, *The Uncivil Wars: Ireland Today*, Belfast: Blackstaff Press, 1983.

— O'Meara, J. J., *Reform in Education*, Dublin: Mount Salus Press, 1958.

— O'Neill, Sir Con, *Britain's Entry into the European Community*, London: Frank Cass, 2000.

— O'Neill, Terence, *The Autobiography of Terence O'Neill, Prime Minister of Northern Ireland, 1963–1969*, London: Rupert Hart-Davis, 1972.

— O'Neill, Terence, *Ulster at the Crossroads*, London: Faber and Faber, 1969.

— Ó Néill, Tomás, and Ó Fiannachta, Pádraig, *De Valera*, Dublin: Cló Morainn, 1968, vol. 1.

— O'Sullivan, Michael, *Seán Lemass: A Biography*, Dublin: Blackwater Press, 1994.

— O'Toole, Fintan, *The Irish Times Book of the Century*, Dublin: Gill & Macmillan, 1999.

— Ó Tuama, Liam, *Jack Lynch: Where He Sported and Played*, Dublin: Blackwater Press, 2000.

— Ó Tuama, Liam, et al., *The Spirit of the Glen: A Glen Rovers Presentation, 1916–1973*, Cork, 1973.

— Ó Tuama, Liam, et al., *The Nicks of Time: A St Nicholas' Gaelic Football Club Presentation, 1901–1993*, Cork, 1993.

— Patterson, Henry, *Ireland since 1939*, Oxford: Oxford University Press, 2002.

— Patterson, Henry, *The Politics of Illusion: Republicanism and Socialism in Modern Ireland*, London: Hutchinson Radius, 1989.

— Pearce, Malcolm, and Stewart, Geoffrey, *British Political History, 1867–1995: Democracy and Decline*, London: Routledge, 1996.

— Peck, John, *Dublin from Downing Street*, Dublin: Gill & Macmillan, 1978.

— Phoenix, Eamon, *Northern Nationalism: Nationalist Politics, Partition and the Catholic Minority in Northern Ireland, 1890–1940*, Belfast: Ulster Historical Foundation, 1994.

— Pierce, David, *Light, Freedom and Song: A Cultural History of Modern Irish Writing*, New Haven and London: Yale University Press, 2005.

— Prager, Jeffrey, *Building Democracy in Ireland: Political Order and Cultural Integration in a Newly Independent Nation*, Cambridge: Cambridge University Press, 1986.

— Prior, Jim, *A Balance of Power*, London: Hamish Hamilton, 1986.

— Rafter, Kevin, *Sinn Féin, 1905–2005: In the Shadow of Gunmen*, Dublin: Gill & Macmillan, 2005.

— Raftery, Oliver P., *Catholics in Ulster, 1603–1983: An Interpretative History*, London: Hurst, 1994.

— Regan, John M., *The Irish Counter-Revolution, 1921–1936*, Dublin: Gill & Macmillan, 1999.

— Riordan, E. J., *Modern Irish Trade and Industry*, London: Methuen, 1920.

— Rose, Richard, *Northern Ireland: A Time of Choice*, London: Macmillan, 1976.

— Rostow, W. W., *The Stages of Economic Growth: A Non-Communist Manifesto*,

London: Cambridge University Press, 1960.

— Rostow, W. W., *The Process of Economic Growth,* London: Oxford University Press, 1953 (second edition, 1960).

— Savage, Robert, *Irish Television: The Political and Social Origins,* Cork: Cork University Press, 1996.

— Sciascia, Leonardo, *The Moro Affair,* London: Carcanet, 1987.

— *Second Programme for Economic Expansion, Part II* (Pr 7670), Dublin: Stationery Office, 1964.

— *Second Programme for Economic Expansion: Progress Report for 1965* (Pr 8703), Dublin: Stationery Office, 1966.

— Shepherd, Robert, *Enoch Powell,* London: Hutchinson, 1996.

— Sinnott, Richard, *Irish Voters Decide: Voting Behaviour in Elections and Referendums since 1918,* Manchester: Manchester University Press, 1995.

— Skelly, Joseph Morrison, *Irish Diplomacy at the United Nations, 1945–1965,* Dublin: Irish Academic Press, 1997.

— Skelly, Joseph, and Kennedy, Michael (eds.), *Irish Foreign Policy, 1919–1966,* Dublin: Four Courts Press, 2000.

— Sloan, G. R., *The Geopolitics of Anglo-Irish Relations in the Twentieth Century,* London: Leicester University Press, 1997.

— Smith, Raymond, *Charles J. Haughey: The Survivor,* Dublin: Aherlow Publishers, 1983.

— Smyth, Sam, *Thanks a Million, Big Fella,* Dublin: Blackwater Press, 1997.

— Spellman, Greg, 'Ireland at the United Nations, 1965–69,' in Michael Kennedy and Deirdre McMahon (eds.), *Obligations and Responsibilities: Ireland and the United Nations, 1955–2005,* Dublin: Institute of Public Administration, 2005.

— Sunday Times Insight Team, *Ulster,* London: Penguin, 1972.

— *Survey of Grant Aided Industry,* Dublin: Stationery Office, 1967.

— Tobin, Fergal, *The Best of Decades: Ireland in the Nineteen Sixties,* Dublin: Gill & Macmillan, 1984.

— Townshend, Richard, *Ireland: The 20th Century,* London: Arnold, 1999.

— Travers, Pauric, *Éamon de Valera,* Dundalk: Dundalgan Press, for Historical Association of Ireland, 1994.

— Travers, Stephen, and Fetherstonhaugh, Neil, *The Miami Showband Massacre: A Survivor's Search for the Truth,* Dublin: Hodder Headline Ireland, 2007.

— Urwin, Derek, *The Community of Europe: A History of European Integration since 1945,* Singapore: Longman, 1991.

— Walker, Brian M. (ed.), *Parliamentary Election Results in Ireland, 1918–1992: Irish Elections to Parliaments and Parliamentary Assemblies at Westminster, Belfast, Dublin, Strasbourg,* Dublin: Royal Irish Academy, and Belfast: Institute of Irish Studies, Queen's University, 1992.

— Walker, Dorothy, *Michael Scott, Architect,* Cork: Gandon Editions, 1995.

— Walsh, Dick, *The Party: Inside Fianna Fáil,* Dublin: Gill & Macmillan, 1986.

— Warner, Geoffrey, 'The Falls Road curfew revisited,' *Irish Studies Review,* 14, no. 3 (1 August 2006), 325–42.

— Whitaker, T. K., *Interests*, Dublin: Institute of Public Administration, 1983.
— Whitaker, T. K., *Retrospect, 2006–1916*, Dublin: Institute of Public Administration, 2006.
— Whitelaw, William, *The Whitelaw Memoirs*, London: Aurum Press, 1989.
— Whyte, J. H., *Church and State in Modern Ireland, 1923–1979*, Dublin: Gill & Macmillan, 1980.
— Wichert, Sabine, *Northern Ireland since 1945*, London and New York: Longman, 1991.
— Wilson, Andrew J., *Irish America and the Ulster Connection, 1968–1995*, Belfast: Blackstaff Press, 1995.
— Wilson, Desmond, *Democracy Denied*, Cork and Dublin: Mercier Press, 1997.
— Young, Hugo, *The Iron Lady: A Biography of Margaret Thatcher*, New York: Farrar, Straus and Giroux, 1989.
— Young, Hugo, *This Blessed Plot*, London: Papermac, 1998.
— Young, J. W., *Britain and European Unity*, London: Macmillan, 2000.
— Young, J. W., *Britain, France and the Unity of Europe*, Bath: Leicester University Press, 1984.
— Ziegler, Philip, *Mountbatten: The Official Biography*, London: Collins, 1985.

INDEX